Enterprise and Social Rights

Studies in Employment and Social Policy

Volume 48

Series Editors

Prof. Alan C. Neal
Prof. Dr Manfred Weiss
Prof. Birgitta Nyström

Launched in 1997, the Studies in Employment and Social Policy series now boasts over forty titles, addressing key policy and development issues in the fields of Industrial Relations, Labour Law, Social Security, and International Labour Regulation.

Under the direction of its General Editors, Professor Alan Neal (Founding Editor of the International Journal of Labour Law and Industrial Relations, and Convenor of the European Association of Labour Law Judges), Professor Manfred Weiss (past-President of the International Industrial Relations Association) and Professor Birgitta Nyström (Professor of Private Law at the Law Faculty, University of Lund, Sweden), Studies in Employment and Social Policy seeks to provide a forum for highlighting international and comparative research on contemporary areas of significance for evaluation and regulation of the world of work.

With contributors from leading figures in the field, Studies in Employment and Social Policy brings together key policy-makers, academics, and regulators, providing a unique context in which to analyse and evaluate the rapid and dramatic work and social policy developments taking place across the globe.

Enterprise and Social Rights

Edited by
Adalberto Perulli
Tiziano Treu

Published by:
Kluwer Law International B.V.
PO Box 316
2400 AH Alphen aan den Rijn
The Netherlands
Website: www.wolterskluwerlr.com

Sold and distributed in North, Central and South America by:
Wolters Kluwer Legal & Regulatory U.S.
7201 McKinney Circle
Frederick, MD 21704
United States of America
Email: customer.service@wolterskluwer.com

Sold and distributed in all other countries by:
Quadrant
Rockwood House
Haywards Heath
West Sussex
RH16 3DH
United Kingdom
Email: international-customerservice@wolterskluwer.com

Printed on acid-free paper.

ISBN 978-90-411-8234-0

e-Book: ISBN 978-90-411-8621-8
web-PDF: ISBN 978-90-411-8622-5

© 2017 Kluwer Law International BV, The Netherlands

All rights reserved. No part of this publication may be reproduced, stored in a retrieval system, or transmitted in any form or by any means, electronic, mechanical, photocopying, recording, or otherwise, without written permission from the publisher.

Permission to use this content must be obtained from the copyright owner. Please apply to: Permissions Department, Wolters Kluwer Legal & Regulatory U.S., 76 Ninth Avenue, 7th Floor, New York, NY 10011-5201, USA. Website: www.wolterskluwerlr.com

Printed in the United Kingdom.

MIX
FSC® C103993

Editors

Adalberto Perulli is Full Professor of Labour Law at the Ca' Foscari University of Venice and Visiting Professor at the University of Paris Ouest Nanterre La Défense since 2000. He is the Director of a First Level Master in Labour Law at the Ca' Foscari University of Venice. He did research and studies for the European Commission and for the International Labour Organization (ILO) of Geneva. Prof. Perulli has been rapporteur to the XVIII World Congress of Labour Law on "Labour Law and productive decentralization" in Paris, on 2006; He is Master EMA Director at EIUC (European European Inter-University Centre for Human Rights and Democratisation) and also member of the scientific and editorial staff of several Italian and foreign labour law reviews. Among his most important publications: Perulli A., Sustainability, Social Rights and International Trade: The TTIP, in International Journal of Comparative Labour Law and Industrial Relations, vol. 32, 2015; Perulli A., Fundamental Social Rights, Market Regulation and EU External Action in International Journal Of Comparative Labour Law And Industrial Relations, vol. 30, 2014; Perulli A., Casale G., Compliance with labour legislation: its efficacy and efficiency, Ginevra, ILO, 2010; Perulli A., Economically dependent / quasi-subordinate (parasubordinate) employment: legal, social and economic aspects, European Commission, Brussels, 2002.

Tiziano Treu is Professor Emeritus of Labour Law, Catholic University of Milan, Law School, and President of ISLSSL – International Society of Labour and Social Security Law. Previously he has been President of the Italian Association of Labour Law and Social Security. During his political experience prof. Treu has been Minister of Transportation and Minister of Labour and Social Security in the Italian Government, and more recently President of the XI Commission (Labour and Wefare) of the Italian Senate. Among his recent publications: Diritto del lavoro dell'Unione Europea (7th ed., with M. Roccella), Labour Law in Italy (4th revised ed.), Verso nuove relazioni industriali (with M. Carrieri, eds.).

Contributors

Takashi Araki is professor of law at the University of Tokyo and former Dean of its Law School. In Japan, he is currently a member of Labor Policy Council in the Ministry of Health, Labor and Welfare, and deputy president of the Central Labor Relations Commission. Internationally, he is the former vice-president of the International Society for Labor and Social Security Law and actively involved in comparative studies in labour law and industrial relations. He has been a visiting scholar and professor at several institutions worldwide, including Harvard Law School (1990–1991, 2013–2014), the Catholic University of Leuven (1991–1992), Columbia Law School (1997), Cambridge University (2000–2001), and Goethe University, Frankfurt am Main (2014, 2015).

Mariachiara Barzotto is a Marie Skłodowska-Curie Research Fellow at the Birmingham Business School (BBS). She obtained her Ph.D. degree from Ca' Foscari University Venice (Italy) in 2014. Before joining BBS, Mariachiara worked as a Post-Doctoral researcher at Ca' Foscari University Venice and was visiting Ph.D. student and research collaborator at Cass Business School – City University London (UK). Her research interests and work experiences focus on regional development, with a particular emphasis on workforce development interventions to overcome skills shortage and imbalances.

Agar Brugiavini is full professor in Economics at Ca' Foscari University of Venice. Her research interest is in household's savings and old age insurance markets, labour supply, and pension reforms. She is in the core-group of the EU SHARE-project (Survey of health, ageing and retirement in Europe), for the section on 'Employment and Pensions'. She is a research associate of the Institute for Fiscal Studies, London, and has taken part to several international projects of the NBER (National Bureau of Economic Research), Boston, USA.

Giuseppe Casale is Deputy Director of the International Training Centre of the ILO, Director of the Turin School of Development and Secretary General of the International Society for Labour and Social Security Law. He is visiting professor at the Cà Foscari

Contributors

University, Venice and lectures in international and comparative labour law in several European universities. He is editorial member of various international journals and reviews. He is the author of several publications in international and comparative labour law, and comparative industrial and employment relations.

Giancarlo Corò is Professor of Applied Economics at Ca' Foscari University of Venice, where he is director of the School of Economics, Languages, and Entrepreneurship for International Trade. His research topics are Industrial cluster economics, Global value chains analysis, and Regional economic policies. He is also director of the Master in Economics of Eastern Europe and he has the scientific responsibility of The Urban Innovation Bootcamp, an action-learning programme involving students, firms and institutions in projects of social and green innovation. Among the last publications: *Territorial Capital as a Company Intangible* (Journal of Intellectual Capital, Vol. 17/2016); *The impact of Foreign Multinational Firms on the Local Labour Market* (WP CMET 2016); *The Governance of Metropolitan Areas in Italy: A Plan to Enhance Competition* (Tafter Journal, 85/2015); *Rethinking the Role of Manufacturing in Global Value Chains* (Industrial and Corporate Change, 2/2014).

Francesco Denozza, Professor of commercial law, Università degli Studi di Milano, Managing editor of the law journal *Orizzonti del diritto commercial, Rivista online*, published by the Italian Association of the professors of commercial law. Member of the managing board of the law journal *Giurisprudenza commerciale*. Member of the Milan Bar Association.

Riccardo Del Punta Born in 1957, he is Full Professor of Labour Law, University of Florence, after previous teaching experiences in the Universities of Pisa, Trieste, Siena. He has numerous publications and essays in the field of Labour Law. He is especially active on the topic of the identity and the perspectives of Labour Law and its relationships with other social sciences. He is member of Italian Association of Labour Lawyers and founding member of Italian Society of Law and Economics. He is member of the advisory board of 'The International Journal of Comparative Labour Law and Industrial Relations' and of the scientific committee of 'Giornale di diritto del lavoro e delle relazioni industriali', 'Rivista italiana di diritto del lavoro', 'Diritto delle relazioni industriali'. He was advisor to the Labour Ministers in the Governments headed by Mario Monti (2012–2013) and Matteo Renzi (2015–2016).

Adrián Goldin, Former full professor at the University of San Andrés (Buenos Aires, Argentina) Adrián Goldin was recently appointed Professor Emeritus of that university. He is also a plenary professor (Profesor titular) in the Law School of the University of Buenos Aires and current Director of the Department of Labour Law and Social Security. He's been the president of the International Society for Labour and Social Security Law (2012–2015), and he is currently its Honorary President. He is a fellow full member ('Academico de Número') of the Academia Iberoamericana de Derecho del Trabajo y de la Seguridad Social, corresponding member of the Brazilian Academy for Labour Law and former president of the Argentinean Association of Labour Law and

Social Security. He is also a member of the editorial board of many international Labour Law reviews. He has authored books, contributed to edited collection, and published some 150 articles and research reports in Argentina and abroad on labour law and labour relations.

Jeff Kenner is Chair of European Law at the University of Nottingham, UK. He is author of *EU Employment Law*, 2nd edn (Hart 2018, forthcoming) and co-editor of Ales, Deinert and Kenner (eds), *Core and Conntingent Work in the European Union* (Hart 2017) and Peers, Hervey, Kenner and Ward, *The EU Charter of Fundamental Rights: A Commentary* (Hart 2014). He is Leader for the University of Nottingham and contributing author of several reports for the EU FP7 project 'Fostering Human Rights among European Policies (FRAME)', 2013–2017.

Sheldon Leader is Professor of Law and Director of the Essex Business and Human Rights Project, University of Essex (UK). He focuses on bringing academics and non-academics together in collaborative projects, aiming to formulate and apply principles linking business activity and human rights standards, often with the tools of legal and political theory. Relevant publications include 'Human Rights and the Constitutionalized Corporation' in *Multinationals and the Constitutionalization of the World Power System* edited by Stephane Vernac et al. Ashgate Publishing Ltd. (2016); 'Coherence, Mutual Assurance, and a Treaty on Business and Human Rights' in Surya Deva and David Bilchitz (eds) *Business and Human Rights: Exploring the Contours of a Treaty* (Cambridge University Press, 2017); 'Collateralism' in R. Brownsword (ed.) *Global Governance and the Search for Justice* (Hart Publishing: 2005); *Freedom of Association: A Study in Labor Law and Political Theory* (Yale University Press, 1992).

Antoine Lyon-Caen President of the 'Institut International Pour les Etudes Comparatives', he is Professor emeritus at the Law School of the University of Paris Ouest Nanterre La Défense, Professor at the Higher School of Social Sciences (Chair: Law, Economy and Enterprise) and Barrister at the Conseil d'Etat and the Supreme Court of cassation. He is Director of *Revue de droit du travail (Labour Law Journal)* since its creation and Member of editorial committees of several European journals as well as Author of various books in Labour Law, concerning European Social Policy, Social Policy and Competition Law, Law and Globalization. Critical approach of Law and Economics (Last book published: Multinationals and the constitutionalization of the world power system, with J.-P. Robé, S. Vernac, Préface J.G. Ruggie, éd. Routledge, 2016).

Andrea Pin (JD, University of Padua; Ph.D., University of Turin) is Associate Professor of Comparative Public Law at the University of Padua, where he teaches also Economic & Social Rights. He is Senior Fellow of the Center of the Study of Law and Religion at Emory University (Atlanta, USA) and a member of the Scientific Committee of Oasis International Foundation. He was visiting fellow at the Kellogg Institute for International Studies at Notre Dame University, and Visiting Professor at the Notre Dame Law School and Emory Law School. His works have appeared on Italian, American, British, French, and Spanish law reviews or books.

Contributors

Orsola Razzolini is associate professor of labour law at the University of Genova, with a Ph.D. in law of Business and Commerce at Bocconi University (Milan). In 2013–2014 she was associate professor in European and International labour law at the University of Luxembourg. She also held visiting fellow positions at the London School of Economics and Political Science and a visiting professor position at the University of Illinois, Urbana-Champaign. Since June 2016, she is a member of the Italian Strike Authority. She is author of one monograph (*Piccolo imprenditore e lavoro prevalentemente personale*, Giappichelli, 2012) and of several articles in Italian and English language.

Jean-Michel Servais Visiting Professor at the Faculty of Law of the University of Gerona, former Director of the International Labour Office (ILO), Honorary President of the International Society for Labour Law and Social Security. Author of a number of publications in various languages on comparative, international and European labour law, including *International Labour Law* (The Hague), Kluwer, 4th revised ed., 2014, *International Social Security Law*, The Hague, Kluwer, 2013, *Droit social de l'Union européenne* (Brussels), 2nd edn, Bruylant, 2011 and *Droits en synergie sur le travail. Eléments de droits international et comparé du travail* (Brussels), Bruylant, 1997.

Valerio Speziale, born In Pescara (Italy) on 24 July 1954, is full professor of Labour Law and teaches at the University 'G. D'Annunzio' of Pescara – Chieti. He is a member of the directive committee of some important Italian Labour Law Reviews and the National Juridical Advisors Committee of the CGIL (the most important Italian Trade Union). He also works as a lawyer specialized in Labour and Civil Law. He has written a book and many essays on Labour Law matters regarding the most important subject (fixed term contracts, individual and collective dismissals, minimum wage legislation, strikes, collective agreements, etc.), some of them connected to general theory, like interpretation or epistemological characteristics of the matter.

Fernando Valdés Dal-Ré Professor of Labour Law, Complutense University (Madrid). Associated Professor of Universities of Paris X (Nanterre) and Lyon 2 (Lumière). General Attorney of State (1986–1990). Co-Director of reviews 'Relaciones Laborales' (2006–2014) and 'Derecho de las Relaciones Laborales' (2014). President of Spanish Association of Labour Law and Social Security (2008–2013). DHC, Valladolild University. Judge of Constitutional Court (2012).

Mario Volpe is professor of Economics at the University of Venice Ca' Foscari, where he teaches in graduate course Economic of Innovation, International Economics, and Tourism, economics. After graduation in Economics, he did post-graduate studies at New York University, where he got a research assistantship with Professor Leontief. His research interests are on applied economics, mainly on internationalization of SME's and local system of production. He was delegate for Ca' Foscari on relationship with Latin America. He acted as research coordinator of different EU- funded projects. He is actually local coordinator of the Horizon 2020 project 'Makers', on the role of SMEs in Industry 4.0.

Manfred Weiss, Emeritus Professor for Civil Law and Labour Law first since 1974 at the University of Hamburg and from 1977–2008 at the Goethe University in Frankfurt. Visiting Professor in many countries. Former President of the International Labour and Employment Relations Association (ILERA). Consultant to the EU Commission, to the ILO and to foreign Governments for many years. Many publications in labour law and industrial Relations.

Summary of Contents

Editors	v
Contributors	vii
Introduction *Adalberto Perulli*	1

PART I
The Enterprise Labour and Commercial Law Analysis — 15

CHAPTER 1
Law, Enterprise and Employers
Antoine Lyon-Caen — 17

CHAPTER 2
The Contractual Theory of the Firm and Some Good Reasons for Regulating the Employment Relationship
Francesco Denozza — 25

PART II
Enterprise Transformations, Externalization Process and Productive Decentralization — 39

CHAPTER 3
Productive Decentralization: An International and Comparative Perspective
Jean-Michel Servais — 41

Summary of Contents

CHAPTER 4
Enterprise Transformations, Externalization Processes and Productive Decentralization
Adrián Goldin 75

CHAPTER 5
Lost in Externalisation: A Regulatory Failure of Labour Law?
Riccardo Del Punta 93

CHAPTER 6
Multinational Firms and Local Development: How Global Value Chains Can Sustain Industrial Commons
Mariachiara Barzotto, Giancarlo Corò & Mario Volpe 99

PART III
Enterprise-Network and Enterprise-Groups: Trends and National/International Experience 119

CHAPTER 7
Enterprise-Network and Enterprise-Groups: Trends and National/International Experiences The Duty of Care
Sheldon Leader 121

CHAPTER 8
Enterprise Networks and Enterprise Groups
Orsola Razzolini 131

CHAPTER 9
Groups of Companies and Employment Contracts
Valerio Speziale 147

PART IV
Enterprise in the Collective Bargaining Process 159

CHAPTER 10
Collective Bargaining at the Transnational Level
Giuseppe Casale 161

CHAPTER 11
Japan's Decentralized Industrial Relations, Internal Flexicurity, and
Challenges Japan Faces
Takashi Araki 173

PART V
Enterprise in EU Law 197

A. Enterprises and the Courts 197

CHAPTER 12
The Enterprise, Labour and the Court of Justice
Jeff Kenner 199

CHAPTER 13
Appeals for Constitutional Protection *"Recurso de Amparo"*
Fernando Valdés Dal-Ré 249

B. Workers Participation in the Enterprise: Information and Consultation
Rights, Codetermination Dynamics and Firms Welfare 269

CHAPTER 14
Workers Participation in the Firm: Trends and Insights
Tiziano Treu 271

CHAPTER 15
Workers' Participation in the Enterprise in Germany
Manfred Weiss 293

CHAPTER 16
Workers Participation in the Enterprise: Welfare and Quality of Work
Agar Brugiavini 311

PART VI
The 'Constitutionalisation' of the Firm: Multinational Regulations in
the Global Context between Hard and Soft Law 333

Summary of Contents

CHAPTER 17
The 'Constitutionalisation' of the Firm: The Corporation as a Legal System
Andrea Pin 335

CHAPTER 18
The Theories of the Firm between Economy and Law
Adalberto Perulli 351

Bibliography 379

Index 409

Table of Contents

Editors	v
Contributors	vii
Introduction *Adalberto Perulli*	1

PART I
The Enterprise Labour and Commercial Law Analysis ... 15

CHAPTER 1
Law, Enterprise and Employers
Antoine Lyon-Caen ... 17

1.1	Power and Enterprise	18
1.2	Employer and Enterprise	21

CHAPTER 2
The Contractual Theory of the Firm and Some Good Reasons for
Regulating the Employment Relationship
Francesco Denozza ... 25

2.1	Introduction	25
2.2	Two Notions of the Firm	26
2.3	The Contractual View and the Mandatory Rules	28
2.4	The Nexus of Contract and the Notion of Entrepreneur	29
2.5	The Implications for the Employment Relationship	31
2.6	In a Contractual View, Is There a Role for Mandatory Rules? (A) A 'Coasean' Answer	32
2.7	Is There a Role for Mandatory Rules? (B) Three Reasons Why the Coasean Reasoning Often Does Not Hold	34

	2.7.1	Myopia or Short-Termism: The Bigger Pie Goes Out of Sight	34
	2.7.2	The Problem of Power: An Even Bigger Pie Is Always Looming on the Horizon of the Powerful	35
	2.7.3	Allocation and Distribution: The Slice, Not the Cake, Matters	36

PART II
Enterprise Transformations, Externalization Process and Productive Decentralization 39

CHAPTER 3
Productive Decentralization: An International and Comparative Perspective
Jean-Michel Servais 41

3.1	Introduction: A Variety of Firms, Production Processes and Forms of Jobs			42
	3.1.1	A Variety of Firms		42
	3.1.2	A Variety of Forms of Work		43
3.2	The Applicability of General Social Provisions to the Various Forms of Employment			44
	3.2.1	In a Particular Country		44
	3.2.2	Covering More than One Country		47
		3.2.2.1	Depending on the Type of Enterprise and on the Production Process	47
		3.2.2.2	Depending on the Modalities of Work	49
			3.2.2.2.1 International Labour Mobility	49
			3.2.2.2.2 Posted Workers	49
3.3	Specific Provisions			50
	3.3.1	Extension of or Assimilation to the Employment Relationship		51
	3.3.2	Special Protection		52
		3.3.2.1	Depending on the Type of Enterprise and on the Production Process	52
			3.3.2.1.1 SMEs	52
			3.3.2.1.2 Subcontracting	53
			3.3.2.1.3 Grouping of Enterprises	55
			3.3.2.1.3.1 Chains of Production	56
			3.3.2.1.3.2 'Complex' Employer	56
			3.3.2.1.3.3 Groups of Enterprises	57
			3.3.2.1.3.4 Common Activities	58
			3.3.2.1.4 Transfer of Enterprises	59
		3.3.2.2	Depending on the Modalities of Work	59
			3.3.2.2.1 Self-Employment	60
			3.3.2.2.2 Parasubodinazione	61

		3.3.2.2.3	Home-Based Work	62
		3.3.2.2.4	Apprenticeship	64
		3.3.2.2.5	Part-Time Work	64
		3.3.2.2.6	Fixed-Term and Temporary Work	66
			3.3.2.2.6.1 The Legal Situation of the Temporary Work Agency	67
			3.3.2.2.6.2 The Legal Situation of the User Company	69
3.4	Concluding Remarks: And Now?			71

CHAPTER 4
Enterprise Transformations, Externalization Processes and Productive Decentralization
Adrián Goldin   75

4.1	The Crisis of the Fordist Enterprise Model and the Process of Productive Decentralization			75
4.2	New Labour Emerging Problems			77
	4.2.1	Generalization of the Phenomenon and Blurring of the Status of the Parties Involved		77
		4.2.1.1	The Problem	77
		4.2.1.2	The Employer Status	78
		4.2.1.3	The Employee Status	80
	4.2.2	Degradation and Precarization		81
	4.2.3	The Effects on Industrial Relations		82
4.3	Productive Decentralization Techniques in MERCOSUR and in Chile			83
	4.3.1	General impact on Labour Law		83
	4.3.2	The Technical Regulations Used in MERCOSUR and in Chile		84
		4.3.2.1	Subcontracting	85
			4.3.2.1.1 Definition	85
			4.3.2.1.2 Attribution of Liability	87
			4.3.2.1.3 Equal Treatment	88
		4.3.2.2	Temporary Work Agencies	89
		4.3.2.3	Groups of Companies	90

CHAPTER 5
Lost in Externalisation: A Regulatory Failure of Labour Law?
Riccardo Del Punta   93

5.1	The Externalisations, That Is the Fragmented Enterprise	93
5.2	A Voice from the USA: The Fissured Workplace	94
5.3	Old Europe Already Knew	95

Table of Contents

5.4	The Equal Treatment Rule	95
5.5	The Vicarious Liability Rule	96
5.6	The Ban on the Subcontracting of Workers	96
5.7	A Regulatory Failure?	97

CHAPTER 6
Multinational Firms and Local Development: How Global Value Chains Can Sustain Industrial Commons
Mariachiara Barzotto, Giancarlo Corò & Mario Volpe 99

6.1	Introduction	99
6.2	Industrial Commons: Definition and Characteristics	102
6.3	How the Opening Up Processes Towards Global Economy Affect the Industrial Commons	104
6.4	The Need to Engage with Local and GVCs	107
6.5	Manufacturing Production and Offshoring Trends	108
6.6	Overview of the Research Methodology	110
6.7	Companies' Awareness of Industrial Commons	111
6.8	Some Conclusions and Questions for Further Research	116
Endnote		118

PART III
Enterprise-Network and Enterprise-Groups: Trends and National/International Experience 119

CHAPTER 7
Enterprise-Network and Enterprise-Groups: Trends and National/International Experiences The Duty of Care
Sheldon Leader 121

7.1	The Problem: Fragmented Responsibility and Integrated Production	121
7.2	New Forms of Accountability Within Corporate Groups	123
7.3	New Forms of Accountability in the Commercial Supply Chain	125
	7.3.1 Supply Chains and Sharing Responsibility for Damage Done to Third Parties	125
	7.3.2 Re-drawing the Boundary Lines: The Position of the Purchaser with 'Leverage'	127
7.4	Conclusion	129

CHAPTER 8
Enterprise Networks and Enterprise Groups
Orsola Razzolini 131

8.1	From the Vertical Firm to the Network Forms of Organization: Introduction	131

8.2	The Firm and the Networks under the Lens of New Institutional Economics, New Contractualism and Constitutionalism	132
8.3	The Search for the Employer in the Networks: The Single, Plural and Functional Pattern	136
8.4	The Italian Case of the Interfirm Network Agreement	140
8.5	Networks, Flexicurity and 'Organised Responsibility'	144

CHAPTER 9
Groups of Companies and Employment Contracts
Valerio Speziale — 147

9.1	Groups of Companies and the 'Group Interest'	147
9.2	Groups of Companies and the Crisis of the Unitary Concept of the Employer	148
9.3	The Absence of a General Legal Discipline of Groups of Companies at European Level	148
9.4	The Labour Discipline of Groups of Companies in Different Countries	149
9.5	The Role of the Jurisprudence Regarding 'Fraudulent Groups'	149
9.6	'Genuine' Groups of Companies and Labour Relations in Different Countries: The Co Employment Approach	150
9.7	The Need for a European Directive Regarding the Employment Contract in Groups	153
9.8	The Role of the Jurisprudence Regarding 'Genuine' Groups and the Co Employment Perspective	154
9.9	Co Employment in Groups of Companies	156

PART IV
Enterprise in the Collective Bargaining Process — 159

CHAPTER 10
Collective Bargaining at the Transnational Level
Giuseppe Casale — 161

10.1	Introduction	161
10.2	Transnational Collective Bargaining	162
10.3	Trade Union Responses at Transnational, Sectoral and Company Level	164
10.4	IFA and EFAs	165
10.5	Legal Framework	166
10.6	European Social Dialogue	167
10.7	The Future of Collective Bargaining at Transnational Level	169
10.8	Conclusion	171

Table of Contents

CHAPTER 11
Japan's Decentralized Industrial Relations, Internal Flexicurity, and
Challenges Japan Faces
Takashi Araki 173

11.1	Introduction: Decentralized Negotiation, Norm Flexibilization and Flexicurity	173
11.2	Legal Tools Regulating Working Conditions and Their Relationship	175
	11.2.1 European Model	175
	11.2.2 Japanese Model	177
11.3	Enterprise Unionism and Decentralized Industrial Relations in Japan	178
	11.3.1 Enterprise Unionism	178
	11.3.2 The Unique Nature of Japanese CBA	179
	11.3.3 Plural Unionism	180
	11.3.4 Japan's Cooperative Industrial Relations Developed under the Enterprise Unionism	181
11.4	Statutory Minimum Labor Standards and Their Flexibilization	182
	11.4.1 Worker Protective Laws	182
	11.4.2 Flexibilization of Minimum Labor Standards: Derogation Through LMAs	183
	11.4.3 Abuse of Derogation Mechanism	184
	11.4.4 Introduction of Works Councils?	185
11.5	Japanese Model of Flexicurity: Employment Security and Flexible Adjustment of Working Conditions in the Internal Labor Market	186
	11.5.1 Labor Contracts	186
	11.5.2 Work Rules	186
	11.5.3 The Duty to Draw Up Work Rules	186
	11.5.4 The Legal Effect of Work Rules and Their Unfavorable Modification	187
	11.5.5 Case Law on a "Reasonable Modification" of Work Rules	188
	11.5.6 Criteria for "Reasonableness"	190
11.6	Conclusion: Decentralized Industrial Relations with Internal Flexicurity	191
	11.6.1 Decentralized Industrial Relations	191
	11.6.2 Internal Flexicurity	192
	11.6.3 A Reconsideration of Statutory Regulations	193

PART V
Enterprise in EU Law 197

A. Enterprises and the Courts 197

CHAPTER 12
The Enterprise, Labour and the Court of Justice
Jeff Kenner 199

12.1	Introduction			199
12.2	Collective Redundancies			202
	12.2.1	Analysis of the CRD		202
	12.2.2	Case Law		204
	12.2.3	Ways Forward		214
12.3	Posted Workers, Public Procurement and 'Fair Competition' in the EU's Single Market			217
	12.3.1	The Posted Workers Directive		217
	12.3.2	Case Law		221
		12.3.2.1	Laval, *Commission v. Luxembourg* and Rüffert: Preventing or Promoting Social Dumping?	221
		12.3.2.2	Bundesruckerei and RegioPost: Posted Workers and Public Procurement – Tilting the Balance Towards the Social?	234
	12.3.3	Ways Forward		242
12.4	Concluding Remarks			247

CHAPTER 13
Appeals for Constitutional Protection *"Recurso de Amparo"*
Fernando Valdés Dal-Ré 249

13.1	A New Configuration of Appeals for Constitutional Protection *"Recurso de Amparo"*			249
13.2	Admissibility Requirements in Appeals for Constitutional Protection			255
	13.2.1	General Considerations		255
	13.2.2	Specific Constitutional Relevance as a Material Requirement or Condition for Admissibility		259
	13.2.3	Comments on the Traditional Requirements of Appeal Claims		260
		13.2.3.1	Deadline and Register Receiving the Appeal	261
		13.2.3.2	Procedural Nullity Incidents	262
		13.2.3.3	Observations on the Exhaustion of the Means of Challenge Foreseen in Procedural Rules: Article 44.1.a) General Public Act of the Constitutional Court (LOTC)	264
		13.2.3.4	Untimeliness of Appeals and Unification of Doctrine	265
13.3	Possible Pronouncements, Enforcement of Appeal Judgments and Irregularities in Processing the Appeal			266

Table of Contents

B. Workers Participation in the Enterprise: Information and Consultation Rights, Codetermination Dynamics and Firms Welfare — 269

CHAPTER 14
Workers Participation in the Firm: Trends and Insights
Tiziano Treu — 271

14.1	Divergent National Patterns and European Harmonization	271
14.2	The Continuum of Workers Participation: From Information to Board-Level Representation	273
14.3	The German Model and Its Foundations	274
14.4	European Harmonization of a Minimum Common Denominator	275
14.5	The Compromise Solution of the SE	277
14.6	Factors Affecting the Effectiveness of Participation	278
14.7	The Impact of the Recent Transformations of Work and of Firms Structure on Workers Participation	280
14.8	Management-Led Forms of Employees Involvement	281
14.9	Specialized and Financial Forms of Workers Participation	282
14.10	Acceptance and Innovation of Workers Participation: The Impact of the Individualization of Employment Relations	283
14.11	The Impact of Changing Enterprise Structures: Group Enterprises and 'Network Contracts'	284
14.12	Participation in the 'Fluid Enterprise'	286
14.13	Participation in the Corporation as 'Commons'	288

CHAPTER 15
Workers' Participation in the Enterprise in Germany
Manfred Weiss — 293

15.1	Introduction		293
15.2	The Works Council System		294
	15.2.1	The Basic Organizational Structure	294
	15.2.2	The Link to the Trade Unions	296
	15.2.3	The Legal Position of the Works Council Members	297
	15.2.4	The Financial Structure and the Basic Duties	298
	15.2.5	The Arbitration Committee	298
	15.2.6	The Works Council's Rights of Participation	299
15.3	Workers' Representation in the Supervisory Board		301
	15.3.1	Three Different Models	301
	15.3.2	The Function of the Supervisory Board	301
	15.3.3	The Model of the Coal, Iron and Steel Industries	302
	15.3.4	The Model of 1952	303
	15.3.5	The Model of 1976	304
	15.3.6	The Legal Position of Employee Representatives	305
	15.3.7	The Implementation in Practice	306
15.4	Attempt of an Assessment		307

CHAPTER 16
Workers Participation in the Enterprise: Welfare and Quality of Work
Agar Brugiavini 311

16.1	Workers Participation	311
16.2	European Participation Index	312
16.3	Literature Review	313
16.4	The Data	314
16.5	Descriptive Analysis	315
16.6	Conclusions	331

PART VI
The 'Constitutionalisation' of the Firm: Multinational Regulations in
the Global Context between Hard and Soft Law 333

CHAPTER 17
The 'Constitutionalisation' of the Firm: The Corporation as a Legal System
Andrea Pin 335

17.1	Introduction	335
17.2	Soft and Hard Law in Global Context and the Role of Firms	339
17.3	Firms as Legal Orders: Theories and Components	344
17.4	The Firm as a Legal Order	344
17.5	The Morality of Firms	345
17.6	Some Possible Consequences of the Constitutionalisation of the Firm	348

CHAPTER 18
The Theories of the Firm between Economy and Law
Adalberto Perulli 351

18.1	The Theory of the Firm: Economic and Legal Perspectives	351
18.2	What Is the Firm? The Incomplete Answers of Economy and Law	354
18.3	Transaction Costs, Relational Contracts, and Neo-hierarchy	359
18.4	Contractual Theory of the Firm	363
18.5	The Theory of the Agency	366
18.6	The Theory of the Firm Beyond the Contract: Reticular and Systemic Theories	369
18.7	The Firm in the Non-standard Economy Researches	372
18.8	Going Back to Law in Order to Reform the Governance of the Firm	374

Bibliography	379
Index	409

Introduction

Adalberto Perulli

This book takes its form from an interdisciplinary confrontation on the enterprise and from its different profiles of economic, political, juridical, and social relevancy. The enterprise is the main actor of the globalisation process that has involved the economic and juridical systems of old nation-states, projecting its activity in differentiated contexts and playing an increasingly important role not only in economic activities, but also in public policies. We are facing a historical period where the enterprise is subject to several solicitations and demands not only in the economic, but also juridical, ethical and social field. The enterprise is a complex structure precisely due to its relevancy and its being at the centre of a system of power spreading globalisation. Therefore, it shows different – and sometimes conflicting – issues and rationalities in its paradigm; for this reason, people expect a balance among the powers existing within the enterprise (shareholders', managers' and workers' power). In its relationship with the 'environment' (with other enterprises, with institutions, with stakeholders), the enterprise is increasingly called for being 'socially responsible'. Unfortunately, this reveals only as something written on codes of conduct, and is not matter-of-factly implemented, especially when the enterprise acquires complex and multinational structure.

Facing this complexity related to the enterprise, the juridical literature – albeit being abundant – has one determined focus: the enterprise as an economic actor, the enterprise as a nexus of contracts, the enterprise as activity and organisation, the enterprise as juridical set of rules, the enterprise as political subject, the enterprise as social community, the enterprise as representative of the industrial relation system, etc. Rarely is the enterprise being unitarily analysed in its multi-disciplinary contents; and even more rarely does the juridical literature satisfactorily answer the question: what is the enterprise? Which are its profiles of economic, social and juridical relevancy?

This volume proposes a research trying to help whoever is interested to know the different aspects that compose the enterprise, without leaving aside the necessity to re-build a cognitive, theoretical and scientifically controlled paradigm.

The Part 1 of this book deals with enterprise theory, with commercial law, law & economic analysis (Perulli, Denozza) and labour law (Lyon-Caen) close examinations. The concept of enterprise has economic origins, and the juridical system attempts to translate this notion into normative terms, which, on the other hand remains widely undetermined. According to part of the doctrine, this notion acts as a sort of 'black box', and can be inflected differently according to how the juridical system conceives the enterprise (company law, labour law, trade law, etc.).

In particular, Perulli's paper analyses the different meanings of the theory of enterprise, starting from the classic question: what is an enterprise with regards to the market? The institutional theory, which dates back to the pioneering work of Ronald Coase, allows us to give the first answer, which lies in the reduction of the transaction costs through the use of hierarchy. The neo-institutional doctrine of the enterprise is largely useful for labour law, because it explains, in different terms but coincident with the ones of the law doctrine, the meaning of the authority (hierarchy) and of the subordination of the employer, highlighting the actual labour relation as an example of contract that allows a considerable reduction of transaction costs. The economic doctrine is significant also because it conceives the enterprise as not a mere 'production function' – according to the neo-classical economy's thought– but as an 'instituted order', which cannot operate without certain normative and regulative processes. However, within the enterprise theory, the neo-institutional approach coexists with other theoretical perspectives, which tend instead to undervalue the juridical and sociological dimension of the enterprise and its organisation. On one hand, the theory of the *nexus of contracts*, on the other hand, the *theory of the agency*: both approaches show evident limits in understanding the phenomenon of the enterprise. The contractual theory (nexus of contracts), the Author claims, excludes all references to the dimension of power, which is, on the other hand, central in order to understand the functioning of the organisation; further, this theory assigns a lowermost role to the juridical regulation, by all means overvaluing the rules freely established among the parties. On the other hand, the theory of the agency considers the labour relation as a mere principal-agent relation, where the main goal is to avoid opportunist behaviours on the part of the agent, ignoring the complexity of the (juridical) regulation within the relations among the various subjects that participate to the organisation. For these reasons, according to Perulli, the juridical theory of enterprise should in part free itself from the analytic method proposed by economic theories, valorising an axiological-juridical dimension where the enterprise – conceived as an entity with numerous and differentiated rationalities coexisting together – is called for activating processes of democratisation and of constitutionalisation in order to found its own social legitimateness.

Also Denozza's paper deals with the problem of the enterprise's juridical nature, and analyses the influence of the definition of enterprise as network on the regulation of labour relations (according to him, firms are not real entities, but social constructions), with special reference to two orders of matters. On one hand, the protection of workers' rights from the employer's attempt to avoid complying with his/her duties; on the other hand, a research on the reasons that may found the recourse to imperative norms guaranteeing special protection to workers. Regarding the first point, the Author claims that the function of employer/entrepreneur in the enterprise theory requires a particular strictness in the prevention of duty-elusion behaviours, since the war to the latter is not only a matter of decency, but also a matter of efficiency. In the second point, Denozza underlines the lack of 'preconceived reasons' in a contractual field in order to define the interests of the parties; on the contrary, from an efficiency point of view, the best result is achieved by common agreement among the parties. This contractual matrix way of thinking results as unsuitable in many cases and for this reason the recourse to imperative norms regulating the labour relation is still justified. Therefore, while crediting contractual theories with understanding that firms are not communities created by involuntary or by an authoritative act of foundation, the relevant role played by imperative norms cannot be underestimated, especially in the cases in which the employer's interests do not match with the ones of the enterprise in general.

In his essay, on the contrary, Antoine Lyon-Caen starts from the assumption that the enterprise (defined as 'social sciences black box'), while having generated a huge literature, is still a substantially obscure matter (either from economic theory, law and social sciences points of view). Therefore, the Author proposes to survey the notion of enterprise, first reflecting on the pair 'power and enterprise' and then on the pair 'employer and enterprise'.

Inside and through enterprises a vast plurality of power is revealed: the ability of autonomous action of a market power is utilised to identify an enterprise and to build a competition law for the enterprise provided with decisional autonomy. The dissociation between 'corporation' and 'enterprise' offers the Author further hints to reflect on the employer's managing power and on the managers' organisational power, defined as 'power on powers'. This meta-power, especially in multinational enterprises, overcomes the national borders, determining a juridical pluralism and a normativity on global scale. Recalling the crisis of the unitary and rigid notion of 'employer' further to the continuous fragmentation and disintegration of enterprises and the consequential multi-polarity and multi-laterality of labour relations which results in the notion of co-employment, Lyon-Caen suggests going back to reason upon the enterprise and on the *functions* of the employer (and no longer on the notion of contractor, by now lacking meaning) in order to study the complexity of the recent evolution of labour law.

The Part 2 faces – through a juridical point of view – some complex enterprise evolutionary aspects, being outsourcing and productive decentralisation. These processes are analysed both from an economic point of view (Corò), and international relations and international law points of view (Servais); both from national and compared law points of view (Goldin, Del Punta), with particular reference to the consequences that these processes determine in the field of labour relations. Corò's article aims to analyse the relationship between the process of internationalisation undertaken by companies and the industrial commons of the regions where enterprises have their seat (human capital, subsidies, usage and supply of networks, institutions). Being committed to local dimension is still important for enterprises competing at a global level, even if they still benefit from having international presence. The Author analyses how leader enterprises may favour local resources' sustainability in order to be involved in the 'glocal value chains'. Through case-studies of mid-to-large manufacturing companies, the article's aim is to detect which may be the territorial stimulus in order to increase competitiveness and how enterprises may enact positive outsourcing, nourishing the territories where they are set. The final aim is to understand which may be the critical factors in order to improve companies and the factors to maintain attractiveness and competitiveness in the attempt to balance and global and local involvement. Local and global relations are not mutually exclusive: on the contrary, the local network can increase the company's international appeal (fundamental is the company's interaction with the network of suppliers and workers, and with local education processes). For this reason, companies can represent an important factor of growth and development of territory – considered as one of the stakeholders – where they have their seat, while deciding to invest capitals abroad.

Servais goes along the rapid technological and economic liberalisation changes that induced to re-plan the processes of production and gave the enterprise a larger freedom in the organisation of labour and in the configuration itself of relations within labour, which is often precarious, also because it has developed outside the classic field of Industrial Relations. In his article, the Author does not aim to deplore this evolution and to invoke the barriers that traditionally protect social rights, since it would be unrealistic and inefficient using them to improve the conditions of whoever may be vulnerable. Servais rather aims to identify which institutions and guarantees are already in use and which are their outcomes in order to improve workers' income, life conditions and bargaining power, with particular reference to European and international scenario (and considering the potential of guarantees to be spread).

In the first part, after an introduction on the different forms of production processes and contractual typologies of labour, the Author examines the applicability of the general social provisions to the various forms of labour organisation and to contracts. In the second part, the Author focuses on the special measures adopted to adjust the protective norms to both workers' and companies' interests, analysing the regulatory and institutional factors that may lead to new forms of security on the workplace, as well.

In the conclusion, the Author states that equal and global social justice is out of reach, since its implementation would require a world sovereign state, which does not exist. However, we may look for actual improvements to be adapted to our modern social-economic context (like Dutch flexicurity). When precarious forms of labour increase, the protection of labour cannot be compared to the one of steady labour relations, and the institution of security regimes must be based on contributors and residents, rather than on the typology of contractual relation. As regards to labour contracts, it is not easy to tell which are subordinate or autonomous: some countries have elaborated and intermediate category like para-subordination, in order to identify their economic features. Other states underline the importance of liable or subsidiary responsibility, in order to remedy the fragmentation of companies and the separation between power and responsibility. Another choice is the strengthening of representation and collective bargaining, to protect precarious workers.

Also Goldin deals with the mutations of the enterprise induced by the substitution of the Fordist model of enterprise with a fragmented and outsourced organised structure. The cycle of production is segmented and constituted by different units coordinated and linked each other. This cooperation led to the development of a network of companies and to a re-conception of the process of outsourcing, once limited only to less strategic and qualified activities. To realise the process of outsourcing, various contractual typologies are used (classic, like transportation or agency contract and new, like franchising and manufacturing), and the responsibility of the enterprise results as blurred in the latter. According to the Author, the new forms of enterprise disorganise labour law. The first problem is represented by the individuation of the 'businessman' who has responsibilities as employer, beyond who actually appears as employer ('pluralisation of businessman'). Outsourcing has led to two typologies of problems: on one hand, the erosion and pluralisation of the contractor's figure, with difficulties in individuating the actual employer; on the other hand, and increase of atypical workers (autonomous and economically dependent) subject to a weakened protection compared to standard workers. So, it is necessary to reduce the different amount of protection that very often differentiates workers in enterprises and workers in outsourced branches. In the last part, the Author analyses how subcontracts and contracts of agency have developed in the Mercosur countries.

According to Del Punta, the fragmentation of the enterprise through increasingly outsourcing activities and the consequent decline of hierarchically organised internal labour have led to complex relations that do not fit to the concept of labour as a bilateral and personal contract. The Author analyses three matters raised by the phenomena of outsourcing; they are apparently separated but results as being linked: how to guarantee a satisfactory implementation of labour standards in the fragmented enterprises; who actually takes on responsibility towards workers; who is the employer. Before opening to flexibility, some systems have tried to protect workers even in case of subcontract or productive outsourcing, forcing the contractor to comply with liable responsibility towards the subcontractor's workers. The ambitious aim of such normative is to discourage fictitious subcontracts, that is to say the ones consisting in a mere supply of workers. Two matters lie unsatisfactorily unanswered: whether liable responsibility should be applied to all productive chain; whether it is right to insist on the defence of the consistency of the system based on subordination, or, rather, to invent new criteria with the aim to select good subcontractors, or, rather, to concentrate on the implementation of labour standards, even if the actual employer is different from the formal one. Anyway, the most relevant problem appears when outsourcing goes beyond national borders: here legislation is unable to adequate. We must take into consideration the possibility that the excess of regulation may drive companies to enter the global market.

In the Part 3, the enterprise is seen in a group and network perspective, which represents the most significant forms acquired by productive structures both to international and internal markets field (Leader). In this perspective, the juridical mechanisms of re-composition of the figure of the employer and of responsibility charges deriving from labour relations are analysed through the instruments of 'co-employment' (Speziale), of social and economic unity of joint-employers.

Leader deals with the problem of the dual movement of contemporary enterprises: the integrated production, which overcomes the boundaries of corporations and the fragmentation of responsibilities. Further, the matter is connected to the tension among forces and production relations and to the evolving framework of responsibility.

In the second part, the Author analyses the on-going transformations, such as the new forms of responsibility inside groups and inside distribution chains.

In conclusion, Leader claims that a synthesis between the fundamental principles of corporation and trade law may be possible, and that the gap between the development of integrated production and the weak protection offered by norms regulating the process of production can be bridged thanks to the notion of 'duty of care'.

Speziale analyses the group of enterprises formed by companies that have juridical autonomy and carry out the same entrepreneurial activity in order to obtain a competitive advantage; each company thus becomes part of the production chain. There is a strong integration among the companies that pursue a group strategy, although carrying out different entrepreneurial activities.

What is missing at European level is a general definition of group of enterprises; at international level, there are big differences in the labour discipline linked to groups of enterprises. The subject responsible for contractual obligation towards workers is not identified.

The aim of the group is to create a unitary enterprise with different levels of specialisation of the product entrusted to the single enterprise.

The bilateral structure of the labour contract is not always suitable to the group, since the difficulty in finding the actual responsible employer. Therefore, a discipline of labour contract within these juridical entities is needed, both at collective and individual level, in order to avoid opportunistic behaviours, to guarantee transparency, to attribute the mandatory effects of the contract to whoever makes use of the activity of workers, equally distributing the responsibilities. The Author observes that within the lack of legal discipline, the role played by jurisprudence is fundamental since, both restraining fraudulent behaviours and defining the hypothesis of co-employment, it has influenced the Italian legislator in founding the groups of enterprises on the concept of 'company carrying out activities of direction and control on another company', whereby the concepts of direction and control within holdings are different from the directional power in the traditional labour contract.

The network forms of organisation are at the core of Razzolini's analysis: they represent a challenge for labour law, since they undermine the idea of employer as single and indivisible entity whose juridical boundaries correspond to the hierarchical enterprise's boundaries, in order to attribute responsibilities. This employer/entrepreneur/enterprise equation and the description in atomist terms derive from the necessity of not considering an entrepreneur as responsible for someone else's actions, thus guaranteeing to entrepreneurs that cooperate within integrated economic processes to maintain distinct juridical personalities in order to attribute responsibilities. This atomist vision reveals as weak and often transforms into an instrument of elusion of responsibilities. Under a labour law profile, the Author wonders to which extent the employer/entrepreneur can freely choose some forms of integration, since this freedom undermines also traditional countermeasures of the enterprise, like public actions and collective bargaining. In particular, these issues arise from the context of networks.

Therefore, according to Speziale the Italian normative on network con tracts can be considered as the first attempt to shift the attention of employment protection from single legal entities to the network's economic activity. If this outcome is thoroughly fulfilled, in the future the network will be an instrument in order to guarantee an organised and transparent responsibility instead of irresponsibility. The Author underlines that the importance the normative attributes to 'common program', 'group interest', 'compensative advantages' represents the first attempt to shift the attention from single entities to the group's economic activity, in order to re-align the legal boundaries of the enterprise with its economic reality. Shifting the attention on the network's economic activity, we face the risk of the creation of a new form of hierarchy, rather than a form of equal collaboration; however, in spite of some weak points, the networks of enterprises can have a positive role if their members share responsibilities (counterbalancing workers' flexibility in the network/security in the workplace).

In the Part 4, the enterprise is analysed through the prism of collective bargaining processes that take place at company level, both with reference to the extent of international and transnational collective agreement with framework agreements on workers' fundamental rights and on the promotion of CSR praxis (Casale), and to national extent, with particular reference to the experience of the systems – like Japan (Araki) – that have historically developed the company level of bargaining.

According to Araki, two of the main contemporary matters related to labour law are the outsourcing of industrial relations and the modalities of adaptation of protection norms suitable to the various typologies of labour contracts.

Outsourcing and flexibility's aim is to make norms more adaptable given the market's fluidity, but at the same time they entail the risk to weaken the bargaining power and to lower social power. Hence, we can observe the fundamental importance to find a balance between flexibility and security. The Author shows how industrial relations have developed in Japan (as a matter of fact, outsourced relations at company level have developed long since, by now) and the level of balance between flexibility and security reached, comparing the development of the two elements in the European framework. Japan shows examples of outsourced industrial relations, of labour protection norms' flexibilisation and a unique model of flexicurity.

In the conclusion, the Author underlines how in Japan the system of industrial relations at company level has led to the application of collective contracts only in single companies, and this allows to satisfy workers' needs in a rapid and flexible way (stability of employment and lowering of working conditions), but it has also led to a lowered bargaining power among parties. The internal flexibility balances the employment security with the flexible regulation of working conditions; therefore, we can state that in any given enterprise we reach equilibrium by balancing the guarantee of the workplace with the flexibility of working conditions. But this type of flexicurity can only be applied to people benefitting of standard labour contracts: for this reason, the system is not balanced for those who have atypical labour contacts, leading us to reconsider the nature and efficacy of State laws.

Casale's essay develops the topic related to the right to international collective bargaining, as linked to freedom of association, a value promoted by the International Labour Organization (ILO) and representing an instrument of governance of labour market. Globalisation influencing the market and the outsourcing of industrial relations are a new challenge to the actual implementation of the right to collective bargaining, since it requires to industrial relations greater transnational cooperation and coordinated answers by employers and workers' unions at company and transnational level. International Framework Agreements (IFA) (IFA between a global and multinational union federation) for example are the result of a negotiation at company level, and are differentiated by form and content, often refer to the ILO's fundamental principles, but there are some uncertainties about their nature and their effects. The Transnational Collective Bargaining (TCBs) are practises of collective bargaining between employers and workers whose aims are reaching international agreements, regardless the contracts' nature; they are not binding, because a specific international juridical framework is missing, so they are unlikely to be actually implemented and respected.

At European level, the Commission has already favoured – since early 2000 – the development of a general framework of action based on a series of rules for employers and workers, underlining their beneficial role for companies and the market. The asymmetry between the totality of enterprises and the territoriality of representatives is, according to the Author, the limit to the future development of efficient industrial relations at global level (companies go global, but workers remain local).

However, we need a legal juridical framework in order to expand the competences of European Union (EU), to regulate the transnational aspects of collective agreements. Such measures would contribute to a better functioning of the common market and would satisfy in a more efficient way the workers' and employers' needs. Eventually, the Author wonders whether the European Commission is ready to promote a juridical framework for Transnational Company Agreements (TCAs).

In the Part 5, the enterprise, while profit-oriented and pursuing free private initiative logics, is analysed in its social dimension, as being conditioned by political and institutional mechanisms such as jurisprudence of Courts (CGE, Constitutional Court) (Kenner, Valdes Del Re), the mechanisms of participation of workers to the management of the enterprise, especially in the Germany system (Weiss) but also, even though with far weaker instruments, in other European countries (Treu), and the 'constitutionalisation' of the firm (Pin). These institutional vectors affect some fundamental aspects of private economic initiative, driving the enterprise also to social aims, creating the conditions for a social vision of the enterprise and for the activation of endogenous mechanisms of social nature, like company welfare systems (Brugiavini).

Kenner's analysis is focused on the detachment between the standard two-dimensional model of labour contract and the multi-dimensional mutations of contractual agreements and of the enterprise's organisation in twenty-first century. European Regulations on labour have been issued when the relations were still two-dimensional. However, in the course of time, enterprises got subject to privatisation, liberalisation and globalisation phenomena, that were permitted also by the market liberalisations set up by the EU. In the Article, the Author faces two matters deriving from the transformations of the relationship between enterprise and workers, focusing on the jurisprudence of the EU Court of Justice.

First, the Author analyses how the Court of Justice interprets and applies the concepts of 'employer', 'enterprise' and 'institution' in articulated company scenarios, included in the range of application of EU directive on collective dismissals. The Author wonders, in the light of the Court's pronouncements, to which extent the directive pursues the goal to protect workers in complex contexts, in which also decisions are adopted at a global level (cases: *AEK v. Fujitsu Siemens Computers, Lyttle, USDAW and Wilson, Rabal Canas*).

Then, the Author examines the sentences of the Court on the validity of collective contracts and national or local laws, as regards to working conditions, which are included in the range of application of the Community directive in matter of seconded workers and/or public contracts. The cases, in particular, are about the application of the secondment directive 96/71 and the public contracts directive 2014/24. On the basis of the analysis of this jurisprudence, the Author wonders to which extent the provisions of such directives may be used in order to protect workers, easing the most harmful effects of social dumping (cases: *Laval, Commission v. Luxembourg, Rüffert*).

In the conclusion, Kenner observes that the analysis of the Court of Justice's jurisprudence in matter of collective dismissals, seconded workers and public contracts shows that the EU's labour law and the Single Market's social protection – initially planned in order to guarantee the protection of workers also in specific cases like transnational reorganisation and subcontract – are by now inefficient. Further, the Single Market has boosted globalisation, opening new alternatives to enterprises (subcontracts, creation of branches, etc.) and this led to a growing labour fragmentation and to gaps in terms of social protection. Along with the EU's territorial expansion, also social inequalities have been spreading among Member States, bringing back the problem of social dumping.

Valdes del Re's article is developed around the proceeding for the constitutional appeal in Spain which, following the 2007 reform of the 'public General Act' of the Constitutional Court, underwent not only formal modifications, but by now it allows the protection of fundamental rights and freedoms so as provided in the Article 154 and section 1, Chapter 2, title 1 of the Spanish Constitution. The acceptability of the appeal is validated by the violation of a right or a fundamental freedom, only if it bears a 'specific constitutional relevance' (constitutional relevance is by now a substantial element and it must always be valid and it precedes the exam on the merit of the appeal). This requirement means that the mere violation of a fundamental right will not be per se enough to validate the appeal: consequently, this new model has transformed the previous configuration of the appeal. Following the legislative news, the discussion is going to deal with the actual margin in order to resort to constitutional protection as instrument for subjective protection of specifically violated fundamental rights. Further, the Author wonders whether this new procedural requirement has changed the substantial nature of the appeal. However, according to the Author, every attempt to modify the constitutional procedure to protect social rights in something different and detached from protection aims would clash with the Constitution; this happens not only if we exclude this type of appeal, but also if the protection is only apparent, or if we have obstacles, or the protection is merely subsidiary or conditioned to other aims of the process. The Author claims that, regardless the appeal's new requirements, the latter must anyway be applied in a coherent way on the basis of the object of the protection one is intended to pursue, in order to avoid that, with the objectification of the appeal, the constitutional protection becomes almost subsidiary or subordinate.

Weiss's paper is specifically about the workers' participation in Germany's enterprises, whose origin dates back to the twentieth century, and it is particularly focused on two topics: the functioning and the right to participation to Work Councils, which includes the access to information, consultation, right of veto, right of co-determination; the participation of workers to supervisory boards of big companies.

Introduction

The Author surveys three different models of representation of workers in the supervisory boards (the model of iron, coal and steel industry; the 1952 model, the 1976 model). Weiss focuses on the status of workers' representatives that benefit of equal rights as regards shareholders' representatives, and on the principle 'the interest of the enterprise', which represents a point of reference for the decision of the supervisory Board, both regarding shareholders' representatives and workers' representatives.

Eventually, the positive aspects and the criticalities of the participative system are assessed in its complex. This offers to German economy a significant advantage compared to other countries, because it is able to contrast the crisis thanks to the trust in the permanent dialogue between company manager and workers' representatives. The German workers' representation system is situated in a context with such historical, cultural and institutional peculiarities, that it could hardly work if exported in other contexts.

According to Treu, the participation of workers in the enterprise has a long and controversial history, which reflects the different positions of the workers' movement and parties upon the role of Unions and workers in democratic Countries. The long controversy on EU directives for the promotion of different forms of participation of workers in the enterprise, which confirms the importance attributed by Europe to the enterprise's internal dynamics and to the promotion of Union relations, is the evidence of the differences among the various European systems. The forms of participation, while being different in the Countries where they are adopted, have common elements and they differ for the modality and the intensity of their influence on the company decisional process, instead: we get even to 'institutional' forms of participation, where representatives are present in the enterprises' directional bodies, like, for example, in Germany and North-Western Europe, where the social and political conditions allowed the rooting and the development of participation.

The European intention to start harmonising national models of participation has faced some obstacles, such as the different national traditions of Member States and the strategies of the national actors, like governments, social parties and the relative public institutions. Therefore, Europe was able to successfully promote only the forms of participation that had already been accepted and were already present in the most part of the states (consultation and information) and that may affect to a relevant extent the company behaviour.

Whatever may be the extent of the participation, the influence of the workers' representatives on the company's choices is limited, since they are a minority in the boards of administration; however, the influence also depends on other factors like the ability of representatives to uphold their reasons before authorities, the ability to create alliances with other stakeholders, but also the structure of the decisional process plays a fundamental role. The transformations of the company structure occurred in the last years have weakened the presence and the Union's cohesion, leading to an 'individualization of labour management relations'. The involvement of workers in the single productive unities has revealed itself as an efficient instrument to promote innovation and productivity and, according to the Author, it's the Union's duty to insert these forms of 'micro participation' in the widest context of industrial relations.

In Brugiavini's essay the attention is focused on factual observations and some data, such as the European Participation Index as a possible measure of the strength of the workers' participation. The A. provides also a graphical analysis of the job quality and workers satisfaction based on the data from the Survey on Health, Ageing and Retirement in Europe (SHARE), which shows that the Nordic countries report higher quality of work vis-à-vis Sothern countries in Europe, possibly also related to the effect of workers' participation in the organisation of the workplace. According to Brugiavini, one important issue is the limitations that women face in the work place, which do not seem to have voice even when participation is advocated.

In Pin's chapter, the topic analysed is the possibility of 'constitutionalisation of the enterprise'. With this term, we allude to the theoretical perspective conceived by Teubner, which is intended to regulate public interests with private regimes (Pin), and to different normative envisioning intended to give the enterprise the sense of responsibility for the social consequences of its behaviour. According to Pin, the hypothesis of enterprise constitutionalisation is to be intended in considering this entity as a 'micro-constitutional system', having inside different groups of interest and developing its own dynamics and mechanisms. The need for constitutionalisation is as much larger nowadays, in the light of the growing trans-nationality involving enterprises, and since, as part of the doctrine claims, 'today is the law that should follow the needs of the economy and of the market'. Constitutionalising enterprises is a complex operation; for this reason, the Author starts by analysing two main aspects characterising enterprises: the variable nature of the term enterprise, which has broadened in the course of time, including an ever-growing series of interests (internationalisation of conflicts of interests); the mutability of the constitution in the course of time and space: we are assisting to global phenomena of constitutionalisation, which crystallise political processes and juridical tendencies, giving them constitutional relevancy.

The process of constitutionalisation of enterprises would be beneficial both from an epistemological and normative points of view. It matter-of-factly can conceptualise the diversity of rights and of the beneficiaries of rights that constitute a common framework in the enterprise; the rights would derive from the enterprise as an institution.

Originally, the idea of constitutionalising the enterprise was linked to sociology, but it should be re-considered also from a more strictly normative point of view (as a matter of fact, according to Teubner, the constitution should be broadened to include enterprises as forms of social constitutions). Only if enterprises go beyond the maximisation of profits, the constitution of states and of enterprises can coincide. Recalling Santi-Romano, we can consider enterprises as juridical systems that work as a system in which their very same institutions produce essential rules for the existence of enterprises themselves.

In conclusion, the constitutionalisation of the enterprise is a useful model, since it would not impose a rigid structure, but it would grant the enterprise itself a larger legal protection (Hobby Lobby USA Supreme Court sentence). The expansion of the protection would regard the nature of the enterprise and the interests that go beyond the merely economic aim (environment protection, working conditions, etc.). The enterprise shifts from being a hierarchy of powers concentrated on the maximisation of profits, to an institutional structure, being composed of different powers and interests.

PART I The Enterprise Labour and Commercial Law Analysis

CHAPTER 1
Law, Enterprise and Employers

Antoine Lyon-Caen

Economic theory has a number of failings that are hard to accept. For example, enterprise has generated a vast literature while remaining a mystery. We can easily believe that *'le statut de l'entreprise est au cœur du problème politique central des ... économies de marché '*.[1] But it should be equally easy to convince ourselves that *'les économies de marché disposent peut être d'une pensée du marché; elles n'ont pas de pensée de l'entreprise'*.[2]

In reality, economic theory is not alone in needing to recognise its failure.

In fact, it would not be an exaggeration to claim that enterprise continues to be a poorly identified scientific subject. Whenever large fields or categories of knowledge are explored in depth, their persistent difficulties in understanding enterprise inevitably become apparent.[3]

In order to discuss enterprise, the dominant economic theory uses notions that only offer a limited understanding of it. When considering the possible coordination mechanisms involved when individuals interact in their economic actions (economic theory), it cannot fail to note that enterprise must coordinate its actions within the market of products, the employment market, and the capital market to mention only a few. This can be described rather evocatively as a way of coordinating within markets.[4] And this is the situation that the dominant economic theory, in its various forms, seems incapable of grasping in full. Thus, today's contract theory conceives each management operation in

---

1. Olivier Favereau, *Quelle gouvernance pour l'entreprise post-crise*, Entreprise et histoire, n°57, 239 (décembre 2007).
2. Olivier Favereau, *Entreprise: la grande déformation*, Paris, Parole et silence, 11 (2014).
3. Blanche Segrestin, Baudoin Roger, Stéphane Vernac (eds), *L'entreprise. Point aveugle du savoir*, Editions Sciences humaines (2014).
4. François Eymard-Duvernay, *Economie politique de l'entreprise*, La Découverte, Collection Repères (2004).

terms of contractual relations but does not take into account the overall production process or the organisation of contractual relations other than by means of a rather vague principle of corporate governance that is barely that of the share value. The powers that can be linked or attributed to enterprise, or to some enterprises also, remain in the shade.

This shadow is not dispersed by the more classic sociology that extends into the collectivity or community of subjects presumed to be enterprises.

As far as the law is concerned, it mainly considers enterprise in terms of the legal personality of the company or other legal form.

The aim of management theory is to study the mechanisms and procedures of enterprise management in depth. Its tendency to borrow and combine concepts and categories developed and used by other sciences is not only a strong point but undoubtedly also a limit to the interpretations proposed.

To sum up, even if this brief overview is almost a caricature, I believe it would be sensible – and I hope you will agree with me – to consider enterprises today as the black box of the social sciences.

In this context, what goal should we pursue here? It might be useful to present and comment on an extensive interdisciplinary work programme that is currently underway, although this is no easy task given its scale.[5] We also put forward a rather unique way to approach this work, which is more limited than the programme and more focused on issues of interest to jurists.

Leaving scholarly considerations aside, it is clear that the concept of enterprise belongs to our everyday language. We all refer to it without worrying about being particularly precise. It may be interesting to find out what changes the enterprise considered urges or obliges us to make, and how it suggests or gradually demands that we revise different categories and their uses.

This brief investigation can be carried out along two pathways, or rather by focusing on two concepts concerning law and the social sciences: *power* and the *employer*.

1.1 POWER AND ENTERPRISE

Jurists find it difficult to speak of enterprise, overcoming the allusive and vague use of the term. To overcome these difficulties we must first identify their origin. One such difficulty derives from the weight of wide-reaching classifications, which the analytical language of jurists cannot easily avoid. One of these wide-reaching classifications limits or even hinders our comprehension of

---

5. The results of this programme are described in Baudoin Roger (eds) *L'entreprise, formes de la propriété et responsabilités sociales*, Paris Collège des Bernardins (2012); Favereau, *supra* n. 2; Segrestin, Roger, Vernac, *supra* n. 3; Jean-Philippe Robé, Antoine Lyon-Caen, Stéphane Vernac (eds), *Multinationals and constitutionalization of the world power system*, Routledge (2016); *see also* Jean-Philippe Robé, *Le temps du monde de l'entreprise*, Paris Dalloz, Coll. A droit ouvert (2015).

enterprise. An enterprise has hardly any substance compared to the classification test between people and things (or goods), because this is what is involved. Given that it is not a person – even though a certain doctrine would like it to recognised as such[6] – the enterprise must be shut up in the category of things. This classification ensures that a company will maintain its obscurity. It is certainly not a set of goods, or company assets.

En route, another source of confusion was mentioned. It derives from the distinction – one that is as necessary as too swiftly forgotten – between propositions that are descriptive and analytical, and those that are prescriptive – for which the definition of doctrine should be reserved. Enterprise has undeniably suffered from the denial of this distinction. In fact, this has given rise to a true doctrine[7] that has ultimately acted as a hindrance to the understanding of enterprise.

At least two of the various analytical propositions deserve a closer look on the basis of the claims they make but also due to the limits that they fail to overcome.

In the field of labour law drawn upon by the former type of analysis, enterprise occupies a particular position. Although not always named and, above all, without corresponding – when named – to a concept of positive law, enterprise is a latent reference, a sort of premise for many rules, an implicit model.[8]

This analysis has a heuristic worth. In particular, it helps us to understand why and to what extent certain systems no longer satisfy the forms of organisation adopted by all or some enterprises. This analysis does, however, have its limits because it puts the enterprise in the background, making it hard to appreciate the movements and tension that can drive it. Moreover, this type of analysis fails to grasp the mechanisms and the sheer range of the powers that appear within and through enterprises.

Power, or rather a certain power, appears in another type of analysis that is based on an observation of positive law, and on the law of competition, in particular. Its texts – beginning with the texts relative to the European Economic Union, and subsequent European Union (EU) – address enterprises. In order to determine what is part of an agreement or what is a body in a dominant position and susceptible to abuse, the judges made a clear distinction between enterprise and company. Enterprise is not defined by its legal status, but as an agent on one or more markets, which has decision-making autonomy. Therefore, what identifies an enterprise is its capacity to act independently in a market, its market power.

---

6. The leading work following this direction in France is by Michel Despax, *L'entreprise et le droit*, Paris LGDJ 620 (1957).
7. For a critical presentation of this doctrine in the French legal literature, *see* Antoine et Gérard Lyon-Caen, *La doctrine de l'entreprise*, in *Dix ans de droit de l'entreprise*, Litec (1978).
8. *See* Elsa Peskine, *Réseaux d'entreprise et droit du travail*, Paris LGDJ (2004).

The European judges seem to have used this definition of enterprise in order to construct a coherent law of competition that meets the objectives assigned to it. The limit of this construction, which adapts well to a specific rationale linked to a policy of competition, is that its overt functionalism does not does not lend itself to a possible generalisation.

When examined with renewed care, the dissociation between company and enterprise opens up interesting perspectives. If we consider the forms of organisation that dispose of production processes, and, more in general, of capital optimisation, it becomes clear that they are not regulated by law. In fact, law is not supposed to do this. It does something else. Law offers those who choose the different forms of organisation a range of means, techniques and instruments, and contributes to establishing and legitimising a power of organisation. The law does not recognise this power as such. It does not regulate it. It accepts it and offers it ways and means of action.

In order to describe this power correctly, we must distinguish between the power of those dealing with employment law, often called 'management power', and the power of those dealing with corporate law, that is, the power of executives or of those responsible for management. The power of organisation is exercised over these powers. It surpasses and organises them because it is expressed through the choice of juridical structures, the choices concerning the distribution of powers between these structures and the relations between them. As a recent publication suggests, it is 'a power over the powers',[9] the power to manage, organise and distribute them. At international level, it is the power to impose one's own justifications upon national legal regimes that nonetheless have supplied it with the means to express and explain itself.

In order to overcome its phenomenology and to attempt to understand this power of organisation, we may consider an analysis that proclaims an enhanced juridical pluralism in the expansion of certain well-known works[10] on the legal order. This allows us to account for the orders established within freely defined spaces, within spaces not defined by States and within rights not limited by national borders. However, the non-state normativity that has sprung up within these orders draws a whole series of resources from state legal orders.

The focus on this power of organisation and its analysis as an expression of private legal orders makes it possible to simultaneously grasp its dimension within the organisation and externally, that is, its relations with the state legal orders. Do these orders limit themselves to receiving such expressions at the price of attempting to impose certain demands concerning method? Or do they strive to correct their effects? Such questions require further investigation.

---

9. See Stéphane Vernac, *Le pouvoir d'organisation. Au croisement du droit du travail et du droit des sociétés*, Paris LGDJ (2016), pending publication.
10. On the expansion by Santi Romano, see Nikitas Aliprantis, *L'entreprise en tant qu'ordre juridique*, in *Le droit collectif du travail. Etudes en hommage à H. Sinay Bâle*, Peter Lang 185 (1994); égal Jean-Philippe Robé, *L'entreprise et le droit*, Paris PUF, coll 'Que sais-je' (1999).

However, such questions concern what has aptly been described as '*la crise de la notion d'employeur*' or the crisis of the notion of employer.

1.2 EMPLOYER AND ENTERPRISE

The majority of observers find themselves in agreement with regard to the existence and importance of a particular movement, and that is the growing complexity of the forms of organisation of enterprises. This is undoubtedly due to a multitude of factors ranging from risk calculation to the financialisation of activities and technological developments.

It is interesting to note how this growing complexity is described, and what terminology is used to make it possible to perceive and interpret this movement. A widely used description refers to the enterprise, underlining the calling into question of its unity and/or of its integrity, by using expressions such as '*désintégration*' (disintegration) or '*éclatement*'[11] (fragmentation); in brief, enterprises are presented as undergoing a process of disintegration and fragmentation.

The results of this process are reflected in the importance of corporate groups, in particular, of the groups that are controlled by finance companies or investment funds, as well as in the diffusion of forms of organisation based on *résèseaux*, or networks relative to production, service supply, distribution, and so on...

Another way of describing this complexity, which emphasises its impact on employment relationships, involves pointing out the relations that have frequently lost their historic bilaterality. Employment, or if preferred, employment relationships have become multipolar and even multilateral – whereby the latter qualification underlines the fact that multiple legal entities exercise prerogatives upon the same employee.

The notion of employer cast by the national labour laws seems rather limited in the face of these complex forms of enterprise organisation and these multipolar or multilateral employment relationships.

In Western Europe, where the notion has frequently been examined in comparative studies,[12] it has been conceived in the shade of the bilateral contractual vision of employment relations and of the limited responsibility of the shareholder associated with the choice of a company form.

In other words, historically, the employer was considered first and foremost as a contractor. The traditional model of contract provides for one contractor, and only one is responsible with regard to an employee. Often this contractor has a company form that allows the shareholders to limit their

---

11. *See* thirty years later *L'entreprise éclatée*, Droit ouvrier (mars-avril 1981) and the new contributions collected under the same title with the subtitle '*identifier l'employeur, attribuer les responsabilités*', Droit ouvrier (mars 2013).
12. Jeremias Prassl, *The concept of the employer*, OUP (2015).

economic and legal risk to the value of their shares, and is the sole entity responsible for the actions and activities carried out in its name.

However, what this conception of employer does not reveal spontaneously is the strange power that it attributes to the employer who can shape it at will. Employers may assume the form that is most convenient, a company form, for example, but they may also split up into several companies, merge with another company or transfer the burden of certain employment contracts to another company. Should we retreat in the face of a kind of obvious fact? Unless they are an individual entrepreneur, employers are a construct, an artefact.

If employers are constructs, and if they have the power to choose the legal forms and relations that they have with others, we need to correct the previous claim, which is a mere simplification of language: an employer, or artefact, may not possess this power. Who has this power then? We would have to be capable of pulling back the veil of the company's legal personality in order to identify the holder of this power.

Historically, the employer was a homogeneous, rigid concept.[13] But the configuration of each employer is potentially the result of various choices that have the effect of managing and distributing the risks of those making such choices. The plasticity of the individual employer, which clashes with the rigidity of the notion, owes everything to what was previously called 'the power of organisation'.[14] This gives rise to a question that is more relevant than ever before: do national laws offer the ways and means to correct the effects of choices of organisation and, for example, to attribute the burden for the correction or distribution of the damaging consequences of their choices to this or that investment fund, to this or that main shareholder?

In some countries the pertinence and acuteness of this question comes forth in the lively debates that give rise to recourse to the notion of *coemploi* or *coemployeur*[15] (co-employment or co-employer) or to the demand to attribute a responsibility to a legal entity other than the employer.[16]

One promising new approach may help us overcome the rigidity of the notion of employer that generally results in powerlessness.[17] This approach invites us to change direction: instead of starting with the notion of employer, we should focus on the functions that this notion fulfils. In fact, it is possible to identify the various functions that it carries out within a legal system.

---

13. *Ibid.*
14. *Ibid.*
15. *See* the most recent work in France by Stéphane Vernac, *L'avenir sauvegardé du coemploi*, Revue de droit du travail 560 (2016).
16. *See* Elsa Peskine, *L'imputation en droit du travail*, Revue de droit du travail 347 (2012); Alexandre Fabre, *La responsabilité délictuelle pour faute au secours des salariés victimes d'une société tierce*, Revue de droit du travail 672 (2014).
17. Prassl, *supra* n. 12; and by the same author, *L'emploi multilatéral en droit anglais. A la recherche du patron perdu*, Revue de droit du travail 236 (2014).

Once this identification has been carried out, we should change perspective, leaving behind the analysis and description of a legal system in order to prescribe an evolution.

The diversity that has been revealed within the functions could actually justify and order that different legal entities meet the obligations laid down by employment law. By way of example, if we agree that one of the functions of the notion is to designate the entity responsible for the management of the people that work, we would have to admit that this entity bears the burden for job cuts, even if traditionally such an entity did not correspond to the employer.

Returning to the enterprise, rediscovering the weakness of the concepts underpinning economic and juridical theories, and uncovering the reasons for this weakness can prove to be a fertile approach – and hopefully we have proved this – to renewing the analysis of major themes.

CHAPTER 2

The Contractual Theory of the Firm and Some Good Reasons for Regulating the Employment Relationship

Francesco Denozza

2.1 INTRODUCTION

This chapter deals with the legal nature of the firm and explores the influence that the definition of the firm as a network of contracts has on the regulation of the employment relationship, with special reference to two problems.

The first problem concerns the protection of the rights of the employee against the attempts of the employer to evade its obligations. That, as is well known, is a plague afflicting the labour contract much more than other contracts and is perpetrated especially through the concealment of the employment relationship under the guise of self-employment or through the concealment of the real employer behind figureheads and shell companies. With regard to this problem the paper maintains that the function assigned to the employer – entrepreneur in the theory of the firm, and especially his role as residual claimant, requires a special severity in preventing any kind of elusion of his obligations. The fight against all circumvention tools, such as those just mentioned, is a matter not only of fairness, but also of efficiency.

The second question asks what reasons, if any, may ground the (in the past widespread, and in many systems still relevant) recourse to mandatory rules, granting special protections to the employees. The problem arises from the fact that in a contractual vision of the firm there are no *a priori* reasons for preferring the interests of one or the other party to the contract and, from an efficiency viewpoint, the best result is presumed to be that which the parties consented to, absent any external interference. The ('Coasean') idea is that whatever the problem, if an efficient solution exists, the parties (in a world with no transaction costs) will find an agreement about it (the efficient solution), with no need of any external compulsion. The paper presents arguments to illustrate the reasons why this reasoning may prove in many situations wrong and concludes in the sense that even from an efficiency viewpoint (i.e., setting aside any concern of fairness) and in a contractual context, many reasons may justify the resort to mandatory rules regulating the employment relationship.

Two opposite notions of the firm are illustrated in section 2.2. The institutional theory is set aside as unacceptable in a market system and the remaining Sections focus on the contractual theories. Sections 2.4 and 2.5 deal with the definition of entrepreneur, employer and employee, while sections 2.6 and 2.7 deal with the possible role of mandatory rules.

2.2　TWO NOTIONS OF THE FIRM

The firm can be understood basically in two ways: as an organism or as an aggregation. I use the term 'understood' to signify that (in my view) firms are not real entities, but social constructions. Real is the bundle of human and non-human elements (labour power and means of production) which the firm consists of. Real are, as it were, the components of the firm. The tie that binds those elements is instead a social construct and may be differently conceived (and carried out) in different societies[1] (and even in the same society, where the nature of the firm can be subject to harsh dissent).

In this perspective, which contrasts firm as organism versus firm as aggregation, we are confronted with an instance of more general oppositions, as that between holism and individualism[2] or, in another language and from another viewpoint, that between *Gemeinscaft* and *Gesellschaft*[3] or, at last, and in 'more legal' terms, that between institution and contract.[4]

In the first perspective (holism) the firm may be considered as an organism and, from a legal viewpoint, as something akin to an institution, in the sense given to the term by the 'old institutionalists' as Maurice Hauriou or Santi Romano.[5] In a modern economic version of the institutionalist conception, the

---

1. The same enterprise, say hunting, is differently conceived, organized and practiced in a tribe of hunters-gatherers (where it is the main societal activity) in a market system (where it is the possible scope of voluntary organizations) or in a planned economy (where the task may be assigned to a public body).
2. Norberto Bobbio, *Organicismo e individualismo: un'antitesi*, in Petroni, Viale (a cura di), Individuale e collettivo. Decisione e razionalità, 179 et seq. (Cortina, 1997).
3. According to the famous opposition valorised by Ferdinand Toennies, *Community and Civil Society* (Jose Harris, Cambridge University Press, 2001).
4. *See*, recently, *Contrat ou Institution: un enjeu de société*, coord. B.Basdevant-Gaudemet, L.G.D.J, Paris (2004).
5. According to Santi Romano an institution is 'any entity or social body that has a stable and permanent pattern and forms a body in itself, with a life of its own', Massimo La Torre, *Law as Institution* (Springer Science + Business Media BV., 2010).

firm may be defined as an organism endowed with its own qualities and capabilities, distinct from that of its human parts.[6]

In my opinion the firms in market systems are usually regulated not as institutions,[7] but as contracts (as a 'nexus of contracts' as it is used to be said today). Leaving aside many complicated issues, the decisive point in favour of the contract theory is that in the market systems the firms are not communities created by involuntary ties (as might be a common language, tradition, culture, etc.) or by an authoritative act of foundation. They are voluntary associations that are created by agreements among all the individuals who participate in the enterprise. Their development and their very survival depend on the decisions taken by a number of market actors, allowed, or even encouraged, to act only out of their own self-interest. The survival of the firms (and of the corporations that are their main legal form) depends, in particular, on the decisions of shareholders and managers, who can discretionally, and legitimately, decide to close down, wind-up, merge, split, transfer, run away, and so forth.

What is protected by the law is not the survival of 'the firm as such'[8] but the autonomy and the economic freedom of the entrepreneur (and of the market actors who transact with him).

In market economies attempts to present the firm, and the rules that govern it, as a harmonious and functional coordination of the parts of a single body, end up legitimizing (consciously or not) mystified images[9] and authoritarian options. Therefore, I do not think that they deserve to be seriously considered.

Currently, the term institution is generally used with the generic meaning of a set of rules whatever their origin, so that even a network of contracts may create an 'institution'.

6. On the so-called 'competence-based evolutionary firm', *see* Olivier Weinstein, *The Current State of the Economic Theory of the Firm: Contractual, Competence-Based, and Beyond*, in Biondi, Canziani & Kirat (a cura di), The Firm as an Entity, 42 (Rouledge, 2007); Goeffry M. Hodgson, *Evolutionary and Competence-Based Theories of the Firm*, 25 *Journal of Economic Studies*, n 1, 25 et seq. (1998), Lars Hakanson, *The Firm as an Epistemic Community: The Knowledge Based View Revisited*, www2.druid.dk/conferences/viewpaper.php?id=500937&cf=43; Nicolai Foss, *Strategy, Economic Organization, and the Knowledge Economy* (Oxford University Press, 2006).

7. 'Organisms whose parts are human beings', borrowing Gierke's well-known definition of associations quoted by Gunther Teubner, *Enterprise Corporatism: New Industrial Policy and the 'Essence' of the Legal Person*, 36 *The American Journal of Comparative Law*, 130, 134 (1988).

8. The 'Unternehmen an sich' theorized by W. Rathenau, on whose thought *see* Philipp Klages, *Die Wiederentdeckung schlafender Alternativen in der Rechtslehre: Der Begriff 'Aktiengesellschaft'*, 18 *Berliner Debatte Initial*, 75 (2007).

9. A mystification, as in the famous episode, narrated by Titus Livius, of the comparison between the human society and the human body by which Menenius Agrippa frightened the plebs to induce them to return to working for the patricians. Quoting from Wikipedia *Agrippa Menenius Lanatus (consul 503 BC)*: 'According to Livy, writing five hundred years after the fact, Menenius was chosen by the patricians during the secession of the plebs in 494 BC to persuade the plebs to end their secession. Livy says that Menenius told the soldiers a fable about the parts of the human body and how each has its own purpose in the greater function of the body. The rest of the body thought the stomach was getting a free

2.3 THE CONTRACTUAL VIEW AND THE MANDATORY RULES

In the second perspective the firm is considered, as noted before, as a network of voluntary relationships, implemented by contract law, among all the individuals who take part in the enterprise. So, not an individual body articulated in many different parts, but many individuals who coordinate themselves by means of agreements.

Two possible misunderstandings of the contract view of the firm must be immediately cleared.

The first clarification is that the contractual (individualistic) view of the firm is not inconsistent with the indisputable fact that firms as such have a social relevance and may be an important factor of social wealth. This theory does not deny that firms may have a social value that goes lost when one of them is dissolved (as we will see, one of the 'most contractual' theories of the firm takes as its starting point the assumption that the main characteristic of the firm is just the fact that its product is more than the sum of the outputs of each cooperating individual). What is denied is that the preservation of this value requires a specific protection by means of mandatory rules.

The idea (here, as elsewhere) is that the interest of the entrepreneur is perfectly aligned with the interest of the whole society, so the decisions regarding the firm that the entrepreneur takes in his own interest will result as the best possible decisions also from the viewpoint of the society. Resorting to a simple metaphor we could say that as any rational person does his best to grow well the goose that lays the golden eggs (at least until the eggs are actually of gold) so the entrepreneur will take care of his business as long as it is worth it, without any need of rules requiring him to do so.

The second possible misunderstanding pertains to the protected interests. The contractual conception of the firm does not imply the prevailing protection of the interest of one of the parties participating in the contracts constituting the institutional structure of the firm. In fact, contract law does not give primacy to either buyer or seller, contractor or owner.[10] In the same way the 'nexus of contracts' conception does not logically imply the primacy of one or the other group of contracting parties.

In conclusion, the contractual conception of the firm is characterized neither by an (obviously unacceptable) undervaluation of the social relevance of the firms, nor by an *a priori* bias in favour of the entrepreneur or any other

---

ride so the body decided to stop nourishing the stomach. Soon, the other parts became fatigued and unable to function so they realized that the stomach did serve a purpose and they were nothing without it. In the story, the stomach represents the patrician class and the other body parts represent the plebs. Eventually, Livy says, an accord was reached between the patricians and the plebs, which included creating the office of tribune of the plebs'.

10. Melvin A. Eisenberg, *The Conception That the Corporation Is a Nexus of Contracts, and the Dual Nature of the Firm*, 24 *Iowa Journal of Corporation Law*, 819, 833 (1999): 'contract law does not give primacy to either buyer or seller, contractors or owners'.

participant in the enterprise. What really and especially characterizes the contractual vision is the rejection of the idea that mandatory rules may be necessary in order to protect the interest of the public or that of one of the parties involved.

2.4 THE NEXUS OF CONTRACT AND THE NOTION OF ENTREPRENEUR

So we arrive at the first relevant question: in a firm conceived as a network of contracts, who, among the many contracting parties, is the entrepreneur? Who is the employer and who the employee? Since in the theory of the firm the idea of employment is based not on the notion of employee, but rather on the notion of employer, the starting point must be: who is the entrepreneur, and, consequently, the employer?

In an institutional conception of the firm the entrepreneur, in the sense of the chief of the enterprise, should be the one able to qualify as the best interpreter of the interests of the community (of the *Gemeinschaft*) which constitutes the firm. Thus the entrepreneur is the gifted individual born to rule, who, for natural vocation, is called to be the leader answering only to an abstract entity: the firm as such, the society at large, the people, etc.

This kind of semi-divine investiture cannot identify and legitimize the entrepreneur in the contractual theories of the firm. Here a different kind of legitimation is needed.

I think that the most important among the contemporary theories of the firm[11] are in this regard (identification of the entrepreneur and legitimation of its role) inspired by a *functionalist* perspective. Each theory emphasizes as essential (for the survival and development of the organization) a specific function and identifies the entrepreneur, consequently, in him who performs this very function.

In the Coase's conception, for example, the 'authority relation' is emphasized as the most efficient means for reducing the transaction costs inherent in some kinds of business relations and as the distinctive feature of the firm. The exercise of this authority naturally becomes the specific function of the entrepreneur.[12] In a similar way the Grossman-Hart-Moore model dictates that the

---

11. A recent survey in Paul Walker, *Contracts, Entrepreneurs, Market Creation and Judgement: The Contemporary Mainstream Theory of the Firm in Perspective*, Journal of Economic Surveys, published online, 7 February (2014).
12. Ronald Coase, *The Firm, the Market and the Law*, 54 (The University of Chicago Press, 1988) 'we thus see that it is the fact of direction which is the essence of the legal concept of 'employer and employee', just as it was in the economic concept which was developed above'. Oliver Williamson, *The Vertical Integration of Production: Market Failure Considerations*, 61 American Economic Review, 112 (1971); Id., *The Economic Institution of Capitalism* (The Free Press, New York-London, 1985).

firm should be owned by those who contribute the most valuable and most asset-specific property to the joint enterprise.[13]

Probably the model which gives the most complete and refined theoretical arrangement to the complex of the relationships between the entrepreneur – employer and the providers of other resources, is that of the so-called 'team production theory', whose roots are in the work of Alchian and Demsetz, but which found integration and development also in legal thought.[14]

The team production theory starts from the view of the firm as an enterprise in which the participants can reach a joint result greater than the sum of the results that everyone can get alone, but where the personal contribution of each participant cannot be measured separately. This last feature entails the risk that each participant seeks to act as a free rider, by minimizing his efforts and relying on others.

In this model[15] the biggest problem facing the firm, conceived of as a team, is the possible free riding by the team's members. The solution is to vest the right to monitor in one of the team members – the entrepreneur- who observes the activity of the others and tries to guess their marginal contributions.

To ensure that the efficient amount of *impartial* monitoring takes place, the individual who takes the task of monitoring is given the status of 'residual claimant'.[16] He has rights only to the residual income of the team, namely, that remaining after the payment of the fixed amounts due to all other members.

---

13. Oliver Hart, *An Economist's Perspective on the Theory of the Firm*, 89 Columbia Law Review, 1757, 1759 (1989); Sanford Grossman, Oliver Hart, *The Costs and Benefits of Ownership: A Theory of Vertical and Lateral Integration*, 94 Journal of Political Economy, 691 (1986), Oliver Hart- John Moore, *Property Rights and the Nature of the firm*, 98 Journal of Political Economy, 1119 (1990), Oliver Hart, *Firms, Contracts, and Financial Structure* (Oxford University Press, 1995).
14. Margaret Blair, Lynn Stout, *A Team Production Theory of Corporate Law*, 85 Virginia Law Review, 247 (1999).
15. According to Armen Alchian, Harold Demsetz, *Production, Information Costs, and Economic Organization*, 62 American Economic Review 779 (1972), team production 'is production in which 1) several types of resources are used and 2) the product is not a sum of separable outputs of each cooperating resource…' and '.. 3) not all resources used in team production belong to one person.'. As underlined by M. Bodie, *Employees and the Boundaries of the Corporation*, in C. Hill & B. McDonnel, Research Handbook on the Economics of Corporate Law (Edward Elgar, 2012), '…the primary concern of team production is making sure that the team members do not shirk their responsibilities to the team. The inability to measure individual contributions to productivity is what makes the firm an efficient alternative to markets, but it is also the firm's central governance problem. Alchian and Demsetz argued that a specialized, independent monitor may be the best way of ensuring that the team members all contribute appropriately and are rewarded appropriately. That central monitor – the recipient of the residual profits – would be the firm'.
16. The *residual claimant* is also the holder of the *residual rights of control*. On the latter notion, Oliver Hart, *Incomplete Contracts and the Theory of the Firm*, in Oliver Williamson & Sidney Winter, The Nature of the Firm, Origins, Evolution Development, 141 (Oxford University Press, 1993).

2.5 THE IMPLICATIONS FOR THE EMPLOYMENT RELATIONSHIP

As we saw, the residual claimant is the one who guarantees to all the participants (all those who provide the firm with the resources it needs) full satisfaction of their claims. Nothing belongs to him until there is anyone's right even partially unfulfilled.

It follows that when the residual claimants are satisfied everyone is satisfied. This feature is very important because it allows focusing on the welfare of the residual claimants. If their well-being is maximized, we can be confident that the overall welfare is equally maximized (this is the ideological root of the theory of shareholder value that has dominated in recent decades). But if the residual claimant can circumvent the rights of some, or transfer risks on others, this reasoning obviously fails. The founding element of the entire construction is put to shake like a house of cards.

What follows from this reasoning is the special importance of preventing any possible evasion of the duties of the entrepreneur. Preventing evasion is obviously a matter of relevance for any kind of obligation, but it has a peculiar significance in regard to the employment relationship, given the frequency with which the entrepreneur – employer tries to escape from its commitments by simulating self-employment relationships or by creating appearances in which another person looks as the employer in his place.

The reference to the role of residual claimant, and to the need of making this role effective, provides the reasons for considering the attempt to prevent the avoidance of the employer's responsibilities not only as a matter of fairness, but also of efficiency.

The emphasis on the *entrepreneurial* function of the employer shifts the focus from the common law paradigm of master – servant, to the principle '*cuius commoda eius et incommoda*'. It is not so much a matter of protecting the 'servant', but more an issue of preventing circumvention of duties and transfers of risks, both of which could result in an inefficient decoupling of the role of entrepreneur from that of residual claimant.

More concretely, I think that this perspective, as far as it regards the crackdown on the *concealment of the status of employer*, provides arguments in favour of rules able to impose the employer's liability towards its employees on all individuals who prove to be the last resort supervisors and beneficiaries of the performances of the latter.[17]

---

17. This argument may justify I think even the most radical solutions, as for example the California's anti-sweatshop law, known as AB 633, '…which makes garment manufacturers guarantors of their subcontractors wage and hour practices. Under this provision, if unpaid wages cannot be collected from the subcontractor due to insolvency, they can be collected from the manufacturer without the need to demonstrate an employment relationship', Timothy Glynn, *Taking the Employer Out of Employment Law? Accountability for Wage and Hour Violations in an Age of Enterprise Disaggregation*, 15 Employee Rights and Employment Policy Journal, 201 (2011).

Instead, with regard to the *camouflage of the status of employee*, the reference to the monitoring function and to the team production theory may recommend, as a criterion for the identification of the employee, a combination of a softened version of the traditional common law 'control' test[18] with the so-called 'entrepreneurial opportunities' test,[19] that focuses not upon the employer's control of the means and manner of the work but instead upon whether the putative independent contractors have a significant entrepreneurial opportunity for gain or loss.

The main focus should shift from the existence of a rigid, hierarchical, control, to the assessment of the existence of a team to which the employees participate. The focus should shift from the role of the employer, to the position of the employee.

This is not to deny the importance of the employer's role in monitoring the joint activity of the team. The point however is that a pattern of generic monitoring is different from an individualized model of command and control (in this sense, I alluded to a 'softened' version of the control test). At the end, in this perspective, what defines the employees is the fact that they are acting together within one unit, as participants to a process of joint production.[20] The fact that they are monitored by the employer is a consequence and, from the viewpoint of an outside observer, a clue.

2.6 IN A CONTRACTUAL VIEW, IS THERE A ROLE FOR MANDATORY RULES? (A) A 'COASEAN' ANSWER

The last issue that I would like to address concerns the function (if any) that can be played by mandatory rules in the contractual conception of the firm.

Mandatory rules, in a contractual perspective sensitive only to efficiency issues, are justified only in case of market failures, cases in which private interests are not aligned with social interests and the possibility exists that total welfare increasing transactions are not implemented, so that suboptimal *equilibria* settle.

Many of the typical causes of market failures (externalities, monopolies, information asymmetries, public goods, etc.) are pervasive and relevant also in the employment relationship. Just think, for example, of the problem of safety in the workplace. We have here to cope with problems of information asymmetry

---

18. 'The principal test of an employment relationship is whether the person to whom service is rendered has the right to control the manner and means of accomplishing the result desired': *Alexander v. FedEx Ground Package System, Inc.*, 27 August (2014), U.S. Court of Appeals for the Ninth Circuit.
19. The determination of the employee status should focus 'not upon the employer's control of the means and manner of the work but instead upon whether the putative independent contractors have a significant entrepreneurial opportunity for gain or loss.' *Corporate Express Delivery Systems v. N.L.R.B.*, 292 F3d 777 (D.C. Cir. 2002).
20. M. Bodie, *Participating as a Theory of Employment*, 89 Notre Dame Law Review, 661 (2013).

Chapter 2: The Contractual Theory of the Firm and Some Good Reasons

(usually, the prospective employees have a poor understanding of the effects that an unsafe workplace can have on their health) cognitive bias (the irrational undervaluation of the probability of an accident) indivisibility (impossibility of offering to each employee the degree of safety precisely matching her preferences) etc., that can all be considered as possible grounds for a peremptory regulation. In these cases the use of mandatory rules may be justified by reasons of efficiency, in addition to reasons of fairness.

All this is in general well known and here is not the place where a list of all the possible relevant market failures can be compiled. Here I would focus instead on another more general problem, that of the treatment of the employment relationship requiring idiosyncratic investments.

The hypothesis is that of a firm in need of special skills ('skills that are acquired in a learning – by – doing fashion and that are imperfectly transferable across employers'[21]) or of the development of a strong corporate culture. This is an example of a situation in which efficiency requires that the employment relationship is *embedded in a protective governance structure*,[22] otherwise, the employee will not make the necessary idiosyncratic investments (investments that she cannot exploit elsewhere). The employee, absent a promise that she will not be fired on a whim, or in the last few years of her working life or for obsolescence of the knowledge that just the firm led her to acquire, etc., will not make the required specific investment in terms of attention, dedicated efforts, willingness to learn, etc.

Is this a good reason for introducing the needed protective structure via mandatory rules? The usual reasoning answers: when productive values as, for example, a special commitment of some employees, can increase the firm's profits, the most interested party is just the entrepreneur. Thus the protective governance structure will be spontaneously offered to the employees, with no need of mandatory rules.

This result is consistent with the so-called Coase's theorem, according to which in a world with no transaction costs all possible efficient transactions will always occur.[23] In terms relevant for our subject, the intuition underpinning the Coase's theorem is the following. If there is a possibility of having a bigger cake (more profits for the firm) the interested individuals (the employer and the employee) will always reach an agreement on the division of the surplus, thereby making possible the production of the (biggest) cake.

---

21. Oliver Williamson, *The Economic Institutions of Capitalism: Firms, Markets, Relational Contracting*, 243 (New York, Free Press, 1985); Oliver Williamson, Michael Watcher, Jeffrey Harris, *Understanding the Employment Relation: The Analysis of Idiosyncratic Exchange*, Bell Journal Economics, 1 (1975).
22. *Id., The Economic Institutions*, 243. On this aspect of Williamson's thought *see* Robert McMaster, Michael White. *An Investigation of Williamson's Analysis of the Division of Labour*, 37 Cambridge Journal of Economics, 1283 (2013).
23. Ronald Coase, *The Firm, the Market and the Law*, 95 et seq. (The University of Chicago Press, 1988).

The division (almost any division, except only that that gives the entire surplus to one party) of the surplus will improve the position of both parties and, therefore, both are interested in reaching an agreement that makes possible the making of the bigger cake.

2.7 IS THERE A ROLE FOR MANDATORY RULES? (B) THREE REASONS WHY THE COASEAN REASONING OFTEN DOES NOT HOLD

There are in my opinion at least three factors that can make unacceptable the reasoning summed up in the previous section.

2.7.1 Myopia or Short-Termism: The Bigger Pie Goes Out of Sight

The first factor which can invalidate the Coasean vision is the myopia, now called short-termism, that is the tendency of corporate managers to sacrifice long-term investments to improve short-term earnings.

This is not the place for discussing the possible causes of the current diffusion of this attitude. It is sufficient to stress that short-termism is almost universally considered the main cause of the financial crisis (and of the following great depression) and the main illness of the current economic system.[24]

From the viewpoint relevant here, short-termism implies an overvaluation of the negative impact of actual expenses and an undervaluation of the benefits associated with future performances. Consequently, one of the negative consequences (as is widely recognized) of short-termism is a substantial reduction in the propensity to invest, especially in R&D. As the costs incurred for creating a corporate culture, for training the workforce, for encouraging dedicated efforts, etc., are all investments in future productivity (as investments in machinery or in R&D are) we can reasonably assume that firms are currently prone to underinvest not only in real, but also in human capital.

In a situation in which firms most likely prefer to monetize the immediate benefits of less protection for workers rather than waiting for the better yields

---

24. This is, I think, a rather complicated issue. The alternative between short and long misses, in my opinion, the point. Indeed, there is nothing inherently positive in a long-term vision. The real important point is planning. If an old man decides to join an insurance plan, that may be considered a long-term decision. But it is a foolish decision if the goal is to employ in a double world tour the benefit that after forty years the insurance will guarantee him, while it is a wise decision if he considers the insurance a way to benefit his grandchildren. The point is that short and long gain a positive, or a negative, sense only within a specific plan. The problem today is not short-termism, but lack of planning. States do not make plans anymore but perhaps for reducing their deficits; CEOs plan only within the time horizon of their tenure (often less than five or six years); households do not plan at all, lacking the resources for planning and employees have ceased to plan, since they have been told that we now live in a flexible world in which planning is useless or even harmful.

obtainable with more investments in a greater protection granted to employees, the coincidence of the private interest of the firm with the general interest of society is not guaranteed and a regulatory intervention may therefore be justified accordingly.

2.7.2 The Problem of Power: An Even Bigger Pie Is Always Looming on the Horizon of the Powerful

The second factor is linked with the phenomenon of power.

Recall that what we are examining here is the possibility of an efficient deal by which the employer accepts a restriction of his right to fire the employees at will, as a means to inducing them to make idiosyncratic (not redeploy able) investments.

A restriction of the right to dismiss at will puts into play one of the fundamental components of the employer's authority and is able to negatively affect his power in a relevant measure. In some sense, it affects the power on which essentially all other employer's powers depend.

That seems not to be a problem in the Coasean perspective. In the analysis of Coase (and Williamson) no special consideration is devoted to the notion and the phenomenon of power. Rights, and the power they confer to the holder, are treated as a resource that can be bought and sold as any other commodity. In this perspective, regardless of the nature and the amount of power involved, the basic assumption remains valid: the parties involved will anyway undertake all available advantageous transactions.

This is in my opinion a shallow and potentially misleading generalization. Power has a dispositional attitude,[25] in the sense that it is oriented towards the future and its value depends on the gains that the holder will be able to collect from a series of acts of exercise of its power that cannot be defined in advance and that will vary according to future concrete unforeseeable circumstances.

One might note that this obviously applies to all the rights whose exercise is projected into the future and which are usually bought and sold without relevant problems. However, I think that a distinction must be made. There are future events that the market is able to easily price. For these events the power to determine them can be bought and sold with no particular trouble. But there are many other events which are so uncertain and remote that no market is able to convincingly evaluate the power of determining or preventing them. Here the phenomenon of power becomes paramount, and the idea that the power holder will treat its power as any other commodity turns out unbelievable.

In the case of lack of markets able to give a price to any future relevant event, power is difficult to evaluate and prone to be overestimated by its holder.

---

25. Francesco Denozza, *Law and Power in a World with No Transaction Costs: An Essay on the Legitimating Function of the Coasian Narrative*, http://ssrn.com/abstract=1361613 or http://dx.doi.org/10.2139/ssrn.1361613 (accessed 17 March 2009).

And it is much more so in a world, as the present labour market, where the watchword is flexibility and where the uncertainty affects not only the life and fate of workers but also that of the firm.[26]

2.7.3 Allocation and Distribution: The Slice, Not the Cake, Matters

The last possible obstacle to the functioning of the mechanism described in the so-called Coase's theorem arises from the impossibility of separating, *in reality*, allocative from distributive issues.

From an analytic viewpoint it is obviously easy to distinguish the effect of a contract on the total welfare (allocation) from the effect on the well-being of each party (distribution). In reality, the parties agree on a given contract's content that has *indivisible* effects on both dimensions (allocation and distribution). Each party is however interested only in the effects on its well-being and does not care of the overall welfare. If a party considers insufficient the size of the gain to which such party is entitled according to the planned contract, the agreement shall not be reached even in case of a contract which would increase the total welfare of the parties.

All that is obvious and well known. To overcome this difficulty (social relevance of the total welfare/parties interested only in their personal well-being) the 'ruse' of the 'Coasean' reasoning is to presume that if a bigger cake is achievable, the parties will always find an agreement on how to divide it. In case of a contract which increases total welfare, but is not satisfactory for one of the parties, we can imagine that the other party, in order to make possible the conclusion of the efficient contract, will yield a portion of its gain, at least up to the point at which the contract remains more beneficial than another contract. The opportunity, for the party potentially more advantaged, of using the surplus created by the contract to 'bribe' the other party, should make certain the conclusion of all contracts actually efficient.

This reasoning supposes a simplicity and linearity that are rarely present in the real world. Keeping the usual metaphor of the cake, we can say that, contrary to which is supposed by the 'Coasean' 'trick', in the real world a loss of efficiency may arise from the fact that one of the parties of the transaction may prefer a bigger slice of a smaller cake, instead of a smaller slice of a bigger cake.

Let me illustrate the point by resorting to a numerical example. We can start from the situation S1 in which the cake (the product of the firm with employee E) is equal to 50 and the slices are 40 to the employer ER and 10 to E. We can imagine two other alternative situations. The situation S2, in which E

---

26. In some sense, by resorting to a rather bold but potentially explanatory comparison, the preference for retaining economic power may be likened to the preference for financial liquidity. Both, power and money, are instruments for hedging against fundamental uncertainty.
    On the link between uncertainty and liquidity preference, s. John Mainard Keynes, *The General Theory of Employment, Interest and Money*, Ch. 13, II.

can improve her performance, so as to cause an increase of the product equal to 10, in exchange for 5, and the situation S3 in which a third party E1 could provide a performance causing an increase of the product equal to 8 in exchange for 2.[27]

It is obvious that from a social viewpoint S2 is better than S3 (the product of the firm is 60 in S2 and only 58 in S3). However, it is equally obvious that the employer will choose S3 (firing E, hiring E1) where his slice is 46, and not S2 (slice 45).

The moral of the story is simple: for society what matters is the size of the cake, for the individual what matters is the size of his slice. Thus the interests and perspectives of the former often do not coincide with those of the latter.[28]

In conclusion, I think that even accepting the contractual theory of the firm and the conceptual framework underpinning it (the functional reconstruction of the role of the entrepreneur, the 'Coasean' attitude in the theoretical structuring of the relations between the various participants, and especially between employers and employees, and so forth) a considerable scope remains for a (potentially efficient) recourse to mandatory rules (protecting the specific investments of the employee, especially by limiting the employer's right to dismiss at will,), in all cases in which the interests of the employer do not coincide with that of the society at large.

---

27. As an actual fact able to ground the numbers of the example given in the text, we can simply imagine that in S2 E should make an effort such as to be considered by him unacceptable for any compensation less than five (because insufficient, unfair, and so forth).
28. From another viewpoint the example illustrates a simple fact remarked especially by John Rawls, *Lectures on the History of Political Philosophy*, 56 et seq. (Harvard University Press, 2007). In examining Hobbes's political philosophy Rawls develops a distinction between *coordination* (bees in a hive, workers on an assembly line, etc.) and *cooperation.* Unlike the former, the last (cooperation) involves some notion of mutuality and of a fair terms division of the advantage among those engaged in cooperation. The conclusion of Rawl's reasoning is in the sense that fair terms impose constraints 'on efficient and productive and coordinated social activity'.

  In the example in the text, the possible conviction of employee E that her greater effort requires a compensation no less than a certain degree, functions as an unsurpassable obstacle to an efficient coordination.

PART II Enterprise Transformations, Externalization Process and Productive Decentralization

CHAPTER 3
Productive Decentralization: An International and Comparative Perspective

Jean-Michel Servais

Rapid technological change and economic liberalization have induced reshaping the processes of production and given enterprises more freedom to change work organization and labour relationships. Precarious forms of employment have developed outside the confines of the classical industrial relations' principles.[1] The structures and functions of trade unions, historically conceived to cater to the needs of a stable and homogeneous labour force, have faced problems to adjust and respond effectively to the varied demands of a growlingly heterogeneous labour force. While job instability as well as firm autonomy are relatively novel traits of today's world of work in many industrialized countries, they have constituted ever since distinct characteristics of the informal economy of many developing countries.

My argument is not to deplore this evolution and to call for barriers protecting the traditional social scene. The large evidence available suggests that it should be a totally unrealistic and probably even not efficient method to improve the lot of vulnerable people. I rather aim at identifying which institutions and legal guarantees are already used, with which results, to enhance their income-earning capacity, living and working conditions, and their bargaining power. I focus on international and European social law and consider the potential of the safeguards to be extended.

This chapter addresses the issues of enterprises transformation, productive decentralization and externalization processes from both the workers and the enterprise perspectives. An introduction gives an overview of the variety of

---

1. ILO, *World Employment and Social Outlook Trends 2016* (Geneva, 2016).

production processes and forms of jobs. A first part briefly reviews the applicability of the general social provisions to the various forms of work organization and contractual arrangements. This should permit to ascertain the cases in which, and the extent of, the relevance of general labour protection to the problems of the new operators. It should help appreciate how far persons with unstable employment actually enjoy the rights recognized by law and the need for more specific rules and strategies. The transnational dimension of the relationships adds to the difficulties.

In a second part, attention is paid to the special measures adopted to better adjust the protective regulation to the interests of both workers and business. The same division between distinct forms of productive decentralization and types of jobs applies. The institutional and regulatory factors, which may facilitate new forms of security at work, are examined. The conclusions underlines the best experiences and propose further steps.

3.1 INTRODUCTION: A VARIETY OF FIRMS, PRODUCTION PROCESSES AND FORMS OF JOBS

The concept of productive decentralization corresponds to a great variety of undertakings structures and work relationships.

3.1.1 A Variety of Firms

The production process may take different forms besides the well-known concentration of all activities within a sole firm. Work may be distributed amongst several enterprises, often Small and Medium-Sized (SMEs). That labour laws have been draft and that governments (France) still conceive their economic policies with the major firms in mind when the SMES remain the main source of employment should be studied in depth. Likewise manufacturing or servicing may be done by a self-employed or a micro-enterprise; in the informal economy, the demarcation line between an employer and a wage-earner becomes blurred.

At the other side of the spectrum, are the big firms and the groups of enterprises legally distinct, but financially integrated. The answer to the question who is the employer could appear unclear. The same holds true for the chains and the networks of firms where the legal plurality may also relate to an economic singleness.[2] Subcontracting is another way to decentralize production and could be plural. The law distinguishes between the subcontracting of goods

---

2. Maria Teresa Carinci (ed.), *Dall'impresa a rete alle reti d'impresa* (Giuffrè, 2015); Jeremias Prassl, *The Concept of Employer* (Oxford University Press, 2015); Luca Ratti, *Réseaux d'entreprise et coemploi, perpectives comparatives*, janvier RDT,72–75 (2015); Antoine Lyon-Caen, Adalberto Perulli, *Transformazioni dell'impresa e rapporti di lavoro* (CEDAM, 2004).

and services and of manpower. Franchise, concession, workers cooperative (Argentina, Colombia, Peru) are close to subcontracting while keeping their own character.

Employers finally group themselves for various purposes even without capital imbrication.

The variety of sizes and production processes creates a number of difficulties with regard to the common representation of the workers. Would they wish to do so, the historical institutions of industrial relations do not normally permit the delegates of the smallest and of the biggest undertakings to speak with one voice. The practice, in European countries, of bargaining collective labour agreements at the sector level does not fit with the plurality of activities in the large firms. This explain, partially at least, their trend to focus the negotiations to the company itself (IBM in Germany). Firms also create other structures to defend their own interests such as clubs, lobbies (Volkswagen); they finance political parties (according to Radio France Culture, French enterprises have significantly participated in the financing of the two main parties, and especially the Republican one, during the last mid-terms elections in the USA).

In the International Labour Organisation (ILO) too, the representation of the enterprises constitutes a serious challenge as major and multinational firms have often no affiliation or influence within the national organizations of employers, the only ones to send delegates to the Organization decision making bodies.

3.1.2 A Variety of Forms of Work

The freedom of contract makes it possible to adapt the work relationships to the 'decentralization' and 'externalization' processes. It permits all kinds of arrangements with regard to the duration of work, up to the most tenuous: crowdworking, on-call or even zero-hours contracts when there is no obligation for employers to offer work and sometimes – but here the naming may be different – for workers to accept it.[3] Some bring along human distress.

Contract of employment is distinguished from the contract for service (based on private or commercial law) by the subordination that relates the worker to the employer. It is, generally speaking, of a legal nature, Even if present human resources policies tend to increase the staff autonomy, the criterion remains clear in most cases. There are however a number of exceptions either when the situation is ambiguous (home-based work) or when the parties hide the subordination dimension of their relations to escape the protection of labour law (the 'false' self-employed). A number of countries have established

---

3. For UK, *see* http://www.acas.org.uk/index.aspx?articleid=4468; More generally, Sophie Robin-Olivier, *Les contrats de travail flexibles. Une comparaison internationale* (Paris, Presses de Sciences-Po, 2015).

an intermediary category of *'parasubordinazione'* which combines legal autonomy and economic subordination.[4]

Unpaid work (household activities, voluntary work, internship, etc.) forms still a distinct category.

3.2 THE APPLICABILITY OF GENERAL SOCIAL PROVISIONS TO THE VARIOUS FORMS OF EMPLOYMENT

A distinction is made between on one hand the ratified or inspiring ILO standards, as well as the domestic and European provisions, applicable in a particular country and 3.2.1, and on the other, the rules identified when the employment relationship covers more than one country 3.2.2.

3.2.1 In a Particular Country

Generally speaking, the national, European and international labour provisions covers at least the wage-earners. The precise scope and the exceptions result from the text. The ILO instruments contain 'flexibility clauses' that give the State the possibility of choosing the extent of their obligations.

Considering the international labour standards, I observe that the ILO Conventions and Recommendations on freedom of association, equality of opportunities and treatment, and the abolition of forced and child labour apply to all workers, regardless of the nature of their contracts; they cover the self-employed. Some, as Convention No. 141 on rural workers' organizations, refer explicitly to people working on their own account. In practice however, those workers as well as the staff of SMEs or with a precarious contract face serious obstacles to organize because of the sometimes temporary nature of their contract, the more individualized relations or the dispersion of working places. The conditions imposed by some legislation further impede certain categories of employees to create or join trade unions. This is the case when the law requires for a minimum number of affiliates within the enterprise to be involved. In brief, the impact of trade unions is generally not felt in those undertakings.

The Employment Policy Convention, 1964 (No 122) and the complimentary Recommendations concern all those who are available and willing to work. They refer to clandestine and seasonal workers, family members and self-employed.[5] Convention n°142 on human resources development, 1975 and Convention n°159, 1983, concerning the rehabilitation of disabled persons apply

---

4. Guy Davidov, Mark Freedland, Nicola Kountouris, *The Subjects of Labor law: 'Employees' and Other Workers*, in Mattehew W. Finkin, Guy Mundlak (eds), *Research Handbook on Labor Law* (Cheltenham, Edward Elgar, 2015); Bernd Waas, *The Legal Definition of the Employment Relationship*, vol. 1 (1) European Labour Law Journal, January 45–47 (2010); Juan Raso Delgue, *La contratación atípica del trabajo*, Montevideo, AMF (2009).
5. Article 1, §2 of Convention no. 122; §12 of Recommendation no. 122 and §§ 8 and 27–29 of Recommendation no. 169.

to both wage-earners and self-employed. Needless to write that the Convention n° 158 on dismissal does not cover independent people and even all employees.

ILO standards regarding labour inspection relate mainly to workers employed in industry, commerce or agriculture. Convention n° 129 provides for the optional extension of the system to categories of agricultural workers, such as tenants, sharecroppers, members of cooperatives or of the operator's family, even if controlling the social legislation in these sectors is difficult.[6] Convention n°150 on Labour administration, 1978 focuses mainly on wage-earners, although it also includes the self-employed, members of cooperatives, tenants, sharecroppers, etc. when national conditions so require; the text refers expressly to self-employed workers 'occupied in the informal sector'. Convention n°160 on labour statistics refers to economically active population.[7]

Conventions on working conditions have been drafted for the workers of industry, commerce, offices or agriculture. Legally, they often cover the self-employed, though this is purely theoretical in such fields as working time. On the contrary the extension of basic safety and health provisions is easier to operate; certain Recommendations say this expressly.[8] Statistics show that temporary workers are more exposed to professional risks than established wage-earners. International labour standards sometimes call for the extension, progressively if need be, of their scope to self-employed workers.[9] Australia and UK have sought to extend Occupational Health and Safety (OHS) law protection to those undertaking remunerated work in a relationship not governed by an employment contract.[10]

The Paid Educational Leave Convention, 1074 (n°140) expressly allows the adoption of special provisions for small enterprises.[11]

The standards on the protection of women workers (the prohibition for women to do certain jobs; maternity guarantees) are conceived for situations where the women are subordinates. Nevertheless Convention No. 183 of 2000 on maternity protection expressly covers women employed 'in atypical forms of

---

6. Article 5 of Convention no. 129 on labour inspection in agriculture, 1969.
7. Articles 7 and 6§2 b) of Convention no. 150, Art. 1 of Convention no. 160.
8. *See* the following ILO Recommendations: the Working Environment (Air Pollution, Noise and Vibration) Recommendation, 1977 (No. 156), para. 1(1); the Occupational Safety and Health Recommendation, 1981 (No. 164), para. 1(1); the Occupational Health Services Recommendation, 1985 (No. 171), para. 2(2); the Asbestos Recommendation, 1986 (No. 172), para. 1(2); the Safety and Health in Construction Recommendation, 1988 (No. 175), para. 2(2) (d); the Chemicals Recommendation, 1990 (No. 177), para. 4. Recommendation No. 192 of 2001 requires that Convention No. 184 on health and safety in agriculture, also adopted in 2001, be extended progressively to self-employed farmers.
9. Such is the case of Convention No. 119 on the guarding of machinery, 1963, Art. 13.
10. Paul Harpur & Phillip H. James, *The Shift in Regulatory Focus from Employment to Work Relationships: Critiquing Reforms to Australian and UK Occupational Safety and Health Laws*, vol. 36 (1) Comparative Labor Law & Policy Journal, 111–130 (fall 2014).
11. Article 9 of Convention No. 140.

dependent work'.[12] Recommendation No. 162 on older workers, of 1980, applies to wage-earners and independent workers. Conventions Nos. 97 and 143 define migrant workers, in terms of the protection they grant, as people who migrate from one country to another with a view to being employed otherwise than on their own account.

Many of the social security conventions adopted since the end of the Second World War offer the possibility of protecting specific categories of residents or of the working population (including, therefore, independent workers); the States also have the choice, however, of covering only wage-earners. Nevertheless most vulnerable workers are among those the instruments make exceptions for; such is the case of casual workers but also, in respect of occupational accidents and diseases, of homeworkers.[13] The supplementary recommendations frequently ask that these restrictions be waived, gradually if needed. Other conventions expressly authorize the exclusion of people working exclusively on their own account[14] or limit their scope to those bound by a subordinate working relationship.[15] Some stipulate that they apply to apprentices.[16]

What is more, these workers find it difficult to meet the conditions to receive benefits, in particular the obligation to have worked or contributed for a minimum period (or worked for a minimum number of hours or paid a minimum amount of contributions). Convention No. 102 on social security (minimum standards), 1952, and more recent conventions, authorize States to impose qualifying periods, although the supplementary recommendations usually suggest that it be waived. Furthermore the amount of the benefits usually depends, in national social security schemes, on the earned salary while among 'atypical' workers that amount is often modest. This is not the only method of calculation, however. Convention No. 102 and the subsequent instruments permit – and themselves use for their 'average' standards for determining the minimum amount – techniques that are not directly related to the wage received.

The rules may contain special adjustments for the specific employment conditions of certain groups of workers. Convention No. 102, for example, has a special provision on unemployment benefits for seasonal workers.[17] Generally speaking, States have to revise the pensions and social insurance systems so that they are no longer tied to continuous employment. In the USA where the pensions are normally contractual, they must be delinked from any particular employer and let the beneficiary keep the acquiring rights when he/she has no job or to transfer them to the new employer.

---

12. Article 2 §1 of Convention 183; §1 of Recommendation No. 162; articles of Convention No. 97 and of Convention No. 143.
13. Convention No. 121, Art. 4 §2 (b).
14. As Convention No. 71 on seafarers' pensions, 1946, Art. 2(2) h.
15. For example, Convention No. 175 and Recommendation No. 182 on part-time work, 1994.
16. Conventions No. 121 (Art. 4), No. 128 (Arts 9 and 22) and No. 130 (Art. 10).
17. Article 24, para. 4.

The fundamental problem is to adapt social security – which is a guarantee of income – to new categories of workers (at least in terms of their numbers) who have few resources and for whom social welfare schemes cannot, for one reason or another, make suitable provision. Sometimes, in order to promote hiring, the State acts as a substitute, at least in part, for the parties concerned when it comes to financing social benefits for these workers. The system can also be financed by general or particular taxes. The Income Security Recommendation, 1944 (No. 67) and the Medical Care Recommendation, 1944 (No. 69) had already established the principle of a comprehensive coverage of the whole population by a social protection scheme associating measures of social insurance, social assistance and public services. The Social Protection Floors Recommendation, 2012 (No. 202) promotes a guaranteed minimum income for the poorest.[18]

3.2.2 Covering More than One Country

Let us again adopt the double perspective of the enterprise and of the worker.

3.2.2.1 *Depending on the Type of Enterprise and on the Production Process*

The main question relates to the law applicable to multinational companies. They must respect the rules and regulations of the countries in which they operate. The social protection of their staff however is far from being always perfect because of the uncertainty about the law applicable and of the weakness, or the lack of transparency, of the domestic legislation.

Multinationals that operate in countries where wages are low are increasingly concerned by the conduct of their subsidies or subcontractors in respect of their staff. In addition to the ethical questions the situation poses, these large corporations are worried about their images and the threats of boycotts brandished at the instigation of unions or human rights organizations. Consumers would undoubtedly be shocked to learn that their clothes were manufactured or their fruit picked by children in abysmal conditions of health and safety, or by workers deprived of the basic right to organize and of collective bargaining. In a positive step forward, this has prompted a number of multinationals to establish a relatively detailed code of good conduct and to have its application monitored by genuine private inspectors hired by them. Thus, the private sector makes up for the absence of adequate protective legislation and for the shortcomings in national supervision.

The same reasons push them to comply with the non-compulsory instruments of international organizations such as the ILO Tripartite Declaration of

---

18. Jean-Michel Servais, *International Labour Law*, §§ 714–719 (4th ed., The Hague, Kluwer, 2014).

Principles concerning Multinational Enterprises and Social Policy, adopted by the Governing Body in 1977, the Organisation for Economic Co-operation and Development (OECD) Guidelines for Multinational Enterprises, the UN Social Compact or the UN Guiding Principles on the Implementation of the 'Protect, Respect and Remedy' framework, which were developed by J. Ruggie and endorsed by the Human Rights Council on 16 June 2011.

While the latter apply to all States and to all business enterprises, both transnational and others, regardless of their size, sector, location, ownership and structure, they are of special relevance for the multinationals. The Guiding Principles insist on the corporate responsibility to respect human rights. Business enterprises may be involved with adverse human rights impacts either through their own activities or as a result of their business relationships with other parties. Guiding Principles 13 and ff. elaborate further on the implications for how business enterprises should address these situations.[19] They contain a human rights duty of diligence which goes much beyond the classical liability regulation, stating that where a business enterprise contributes or may contribute, directly or through their business relationships with other parties, to an adverse human rights impact, it should take the necessary steps to cease or prevent its contribution and use its leverage to mitigate any remaining impact to the greatest extent possible. The French Parliament has adopted an act to give effect to these Principles.[20] The Performance Standards on Environmental and Social Sustainability of the International Finance Corporation (World Bank group) also requires that the client will take commercially reasonable efforts to ascertain that the third parties who engage these workers are reputable and legitimate enterprises and have an appropriate environmental and social management system that will allow them to operate in a manner consistent with the requirements of Performance Standard 2 (on labour and working conditions).

More generally, the voluntary commitment to a Corporate Social Responsibility (CSR) may lead major enterprises to extend their labour obligations. The European Union (EU) directives no 2005/29/CE of 11 May 2005 on unfair business-to-consumer commercial practices and no. 2014/95 of 22 October 2014 on disclosure of non-financial and diversity information by large undertakings and groups further stimulate them to do so. The last one includes among the required information a description of the policies pursued by the undertaking in relation to social and employee matters and respect for human rights, including due diligence processes implemented.

---

19. United Nations, General Assembly, *document A/HRC/17/31* of 21 March 2011.
20. No 2017/399 of 27 March 2017. *See also* Isabelle Vacarie, *Le travail dans un marché sans frontières*, 10 Revue de droit du travail, 634–64 (October 2015). For an analysis of recent cases in England, the Netherlands and Canada in this regard, *see* Renée-Claude Drouin, *Le développement du contentieux à l'encontre des entreprises transnationales : quel rôle pour le devoir de vigilance ?* 3 Droit social 246–255 (2016).

3.2.2.2 *Depending on the Modalities of Work*

3.2.2.2.1 *International Labour Mobility*

When the employment relationship includes a transnational dimension, the private international law of each country normally applies. The EU has coordinated the rules for their Member States with European Regulation 593/2008 of 17 June 2008, known as 'Rome I' according to which in most cases, employment contracts shall be governed by the law of the country where the employee habitually carries out his work.[21]

This however only applies to individual employment contracts. Collective agreements come under the general provisions of the instrument, which cover all acts that give rise to contractual obligations. Article 3 states that the parties must have the freedom to choose the applicable law. If they do not, Article 4 requires that the applicable law be that of the country in which the party required to effect the characteristic performance of the contract has their habitual residence, that is to say (Article 19), the place of central administration for companies, employers' organizations or trade unions. This solution also corresponds to parts of certain directives that cover other areas, such as worker information, consultation and participation. It is only really suitable for company or group-wide agreements. Nevertheless no overall solution clearly emerges with regard to agreements reached between employers' and workers' organizations from more than one country or at European level, and when it comes to applying national collective agreements to international employment relationships.[22] Indeed, it is by no means easy to determine, as Article 4 stipulates, the law of the country with which the contract is most closely connected.

Last but not least, major differences exist in domestic laws concerning labour law, in particular with regard to the regime of collective bargaining and strikes. Coordination of collective activities at transnational level may therefore appear rather uneasy.[23]

3.2.2.2.2 *Posted Workers*

The EU directive no 96/71 of 16 December 1996 applies, in the framework of the provision of services, to undertakings that take one of the three following

---

21. Articles 8 et seq.
22. On this second point *see* Fabienne Jault-Seseke, *La détermination des accords collectifs applicables aux relations de travail international*, in *Le droit international privé : esprit et méthodes. Mélanges en l'honneur de Paul Lagarde*, Paris, 455–473 (Dalloz, 2005).
23. Michael E. Gordon, Lowell Turner (eds), *Transnational Cooperation among Labor Unions* (ILR Press, Ithaca, NY, 2000).

transnational measures: (i) post their employee to the territory of another Member State, under a contract concluded between the undertaking making the posting and the party for whom the services are intended; (ii) post their employee to an establishment or to an undertaking owned by the group in the territory of a Member State; (iii) being a temporary employment undertaking or placement agency, hire out an employee to a user undertaking established or operating in the territory of a Member State.

These undertakings must guarantee workers posted the terms and conditions of employment covering a limitative list of core provisions laid down in the Member State where the work is carried out. As the European legislation is interpreted restrictively by the EUCJ,[24] there is a serious danger that the posting of workers be used to skip the labour law and free movement of workers law protection. The ILO supervisory bodies have expressed their concern about the civil liability of the trade unions in case of strike and its compatibility with the ILO freedom of association conventions (Case *Laval un Partneri* C-341/05 of 18 December 2007) and the consequences of the Rüffert case (C-346/06 of 3 April 2008) on the application of the ILO Labour Clauses (Public Contracts) Convention, 1949 (No. 94). Under EU Regulations 883/2004 of 29 April 2004 on the coordination of social security systems, a posted person shall in principle continue to be subject to the legislation of his/her State of origin.[25]

The EU directive no 2014/67 of 15 May 2014 complements Directive 96/71. It represents the limited result of a largely failed attempt to revise the main rules.[26] Article 5 asks Member States to ensure that the information on the terms and conditions of employment which are to be applied and complied with by service providers is made generally available free of charge in a clear, transparent, comprehensive and easily accessible way at a distance and by electronic means.[27]

3.3 SPECIFIC PROVISIONS

Specific regulations regarding certain categories of persons deal with issues of fundamental importance to them such as wages, employment stability, safety and health at work, social security. They broaden the concept of subordination by extending its meaning or integrating on their own authority other types of relations into the employment relationships 3.3.1. They also elaborate particular forms of labour protection 3.3.2. In brief, they adjust the general rules to situations in which those rules have difficulties to apply.

---

24. See in particular the case *Commission v. Luxembourg* C-319/06 of 19 June 2008 and the two sentences mentioned later on in the text.
25. Article 12.
26. The European Commission has proposed again in March 2016 another revision of those rules.
27. *See also* the CJEU case *Arblade and Leloup* C-369/96 and C-376/96 of 23 November 1999.

3.3.1 Extension of or Assimilation to the Employment Relationship

The ILO Recommendation No. 198 on Employment Relationship, 2006 focuses on the demarcation line between the contract of services and the contract for services. Specific indicators of the existence of an employment relationship should be defined[28] and incentives to disguise an employment relationship be removed. The qualification should be guided primarily by the facts relating to the performance of work and the remuneration of the worker, notwithstanding how the relationship is characterized in any contrary agreed arrangement The abusing recourse to civil or commercial contracts with a view to skipping the labour protection is regularly denounced, as in some Eastern Europe countries or in Portugal ('recibos verdes').[29]

In line with the recommendation, a broad range of means should be allowed for determining the subordination. The Courts may first adopt an extensive definition of the dependence. In the USA or in UK, they take more into account the economic reality.[30] In Belgium and in Italy, administrative bodies have been created to decide on the type of relationship. The domestic law may also proceed by assimilation of certain situations into the employment relationship. It could be done by an authoritative decision to extend the labour law protection beyond the employment relationship (as in France, Germany, the Netherlands, and Sweden). Countries can also use presumptions of subordination or of self-employment (with or without the possibility to prove the

---

28. The text mentions a number of indicators that can be seen in domestic case-laws:
    - the fact that the work is carried out according to the instructions and under the control of another party, involves the integration of the worker in the organization of the enterprise, is performed mainly for the benefit of another person, must be carried out personally by the worker, is carried out within specific working hours or at a workplace specified or agreed by the party requesting the work, is of a particular duration and has a certain continuity, requires the worker's availability, or involves the provision of tools, materials and machinery by the party requesting the work;
    - periodic payment of remuneration to the worker; the fact that such remuneration constitutes the worker's sole or principal source of income; provision of payment in kind, such as food, lodging or transport; recognition of entitlements such as weekly rest and annual holidays; payment by the party requesting the work for travel undertaken by the worker in order to carry out the work; or absence of financial risk for the worker.
29. *See also* EUCJ case C-413/13 *FNV KunstenInformatie en Media* of 4 December 2014. The German Government has submitted at the end of 2015, a bill that provides new rules for identifying contracts of employment; a new s. 611a should be inserted into the Civil Code, introducing criteria that qualify contracts as contracts of employment (*ELLN Newsletter*, vol. 4, no. 12, December 2015).
30. Raffaele De Luca-Tamajo, Adalberto Perulli, *Productive Decentralisation and Labour Law (Individual and Collective Dimensions)*. World Congress of the ISLLSS, Paris, 5–8 September 2006, General Report. For a functional approach of the definition of the employer, *see* Jeremias Prassl, Martin Risak, *Uber, TaskRabbit, & Co: Platforms As Employers? Rethinking The Legal Analysis of Crowdwork*, Comparative Labour Law and Policy Journal (May 2016).

contrary), like in France, Germany, Belgium, Portugal and South Africa.[31] The obligation of the employer to inform the workers on their working conditions, under the European directive n° 91/533 of 14 October 1991, indirectly permits a recognition of the employment relationship

3.3.2 Special Protection

I have underlined the technical difficulties to extend the scope of the labour protection to all forms of work. A number of provisions therefore provide special protection for certain types of enterprises organization and for certain categories of workers. The ability of the public authorities to control the rules and regulations applicable may also be doubtful. Beyond the law in force, there is in both cases a need to rethink workplace regulation.[32]

3.3.2.1 Depending on the Type of Enterprise and on the Production Process

I will examine the special social rules applicable in the small and in the large firms, leaving the micro-enterprises and the self-employed for the second section as they appear much closer to the worker and his problems. The first paragraphs will deal with SMEs, the following ones with successively the subcontracting and the groupings of enterprises, including the integrated groups.

3.3.2.1.1 SMEs

The ILO considers that SMEs are responsible for the creation of numerous jobs throughout the world and 'provide the potential for women and other traditionally disadvantaged groups to gain access under better conditions to productive, sustainable and quality employment opportunities'.[33] The Organization adopted, in 1998, a recommendation No. 189 on the job creation in those undertakings. The preamble insists on the respect of the conventions on freedom of association, abolition of forced and child labour, and of discrimination.

The text considers the policy dimension and the legal framework, the development of an enterprise culture and of an effective service infrastructure and – two topics dear to ILO – the roles of employers' and workers' organizations and international cooperation.

---

31. Giuseppe Casale (ed.), *The Employment Relationship: A Comparative Overview* (Geneva, ILO, 2011); ILO, *The Scope of the Employment Relationship*, Report V, International Labour Conference (91st session) (Geneva, 2003); ILO, *The Employment Relationship*, Report V (I), International Labour Conference (95th session, 2006) (Geneva, 2005); ILO, *Non-standard Forms of Employment*, Document MENSFE/2015 (Geneva, 2015).
32. Katherine V.W. Stone, Harry Arthurs (eds), *Rethinking Workplace Regulation: Beyond the Standard Contract of Employment* (New York, Russell Sage Foundation, 2013).
33. *See* the considering of Recommendation no. 189 (1998).

Provisions allow derogations (exclusions or special rules) for small undertakings or, in the maritime and fishing sectors, for small boat. These undertakings (and boats) are often family undertakings (or vessels) which are thereby excluded from the benefits of the instruments or subject to special provisions.[34]

More generally the expression 'family work' covers two hypotheses: work in family undertakings, i.e. usually in establishments where the only employees are members of the same family, and the work of a special category of workers, the members of the employer's family, no matter what the undertaking. Many of ILO's earlier instruments on labour conditions (hours of work, weekly rest, paid leave, work of women, of young people) do not apply to family undertakings or, more flexibly, authorize the exclusion of those undertakings. Such exceptions are usually not to be found in the conventions on occupational safety and health. Other instruments[35] explicitly stipulate that they apply, on terms and conditions that vary, to family work.

The social security exemptions allowed are aimed more often than not at members of the employer's family, usually on condition that they live under the same roof as he does and work for him. Similar possibilities for exemptions exist in other fields. In some cases, however, the ILO recommendation drafted to supplement a convention on a given subject expressly suggests that the same protection be granted to this specific category of worker.[36]

3.3.2.1.2 Subcontracting

Subcontracting is a usual method to decentralize production,[37] either in the same country or in another one. It has much in common with the regulation of temporary-work agencies that I will deal with later as both establish triangular relations. Subcontracting is of two types, one regarding goods and services, the other, manpower.

In the last case, an enterprise either provides staff, on a temporary basis or not, or loans personnel. The notion covers the intermediaries that recruit persons to work for other. This last formula, which supposes a transfer of

---

34. See for example: the Paid Educational Leave Convention, 1974 (No. 140), Art. 9; the Plantations Convention, 1958 (No. 110) and its Protocol of 1982, Art. 1 (which refers to both family and small-scale enterprises) and a number of maritime conventions (in particular Conventions Nos 53, 71, 73, 91, 92, 133, 147, 165) and Recommendation No. 140. With regard to fishing, *see in particular* the Conventions Nos 113, 125, 126.
35. Convention No. 153 on hours of work and rest periods (road transport), 1979, Recommendation No. 132 on tenants and sharecroppers, 1968, and Recommendation No. 170 on labour statistics, 1985.
36. Examples are Recommendation No. 79 on medical examinations of young people and children, 1946, and, in the field of social security, Recommendations Nos 131 and 134. Convention No. 129 on labour inspection (agriculture), 1969, also expressly provides for this possible extension.
37. Antonio Ojeda Avilés, *La 'externalización' del derecho del trabajo*, vol. 148, núm. 1–2, Revista Internacional del Trabajo, 49–70 (2009).

authority, is totally or partially prohibited as trafficking in a number of countries, except in the case of employment agencies (Belgium, France, if mercantile, Australia, Spain). It is permitted in others (Germany, Austria, Switzerland, UK, and the Netherlands).[38] The ILO Convention (No. 181) on private employment agencies 1997 considers both options; the text allows the operation of private employment agencies and asks for the protection of the workers using their services.

When the activity is illegal, national laws normally imposes penal sanctions. Legislation may charge the user company for the civil obligations deriving from the employment relationship or establish a joint and several liabilities to the user and the provider. The Finnish legislation on employment contracts promotes the right to bargain collectively in favour of the workers placed at the disposal of an undertaking; every employer must comply at least with one national collective agreement; if the provider is not committed to any, the collective agreement applicable to the user company would apply.[39]

With regard to the subcontracting of goods and services, various domestic statutes or collective agreements (as in the USA) make the two employers jointly liable with regard mainly to security and health in line with the international labour standards,[40] but also to wages and/ or social benefits (Austria, France, Italy, Spain, and Finland)[41] or fundamental rights (Finland). The OECD requires corporations to encourage their suppliers and subcontractors to comply with their Guidelines for Multinational Enterprises. Such a commitment may also be part of a social corporate responsibility policy adopted by a company. Some legislation has developed a civil liability based on the fault, on the ownership or on principal business, especially in their safety and health legislation (Italy[42]). A written contract is required in Switzerland between the two firms. The establishment of internal inspections on subcontractors exemplifies the need for sharing social risks.[43]

---

38. Thomas Chaudron, *Les tiers employeurs ou comment conjuguer compétitivité et responsabilité dans la France du XXIème siècle*, Report to Mr. Brice Hortefeux, French Ministry of Labour, Social Relations, Family, Solidarity and City (February 2009); Alain Supiot (ed.), *Au-delà de l'emploi. Transformations du travail et devenir du droit du travail en Europe*; R. De Luca-Tamajo, A. Perulli, *supra*; ILO, *The Employment Relationship, supra*.
39. ILO, *supra*.
40. ILO Convention no. 174 on the prevention of major industrial accidents, 1993, Art. 9c; Convention no. 155 concerning occupational safety and health, 1981, Art. 6.
41. European Industrial Relations Observatory on-line, *Temporary Agency Work and Collective Bargaining in the EU*, http://www.eurofound.europa.eu/eiro/studies/tn0807019s, (28 May 2009); Marie Laure Morin, *Labour Law and New Forms of Corporate Organization*, vol. 144 (1) International Labour Review (2005).
42. Davide Casale, *Joint Responsibility of Enterprises for the Health and Safety of Their Contractor's Workers: Recent Trends in Italian Law*, vol. 36 (1) Comparative Labor Law & Policy Journal, 131–148 (fall 2014).
43. Renée-Claude Drouin, *Responsabiliser l'entreprise transnationale: portrait d'une normativité du travail en évolution*, in PierreVerge (ed.), *Droit international du travail. Perspectives canadiennes*, Cowansville, 306 (Ed. Yvon Blais, 2010).

According to the EU directive no 2014/67 enforcing the directive 96/71 on the posting of workers (Article 12), the State may provide joint liability in the chains of subcontracting. The Court of Justice of the EU (CJEU) had already decided that directive 96/7 does not preclude a domestic legislation imposing to a (building) enterprise, established on its territory, becomes liable, in the same way as a guarantor who has waived the defence of prior recourse, for the obligation on another undertaking, established in another Member State, to which it has subcontracted the conduct of building work or that undertaking's subcontractors to pay the minimum wage to a worker employee by the latter.[44]

Article 4 of the EU directive 2002/14 of 11 March 2002 states that the information to and consultation with staff representatives must include the situation and the likely evolution of the employment within the enterprise as well as any decision which could change substantially the work organization and the employment relationships. This clearly cover information and consultation on subcontracting.

The subcontracting companies are generally small and may therefore escape obligations when the rules provide for a minimum threshold of staff for their application. Example are the obligations to prepare a social plan in France in case of collective redundancies or to establish a collective representation of the employees (European countries). French Courts consider however that the workers of external enterprises that participate in the activities necessary to the functioning of the user company must be included in the workers to be taken into account for staff elections purposes.[45]

Some collective agreements require equality of working conditions between the staff of the subcontracting and the user companies, or at least impose guarantees to both (Spain[46]).

The franchise or the concession appears as a form of subcontracting. The subcontractor may be seen as an independent unit, even if the persons concerned are sometimes assimilated to employees (France) or to 'workers' (United Kingdom) for the application of labour regulations.[47]

3.3.2.1.3 Grouping of Enterprises[48]

Employers 'associations are known as extremely reluctant to any labour regulations regarding the grouping of enterprises. The question has led to chilly debates in the ILO and to a lot of controversies within the EU.

---

44. Case *Wolff* and *Müller* C-60/03 of 12 October 2004.
45. Morin, *supra*.
46. *El País*, 65 (30 January 2006).
47. Raso Delgue, *supra*, pp. 237–241; De Luca-Tamajo, Perulli, *supra*.
48. Pierre Fadeuilhe, France Joubert, *Quelle utilité des groupements d'employeurs?* Revue de Droit du Travail, 84–90 (février 2015).

Some domestic laws do not integrate the notion of groupings in labour law, focusing on the single undertaking as a legal independent entity. Others give relevance to it. A variety of options exist between the two poles, with a varying influence of trade and commercial law on work situations. In Switzerland and the USA, the Courts only sanction frauds.[49] The French and the German systems establish a more significant coordination in this regard between trade and labour law.

3.3.2.1.3.1 Chains of Production

The constitution of chains of production includes, but is not limited to, the recourse to subcontracting. Different contractual arrangements link enterprises for the final delivery of goods, with or without cross-participation in their respective capital. The ILO is involved, with public and private partners, in research and technical cooperation projects aiming at achieving sustainable improvement of labour standards in global supply-chains.[50] The Organization also holds a general discussion on 'decent work in global supply chains' at the 105th Session (2016) of its yearly Conference. In the United States, collective bargaining has occurred at the chain level (multi-employer unit).[51]

3.3.2.1.3.2 'Complex' Employer

Canadian provinces, and to a certain measure the USA, have elaborated the legal institutions of sole (as in the case of a brand demonstrator) or joint employer for the purpose mainly of staff representation.[52] National Courts in Europe have more than once identified the figure of co-employer when it can be proved that the worker is subordinated to two firms.[53]

---

49. De Luca-Tamajo, Perulli, *supra*.
50. This is the case for example of the Child Labour Platform and the Global Business and Disability Network: www.businessanddisability.org.
51. François Gaudu, *Entre concentration économique et externalisation : les nouvelles frontières de l'entreprise*, 5 Droit social, 471–477 (May 2001). More generally, see Kevin Kolben, *Dialogic Labor Regulation in the Global supply Chain*, vol. 36 (3) Michigan Journal of International Law, 425–465 (2015).
52. Pierre Verge (with the collaboration of Sophie Dufour), *Configuration diversifiée de l'entreprise et droit du travail*, (Saint Nicolas (Québec), P U Laval, 2003). See also Judy Fudge, *The Legal Boundaries of the Employer, Precarious Workers and Labour Protection*, in Guy Davidov, Brian Langille (eds), *Boundaries and Frontiers of Labour Law*, International Institute for Labour Studies (Oxford and Portland, Oregon, 2006).
53. Luisa Corazza, Orsola Razzolini, *Who is an Employer?* Centre for the Study of European Labour Law Massimo D' Antona, Working Paper, INT – 110/2014; Yannick Pagnerre, Regard comparatiste sur le co-emploi, *Revue de droit compare du travail et de la sécurité sociale* 1, 84–90 (2016).

3.3.2.1.3.3 Groups of Enterprises

No consensus has been reached within the ILO on the involvement of the groups of enterprises in the protection of labour, with one main exception: the Tripartite Declaration of Principles concerning Multinational Enterprises and Social Policy adopted by its Governing Body in 1977. A Multinational Enterprises Helpdesk provides advice to a variety of users, in particular company managers and workers, to foster the implementation of the document in company operations. Being far from the local conditions, it has, however, been criticized for the extremely general character of some of its opinions.

Not always does the EU Law take the group into account to extend the protection. Interpreting the directive no 86/653 of 18 December 1986 on self-employed commercial agents, the CJEU has decided, where the principal belongs to a group of companies, that benefits accruing to other companies of that group are not, in principle, deemed to be benefits accruing to the principal and, consequently, do not necessarily have to be taken into account for calculating the indemnity to which a commercial agent is entitled.[54]

The EU has however promoted CSR. The adoption of codes of conduct and other social initiatives may be common to all enterprises of the group. The codes in particular may include provisions on fundamental rights at work, on health and safety and the determination of wages.

The EU directive no 2009/38 of 6 May 2009 on European Work Councils has timidly laid the foundations for a European system of labour-management relations. It applies to UE-scale undertakings and groups of undertakings, a group meaning an institution composed by a controlling undertaking and one or more controlled undertakings which are submitted to its dominant influence 'by virtue, for example, of ownership, financial participation or the rules which govern it'. It does not matter whether the central management of the group is located or not in the EU. The CJEU has decided in the *Bofrost* case that an undertaking which is part of a group is required to supply information to the internal workers' representative bodies, even where it has not yet been established that the management to which the workers' request is addressed is the management of a controlling undertaking within the group.[55]

The directive imposes the establishment of a European Works Council or another procedure for informing and consulting employees; it doesn't' include any obligation to negotiate. Some multinationals however have taken advantage of that institution to do so at the group level. A few domestic laws (France, Germany, and Spain[56]) contain a reference to such collective bargaining.

---

54. Case C-348/07 Turgay Semen of 26 March 2009.
55. Articles 2–4 of the directive; case C-62/99 *Bofrost* of 29 March 2001; case C-440/00 *Kühne & Nagel* of 13 January 2004.
56. Morin, *supra*; Manfred Weiss, *Négociation collective et groupe de sociétés en Allemagne*, Working paper (Bordeaux, April 2009); José Luis Gil y Gil, *La negociación colectiva en los grupos de empresas:marco jurídico*, Working paper (Bordeaux, April 2009).

The EUCJ has decided that directive no. 2001/23 of 12 March 2001 on transfer of enterprise also applies to a transfer between two companies in the same group which have the same ownership, management and premises and which are engaged in the same works.[57] This notion of group differ from the one used in European anti-trust law where the agreements restricting competition must be concluded between independent market operators or firms that hold a dominant position on a given market.[58]

I will still mention another sentence demonstrating how the European Court integrates the group within the scope of the directive. When, within a group of companies, there are two employers, one having contractual relations with the employees of that group and the other non-contractual relations with them, the EUCJ has considered possible to regard as a 'transferor' the employer responsible for the economic activity of the entity transferred which, in that capacity, establishes working relations with the staff of that entity, despite the absence of contractual relations with those staff.[59]

The EUCJ has also considered the group of undertakings in relation with the EU Directive no 98/59 of 20 July 1998 on collective redundancies. The adoption, within a group of undertakings consisting of a parent company and one or more subsidiaries, of strategic decisions or of changes in activities which compel the employer to contemplate or to plan for collective redundancies gives rise to an obligation on that employer to hold consultations with workers' representatives. Where the parent company adopts decisions likely to have repercussions on the jobs of workers within the group, it is for the subsidiary whose employees may be affected by the redundancies, in its capacity as their employer, to start consultations with the workers' representatives. It is therefore not possible to start such consultations until such time as that subsidiary has been identified.[60]

An obligation to try to relocate the staff within the group in case of collective termination of employment exists in some countries (France[61]).

3.3.2.1.3.4 Common Activities

France has conceived the 'Economic and Social Unit' in order to ensure that employees received better representation when several legally independent

---

57. Case *Allen* C-234/98 of 2 December 1999. *See* also case *Amatori* C-458/12 of 6 March 2014.
58. Articles 101 and 102 of the Treaty on the functioning of the EU. *See* Pierre Rodière, *Droit social de l'Union européenne*, § 406 (Paris, LGDJ, 2002).
59. Case *Albron Catering* c-242/09 of 21 October 2010.
60. Arrêt *AEK (Futjistsu Siemens)* C-44/08 du 10 septembre 2009.
61. Code français du travail, Art. L.1233-4. Concerning, more generally, the complex issues relating to the existence of groups of enterprises in domestic labour law, see with regard to Spain: Juan Carlos García Quiñones, *El impacto laboral de los grupos de empresa: una asignatura pendiente en el Derecho del Trabajo español*, vol. 4 (1) Revista Internacional y Comparada de relaciones laborales y derecho del empleo (January–March 2016).

undertakings carry out similar or complementary activities and one single entity concentrate in practice all power. The institution does not seem to have much impact in practice.[62] This country has established two more institutions. The first is called 'employers 'groupings' whose purpose is to share manpower; they organize common services like child-care, vocational training, etc. and share liability on the debts of the grouping vis-à-vis their employees and creditor institutions of compulsory contributions. The second consists of time-shared companies, established by the French labour code, to share staff.[63]

The work site is another hypothesis where responsibilities may be shared between several employers, especially for security and health purposes. Where several undertakings are present on the same location, the EU Directive no 89/391 of 12 June 1989 on health at work obliges employers to cooperate in implementing the relevant provisions and to coordinate their actions; they shall inform one another and their respective workers and/ or workers' representatives of occupational risks.[64] In the same manner, the ILO Recommendation no. 164 on occupational safety and health, 1981 urges undertakings engaged in activities simultaneously at one workplace to collaborate.[65]

The French Labour Code again provides for a representation of the employees at the site level.[66] More generally, the negotiations of collective agreements at the branch, district (Italy) or national level, as is still the practice in a number of European countries, make it easier in practice for the trade unions to obtain better working conditions for the precarious workers.

3.3.2.1.4   Transfer of Enterprises

Following the EU directive no 2001/23 on the transfer of enterprise, Member States may provide that, after the date of transfer, the transferor and the transferee shall be jointly and severally liable in respect of obligations which arose before the date of transfer from a contract of employment or an employment relationship existing on the date of the transfer.[67]

3.3.2.2   Depending on the Modalities of Work

Self-employment or independent work, 'parasubordinazione', home-based work, apprenticeship, part-time, fixed-term and temporary work are examined

---

62. Elsa Peskine, Cyril Wolmark, *Droit du travail 2013*, §§986–993 (Paris, Dalloz, 2013).
63. French Labour Code, Art. L1253-21 and Arts L1252-1–L1252-13. See Irene Mandl, *New forms of employment: Developing the potential of strategic employee sharing*, Luxemburg, European Publication Office (Eurofound), 2016.
64. Article 6§4.
65. Paragraph 11.
66. Article L2312-5.
67. Article 3§1.

successively. Voluntary activities and the activities in his/her own household are normally unpaid. They will not be dealt with here.

3.3.2.2.1 Self-Employment

Labour law was developed for the protection of wage-earners; it did not apply to workers subordinate to no one. However, the situation has gradually changed. The word 'social' in 'social question' has got another connotation. Historically it referred to the division of society into classes and especially to the proletariat and its relations with a dominant, property-owning middle class.[68] The social question facing industrial societies and developing countries today concerns the impoverishment, not of the working class but of all those, wage-earners and the self-employed, swept up, usually because of their forced inactivity but also because of their inadequate salary or precarious employment, in a current that is carrying or keeping them away from established structures.

Trade in services is challenging the standard application of labour law, including at the transnational level.[69] A growing number of persons try to find a job managed via the so-called 'sharing economy' platforms such as Uber, TaskRabbit or Handy that lead workers to compete against each other.[70] It has become clear that there was a need to extend at least some of the guarantees to the self-employed.[71]

Codes of commerce and branches of activities regulations include provisions for the protection of independent workers such as standard contracts in agriculture and commercial distribution[72] or rules on remuneration, social security, termination of contract, including for the grantees (Belgium[73]), or

---

68. See for example André Lalande, *Vocabulaire technique et critique de la philosophie*, 998 (Paris, PUF, 1962).
69. Tonia Novitz, *Trading in Services: Commmodification and Beneficiaries*, in Adelle Blackett, Anne Trebilcock, *Research Book on Transnational Law*, 497–508 (Cheltenham, E; Elgar, 2015).
70. See Valerio De Stefano, *Introduction: Crowdsourcing, the Gig-Economy and the Law*, Comparative Labour Law and Policy Journal, 10, 14 (May 2016) and the Joint study by the Foundation for European Progressive Studies (FEPS) and UNI Europa, carried out by the University of Hertfordshire and Ipsos MORI: http://www.feps-europe.eu/en/publications/details/363.
71. *Shaping the new world of work. The impacts of digitalisation and robotisation*, Conference report — ETUI-ETUC Conference Brussels, 27-29 June 2016, pp. 16, 32-33. See already Gérard Lyon-Caen, *Le droit du travail non salarié* (Paris, Sirey, 1990) and also for example Alain Supiot, *L'avenir d'un vieux couple: travail et sécurité sociale*, Droit social, Nos 9–10, 823–831(September–October 1995); Brian Langille, Guy Davidoff (eds), *Boundaries and Frontiers of Labour Law* (Oxford, Hart Publishing, 2006). Another approach would be to adopt a more functional definition of the employer: see footnote 30.
72. Alain Supiot, *Les nouveaux visages de la subordination*, no 2 Droit social, 131–145 (February 2000).
73. J.L. Monereo Pérez, 'El trabajo autónomo, entre autonomía y subordinación', *Aranzadi Social*, no. 5/2009 (Estudio).

parental leave (Canada⁷⁴). The ILO Recommendation No. 132 of 1968 concerns the improvement of conditions of life and work of tenants, sharecroppers and similar categories of agricultural workers.[75] The EU Directive no 86/653 of 18 December 1986 on independent commercial agents has already been mentioned.

Many ILO instruments, as we have already pointed out, use the word 'worker' without qualifiers, i.e. without limiting the meaning, directly or indirectly, to wage-earners. The United Kingdom distinguishes between employees, self-employed and 'workers', granting some protection to the latter. Australia and UK have sought to extend OHS law protection to those undertaking remunerated work in a relationship not governed by an employment contract. Some of those workers fulfil the criteria to be considered in some countries as *parasubordinati*.[76]

3.3.2.2.2 Parasubodinazione

The ILO Recommendation No. 198 on Employment Relationship Recommendation does not deal with the grey area between the contract of services and the contract for services, the relationships called *parasubordinazione* by the Italians, where the dependence is more economic than legal. Germany, Spain, and some other countries know this intermediate category of workers; the persons concerned received some protection in line with the waged employees, with regard to their employment conditions and social security.[77] According to their Spanish Federation, 77% of the new 'autonomous' workers are foreigners.[78] A first attempt to protect persons working through electronic platforms can be seen in Articles L-7342-1 to L-7342-6 of the new version of the French Labour Code.

The criteria and conditions of economic dependency (forms of work: alone, autonomy, etc.; percentage of the total resources from the clients) depend on each domestic law. The weakness of the worker vis-à-vis his client varies according to the major characteristics of this form of work, i.e. the duration of

---

74. Urwana Coiquaud, *Le droit du travail : générateur de pauvreté ? Le cas du Canada*, in Philippe Auvergnon (ed.), *Droit social et travailleurs pauvres*, 334–335 (Brussels, Bruylant, 2013).
75. The scope of the Recommendation is indicated in paras 1–3.
76. Felicia Rosioriu, *Legal Acknowledgement of the Category of Economically Dependent Workers*, vol. 5 (3/4) European Labour Law Journal, 279–305 (2015).
77. Guy Davidov, Brian Langille (eds), *Boundaries and Frontiers of Labour Law*, International Institute for Labour Studies (Oxford and Portland, Oregon, 2006); Deirdre McCann, *Regulating Flexible Work* (Oxford University Press, 2006); Arturo Bronstein, *Current Challenges of Labour Law* (Geneva, ILO/Palgrave, 2009); Leah Vosko, *Managing the Margins:Gender, Citizenship and International Regulation of Precarious Employment* (New York (NY), Oxford University Press, 2010). *See also* Guy Davidov, *The Goals of Regulating Work: Between Universalism and Selectivity*, Labour Law Research Network (December 2012).
78. http://www.efeempresas.com/noticia/el-77-de-los-nuevos-autonomos-en-espana-en-2015-son-de-origen-extranjero-segun-ata.

the relationship and of the lack of freedom in the organization of the production.[79]

The protection also changes from one country to another. The Spanish Act no 20/2007 of 11 July 2007 – el 'Estatuto del Trabajo Autónomo' – requires written contract and regulates the termination of contract and health at work. In Germany, provisions on social protection, working conditions (leaves, safety and health, harassment) and collective agreements are applicable to *Arbeitnehemeränliche Person.*[80]

3.3.2.2.3 Home-Based Work

Home-based workers can be employees or self-employed. We have seen that some legislation assimilate their contract to a contract of employment or presume that they are linked by an employment relationship with a view to apply whenever possible the general labour legislation.

The vulnerability of many homeworkers has lead countries to elaborate new rules of protection and the ILO, the Home Work Convention (No. 177) and Recommendation (No. 184), 1996 which do not apply however to independent workers.[81]

The Convention aims at promoting equality of treatment between homeworkers and other wage-earners and, at the same time, at taking into account the characteristics of their activities. Difficulties to implement some rules on working conditions (as on hours of work) seem obvious. Others remain a priority because of the incidence of certain practices on the life and health of the worker, his spouse and his family. The Convention mentions regulations on safety and health at work and asks States to establish conditions under which certain types of work and the use of certain substances may be prohibited in homework. As concerns hours of work, Recommendation No. 184 simply requests that the deadline to complete a work assignment not deprive a homeworker of the possibility to have daily and weekly rest comparable to that enjoyed by other workers; national laws and regulations should establish the conditions under

---

79. Paul Henri Antonmattei, Jean-Christophe Sciberras, *Le travailleur économiquement dépendant: quelle protection?* Report to the French Minister of Labour, Social Relations, Family, Solidarity and City (November 2008).
80. Marita Körner, *La transformation du contrat de travail*, in *Tendances actuelles du droit social allemand*, Bulletin de droit comparé du travail et de la sécurité sociale, 29–30 (1998); R. Wank 'Germany' in the first part of Roger Blanpain, Takashi Araki, Shinya Ouchi (ed.), *Labour Law in Motion. Diversification of Labour Force and Terms and Conditions of Employment*, vol. 53 Bulletin of Comparative Labour Relations (2005); De Luca-Tamajo, Perulli, *supra*.
81. Article 1(a) of the Convention and para. 1 of the Recommendation. with regard to telework, *see* Tatsiana Ushakova, *Derecho de la OIT para el trabajo a distancia: ¿una regulación superada o todavía aplicable?* vol. 3, no. 4 Revista Internacional y Comparada de Relaciones Laborales y Derecho del Empleo 74–92 (October-December 2015).

which homeworkers are entitled to benefit, as other workers, from paid public holidays, annual holidays with pay and paid sick leave.[82]

A further difficulty comes from the supervision of the applicable rules. Admission to inhabited premises is normally subject to the authorization of the person occupying those premises; that person can refuse entry to controllers, perhaps because of an ill-defined fear of supervision. This is why the Recommendation insists[83] that labour inspectors be allowed to enter the parts of the home in which the work is carried out. Quite often more than sanctions, information on or awareness of the risks to health and the usefulness of protective rules are of signal importance. Several countries have set up bodies of inspectors specially trained for this kind of employment, such as the *Entgeltprüfer* for homework in Germany.

Recommendation No. 184 suggests a number of means of reinforcing the effectiveness of inspection. The home worker should be kept informed of the specific conditions of employment in writing or by other means;[84] employers, or the intermediaries used by them, should be registered (and provide the information requested); they should be required to notify the competent authority when they give out homework for the first time and should keep a register of all home workers to whom they give work; they should also keep a record of the time allocated for a given task and of the rate of remuneration.[85] The inspector then has to supervise, not only compliance with the applicable rules but also, in a way, the validity of the contract and the respect for its content.

The Recommendation deals with other matters, as well: the right to organize and to collective bargaining and the settlement of disputes; remuneration, minimum age, OHS, protection in the event of dismissal, protection of maternity and social security. The laws of some countries have original mechanisms, such as ad hoc committees, to make up for the inevitable defects in this sector of collective bargaining of employment conditions, in particular wages. The Recommendation further encourages information and training programmes and access to the necessary facilities. The Convention requires that labour statistics cover this kind of employment.[86] When the use of intermediaries is permitted, the respective responsibilities of employers and intermediaries must be determined; where such an intermediary is used, the latter and the employer should be made jointly and severally liable for payment of the remuneration due to home workers.[87]

At the EU level, the social partners have signed a framework agreement on telework on 16 July 2002. It deals with equality, the protection of privacy and of data, work organization, equipment, training and health. A directive no 90/270

---

82. Articles 4 and 7 of the Convention, paras 23 and 24 of the Recommendation.
83. Paragraph 8 in addition to Art. 9 of the Convention whose wording is not very specific.
84. Paragraph 5.
85. Paragraphs 6 and 7.
86. Article 6.
87. Article 8 of the Convention and para. 18 of the Recommendation respectively.

of 29 May 1990, as amended, imposes minimum safety and health requirements for work with display screen equipment.

3.3.2.2.4 Apprenticeship

Few instruments exclude from their scope apprentices or other people undergoing practical training.[88] The provisions on minimum age usually allow for obvious reasons, exceptions to the prohibition to work before having attained a given age for tasks performed in the framework of vocational training.[89]

With the high unemployment rate of youth unemployment, what is at stake is every individual's ability successfully to manoeuvre the passage from the school to the workshop or office. Distinct kinds of apprenticeships have been put in place to facilitate their entry into the world of work considering that young people need to alternate between classroom learning and company internships as they approach the end of their vocational training period. The tendency is to integrate the two, to bridge the gap between training and employment, to start work before the training is over and to continue training after work has started. Countries still adjust these new forms of contract to make them more successful (Luxembourg, Spain[90])

3.3.2.2.5 Part-Time Work

Part-time work is the subject of Convention No. 175 and Recommendation No. 182 of 1994. The Convention seeks to facilitate access to this modality of work which may meet the needs of both employers and workers and to provide the persons concerned with the same protection as that granted to full-time workers. The Recommendation suggests that part-time workers benefit on 'an equitable basis' from the facilities and services intended for their welfare. Several provisions of both instruments deal with facilities of access to this form of employment (and the review of the obstacles to the access) and with the transfer from full-time to part-time work and vice versa.[91]

The Recommendation provides part-time workers with a similar guarantee as home workers, namely to be informed of their specific conditions of employment in writing (or by another means). It also discusses how to count part-time

---

88. Convention No. 114 on fishermen's articles of agreement, 1959, excludes from its definition of the term 'fisherman' cadets and 'duly indentured' apprentices (Art. 2). The same holds true for Convention No. 22 on seamen's articles of agreement, 1926 (Art. 2).
89. *See* the Minimum Age Convention, 1973 (No. 138), Art. 6.
90. *Newsletter European Labour Law Network*, vol. 4, no. 12 (December 2015); Francisco Andrés Valle Muñoz, *El contrato en prácticas incentivado como mecanismo de inserción laboral*, 42 Revista General de Derecho del Trabajo y de la Seguridad Social (January 2016).
91. *See also* Jill Murray, *Transnational Labour Regulation: The ILO and EC Compared*, 156 et seq. (The Hague, Kluwer, 2002).

workers in the total number of company wage-earners (for the purposes of certain social laws). As observed before, those workers can find themselves excluded from the social security schemes promoted by Convention No. 102 and later ILO instruments. They may not fit the definition of people covered or meet the conditions to qualify for benefits (minimum period of work or earnings). Both these instruments and those on part-time work nevertheless propose that, if the country's financial resources permit, certain requirements be waived, thresholds lowered, minimum allowances established and other means adopted to circumvent such limits.

The EU directive no 97/ 81 of 15 December 1997 endorsing the framework agreement on part-time work of 6 June 1997 has same purpose: to facilitate the development of voluntary part-time work, contributing in this manner to the flexible organization of working time in a manner which takes into account the needs of employers and workers, and to provide for the removal of discrimination against part-time workers and for the improvement of the quality of part-time work. Clause 4 §2 refers to the principle of pro rata *temporis*.

Clause 3 defines broadly the part-time worker as an employee whose normal hours of work, calculated on a weekly basis or on average over a period of employment of up to one year, are less than the normal hours of work of a comparable full-time worker. Clause 2 authorizes nevertheless Member States, for objective reasons, to exclude wholly or partly part-time workers who work on a casual basis. In the same manner, Article 3 of Convention no 175 gives the ratifying States the possibility to exclude wholly or partly particular categories of workers or of establishments 'when its application to them would raise particular problems of a substantial nature'. Article 8 adds that part-time workers whose hours of work or earnings are below specified thresholds may be excluded from any of the statutory social security schemes, except in regard to employment injury benefits and from any of the measures taken in the fields of termination of employment, paid annual leave and paid public holidays, sick leave, and the maternity protection measures provided under statutory social security schemes.

In those conditions, the most flexible forms of employment relationships, as on-call and zero-hours contracts may remain outside the protection of international and European labour law. The question has been raised whether the protection of the European framework agreement could be extended to contracts where the working time is not fixed in advance, but depends on the demand (*quantitative requirements*). In a case *Wippel*[92] where a contract of part-time employment according to need makes provision for neither the length of weekly working time nor the organization of working time, the CJEU has decided that there was no full-time worker comparable within the meaning of the Framework Agreement; according to the Court, it follows that the contract does not result in less favourable treatment within the meaning of Clause 4.

---

92. Case *Wippel* C-313/02 of 12 October 2004.

3.3.2.2.6 Fixed-Term and Temporary Work

Fix-term contracts includes an element of insecurity, the completion of the relations. The European social partners have signed in this respect a framework agreement implemented by the Directive no 1999/70 of 28 June 1999. The text aims at reaching a balance between flexibility and security on the one hand and, on the other, at ensuring the application of the non-discrimination principle and preventing abuses arising from successive fixed-term employment relationships.

The text affirms, in the general considerations, an extremely important guarantee: contracts of an indefinite duration are the general form of employment relationship. To prevent abuse, the end of the fixed-term employment relationship should be based on objective conditions (clause 3.1). Member States are requested to introduce one or more of the following measures: the obligation to justify objectively the renewal of such relationships; the determination of the maximum total duration of those successive relationships; the limitation of the number of renewals. They determine under what conditions fixed-term employment relationships shall be deemed to be of indefinite duration (clause 5). The ILO Recommendation no 166 on the termination of employment suggests similar measures.[93]

The Framework Agreement lays down the principles of non-discrimination with regard to comparable permanent workers and of pro rata *temporis*. Employers must inform fixed-term workers about vacancies available to ensure that they have the same opportunity to secure permanent positions as other workers. Management should, as far as possible, facilitate their access to appropriate training opportunities. They shall be taken into consideration in calculating the threshold above which workers' representative bodies may be constituted in the undertaking. The employers must provide as far as possible suitable information on the use of fixed-term staff.[94]

Interim and temporary workers (up to a precise date, the completion of a certain work – a harvest – the end of the season) are in the most precarious situation. They may even be afraid to defend their most basic rights. The Directive no 91/383 of 25 June 1991 concerning the safety and health of workers with a fixed-duration or a temporary employment relationship provides safeguards for all of them, but adds further obligations for the temporary employment relationships.

Focusing on private employment agencies, the ILO has adopted in 1997 a Convention No. 181 and a supplementary Recommendation No. 188. The instruments admit the role which they may play in the labour market but bring to the workers concerned protection from abuses. EU Directive no 2008/104 of 19 November 2008 on temporary agency work has basically the same purposes. It puts more emphasis on the need for the development of flexible forms of

---

93. Paragraph 3(2).
94. Clauses 4, 6 and 7.

activities by limiting the cases of prohibitions and restrictions of temporary agency work (Article 4).

The triangular relations between the temporary-work agency, the user company and the worker need to be clarified. In most cases, the two enterprises share the management power so that the subordination link again is not easily identifiable. The instructions about the work are given and, the remuneration normally paid, by the user company. The ILO Convention considers the two hypotheses, the one in which the employer is the private agency itself and, the one in which it is the user enterprise. It asks ratifying States to allocate the respective responsibilities of both undertakings in relation to the working conditions, including minimum wages, collective bargaining, social security and training.[95] The European Directive goes further and considers that the recognition as employers of the agencies ensures the protection of the concerned workers and improves the quality of the work.

I detail below the legal situation of the agency and of the user company.

3.3.2.2.6.1 The Legal Situation of the Temporary Work Agency

Article 13 of the Convention no. 181 promotes cooperation between the public employment service and private employment agencies that must provide information on their structure and activities. Recommendation no 188 proposes concrete measures in this regard.

National legislation seeks to prevent unscrupulous agencies from having recourse to reprehensible practises; they stipulates, for example, the conditions for delivering and withdrawing operating licences; they give legally recognized agencies the possibility to form an association or federation. Some domestic laws appear rather restrictive on the recourse to temporary employment agencies (Belgium, France, Portugal, Spain), while others are more liberal (Australia, the Netherlands, UK, USA).[96] Article 3 of the ILO Convention states that the conditions governing the operation of private employment agencies are in principle determined in accordance with a system of licensing or certification.

The Netherlands have invented the term 'flexicurity', meaning a policy seeking a balance between work flexibility and the necessary protection of the employees: It has been used in an Act of 1 January 1999, based on an informal agreement between the social partners, whose purpose has been to stabilize the position of temporary workers. Interesting enough, the formula provides some security to the employees concerned, in the sense that they may after a time benefit fully from labour and social security law, including a contract with no

---

95. Article 12 of the ILO Convention, Art. 2 of the Directive.
96. Chris Engels, Sophie Maes, *La mise à disposition de travailleurs en Europe*, in Thomas Chaudron, *Les tiers employeurs ou comment conjuguer compétitivité et responsabilité dans la France du XXIème siècle*, Report to Mr. Brice Hortefeux, French Ministry of Labour, Social Relations, Family, Solidarity and City (february 2009); De Luca-Tamajo, Perulli, *supra*; European Industrial Relations Observatory on-line, *supra*.

limit of time, while maintaining the required mobility. It seems well accepted by all parties involved.[97]

The ILO instruments focus on some well-known abuses. Convention no. 181 states that migrant workers must be given sufficient safeguards. Recommendation no. 188 calls on States to combat unfair advertising practices and misleading advertisements, including advertisements for non-existent jobs, and requires the agencies not knowingly to recruit workers for jobs involving unacceptable hazards or risks. It recommends that the contract be written.[98] Once again EU directive n° 91/533 of 14 October 1991 provides an important guarantee in obliging the employer to inform the worker on the working conditions.

The ILO Convention and the Directive no 2008/104 requires that the agencies do not charge directly or indirectly, in whole or in part, any fees or costs to workers.[99] The Directive adds that any clauses prohibiting or preventing the conclusion of an employment relationship between the user undertaking and the temporary agency worker after his assignment should be null and void. The Recommendation also prohibits such clauses. It urges private agencies, as do a number of European legislations and Directive,[100] not to make available to enterprises staff to replace strikers.

Several articles of the Convention deal with the protection of the workers recruited by the agency. These guarantees concern fundamental labour rights (freedom of association and right to collective bargaining, equality of opportunity and treatment, no child labour) and the processing of personal data (which should be limited to matters related to the qualifications and professional experience of the workers and any other directly relevant information). The Recommendation specifies that the agencies should store such data only for so long as justified; the workers should be able to obtain and examine a copy, and to correct any errors. The agencies should not require, maintain or use information on the medical status of a worker, except, with the express permission of the worker, if they are directly relevant to the requirements of a particular occupation and concerned.

The difficulties for the precarious workers in general to exercise their rights to freedom of association and to bargain collectively have been underlined.

---

97. Gustav Heerma van Voss, *The 'Tulip Model' and the New Legislation on Temporary Work in the Netherlands*, vol. 15 (4) The International Journal of Comparative Labour Law and Industrial Relations, 80–84 (1999); Teun Jaspers, *Flexiguridad:? es la respuesta acertada a la modernización del Derecho del Trabajo? Una perpectiva holandesa* in Juan Pablo Landa Zapirain (ed.), *Estudios sobre la estrategia europea de flexiseguridad: una aproximación crítica*, 25–56 (Albacete, Ed. Bomarzo, 2009); ILO, *Combining flexibility and security for decent work*, Document GB.306/ESP/3/1, §4 (Geneva, November 2009).
98. *See also* Art. 19 of the Swiss Act of 6 October 1989 on public employment placement and private agencies.
99. Articles 7 of the Convention and 6 of the Directive.
100. European Industrial Relations Observatory on-line, *supra*; para. 20 of the Preamble of the Directive.

Sometimes (Malaysia), law hinders agency workers from joining trade unions because they works in different sectors. The European Directive and some domestic legislations provide however some measures to strengthen the collective defence of their interests.

According to Article 7 of the Directive, they shall count for the purposes of calculating the threshold above which bodies representing workers are to be formed at the temporary-work agency. In various Western European Countries, collective bargaining plays a significant role in the regulation of their working conditions, but also for the limitation of temporary work by collective agreement (Spain, Sweden). In France, Greece or Italy, those workers have their own trade unions. In others (Belgium, Ireland, Poland, Spain, even UK), national intersector collective agreements apply. The negotiations take place either in the sector of employment agencies or at branch or workplace level concerned.[101]

3.3.2.2.6.2 The Legal Situation of the User Company

Three questions have a direct bearing for the concerned workers: the liability of the user company, the equality of rights with its staff, and, if any, the collective representation of the interests of the temporary workers.

Convention 181, as we have seen, asks the State to allocate the responsibilities of the agency and of the user enterprise. Other ILO standards refer to the determination of responsibilities with regard to health and safety at work.[102] More precise, Directive no 91/383 obliges the user company to specify in advance the occupational qualifications required and the specific features of the job to be filled to the temporary employment agency which shall bring these facts to the attention of the workers concerned. It makes the user undertaking responsible, during the assignment, for the conditions of the work safety, hygiene and health at work without prejudice to the responsibility of the agency.[103]

Even in the absence of any particular legislation, the national courts use private law rules relating the joint and several or the individual liability based on the fault (lack of diligence, fraud, pollution of the environment), on the ownership or on principal business (Occupational Safety & Health (OSH): responsibility for the risk assessment). The joint liability in the field of labour seems more difficult to be accepted in common law countries, as it appears from the Canadian experience.[104] Judges refer mainly to a framework of bilateral employment relationships and resist imposing such a common responsibility in

---

101. European Industrial Relations Observatory on-line, *supra*.
102. Convention no. 174 on the prevention of Major Industrial Accidents Convention, 1993, Art. 9 c); Convention no. 155 on occupational safety and health, 1981, Art. 6.
103. Articles 7 and 8 of the Directive.
104. Geraldo von Potobsky, 'Modalidades laborales y su encuadramiento normativo (Tendencias en Europa y en América Latina)', *Documento de trabajo*, 2009, p. 6.

the absence of a direct control of the work within a triangular structure.[105] The concept of co-employer could be of some help in that case.

Austria, France,[106] Italy, Spain recognize, with differences, the joint and several responsibility of both companies with respect to working conditions, wages, and the cost for security at work. In the case of the remuneration especially, the justification lies in the possibility for the users to benefit from the work and be enriched without cause if wages are not paid. Poland imposes joint and several liabilities for safety and health at work. In the same field, the United States imposes the main responsibility to the user[107] and the Netherlands, an exclusive liability if the user firm does not comply with its obligations.[108]

A second question concerns the equality of treatment with the staff of the user company. The ILO Recommendation only mentions that 'private employment agencies should be encouraged to promote equality in employment through affirmative action programmes'. On the contrary, Article 5 of the European Directive establishes the principle of equal treatment of temporary agency workers with the other workers: for the duration of their assignment at a user undertaking, their basic working and employment conditions shall be, at least those that would apply if they had been recruited directly by that undertaking to occupy the same job. It permits exceptions in two cases: (i) with regard to pay, where temporary agency workers who have a permanent contract of employment with a temporary-work agency continue to be paid in the time between assignments; (ii) if the social partners choose the option of upholding or concluding collective agreements which may differ, while respecting the overall protection of temporary agency workers.

Article 6 guarantees access to employment, collective facilities and vocational training. Temporary agency workers are informed of any vacant posts in the user undertaking to give them the same opportunity as other workers in that undertaking to find permanent employment.

Collective agreements have been concluded in a number of countries (such as Denmark, Spain, and Sweden) on temporary work; they normally provide equality of treatment with the staff of the user company. On the contrary, they

---

105. Judy Fudge, *The Legal Boundaries of the Employer, Precarious Workers and Labour Protection*, in Guy Davidov, Brian Langille (dir. de publ.), *Boundaries and Frontiers of Labour Law*, International Institute for Labour Studies (Oxford and Portland, Oregón, 2006).
106. Morin, *supra*.
107. Arturo Bronstein, *La subcontratación laboral*, report presented in the International Seminar on the Labour Law in the New Millennium, Dominican Republic, April 1999, ILO, San José, Costa Rica.
108. OIT, La relación de trabajo, *supra*; De Luca-Tamajo, Perulli, *supra*. To what concern Latin America *see also*, in particular Arturo Bronstein, *La subcontratación laboral*, ponencia presentada en el Seminario Internacional sobre Derecho del Trabajo ante el nuevo Milenio, Rep. Dominicana, abril, 1999. On-line reviewed on June 2007: www.oit.or.cr/oit/papers/subcontrat.pdf.

authorize deviations from the legal requirement of equal treatment in the Netherlands and in Germany.[109]

As to the collective representation of the interests, only some countries however recognize, in a limited manner, the collective rights of the temporary workers in the user company (Austria, France, Germany, Italy, Spain). In the United States, the National Labour Relations Board (NLRB) has decided that they cannot be part of the same contractual category of workers.[110]

The European Directive no 2008/104 gives the Member States the option to count the temporary agency workers in the user undertaking rather than in the temporary agency, for calculating the threshold above which institutions representing workers are to be formed. While those workers are only represented in the temporary employment agency in Spain and in Sweden, they may be represented in both companies in Denmark, France, Portugal, and the Netherlands. In Belgium, they are mainly represented in the user company.[111] The latter must in any case provide suitable information on the use of temporary agency workers, when providing information on the employment situation to bodies representing workers set up in accordance with national and EU legislation as Directive 2002/14.[112]

In some countries (the Netherlands, Sweden), the trade union protection seems to focus on the control and the regulation of the recourse by the user company to employment agencies. Swedish law refers to collective bargaining that has the possibility to limit it; so do group collective agreements in Spain.[113]

3.4 CONCLUDING REMARKS: AND NOW?

Certain categories of workers appear to be at the extreme margin of the labour law protection.[114] The latest estimate of the number of people who are in the UK, employed on 'zero-hours contracts' in their main employment is 744,000 for April to June 2015, representing 2.4% of people in employment. This latest figure is higher than that for April to June 2014 (624,000 or 2.0% of people in employment). People on 'zero-hours contracts' are more likely to be women, in full-time education or in young or older age groups when compared with other

---

109. Eurofound, *Private employment agencies*, Dublin, European Foundation for the Improvement of Living and Working Conditions, 23, 34 (2008).
110. Luca-Tamajo, Perulli, *supra*.
111. European Industrial Relations Observatory on-line, *supra*.
112. Article 8 of Directive no 2008/104.
113. De Luca-Tamajo, Perulli, *supra* ; Edardo López Ahumada, *Le contenu des conventions collectives des groupes d'entreprises*, Working paper, Comptrasec, Montesquieu-Bordeaux IV University, April 2009.
114. Eurofound, *New Forms of Employment* (Luxembourg, EU publications office, 2015); European Labour Law Network, *New Forms of Employment and EU Law*, 7th Annual Legal Seminar, The Hague, 27–28 November 2014.

people in employment.[115] New Zealand has prohibited such a contract.[116] A recent study finds that those contracts are not extensive in Ireland. However, concern is raised at the prevalence of 'if and when contracts'. The difference between the two forms of contracts lies in the fact that workers engaged under the former are contractually obliged to make themselves available for work, whereas workers engaged under the latter are 'free' to be unavailable for work. The Government has now engaged in a consultation process with the relevant stakeholders.[117]

There is no doubt that a perfect and universal Social Justice, based on a totally equitable institutional framework, is out of reach. If discovered, such a system would require for its implementation a sovereign World State that does not exist.[118] This does not mean that one cannot search for serious improvements which fit well with the present global socio-economic environment, to propose new forms of work security which better adjust to the present instability of employment. The Dutch act on 'flexicurity' is an example. The method implies more often than not to identify existing legal techniques and institutions for new purposes.

When self-employment and precarious forms of wage employment are growing, the protection of work can no longer be based, in the same manner, on the permanent labour relationship. The establishment of social security schemes should therefore more and more be based on tax-paying and residence rather than on the type of relationship.

With regard to employment contracts, it may be difficult to decide whether persons such as home-based workers, sportsmen or women, artists, professional journalists, lorry or taxi drivers should be considered as employees or rather self-employed entrepreneurs. We have seen that various legislations extend the application of labour provisions to some of those workers. In others, law goes further on and presumes either their subordination to an employer (or on the contrary their independence). They are in line with the ILO Recommendation No. 198 on Employment Relationship, 2006. A few laws have gone further and elaborated an intermediary category, often called by its Italian name 'parasubordinazione'. It covers workers who are not legally employees of an employer, but depends economically of one or few contractors.

We have also observed the use, in some countries of joint and several or subsidiary liability, i.e. the liability of the principal enterprise in case of subcontracting and temporary supplying or loan of staff, and timidly of groups of

---

115. http://www.ons.gov.uk/ons/dcp171776_415332.pdf. It is however not possible to say how much of this increase is due to greater recognition of the term 'zero-hours contracts' rather than new contracts.
116. *The guardian*, 17 March 2016.
117. *Newsletter European Labour Law Network*, vol. 4, no. 12 (December 2015).
118. Amartya Sen, *The Idea of Justice* (London, Penguin Books, 2009).

corporations. The technique constitutes an answer to the fragmentation of the firms and the separation it implies between power and responsibility.[119] It has allowed in particular strengthening the guarantees of the persons concerned that have precarious work relations including if they have activities in more than one firm. While the purpose appears quite similar, some law has elaborated distinct figures, in particular the legal institution of co-employer, whatever is its name.[120] Furthermore the responsibility of the leading enterprise could still be extended[121] as shown in the Ruggie's principles which asks firms, in case of adverse human rights impacts, to cease or prevent its contribution with business relationships or even to use their leverage to mitigate any remaining impact[122].

The broadening of the liability corresponds finally to a very basic idea: is it not morally and politically acceptable that the person or the enterprise that benefits from the work be charged with some obligations vis-à-vis the worker that has provided a profit or permitted otherwise an enrichment? This line of thoughts would lead to extend social protection to the gig economy and to all situations where the demarcation line between the dependent worker and the real self-employed is blurred.

The approach to the protection of labour should open to other legal disciplines such as civil and commercial law. Competition law often keeps the double aims of economic freedom and anti-social dumping policies. In EU law, it has an influence on labour law development, in a direction that not always favours the employer. Some European directives request States to consider the principal firm, with a ruling position, in the hypothesis of a group of companies or of triangular relations of the types we may find in temporary and in subcontracted work. Beyond, the notion of enterprise and its different meanings in European Law has to be examined in depth. Economic law inspires the requirements of transparency and accessibility of the information imposed in the European directive no 2014/67 of 15 May 2014 on the posting of workers.

Another important track of thoughts is the development of collective representation and bargaining in such a way that the precarious workers with or without a contract of employment would be better covered in practice. We have

---

119. Isabelle Martin, *Corporate Governance Structures and Practices: From Ordeal to Opportunities and Challenges for Transnational Labour Law*, in Blackett, Trebilcock, *supra.*, at 51–64.
120. Gilles Auzero, *Coemploi: en finir avec les approximations*, 1 Revue de droit du travail, 27–31(2016).
121. Renée-Claude Drouin, *Responsabiliser l'entreprise transnationale: portrait d'une normativité du travail en évolution* in Pierre Verge (ed.), *Droit international du travail. Perspectives canadiennes* (Cowansville, Ed. Yvon Blais, 2010); Guy Davidov, *Indirect Employment: Should Lead Companies Be Liable?* vol. 37 (1) Comparative Labor Law and Policy Journal 5–36 (fall 2015).
122. Such a responsibility has been introduce in the French law by an act no 2017-399 of 27 March 2017.

seen the timid effort made by some countries and by European law in this respect. The possibility to negotiate at a level higher than the enterprise (branch or inter-sector) gives more chance for trade unions to reach this objective.[123]

---

123. *See also* Aristea Koukiadi, Isabel Távara, Miguel Martinez Lucio, *Joint Regulation and Labour Market Policy in Europe During the Crisis* (Brussels, ETUI, 2016).

CHAPTER 4
Enterprise Transformations, Externalization Processes and Productive Decentralization

Adrián Goldin

4.1 THE CRISIS OF THE FORDIST ENTERPRISE MODEL AND THE PROCESS OF PRODUCTIVE DECENTRALIZATION

The economic crisis of the 1970s problematized the twentieth century's predominant enterprise model: the vertically integrated Fordist enterprise, which controlled the whole production cycle- organizationally subject to the so-called scientific organization of work.

Mainly due to – among other factors – the development of information technologies that allowed companies to spread out throughout different geographical locations and to access international markets of developing countries now empowered to compete in terms of relative equality, the Fordist model tends to be replaced by an organizational structure featured by the fragmentation and the decentralization of the production cycle[1] which is now conducted by several business units that are coordinated and connected among themselves. Each unit specializes and focuses on the functions which correspond to that unit's core competences which involve its most effective and cost efficient activities. All other functions are 'driven' out, for such purpose the principal

---

1. Cf. Antonio Loffredo, *Sobre las transformaciones de la figura del empresario: entre contractualismo y sugerencias institucionalistas*, in *Los empresarios complejos; un reto para el Derecho del Trabajo*, Lorenzo Gaeta, Rosario Gallardo Moya (coords) (Bomarzo, 2010).

company relates to the business units that will supply them, in a new organizational structure characterized by relations of cooperation, coordination or even dependence.[2]

In order to participate in this scheme, medium and small specialized and high technology equipped enterprises are created that occupy and exploit market niches related to a specific segment of the production process. This has led to a scheme of *network companies or network of companies,* composed of affiliates and, particularly, completed by external contractors and suppliers who take over duties which, under the Fordist enterprise model, were usually undertaken by the direct employees of the company.

This new scheme involves *a profound change in the externalization process,* previously restricted to less qualified and strategic tasks. Under the former enterprise model, externalization – at least for Labour Law's protective approach – was deemed to be an anomaly. In this new stage, externalization expands first to the company's internal management services (storage, maintenance, cleaning, surveillance, public relations, IT and advice). Subsequently, as an expression of labour's division most modern approach[3] and through the aforementioned specialization process of each unit in its core competences, the dominant company – if any within the network – keeps control of the overall production process, whilst the decentralized units, in turn, add up their own functions, each preserving a certain degree of management autonomy.[4]

The referred technological innovation – particularly in the field of telecommunications – and *the renewal of contractual technology,* were some of the factors that enabled companies to become an aggregate and articulation of contracting and subcontracting.[5] In order to materialize this decentralization process different contractual categories are used, some classic, some amended and some new. Classic contracts, such as lease of services, contract of deposit, transportation contract, commission and agency contract are currently used to externalize business activities. However, new contractual structures also appear in this scenario, such as franchise agreements, factoring, merchandising, facilities management, logistics or maintenance agreements and IT supply contracts.[6] Some of these new contracts blur business co-liability, such as those that involve

---

2. *See,* Wilfredo Sanguinetti Raymond, in *Las transformaciones del empleador y el futuro del derecho del trabajo,* published in No. 1 Relaciones laborales 389–416 (Madrid, 2009).
3. Accordingly, Blat Gimeno, Francisco, *El marco socioeconómico de la descentralización productiva,* in *Descentralización productiva y protección del trabajo en contratas. Estudios en recuerdo de Francisco Blat Gimeno* (Valencia Ed. Tirant lo Blanch, Valencia, 2000), particularly, s. 3.3., 'Una nueva división del trabajo entre las empresas'.
4. A scheme that allows a group to adapt and align swiftly to market changes.
5. *See* J. Rivero Lamas, *La descentralización productiva y las nuevas formas organizativas del trabajo,* published in Asociación Española de Derecho del Trabajo y de la Seguridad Social, X Congreso Nacional Español de Derecho del Trabajo y de la Seguridad Social, Ministerio de Trabajo y Asuntos Sociales, 22 (Madrid, 2000).
6. The combination of some of these contractual structures allow for the so-called 'hollow corporation' that acts as intermediary of financing, production and marketing organized around a trademark.

managing third party services, those contracts which subject matter consists in *giving something instead of doing something* (supply of goods), those which subject matter involves doing something but where the affirmative duty is not a result but an activity (facilities management or IT maintenance).

The network of companies so created involves reducing the structure of large companies but, correlatively, increasing the size of the *enterprise network organization*. The decentralization process may be either *internal*, by means of direct employees who are seconded to self-organized units (affiliation process) or *external*, when the functions are outsourced all together to be catered by non-affiliate companies or individuals. It may be merely *operative*, if secondary or supplementary activities are outsourced, or *strategic* if some of the company's principal activities are allocated to other contractually tied companies. Finally, it may be *vertical* if the principal company acts as a dominant entity of other subordinate companies or *horizontal* if the network involves cooperative relations at a relatively balanced and equal level.

Only one thing to add to this brief introduction, these decentralization processes are currently generalizing, and thus, they are no longer restricted to developed countries or contingent production economic activities such as civil construction and shipbuilding.

4.2 NEW LABOUR EMERGING PROBLEMS

4.2.1 Generalization of the Phenomenon and Blurring of the Status of the Parties Involved

4.2.1.1 The Problem

The referred company resizing process (i.e., large companies downsizing, network broadening) would not necessarily imply a net loss of jobs actually equivalent to the number of employees released by such companies; in many cases substitution will come into play – and therefore trigger an offset – in two ways: work subcontracting and conversion of former salaried employees into self-employed workers.

However, the process is far from being framed into renewed and modern formats that may be deemed innocuous from a social perspective.

It must be said, first, that globalization has allowed capital and work centres to migrate to countries and places with less protection and lower costs that operate in highly unfavourable contexts for the effectiveness of the labour protection system.[7]

---

7. This phenomenon appears in the transnational field through the so-called '*maquiladora companies*' frequently used as vehicles of the decentralizing strategy of developed countries to drastically reduce labour costs. On the harsh working conditions in maquiladora companies in Central America, see the ILO survey *La situación sociolaboral en las zonas francas y en las empresas maquiladoras del istmo centroamericano y República Dominicana*

Through these and other decentralization means, such new forms of production organization *disorganize Labour Law* and lead to a certain deconstruction of the labour arrangements used by Labour Law to allocate the consequences of its rules.[8] The regulatory prototype of the employer and the businessman fades away as well as their counterpart, the defining paradigm of the employee, both in its capacity as party to the employment relationship and member of his/her professional group.

4.2.1.2 The Employer Status

One crucial phenomenon resulting from this reform process undergone by enterprises is the increasing difficulty involved in identifying who is the businessman upon whom to pinpoint employer's prime responsibility. In fact, the identity and uniqueness of the employer is jeopardized when, in addition to the contractor who formally undertakes the capacity as employer, the final addressee of the work/service is another person upon whom the usefulness of such work/service reverts. Although it is likely that in such context the contents of the protection will not be invalidated, this *pluralisation* of the businessman hampers the attachment of liability for its performance.

The distinctly binary feature that has historically characterized the employment relationship is thus altered. In this scenario, problems arise when trying to identify the employer and, consequently, to pinpoint who is or are liable for ensuring the effective enjoyment of workers' entitlements, beyond those who formally appear as parties to the employment contract. The fact is that, as I highlighted earlier, the decentralization of production, by multiplying the centres for the allocation of duties and liabilities and by diversifying the organization powers, has disorganized the classic standard of the employer's legal status, that tends to blur or, at least, to lose its historical sharpness.

In this context, companies – constantly striving to make their costs variable so as to cope with product market fluctuations- shall avail of the referred erosion and pluralization of the employer's legal status – and not only of the flexibilization of working conditions themselves-to try to avoid some of these costs. This is another means to make them variable, and thus, cut labour costs (*'abaratar la*

(1996). See also Adrián Goldin, *La libertad sindical y las iniciativas voluntarias; el caso de Jerzees de Honduras* in the article *El Derecho a la Negociación Colectiva*, Liber Amicoru Profesor Antonio Ojeda Avilés (Juan Gorelli Hernández, Coordinador) Colección Monografías de Temas Laborales, Consejo Andaluz de Relaciones Laborales, 191 (Junta de Andalucía, 2014), where I outline the Jerzees case in Honduras, where I participated as an expert retained by the Fair Labor Association.

8. Cf. Spiro Simitis, *Il diritto del lavoro ha ancora un futuro?* 79 Giornale di Diritto del Lavoro e di Relazioni Industriali 617 (1997), cited by Fernando Valdes dal Re in the paper *Descentralización productiva y desorganización del Derecho del Trabajo*, published in 2 Revista Universitaria de Ciencias del Trabajo, 41–63 (2002).

laboralidad').⁹ The fragmentation of companies and of the employer's status allows misbalancing protections, thus posing problems for Labour Law.

In fact, employment costs and the resulting responsibility are shifted on to the business units upon which the production process is decentralized – affiliates, subcontractors and suppliers¹⁰ – however, the principal company (in the *vertical* network) withholds the right to impose the contractual arrangement, the working day and time schedules and the allocation of shifts and holidays upon such units. In other words, the parent company imposes the contractual conditions, and yet, it undertakes no liability as a party to the relation or as regards the consequences arising therefrom.¹¹

This split of roles, authority and powers among the different players who hold the role of businessmen and who try to avoid, instead, being labelled as employers, involves a certain evanescence of the contractual party status hindering its identification, preventing its easy individualization and obstructing the attachment of responsibility. The latter is aggravated by what I once termed -when defining the contractor as the responsible party- the *employer's inconsistency*, that arises from the fact that in many cases the employer is not the owner of the bulk of assets for which the worker actually renders services, thus severing the relation or ratio that normally exists between the number of employees that the employer hires and the fixed capital allocated to production.¹² The employer status is difficult to pinpoint: as regards its functions and the exercise of the right to control work performance, the condition as ultimate recipient of the utility stemming from the employee's work and the resulting responsibility for ensuring employees' effective enjoyment of their entitlements.¹³

In this context, the employer-businessman status has been put into challenge mainly by the *internal* decentralization trends –particularly agency work. This contractual arrangement challenges the unity and uniqueness of the obligation relationship resulting from an employment contract, since it is the

---

9. Spanish term coined some time ago by Antonio Ojeda Avilés.
10. Cf. Alain Supiot, in his inaugural address at the XXI World Congress of Labour Law and Social Security, Cape Town, 15–18 September 2015.
11. Cf. Antonio Loffredo, *supra* n. 1.
12. Cf. my communication to the Seminar on Freedom of Enterprise and Labour Relations (*Seminario sobre Libertad de empresa y Relaciones Laborales*), La Toja-Santiago de Compostela 12–16 April, 1993 on the issue *Las empresas de trabajo temporal en la Argentina*, 1031 (published in DT LIII B).
13. In continental European legal systems, 'the prohibition of the separation between the formal employer, who bears the employment risks and liabilities, and the employer who effectively owns the firm and exercises control and direction over the working activities, derives from the traditional hostility toward any form of labour intermediation (*merchandeur, meister, caporale*) whereas 'a general acceptance of this phenomenon took place in the United Kingdom' (Luisa Corazza, Orsola Razzolini, *Who is an Employer*, in Comparative Labor Law (Matthew V. Finkin and Guy Mundlak eds) Research Handbooks in Comparative Law, 132–152 (Edward Elgar Publishing, Cheltenham, IK, Northampton, Ma. USA, 2015).

agency who –as in other contractual arrangements, such as subcontracting-formally undertakes the status as the employer of the temporary worker, *but neither exercises the integral powers arising therefrom nor necessarily bears the labour responsibilities, which tend to be apportioned between the Agency and the user company.*

4.2.1.3 *The Employee Status*

This process involving the *deconstruction* of the single employer status[14] and the decentralization towards – in many instances – several individuals (external collaborators who render their work personally and directly with their own resources) fosters the presence of real or alleged autonomies, coordinated – however – in line with the principal organization's production needs; self-employment becomes one of the instruments for the externalization of activities, since it allows reducing workforce and payroll volumes and shifting risks to the workers themselves. Resorting to these arrangements serves the purpose of avoiding as well as of disguising the existence of employment relations.

Accordingly, in the *continuum* going from self-employment) to work under an employment relationship, a grey area is growing and developing by way of the so-called semi-self employment or *parasubordinated* (in the term- lavoro parasubordinato – coined by Italian academics) engaged to the principal company by means of civil or commercial law governed contracts, thus expanding the grey area that always existed in the interior of such *continuum*. This is the main – however not single – reason for the recent creation and development of what has come to be known within the ILO as 'ambiguous employment relationships';[15] reflecting work that is dependent in economic terms (although it may appear as self-employment), that calls for realigning the responsibility standards traditionally used. On the one hand such workers are, in fact, more independent[16] and as such entitled to less labour guarantees, whilst on the other hand they are allocated more responsibility, such as the duty to supervise and correct their own mistakes.[17]

These outsourcing arrangements amount to transformations in production that, in the words of D'Antonna, make it possible for the same professional tasks to be hired indistinctly either under an employment relation basis or under a

---

14. Cf. Fernando Valdés dal Re, *supra* n. 8.
15. Central idea that led to the adoption of 2006 ILO Recommendation (No. 198) concerning the Employment Relationship in the 95th ILO Conference; *see*, particularly, report V (1) prepared by the ILO on the Employment Relationship in http://www.ilo.org/public/spanish/standards/relm/ilc/ilc95/pdf/rep-v-1.pdf .
16. And not always in fraud of the law. Accordingly, Wilfredo Sanguinetti Raymond, *La dependencia y las nuevas realidades económicas y sociales: ¿un criterio en crisis?* published in no.2 Doctrina Judicial Laboral (Rosario, Argentina), 5 et seq. (July 2000).
17. These collaborators establish in many occasions exclusive, stable and durable relations, with technical and functional independence but with net material unequal positions.

self-employment scheme.[18] The referred larger responsibility and independence allows suppressing, with the resulting cost savings, certain intermediate hierarchical levels. Contractual arrangements, which not always take the form of labour law governed arrangements, are used to render services, thus new contractual arrangements arise such as telecommuting and other types of home-based work and subordination adopts new faces in the attempt of eluding such condition.

Does this trend involve that enterprises give up any of their powers? As has been rightly said, this does not involve a retreat of such powers or more democracy in the enterprise, since the diligence and submission of those workers is ensured by their concerns for keeping their jobs. It involves, actually, extending the grey zone existing between subordinated work and self-employment, occupied by an intermediate category of players, formally independent but who are economically and materially dependent of the activities of the principal company. The progressive use of these arrangements – truly 'ambiguous' relations or the outright use of fake self-employment[19] – has led several legal systems to conceive special regulations for economically-dependent self-employed workers.[20]

Such model obtains payroll savings by resorting to this type of working arrangements (either directly or through subcontracting) which involve precarious employment – temporary contracts, part time work – and the correlative salary undermining. *In other words, the externalization phenomena is in the base of the expansion and spread of the different working arrangements by way of temporary work and part-time work, and also explains – as earlier stated – the rising ambiguity of the contractual arrangements currently in use.*

4.2.2 Degradation and Precarization

If Labour Law relies on the general technique of diverting basic labour conditions from the phenomenon of business competition, the productive decentralization process has reinstalled such competition by shifting functions from large to smaller companies and, thus precisely, less controllable.

Productive decentralization reduces the security, stability and guarantees that labour legislation has been affording in the past to employees under an employer-employee subordinated relation. In addition to the indefinition of the status of the parties involved, there is a transit towards precariousness and temporariness. In this frame, auxiliary companies – affiliates, subcontractors,

---

18. Cf. Massimo D'Antona, *La subordinazione e oltre. Una teoria giuridica per il lavoro che cambia*, in *Lavoro subordinato e dintorni. Comparazione e prospettive* (a cura di) Marcello Pedrazzoli, 43 (Ed. Il Mulino, 1989).
19. The remarkable expansion of self-employment (*trabajo autónomo*) in productive decentralization reflects the lack of legal protection of such working arrangement and, once again, reintroduces the need of considering the enactment of a statute for its protection.
20. Such are the cases of Spain, Italy, UK, Germany and Hungary, among others.

suppliers – justify their engagement of temporary workers not on the nature of the tasks involved but on the nature of the business relationship to which the contract of employment is associated. Job stability no longer depends on the development of the principal company's activities, to which production cycle such temporary workers are ultimately integrated, to depend exclusively on the contents and duration of the relationship between the subcontractor employer and the principal company, even when the ordinary and permanent needs of the principal company are catered through such temporary workers.[21]

Detached in this way from the principal company, the labour terms and conditions of workers of decentralized units are not in line with those enjoyed by the direct employees of the principal company, which collective bargaining agreements are not applicable to the former, and even which are sometimes replaced by other agreements affording a lower protection. Thus, the existence of precarious employment is accompanied by *salary erosion or undermining*.[22] Its economic justification lies in that contractors only maintain such capacity to the extent that they offer, through their own workforce, work/service that is cheaper than the one that would be provided through direct employment. Such use of productive decentralization processes actually involves a lowering of the statutory rights afforded to workers by legislation, without the need of amending such legislation.

4.2.3 The Effects on Industrial Relations

This process involving the blurring of the worker's status as a contractual party, which generally reflects progressive erosion and undermining of working conditions –salaries, work quality, social security protection – extends also to the worker's condition as member of a professional category and alters the rules regarding industrial relations.

The decentralization of production and, particularly, the delocalization of companies resulting from progressive market internationalization, its displacement and resizing, particularly, the growth of small companies, the relative downsizing of large companies, the organization dismemberment, the corresponding reduced dimensions of contractors, the reduction of payroll –together with the emergence of new functional scenarios (groups and networks of companies, decentralized sectors, auxiliary companies), are *organizational expressions which are lacking in their interior the traditional landmark of solidarity, cohesion and social power of workers that is the rationale for industrial action and collective bargaining* and therefore significantly hinder the implantation of trade unions; difficulty that is aggravated by the trends towards a greater individualization, the shifting of functions to auxiliary companies that resort to

---

21. On this issue, Jesús Mercader Uguina, *La contratación temporal en la jurisprudencia del Tribunal Supremo*, 29 et seq. (Valencia, Tirant lo Blanch, 1999) and Luis Miguel Camps Ruiz, *La contratación laboral temporal*, 31 et seq. (Valencia, Tirant lo Blanch, 1995).
22. Accordingly, Loffredo, *supra* n. 1.

workers of different conditions (subordinated, members of cooperatives, economically-dependent self-employed workers and outright self-employed workers), many times under a precarious work arrangement. Additionally, as result of the foregoing, the scope of collective bargaining and the ensuing bargaining unit is blurring.

As noted above, as result of these difficulties collective bargaining agreements effective in user companies are not applicable to decentralized units, and in some cases, such bargaining agreements are even replaced by others affording less labour guarantees. This owes to the fact that both the principal company and its direct employees will try to avoid a bargaining unit from establishing a certain degree of uniformity in the employment terms to be applied to both direct employees and workers of decentralized units; neither is the user company willing to pay better conditions nor are its direct employees willing to distribute the benefits they enjoy. *This is the problem that arises whenever the trade union does not represent externalized workers, who are deemed to be outsiders by the direct employees of the user.*

4.3 PRODUCTIVE DECENTRALIZATION TECHNIQUES IN MERCOSUR AND IN CHILE

4.3.1 General impact on Labour Law

In view of the above, it can be said that Labour Law has been seriously affected and that it is facing problematic issues which are not easy to resolve.

Thus, *the progressive narrowing of its scope of application, as a consequence of the growing replacement of employment contracts by working arrangements that involve disconnecting services rendered from the production process*, all of them characterized by combining independence, at least formally, regarding the performance of the activities, with more or less intense degrees of relation to the strategic goals of the companies for which services are rendered. Also, *the degradation of the protective and homogenization role traditionally played by labour rules, arising from either statutory or contractual sources, as regards working terms and conditions* resulting from the upsurge of precarious working arrangements to hire employees. Arrangements that are generally subject to rules applicable to work on an independent contractor basis or to collective bargaining agreements less favourable than those that would apply to non-precarious employment contracts.

In the frame of the Fordist enterprise, shifting duties and functions to different players would have been regarded fraudulent and legal regulations would have sought to recouple the traditional binary employee-employer relationship, the generalization of externalizations no longer allows such alternative. What in the former model would have only introduced some crevices and preventions in the social protection system, today's widespread implantation constitutes a core problem in Labour Law. This raises the question of whether *the mechanisms used to resolve the past marginal problem that externalization posed to the operation of the protection system, are still effective even in the face of such a complex, varied and extended myriad of decentralization strategies.*

However, one has to admit that decentralization and its subsequent externalization of activities has turned into a production organization arrangement that, alongside entrepreneurial freedom,[23] cannot be suppressed. There are no rules, except for a few exceptions,[24] preventing a businessperson from outsourcing to perform production processes or mandating it to cover all its work posts by directly employed workers,[25] thus, the unfavourable projections resulting from the decentralization and externalization processes must find other solutions.

4.3.2 The Technical Regulations Used in MERCOSUR and in Chile

It should be noted, once again, that in the early times of the history of Labour Law in civil legal systems – such as the sub region subject matter of this document – the law was hostile to externalizations. The 'legitimate' employment relationship was exclusively that held by employees with the *real businessman* (this was the term used to refer to the user or principal company) and not with the merely *formal* one; the *employment relationship* would therefore prevail over the contractual formality and the relationship was governed by the so-called *principle of primacy of reality*. Externalization processes were admitted as mechanisms of exception in the attachment of liability, the purpose of such a restrictive perspective was to prevent fraud to the law.[26]

The generalization of the productive decentralization process as a nearly universal mechanism of production organization – which, as earlier said, legal systems are unable to prevent today – tends to reduce the security, stability and equality guarantees provided in the past by labour protective legislation at a time

---

23. Freedom that is not restricted to the time of incorporation of the company, but that extends to the determination of its purposes and the establishment of its organizational structure as it may adequate to place it a competitive position within the market.
24. This is the case of Brazil, where – as described below – subcontracting is forbidden for the so-called 'activities-end'. *See* footnotes 35 and 36 below and the text from which they originate.
25. Accordingly, in Argentina, as strictly held in an opinion issued by the Attorney General of the Labour Appellate Court (*Fiscal General de la Cámara Nacional de Apelaciones del Trabajo*) (Dictamen N° 33.888 del 17/5/2002, *in re* 'Nemen, Ricardo c/ Aguas ArgentinasS.A.', *'the company is entitled to the undisputed authority to organize the company (art. 64 LCT), as an expression of its property and freedom of contract rights'*.
26. As stated by Luisa Corazza, Orsola Razzolini 'the continental European legal systems the prohibition of separation between the formal employer, who bears the employment risks and liabilities, and the employer who effectively owns the firm and exercises control and direction over the working activities, derives from the traditional hostility toward any form of labour intermediation whenever the subcontractor (the service provider) appears to be neither a "genuine" entrepreneur nor a "real" employer and, at the same time, is not a licensed intermediary agency' (*supra* n. 13).

when full-time employment in a specific company was the nearly exclusive working arrangement to hire human services.[27]

The idea is, therefore, for Labour Law to protect the economic and social conditions of workers who fall outside the scope of protection afforded by user companies, of workers whose unfavourable legal and economic situation contrasts with the job security and availability of social protection mechanisms enjoyed by direct employees covered under stable rules with principal companies. It is thus necessary, *to reduce the distance currently existing between the direct employees of the user company and those who are related to such company either by way of subcontracting or as allegedly self-employed workers,*[28] by providing socially equitable solutions that will give an adequate answer in view of the impossibility or impracticability of attempts to limit the spread of such organization form.

MERCOSUR countries make an exception to this latter restriction – and have generally implanted the prohibition of *workers supply*, except for the supply of temporary workers in the usually regulated scope of temporary *agency work* (permanent leased personnel is only allowed in Uruguay, subject to the conditions I will mention later). Upon infringement on this prohibition, the most widespread solution is, as we will see below, disregarding such agency's intermediation and treating the relationship as a direct employment between the employee and the user or principal company.[29]

The prevailing refusal of permanent workers supply arises from the fact that lawmakers of the region *reluctantly* prefer *subcontracting*, which although problematic and subject to regulations, does not create such application problems.

4.3.2.1 *Subcontracting*

4.3.2.1.1 *Definition*

Subcontracting is a business practice where the subcontractor is a real entrepreneur or businessman who conducts activities by means of its own organization, undertaking risks and liabilities and acting as an employer who exercises the rights of organization and direction of its companies. If such conditions are not met, the alleged subcontractor is either a *work supplier* (as earlier stated, this

---

27. It must be said also, since it is highly explanatory, that decentralization also served as a mechanism of external flexibility (payroll reduction and corresponding cost reduction); accordingly, see G. Barreiro González, *Notas sobre la descentralización productiva en la empresa y su escisión interna*, 94 Revista Española de Derecho del Trabajo 168 (1999).
28. J. Rivero Lamas, *supra* n. 5, at 34.
29. Instead, in the case of a worker supplied by a temporary work agency and the temporary nature of the work would be breached, the consequence tends to be that such relation, apart from being treated as a direct employment with the user company, will be deemed of permanent and indefinite duration.

practice is outrightly prohibited) or merely a fraudulent 'straw man'. In this latter case it would be, in my own words,[30] a *weak intermediation*, since the law fails to acknowledge it and disregards it; this disregard amounts to disregarding the intermediation act – as if it had never existed – and involves establishing a direct employment relation between the employees of the alleged intermediary and the user company.[31]

This is the treatment afforded to subcontracting in the new and prevailing context in MERCOSUR and Chile:[32] the described illegitimacy of subcontracting carries the consequences attributed to instances of what I have called *weak decentralization* by application of the so-called disregard of the intermediary technique.[33] Additionally, in Argentina and Chile the law imposes joint and several liabilities on the intermediary (disregarded as employer) and the user company. As earlier stated, only Uruguay allows for the arrangement of permanent workers supply, provided that the intermediary is the *one who organizes the tasks and delivers it to the user company* since it is also disregarded if it only acts to attach liability upon himself/herself on account of the rights of the workers who carry out the work.[34] In Brazil, conversely, the cases decided by the Superior Labour Tribunal distinguish between the so-called 'activities-means'[35] as regards which subcontracting is deemed legitimate and 'activities-end'[36] as regards which subcontracting is not admitted.[37]

If there is an admissible intermediary – a person who meets the conditions that are *proper of a genuine entrepreneur and employer* – the subcontracting shall

---

30. *See* my paper *Normas laborales y mercados de trabajo argentino: seguridad y flexibilidad*, CEPAL, División de Desarrollo Económico Santiago de Chile, 32 (December 2008).
31. This rationale is aligned with the rest of the continental systems, that try to prevent decoupling the formal employer, who undertakes risks and responsibilities, from the employer, who is the actual owner of the company and exercises direction and control of the work (*see supra* n. 13).
32. As regards Chile, *see* Francisco J. Tapia Guerrero, *Descentralización empresarial y responsabilidad laboral en Chile*, included in *La descentralización empresarial y la responsabilidad laboral en América Latina y España* (coordinators Tomás Sala Franco, Cristina Mangarelli & Francisco J. Tapia Guerrero), 85–118 (Ed. Tirant lo Blanch, 2nd Ed. Valencia 2011).
33. *See supra* n. 13.
34. On productive decentralization in Uruguay and, particularly, its legal treatment, *see* Cristina Mangarelli, *Descentralización empresarial y responsabilidad laboral en Uruguay*, included in *La descentralización empresarial*, supra n. 32, at 349–396.
35. Such being understood as the activities that are auxiliary or supplementary to the economic activities of the user company (which includes temporary work, private security and cleaning services).
36. Such being understood as activities inherent in the economic activities of the user company.
37. A 2004 bill proposed suppressing the distinction between 'activities-means and activities-end' so as to allow the subcontracting of any activity. There were strong reactions against such bill, even from the Labour Superior Tribunal), which held that the approval of such regime would severely damage workers' rights. The bill has not been approved yet (Cfr., Sean Cooney, Darcy du Toit, Roberto Fragale, Roger Tonnie & Kamala Sankaran, *Building BRICS of Success?* also included in *supra*. in footnote 13, pages 440–473).

be real. In such case, *the guarantees of the claims held by subcontracted workers should not be different from those enjoyed by direct employees under the employment of the user company.* This is secured by imposing joint and several liabilities upon the user company that is the ultimate addressee of the activities rendered by the employees of the subcontractor.[38] Such guarantees cover both the workers' access to salaries and further labour claims as well as timely registration with social security agencies and further obligations undertaken by the contractor company.

4.3.2.1.2 Attribution of Liability

However, it should be noted that not every subcontracting triggers the user company's joint and several liability. In general, *the subcontracting of works or services outside the scope of the principal company's activities* will not trigger such liability, in the understanding that in such case the user company does not intend to shed duties and liabilities, but the objective need of obtaining work/services in the market that the user company would be unable to perform with its own means; it would be, what I have designated as, a 'strong intermediation', that is one that does not transfer responsibilities onto the user or principal company.

Conversely, liability will be extended to the user company in the case of subcontracting services which fall within the scope of the *normal and specific activities conducted* by the user company (Argentina) or whenever *the activities belong to the organization of the principal company, either within or outside such company* (Chile), or *forms part of the normal or proper activities of the establishment, whether principal or accessory,* also within or outside the establishment (Uruguay). In Brazil, the Labour Superior Court decisions have created a subsidiary liability of the user company in case non-performance of the contractor's obligations, such liability being only applicable to the so-called 'activities-means' since, as earlier mentioned, subcontracting in the case of 'activities-end' is forbidden.

Admittedly, such treatment imposes the need of determining what can be considered to be part of *the activity proper of the principal company*. Do these activities include auxiliary, secondary or ancillary activities, permanent or temporary? A restrictive approach that, to some extent, would place the latter out of the scope of liability, excludes precisely the most vulnerable collectives, more prone, thus, for subcontracting to result in the degradation of their working terms and conditions.[39]

What is the type of liability imposed in MERCOSUR member countries and Chile? In Chile and Uruguay, the user company is entitled to information rights,

---

38. *See*, accordingly, Juan Rivero Lamas, *supra* n. 5.
39. These are workers who render services in certain service companies (cleaning, security and surveillance, for instance) who have no other resource than their unskilled labour.

and if used, its liability is only *subsidiary*; conversely, it will be jointly and severally liable. In both countries, and also in Argentina, the user company is also entitled to withholding rights if the contractor fails to evidence performance of its obligations *vis-à-vis* workers. In Chile the *subsidiary or joint and several liability* refers to affirmative and negative obligations- both involving doing and giving something- such as the obligation imposed on the contractor to reinstate a dismissed employee in the case of a null dismissal.

In Argentina, where the principal enterprise has the duty of exercising controls over its contractors, the liability, when triggered, is always joint and several, since the mere breach of the rights of subcontracted workers must be understood as sufficient evidence of failure to conduct such controls in due form. In Brazil, the liability of the user is subsidiary in case of default by the contractor, without the need of the contractor's bankruptcy. In Uruguay, the user company must also collaborate in the enforcement of employment safety regulations.[40]

In Paraguay, it is the intermediary – that is the person who hires the services of another person or persons to render services for the benefit of an employer, even when he appears as an independent businessman – *the one who has to declare the capacity in which he acts and the name of the employer for the account of whom he acts upon executing employment contracts. Conversely, the intermediary shall be jointly and severally liable with the employer for the relevant statutory and contractual obligations* (Article 25 of the Labour Code). However, those who *perform services that fall outside the scope of the activities conducted by the person who commissions the work* do not qualify as intermediaries (Article 16), but are employers instead. Therefore, in Paraguay both conditions seem to be necessary to avoid the extension of liability to the user company: (a) perform work for the benefit of a third party, undertaking all the risks involved in performing such work with its own elements and direct and technical independence and (b) that such services or works fall outside the scope of the activities conducted by the person who commissions the work.

4.3.2.1.3 Equal Treatment

In order to place the subcontractor's employees on a comparable footing with the employees of the user company, the enjoyment of identical benefits should be guaranteed, e.g. to be included within the scope of the same collective bargaining agreements and, particularly, to be paid the same salaries. However, this is not the case throughout the MERCOSUR member countries, where equal treatment is reserved only to employees subject to the direction of the same employer (it is, as we will analyse herein below, the case of *agency work*), and not when they act under the control of another person (in this case, the

---

40. This is so pursuant to Art. 17 of ILO Convention No. 155 whereby whenever two or more undertakings engage in activities simultaneously at one workplace, they shall collaborate in applying the requirements of this convention.

contractor) even when they are part of the same production or services process. Non-compliance with this equal treatment standard allows for and fosters the use of subcontracting for the mere purpose of reducing labour costs.

To conclude it must be said that admitting subcontracting as one of the most relevant expressions of productive decentralization tends to create certain dualism or fragmentation of labour markets: one of them composed of the direct employees of the principal company, who enjoy stability and labour conditions usually framed under collective bargaining agreements, and a second market composed of the workers of contractors and subcontractors, who have less stability and are worse paid, lowly skilled and usually under precarious arrangements and temporary work arrangements which duration is not related to the nature of the work but to the duration of the contract of the company to which they are adscribed.

4.3.2.2 Temporary Work Agencies

MERCOSUR countries and Chile regulate agency work, formerly banned as prescribed by ILO Convention 34.

Under regulations in force, temporary work agencies must obtain qualification from the regulatory agency and, both in Argentina and in Chile, they must post a bond securing payment of their workers claims. In Chile the amount of the bond increases in proportion to the number of temporary workers that the agency supplies. Chile, Argentina and Brazil require temporary work contracts to be in writing. Additionally, in Argentina, *the corporate purpose of temporary work agencies must exclusively consist in the supply of temporary workers.*

In the countries of the region, these agencies are only authorized to supply workers for the performance of contingent and extraordinary services or to provide replacements in case of absence, occasional spikes in the activity, organization of conferences, seminars or fairs and the execution of urgent works that cannot be postponed in order to prevent accidents. Conversely, clients cannot resort to work agencies to provide for the replacement of employees who are exercising their right to strike (Chile and Argentina), or to cover posts of workers who have been suspended on the grounds of lack of work (Argentina). In Chile clients may resort to work agencies to kick-off new companies for a term of up to 180 days. In Brazil, the agencies can only supply workers to cater for transient needs to replace regular and permanent personnel of the client company or needs resulting from an extraordinary spike of the client company's activities.

Although the employment relation of temporary workers with the intermediary agency is acknowledged (this is the case of Argentina and Chile), several types of co-liability of the user companies are provided. In Argentina, the user company is jointly and severally liable for the claims of workers supplied by the agency, and is directly liable for withholding and paying their social security contributions. In the case of Uruguay, the user company is jointly and severally liable or secondarily liable, depending on whether it exercises or not its information right as regards the status of compliance of labour obligations and social security contributions, its liability extends for the period of duration of the supply. In the case of Brazil, decisions of the Superior Labour Tribunal have established the secondary liability of the user company in case of default by the agency, without the need of checking the bankruptcy status of the agency. The user company is also jointly and severally liable for social security contributions, remunerations and compensations, in the case of bankruptcy of the agency.

As early stated, agency work is, among the different types of outsourcing, the only one that affords the worker with the right to receive a remuneration equal to that of the direct employees of the user who render the same services. This is provided in the case of Argentina –where temporary workers are also entitled to the protection of the collective bargaining agreement, trade union representation and health coverage in force in the user company where such worker renders services; this is also the case in Brazil, Chile and Uruguay, in the latter, only in the case of supply of temporary work.

4.3.2.3 Groups of Companies

Groups of companies in Argentina include affiliates integrated both vertically to a common parent company and horizontally among them. The law imposes joint and several liability upon all the companies of the group, 'when the group is permanent and fraudulent or reckless actions have been committed'.[41]

In Chile, groups of companies are made up of companies that are not only related by property, but also by their subordination, coordination or supplementariness of their operations; this relation entails the indistinct liability of all the companies' members of the group. At any event, it should be noted that, as in the case of Argentina, groups of companies may be composed through ties of subordination and control or through horizontal coordination.[42]

In Uruguay legal scholars have elaborated the concept of an economic group which presence – insofar all companies members thereof are *subject to a single direction* – triggers joint and several liability upon the companies that are members of the group. Court decisions, conversely, do not require such a *vertical*

---

41. However, under Argentine commercial law, the companies in an economic group are jointly and severally liable regardless of whether any fraudulent or reckless action was committed or not.
42. Court decisions have established that although the members of a group are legal entities with existence and personality of their own, whenever the antecedents show the existence of an organization of companies with elements such as organization unit or management unit, or have shared administrations or corporate domiciles, it must be understood that they are one single company, with the corresponding single and indistinct liability of all of them.

hierarchical integration, thus, the idea of economic group in the court's perspective broadly encompasses two or more legally independent companies, however subject to a single and exclusive direction or sharing a common economic interest. As in Argentina, the consequence allocated to this organization arrangement is the imposition of joint and several liability, the group being treated as the sole employer, thus workers may address their claim against one or all of the companies of the group, although such employee may have formally worked in only one of them. In these terms, liability is not apportioned on the grounds of joint and several but as results of the fact that the group is treated as the single employer.

In Brazil the *Consolidação das Leis do Trabalho* (CLT), is the rule that defines the group of companies as such where two or more companies, each one with its own legal personality, is under the direction, control or management of another, thus constituting an industrial or commercial group (for some legal scholars, an economic group also exists when parties are related and maintain among them merely coordination relations). In such case, the principal company as well as each and all subordinate companies are jointly and severally liable for the obligations resulting from the executory employment contracts; the employee may, therefore, file an action seeking enforcement of the contract either against all the companies in the group or against any one of them. Each company member of a group of companies may exercise powers as an employer without the need of entering into new employment contracts.

In Uruguay and Argentina courts have created the concept of *plural or complex employer,* where in the absence of an economic group, the employer powers are exercised by several companies, thus triggering the liability of all the companies involved.

CHAPTER 5

Lost in Externalisation: A Regulatory Failure of Labour Law?

Riccardo Del Punta

5.1 THE EXTERNALISATIONS, THAT IS THE FRAGMENTED ENTERPRISE

The phenomenon is well-known in all the advanced economic systems: the fragmentation of the enterprise through the externalisation of a growing number of activities and the consequent decline of hierarchically organised internal labour markets have led to more complex relationships that do not fit with the concept of employment as a bilateral and personal contract.

A wide range of situations is involved by these trends, in which the different functions involved in employing labour are distributed among a number of different entities: for example, employment agencies, franchising, subcontracting, labour-only contracting and so forth.

For the sake of this paper, three separate but interrelated questions are posed by externalisation:

(a) How to guarantee a satisfactory enforcement of labour standards in the fragmented enterprises?
(b) Who bears the responsibility towards the employees?
(c) Who is the employer?

Some short reflections will be made on these topics in the following pages.

5.2 A VOICE FROM THE USA: THE FISSURED WORKPLACE

Even the Americans[1] have discovered that the employment relationships in a growing number of industries with large concentrations of low-wage workers have become 'fissured', where the lead firms that determine the product market conditions in which wages and other conditions of work are set have become separated from the actual employment of the workers who provide goods or services.

Employment fissuring therefore represents the intersection of at least two business strategies, one focused on increasing revenues, one on diminishing costs.

The 'external workers' operate in much more competitive markets that create the conditions for non-compliance with labour standards. This point is stressed by Weil in the following terms: 'As major companies have invested in building well-known products as cornerstones of their business strategy, they have also shed their role as the direct employer of the people responsible for providing those products and services. In many cases, the jobs have been shifted to employers who pay low wages, seldom provide benefits, and frequently subject their workforce to conditions that violate wage and overtime, health and safety, and other workplace protection standards. *These conditions are not the inevitable result of the nature of those jobs, but a result of how those sectors are organised*'.

In other words, Weil appears to be concerned exclusively with the higher rate of violations of labour standards which occurs in these industries, and so with the problem of enforcement of labour standards (issue no. 1: *see* above). The externalisation of labour is not considered as negative in itself, but as soon as it determines a slackening of the main labour standards.

Consequently, the principal remedy proposed by the author is a reinforcement and a refocusing (also on the lead firm, which is at the top of the decision-making chain) of the inspections of the Wage and Hour Division (which honestly does not sound as a particularly strong solution from a Continental European viewpoint).

In the second place, his suggestion is to exert pressure on the lead firm through the threat of damage to reputation (as if we were speaking of Corporate Social Responsibility, and this too is quite dissatisfying for a Continental lawyer).

Only in the third place does Weil finally wonder whether, in terms of a stronger policy response in the medium term, the legal regime of employer's liability should be reconsidered, a possible reference for such reappraisal being found in the 1938 Fair Labor Standards Act, which established a broad definition of employer which 'required only that the business owner has the reasonable ability to know that the work was being performed and the power to prevent it'.

---

1. *See* David Weil, *The Fissured Workplace. Why Work Became So Bad for So Many and What Can Be Done to Improve It* (Harvard Univ. Press, 2014).

Nonetheless the issue of subordination, which underlies that regarding the employer, still remains on the margins of US regulation in this field.

5.3 OLD EUROPE ALREADY KNEW

The lost innocence of American scholars is somehow surprising for a Continental European labour lawyer.

I will take as an example a typically Southern European system of Labour Law, such as the Italian one, which has long been very protective and structured, before being deeply amended by a number of reforms adopted in the name of flexibility, as it has happened in most Western countries.

As far back as the 1960s Italian legislation passed a very rigorous law (no. 1369/1960) concerning the situation of workers involved in processes of subcontracting.

Then in the 1970s, long before outsourcing was outsourcing, Italian doctrine[2] had explored the phenomenon known as 'productive decentralization' in order to stress the risks that it entailed for workers' protection and to envisage counter-measures.

Since that period, and along all its course, Italian Labour Law has tried to chase after the processes of externalisation, exploiting different techniques of regulation, sometimes quite invasive (starting with the aforementioned Law no. 1369/1960) with regard to the employer's prerogatives.

The aims of such regulation have been multiple: not only compliance with labour standards (issue no. 1: *see* above), but also the extension of the sphere of liability for obligations towards the subcontractors' employees (issue no. 2) and the establishment of a principle of coincidence between the official employer and the real one (issue no. 3).

Have these various regulations succeeded?

5.4 THE EQUAL TREATMENT RULE

The answer to the previous question is certainly negative for what concerns the rule, provided by the original Italian legislation (but then abolished), under which subcontractors' employees should be treated in exactly the same way as the contractor's employees, since their activity was performed 'inside' the contracting-out enterprise.

This rule was very ambitious but was totally lacking of realism, which should have suggested that it is impossible, and also senseless, to impose an equal treatment among workers normally belonging to different productive sectors. So the equal treatment rule couldn't work and it hasn't worked, as it has been showed by its notoriously high rate of infringement.

---

2. For example, Luigi Mariucci, *Il lavoro decentrato. Discipline legislative e contrattuali* (Franco Angeli, 1979).

At the end the rule was therefore ingloriously abolished by the Biagi Decree (no. 276/2003) and it has survived only in relation to the employees of temporary employment agencies, who are entitled to the same treatment as the employees of the enterprise where they are sent on a mission.

5.5 THE VICARIOUS LIABILITY RULE

The most important rule provided by Italian law, and by other European legislations, concerns the vicarious liability of the contractor towards the subcontractor's employees in the event that their credits are not honoured by the employer.

It is important to remark that this liability concerns not only the immediate subcontractor, but all the other subcontractors that may form the production chain, in that the first subcontractor is responsible towards the ulterior subcontractors, and so on up to the end of the chain.

The rule of vicarious liability does not affect the level of the standards applied to the employees, but only liability for the credits they have acquired during the period in which they were employed in the subcontracting.

This is undoubtedly an important rule, even though its extension to the entire production chain, whatever long it is, can make some contractors responsible for conduct that they are unable to control (e.g., in relation to health & safety). In particular, when the subcontractor obstructs the contractor's control or conceals essential information, the rule seems to entail dysfunctions.

A possible rationale of this discipline could therefore be that of discouraging contracting-out when it spreads beyond any reasonable possibility of control.

5.6 THE BAN ON THE SUBCONTRACTING OF WORKERS

The most ambitious goal pursued by the Italian legislation since its beginning in the 1960s (even though with amendments along the time) is that of discouraging fictitious subcontracting, as soon as it actually consists of a mere supply of workers and not of a service.

This has been realised through imposing a legal ban on the so-called *'appalto di manodopera'*, that is on a mere subcontracting of workers. The Article 29 of the Biagi Decree (no. 276/2003) actually establishes that when the subcontractor does not have an independent organisation, and/or the contractor exerts managerial authority over the subcontractor's employees, such employees can sue the contractor asking a judge to state that they are in effect employed by him/her.

The principle that the real employer must coincide with the official one has been therefore solemnly upheld, consolidating and to some extent expanding the notion of subordination.

The described rule indeed assures the coherence of the Labour Law system since it is based on the notion of subordination as referred to a certain factual modality of work, under the Article 2094 of the Italian Civil Code: in effect, when an analogous modality of work occurs within a trilateral situation, why shouldn't the legal consequence be the same, that is the legal consolidation of a subordinate work relationship?

However the dividing line between genuine subcontracting and a mere supply of workers is extremely fine and often blurred, especially in labour-intensive activities. For example, consultants are in the habit of suggesting to their subcontracting clients the expedient of obliging the subcontractor to ensure the stable presence of a reference person in the workplace, so as to prevent direct contact with the subcontractor's employees: but this tends to be a fig leaf.

It therefore makes no surprise that the rule in question, although rendered more flexible by the Biagi Decree compared to the original version of 1960, is still characterised by a high rate of violation.

A further question must be posed: this discipline evidently discourages integration between the employees of the contractors and those of the subcontractors.

One could say, conversely, that such integration ought to be encouraged in order to allow the contractor and the subcontractor to learn by working together and to develop their respective know-how and professional skills. If this were true, the current discipline would be clearly inefficient.

So, would it be possible to imagine an alternative discipline that could differently distinguish the good subcontractor from the bad one, on the basis of appropriate criteria, without discouraging organisational integration in the performance of the shared activity?

However, once the feasibility of such a discipline was admitted, the temporary employment agencies might not be very happy about it. Indeed the current discipline also has the function of regulating the market of professional supply of workers: given this, who would resort to employment agencies anymore if the supply of work could be de facto performed (as it is already performed), in a much cheaper way, by subcontractors?

5.7 A REGULATORY FAILURE?

At least two questions remain, at the end, without a satisfactory answer.

In the first place, even though the rule of vicarious liability remains reasonable in itself – as soon as it pushes the leading firm to have control over the process of externalisation, and in particular to take care of the subcontractors' reliability -, should it be applied to the entire production chain?

In the second place, should we insist on defending the coherence of the system centred on subordination, or invent new criteria aimed at selecting the good subcontractors, or instead concentrate solely on the application and enforcement of the labour standards, even if the real employer is someone else (i.e., the American way)?

However if these questions point out regulatory dilemmas which must be dealt with depending on the characteristics of each system, the possibly biggest failure of all is still another one: when outsourcing becomes offshoring, that is when it goes beyond the national borders, both inside and particularly outside Europe, legislation is totally unable to follow it.

Therefore the possibility that certain excesses of national regulations can push the enterprises to escape in the unregulated global market must be realistically taken into account.

As a conclusive remark, if in the USA the regulation goes on lagging behind, European regulation, although it is certainly more advanced, does not feel much better, as externalisation continues to prove itself a very difficult reality to deal with.

CHAPTER 6

Multinational Firms and Local Development: How Global Value Chains Can Sustain Industrial Commons[*]

Mariachiara Barzotto, Giancarlo Corò & Mario Volpe

6.1 INTRODUCTION

In the last decades, economic activity has become international, not just in terms of trade, but increasingly in the organisation of production.[1] We have been witness to a reorganisation of economic activities that has led to the fragmentation of production processes on a global scale and accordingly to the formation of Global Value Chains (GVCs). This phenomenon has affected many sectors, particularly the manufacturing ones, which still play a crucial role in worldwide economic development.[2]

The international fragmentation of production has emerged through the offshoring processes undertaken by multinational companies. These processes consist of the transfer of activities of the value chain to regions with lower

---

[*] This work was supported by the European Social Fund under Grant Cod. 2120/101/21/1148/2013 – Dgr 1148. We gratefully acknowledge the support of the companies' management and S.VE.C. Core Consulting Group (Vicenza, Italy).
[1] Gary Gereffi, John Humphrey, Raphael Kaplinsky & Timothy J. Sturgeon, *Introduction: Globalisation, Value Chains and Development*, IDS Bulletin, 32.1 DOI: 10.1111/j.1759-5436.2001.mp32003001.x (2001).
[2] Suzanne Berger, *Making in America. From Innovation to Market* (Cambridge, Massachusetts: The MIT Press 2013).
  European Commission, *European Commission Competitiveness Report 2013: No Growth and Jobs Without Industry*, MEMO/13/815 25/09/2013, http://europa.eu/rapid/press-release_MEMO-13-815_en.htm (accessed 10 September 2013).

operating costs or specialised skills, and/or even to the widening of markets.³ Many companies have moved lower value-added activities to low-labour cost countries, maintaining in the domestic market the upstream (research and product development, marketing, and finance) and downstream (logistics and distribution) activities considered less replaceable and able to capture larger shares of economic value.⁴ The extensive pursuit of this strategy of commoditising manufacturing by companies in industrialised countries has produced effects on the resource endowment of the areas involved in GVCs, both in advanced and in emerging economies. Specifically, this labour division has led companies more open to international networks to drift progressively apart from their domestic productive ecosystem. This move away from the domestic environment has generated, in the territories in question, a gradual dissipation of the 'industrial commons', defined as the set of external economies of localisation that companies widely employ, albeit often unconsciously, such as 'R&D and manufacturing infrastructure, know-how, process-development skills, and engineering capabilities embedded in firms, universities, and other organisations that provide the foundation for growth and innovation in a wide range of industries'.⁵ Indeed, the relocation of operations to companies in emerging economies has led – in the domestic base – to the hollowing out of specialised supplier networks, competitors and qualified workforces, as well as experienced managers. The fading of this system of resources has accompanied the contraction of the knowledge spillovers⁶ needed to keep the local manufacturing fabric engaged with production activities. As has been widely shown by previous studies, especially in the economic geography literature, spatial proximity⁷ and the interplay of other dimensions of proximity (such as cognitive, organisational, social and institutional ones) are closely connected to knowledge

---

3. Gary Gereffi & Timothy J. Sturgeon, *Globalization, Employment, and Economic Development: A Briefing Paper*, Sloan Workshop Series in Industry Studies, Rockport, Massachusetts, 1, 2 (2004).
4. For example, Donna Everatt, Terrence Tsai & Bor-Shiuan Cheng, *The Acer Group's China Manufacturing Decision*, Version A. Ivey Case Series #9A99M009, Richard Ivey School of Business, University of Western Ontario (1999).
    Ram Mudambi, *Location, Control and Innovation in Knowledge-Intensive Industries*, 8.5 Journal of Economic Geography, 699 (2008).
    For a critical perspective, *see* Giulio Buciuni, Giancarlo Corò & Stefano Micelli, *Rethinking the Role of Manufacturing in Global Value Chains. An International Comparative Study in the Furniture Industry*, 23.4 Industrial and Corporate Change, 967 (2014).
5. Gary P. Pisano & Willy C. Shih, *Producing Prosperity. Why America Needs a Manufacturing Renaissance*, 2 (Boston: Harvard Business School Press 2012).
6. For example, Roberta Capello & Camilla Lenzi, *The Knowledge–Innovation Nexus. Its Spatially Differentiated Returns to Innovation*, 46.3 Growth and Change, 379 (2015).
7. Among others, *see* Ash Amin & Frank Wilkinson, *Learning, Proximity and Industrial Performance: An Introduction*, 23.2 Cambridge Journal of Economics, 121(1999).

exchange,[8] interactive learning and, consequently, to innovation.[9] The geographic separation from production activities seems to lead advanced economies to a severe reduction in the know-how circulation necessary to create new products, to improve and innovate the existing ones, and to be competitive in the long run.[10] Conversely, the relocation of manufacturing activities enables suppliers in emerging economies to gradually develop this know-how, through so-called processes of 'learning by supplying'.[11]

The advantages arising from being part of a GVC, as well as the role of external economies for the competitiveness of the firm, have been long noticed. Nevertheless, the interplay between these two aspects is still overlooked. Recent works have started to shed light on how the combination of local and non-local skills shapes new 'cluster dependent' knowledge.[12] However, there is still scant evidence for the link between companies' international presence and the reproduction of local factors sustaining manufacturing, such as home-country employment and productivity growth.[13] Exploring this relationship would provide policymakers with a deeper understanding of both local and non-local environments and of which externalities can positively affect development by, for instance, attracting Foreign Direct Investments (hereinafter, FDIs) by multinational companies complementing the resources of a socio-economic environment.

In light of this limitation of the existing literature, the following research question emerges as an interesting and relevant, yet under-studied, issue: *how could lead firms foster the sustainability of their domestic industrial commons through engagement with glocal value chains?*

The present work aims to contribute to addressing this issue by providing empirical evidence to identify possible actions that a lead firm can undertake to sustain its home-base industrial commons, by jointly leveraging foreign economic actors' networks and localised external economies. We focus on lead

---

8. For example, Stig-Erik Jakobsen & Knut Onsager, *Head Office Location: Agglomeration, Clusters or Flow Nodes?* 42.9 Urban Studies, 1517 (2005).
9. Ron Boschma, *Proximity and Innovation: A Critical Assessment*, 39.1 Regional studies, 61 (2005).
10. Berger, *supra*.
    Mikko Ketokivi & Jyrki Ali Yrkkö, *Unbundling R&D and Manufacturing: Post-Industrial Myth or Economic Reality?* 26.1–2 Review of Policy Research, 35 (2009).
    Pisano & Shih, *supra* (2012).
11. Juan Alcacer & Joanne Oxley, *Learning by Supplying*, 35.2 Strategic Management Journal, 204 (2014).
12. Jose-Luis Hervas-Oliver & Rafael Boix-Domenech, *The Economic Geography of the Meso-Global Spaces: Integrating Multinationals and Clusters at the Local–Global Level*, 21.7 European Planning Studies, 1064, 1077 (2013).
13. For exception, *see*: Davide Castellani & Fabio Pieri, *Outward Investments and Productivity: Evidence from European Regions* (ahead-of-print) Regional Studies, 1 (2015).
    Stefano Elia, Ilaria Mariotti & Lucia Piscitello, *The Impact of Outward FDI on the Home Country's Labour Demand and Skill Composition*. 18.4 International Business Review, 357 (2009).

firms, as they are crucial players within an economic system, able to affect the system of local socio-economic resources.

The remainder of the chapter is organised into four sections. The next section outlines the concept of industrial commons, devoting particular attention to the effects of offshoring processes on local assets. In the second section we describe the case studies, consisting of ten manufacturing companies based in the northeast Italian region of Veneto, characterised by a significant international presence. The chapter then discusses the empirical evidence gathered through in-depth interviews on the use of the domestic industrial commons undertaken by the companies investigated, and the possible actions that lead firms can take to block the erosion of this system of local resources. The chapter closes by drawing some theoretical and policy implications.

6.2 INDUSTRIAL COMMONS: DEFINITION AND CHARACTERISTICS

Each territory is characterised by the endowment of a specific set of resources, distinct from the ones available in other areas. In principle, the openness of the economy to global trade and the mobility of factors (such as capital and labour) do not reduce these differences, but might actually contribute to boosting them. On the one hand, we observe that resources have not the same degree of spatial freedom; goods more so than services, information more than idiosyncratic knowledge, financial more than human capital and, in general, companies more than institutions. On the other hand, the development of trade tends to increase the comparative advantages of territories, promoting processes of industry as well as functional specialisation.[14] This specialisation has become more and more intensified with the 'ever-finer slicing-up-of-the-value-chain' that has enabled countries to develop comparative advantages in certain fragments of the production process instead of in complete sectors.[15] Thus, the territorial contexts in which companies operate increase their importance, as factors attracting investments emerge more clearly. The set of elements that distinguish these contexts has been defined in several ways: external economies,[16] innovation systems,[17] innovation ecosystems,[18] the determinants of competitive

---

14. Richard E. Baldwin & Simon J. Evenett, *Value Creation and Trade in 21st Century Manufacturing*, 55.1 Journal of Regional Science, 31, 31 (2015).
15. Steven Brakman, Charles Marrewijk & Mark Partridge, *Local Consequences of Global Production Processes*, 55.1 Journal of Regional Science, 1, 2 (2015).
16. Alfred Marshall, *Principles of Economics* (London: Macmillan and Co. 1890).
17. Christopher Freeman, *Technology Policy and Economic Performance: Lessons from Japan* (London: Frances Printer Publishers 1987).
18. Ron Adner, *Match Your Innovation Strategy to Your Innovation Ecosystem.* 84.4 Harvard Business Review, 98 (2006).
   James F. Moore, *The Death of Competition: Leadership and Strategy in the Age of Business Ecosystems* (New York: Harper Business 1996).

advantage,[19] untraded interdependencies,[20] economies of proximity,[21] territorial capital,[22] and industrial commons.[23]

In its 'Territorial Outlook' report, the Organisation for Economic Co-operation and Development (OECD)[24] tried to integrate some of these theoretical contributions, providing an accurate description of the composition of the system of local resources. Among the factors cited by the document are the location and size of a geographical area, production factor endowment, climate, natural resources, quality of life, and the agglomeration economies provided by the cities in the territory, industrial districts or other business networks which limit transaction costs. Among other factors that the OECD report claims to constitute local resources are untraded interdependencies, such as traditions and informal rules enabling economic actors to work together under conditions of uncertainty; solidarity and mutual assistance; as well as the co-generation of ideas that usually grows in clusters of small and medium-sized enterprises operating in the same sector. Finally, taking the well-known definition of Marshall, the report points out that the set of local resources consists of that 'something in the air' emerging from the combination of institutions, practices, attitudes and knowledge that make innovation possible. The aforementioned definitions highlight how the economic environment is endowed with *material* and *immaterial* territorial assets. While material elements, for example infrastructures such as highways, railways, airports and broadband networks, can be funded, ruled and sustained by public authorities, the development of immaterial assets is characterised by an intertwining of local resources which is difficult to reproduce. Given the distinctive nature of the latter elements, we focus on the five immaterial resources, which seem to emerge as the most critical and relevant factors: (1) labour pools and distinctive skills, (2) suppliers and users networks, (3) education and research systems (including universities, higher education, lifelong education, and public and private research centres), (4) public, private and associative institutions, and (5) the financial system and its ability to provide capital and information to companies.

The exchange of resources between companies and the territory has a two-way structure: on the one hand, the locational context influences a firm's ability to compete in international markets; on the other, the features of this context are largely the outcome of enterprises' competitive strategies. In any case, several local resources from which firms benefit constitute a common good

---

19. Michael E. Porter, *The Competitive Advantage of Nations* (New York: The Free Press 1990).
20. Michael Storper, *The Resurgence of Regional Economies Ten Years Later: The Region as a Nexus of Untraded Interdependencies*, 2 European Urban and Regional Studies, 191 (1995).
21. Jean-Pierre Gilly & André Torre, *Dynamiques de Proximité* (Paris: L'Harmattan 2000).
22. Roberto P. Camagni, *Regional Competitiveness: Towards a Concept of Territorial Capital*, 33 (Roberto P. Camagni, Roberta Capello, Barbara Chizzolini, & Ugo Fratesi eds, Modelling Regional Scenarios for the Enlarged Europe, Springer Berlin Heidelberg 2008).
23. Pisano & Shih, *supra* and Gary P. Pisano & Willy C. Shih, *Restoring American Competitiveness*, 87.7-8 Harvard Business Review, 114 (2009).
24. OCED, *Territorial Outlook 2001*, 15 (2001).

produced by the interaction of a number of local actors, both public and private.[25] Consequently, entrepreneurial activities are essential in influencing the dynamics of agglomeration. Indeed, it is the use of local resources by companies that contributes to the accumulation process of territorial capital. The actions undertaken by local actors can either reinforce or, on the contrary, weaken the formation of the local resources system.

The industrial commons can be classified as goods whose use is difficult to exclude from potential beneficiaries, but with a certain degree of rivalry, especially when the allocation of these resources falls below a critical threshold. Given the nature of the positive externality of the industrial commons, from the point of view of economic analysis two important aspects can be identified: first, the existence of a social benefit coming from the fact that the company can draw from the overall local common assets without having to pay a price; second, the absence of property rights that can easily give rise to a market equilibrium lower than the social optimum. Depending on the type of local common resources, the imbalance arising from their under/over-exploitation can lead to the rapid disappearance of goods. The fact that people do not pay for the consumption of a common good leads actors to use the resource at a higher rate than it can be produced (over-exploitation imbalance of a tangible asset), eventually leading to its depletion. Hardin (1968)[26] defines this phenomenon as a 'tragedy of the commons'. It might be also the case that common good under-use weakens the regeneration of the resource, determining its gradual disappearance. This is most likely to happen if the common good is an intangible resource. Nevertheless, as shown in the masterful work of Elinor Ostrom,[27] we do not lack evidence and models of successful governance of the use of the commons, which have significant similarities with the system of local resources to which we refer. This chapter attempts to make a contribution to this discourse by exploring how lead firms can boost the regeneration of their domestic industrial commons through engagement with the local value chain(s) and ineluctable involvement in GVCs.

6.3 HOW THE OPENING UP PROCESSES TOWARDS GLOBAL ECONOMY AFFECT THE INDUSTRIAL COMMONS

Technological changes (mainly in digital innovation and integrated logistic developments) have enabled global openness in trading goods, services, information and production, giving manufacturing firms the 'perception' of being

---

25. Camagni, *supra*, 42.
26. Garrett Hardin, *The Tragedy of the Commons*, 162(3859) Science, 1243 (1968).
27. Elinor Ostrom, *Governing the Commons: The Evolution of Institutions for Collective Action* (Cambridge: Cambridge University Press 1990).
    Elinor Ostrom, *Beyond Markets and States: Polycentric Governance of Complex Economic Systems*, 2.2 Transnational Corporations Review, 1 (2010).

'footloose' companies.[28] Supra-local organised relations (such as global networks of firms) might take place even in the absence of geographical proximity, as actors can coordinate themselves by sharing rules and standards, as well as by the development of long-distance mobility of individuals and information.[29]

Although the globalised economy is characterised by an 'increasing nomadism of firms',[30] GVCs are not borderless and a-territorial networks. They are, instead, networks whose nodes are places where socio-economic-institutional activities are embedded.[31] By reshaping the organisation of economic activity through the creation of GVCs, globalisation has led to a redefinition of the international networks of places, each of which is characterised by a specific economic task that still allows firms to exploit the competitive advantage of locations.[32]

The extensive offshoring of low value-added operations from advanced economies to low-labour cost ones has contributed to a significant change in the resource endowment of the economies involved in the GVC, determining different consequences in emerging countries compared to advanced ones. The relocation of production to enterprises based in emerging economies has made the undertaking of upgrading strategies possible for these companies.[33] In other words, the decentralisation of production has started learning processes even in economies with low-labour costs, therefore raising the ability to offer better goods and services, produce more efficiently, or move towards activities that require the provision of more skills.[34] The upgrading activities in emerging economies are undermining the competitive advantage of industrialised countries. Indeed, in high-income countries, the hollowing out of manufacturing activities has negatively impacted on their home-region productivity growth[35] and new job creation.[36] The drop in the critical mass of specific ties in the domestic socio-economic environment has contributed to the poorer performance of firms and their surrounding environment, a phenomenon known in the literature as erosion of the industrial commons.[37] Despite the relocation of

---

28. Richard E. Baldwin & Simon J. Evenett, *Value Creation and Trade in 21st Century Manufacturing*, 55.1 Journal of Regional Science, 31, 31 (2015).
29. Andre Torre & Alain Rallet, *Proximity and Localization*, 39.1 Regional studies, 47 (2005).
30. Jean-Benoît Zimmermann, *L'Ancrage Territorial des Activités Industrielles et Technologiques: Une Approche Méthodologique* (Commissariat Général du Plan, Paris 1995).
31. Lisa De Propris, *Re-territorialising Production: Global Value Chain*, Paper presented at the Annual Meeting of the SASE Annual Conference, held in Philadelphia, PA, USA (2010).
32. Baldwin, Evenett, 2015, *supra*, 31.
33. Gary Gereffi, *International Trade and Industrial Upgrading in the Apparel Commodity Chain*, 48.1 Journal of International Economics, 37 (1999).
34. John Humphrey & Hubert Schmitz, *How Does Insertion in Global Value Chains Affect Upgrading in Industrial Clusters?* 36.9 Regional Studies, 1017, 1017 (2002).
35. Castellani, Pieri (2015), *supra* 2.
36. David Bailey, Marco Bellandi, Annalisa Caloffi & Lisa De Propris, *Place-Renewing Leadership: Trajectories of Change for Mature Manufacturing Regions in Europe*, 31.4 Policy Studies, 457 (2010).
37. Pisano & Shih (2009), *supra*.

operations to companies in emerging economies, with the aim of concentrating resources in the development of activities with high value-added, it emerges that even the functions that require the involvement of highly skilled workers are increasingly the object of offshoring.[38] As shown by Pisano and Shih[39] in their study on the offshoring of US industry, if the production system falls below a critical threshold of productive activity, the economy runs the risk of weakening the foundation of skills and knowledge which support the most innovative activities, such as research. Examining the effects of the transfer of production by multinational companies to foreign subsidiaries located both in low-labour cost countries and in industrialised ones, Elia et al.[40] (2009) report three major production substitution effects on domestic employment when production is transferred to foreign affiliates: (1) a reduction in the domestic low-skilled workforce; (2) a loss of market share from local suppliers and loss of the opportunity to learn and grow through the relationship with the leader firm; and (3) the sign-out of subcontracting agreements.

The depletion of the economic fabric in advanced economies has triggered a significant reduction of knowledge circulation within domestic localised networks and, as a consequence, a shrinkage of knowledge spillovers. As widely shown by previous studies, knowledge externalities and local informal knowledge and capabilities are crucial for the survival of an innovative ecosystem.[41] Labour mobility and social networks[42] have been identified as different mechanisms channelling knowledge flows, especially in the contexts of limited R&D intensity.[43] The importance of informal local knowledge flows is even more critical in traditional sectors, such as low-tech manufacturing, where actors 'rely

---

38. Alan S. Blinder & Alan B. Krueger, *Alternative Measures of Offshorability: A Survey Approach*, Part 2, 31.2 Journal of Labor Economics, S97 (2013).
39. Pisano, Shih (2009), *supra*.
40. Elia et al., *supra*, 359.
41. Luc Anselin, Attila Varga & Zoltan Acs, *Local Geographic Spillovers Between University Research and High Technology Innovations*, 42(3) Journal of Urban Economics, 422 (1997).
    David B. Audretsch, Maryann P. Feldman, *R&D Spillovers and the Geography of Innovation and Production*, 86.3 The American Economic Review, 630 (1996).
    Phil Cooke, *Regionally Asymmetric Knowledge Capabilities and Open Innovation: Exploring 'Globalisation 2' – A New Model of Industry Organisation*, 34.8 Research Policy, 1128 (2005).
    Glenn Ellison, Edward L. Glaeser & William R. Kerr, *What Causes Industry Agglomeration? Evidence from Coagglomeration Patterns*, 100.3 The American Economic Review, 1195 (2010).
42. Ajay Agrawal, Devesh Kapur & John McHale, *How Do Spatial and Social Proximity Influence Knowledge Flows? Evidence from Patent Data*, 64.2 Journal of Urban Economics, 258 (2008).
    Stefano Breschi, Francesco Lissoni, *Mobility of Skilled Workers and Co-invention Networks: An Anatomy of Localized Knowledge Flows*, lbp008 Journal of Economic Geography (2009).
43. Capello, Lenzi, *supra*.

more on technologies embodied in machinery and equipment' and 'informal knowledge embedded in professionals'.[44]

6.4 THE NEED TO ENGAGE WITH LOCAL AND GVCS

The competitiveness of a company and the health of the communities around it are closely intertwined. As Porter & Kramer highlighted: 'A business needs a successful community, not only to create demand for its products but also to provide critical public assets and a supportive environment. A community needs successful businesses to provide jobs and wealth creation opportunities for its citizens'.[45] As this synergy occurs, territories need to connect local resources with non-local ones. Drawing on international business and economic geography literature, local companies could boost innovation and competitiveness by generating unique repositories of knowledge or 'knowledge domains',[46] combining local and non-local knowledge. Lead firms are pivotal actors that connect territories, convey information and knowledge, and articulate global pipelines.

The intense reorganisation of economic activity was driven crucially by multinational firms' offshoring strategies, which have led to the emergence of global production networks. Multinational firms have considered the creation of GVC an indispensable move in seeking to maintain their competitiveness vis-à-vis very price-aggressive competitors; this has especially been the case in the manufacturing sector.[47] Indeed, for lead firms in advanced economies, being involved in GVCs is a necessary condition for survival and, to a certain extent, their international presence is beneficial not just for the companies themselves, but also for home-region productivity. As the international business literature has shown, outward FDIs are positively associated with a sales increase for investing firms and their suppliers.[48] Notwithstanding this, also according to Castellani and Pieri (2010),[49] FDIs show positive effects on regional productivity, but when multinationals develop a 'too' high volume of cross-border activities, substitution effects with investments in the domestic base are created,

---

44. As cited in Capello, Lenzi, *supra*, 3: Andrea Conte & Marco Vivarelli, *One or Many Knowledge Production Functions? Mapping Innovative Activity Using Microdata*, IZA Discussion Papers, 1878 (2005).
    Roberta Piergiovanni, Enrico Santarelli & Marco Vivarelli, *From Which Source Do Small Firm Derive Their Innovative Inputs? Some Evidence from Italian Provinces*, 12 Review of Industrial Organization, 243 (1997).
45. Michael E. Porter & Mark R Kramer, *Creating Shared Value*, 89.1/2 Harvard Business Review, 62, 6 (2011).
46. Phil Cooke, *Global Bioregions: Knowledge Domains, Capabilities and Innovation System Networks*, 13.4 Industry and Innovation, 437 (2006).
47. Paulina Ramirez & Helen Rainbird, *Making the Connections: Bringing Skill Formation into Global Value Chain Analysis*, 24.4 Work, Employment & Society, 699 (2010).
48. Castellani, Pieri, *supra*, 2.
49. Davide Castellani & Fabio Pieri, *Investimenti Esteri e Produttività: Le Regioni Italiane nel Contesto Europeo* (Eds Alberto Zazzaro, Reti di imprese e territorio, Il Mulino 2010).

threatening the sustainability of the growth process of the territory. Indeed, companies need to be embedded in their home-country territory. As Torre and Rallet (2005)[50] claim, geographical proximity increases the likelihood that economic actors interact but by itself does not enable coordination between subjects and the generation of synergies at the local level.

Hence, it is important to re-think the role of lead firms and how they could sustainably use their local and global networks. Given the strategic decision-making power of multinational companies, lead firms should be elected as integrators of global and local value chains. Both multinational companies and their domestic bases would benefit from the simultaneous use of these chains. In the following section we discuss some of possible simultaneous uses of global and local value chains undertaken by lead firms, which would benefit the multinational companies themselves, as well as the economic environment around them.

6.5 MANUFACTURING PRODUCTION AND OFFSHORING TRENDS

The manufacturing share of western European economies has been decreasing since 2000, falling by 3.3 percentage points of Gross Domestic Product (GDP) over the period 2000–2012. With a small increase of 0.1 percentage points, Germany was the only western European country showing a manufacturing share of Gross Value Added (GVA) higher in 2012 compared to 2000. In the same period (2000–2012), Finland reported the largest decrease in Western Europe (–10.2 percentage points), followed by Belgium (–5.9 percentage points), the United Kingdom (–5.6 percentage points), Sweden (–5.6 percentage points), France (–5.2 percentage points), Denmark (–4.7 percentage points), Spain (–4.6 percentage points) and Italy (–4.5 percentage points).[51]

International fragmentation has affected many production activities. In particular, with respect to the case of Italy, outsourcing has been crucial in the economic systems of the north-eastern region of Veneto, as well as the whole country since 1999. As shown by Corò, Schenkel and Volpe (2013),[52] in the period 1999–2011 the offshoring index – defined as the share of imports of manufacturing goods over value-added in manufacturing – exhibits an upward trend (*except* 2009), both at the national level and in Veneto. The authors claim that the lower value of the index in Veneto compared to the value reported in

---

50. Torre, Rallet, *supra*.
51. Eric Heymann & Stefan Vetter, *Europe's Re-Industrialisation. The Gulf Between Aspiration and Reality*, Frankfurt: Deutsche Bank EU Monitor (2013). Further details can be found at Eurostat, Industrial production (volume) index overview, European Commission (2016), http://ec.europa.eu/eurostat/statistics-explained/index.php/Industrial_production_(volume)_index_overview (accessed 7 September 2016).
52. Giancarlo Corò, Marina Schenkel & Mario Volpe, *International Offshoring, Local Effects: An Inquiry on Italian Firms*, 2 Symphonya, 1 (2013).

Italy can be explained by the strong specialisation of Veneto in manufacturing sectors.

Notwithstanding the fact that the manufacturing industry is the sector that has mainly suffered the impact of the offshoring processes, the importance of this industry is still particularly relevant in advanced economies. For instance, in Europe the manufacturing sector accounts for over 15% of European GDP (EU-27), but the overall impact on the economy is much greater, especially in terms of jobs: Rueda-Cantuche et al. (2012)[53] have estimated that for every new job in manufacturing up to two jobs in other sectors will be created in Europe. Indeed, a solid industrial base not only generates the need for highly skilled workers, but also fosters labour markets in other sectors by inducing demand for related business functions and services. Moreover, a strong manufacturing industry contributes to sustaining as well as stimulating new export channels, as manufacturing exports on average account for over 50% of total exports in Western Europe.[54]

A balanced economy may be a powerful tool to better face economic downturns; for this reason European policy makers are promoting a manufacturing renaissance by: (1) establishing 'an industrial policy creating the best environment to maintain and develop a strong, competitive and diversified industrial base in Europe...';[55] and, (2) reversing the declining role of industry in Europe by targeting an increasing share of the manufacturing sector of up to 20% of GDP by 2020.[56]

In 2012, Italy was the second-largest industrial country in the EU, after Germany. In the same year, it generated 12.5% of the total industrial GVA within the EU, preceded only by Germany, with 30.5% of the total EU GVA.[57]

Despite the decline in the manufacturing sector and the job losses, the northern Italian region of Lombardia (including the city of Milan) and the French capital city region of Île de France recorded the highest number of persons employed in manufacturing in 2012 at the NUTS-2 level within the EU-28. The regions with the next largest manufacturing workforces were Stuttgart (Germany) and the north-eastern Italian region of Veneto, with just over half

---

53. José M. Rueda-Cantuche, Nuno Sousa, Valeria Andreoni & Iñaki Arto, *The Single Market as an Engine for Employment Growth Through the External Trade*, Joint Research Centre, IPTS, Seville (2012).
54. As cited in Heymann and Vetter, *supra*, 2: Rolf Kroker & Karl Lichtblau, 'Industrieland Europa': Die europäische Industrie im internationalen Vergleich (Eds Cologne Institute for Economic Research, Die Zukunft der Industrie in Deutschland und Europa, IW-Analysen No. 88, Cologne 2013).
55. European Commission, *Europe 2020: A Strategy for Smart, Sustainable and Inclusive Growth* (2010).
56. European Commission, *Communication from the Commission to the European Parliament, the Council, the European Economic and Social Committee and the Committee of the Regions* (2012).
57. Eurostat, as cited in Heymann & Vetter, *supra*.

a million people employed in manufacturing.[58] In 2012, among the top twenty list of regions with the highest workforce share in the manufacturing sector, Eurostat (2016) reports eight German regions, followed by five regions in Italy, three regions in Poland, two in France, and one each in Spain and Portugal.

6.6 OVERVIEW OF THE RESEARCH METHODOLOGY

Building on Yin's (2003)[59] work, we adopt a multiple case-study approach, as it represents a suitable research method given the exploratory nature of the analysis.[60] The in-depth investigation implied in this method allows the researcher to acquire a finer understanding of the specific phenomenon under analysis[61] and at the same time provides grounded evidence on whether the findings are idiosyncratic to a single case or generalisable, as they are consistently replicated in several cases.[62] Thus, drawing on previous qualitative studies underlining the need to examine cases showing differences,[63] we have selected ten medium-large sized companies belonging to the manufacturing sector located in Italy which differ in sector and internationalisation process. These companies have been chosen primarily on the basis of four criteria:

- They operate in industries that are facing considerable pressure from the global opening up processes.
- They are based in Italy and, in particular, in the Veneto region. The rationale for this choice is three-fold. First, Italy is the second-largest industrial country in the EU and Veneto recorded the highest number of persons employed in 2012 in the manufacturing sector. Second, Italy has a long and renowned worldwide tradition in manufacturing. Finally, keeping the industrial location constant[64] enables us to control for legal, cultural, and socio-economic frameworks.

---

58. Eurostat, *Manufacturing statistics – NACE Rev. 2 – Data extracted in November 2015*, http://ec.europa.eu/eurostat/statistics-explained/index.php/Manufacturing_statistics_-_NACE_Rev._2 (Last modified on 24 February 2016).
59. Robert K. Yin, *Case Study Research: Design and Methods* (Newbury Park, CA: Sage Publications, 3/e 2003).
60. Jean F. Hartley, Case Studies in Organizational Research, 208 (Eds Cathy Cassell & Gillian Symon, Qualitative Methods in Organizational Research, London: Sage 1994).
    Riccardo Silvi & Suresh Cuganesan, *Investigating the Management of Knowledge for Competitive Advantage: A Strategic Cost Management Perspective*, 7.3 Journal of Intellectual Capital, 309 (2006).
61. Kathleen M. Eisenhardt, *Building Theories from Case Study Research*, 14.4. Academy of Management Review, 532 (1989).
62. Kathleen M. Eisenhardt & Melissa E. Graebner, *Theory Building from Cases: Opportunities and Challenges*, 50.1 Academy of Management Journal, 25 (2007).
63. Eisenhardt & Graebner, *supra*.
64. Lizbeth Navas-Alemán, *The Impact of Operating in Multiple Value Chains for Upgrading: The Case of the Brazilian Furniture and Footwear Industries*, 39.8 World Development, 1386 (2011).

- They belong to sectors in which Italy, and more specifically Veneto, is traditionally renowned to have a competitive advantage; such as technology-intensive and medium-tech industries (such as high-quality mechanical engineering, automation, pharmaceuticals) and traditional manufacturing ones (such as textiles and apparel).
- The sampled companies are multinationals, as they are, by definition, multi-located, which means they choose territories where to develop their value chain. Hence, these companies have available tools to evaluate where to perform the activities and how to undertake strategies of integrated production.

The in-depth study of the ten cases is the result of the collection of primary and secondary data, through semi-structured interviews and archival research. Specifically, the research aimed to collect quantitative data through analysis of published corporate reports, financial reports, and companies' websites. The information gathered was subsequently supplemented by qualitative data obtained through in-depth interviews, mainly with human resource managers or CEOs. During the interviews we obtained information on the organisation's international production activities, as well as the business functions that the company performs and where they take place. The specific links the company has established with the home-base socio-economic environment in which it is embedded were also investigated. To guarantee the anonymity of the ten companies, we list them under pseudonyms.

6.7 COMPANIES' AWARENESS OF INDUSTRIAL COMMONS

From the analysis of companies presented in this research, it has been clearly shown that the presence of critical skills, suppliers, and educational/training programmes play an important role for companies and, in general, for economic area international growth.

The match between skills demand and supply, particularly those necessary for operations management, has allowed companies to develop high-quality products, customising the offering according to demand needs and maintaining control over the innovation processes. As claimed by *Heat*'s General Manager:

> The territory in which the company was funded and has grown is endowed with such a strong and qualified human capital that it has allowed the company to reach its goal over time. ... There is no application area in which we operate that cannot be supplied with the local human resources.

From this perspective, an important role is played by the technical and vocational educational system, in which companies recognise the ability to have created a pool of technical skills and attitudes necessary to constantly develop new viable products. In this respect, *Power*'s HR Manager states:

We benefit from a local higher education (as well as vocational) presence which is extremely qualified. For instance, the local university shapes a basin of knowledgeable graduates. There is no obstacle in employing a mechanical engineer; the university trains professional profiles that absolutely meet our needs.

Over the years, the supply and customer networks have become increasingly global. In particular, the proximity of suppliers is now defined in terms of macro-areas. The Italian bases of the investigated companies mainly use suppliers located in Europe. The cases in which companies use local suppliers refer to a few special needs, such as commodities (e.g., standard solvents used in the chemical industry in *Pharma*'s case) or goods which involve an intensive interchange between producer and consumer. As reported by *Sport*'s CEO:

> The district is fundamental for our supply, for two main reasons: first, the typology of the product they make; second, which is the most important, they own a distinctive competence in the treatment of the raw material that nobody else in the world has. We have to buy this product here because of their knowledge.
> On the one hand, local resources have allowed and supported the growth of the companies analysed; on the other, their different use over time has led to different (re)production capabilities. Indeed, to ensure the existence of these territorial levers, it is necessary for tenants to constantly nourish a critical mass of talented labour force, educational/research centres and specialised firms. Conversely, as happened in sectors where many companies outsourced most of their manufacturing operations to low-labour cost countries, the availability of skilled workers and technicians has been significantly reduced.Because of the high production cost, the technology has - by now - disappeared from Italy. It will be difficult even to keep in Italy the manufacture of the top-quality products (*Sport*'s CEO).

As well as the influence of the local resource system on companies' performance, at the same time the activities undertaken by them contribute to the generation of a set of resources present in a territory. The actions that the companies investigated have taken in favour of the local industrial commons are different, although very often there is an indirect effect (outcome), not intentionally directed to that goal.

Here are some examples drawn from the empirical evidence gathered, where the pivotal role that lead firms may play in sustaining and fostering knowledge specialisation and resources agglomeration emerges. More specifically, they can act as 'anchor tenant',[65] triggering positive externalities by attracting a critical mass of suppliers as well as a skilled labour force.

The evidence shows that, when lead firms perceive the domestic territory as a strategic base performing high added-value business functions, they further

---

65. Maryann Feldman, *The Locational Dynamics of the US Biotech Industry: Knowledge Externalities and the Anchor Hypothesis*, 10 Industry and Innovation, 3 (2003).

stimulate the agglomeration of investments, expertise and specialised companies. As shown in the interviews, Italian plants are places dedicated to the development of strategic products:

> We have made significant investments in Italy to develop [new equipment]. Last year we increased investment to strengthen the group's innovative capacity by enlarging the testing room for new high-technological products (*MotorTwo*'s Chief HR and Organisation Officer).

The analysis shows that the local resources system benefits from the presence of the 'anchor tenant', leaders in the sector in which they operate at the international level. Indeed, the 'catalyst'[66] function performed by the anchor tenant also clearly arose during the interviews with *Heat*'s General Manager and *System*'s HR Manager:

> We manufacture our product in Italy and, moreover, we approved a further expansion in this territory. ... We will employ more than 150 workers (both low- and high-skilled profiles) to supply one of the biggest automobile players.... We absorb workers from those companies - located in this territory - that experienced a downshift (*Heat*'s General Manager).

System's HR manager posits that the company attracts high-qualified workers thanks to the role of technological leader that they play in the sector.

In a few cases, lead firms intentionally act as an anchor tenant in order to be loyal to the territory and to support the accumulation of knowledge as well as expertise. Building on the historical specialisation of the socio-economic environment around which the company is set, *Power* supports the accumulation of knowledge and the agglomeration of expertise by training future workers. Indeed, the company constantly employs intern students enrolling in local technical schools. According to the company's HR Manager, *Power* decided to undertake this action as a tribute to the territory that has allowed (and still allows) it to become (and be) an international player.

Lead firms cannot only act as anchor tenant but they may undertake an 'anchoring role' to 'dovetail the local circuits of embedded and cumulative competences and specialisations with the global circuit knowledge creation and transfer'.[67] Lead firms simultaneously engage both with local and global networks, enabling the pollination of the local socio-environment with new inputs, ideas and innovations.[68] The following quotation reveals evidence of how the

---

66. Maryann Feldman & Nichola Lowe, *Consensus from Controversy: Cambridge's Biosafety Ordinance and the Anchoring of the Biotech Industry*, 16.3 European Planning Studies, 395 (2008).
67. Lisa De Propris & Olivier Crevosier, *From Regional Anchors to Anchoring*, 167, 171 (Eds Phil Cooke, Bjorn T. Asheim, Ron Boschma, Ron Martin, Dafna Schwartz & Franz Tödtling, Handbook of Regional Innovation and Growth, Edward Elgar Publishing 2011).
68. Majella Giblin, *Managing the Global–Local Dimensions of Clusters and the Role of 'Lead' Organizations: The Contrasting Cases of the Software and Medical Technology Clusters in the West of Ireland*, 19.1 European Planning Studies, 23 (2011).

mobility to float whilst still having a firm anchor in the home place[69] can be beneficial to the domestic base (passive internationalisation, foreign collaboration and active internationalisation, respectively):

> Thanks to the investment fund that acquired us, we have been able to absorb expertise of international sales as well as use their knowledge and networks to penetrate new markets. ... The financial resources and know-how of international markets provided by the fund enabled us to boost our locally grounded technical competencies and become one of the major international players in our sector (*MotorTwo*'s Chief HR and Organisation Officer).

To complement and foster local resources with global ones, *System* and *GlassTwo* employ foreign technicians in R&D activities within the Italian branch in order to facilitate the activation of collaborations with research institutions abroad, integrating and thus increasing the knowledge stock in the area. New inputs and innovations also arise from the collaboration with international universities and research centres (such as *Sport*), and with international artists in the case of the fashion/design sector (*GlassOne*):

> We signed partnerships with several international research centres and universities. We collaborated with and for [omitted] university [in the USA]. They paid us to develop [clothes for specific activities]. A small group of students came here to work with our experienced modelers (*Sport*'s CEO).
>
> We collaborate on a continuous basis with leading architects and designers (*GlassOne*'s HR manager).

Following a technology seeking strategy, lead firms may acquire companies in related sectors to upgrade their products and boost parent company innovation capabilities, as occurred in *Power* and *Heat*:

> Our acquisitions have been the outcome of a strategic choice, aiming to become an international player. ... In Europe and other advanced markets, the goal of acquisitions was to internalise specific technologies. The acquisition path has been coherent with our core business, to complement our know-how and develop new strategic products (*Power*'s CEO).
>
> The acquisitions in high-income countries have been mainly driven to acquire technologies. ... We became an application driven company, from a technology driven company. Now we are able to offer a functional subsystem to our clients (*Heat*'s General Manager).

Lead firms are one of the territorial actors that can play the role of anchor tenant in a regional system of innovation; universities and public laboratories might assume this role as well.[70] The exploitation of synergies and interdependencies amongst the business community, government and universities (the

---

69. De Propris, Crevosier, *supra*, 176.
70. Feldman, *supra*.

triple helix[71]) would enhance the sustainability of the regional innovation systems.[72] Thus, the impact of a lead firm acting as 'anchor tenant' on the reproduction of the local resources system can be fostered by initiating partnerships between companies and technical institutes/universities in the region. The companies investigated have implemented several local channels to constantly increase workers' skill endowment, trying to integrate the technical knowledge that employees already own thanks to the local education system, with managerial skills and behavioural ones. The partnerships with universities are mostly made with institutions located close to the companies, in the same region and/or in neighbouring regions. The partnerships established with technical schools highlight a more pronounced local nature; they tend to be created within the same region, and often the same province or district. The collaborations between the companies investigated and the educational system are heterogeneous. They differ in terms of intensity and duration, as well as in the types of programmes. In *Pharma*, *MotorTwo* and *System*, the collaborations with universities are structured and continuous. Collaborations with universities established to meet specific company needs are more common. A possible result of the synergy between higher education institutes and companies is evidenced by the experience revealed by *MotorTwo*'s Chief HR and Organisation Officer of actions undertaken by the firm to develop its corporate workforce. *MotorTwo* has established a continuous collaboration with at least one Italian university. In *MotorTwo*'s plants and offices, courses are constantly organised for high-skilled workers in order to enrich and complement their soft skills to enable the company to be more efficient and integrated at the international level.

Although a local system can benefit from the collaboration within the triple helix, the interdependencies amongst the three key actors is still not completely exploited in the territory. According to the companies investigated, the lack of continuity and an on-going commitment are usually due to bureaucratic constraints. *MotorOne* has collaborated with some Italian universities, in particular by establishing internships and/or projects related to specific student thesis themes. They state:

> It is difficult to put companies in contact with the educational world. A simplification of the bureaucratic procedures would be useful. ... We should invest more in the relationship between academia and industry. We have done internships and theses. ... There is not a continuous and constant relationship. It has mainly been left to personal initiatives (MotorOne's HR manager).
>
> There are also collaborations with local Italian universities but they are extemporaneous. ... We have re-activated our channels with the education world, with specialised technical institutions because we needed to deal with a shortage of workers in the operations activities (*Yarn*'s HR manager).

---

71. *See* Henry Etzkowitz & Loet Leydesdorff, *The Dynamics of Innovation: From National Systems and 'Mode 2' to a Triple Helix of University–Industry–Government Relations*, 29.2 Research Policy, 109 (2000).
72. De Propris & Crevosier, *supra*.

6.8 SOME CONCLUSIONS AND QUESTIONS FOR FURTHER RESEARCH

The objective of this research was to shed light on the relationship between multinational companies' internationalisation processes and the use of local industrial commons. The analysis helps explore what are the critical factors to upgrade the manufacturing base in advanced economies as well as to maintain the attractiveness and competitiveness of these countries in the new global division of labour.

Comparing previous studies on international business and economic geography, there emerges a need to balance the local and global involvement. Being at the edges of the local and global continuum might generate detrimental effects. Delocalising many business functions might lead to losing core knowledge; conversely, sharing many proximity dimensions can be disadvantageous because being too involved in a territory can inhibit cross-pollination through the 'lock-in'. The information collected confirms that local relationships are not an alternative to global ones. Conversely, the ability of a manufacturing company to develop strong links with the local labour market and suppliers' networks is a condition to increase its international projection. The intense use of local resources integrated with external factors eases the maintenance of a local industrial common, which, in turn, contributes to improving both companies' competitiveness and local resource quality. The influence of local resources in supporting the strategies of internationalisation has been clearly shown in all the investigated companies, in particular in the matching of supply/demand in the labour market, local suppliers' networks and the education system. The programmes provided by the education system have been evaluated as corresponding to the companies' needs. Knowledge and skills, both technical and manufacturing in nature, seem to be the factor that has greater territorial impact on the companies' results and, more specifically, on the conditions that make it possible to maintain some degree of GVC governance. Evidence from the present work highlights how local supplier networks continue to be relevant factors of the territory, especially when there is a need for a company to exchange strategic information continuously and with high frequency. This requires close contact with actors spatially and culturally.

The results show some examples on how territorial competitiveness can rely on the local capacity to be part of long-distance interactions, through foreign investments carried out by lead firms, their actions as anchor tenants and their anchoring role. Companies can contribute to the development of local resources even through their foreign investment decisions. Indeed, up to a certain extent, foreign investment decisions by local companies could be beneficial for the development of local resources. They are desirable if lead firms undertake them not to weigh anchor but to leverage the domestic-base resources. The presence of lead firms acting, both intentionally or not, as anchor tenant in the territory and representing international excellence is an extraordinary factor in attracting talent and resources outside the local system. Moreover, thanks to the 'anchoring role' performed by these companies, the local dimension can take advantage of the diversity and complementarity of these external inputs, integrating them with the existing 'local circuits of embedded and cumulative competences'.[73]

The findings also provide suggestions to conceptualise sustainable growth models, enabling territories to attract and retain specialised workers and firms. A better knowledge of local resources affecting the competitive advantage of firms willing to engage with global networks is a condition for defining the most appropriate interventions for local development policy and, more generally, for industrial policy intervention. To enhance lead firms' anchoring role, it is necessary to increase companies' awareness of the critical function played by the industrial commons in sustaining their growth and innovation capability. Only some of the investigated companies are aware of the critical role played by the local resources system. Paradoxically, foreign companies or foreign funds acquiring Italian firms have a better perception of this economic value. This value can be expressed by a certain degree of local stickiness in term of manufacturing activity, which is the maintenance or the increase in specialised manufacturing activities in the Italian base, as an implicit acknowledgement of the importance of the local industrial common. To conclude, the chapter focuses on possible actions that the main private economic players, such as multinational companies, can undertake to foster a successful governance of the industrial commons. To increase this awareness, the territory should be considered as one of the company's stakeholders. Concepts such as 'territorial loyalty' should be promoted by a supportive political system or, as suggested in Ostrom's work, by the resource users (not only companies, but also institutions and local communities). That means complex relationships between different actors: not only multinational companies, but also institutions and local communities, all involved in maintaining a shared value. Further analysis has to be made to establish precise policy interventions; there is need for further evidence on institutional behaviour field of research, identifying institutional designs of sustainable use of the local industrial commons, investigating institutional regularities in effectively managing the local and GVCs involvement, and finally suggesting possible governance models. The findings of the present research suggest that another promising research line is to study models of 'synergistic governance' as sustainable ways of upgrading, both economically and socially.[74]

This chapter is not free from limitations. The generalisability issue, due to the sole focus on Italian companies, represents the first shortcoming. The second is that the use of a qualitative methodology does not allow the identification of an industrial common measure. Future studies should provide an indicator of the use of the global and local resources necessary to maintain a critical mass of manufacturing resources, able to promote an increase in domestic-base productivity without threatening productive local resources.

---

73. De Propris, Crevosier, *supra*.
74. Gary Gereffi & Joonkoo Lee, *Economic and Social Upgrading in Global Value Chains and Industrial Clusters: Why Governance Matters*, 133.1 Journal of Business Ethics, 25 (2016).

ENDNOTE

Verbatim data has been collected in Italian and translated in English by the authors.

PART III Enterprise-Network and Enterprise-Groups: Trends and National/International Experience

CHAPTER 7

Enterprise-Network and Enterprise-Groups: Trends and National/International Experiences The Duty of Care

Sheldon Leader

7.1 THE PROBLEM: FRAGMENTED RESPONSIBILITY AND INTEGRATED PRODUCTION

Contemporary enterprise is a site of a dual movement: one occurs at the level of patterns of production and another at the level of responsibility for the impacts of that production. One is a domain undergoing incessant integration, and the other continues to display fragmentation. The first domain is evident to any observer of corporate activity. Lines of production are increasingly integrated. The division of labour worldwide intensifies as tasks are subdivided and outsourced to far-flung locations. At the same time, these different stages and types of production are ever more tightly coordinated. Multinational corporations in sectors ranging from clothing to oil and gas are happy to announce the tight control that they exercise over the timing and quality of the goods and services they produce and which they also source from outside the company.

This integration of production spreads out and crosses the borders between companies, which are – in legal theory – independent entities. This formal independence sets the stage for the functioning of the second domain: the fragmentation of responsibility. Parent companies are able to avoid liability for the actions of their subsidiaries on the ground that, as separate companies, the former has no responsibility to supervise the operation of the latter. The parent company's tight control over the process of production carried out by its subsidiaries is not followed by the parent's liability in the event that the subsidiary goes wrong and does damage. The parent is responsible for its mistakes in carrying out its portion of integrated production lines, but is not responsible for the mistakes of others in the corporate group. Separate corporate personality frames separate and isolated responsibility.

When we move from the inner workings of a single corporate group to the wider relations between different corporate groups in a supply chain, the gap continues between conditions of production and responsibility for those conditions. Here, stages and types of production along a supply chain are often made to fit in with one another optimally. Integration reigns – so tightly that it is sometimes difficult to distinguish the supplier of a component of a car, or an element of clothing, from the purchaser of those goods. Commands about methods of production are sometimes given by the purchaser and obeyed by the supplier in such a way that it looks and feels as if both were parts of the same company.

But looks can deceive. As is true between parent company and subsidiary, each party to the contract of sale is formally responsible for the way it behaves as e.g. an employer towards its workers, but does not take on responsibility for behaviour of the other party. The supplier of goods and services is responsible for the way in which it carries out the production of what it sells, but any damage done by it in the process does not carry through to affect the responsibility of the purchaser: the purchaser is not responsible for the way the supplier manages the good or service that it produces, and the supplier is not responsible for the way the producer uses what is supplied.

These are well known features of the modern commercial relationships both within and between enterprises.[1] Fragmented responsibility frames integrated production in both the corporate group as a matter of corporate law, and within the network of purchasers and suppliers as a matter of commercial law.

What is less well known is the way in which this picture is being altered. We are moving into a tension between what Marx called forces and relations of production.[2] Forces of production are factors which push the integration of production that goes along with the intensified division of labour referred to earlier. This is propelled by developments in technology and developments in the deployment of that technology in the on-going worldwide division of labour. Relations of production provide the normative framework within which these patterns of production function and evolve. For a time, these relations provide a suitable framework for forces. But there comes a point at which norms which enable forces to flourish turn into their fetter. There then begins a period in which classical principles are challenged: a new framework of responsibility

---

1. The phenomenon has been analyzed by a range of thinkers, including Adolf Berle and more recently Gunther Teubner. *See* Adolf Berle, *The Theory of Enterprise Entity*, Columbia Law Review (1947), http://www.shiftproject.org/resources/publications/the-corporate-respon sibility-to-respect-human-rights-an-interpretive-guide/ and Gunther Teubner in his important work on networks of production and responsibility *infra* n. 10.
2. Karl Marx, *Preface to Critique Political Economy* (London: Lawrence and Wishart, 1968).

becomes a fresh area of social and political, and ultimately legal, confrontation and development.³

What are the transformations that we can observe?

7.2 NEW FORMS OF ACCOUNTABILITY WITHIN CORPORATE GROUPS

Courts are penetrating the corporate group and widening the net of a parent company's responsibility for the actions of its subsidiaries. The longstanding frustrations with trying to pierce the corporate veil – which protects the parent company from liability despite its power to determine key decisions for members of the group – are being sidelined via the development of different legal principles. Advocates and courts are developing a different ground of liability that is far more suited to the facts of corporate power and equally suited to the drive to alter the profile of that power – a drive exemplified in the UN Guiding Principles on Business and Human Rights.

This legal innovation moves beyond the tradition of asking whether the parent has transgressed the boundary between itself and the subsidiary by exercising *too much* detailed control over the latter's decisions – inviting the piercing of the corporate veil. Instead, the new approach asks whether the parent has displayed *enough control of the right sort* over the subsidiary's actions. If parent and subsidiaries are in the same line of business – in pharmaceuticals, or oil and gas, etc., the parent is called on to become aware of any dangers to safety in the subsidiary's system of operation; to make use of any superior technical knowledge it has of ways in which the subsidiary's operation might improve – or and indeed if it does not have such superior knowledge appropriate to the sector, to acquire it. If the parent fails along any of these dimensions, it lays itself open to substantial claims for damage from victims. This development is grounded on an extension of what tort lawyers call a 'duty of care'.

This duty of care has found its scope of application recently expanded in a highly significant decision by the UK Court of Appeal, *Chandler v. Cape Industries*.⁴ In this case, Mr Chandler, an employee of a subsidiary of Cape Industries, had contracted cancer from working with asbestos in conditions that had, the court found, been negligently supervised by the subsidiary. The subsidiary had ceased to exist by the time Mr Chandler became ill. According to classic corporate law principles, his only recourse would have been against his employer, which would have left him with nothing. However, the Court found that the parent company had put itself in a position of special responsibility for the health and safety of those individuals, even though they were not its employees, by having deployed one of its own employees – a medical

---

3. *Ibid.*, at 182–183.
4. See *Chandler v. Cape Industries Plc*, Court of Appeal, para. 80 [2012] EWCA Civ 525.

officer – to superintend the conditions of work. On this basis, the parent company was held liable for its failure to adequately follow through with exercise of its responsibilities: it had not simply let down its subsidiary, but it violated its own duty of care to Mr Chandler.

This decision did not contradict the principle entrenching the separate legal personalities of the two companies. Instead it reached into a different area of law and added considerably to the lines of responsibility that parent companies have. From now on corporations in the UK will have to see if they meet the following conditions set down by the Court. A duty of care will arise, it said, if (1) the businesses of the parent and subsidiary are in a relevant respect the same, (2) the parent has, or ought to have, superior knowledge on some relevant aspect of health and safety in the particular industry, (3) the subsidiary's system of work is unsafe as the parent company knew, or ought to have known, and (4) the parent knew or ought to have foreseen that the subsidiary or its employees would rely on its using that superior knowledge for the employees' protection.

There is now on-going litigation against multinational and national commercial companies for damage done in the Niger Delta that draws on this development of the duty of care.[5] In addition there are jurisdictions such as France that are linking the duty of care to parent companies by legislation – at the moment in draft form.[6]

Standing away from the detail of cases, one sees here two different streams of principle in corporate law that can address the problem of fragmented responsibility for integrated production: principles that are capable of crossing the barrier of immunity between a parent company and its subsidiary.

On one longstanding approach, liability for a parent company varies with the degree of its power over the subsidiary. If, behind the formality of separate legal personality, there is in reality an exceptionally extensive and penetrating degree of control that the parent exercises over decision making by its subsidiary, then there will come a point at which the judiciary will decide that the subsidiary has in effect lost its distinct legal existence. Its acts and omissions are then treated as if they were the acts of the parent – and the wrongs done are deemed to have a new perpetrator. Courts are normally reluctant to take this course.

On the second more recent approach, grounded on the duty of care, the concern is the opposite: parent company accountability does not flow from an

---

5. For the implications of the duty of care jurisprudence for issues governing Shell Petroleum's liability for pollution in the Niger Delta, *see Corporate Liability in a New Setting: Shell and the changing legal landscape for the multinational oil industry in the Niger Delta* (2011) by the Essex Business and Human Rights Project https://www.essex.ac.uk/ebhr/documents/niger-delta-report.pdf.
6. Loi n° 2017-399 du 27 mars 2017 relative au devoir de vigilance des sociétés mères et des entreprises donneuses d'ordreFor an analysis of the issues *see* Antoine Lyon-Caen and Tatiana Sachs, *Multinationals and the Constitutionalization of the World Power System*, 204 (Routledge, 2016).

unusually strong degree of control, but rather on a failure to exercise adequate control. The key enquiry is not into the power of the parent but rather into whether or not there is between parent and subsidiary a 'special relationship'. In situations covered by the principles in *Chandler*, for example, that will arise if the four features of a corporate relationship exist: the companies are in the same line of business – which is not always so of corporate groups, since many bring together disparate commercial activities; that the parent has superior knowledge that important to prevent damage; that the parent knew or ought to have known that the subsidiary was operating dangerously; and that it was reasonable for the subsidiary to rely on the parent's expertise.

There is no issue in this second alternative of the parent exercising unusually strong and comprehensive power. Its special responsibility can arise even though it approaches the subsidiary with a light touch. The parent company is responsible for not having followed through with monitoring, and not demanding changes in its subsidiary's practice. The focus is one in which the parent is called on to raise its standards. It is a reforming branch of principle: designed to oblige the parent to pull itself and its subsidiary to a higher level of conduct. It marks a shift in the normative relations of production, to better reflect the reality of integrated forces of production.

How might this development be applied to that second domain of fragmented responsibility, the supply chain?

7.3 NEW FORMS OF ACCOUNTABILITY IN THE COMMERCIAL SUPPLY CHAIN

7.3.1 Supply Chains and Sharing Responsibility for Damage Done to Third Parties

At first glance, the relationship between purchaser and supplier looks to be fundamentally different from the relationship between a parent company and its subsidiary. However, they can resemble one another in crucial ways. To see this, it is best to begin with their formal differences before looking at their convergence. The two seem to engage distinct instincts about social accountability of business. The parent company's potential liability resides in the *special* forms of control – not just control per se – that it has over its subsidiary.

In the supply chain situation, on the other hand, the ingredients of responsibility seem to be quite distinct. It can arise, for example, when the purchaser plays a substantial role in the perpetration of the wrong, as when an order for a good or service is based on a low price only possible due to abusive labour practices. The enquiry is causal. The purchaser's liability for its contribution to the supplier's wrongs does not seem to be made of the same ingredients as are present when a duty of care arises for parent companies. The 'special relationship' between two parties – *this particular* parent company and *this particular* subsidiary – a relationship not necessarily shared with others, is missing in the reasoning about the standard purchaser/supplier relationship. There is, for example, no requirement before liability can arise that the purchaser's knowledge be superior to that of the supplier, nor indeed that they be in the same line of business, nor finally that the supplier relies on the purchaser for guidance.

The *range* of purchasers potentially liable for sharing in damage done by their suppliers is wider than is the range of parent companies potentially liable for sharing in the damage done by their subsidiaries. However, the *ground* of that liability for each purchaser is narrower as compared with the liability of the parent company:

> *Range*: The group of potentially liable purchasers is larger than the group of parent companies, since victims pursuing the former have no need to establish the ingredients of a pre-existing special relationship. A purchaser might come for the first time on a violating supplier, and have no knowledge which is superior to that of the supplier regarding the standards that should govern the latter's behaviour, and could still – if the other elements of the wrong are satisfied – be liable for its contribution to the damage done.
>
> *Ground*: Purchaser liability can also be narrower than that of the parent in that, in the standard case, the purchaser is not liable for violating the terms of a special relationship it has with the supplier. One purchaser does not have an extra layer of responsibility, corresponding to a duty of care, that another purchaser does not have on the ground that the former has a prior relationship to which special responsibilities attach. All purchasers, unlike all parent companies, are in the same boat.
>
> *The threat to victims:* One practical result of separating the basis of liability for parent companies and for purchasers emerges if one were to attempt to transform the former into the latter. When, for example, a subsidiary produces a good or service that is then transferred for an internal charge to the parent as part of a larger process of bringing the various stages in the company's production together into the final product, this might be re-described in the language of purchase and sale and not as that of coordinated parts of a corporate whole. The hope of the lawyers engaged in this re-configuration is that the prospect of liability of the parent for damage done by its subsidiary will shrink to the dimensions appropriate to purchasers for damage done by their suppliers. The risk to potential victims of such a manoeuvre is that the growing duty of care for parts of corporate groups that the courts are developing might be avoided. This can only be resisted if one reaches into certain purchaser – supplier relationships and strengthens the ground of responsibility that they can generate. It might then be possible to draw from developments in corporate liability so as to apply them to purchasers.

7.3.2 Re-drawing the Boundary Lines: The Position of the Purchaser with 'Leverage'

Advocates in various jurisdictions are beginning to lose patience with these formal separations between supplier and purchaser responsibility, and lawmakers are beginning to listen. Policy makers are looking inside these supply chain relationships, and attaching liability to what is often called 'leverage'.[7] This notion can be understood in two ways – parallel to the two ways in which we have seen a parent company can have leverage over its subsidiary. These are (1) accountability for a purchaser in a supply chain that can be correlated with the degree of its power over the supplier, and (2) accountability can emerges from a special relationship between purchaser and supplier:

(1) *Leverage as power in the supply chain*: The factors relevant here are those evoked by the UN Guiding Principles. The Interpretive Guide to the Principles defines leverage as '... the ability to effect change in the wrongful practices of the party'[8] Purchasers in a supply chain are encouraged, by the Principles, to bring their leverage to bear to effect respect for human rights. The central questions put to purchasers are 'do you have the power to get a supplier to listen to you by e.g. threatening to withdraw your custom if it does not comply? The company is called on to balance the gain in human rights terms of bringing its pressure to bear against, in some instances, the potentially drastic cost of losing a relatively unique source of supply.[9]

(2) *Leverage as a special relationship in the supply chain*: Here, it is possible to design a strategy of increasing accountability that is distinct from that set out in the Guiding Principles, and builds on the characteristics that are shared between certain parent/subsidiary relationships and a certain purchaser/supplier relationship. They are characteristics that attract the special responsibility associated with the 'duty of care'.

How does this duty of care function in this context of a supply chain? It is clear that there are certain purchasers that have integrated the timing and quality of the products of their suppliers into an integrated network. It is a network that not only controls the qualities of the ultimate *product*, but also the qualities of the *process* of production, including labour standards. The whole might be distributed across several legally independent commercial entities, labelled 'purchaser' and 'seller', but they are in fact so integrated that they amount to

---

7. For a seminal statement see the *UN Guiding Principles on Business and Human Rights*, at 21 ff http://www.ohchr.org/Documents/Publications/GuidingPrinciplesBusinessHR_EN.pdf.
8. *See The Corporate Responsibility to Respect Human Rights, An Interpretive Guide* p. 48 http://www.shiftproject.org/resources/publications/the-corporate-responsibility-to-respect-human-rights-an-interpretive-guide/.
9. *Ibid.*, at 50–51.

entities in what the Court in *Chandler* calls the 'same line of business'. They could well fit a criterion for network responsibility formulated by Gunther Teubner. This is that the members of the network share, in content, the same functional objectives in pursuing their commercial relationship.[10]

However, it is important to see this as not simply a link via a network of linked implied or explicit contracts. It is also a link in tort, connecting purchaser, supplier, and victim in certain situations via a duty of care. Certain purchasers which use a wide range of suppliers in, for example, the textile industry are often better placed than is the supplier itself, standing alone, to assess the adequacy of the standards of e.g. health and safety that the supplier follows. In this situation, it is easy for a supplier that adopts dangerous labour practices to be lulled into a false sense of adequacy if the dominant producer does not act to ensure quality: if, that is, the purchaser tolerates the sub-standard performance.

This link becomes compelling when the purchaser publicly formulates and publishes standards of responsible sourcing of goods, which it claims to insist upon when announcing to the world, and to its suppliers, its commitments. At that point, the supplier which knows of this commitment by its purchaser, and which sees that its own labour practices are tacitly deemed acceptable by that purchaser, might well rely on that toleration as part of an indication that its own production processes are acceptable. A 'special relationship' may well arise – directly comparable to the internal workings of certain parent/subsidiary relationships that, as has been seen, may carry a duty of care.

A case being litigated on these issues at the time of writing is *Jabir and others v. KiK Textilien und non-food GmbH*.[11] KiK Textilien (hereafter KiK) was the major buyer of the apparel produced in Pakistan at a factory owned by a separate company registered in Pakistan, Ali Enterprises (hereafter AE). A fire broke out on the premises of AE, killing close to 300 employees. According to evidence adduced, the high number of deaths and injuries could in part be traced back to the heavy iron bars on the windows and to the lack of emergency exits. KiK is being sued *inter alia* on the ground of its breach of a duty of care, along with the breach by AE of its own duty, towards the victims. In making the central arguments on behalf of the victims, it has been essential to distinguish this species of purchase/supply relationship from others. In the latter no duty of care exists, whereas in the former there is such a duty.

Several of the elements present in the decision in *Chandler*, governing parent/subsidiary relations, were also present here. Both AE and KiK were in the same line of business; KiK had, via its extensive network of involvement in assessing production conditions from its suppliers around the work, a superior ability to evaluate whether AE's system was unsafe: a lack of safety which it either knew about or ought to have known about. Finally, AE's system of work

---

10. Gunther Teubner, *Networks as Connected Contracts*, 57 (Oxford: HartPublishing, 2011).
11. https://www.ecchr.eu/en/our_work/business-and-human-rights/working-conditions-in-south-asia/pakistan-kik.html.

was unsafe, which KiK either knew about or ought to have known about; and KiK's toleration of the unsafe conditions.

The outcome of deliberation in this case could mark a decisive modification of the norms governing responsibility in the supply chain.[12]

7.4 CONCLUSION

The concept of a network is beginning to traverse corporate law and wider realms of commercial law. A synthesis between the core principles governing both domains is possible. If suitably shaped by the dynamic notion of a duty of care, the potential is there to close the gap between the practice of integrated production and the weak protection offered by the norms governing that production process. It is a gap into which many victims fall, and which robust development in the law can help to close.

---

12. *Ibid.*

CHAPTER 8
Enterprise Networks and Enterprise Groups
Orsola Razzolini

8.1 FROM THE VERTICAL FIRM TO THE NETWORK FORMS OF ORGANIZATION: INTRODUCTION

The network forms of organization[1] – groups of companies and other forms of contractual integration among firms – represent a big challenge to labour law as they seriously undermine the idea of the employer as a single indivisible entity whose legal boundaries correspond closely to the boundaries of the vertical firm/entrepreneur for the purpose of ascription of legal responsibilities.

In the European legal systems it is a common trend to draw the boundaries of the legal concept of employer as to coincide with the boundaries of the vertical firm within which the employee performs her tasks.[2] In turn, the legal concept of firm, meant either as economic activity or as economic organization, can be ascribed only to one entrepreneur, viewed as a discrete legal entity. The strong equation employer-entrepreneur-firm as well as their description in *atomistic* terms stem from the need to guarantee the principle that 'I should not be responsible for another's action' or for another's employees.[3] Notably, it ensures to entrepreneurs, who enter into complex patterns of business integration and business transactions, that they will retain separate legal personalities for the purpose of the ascription of legal responsibilities.

---

1. On the meaning of this expression *see* Walter W. Powell, *Neither Market Nor Hierarchy: Network Forms of Organization*, in B.M. Straw, L.L. Cummings, *Research on Organizational Behavior*, 295 (JAI Press, Greenwich (Conn.) (1990)).
2. *See*, for a recent and synthetic comparative overview, Luisa Corazza, Orsola Razzolini, *Who Is an Employer*, in Matthew W. Finkin, Guy Mundlak (eds), *Comparative Labor Law*, 132 (Edward Elgar 2015).
3. Hugh Collins, *Ascription of Legal Responsibility to Groups in Complex Patterns of Economic Integration*, 53 Mod. L. Rev., 731, 744 (1990).

This basic legal representation suffers of a number of weaknesses. One of the most relevant has been described in terms of 'capital boundaries problem' or, more recently, 'organised irresponsibility':[4] 'When in reality these separate legal personalities constitute an integrated productive organization, the freedom to determine the boundaries of a capital unit turns into a licence to evade legal responsibilities towards others.'[5] From a labour law perspective, the capital boundaries problem leads one to ask to what extent should firms/entrepreneurs be able and free to choose forms of economic organization and integration that preclude the ascription of employment risks and liabilities simply by going beyond the boundaries of the discrete legal entity.[6] The freedom to determine the capital boundaries, when exercised in the global market, also undermines the traditional counterbalances to corporate power: namely, public actions and collective bargaining.

These problems particularly emerge in the context of network forms of production, where the boundaries of economic activities and economic organizations are spread throughout a number of discrete legal entities that share a common business project or interest. As Douglas Baird pointed out, in this case we should resist the general idea that 'the locus of economic activity rests with a discrete legal entity'[7] and we should focus in the future on regulating economic activity, 'rather than on regulating discrete legal entities'.[8]

In this contribution I will try to show (*infra* §§ 8.4–8.5) that the Italian regulation of the 'interfirm network agreement' might be understood as one first step towards this direction. More precisely, the Italian regulation of the 'interfirm network agreement' is an attempt to shift the focus of the employment protections from the discrete legal entities to the economic activity of the network. If this result will be achieved, in the next future, the networks might become a tool by which ensuring transparent 'organised responsibility' rather than 'organised irresponsibility'.

8.2 THE FIRM AND THE NETWORKS UNDER THE LENS OF NEW INSTITUTIONAL ECONOMICS, NEW CONTRACTUALISM AND CONSTITUTIONALISM

The closed correspondence between the concepts of firm/entrepreneur and the concept of employer was also outlined in the Ronald Coase's pivotal work 'The

---

4. Hugh Collins, *A Review of the Concept of Employer by Dr. Jeremias Prassl*, available at https://www.law.ox.ac.uk/content/labour-law-0/blog/2015/11/review-concept-employer-dr-jeremias-prassl.
5. Collins, *supra* n. 3, at 744.
6. *See* David Weil, *The Fissured Workplace: Why Work Became So Bad for So Many and What Can Be Done to Improve It* 183 ff. (Harvard University Press 2014).
7. Douglas G. Baird, *In Coase's Footsteps,* 14 (Chicago John M. Olin Law & Economics Working Paper No. 175, 2003).
8. *Ibid.*

Nature of the Firm'. According to Coase, both the firm and the employer are characterized by the 'fact of direction': the firm is an hierarchical organization of productive resources left to the direction of a private authority (the entrepreneur) to save in market transaction costs;[9] the employer (master) has the right to control the servant's work.[10] However, Coase himself, in 1988, tried to mitigate the value of his statement that, in his opinion, had led to overemphasize the employer-employee relationship as the archetype of the firm to the detriment of other commercial long-term relations.[11] A firm exists whenever the organization and cooperation of productive resources is not left to the price mechanism but to a form of private governance structure or authority; the employer-employee relationship is only one possible example.

To remedy to what Coase defined a 'weakness' of his work, Oliver Williamson enlarged the spectrum of the analysis to a number of commercial long-term relations (such as franchising contracts and supply partnerships) that, when characterized by incompleteness and asset-specificity, might be aligned with hybrid forms of governance of the economic activity that can be located along the continuum running from market to hierarchy.[12]

The weight placed on the 'authority' and on the need for mechanisms of governance of productive relations represents the line drawn between the new institutional economics, fathered by Coase and Williamson,[13] and the new contractualism, fathered by Alchian and Demsetz, Jensen and Meckling. The new contractualism regards the firm as a network of contracts; it rejects the assumption that the distinction between firms and markets depends, respectively, on the existence or on the absence of a 'private authority' and that contracts inside a firm have different characteristics from contracts outside the firm.[14] According to this theory, the central role played by the shareholders and

---

9. Ronald H. Coase, *The Nature of the Firm*, 4 Economica 392 (1937).
10. *Ibid.*, at 404. When Ronald Coase suggests the 'fact of direction' as the essence of both the legal and economic concepts of employer and employee, he relies on Professor Batt's The Law of the Master and the Servant (R. Batt, *The Law of the Master and the Servant* (London: Sir Isaac Pitman and Sons Ltd., First Edition, 1929), 6 et seq. quoted by R. H. Coase, at 404).
11. Ronald H. Coase, *The Nature of the Firm. Influence*, 4 J. L. Econ. & Organizations 33 (1988) at 37 says: 'I consider that one of the main weaknesses of my article stems from the use of the employer-employee relationship as the archetype of the firm. It gives an incomplete picture of the nature of the firm. But more important, I believe it misdirects our attention ... And in my notes written around 1934, I said that the employer-employee contract approaches the firm relationship but that the full firm relationship will not come about unless "several such contracts are made with people and for things which cooperate with one another"'.
12. *See*, among others, Oliver E. Williamson, *Transaction-Cost Economics: The Governance of Contractual Relations*, in Peter J. Buckley, Jonathan Michie (eds), *Firms, Organizations and Contracts*, 168 (Oxford University Press 2001).
13. *See*, on the origin and development of the new institutional economics, Ronald H. Coase, *The New Institutional Economics*, 88 Am. E. R., 72 et seq. (1998).
14. *See* Arme A. Alchian, Harold Demsetz (1972). *Production, Information Costs, and Economic Organization*, in Peter J. Buckley, Jonathan Michie (eds), *Firms, Organizations*

by the shareholder interest is central simply because, among the different parties involved in the nexus, they are the residual claimants.[15]

A recent interesting development of this perspective is the 'Team Production Theory' framed by Blair and Stout.[16] Broadly speaking, the team production theory questions the idea that shareholders are entitled to all the profits. In a knowledge economy it is no longer possible to be the sole 'owners' of a corporation consisting largely of intangible assets and knowledge; rather, economic production requires a team, while corporations are better understood as a 'nexus of team-specific assets' including both stakeholders and shareholders.[17] In this perspective, the control of the corporation should rest with a board of directors – since team members do not always trust each other – which needs to ensure that the *all* team members receive enough of a return to ensure that they stay in the team.[18] As Blair and Stout argue:

> the primary job of the board of directors of a public corporation is not to act as agents who ruthlessly pursue shareholders' interests at the expense of employees, creditors, or other team members. Rather, the directors are trustees for the corporation itself, mediating hierarchs whose job is to balance team members' competing interests in a fashion that keeps everyone happy enough that the productive coalition stays together.[19]

These new economic conceptualizations of the firm, more closed to the stakeholder paradigm than to the shareholder one, might be aligned, to some extent, with interesting recent French proposals about the 'constitutionalization' of the firm.[20] According to this perspective, the firm needs to be regarded as a power system which is strongly embedded into a broader power system, the legal, economic and political order. Constitutionalizing the firm means to accept that the goals of the firm cannot be determined solely by one of its constituencies (the shareholders) thereby recognizing fundamental substantial and procedural rights also to the other firm's constituencies.[21] This leads to reconsider the

---

       and Contracts, 75 (Oxford University Press 2001); Michael C. Jensen, William H. Meckling (1976). *Theory of the Firm: Managerial Behaviour, Agency Costs and Ownership Structure*, in *ibid.*, at 103; Frank H. Easterbrool, Daniel R. Fischel, *L'Economia delle Società per azioni* (Giuffrè, Milano, 1996). On a recent application of the nexus of contracts theory to the employment contract, *see* Francesco Denozza, *Il rapporto di lavoro subordinato nell'impresa neoliberale*, Riv. it. dir. lav. 41 (2015, I).

15. See Alchian, Demsetz, *supra* n. 14, at 81. The concept of 'residual claimant', that should be provided with monitoring powers, to some extent recalls the concept of 'private authority' framed by Coase and Williamson.
16. Margaret M. Blair, Lynn A. Stout, *A Team Production Theory of Corporate Law*, 85 Va. L. R. 248 (1999).
17. *Ibid.*
18. *Ibid.*
19. *Ibid.*, at 280.
20. See Jean-philippe Robé, *La constitutionnalisation du système-monde de pouvoir* (College de Berardin. Département économie, homme et societé, 2011). *See also* the contributions to this volume by T. Sachs, S. Vernac, A. Pin. Jean-philippe Robé.
21. *Ibid.*, at 22. *See also* the Introduction of Adalberto Perulli, in this volume.

values and goals of the firm in the global arena, though rejecting any form of 'functionalization' of the private activity.[22]

The team production theory is an interesting economic paradigm to apply to network forms of organization. First, the case of groups of companies might be taken into account. Groups of companies represent a process of 'recomposition' of the firm. Here, the share or contractual integration among separate legal entities is so intense that it becomes possible to retrace the boundaries of a 'firm' beyond the boundaries of the discrete legal entities.[23] In groups of companies, separate legal entities are managed under the unified direction and coordination of the lead company (the holding); therefore the multiplicity of companies coexists with the unity of the group.[24] An interesting legal regulation is provided by the Italian civil code Articles 2497 and seq., according to which the exercise of a unified direction is a lawful economic activity to the extent that it is counterbalanced by 'compensative advantages' for all companies belonging to the same group.[25] To put it in another way, the unified direction is lawful to the extent that it is oriented towards the 'interest of the team'[26] and not towards the sole interest of the lead organization. Through the theory of compensative advantages, the law then gives a specific legal value to the interest of the group.

Along with groups of companies, contractual network forms of organization can be better understood under the lens of the team production theory. Similarly to the French industrial system,[27] the Italian one, particularly in the garment and apparel industry sector, is largely based on SMEs that seek to

---

22. *See* the Introduction of Adalberto Perulli, in this volume.
23. *See* François Gaudu, *Entre concentration économique et externalisation: les nouvelles frontières de l'entreprise*, Droit Social 474 (2001).
24. *See* Gunther Teubner, *Unitas Multiplex: Corporate Governance in Group Enterprises* 67 (Bremen/Firenze 1988); Gaetano Vardaro, *Prima e dopo la persona giuridica: sindacati, imprese di gruppo e relazioni industriali*, Giorn. dir. lav. rel. ind. 211 (1988).
25. The theory of 'compensative advantages' (Teoria dei vantaggi compensativi) was first framed in Italy by Paolo Montalenti, *Conflitto di interessi nei gruppi di società e teoria dei vantaggi compensativi*, Giur. comm. 710 et seq. (1995, I).
26. *See* P.G. Jaeger, *Direzione unitaria» di gruppo e responsabilità degli amministratori*, Riv. soc. 817 (1985); Ariberto Mignoli, *Interesse di gruppo e società a sovranità limitata*, Contratto e impresa 730 (1986); Paolo Ferro Luzzi, Piergaetano Marchetti, *Riflessioni sul gruppo creditizio*, Giur. comm. 419 ff. (1994, I); Montalenti, *supra* n. 25; Francesco Galgano, *Le società. Trattato diretto da F. Galgano. I gruppi di società* (Utet, Torino, 2001). More recently, Sergio Gilotta, *Interesse di gruppo e nuove regole sulle operazioni con parti correlate: una convivenza difficile*, Giur. comm. (2012) 254; Marco Maugeri, *Interesse sociale, interesse dei soci e interesse del gruppo*, Giur. comm. (2012) 66. With regard to Italian judgments, *see*, among others, Cass., 26 February 1990, n. 1439, Giur. Comm. (1991, II) 360, with comment of Rondinone; C. App. Milano, 30 March 2001, Giur. Comm. (2002, II) 200; Cass. 24 August 2004, n. 16707, Giur. Comm. (2005, II) 246 ss.; Cass. 4 August 2008, n. 17696.
27. *See* Bruno Courault, Peter B. Doeringer, *From Hierarchical Districts to Collaborative Networks: The Transformation of the French Apparel Industry*, 6 Socio Econ. Rev. 261 et seq. (2008).

achieve productivity gains by means of hierarchical or collaborative production long-term relationships in order to take advantage of scale economies, incompleteness and asset-specificity. In recent years, the perception that these networks have been experiencing a change from an hierarchical to a more collaborative pattern of integration has led the introduction by the Italian legislator of a new kind of contract between firms, the interfirm network agreement (*contratto di rete*). According to Article 3, Act no. 33/2009, an interfirm network agreement is a contract whereby two or more undertakings agree to cooperate on the basis of a common programme, to achieve goals such as increasing innovation and competitiveness, exchanging information, technical and industrial knowledge.

As the team production theory points out, the interfirm network agreement is a 'nexus of team-specific assets' so that it becomes fundamental for the network to be oriented towards a 'common programme' or a 'common interest' in order to ensure that the *all* team members receive enough of a return to ensure that they stay in the team.[28] Insofar as the network is based on collaborative rather than hierarchical relations and no one plays the role of lead organization, exerting control and direction over the others, there is no need to apply a theory of compensative advantages. However, some recent Italian examples of interfirm network agreements – for example the Gucci case – cast doubts on whether the network should be always aligned with a peer-to-peer form of collaboration among firms.[29]

In my view, to some extent, the weight placed by the abovementioned Italian regulations on the 'common programme', on the 'interest of the team' and on 'compensative advantages' represent a first attempt to shift the legal focus from the discrete legal entities to the economic activity of the network (or team) as to realign the legal boundaries of the firm with its economic reality.[30]

8.3 THE SEARCH FOR THE EMPLOYER IN THE NETWORKS: THE SINGLE, PLURAL AND FUNCTIONAL PATTERN

How does the shift from discrete legal entities to the economic activity of the network affect the legal concept of employer?

As said above, the network forms of organization challenge the classical single pattern of employer, which is endorsed in most continental European legal system and which is based on a closed correspondence of the boundaries of the employer to the boundaries of the discrete legal entity for the scope of ascription of the employment risks and responsibilities.

A first well known technique to overcome this problem is represented by the 'lifting of the corporate veil'. Almost in all countries, it is largely accepted

---

28. *See again* Blair, Stout, *supra* n. 16.
29. *See infra* § 4.
30. *See also infra* § 3.

that the principle of formal separation of personalities and responsibilities between different legal entities should be overcome in the event of the allegation of a fraud, through the doctrine of piercing the corporate veil.[31] To put it in another way, formally separated legal entities can be considered as one for the scope of the application of some employment protections or for collective bargaining purposes, in presence of a number of factual indicia that vary from country to country.[32] The doctrine of the piercing of the corporate veil might be aligned with a 'single pattern' of employer insofar as it simply re-composes the boundaries of the concept of employer in accordance with the boundaries of the group, regarded as a single economic entity. Further, this doctrine is based on the allegation of a fraud, while the fact that an economic activity is carried through a number of legal entities cannot be anymore explained only in pathological terms.

The plural employer pattern, originally developed in common-law countries, acknowledges the idea that the entrepreneurial power of management and control can be shared by a number of legal entities. For instance, the American concept of 'joint employer', which traditionally has no counterpart in Continental Europe, allow the courts to consider as the employer, for the purpose of ascription of certain employment responsibilities, two or more firms sharing or co-determining the matters governing the essential terms and conditions of employment or that are closely linked via commercial relations. In his recent work, David Weil pointed out that a more expansive application of the definition of joint-employment could turn out to be used 'to challenge fissured structures that seem designed in some sense to subvert it';[33] however, further steps towards this direction find an obstacle in the hostility of multinationals and other business organizations whose central role in the policy making process cannot be denied nor ignored. Also British statutory law provides for a definition of 'associated employer' (ERA 1996, section 231) that allows for a limited lifting of the corporate veil in a few number of cases, the most important of which relates to continuity of employment.[34]

In a comparative perspective, it is worth noting that the concept of joint-employment has been developed, among others, by Spanish, Italian and French courts in the context of groups of companies.[35] Notably, the French courts give weight to three factors: *'confusion d'intérêts, d'activités et de direction'*. In the presence of all these factors, the French courts ascertain the

---

31. Collins, *supra* n. 3, at 740 et seq.
32. *See* the contribution to this volume by Valerio Speziale.
33. David Weil, *supra* n. 6, at 207.
34. *See*, for instance, Simon Deakin, *Labour Law. Fourth Edition*, 213 ff (Hart Publishing, 2005); *see also* considerations drown by Luca Ratti, *Intorno al concetto di datore di lavoro. A proposito di The concept of employer di Jeremias Prassl*, forthcoming in 3 Giornale di diritto del lavoro e delle relazioni industriali (2016).
35. *See* the contribution of Valerio Speziale, in this volume.

existence of *co-employeurs* (joint-employers) who become jointly liable for the employment obligations and, particularly, for the *obligation de reclassement*.[36]

Italian courts are becoming more and more familiar with the idea of *'codatorialità'* or *'contitolarità'* in groups of companies. The Italian Supreme Court, by relying on company law Articles 2497 et seq. of the Italian civil code, has developed the idea that it is legitimate to use the employee's tasks and abilities in the interest of the group, while it is illegitimate to use the employee's tasks and abilities in the interest of solely one legal entity which is different from the employer.[37] In some cases, the Italian courts focus on the joint exercise of the employer's powers over the employee as to hold for joint-employment to exist;[38] in other cases, they place weight on the fact that the working activity of the employee has been oriented towards the interest of the group shared by a number of legal entities.[39]

In a different perspective, it is also possible to ascribe to the plural employer pattern the common and civil law technique of involving a third party in the employer's liabilities by means of vicarious liability based on the *respondeat superior* rule.[40] Notably, in British tort law, a dual vicarious liability is (and must be) a legal possibility insofar as it is possible and conceivable that the right to control is shared by two or more legal entities.[41] A recent critical line of judicial thinking developed by French courts rejects the doctrine of *'co-emploi'* and considers more appropriate to speak of tort liability, by finding the lead company and the other subsidiaries' liable on the basis of *résponsabilité delictuelle* (Article 1382, French Civil Code).[42]

However, it is worth noting that the vicarious liability doctrine was first framed as to involve the company that retains substantial control over another company in liability for torts committed against third parties rather than against employees. Thus, expanding its field of application from the costumer-client

---

36. *See* Cass. Soc., 9 September 2012, no. 11-12.845; Cour d'appel Rouen, Chambre Social, 4 May 2010, no. 09/00946, 09/00975, 09/01450.
37. Cass., 20 November 2011, n. 25270.
38. C. App. Milano, 3 March 2014, n. 1597/2013; *see*, on this perspective, Gisella De Simone, *Gruppi di imprese*, in Marina Brollo (ed.), *Il mercato del lavoro. Trattato di diritto del lavoro diretto da Mattia Persiani e Franco Carinci*, vol. VI, 1509 (Cedam, Padova, 2012).
39. Trib. Cagliari, 6 June 2013, n. 23.
40. *See*, in the UK, *Viasystem (Tyneside) Ltd v. Thermal Transfer (Northern) Ltd* [2005] IRLR 983. *See also Biffa Waste Services Ltd v. Maschinenfabrik Ernst Hese GmbH* [2008] EWCA Civ 1257; [2009] B.L.R. 1; 122 Con. L.R. 1; [2009] P.N.L.R. 12; (2008) 152(45) S.J.L.B. 25. *See* Patrick S. Atiyah, *Vicarious Liability in the Law of Torts* (Butterworths, 1967) Ch. 3. For a comparative analysis, *see* Luca Ratti, *Agency Work and the Idea of Dual Employership: A Comparative Perspective*, 30 Comp. L.L. & Pol'y J., 835 (2009); *Id.*, *Réseaux d'entreprises et coemploi*, Rev. dr. tr. 72 (2015). With regard to the US, *see* again David Weil, *supra* n. 6, at 186 et seq.
41. *Viasystem (Tyneside) Ltd v. Thermal Transfer (Northern) Ltd* [2005] IRLR 983, para. 12.
42. *See* Jean-François Cesaro, Elsa Peskine, *Le coemploi sur la sellette*, Rev. Dr. Tr. 661 (2014).

relationship to the employer (formal or substantial)-employee relationship does not seem to capture the 'special' nature of the latter. Vicarious liability is rooted in an *ex post* 'compensatory logic' (*logique de réparation*)[43] and it cannot aim to allocate *ex ante* on more legal entities some of special duties owed by the employer to the employee.

The *Newton-Sealey v. ArmorGroup Services Ltd* judgment moves more in this direction;[44] a worker, a formal employee of one company belonging to the ArmorGroup, was seriously injured while working in Iraq under the control and the direction of a subsidiary. According to the High Court of Justice, Queen's Bench Division, although the employee had an employment contract with one company within the group, the other parts of the ArmorGroup had behaved in such a way as to voluntarily enter into a special relation of 'proximity' with the employee whereby they owe the employee a duty of care.[45]

Along with the single and plural pattern of employer, a 'functional pattern of employer' has been recently outlined.[46] This pattern suggests to adopt a targeted or 'functional' approach to identify the employer, which strongly recalls the targeted or functional approach which is usually adopted in common-law countries to identify the employee.[47] The employer is regarded as 'the entity or combination of entities playing a decisive role in the exercise of relational employing functions, and regulated and controlled as such in each particular domain of employment law' (for instance, economic dismissal, information and consultation rights).[48] As has been observed, the implications of 'functional employer' are that 'a worker may have multiple employers, that one particular entity may be an employer for some purposes and not others, and that the tests for determining who is the employer will vary according to the employment right

---

43. *See* Elsa Peskine, *L'imputation en droit de travail*, Rev. Dr. Tr. 347 ff. (2012).
44. High Court of Justice, Queen's Bench Division, 14 February 2008, *Newton-Sealey v. ArmorGroup Services Ltd.* [2008] EWHC 233 (QB).
45. For a similar perspective, *see* in Italy Carlo Castronovo, La nuova responsabilità civile, 122 ff. (Giuffrè, Milano, ed. 2006) who outlines the concept of 'responsabilità da contatto sociale' (liability deriving by social contact) later employed, in the specific context of group of companies, by Enrico Raimondi, Il datore di lavoro nei gruppi imprenditoriali, in Giorn. Dir. Lav. Rel. ind. 287, 307 et seq. (2012).
46. This pattern of employer has been framed in particular by Simon Deakin, *The Changing Concept of the 'Employer' in Labour Law*, 30 Ind. L. J. 72 (2001); Marzia Barbera, *Trasformazioni della figura del datore di lavoro e flessibilizzazione delle regole del diritto*, in *La figura del datore di lavoro. Articolazioni e trasformazioni. Atti del convegno nazionale A.i.d.la.s.s., Catania, 21-23 maggio 2009*, 5 (Giuffrè, Milano, 2010); Jeremias Prassl, *The Concept of the Employer* (Oxford Monographs of Labour Law, Oxford University Press 2015).
47. Jeremias Prassl's work is also based on the functional typological approach framed by Luca Nogler in order to identify who is the employee (*see* Luca Nogler, *Metodo tipologico e qualificazione dei rapporti di lavoro subordinato*, Riv. it. dir. lav. 182 (1990, I).
48. Jeremias Prassl, quoted above n. 46, at 6.

concerned'.[49] This might lead to contradictions and confusions thereby compromising legal certainty.

Furthermore, the targeted functional approach does not seem to offer an adequate solution to the problem of 'organised irresponsibility' that arises in contexts in which an economic activity and entity is in practice shared by a number of discrete legal entities, no one exerting the employer's functions nor a substantive or 'manifest' control over the others in order to avoid the risk to be involved in the employment liabilities.[50]

In my view, the main criterion by which redefining the boundaries of the employer's responsibilities for compliance with labour law standards should be the economic entrepreneurial interest that the working activity of the employee is intended to satisfy.[51] In whose interest the employee is working? The interest of the formal employer? The interest of a legal entity that is not the party to the contract of employment? The interest of a network or team of legal entities? The answer to this question seems to me to be fundamental to redefine the boundaries of the firm and, ultimately, the boundaries of employment responsibilities. It is not a case that the identification of the entrepreneurial interest was at the basis of the Italian legal concept of firm (meant either as an economic activity or as an economic organization),[52] as is the understanding of the role played by the employer/entrepreneur's interest in the structure of the employment contract that allowed to better specify the concept of subordination and the limits to the employer's powers.[53]

8.4 THE ITALIAN CASE OF THE INTERFIRM NETWORK AGREEMENT

As seen above, the Italian Interfirm network agreement shifts the legal focus form discrete legal entities to the economic activity of the network. It acknowledges the idea of the firm as a nexus of relational contracts or as a 'nexus of

---

49. Collins, *supra* n. 4. This result is different from that one achieved by Luca Nogler whose 'functional typological approach' was meant to select a number of different indicia that may be regarded as functionally 'equivalent' for the scope of identifying a 'unitary' concept of employee.
50. As David Weil, *supra* n. 6, at 189 ff., pointed out with regard to vicarious liability, vicarious liability 'creates very complicated and – as usual – contradictory incentives. Shielding itself from vicarious liability creates incentives for the lead organization to exert a little control over its agents as possible, even in cases where it would be more socially efficient for it to do so'.
51. With regard to group of companies, *see*, for this perspective, Orsola Razzolini, *Impresa di gruppo, interesse di gruppo e codatorialità nell'era della* flexicurity, Riv. giur. lav. 29 (2013).
52. *See* Giuseppe Fanelli, *Introduzione alla teoria giuridica dell'impresa*, 75, 116 (Giuffrè, Milano, 1950); Paolo Grossi, *Scienza giuridica italiana. Un profilo storico 1860–1950*, 306 et seq. (Giuffrè, Milano, 2000).
53. *See* Luigi Mengoni, *Contratto e rapporto di lavoro nella recente dottrina italiana*, Riv. Soc. (1965 I) 684 et seq.; Mattia Persiani, *Contratto di lavoro e organizzazione*, 45, 264 (Cedam, Padova, 1966).

team-specific assets'[54] tied together by a 'common programme' or a 'common interest' to which the statutory law gives value.

In the reality, the interfirm network agreement might correspond to a new form of hierarchy rather than to a peer-to-peer form of collaboration, with one firm playing as the lead organization. This is the case of the Gucci interfirm network agreements. The Gucci organizational structure is based on 'first line' contractors and 'second line' subcontractors, who are closely coordinated by the first line contractors through a number of supplier partnerships. After the global economic crisis of 2008, Gucci persuaded its first line contractors to enter into a number of interfirm network agreements with its second line subcontractors as to allow the formers to exert a stronger influence and support of the latters, unable to face the harsh economic conditions imposed by the global market.[55] The interfirm network agreement, with its open and flexible contents and functions, allowed the contractors to increase their influence and control over the subcontractors, providing them with the tools for upgrading their business capabilities[56] and surviving the crisis. Thus, beyond appearances, the interfirm network agreements do not always conceal a form of peer-to-peer collaboration. A proof lies in the fact that the management of the network is often assigned to one of its members – the lead organization – while, as the team production theory suggests, it should better remain with an independent board.[57]

Were it a form of peer-to-peer collaboration or a form of hierarchy or quasi-hierarchy, the labour law question should be, in my view, in whose interest the employee is working? In the interest of one single team member? In the interest of the 'common programme' carried out by the team? If the employee is working in the exclusive interest of one team member – for example a personal assistant, accountant and so on –, then the question is whether this team member is also the party to the contract of employment; in the negative, the law should regard it as the real employer, according to the principle 'substance prevails over the form'. On the contrary, if the employee's working activity is used to achieve the common programme of the team – for example the so-called 'network manager', IT engineers employed for contributing to realize the

---

54. See Blair, Stout, *supra* n. 16.
55. *See*, for the analysis of the Gucci and Ribes interfirm network agreements, Silvana Sciarra, Luisa Corazza, *Reti di imprese e sostenibilità sociale della filiera* (2013), available at www.nelmerito.com/index.php?option=com_content&task=view&id=1906&Itemid=1; Orsola Razzolini, *Network Forms of Organisation and Network Agreements in a Labour Law Perspective: Two Tuscan Case Studies*, in Edoardo Ales et al. (eds), *Employment Relations and Transformation of the Enterprise in the Global Economy*, 67 et seq. (Giappichelli, Torino, 2016).
56. For instance, the network agreement allowed subcontractors to negotiate more favourable conditions with banks and other suppliers, to share knowledge and technical information, and to obtain European or national funds by presenting collaborative research projects. *See*, for this economic analysis, Marika Macchi, *Le reti Gucci ed Esaote: un'analisi economica*, Giorn. dir. lav. rel. ind. 79 et seq. (2016).
57. See *supra* § 2.

strategic plan of the network –, then the employment responsibilities and risks should be split between the team members.

According to Italian Article 30.4*ter* of the Legislative Decree 276/2003, as amended by the Act no. 76/2013, the 'joint-employment' *(codatorialità)* has become a legal possibility in the interfirm network agreements, thereby endorsing, for the first time, a plural employer pattern in contractual networks forms of production.[58] The 'joint-employment' is defined in very flexible terms: for firms that have entered into an interfirm network agreement 'joint-employment of the employees is possible and is regulated by the interfirm network agreement's contractual provisions' (Article 30.4*ter*). The wording responds to the warning that we should be very cautious in introducing the joint-employer pattern in this new flexible form of organization and that the team members' contractual freedom should play a central role.[59] A Ministerial Circular (no. 35/2013) goes even further: the contractual provisions of the interfirm network agreement are to be taken into account to determine the allocation between the team members of criminal, civil and administrative liabilities, including joint liabilities.

All of this is rather ambiguous. The interfirm network agreement permits the contracting parties the discretional allocation of employment and even criminal responsibilities between them. This *'laissez-faire'* approach might work successfully if all the contracting parties play as socially responsible economic actors; for example, they could decide to drive risks and responsibilities to the contracting parties that 'can achieve compliance with labour standards at the least cost'.[60] If this is not the case, however, the interfirm network agreement could turn to be the tool to ensure 'organised irresponsibility' to the strongest contracting parties, by shifting risks and responsibilities on the weakest.[61] Further, the interfirm network agreement could permit the partners a joint regulation or deregulation of employment terms and conditions, without the participation of trade unions or other workers' representatives.

---

58. In Italy, the need for a joint-employer pattern in contractual network forms of production has been first framed by Valerio Speziale, *Il datore di lavoro nell'impresa integrata*, in *La figura del datore di lavoro. Articolazioni e trasformazioni. Atti del convegno nazionale A.i.d.la.s.s., Catania, 21–23 maggio 2009*, 77 et seq. (Giuffrè, Milano, 2010). The need and legal justification of joint-responsibilities in forms of contractual integration had been previously investigated by Pietro Ichino, *Il diritto del lavoro e i confini dell'impresa*, in *Diritto del lavoro e nuove forme di decentramento produttivo. Atti delle giornate di studio di diritto del lavoro, Trento, 4–5 giugno 1999*, 3 (Giuffrè, Milano, 1999); Luisa Corazza, 'Contractual Integration' *e rapporti di lavoro. Uno studio sulle tecniche di tutela del lavoratore* (Cedam, Padova, 2004).
59. Tiziano Treu, *Trasformazioni delle imprese: reti di imprese e regolazione del lavoro*, Merc. conc. reg. 19 (2012).
60. *See* Collins, *supra* n. 4.
61. In this respect, it has been pointed out the 'ambivalence' of the concept of joint-employment: originally, regarded as tool by which strengthening workers' protection, it can turn out to be a tool by which firms can achieve a higher level of flexibility. *See* Luca Ratti, *Réseaux d'entreprises et coemploi, perspectives comparatives*, Rev. Dr. Tr. 72 (2015).

Notwithstanding, labour law is predominantly based on *ius cogens* withdrawn from contractual freedom.[62] Thus, one should ask what is the real margin of discretion enjoyed by the contracting undertakings in the definition of joint-employment and its legal effects? In the Italian legal system, the *lex contractus* (contractual freedom) can operate within strict limits. In particular, it cannot regulate (or deregulate) legal effects which are mandatorily related to the exercise of the employer's powers and withdrawn from contractual freedom. Whatever the wording in the contract, if the contracting party acts as an employer and exercises the employer's powers and functions, she must bear the employment risks and responsibilities.[63] In this respect, the new regulation of the interfirm network agreement appears to promise more than it can actually keep. This increases legal uncertainty and, in the facts, discourages business undertakings from adopting the new legal instrument.

The Italian law also provides for specific rules governing the posting of workers within the network. Notably, it allows for a greater flexibility in workers' mobility, by freeing the employers making the posting from the burden to prove to have own specific interest in the posting.[64] The network agreement allows this interest to be presumed. One should ask whether this conclusive presumption applies only to the existence of this interest, or also to its temporary nature, which is a second essential requirement in Italian employment law. The second interpretative solution appears to be more consistent with the need of flexibility of the network, whilst the former runs into contradiction and nonsense when it frees the business undertaking from the proof to have an interest in the posting but not from the proof that such interest is temporary. Also, the second interpretative solution is supported by a significant body of case law, according to which the word 'temporary' does not mean 'short period of time', but, rather, that the duration is 'limited' or 'defined'; notably, it ends at the end

---

62. See Otto Kahn-Freund, *A note on status and contract in British labour law*, 30 Mod. L. R. 635 et seq. (1967).
63. Adalberto Perulli, *Contratto di rete, distacco, codatorialità, assunzioni in agricoltura*, in Luigi Fiorillo, Adalberto Perulli (eds), *La riforma del mercato del lavoro*, 463, 503 (Torino, Giappichelli, 2014); Maria T. Carinci, *Introduzione. Il concetto di datore di lavoro alla luce del sistema: la codatorialità e il rapporto con il divieto di interposizione*, in Ead. (ed.), *Dall'impresa a rete alle reti d'impresa. Scelte organizzative e diritto del lavoro*, 1, 39 (Giuffrè, Milano, 2015).
64. Comments of this legal provision are to be found in Ilario Alvino, *Il lavoro nelle reti di imprese. Profili giuridici* (Giuffrè, Milano, 2014); Marco Biasi, *Dal divieto di interposizione alla codatorialità: le trasformazioni dell'impresa e le risposte dell'ordinamento*, in Gaetano Zilio Grandi, Marco Biasi (eds), *Contratto di rete e diritto del lavoro*, 117 (Wolters Kluwer, Cedam, Padova, 2014); Valentina Cagnin, *Il distacco intra-gruppo alla luce delle novità sul contratto di rete* (2014) available at http://www.diprist.unimi.it/Reti_impresa/papers/21.pdf; Marco Peruzzi, *Il distacco di personale tra imprese che hanno sottoscritto un contratto di rete. Nozione di codatorialità e questioni aperte* (2014), available at http://www.diprist.unimi.it/Reti_impresa/papers/11.pdf.

of the network programme.[65] In this respect, it is also worth noting that Article 4.3, *let. a* and *b* of Dir. 2014/67 (on the enforcement of Directive 96/71/EC concerning the posting of workers in the framework of the provision of services) suggests that, in the genuine posting, the work must be carried out for 'a limited period of time' (not temporary).[66]

Despite several weaknesses and legal uncertainties, the Italian regulation of the interfirm network agreement acknowledges for the first time that it is a legal possibility to focus on the network, its common interest and economic activity in order to draw the boundaries of the employment responsibilities, thereby overcoming those of the discrete legal employing entity.

8.5 NETWORKS, FLEXICURITY AND 'ORGANISED RESPONSIBILITY'

The network forms of production might play, in the future, a positive role in the protection of workers' interests, by safeguarding workers' expectation in job and income stability.

By establishing that members of the network share responsibilities for wages and social contributions owed to the network's employees, the employees' income stability will be increased. In the meantime, the greater degree of flexibility which is expected from the network's employees should be counterbalanced by greater job security and employability.[67]

In a recent communication from the EU Commission to the European Parliament, the Council, the European Economic and Social Committee of the Regions, launching a consultation on a European pillar of social rights,[68] President Juncker tried to better specify the meaning of 'flexicurity' in practice. On one hand, firms have an interest in 'being able to attract skilled and productive workers but also to adjust to fast-changing market realities'. On the other, 'workers have an interest in job and income security, to be able to reconcile work and private life, but also to take up new challenges and adapt throughout their careers, and to keep accumulating skills, in a lifelong perspective'.[69]

---

65. *See* Cass., 28 November 2010, no. 23933; Cass., 15 May 2012, no. 7517; Cass., 6 November 2011, no. 24942. *See also* the Ministerial Circular no. 3/2004.
66. On the contrary, in the agency work Directive 2008/104, it is used the word 'temporary' and not the wording 'limited period of time', whose meaning might therefore distinguished from that of temporariness.
67. For instance, the Gucci network agreements are characterized by a stronger job stability and employability of workers who find several employment opportunities in the network. The network also provides for artisans' training and education as to preserve the fundamental knowledge and skill of the Italian garment sector. In turn, this increases their employability within the network. *See* Macchi, *supra* n. 56.
68. 8 March 2016 COM (2016) 127 final.
69. *Ibid.*, at 5.

Network forms of production might serve both these interests. The networks might become 'internal labour markets'[70] where firms are able to attract and 'preserve' skilled and productive workers and workers can find employment and training opportunities which improve their employability and safeguard their expectations about job and income security.

If this result will be achieved, the network forms of production shall become a tool by which ensuring 'organised responsibility', rather than 'organised irresponsibility',[71] and promoting constitutional social values and goals other than profit maximization (e.g., an increased protection of human dignity, human security, human capabilities).[72]

As said above, in my view, an important step in this direction is represented by the acknowledgment of the legal value of the interest of the network (or of groups of companies) as to render transparent and legally relevant the productive and employment relations embedded into the enterprise groups and networks. This recognition will make, and has made, it possible to free the legal concept of employer and the boundaries of labour standards and protections from the boundaries of the discrete legal entity as to capture those of the network.

---

70. *See*, Treu, *supra* n. 59.
71. *See* Collins, *supra* n. 4.
72. *See* Robin, *supra* n. 20.

CHAPTER 9

Groups of Companies and Employment Contracts

Valerio Speziale

9.1 GROUPS OF COMPANIES AND THE 'GROUP INTEREST'

Groups of companies are a fundamental characteristic of the market economy. They are a complex phenomenon which includes different economic and organizational entities, like property, financial, industrial or entrepreneurial groups.

The group of companies I am examining is formed by many companies which keep their juridical autonomy and carry out the same entrepreneurial activity to get a competitive advantage. In order to obtain this result, each company is a ring of the 'value chain' which the companies have to develop.

In this case there is a strong integration between the companies which pursue a group strategy even though they manage different entrepreneurial activities. We can have hierarchical or equal status groups. In the hierarchical groups the holding has a primary role and looks after the activities of strategic planning and control, defining the financial mechanisms and dealing with the training, development and distribution of the managerial resources in the group.

In the equal status groups each company has equal powers and the decisions regarding the organization and the aims of the group are shared by the directors of each company.

In both cases, the group of companies is characterized by a 'group interest' which must be pursued by the group and is different from the economic and organizational interest of each company. In addition, the group can be defined as a single enterprise collectively exercised by many entrepreneurs.

9.2 GROUPS OF COMPANIES AND THE CRISIS OF THE UNITARY CONCEPT OF THE EMPLOYER

In the case of the group of companies the traditional link between an employer and a firm can be confirmed, but the boundaries of the firm have to be re-drawn so as to represent a situation in which the firm and the employment are shared by a number of separate legal entities. Here, the separate personalities of companies do not coincide with the real boundaries of the firm as an individual employer. The group overcomes the boundaries of the legal person as well the boundaries of the unitary concept of the employer. This particularly happens when the employee is working on behalf of more than one company of the group or when the performance of his/her job satisfies the interest of the group and not of a single company. In these cases, the question is to identify who is the real employer and if it is possible to define a 'joint employment' relationship.

9.3 THE ABSENCE OF A GENERAL LEGAL DISCIPLINE OF GROUPS OF COMPANIES AT EUROPEAN LEVEL

At European Union level we do not have a general legal definition of groups of companies. This is true in Commercial Law. In this case we have some sectorial legal definitions, linked, for example, to antitrust legislation and registered trademarks. In the first case, the European Court of Justice (ECJ) set up a series of tests which condition the application of this legislation. The main test is the presence of a 'single direction' of the companies, which means that there is a holding exercising a centralized power of direction and control which can be expressed through the ownership of the totality or majority of the shares, or with the power to appoint at least half of the members of the board of directors (but also other tests can be used).

This jurisprudence strongly influenced the Italian legislation about groups of companies, based on the concept of a company which exercises the 'activity of direction and control' over other companies (Article 2497 of the Italian Civil Code).

As regards Labour Law we are in a similar situation. We do not have a general legal discipline of the employment contract in the groups. There are sector regulations in which groups of companies are expressly taken into consideration. This is the case with the European Works Council (Directive 2009/38/EC) and in the discipline of collective dismissals (Directive 98/59/EC).

Generally speaking, from an individual employment contract point of view, European Union law does not apply to groups of companies and in this case employment contracts are established with the individual companies which make up the group.

9.4 THE LABOUR DISCIPLINE OF GROUPS OF COMPANIES IN DIFFERENT COUNTRIES

In the international context and not only at a European level, there are great differences in the Labour discipline regarding groups of companies.

In some countries there are no specific regulations. In these cases the fundamental principle is that 'there is nothing intrinsically fraudulent about deciding to incorporate or about dividing a single enterprise into multiple corporations, even when it is done solely to get the benefit of limited liability'.[1]

In these countries (Spain, Austria, Sweden, Turkey, Israel, and the USA) the group has importance only from an economic and not from a juridical point of view. The group is not a legal entity and employment contracts can be attributed only to the company which has formally employed the worker. Employment contracts cannot be attributed to the group and the group is not responsible for the rights and obligations of the employment contract.

Italy is one of these countries. Italian Labour law does not have a specific discipline for individual and collective employment contracts in groups of companies. The group is taken into consideration for some specific disciplines (collective dismissals, bureaucratic procedures regarding employment contracts and social security) but these rules do not influence the identification of the subject responsible for the contractual obligations of the worker or collective bargaining.

9.5 THE ROLE OF THE JURISPRUDENCE REGARDING 'FRAUDULENT GROUPS'

In some of these countries, however, the jurisprudence has decided to go beyond the corporate veil in the case of 'fraudulent groups of undertakings'. This regards those situations in which the enterprise is artificially segmented into a number of different companies in order to avoid the protection imposed by labour law (such as the protection linked to the number of employees hired by the employer) or to reduce the responsibilities linked to the managing of the labour contract (payment of salaries, safety obligations etc...)

The jurisprudence uses different criteria to identify a fraudulent group. In Italy and Spain tests have been established which, irrespective of the company's intention to avoid its obligations, reveal the illicit fragmentation of the enterprise.

In Italy they are (a) the indivisibility of the organizational and productive structures, (b) the integration of the various activities of the companies of the group with the aim of satisfying a common interest, (c) the technical, administrative and financial co-ordination with a single subject directing the work,

---

1. Stephen M. Bainbridge, *Abolishing veil piercing*, Oklahoma law review, p. 497 ff.(1998).

(d) the undifferentiated and contemporary use of workers by various entrepreneurs.

In Spain there are similar criteria (the management on a unified basis of labour organization and performance leading to a 'workforce confusion', economic and financial connections between integrated companies so as to determine a situation of 'commingling of social patrimony', the presence of companies apparently without an effective productive organization; the abusive use of the unified direction of the group to the detriment of the workers' rights. The jurisprudence requires the presence of some of these conditions but not necessarily all of them.

In Israel the fraudulent group is identified by the following elements: (a) the lack of 'good faith' by the employer, (b) the commingling of assets, (c) criminal activity, (d) the false representation of the employer's identity.

In Argentina the principle of the juridical autonomy of the companies of the groups does not apply when relations between companies are used as instruments to avoid the protection obligations of subordinate work and social security through 'fraudulent manoeuvres' or 'a reckless and unscrupulous management' of business by the holding or the parent company.

In Canada, the Courts impose responsibility jointly and severally among different corporations, sweeping aside corporate veils in situations in which the enterprise is conducted through a series of corporations that are commonly owned. This happens when there is both a common ownership of the group of corporations and there is some integration of the different functions in a common enterprise.

The lifting of the corporate veil implies that the employment contract is attributed to the whole group (or holding) which is considered a single employer.

In Italy, in particular, the fraudulent group is considered a single enterprise to calculate the number of employees for the application of the discipline regarding job reinstatement or the fulfilment of *repechage* obligations.

In this case, before dismissing the employee for economic reasons, the employer is bound to verify the possibility of redeploying the worker in the undertaking. Furthermore the enterprise is considered a single structure for the evaluation of the technical and organizational justifications for the economic dismissal, the application of the discipline on collective dismissals (including choice criteria) and the analysis of the phenomenon of posted workers.

9.6 'GENUINE' GROUPS OF COMPANIES AND LABOUR RELATIONS IN DIFFERENT COUNTRIES: THE CO EMPLOYMENT APPROACH

The situation I have described, however, regards only a partial aspect of the subject of groups of companies. The groups are economic and juridical realities through which strategies for the integration and diversification of production activities are carried out. The aim is to create a single enterprise with different levels of production specialization entrusted to individual companies for a number of purposes (the capacity to work in different markets with different levels of competence, cost reduction, organizational flexibility, production diversification etc.).

In these cases the companies are genuine from an entrepreneurial point of view (capitalization, financial resources, assets, production organization etc.), but are strictly connected to the pursuit of a strategy of a unified and strongly integrated group from an organizational point of view.

These integration processes may also have consequences on labour relations. In fact a worker who is formally an employee of a company of the group, may also be managed and co-ordinated by the parent company of the group or by other companies which are not his formal employer. His work may also be finalized to satisfying the interests of the whole group and not only his company.

In such situations the traditional bilateral structure of the labour contract may not be suited to regulating the ways in which the employee carries out his working activity.

It may also be difficult to identify who is the real employer 'responsible' if the obligations of the employment contract are not fulfilled or which company the juridical effects of business choices (such as dismissals) should be attributed to.

In these cases many legal systems go beyond the traditional approach of the 'corporate personality' of the single companies and attribute juridical importance to groups of companies. The techniques used are very different from each other. In some cases the law is limited to guaranteeing the joint and several liability of the group (or holding) for workers' credits.

In other cases the group of companies is taken into consideration for the application of specific legal disciplines. Finally, there are situations in which the legal system or the jurisprudence codifies situations of real co-employment or joint employment.

In France, for example, the work code establishes that the obligation of *reclassement* (reemployment of the worker in the undertaking) refers to the company or to the group of companies to which it belongs, including those located abroad.

The code also establishes that a worker dismissed by a foreign subsidiary can be repatriated and reintegrated in the parent company, attributing a part of the responsibility to the company even though the subsidiary is really the company which exercises directive power over the worker.

The French jurisprudence has created the notion of social and economic unity, which brings together a plurality of juridically different entities. In the presence of certain conditions (a concentration of directive power exercised by the same subject; the overlapping of financial participations; the directive power of one company exercised over the others; the interchangeability of the workers in the various companies of the group), the economic and social community is considered a single structure in which there may be workers' representatives and union delegates common to all the companies. This interpretation has been codified by law with the possibility of setting up a joint undertaking committee.

French jurisprudence has also developed the idea of co-employment.

In the presence of a series of tests (financial control; a lack of independence in the strategic definition and the fixing of prices; the centralization of human resources; a lack of industrial, commercial and administrative autonomy), French judges believe there is a state of 'triple confusion', that is, a confusion of activity, interests and direction).

In these cases the parent company can be defined as a 'joint employer' together with the company which formally employed the worker.

Thus the parent company assumes direct responsibility with regard to various obligations such as the obligation of *reclassement,* a participation in the contribution towards the financing of labour protection and also a joint liability in the case of illegitimate dismissal or violation of regulations regarding safety at work.

Moreover, in the French legal system, responsibility for debts (including those in favour of workers) can be based on the business notions of company control (ownership of shares, majority voting rights, power to nominate or revoke the majority of the members of the board of directors, exercising a dominant influence, existence of a joint control, and so forth).

In the United Kingdom Labour law legislation (the Employment Rights Act 1996) allows two or more companies to consider themselves 'associated' when one of them has control, either directly or indirectly, of the other company or companies.

The English courts define a controlling company either as one which possesses 51% of the shares of another company, or when many subjects act in a co-ordinated way determining an equivalent vote of control. In these cases the number of employees needed to exercise some rights of workers is calculated with reference to all the employers.

When a worker moves from one company of the group to another the employment contract is considered continuous. Moreover, in the case of unjustified dismissal, the judge can order the re-engagement of the worker by the original employer or by the associated employer. Finally, with regard to the Equal Pay Act, the term of comparison from the definition of the retribution can also refer to the joint employers.

Similar techniques are used in Canada, in the case of associated employers, defined as such on the basis of a series of tests (sharing of management, property, trademarks and assets, sharing of the same market and customers, mobility of workers between the different companies of the group). The entrepreneurs, who are formally separate entities, are jointly and severally responsible for obligations arising from employment contracts.

In Spain, in cases in which the group acts as a 'single business organization' and the workers carry out their activities for a plurality of employers, the co-ownership of the employment contract is confirmed.

Moreover, in these cases and with reference to collective dismissals, Spanish judges have declared that the existence of a crisis or of a negative economic situation that justifies economic dismissals must be ascertained with regard to the group as a whole.

German judges have occasionally admitted the 'double employer' situation in which an employee has worked for a number of firms integrated to such an extent that it is possible to consider the existence of a single employment relationship, rather than a number of separate employment relationships, with a plural employing entity.

In many Latin American countries (Chile, Costa Rica and Uruguay) the jurisprudence declares that in groups of undertakings the individual companies have a joint responsibility towards the workers.

In Brazil the law establishes that when one or more companies are under the direction, control and administration of another undertaking or when they are integrated into a financial economic group of an industrial, business, rural or any other nature, they will be jointly responsible for any obligations arising from employment contracts in the group.

9.7 THE NEED FOR A EUROPEAN DIRECTIVE REGARDING THE EMPLOYMENT CONTRACT IN GROUPS

The development of 'genuine' groups and their growing importance in the European and international context call for a regulation of the discipline of employment contracts in these juridical realities both at an individual and a collective level.

The need for regulations stems above all from the necessity to avoid opportunist behaviour within the group.

This is the case with a company which systematically uses the performances of a worker who is formally an employee of another employer. As this company is not the subject who signed the contract, it can avoid the application of all the regulations regarding employment relationships with all the benefits of work performed to its advantage.

In these situations there is also the need for a more incisive protection of the worker, who risks undergoing the economic and juridical consequences of essential choices which affect his contract (professionality, salaries, work safety and dismissals) but which are made either by a company different from his formal employer or jointly by his formal company and the one he is working for.

However, a legal discipline for work in groups also has the aim of establishing transparency (identifying the real subjects who benefit from the work) in order to attribute the effects of the employment contract to all those who actually use the work performance so that the rights and duties linked to the employment relationships are distributed in an equal and coherent way with the juridical reality.

From a collective point of view too, even though there are regulations dealing with the matter, it would be advisable to define a legal discipline also for groups of a smaller size, both regarding the definition of the area of collective bargaining and relating to requisites to identify union representatives who operate at a group level and have the right to information, consultation and intervention on choices which regard the group but also affect the performance of the individual companies.

It is thus time for a European Directive which regulates the employment contract in groups. The Directive should regulate, in the 'genuine groups', work activities performed in favour of more companies or in which the economic and organizational decisions of the holding (or the main undertakings of the group) are such as to influence the content and performance of labour relations also in the company in which the worker is formally employed.

Different techniques could be used depending on the degree of integration of the various companies and the extent to which the worker is used by the group or by the companies belonging to it. In some cases joint responsibility for the workers' credits could suffice.

In other cases the group would be taken into consideration for some specific parameters (evaluations of the economic and organizational reasons for dismissals, the calculation of the number of employees needed for the application of legal disciplines and collective contracts, the obligation to redeploy the worker in the group in case of non-disciplinary dismissal, mobility between the companies of the group, the discipline of employment benefits, and so forth).

Finally, in situations in which some requisites are present, real forms of co-employment could be identified with which the employment contract is attributed to two or more employers (e.g., the holding and the company which formally employs the worker).

In this case the directive should regulate in detail the structure of the employment contract with its relative rights and obligations. It should not be forgotten, in fact, that the employment contract, in all juridical systems, is considered a 'binary' contract and the introduction of more employers could create situations which are difficult to manage with the rules traditionally conceived for a single employer.

In this area the jurisprudence and European regulations of the other countries previously described could be an important point of reference for a regulation at European level.

9.8 THE ROLE OF THE JURISPRUDENCE REGARDING 'GENUINE' GROUPS AND THE CO EMPLOYMENT PERSPECTIVE

In the absence of this European discipline and national laws which regulate the employment contract in groups of companies, an essential role can be played by jurisprudence. In this case, apart from the traditional role of repressing the fraudulent segmentations of the company aimed at bypassing the protection of the workers, jurisprudence, through interpretation, can try to go beyond the corporate veil and define cases of co-employment.

As well as the experiences which I have already examined, I should also point out that the attribution of employment contracts to more employers also appears in a sentence of the Court of European Justice regarding transfers of undertakings.

In the *Albron case* (21 October 2010, C-242/09) the Court considered as a 'transferor', within the meaning of the Transfer of Undertaking Directive 2001/23 'the employer responsible for economic activity of the entity transferred which, in that capacity, establishes relations with the staff of that entity, despite, the absence of contractual relations with those staff'. It has been quoted that 'by stressing the legal possibility for an employee to have a contractual relation with a formal employer and non contractual relation with a substantial employer to which the employee is permanently assigned, the ECJ's approach comes closer to the British perspective, rather than to the continental European perspective'. In fact 'British judges hold that a dual vicarious liability is a legal possibility when the right to control the working activity is shared by two legal entities'.[2]

Regardless of the specific legal context in which the sentence was emitted, there is no doubt that it expresses a trend which tends to extend the notion of the employer beyond the subject who formally employed the worker and signed the contract.

Also Italian jurisprudence has, in some decisions, expressed itself in different forms from the traditional ones.

With regard to the phenomenon of groups of companies, the Italian Court of Cassation stated that 'in the presence of certain circumstances, it is juridically possible to conceive a single undertaking which supports various activities formally entrusted to different subjects, which does not always entail the need to go beyond the corporate veil or deny the plurality of those subjects, as there may well be an employment contract with a single person in the position of the worker and more subjects in the position of the employer so creating a joint and several obligation of the employer'.[3]

In more recent times the Italian Supreme Court has declared that 'in the presence of genuine but strongly integrated groups', the interference of the parent company may 'determine the destination of the work performance to all the operative companies of the group according to the well known forms of cumulative performance or alternative work'.[4]

The possibility of identifying a case of co-employment within the groups implies the application of 'employment tests' elaborated by the jurisprudence on the basis of legal notions used by each country to define subordinate work.

---

2. Luisa Corazza, Orsola Razzolini, *Who Is the Employer?* WP C.S.D.L.E. 'Massimo D'Antona'.INT, 11072014, in http://csdle.lex.unict.it/workingpapers.aspx, 22 (2014).
3. Cassation 24. 3. 2003 n. 4274.
4. Cassation 29.11.2011 n. 2527.

From this point of view it is important to underline that the notions elaborated in Company Law for the definition of groups of companies cannot have a determining function in identifying a situation of co-employment.

This conclusion is derived from the specific norms typical of Company Law, which identifies a notion of groups of companies strictly connected to the aims of this sector of law which are completely different from Labour Law.

An example may be useful. As we have already seen, the ECJ set up a series of tests which condition the application of some specific legislations regarding antitrust or registered trademarks. The main test is the presence of a 'single direction' of the companies, which means that there is a holding exercising a centralized power of direction and control which can be expressed through the ownership of the totality or majority of the shares, or with the power to appoint at least half of the members of the board of directors (but also other tests can be used).

9.9 CO EMPLOYMENT IN GROUPS OF COMPANIES

This jurisprudence strongly influenced the Italian legislation regarding groups of companies, based on the concept of a company which exercises the 'activity of direction and control' over other companies (Article 2497 of the Italian Civil Code).

In the Italian notion of employment contract and in that of other countries not only European, the direction and control of the activity of the subordinate worker are some of the essential tests of subordination.

However, it is evident that direction and control carried out by the holding over the companies is a power completely different from the directive power which characterizes the employment contract. In the first case, direction and control regard the strategic choices of the company in pursuing its company objectives and they are expressed with directives or with the power to appoint the members of the board of directors. In the second case the directives concern the orders regarding the fulfilment of the single job performance in relation to 'if', 'how' and 'when' to work. In some situations the holding's directives over the controlled companies can also *indirectly* affect the performance of the jobs. However, the two powers (the 'single direction' of the companies from a financial, commercial and strategic point of view, the direction of the single performance of the worker) are completely different and cannot be confused.

The forms of co-employment I want to point out imply that the employment contract is at least characterized by: (a) the power of the employer to give directives over job performance and to control it, (b) the integration of the worker into the productive organization of the employer, (c) the circumstance that the job performance satisfies the juridical interest of the employer to receive the work and to coordinate it with the other workers and with the other productive factors.

Co-employment could be identified when the employer's directives over the job performance ('if', 'how' and 'when' to work) are jointly carried out by the holding and the company which hired the worker or when they are alternately expressed by the companies which are interchangeable from this point of view. The same characteristics should be present as regards the power of the employer to control the performance of the work.

In addition, the job performance must satisfy not only the juridical interests of the company which hired the worker but also the interests of the whole group or of the holding. In these cases, however, the interest the job performance has to satisfy is that linked to the fulfilment of the worker's obligation. This is the case of an engineer who carries out a project whose execution satisfies at the same time the juridical interest of the employer and of the holding or of the whole group which are directly involved in the fulfilment of the performance of the worker regarding the project.

This interest in the performance of the work must be distinguished from the 'interest of the group of undertakings'. In fact, in Company Law the latter coincides with the economic interests of all the companies of the group and it is different from the economic interests of the single undertakings which make up the group.

A clear case of co-employment is the common utilization of the worker by two or more companies of the group, when the performance of the job is done such in a way that it is impossible to distinguish what work activity is performed in favour of one company or in favour of another. In this situation there is a coincidence between the 'formal employer' and the other which is receiving the work, because they are both using the performance of the work at the same time or at different moments.

The co-employment could also be identified when the co-determination of the performance of the job is realized without specific and detailed orders but through the co-determination of the part of the productive structure in which the job is integrated. In fact, in these cases the identification of the part of the organization can strongly influence the performance of the job and could be equivalent to the direction of the work.

This can happen when one company (for instance, the holding) gives 'technical specifications' which are so detailed that they really shape the content of the work performance which must be carried out in that part of the enterprise.

When these conditions are present, we can say that the employment contract can be co-attributed to the formal employer and to the holding or the whole group of undertakings depending on the manner in which the employment is performed and the presence of the essential elements I have described above (exercise of the power of direction and control of the work; satisfaction of the juridical interest of the group or of the holding as the creditor of the job performance etc.). As I have already noted, in these cases the legal discipline of the employment contract – shaped on a bilateral structure – could be inadequate to rule a situation in which there is more than one employer. However, as concerns the Italian system, the difficulties are not insurmountable.

From a legal point of view, we could have a 'joint consideration' of the co-employers as regards the number of the workers employed, the economic and organizational reasons used to justify the economic individual and collective dismissals, the intra-group mobility, the duty to redeploy the worker as an alternative to the economic dismissal, the joint and several liability for workers' credits and for the safety obligations, the evaluation of diligence in performing the employment contract, the evaluation of the duty of loyalty of the worker, and so forth.

The jurisprudence definition of co-employment, even though it raises some problems, can urge the European and national legislators to rule this new frontier of the Labour Law. In any case, the role of judges would be essential in defining a juridical framework for situations which by now are a constant reality in our legal systems and require norms able to combine the company's needs for specialization and productive integration (of which the group is one of the clearest examples) and the protection of the workers.

PART IV Enterprise in the Collective
         Bargaining Process

CHAPTER 10
Collective Bargaining at the Transnational Level

Giuseppe Casale

10.1 INTRODUCTION

The right to bargain collectively is a core International Labor Organization (ILO) value and is inextricably linked with freedom of association. Both represent key tools of labour market governance. As a foundational element of the broader concept of social dialogue, collective bargaining contributes to the strengthening of democratic principles all over the world.[1]

Today globalization, advanced technologies, changes in the structure and composition of the labour force, new forms of employment, new production methods, evolving business relations, combined with political and economic changes have profoundly affected national and international labour markets.

---

1. 'Collective bargaining' is defined by reference to the relevant ILO instruments as the process and activities leading to the conclusion of a collective agreement. Art. 2 of the ILO Collective Bargaining Convention, 1981 (No. 154) defines collective bargaining as follows: 'the term collective bargaining extends to all negotiations which take place between an employer, a group of employers or one or more employers' organisations, on the one hand, and one or more workers' organisations, on the other, for: (a) determining working conditions and terms of employment, and/or (b) regulating relations between employers and workers, and/or (c) regulating relations between employers or their organisations and a workers' organisation or workers' organisations. In addition, the ILO Collective Agreements Recommendation, 1952 (No. 91), para. 2(1.) defines collective agreements as: 'all agreements in writing regarding working conditions and terms of employment concluded between an employer, a group of employers or one or more employers' organisations, on the one hand and one or more representative workers' organisations, or, in the absence of such organisations, the representatives of the workers duly elected and authorized by them in accordance with national laws and regulations, on the other.

These developments, together with the impact of the political choices involved in the liberalization of capital and trade markets accompanied to the decentralization of industrial relations, have created new challenges for the effective implementation of the right to bargain collectively.[2]

The internationalization of production and of the exchange of goods and services has undergone different cycles of intensification and transformation. In recent years, a new emerging move towards the transnational level of labour relations is characterizing industrial relations. The so-called International Framework Agreements (IFA), which are agreements between a Global Union Federation (GUF) and a Multinational Enterprise (MNE), are the result of negotiation at company level. Companies headquartered in France, Germany, Italy and the Nordic European countries are represented in this process, together with US companies operating in Europe. The current IFA are various in terms of form, procedure and context. Their content also varies. Many of them make a direct reference to core labour rights linked to the relevant international labour standards of the ILO. A number of IFA deal with additional issues such as employment, wages, and working time, although not so specific when setting conditions relying more on the broad provisions of relevant national legislation. When health and safety, training or restructuring issues are covered, they are dealt with in a different manner depending on the circumstances of the company and the nature of the agreement itself. In this regard, there are increasing discussions on the legal nature of such agreements and their consequential legal effects.

At another level, one could also observe that the European Works Councils (EWCs) are increasingly going beyond their information and consultation role. In fact, either with or without the national, European and international trade union organizations, the agreements are drawing up transnational texts that are intended to apply in several European countries, notably on health, safety and the environment, data protection, equal treatment at work, mobility management, mergers, closures, relocation and restructuring. Recently, agreements have been negotiated between companies and parties representing the workers at European and/or international level on issues related to Corporate Social Responsibility (CSR), notably on fundamental rights, and which in scope go far beyond Europe.

10.2 TRANSNATIONAL COLLECTIVE BARGAINING

The traditional role of collective bargaining as a mechanism for setting working and employment conditions within the scope of a single country has changed.

As pointed out by the ILO, the economy is becoming increasingly global, while social and political institutions remain largely local, national and regional.

---

2. Director-General's Report to the 2006 International Labour Conference (ILC), Changing patterns in the world of work.

None of the existing institutions provide adequate democratic oversight of global markets, or redress basic inequalities between countries. The imbalances point to the need for better institutional frameworks and policies if the promise of globalization is to be realized.[3]

Increasing market internationalization and mobility of capital have become great challenges for the labour movement. The organization of labour is currently in difficulty due to a constant decline in trade union membership as well as to trade unions' lack of willingness and possibly capacity to mobilize resources to act at a transnational level.

Such a new industrial relations scenario increasingly calls for cross-border, coordinated responses and initiatives by workers and their organizations at transnational and company levels. These include the forms of Transnational Collective Bargaining (TCB).

The term TCB refers to all those collective bargaining practices between employers' and workers' representatives that aim at reaching transnational agreements (European, global) regardless of the legal nature of the agreements.[4]

In this context, it has both a wide scope encompassing all developments, including social dialogue, the coordination mechanism of collective bargaining levels at national level, EWCs, and a narrow one limited to transnational company-level agreements both at the European and global level.

At a closer look, the former scope refers to traditional and well established instruments and procedures of collective bargaining. The latter one refers more to a new phenomenon which is currently underdeveloped in European industrial relations. That is to say, the intensification of cross-border cooperation among workers' organizations with a view to promoting collective bargaining with MNEs.[5]

In addition, TCB is not limited to one specific type of trans-border collective negotiations, but it can take the form of either sectoral or company-level bargaining. It can also take the form of cross-border information exchange of bargaining-relevant data, by either employers or trade unions, with the aim of setting the context for the national and local negotiations which could eventually take place in sectors and companies or it could take the form of transnational negotiations resulting in the adoption of joint texts and framework agreements of varying degrees.[6]

---

3. See ILO, *A fair globalization: the role of the ILO. Report of the Director-General on the World Commission on the social dimension of globalization.*
4. See Kostantinos Papadakis, Giuseppe Casale & Katerina Tsotroudi, *International Framework Agreements as elements of a cross-border industrial relations framework*, in Kostantinos Papadakis, *Cross-border social dialogue and agreements: An emerging global industrial relations framework?* International Institute for Labour Studies, Ch. 3. (ILO, 2008).
5. Romuald Jagodzinski, *Transnational collective bargaining: a literature review*, in Isabelle Schömann, Romuald Jagodzinski, Guido Boni, Stefan Clauweart, Vera Glassner & Teun Jaspers, *Transnational collective bargaining at company level. A new component of European industrial relations?* (ETUI aisbl 2012).
6. Ibid.

10.3 TRADE UNION RESPONSES AT TRANSNATIONAL, SECTORAL AND COMPANY LEVEL

At the transnational level, trade unions negotiate with individual transnational enterprises rather with employers' associations. MNEs pursue their own interests, seeking agreements tailored to their needs instead of taking collective, sectoral (or national) interests into account, as is usually the case with employers' associations.

One of the big challenges for trade unions is that they have not yet acquired sufficient transnational leverage to start an efficient process on this, especially how to negotiate effectively with MNEs on the core global issues of MNEs strategies and how to come to grips with the shift of work-related decision making away from trade unions traditional national level. In addition, there is no general trade union consensus on whether TCB is the right way forward.

The conceptual resistance of trade unions – European Trade Union Federations and national unions – to a supranational level of negotiation is perceived as the main obstacle preventing transnational negotiation from developing. Other obstacles are the very different development patterns of TUs in Europe and in the world, giving rise to a variety of trends in industrial relations systems. Yet there are also other more concrete obstacles, such as language barriers, the lack of sufficient preparation and not adequate training for workers' representatives in European Work Councils or Global Work Councils.

Against this background there is a growing debate on the need for introducing concrete measures for further developing industrial relations at international level. This would restore the transnational social balance through coordinated TU responses at transnational, sector and company level.

At the European Union (EU) level, the Commission has already fostered the development of a general framework of action based on a clear set of rules for both workers and employers. In its report of March 2002, the Commission's High-Level Group on Industrial Relations identified globalization as one of the new challenges for industrial relations in Europe emphasizing the role and potential of transnational company agreements to manage the process of globalization in a balanced way.[7] As a consequence, in 2005, the Commission DG for Employment, Social Affairs and Equal Opportunities provided to a group of experts on industrial relations the task of conducting a study on TCB with a view to preparing an analysis and assessment of the possibility of introducing an (optional) legal framework for TCB.[8] The Commission argued that the legal framework could benefit both companies and workers by extending the social partners' capacities and adapting them to the changing circumstances. In the Commission's view, the introduction of a legal framework for TCB represented a further step towards completion of the common market.

---

7. European Commission (2002).
8. European Commission (2005).

The study team adopted a research method based on the analysis of instruments and field experiences of transnational dialogue at sectoral and company level. The TCB Report of 2006 came out in favour of an (optional) legal framework to be adopted at EU level which could then be used by the social partners to guarantee legal certainty. However, no concrete result was achieved and no final decision has been taken until today.[9]

10.4 IFA AND EFAs

As mentioned earlier, globalization has generated an asymmetry between the scope of the activities of global actors (such as MNEs), which is increasingly transnational, and the scope of action of social actors (such as trade unions, social movements, non-governmental organizations), which remains largely embedded at national level.

In this regard, the IFA represent another emerging form of TCB. The negotiation of IFA can potentially be seen as the start of a bargaining procedure at transnational level, since they are by definition bilateral agreements and are negotiated between transnational enterprises and GUFs, with the main aim of ensuring application of and compliance with international labour standards.[10]

IFA have a global scope of application, whereas European Framework Agreements (EFAs) have a regional (European) scope of application and are signed by European Industry Federations (EIFs), EWCs and/or national unions and central management.

IFA are mainly based on ILO core labour standards, dealing with freedom of association and the right to collective bargaining (ILO Conventions no. 87 and no. 98). Sometimes they go beyond the minimum requirements contained in the ILO Conventions (some of them address other issues such as health and safety, training or restructuring) and in some cases they are used as tools to extend human resource management policies and cooperative industrial relations in those local contexts where MNCs operate.

EFAs are more heterogeneous than IFA, both in terms of content and procedure. EWCs play an important role not only in the negotiation and signature of these agreements (they have signed a large majority of them), but also in the implementation and monitoring processes of a growing number of them. EFAs cover a great variety of issues, including restructuring, social dialogue, health and safety, human resources management and data protection.

---

9. *See* Edoardo Ales, Samuel Engblom, Teun Jaspers, Sylvaine Laulom, Silvana Sciarra, André Sobczak & Fernando Valdés Dal-Ré, *Transnational collective bargaining: past, present and future. Final report*, European Commission (Brussels 2006).
10. Isabelle Schömann, *The impact of transnational company agreements on social dialogue and industrial relations*, in Isabelle Schömann, André Sobczak, Eckhard Voss & Peter Wilke, *Codes of conduct and international framework agreements: new forms of governance at company level*, Publications Office of the European Union (Luxembourg, 2008).

Fundamental social rights also play a role in EFAs, but they are more prominent in IFA.[11]

10.5 LEGAL FRAMEWORK

One of the major problems pointed out when discussing TCB in the form of agreements is their enforceability and legal binding effect. This is due to the lack of a specific international legal framework for such agreements, and to legal concerns about the mandate and acceptance of any binding results of TCB by national trade union organizations affiliated to the negotiating parties.[12]

EFAs and IFA have considerable difficulties regarding their actual implementation and compliance, since they cannot rely upon before national courts and do not lead to enforceable decisions or the adoption of legal sanctions in the case of non-implementation.

In the absence of any legal framework, trade unions and management have established new mechanisms for transnational framework agreements (TFAs), inspired by domestic and European collective labour law. The mismatch between structures and practices within MNCs and national collective bargaining is particularly pronounced in the multi-employer bargaining arrangements prevailing in the majority of EU member States. Alongside organized labour, supranational trade unions and workers' representation bodies have to aggregate the differing, and sometimes contrasting, interests of members and workers from different countries. From here the difficulty in having legal binding effects and hence IFA are only binding in honour among the parties which have subscribed them in good faith.[13]

Such a phenomenon of asymmetry between global companies and local workforces'/workers' representatives represents the limitation for the future of developing effective industrial relations at the global level which are consonant with the current changes. In a nutshell, companies go global, but workers remain local.

One way forward is to further promote collective barging at transnational level by equipping workers with the decent work agenda of the ILO. This could prove the relevance of the international labour standards and make sure that workers participate effectively in the decision making process concerning their working and employment conditions.

---

11. Kostantinos Papadakis (ed.), *Cross-border social dialogue and agreements: an emerging global industrial relations framework?* ILO (2008).
12. Ales E. et al., *supra* n. 9, at 23–24.
13. Vera Glassner, *Transnational collective bargaining coordination at the European sector level. The outlines and limits of a 'European' system'*, in 1 (2) International Journal of Labour Research 113–129 (2009).

10.6 EUROPEAN SOCIAL DIALOGUE

European social dialogue could be interpreted as a form of TCB in its widest sense. There are examples of results achieved by cross-industry and sectoral social dialogue at the European level. While at the enterprise level, a major role has been played by the EWC. In this regard, the EWCs play a stronger role in initiating, negotiating, signing and implementing EFAs. They are commonly identified as facilitators in transnational procedures, providing an institutional structure of information and consultation for MNC workforces.

Already in 1996, the European Commission emphasized the growing need to support the development of new levels of social dialogue, referring specifically to social dialogue in transnational companies at regional level, particularly in cross-border European regions.

At a closer look, the EWCs are the only form of workers' representation at transnational company level, thus providing to workers a tool for conducting TCB.[14]

Nonetheless, the uncertainty on the legal framework of TCB and TFAs limits their operative implementation. As mentioned above, the introduction of a legal framework would make the agreements resulting from TCB more effective, otherwise they would remain private norms based on customary rules of adoption and enforcement. The idea is to establish the conditions under which transnational collective agreements (TCAs) can have binding effects in legal terms and this would guarantee the effective application of TCA provisions uniformly in all MNE subsidiaries in countries through granting direct effect to subjective rights and duties laid down in a TCA. Although this could be seen as a solution, at the same time such a solution is confronted with substantive differences in the legal systems governing collective agreements in the EU Member States, and hence its difficulty in the application.[15]

Ideally, there should be the adoption of a legal framework at the EU level for the provisions of uniform legal effect on TCAs, since the TCB is steadily increasing and should be supported by a harmonious legal framework. In this regard, the European Commission in collaboration with the ILO should promote TCB accompanied by the protection of workers' rights, especially during economic crisis.

The European institutional and legal framework shaping industrial relations in the EU remain incomplete. Articles 152–155 TFEU partially define the European collective bargaining system through organizing the European social dialogue. Yet this framework appears unsuitable for addressing the effective implementation of such agreements, since the EFAs resulting from sectoral

---

14. European Commission (1996).
15. Isabelle Schömann, I., *Transnational collective bargaining: in search of a legal framework*, in Isabelle Schömann, Romuald Jagodzinski, Guido Boni, Stefan Clauweart, Vera Glassner & Teun Jaspers, *Transnational collective bargaining at company level. A new component of European industrial relations?* (ETUI aisbl 2012).

social dialogue are the same to the ones encountered with TCAs. At the same time, the legal framework establishing a EWC or a procedure for informing and consulting employees in a community scale undertaking or group of undertakings (Recast Directive 2009/38/EC) does not foresee the EWC involvement in TCB. In other words, the question remains over the legal capacity of EWCs to negotiate but de facto they are already involved in bargaining, signing and monitoring TCAs.

TCAs are evolving and influencing existing industrial relations. For example, TCAs are introducing innovative alternative dispute resolution mechanisms developed by the parties themselves for ensuring effective implementation and monitoring of the TCA.

TCAs do not fit in any of the existing legal categories of CB outcomes defined in national, European or private international law. They represent a new form of collective (private) regulation by adding a new dimension to European industrial relations. Both workers and employers seek legal rules that would allow TCAs to gain in legitimacy and credibility. In this regard, both private international law and national legislation could provide legal direction and solutions in support of TCB. Yet significant differences among EU member States and between the EU and non EU-legal systems cannot provide the required uniformity in the implementation and enforcement of TCAs. Needless to say, uniformity of treatment is needed by both parties to an agreement for legal certainty and predictability.

Selected Global/European trade union federations have developed 'model agreements' to support their affiliated workers' organizations in negotiating, signing and implementing TCAs. Model agreements are not mandatory but provide a working structure and guidance on existing TCB practices. Based on such an experience, it has been advanced the idea of a European legal initiative in the form of either a directive or a European rule filling the gap with regard to TCA implementation and enforcement. This would assist in the rounding off the European industrial relations together with the introduction of alternative dispute resolution mechanisms. Such an initiative would give uniform TCA application by giving TCAs direct legal effect and would avoid the undesirable development of TCAs parallel legislation and help avoid disputes over who (TUs and/or EWCs) has the mandate to negotiate and implement TCAs. At the same time, it would clarify coordination between TCB levels and outcomes and would propose a typology of TCB and European social dialogue instruments building on the experience gained under the current EU social dialogue (Articles 152–155 TFEU).

From a comparative point of view, this would further promote the capacity of workers' organizations to act at transnational level and would foster transnational solidarity and capacity building initiatives with a view to addressing the fundamental issue at stake (the future role of industrial relations) and redressing the unequal balance of power between globally operating management and nationally rooted workers.

10.7 THE FUTURE OF COLLECTIVE BARGAINING AT TRANSNATIONAL LEVEL

At EU level, the European social partners have already been given the chance to conclude European collective agreements within the so-called 'European social dialogue'. The latter can be considered a form of TCB whose agreements cover (have in force) more than one jurisdiction. However, these agreements are not truly European ones, because they do not have Community legal effects, but only national ones. Consequently, they are:

> 'national' transnational collective labour agreements' which 'satisfy the national requirements that collective labour agreements need to satisfy for the country concerned, having a scope of application covering several jurisdictions.' leaving TCB unregulated will not only represent a 'missed opportunity', but that it is indeed of crucial importance for the interests of the EU, as further uncertainty regarding cross-border negotiations poses a 'danger of distortion of competition' which 'has been, since the very beginning, a common ground for intervention by the EEC in the social field.[16]

Article 6 of the European Social Charter does list what parties should undertake to ensure that the right to bargain collectively is exercised effectively: (1) promoting consultations between workers and employers, (2) promoting machinery for voluntary negotiations between employers or employers' organizations and workers' organizations with a view to the regulation of terms and conditions of employment by means of collective agreements, (3) promoting conciliation and dispute settlement solutions, and (4) recognizing the right to collective action in case of conflicts of interest.

Interestingly, both the said consultations and 'voluntary negotiations' are mentioned only in conjunction with employers and their organizations and workers' organizations which point towards a limited scope of parties – that is excluding employee representation bodies – eligible to engage in collective bargaining. Despite the fact that the European Social Charter does not deal extensively with collective bargaining (apart from acknowledging the right of workers to collective bargaining in Article 6), it does recognize the 'right of workers to take part in the determination and improvement of the working conditions and working environment in the undertaking.' (Part I, Article 22). In view of a lack of any further specification of collective bargaining, it remains unresolved whether the transnational level is also included alongside the traditional national level. Though Article 22 of the European Social Charter does not specify any level, it does make reference to an undertaking (i.e. company level). If we take into account the fact that companies operate at transnational level, this means that collective bargaining, at least with regard to working conditions, can take place in all companies, independent of their scope of operations. In sum, the ILO Conventions and the European Social Charter do not

---

16. Ales *et al.*, *supra* n. 9, at 34.

limit the right to collective bargaining; therefore one can conclude that there is nothing preventing the use of collective bargaining in a transnational context.

Another issue concerning transnational negotiations to which ILO sources (but not the European Social Charter) provide a reply is the one about the parties competent to bargain collectively. There are two key aspects to this question: the level at which they are eligible to operate and whether workers' representatives are eligible as bargaining agents, alongside with workers' organizations.

Regarding the first aspect, the views expressed by the ILO Committee of Experts stating that 'the determination of the bargaining level is essentially a matter to be left to the discretion of the parties' (ILO 1985, paragraph 632) make it clear that there is no limitation of collective bargaining only to national or any other specific level. Consequently, it is up to the bargaining parties to determine the appropriate level that is most effective in terms of handling the content of collective negotiations.

The ILO Conventions and Recommendations do not prevent EWCs concluding TCAs and they provide a sufficient legal framework to accommodate TCB as an eligible level of collective bargaining. Moreover, they foresee the possibility for workers' representatives to engage in collective negotiations, in addition to workers and employers and their organizations.

Article 28 of the EU Charter of Fundamental Rights which, with regard to the right to negotiate and conclude collective agreements, stipulates that 'workers and employers, or their respective organization, have, in accordance with Community law and national laws and practices, the right to negotiate and conclude collective agreements at the appropriate levels'. So the level of collective bargaining should be 'appropriate' which can be interpreted as a level satisfying the needs of the contractual parties (*see* ILO Committee of Experts, 1985 paragraph 632).

This explanation shows that Article 28 might indeed be considered a sufficient legal basis for adopting a framework for TCB in the EU. One could conclude that this expansion of collective bargaining can already be accommodated within the current *acquis communitaire* which further supported by Article 155 of the Treaty on the Functioning of the EU (TFEU) which stipulates: 'should management and labour so desire, the dialogue between them at Community level may lead to contractual relations, including agreements'.

Article 28 provides for EWCs to play a role in TCB: the one regarding the actors or parties eligible to sign such agreements. It covers all possible collective bargaining parties (i.e., workers and employers, or their respective organizations). It also reflects the various national solutions in place which entitle, on the part of labour, the trade unions, representatives of workers, employees' associations or their respective organizations to conduct negotiations.[17]

---

17. Roger Blanpain (ed.), *The actors of collective bargaining: a world report. XVII World Congress of Labour Law and Social Security, Montevideo, September 2003*, Kluwer Law International, The Hague, 20 (2004) and Bruno Veneziani, *Right of collective bargaining*

The EU Charter of Fundamental Rights lacks clarity due to its inconsistent wording across its various articles. Article 27 refers to workers' representatives and Article 28 refers to workers' organizations. Sticking to the exact wording of each article does however allow us to draw the conclusion that the existing EU sources on TCB accommodate the transnational level of negotiations. In other words, it seems that the current acquis provides enough legal basis to accommodate TCB as a lawful form of collective negotiation at transnational level and flexible enough to allow any future more specific legal framework to be developed. Furthermore, with regard to the issue of the legality of EWC involvement in collective bargaining, one could say that the treaty-level provisions do not limit the scope of eligible parties to trade unions only, implying that the signing of such agreements by non-trade union organizations of workers is not forbidden. The EWCs as bodies representing workers could be considered as parties eligible to lawfully sign agreements at transnational level.[18]

Nonetheless, there are further problems concerning EWC involvement in signing TCAs. First of all there is the question whether they have a sufficient mandate to negotiate. As already mentioned, the EWCs were originally intended as bodies for information and consultation and it was for this purpose that delegates were elected at individual sites.

Traditionally, national trade unions have been involved in corporate-level collective bargaining in individual member States. Somehow the future of EWCs will be the one of triggering collective bargaining, although they have no mandate to unilaterally start and engage in transnational negotiations with management.

10.8 CONCLUSION

As long as there is no legal framework for TCB, EWCs engaged in this area will continue to operate on the verge of legality.

EWCs do have an important role to play in TCB, either as the key negotiating party, or, should European trade union federations dominate TCB, through officially recognizing and appreciating their experience through involving them in selected subsidiary functions.

The European Commission needs to take the initiative in establishing a European level of collective bargaining. Such legislation would contribute to the improved operation of the common market and would better respond to the needs expressed by management and workers.

---

and action, in Brian Bercusson (ed.) *European labour law and the EU Charter of Fundamental Rights*, Nomos, Baden-Baden, 314 (2006).

18. Romuald Jagodzinski, *European Works Councils and transnational company agreements – balancing on the thin line between effective consultation and overstepping competences*, in Isabelle Schömann, Romuald Jagodzinski, Guido Boni, Stefan Clauweart, Vera Glassner & Teun Jaspers, *Transnational collective bargaining at company level. A new component of European industrial relations?* (ETUI aisbl 2012).

Either to extend EWC rights in the direction of (collective) negotiations by creating a framework providing legal recognition and support for TCAs (legality, execution, binding effect, monitoring, sanctions), or to expand the EU's competence to regulate transnational aspects of collective bargaining – an issue which is traditionally of national nature.

In the end, the most important questions still remain to be answered: is the European Commission ready to promote a legal framework for TCAs? And if so, which solutions will be adopted?

CHAPTER 11
Japan's Decentralized Industrial Relations, Internal Flexicurity, and Challenges Japan Faces

Takashi Araki

11.1 INTRODUCTION: DECENTRALIZED NEGOTIATION, NORM FLEXIBILIZATION AND FLEXICURITY

Decentralization of industrial relations, flexibilization of labor law, and striking a good balance between flexibility and security (flexicurity) are three major contemporary issues of labor law in many countries.

In European countries, Collective Bargaining Agreements (CBA) between labor unions and employers' organizations have traditionally been concluded at the national or sector level. However, the decentralization of negotiation is conspicuous. More labor unions and employers' organizations give their regulatory power to the decentralized parties, such as works councils and individual companies.[1]

The second challenge many countries face is how to adapt uniform labor protective norms to diversified employment relations at workplaces. Traditionally, the most important purpose of state law has been to provide minimum labor standards for all workers across the state. However, state laws establish legal

---

1. *See* Roger Blanpain, Shinya Ouchi & Takashi Araki (eds), *Decentralizing Industrial Relations and the Role of Labour Unions and Employee Representatives*, Bulletin of Comparative Labour Relations, no. 61 (Kluwer Law International, 2007); European Commission, Industrial Relations in Europe 2014 (2015); Nils Braakmann & Bernd Brandl, *The Efficiency of Hybrid Collective Bargaining Systems: An Analysis of the Impact of Collective Bargaining on Company Performance in Europe*, https://mpra.ub.uni-muenchen.de/70025/1/MPRA_paper_70025.pdf.

norms at the most centralized level and do not necessarily fit to the diversified interests of the diversified workers at the workplaces. Therefore, in many European countries, state laws started to allow derogation or deviation from their mandatory norms under certain conditions. For instance, if a CBA concluded by social partners (labor unions and employers' associations) allows derogation from the minimum labor standards, working conditions lower than the statutory norms become permissible. Such derogatory power previously conceded only to the sector-level labor unions and employers' organizations tends to be given to further decentralized parties like works councils and individual employers recently. Such flexibilization of labor protective norms by the decentralized parties provides various legal and political questions.

Both decentralization of negotiation and flexibilization of statutory norms are required to accommodate the grassroots needs of individual companies and workers' interests in a fluctuating market and to make universal norms more adaptable in the workplace with diversified workers. However, decentralization and flexibilization entail the risk of the weakening of negotiative power and a decrease in social protection.

The third major issue in contemporary labor law policy is to strike a better balance between flexibility and security. In the mid-2000s, the Danish model flexicurity was highly recommended by Organisation for Economic Co-operation and Development (OECD) and EU. However, the Danish model is the external market oriented flexicurity (external flexicurity) consisting of numerical flexibility relaxing dismissal regulations and state-provided security of unemployment benefit and training programs.

Making a striking contrast to the situations in Europe, Japan has developed decentralized industrial relations for more than half a century. Most labor unions in Japan are enterprise-based. Collective bargaining takes place between an individual company and its enterprise union. CBAs are thus concluded by those parties at the company level. Enterprise-based unions continue to dominate to date in Japan because they have functioned well to respond swiftly and properly to the workers' demands and needs in the internal labor market which highly developed under the Japan's long-term employment practice.

Japan also faces problems how to adapt uniform norms established by the state labor protective laws to the diversified workplaces. The Japanese law gives the derogatory power not only to labor unions but also to a single worker who is elected as the majority representative in the establishment. This extremely flexible derogation scheme causes various problematic cases in terms of worker protection.

As to balancing flexibility and security, the Japan law has developed the unique model of flexicurity combining flexible adjustment of working conditions and security in employment in the internal labor market (internal flexicurity). First, employment security was established by the case law prohibiting abusive dismissals. But employment security means the lack of numerical flexibility. Therefore, to compensate for the rigidity, the Japanese Supreme Court created a unique rule allowing an employer to unilaterally change working conditions by modifying work rules on the condition that such modification can be regarded as reasonable. Both case law rules concerning prohibition of abusive dismissals and reasonable modification of work rules were incorporated in the 2007 Labor Contract Act.

Therefore, the Japanese law provides an interesting example of decentralized industrial relations, flexibilization of labor protective norms, and unique flexicurity model.

This paper first clarifies the Japanese system of regulating working conditions in comparison with the European system. Second, it deals with statutory minimum labor standards and their flexibilization. Third, it gives an overview of Japan's enterprise unionism that represents decentralized industrial relations. Fourth, Japan's unique flexicurity model utilizing reasonable modification in work rules will be examined. Finally, after summarizing the discussion, the paper will propose a reconsideration of the nature and methods of the statutory regulations applicable to current employment relations that comprise a small number of union members and a diversified workforce.

11.2 LEGAL TOOLS REGULATING WORKING CONDITIONS AND THEIR RELATIONSHIP

11.2.1 European Model

In order to clarify the Japanese system, let me first confirm the European model for regulating working conditions.[2] In almost all countries with a collective bargaining system, there are three legal tools: state law, CBA, and an individual labor contract. In countries with works councils, Works Council Agreements (WCA) might be added as the fourth legal tool, as is typical in Germany (*Betriebsvereinbarung*). When we analyze these tools according to their effects and regulation level, the European model could be described as presented in Figure 11.1.

---

2. The following parts rely heavily on the author's article appeared in György Kiss (ed.), *Recent Developments in Labour Law* (Akademiai Kiado, 2013).

Figure 11.1   European Model

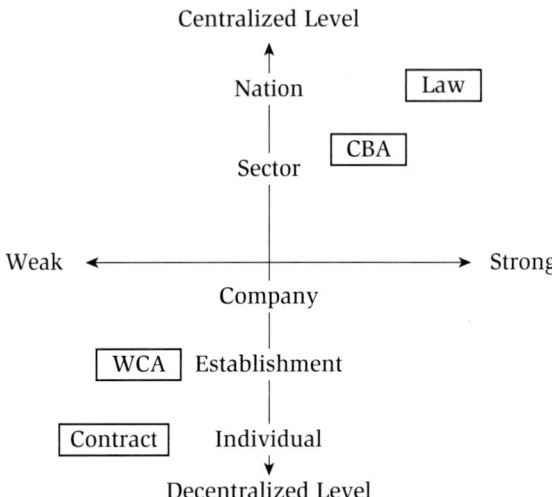

The distinctive feature of the European model is that labor unions are organized at the national or sector level, and thus collective bargaining has traditionally taken place at the national or sector level. However, there is a conspicuous tendency of the decentralization of bargaining structure from national or sectoral multi-employer negotiation to individual firms or workplaces.

The legal effect order of the said four tools is as follows: (from strong to weak) Law > CBA > WCA > Contract. Derogation or deviation from the statutory norms is the exception to this order. When derogation is allowed, for instance, a weaker legal tool such as CBA can violate or alter the statutory minimum labor standard unfavorably to workers.[3] The controversial issue for some European countries is whether, together with the decentralization of bargaining levels, such derogatory power can also be delegated to parties at the more decentralized level, such as labor unions at the company level, works councils at the establishment level or even to individual workers.[4]

---

3. It is known that much of Swedish labor legislation allows for deviation, both to the advantage and detriment of employees, from the statutory provisions by means of CBAs. *See*, Mia Rönmmar, Labour *Policy on Fixed-Term Employment Contracts in Sweden*, Bulletin of Comparative Labour Relations, no. 76, 159 (2010).
4. The UK law that allows derogation from the EC Working Hours Directive by individual employee's consent is one such example. *See* Simon Deakin & Gillian Morris, Labour Law, 347 (6th ed., 2012).

11.2.2 Japanese Model

In Japan, there are four legal tools regulating working conditions. Three of them are common with the European model: law, CBA, and individual labor contract. But the fourth tool in Japan is different: not a works council agreement but work rule or rules of employment (*shugo kisoku*). Work rules (rules of employment) comprise a document drawn up by an employer to regulate working conditions and discipline in the workplace. In drawing up the work rules, the Labor Standards Act, Article 90 requires an employer to seek opinions from a majority representative of workers in the establishment.[5] However, the representative's consent is not required. In this sense, Japanese employers can unilaterally establish and modify work rules. To enable flexible adjustment of working conditions, the Japanese case law established a unique rule that reasonably modified work rules have binding effect on all workers including those opposed the modification. The case law was incorporated in the Labor Contract Act of 2007.

The legal effect order of these four legal tools is as follows: (from strong to weak) Law > CBA > Work Rules (WR) > Contract. A labor contract cannot violate norms established in work rules. Therefore, any portions of a labor contract that violate work rules are deemed invalid, and are governed by the standards stipulated in the work rules.[6] Work rules violating a CBA are also considered to be invalid, and working conditions established by the CBA will prevail. As a principle, CBAs, work rules and labor contracts cannot violate labor standards established by mandatory labor protective laws such as the Labor Standards Act and the Minimum Wages Act. However, derogation of the statutory minimum labor standards is also allowed in Japan. The characteristic feature of Japanese derogation is that it is widely permitted by the decentralized parties' agreement, known as the 'Labor-Management Agreement (LMA)' (*Roshi Kyotei*), between the individual employer and the majority representative of workers[7] in the establishment.

---

5. "A majority representative" is a union that organizes the majority of workers in the establishment or, if such a union does not exist, an individual who represents the majority of workers in the establishment.
6. Article 12, LCA: "A labor contract that stipulates any working conditions that do not meet the standards established by the rules of employment shall be invalid with regard to such portions. In this case, the portions which have become invalid shall be governed by the standards established by the rules of employment."
7. *See supra* n. 5.

Figure 11.2 Japanese Model

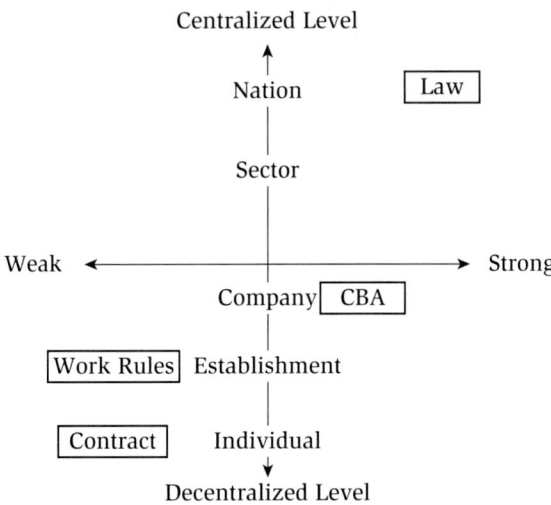

Thus, the Japanese model can be described as in Figure 11.2. Compared with the European model, the features of the Japanese model are as follows: (1) CBAs are concluded not at the sector level but at the company level, between individual companies and enterprise-based unions, since most Japanese labor unions are organized at the enterprise level; (2) Derogation of minimum labor standards is allowed by the decentralized parties' agreement in the establishment; (3) Japan does not have a works council system, and work rules established by the employer play an important role in regulating working conditions. The following parts of this paper deal with these three features of the Japanese labor law system.

11.3 ENTERPRISE UNIONISM AND DECENTRALIZED INDUSTRIAL RELATIONS IN JAPAN

11.3.1 Enterprise Unionism

Enterprise unionism is a system in which unions are established within an individual company. It organizes workers in the same company irrespective of their jobs, bargains collectively with a single employer, and concludes collective agreements at the company level. Currently, more than 90% of Japanese labor unions are enterprise-based.[8] However, enterprise unionism in Japan is not the

---

8. According to the Basic Survey on Labor Unions in 2015, 93.5% of labor unions in private sector are enterprise-based unions and they organize 88.7% of union members. *See* Takashi Araki, *Rōdō-hō* (Labor Law) (3rd. ed.), 567 (Yuhikaku, 2016).

creation of the Labor Union Act (LUA). The Act allows any forms of labor unions. Not only enterprise unions, but also industrial unions, craft unions and local unions that organize workers across companies, are all legitimate unions under the Act.

The main reason that enterprise unionism has taken root and continued to dominate this far, lies in its functional excellence within Japan's highly developed internal labor market. Under the lifetime or long-term employment system, Japanese workers tend to stay at a particular company, develop their working careers, and be subject to flexible adjustments of working conditions in accordance with the company's economic performance. In such an internalized labor market, industrial-level or national-level collective bargaining has made little sense. Enterprise-based unions and enterprise-level collective bargaining have been the most efficient mechanisms to respond to the demands of such workers who develop their working careers in a particular company.

11.3.2 The Unique Nature of Japanese CBA

A collective bargaining agreement is a contract between a labor union and an employer (or employers' organization, which is very rare in Japan). The CBA has two types of legal effect: an "obligatory effect" which means the contractual effect between the labor union and the employer; and a "normative effect" which governs the content of the individual labor contract between the workers who are the member of the union concerned and the employer (Article 16, LUA[9]). The Japanese LUA took the German collective agreement law (*Tarifvertragsgesetz*) as a model. Thus, CBAs in Japan apply to the union members only as a principle.

Because of the decentralized industrial relations, however, the nature of collective bargaining and collective agreements in Japan are very different from those in European countries. European CBAs concluded at the sector level establish minimum standards that are applied across companies. Therefore, more favorable working conditions agreed between individual workers and employers remain valid (*Günstigkeitsprinzip* or "favorability principle"). By contrast, Japanese collective agreements are concluded between a single employer and an enterprise union. Therefore, working conditions prescribed in the CBA are usually interpreted not only the minimum but also the maximum conditions to be held. Individual labor contracts that stipulate not only less favorable conditions but also more favorable conditions than those prescribed in

---

9. Article 16, LUA: "Any part of an individual labor contract contravening the standards concerning working conditions and other matters relating to the treatment of workers provided in the collective agreement shall be void. In such a case, the invalidated part of the individual labor contract shall be governed by those standards. With respect to matters as to which the individual labor contract does not provide, the same shall apply."

the collective agreement are construed as null and void unless the collective agreement explicitly allows more favorable contracts.[10]

Decentralized industrial relations also affect the extension system of CBAs. The LUA has two types of extension systems: plant level (Article 17, LUA[11]) and regional level extension (Article 18, LUA[12]). The regional extension system, which was modeled on the German "general binding effect" (*Allgemeinverbindlichkeit*) system, is rarely used in Japan because it relies on the unusual condition in which a majority of the workers of the same kind, in a particular locality, are covered by a particular collective agreement. In this sense, collective agreements in Japan cannot create a social norm. There is also no practice to refer the CBA as a model of individual labor contract in Japan. As a result, the coverage of CBAs is generally confined to union members.[13]

11.3.3 Plural Unionism

Although Japan introduced the unfair labor practice system modeled after the American Wagner Act of 1935, Japan did not adopt the American exclusive representation system. As a result, more than one union can exist in one company. Under the Constitutional guarantee[14] of the right to organize and to bargain collectively, it is construed that a minority union in a company that organizes very few numbers of workers, can enjoy an equal right to bargain collectively and go on strike in the same manner as a majority union. Under these circumstances, Japanese case law has developed a unique notion of the duty of employers to maintain neutrality toward all unions.[15] Discriminatory

---

10. See Kazuo Sugeno, *Japanese Employment and Labor Law*, 589 (Carolina Academic Press, 2002); Takashi Araki, *Labor and Employment Law in Japan*, 175 (Japan Institute of Labor, 2002); Tadashi Hanami, Fumio Komiya & Ryuichi Yamakawa, Labour Law in Japan (2nd. ed.), 185 (Wolters Kluwer, 2015).
11. Article 17, para. 1, LUA: "When three-fourths or more of the workers of the same kind regularly employed in a particular factory or workplace come under application of a particular collective agreement, the agreement concerned shall also apply to the remaining workers of the same kind employed in the factory concerned or workplace."
12. Article 18, LUA: "When a majority of the workers of the same kind in a particular locality come under application of a particular collective agreement, the Minister of Health, Labor and Welfare or the prefectural governor may, at the request of either one or both of the parties to the collective agreement concerned and, pursuant to a resolution of the Labor Relations Commission, decide that the collective agreement concerned (including an agreement revised pursuant to the provisions of paragraph 2) should apply to the remaining workers of the same kind employed in the same locality and to their employers."
13. Therefore, the CBA coverage generally coincides with union density (around 17%). See ILO (Jelle Visser, Susan Hayter, and Rosina Gammarano), *Labour Relations and Collective Bargaining Coverage: Stability, Erosion or Decline?* 5 (2015) http://www.ilo.org/public/english/iira/pdf/labourrelations.pdf.
14. Article 28, the Japanese Constitution reads "The right of workers to organize and to bargain and act collectively is guaranteed."
15. The *Nissan Motor Co.* Case, Supreme Court, 39 Minshu 730 (April 23, 1985).

attitudes towards a minority union, especially in the course of collective bargaining, are prohibited as one form of unfair labor practices.

In practice, the majority union who bears responsibilities for the majority of workers usually takes a pragmatic attitude over an ideological stance in order to reach an agreement with the employer. By contrast, the minority union who needs to demonstrate its *raison d'etre* tends to require what the management hardly affords to accept, and they cannot reach an agreement. For instance, the majority union agreed to demands for overtime work with paid overtime premiums. By contrast, the minority union refused to agree to overtime, thus minority union members did not engage in overtime and received no overtime premiums. It should not be reprehensible for such a different treatment between majority and minority union members as a result of truly free bargaining. However, if such a difference is caused by the employer's discriminatory intention against the minority union disguising the outcome of the collective bargaining, that may well constitute unfair labor practice. Given the blurred nature of this demarcation, the Labor Relations Commission, an administrative organ in charge of adjudicating unfair labor practice cases, faces a number of difficult interpretative questions.

11.3.4 Japan's Cooperative Industrial Relations Developed under the Enterprise Unionism

Currently, Japan is famous for its peaceful industrial relations. The number of strikes in 2014 was only eighty in Japan.[16] However, this is not because the Japanese people are characteristically peaceful, or Japanese culture favors harmonization. Until 1960 in the private sector and 1975 in the public sector, Japan experienced a very harsh period of friction between labor and management in the same manner as elsewhere. The number of strikes in 1974 was 9581, hundred times more than today.

Severe confrontations between labor and management ensued from the end of WWII until the 1950s.[17] During this period, labor movement was closely tied with political, especially communist movements amid the cold war. From the mid-1950s to the mid-1960s, when Japan embarked upon its rapid economic growth, Japan's industrial relations experienced a gradual but significant transformation. Adversarial labor relations subsided, making way for cooperative relations to emerge in accordance with the spread of joint labor-management consultation practices.

Joint labor-management consultation was not required by law. It was voluntarily established by both labor and management who were disappointed with the adversarial labor relations led by radical leftists. In order to promote the

---

16. Ministry of Health, Labor and Welfare, "Heisei 26-nen Rodo Sogi Tokei Chosa (Survey on Industrial Actions in 2014)" http://www.mhlw.go.jp/toukei/list/dl/14-26-08.pdf.
17. See Araki, *supra* n. 10, at 206.

Productivity Increase Movement, the Japan Productivity Center, an organ established by business circles under the auspices of the Ministry of International Trade and Industry (MITI) and the US Government, together with the SODOMEI, the national confederation of moderate unions, confirmed the movement's three basic principles: (1) maintenance of employment, (2) industrial cooperation through labor-management consultation, and (3) fair distribution of the fruit of the Movement among workers, management and consumers. According to the second principle, joint labor-management consultation was encouraged.

In joint labor-management consultation, employers provided various sets of information to their unions, and unions cooperated with management in order to increase productivity. Employers kept their promise not to dismiss workers who were made redundant through company restructuring or rationalization. Redundant workers were instead transferred to other sections and retrained to settle in new positions. Through labor-management cooperation during the period of rapid economic growth in the 1950s and 60s, Japanese corporations increased their profits and distributed this increased profit fairly among their workers. This led the labor side to confirm the merits of cooperative labor relations based upon long-term relations with mutual trust. In this manner, Japanese labor and management gradually changed the nature of labor relations from a zero-sum game into a win-win situation.

In this context, Japanese enterprise unions developed two unique roles in collective labor relations: First, they engaged in collective bargaining as a traditional labor union, and second, they consulted with employers in the process of joint labor-management consultation. Compared with the European practice whereby consultation is carried out by a single employer and a works council at the decentralized level, Japanese enterprise unions also play the role of works councils. Japan's cooperative industrial relations that have developed since the early 1960s might, therefore, be seen as an outgrowth of the works council aspect of enterprise unions.

This explains why proposals to introduce a works council system (*see* 11.4 below) have generated opposition from the side of labor unions. For the enterprise-base unions, works councils appear to be nothing but rival organizations that deprive them of their function on the same level by the financial support from the employers.

11.4 STATUTORY MINIMUM LABOR STANDARDS AND THEIR FLEXIBILIZATION

11.4.1 Worker Protective Laws

In Japan, the individual employment relationship between an employer and a worker is regulated by labor protective laws such as the Labor Standards Act, the Minimum Wages Act, the Security of Wage Payment Act, the Industrial Safety and Health Act, the Workers' Accident Compensation Insurance Act, the Equal Employment Opportunity Act, the Worker Dispatching Act, and so forth.

The most fundamental and important law is the Labor Standards Act which establishes minimum working standards, including employers' duties to ensure full payment of wages (Article 24), abide by maximum working hours (eight hours a day, forty hours a week, Article 32), provide paid leave (ten-twenty days a year, Article 39), give special protection to young workers (Articles 56-64) and pregnant women (Articles 64-2-68), compensate workers for work-related accidents (Articles 75-88), establish work rules (Articles 89-93). The Act also establishes the government's enforcement machinery such as supervision (Articles 97-105), and penalties against any violations (Articles 117-121).

The Labor Standards Act applies to all establishments who employ a workforce, irrespective of the number of workers. The exemptions are limited to family businesses that employ family members only (Article 116 paragraph 2), domestic workers (Article 116 paragraph 2) and other employment relations for which special regulations apply, namely seamen (Article 116 paragraph 1) and some civil servants. From a comparative perspective, the Labor Standards Act is very broad in its coverage.

Working conditions set forth by labor contracts, work rules and collective agreements that are inferior to the standards set by the Labor Standards Act, are rendered void and replaced by the Act's mandatory legal norms (Article 13, LSA[18]). Minimum standards prescribed in worker protection laws are enforced by Labor Standards Inspection Offices, as well as by sanctions imposed by criminal penalties.

Thus, as a principle, statutory minimum labor standards constitute mandatory norms, and lowering them by agreements between private parties is not allowed.

11.4.2 Flexibilization of Minimum Labor Standards: Derogation Through LMAs

Along with diversification of the workforce and employment relations, statutory minimum labor standards fixed by the national level do not necessarily fit into actual employment relations in a particular industry or company. Therefore, adaptation of statutory norms to the workplace needs is required. This is why in many countries, a certain degree of derogation or deviation from statutory norms is admitted. Japan also employs such a derogation mechanism for norm flexibilization.

However, this Japanese mechanism is very different from those found in European countries. In Europe, derogation from the mandatory norms has been

---

18. Article 13, LSA: "A labor contract which provides for working conditions which do not meet the standards of this Act shall be invalid with respect to such portions. In such a case the portions which have become invalid shall be governed by the standards set forth in this Act."

allowed in exceptions when sector-level labor unions have agreed to it. However, Japan gives such derogatory power even to the individual who is chosen to represent all workers in the establishment. This mechanism certainly makes the adaptation of mandatory norms to the workplace easier, but at the same time it entails the risk of abusive derogation and the deprivation of workers' minimum rights.

The Labor Standards Act allows derogation from the minimum labor standards based upon a "labor-management agreement" when the Act explicitly prescribes such derogation. For instance, the Labor Standards Act requires a LMA for the deduction of wages, hours-averaging schemes, or overtime work.

A LMA is a written agreement between an employer and the majority representative of workers at an establishment.[19] The majority of workers are represented by a union who organizes the majority of workers in the establishment, or by an individual who represents the majority of workers in the absence of a majority union. Where a majority union exists, fewer problems arise because the majority union is strong enough to negotiate with the employer. However, where no such union exists, an individual worker chosen to represent the majority of workers bears the important responsibility of deciding whether to sign LMAs, such as agreements for overtime. In spite of such a significant responsibility, for years the Labor Standards Act and its bylaws did not provide any provisions concerning the qualifications of any person who stood to represent the majority of workers, or the procedures to select such a person.

11.4.3 Abuse of Derogation Mechanism

Criticism has been launched against this process of appointing individuals controlled by the management to be majority representatives, and the fact of employers' derogation proposals being rubber stamped in practice. Faced with such criticism, the Ministry of Labor issued administrative guidance concerning the proper selection of the majority representative in 1988. Ten years later, the 1998 revision of the Labor Standards Act explicitly incorporated the contents of the guidance into the Ordinance for Enforcement of the Labor Standards Act

---

19. A labor-management agreement concluded between an employer and a majority representative is completely different from a collective agreement concluded between an employer and a labor union. A labor-management agreement is a written agreement that simply allows derogation from the minimum labor standards. It has no normative effect on the labor contracts of individual workers in the establishment. In other words, when a labor-management agreement allows, for instance, overtime, it merely provides the employer with immunity from criminal sanctions when the employer orders his/her workers to work overtime. It does not create any contractual obligation for workers to obey overtime order. Since a majority representative who concludes a labor-management agreement has no mandate to establish terms and conditions of employment of workers, the agreement has no normative effect on workers' labor contracts. Therefore, in order to compel workers to work overtime, an employer is required to establish contractual grounds through an individual agreement, work rules or a collective agreement.

(Article 6-2). The revised Ordinance requires that the majority representative cannot be a person in a position of supervision or management, and such person must be elected by voting, a show of hands, and other procedures, only after all participants have been clearly informed of the election's purpose to choose a representative who will conclude agreements provided by the Act.

Despite these provisions in the Ordinance, it is still highly questionable that such an elected individual has equal power in negotiations with their employer. Many cases are reported in which majority representatives have signed LMAs without fully comprehending the meaning of the agreement. Even if the representative knows the effect of a derogatory agreement, he/she cannot afford to reject to sign the documents because he/she is a single individual without any organizational support for their decision.

Although derogation and flexibilization is necessary to make statutory labor protective norms adaptable to diversified employment relations, the Japanese experience tells that derogatory powers should not be given to a party that the employer can easily manipulate. In order for the derogation scheme to function properly, it is important to establish a legitimate mechanism that can fairly represent workers opinions, and that is strong enough to resist control and intervention by employers.

11.4.4 Introduction of Works Councils?

In order to improve the current situation, therefore, Japanese scholars have proposed to introduce genuine employee representation systems, like the works councils adopted in Europe. However, this proposal has not been welcomed by Japanese labor unions. As mentioned above, the reason lies in the Japanese enterprise unionism.

In Europe, where labor unions are organized at the sector or industry level, the introduction of employee representatives at the establishment does not necessarily cause rivalry issues between unions and employee representatives.

In Japan, by contrast, most labor unions are organized at the enterprise or plant level. Consequently, establishing a new employee representation system like works councils at the same level means intruding onto the labor unions' territory. Labor unions fear that the new system could erode and replace their own existence. Whereas labor unions are financially supported by the collected union dues from their members, employee representation systems required by law would run on financial support from employers, and workers do not have to pay dues. Thus, labor unions see employee representation systems, such as works councils, as rival organizations, and oppose the proposal to introduce works council system.

One practical solution would be to introduce works council systems where enterprise-based unions do not exist yet. However, labor unions seem to be still skeptical of even such proposals.

11.5 JAPANESE MODEL OF FLEXICURITY: EMPLOYMENT SECURITY AND FLEXIBLE ADJUSTMENT OF WORKING CONDITIONS IN THE INTERNAL LABOR MARKET

As mentioned already, CBAs in Japan concluded at the company level cannot be extended to workers employed by another company. The rate of unionization in Japan has continuously decreased since 1975 and standing at 17.4% in 2015. As a result, more than four out of five Japanese workers are not covered by CBAs. Their working conditions are mainly governed by individual labor contracts and work rules.

11.5.1 Labor Contracts

The Labor Standards Act requires the employer to clarify the working conditions to the worker when concluding a labor contract (Article 15, LSA). Article 5 of the Enforcement Order of the Labor Standard Act (LSA) enumerates those matters to be clarified. In particular, the clarification of conditions pertaining to the place of work, content of work, working hours, payment of wages, and retirement, must be made in writing (Article 5, paragraph 2, EOLSA).

It is, however, rather rare for an employer and a worker in Japan to make a written contract and prescribe concrete working conditions in detail. Workers merely agree orally that they will work for the company. To satisfy the requirement to clarify working conditions, the employer usually presents the worker with the work rules, which cover most of the items to be clarified. As long as the worker raises no objection to the content of the work rules, he is regarded as having agreed to the conditions. Thus, the conditions stipulated in the work rules become the substantive content of labor contracts.

11.5.2 Work Rules

Work rules are the most important legal tools to regulate terms and conditions of employment in Japan.

11.5.3 The Duty to Draw Up Work Rules

Work rules are a set of regulations drawn up by an employer for the purpose of establishing uniform rules and conditions of employment at the workplace. Article 89 of the Labor Standards Act prescribes that an employer who continuously employs ten or more workers[20] must draw up work rules on the following matters (Article 89, LSA):

---

20. Though it is not clear from the provision, it is generally interpreted that "ten or more workers" should be calculated not in the enterprise but in the establishment, on the

(1) the time at which work begins and ends, rest periods, rest days, leave, and work shifts;
(2) the method for determination, computation and payment of wages, the date of wage payments, and wage increases;
(3) retirement including dismissals reasons;
(3-2) retirement allowances;
(4) interim wages and minimum wages;
(5) cost of food or supplies for work;
(6) safety and health;
(7) vocational training;
(8) accident compensation;
(9) commendations and sanctions; and
(10) other items applicable to all workers at the workplace.

Items 1–3 are absolutely mandatory matters which must be included in the work rules. Items 3-2–10 are conditionally mandatory matters which must be included in the work rules when the employer wants to introduce regulations concerning these matters.

When an employer institutes the work rules for the first time, or when the work rules are altered, the employer must submit those new rules to the competent Labor Standards Inspection Office. Workers must also be informed of the new rules by means of conspicuous posting, distribution of printed documents or setting up accessible computer terminals (Article 106, LSA, Article 52-2, EOLSA). The duties for drawing up, submitting and displaying work rules are sanctioned by criminal provisions (Article 120, LSA).

In drawing up or modifying the work rules, the employer is required to ask the opinion of the majority representative of the workers at the workplace. However, a *consensus* is not required. Even when the majority representative opposes the content of the work rules, the employer may submit the work rules to the Labor Standards Inspection Office with the document citing the opposition's opinion, and the submission will still be accepted. In this sense, the employer can unilaterally establish and modify work rules.

11.5.4 The Legal Effect of Work Rules and Their Unfavorable Modification

The work rules apply to all workers in a given workplace or establishment. Work rules cannot violate enacted laws or collective agreements applicable to the establishment (Article 92, paragraph 1, LSA). The Labor Contract Act endows work rules with an imperative and direct effect on individual labor contracts. Namely, the Act states that labor contracts that stipulate working conditions

---

rationale that work rules apply in each establishment and procedures for drawing up work rules presuppose each establishment as a unit (LSA Art. 90).

inferior to those provided in the work rules shall be invalid and that such conditions are to be replaced by the standards in the work rules (Article 12, LCA).

However, until 2007, the enacted law remained silent regarding the effect of work rules when they set inferior standards to those in individual labor contracts. This led to a difficult legal question when an employer facing economic difficulties modified work rules unfavorably *vis-à-vis* its workers. The binding effect of such modified work rules was challenged in courts.

The majority of scholars in the 1950s and 1960s argued that such unilaterally modified work rules without obtaining workers' consent could not have a binding effect on individual labor contracts. This was the natural interpretation according to the contract theory.

11.5.5 Case Law on a "Reasonable Modification" of Work Rules

However, in 1968, the Supreme Court Grand bench took a different position and established a unique rule governing the effect of unfavorable modifications in the work rules. According to the Supreme Court, when the modification is reasonable, the modified work rules have a binding effect on all workers, including those opposed to the modification.[21] In spite of severe criticism asserting that there was no legal ground for recognizing such a binding effect, the Supreme Court has adhered to this rule and repeatedly confirmed its position.[22] This rule has accordingly become the established case law.

Underlying this ruling is a consideration for employment security and the need for flexible adjustment of working conditions. Traditional contract theory dictates that a worker who opposes any modifications made to the future terms of employment can be discharged. However, according to the strict restriction on dismissals by the prohibition of abusive dismissals in Japan,[23] such a dismissal may well be regarded as an abuse of the right to dismiss, and thus, rendered null and void. However, since the employment relationship is a continuous

---

21. The *Shuhoku Bus* case, 22 *Minshu* 3459 (Supreme Court, December 25, 1968).
22. The *Takeda System* case, 1101 *Hanrei Jiho* 114 (Supreme Court, November 25, 1983); The *Omagari-shi Nokyo* case, 42 *Minshu* 60 (Supreme Court, February 16, 1988); The *Dai-ichi Kogata Haiya* case, 1434 *Hanrei Jiho* 133 (July 13, 1992); The *Asahi Kasai Kaijo Hoken* case, 50 *Minshu* 1008 (March 26, 1996); The *Daishi Ginko* case, 51 *Minshu* 705 (Supreme Court, February 28, 1997); The *Michinoku Ginko* case, 54 *Minshu* 2075 (Supreme Court, September 7, 2000).
23. Article 16, LCA: "A dismissal shall, if it lacks objectively reasonable grounds and is not considered to be appropriate in general societal terms, be treated as an abuse of right and be invalid." The prohibition of abusive dismissals was established by case law and the rule was incorporated in the Labor Standard Act in 2003 (Art. 18-2, LSA). When the Labor Contract Act was enacted in 2007, the provision (Art. 18-2, LSA) was transferred to the Labor Contract Act as Art. 16.

contractual relationship, modification and adjustment of the working conditions is inevitable.

In light of these circumstances, Japanese courts have struck the balance between employment security and the need for flexible adjustment of working conditions by allowing unilateral work rules modifications, on the condition that the desired modification can be regarded as reasonable.[24] This is one manifestation of the Japanese version of "flexicurity" that combines employment security and flexibility in adapting working conditions to fit with economic fluctuation. In 2007, the Labor Contract Act incorporated this case law into its provisions (Articles 9 and 10, LCA[25]) and it became the statutory rule.

Flexicurity in Japan is different from the Danish type of flexicurity, which is best known worldwide. Danish flexicurity combines flexibility in the external labor market created by relaxing economic dismissal regulations, with state-provided security for the unemployed and retraining programs. If we can term the Danish model "external market oriented flexicurity (external flexicurity)," the Japanese model might be defined as "internal market oriented flexicurity (internal flexicurity)," since flexibility and security are balanced in the internal labor market, or within a particular firm, without resorting to dismissals.

Japan has long been known for its lifetime or long-term employment system that holds employment security in high esteem. The practice of lifetime employment has been eroded gradually in recent years, yet it still remains the cornerstone of the Japanese employment system. Therefore many Japanese labor law rules have been devised with employment security in mind. The rule of "reasonable work rules modification" is one such example.

---

24. Takashi Araki, *Accommodating Terms and Conditions of Employment to Changing Circumstances: A Comparative Analysis of Quantitative and Qualitative Flexibility in the United States, Germany and Japan*, in C. Engels & M. Weiss (ed.), *Labour Law and Industrial Relations at the Turn of the Century, Liber Amicorum in Honour of Prof. Dr. Roger Blanpain*, 509 (Kluwer Law International, 1998).
25. Article 9, LCA: "An employer may not, unless an agreement has been reached with a worker, change any of the working conditions that constitute the contents of a labor contract in a manner disadvantageous to the worker by changing the rules of employment; provided, however, that this shall not apply to the cases set forth in the following Article."

  Article 10, LCA: "In cases where an employer changes the working conditions by changing the rules of employment, if the employer informs the worker of the changed rules of employment, and if the change to the rules of employment is reasonable in light of the extent of the disadvantage to be incurred by the worker, the need for changing the working conditions, the appropriateness of the contents of the changed rules of employment, the status of negotiations with a labor union or the like, or any other circumstances pertaining to the change to the rules of employment, the working conditions that constitute the contents of a labor contract shall be in accordance with such changed rules of employment; provided, however, that this shall not apply to any portion of the labor contract which the worker and the employer had agreed on as being the working conditions that are not to be changed by any change to the rules of employment, except in cases that fall under Article 12."

11.5.6 Criteria for "Reasonableness"

The principal test for "reasonableness" is to weigh the disadvantage to the worker by the modification against the business's need to change the working conditions. Simultaneously, courts take other matters surrounding the modification into consideration, such as whether compensatory measures to mitigate the disadvantages to the workers were or are being taken, whether similar treatment is common in other companies in the same industry, or whether the majority union or the majority of the workers are in agreement with the modification.

Some Supreme Court cases[26] suggest that the consent of the majority union weighs heavily in a court's decision over whether or not a work rules modification should be regarded as reasonable. This position respecting the consent of the majority workers is supported by commentators for the following reasons.[27] First, the nature of the issue of work rules modification is more a dispute of interests than it is a dispute of rights, since the modified work rules establish new terms and conditions of employment for the future. Thus, it is more appropriate to respect the negotiating parties' attitude than for the court to intervene and review the reasonableness of the substantive content of newly established working conditions from the judges' standpoint. Second, the most significant defect of the case law rule is its lack of predictability of reasonableness. A position that presumes reasonableness when a majority union agrees on the modification is an attempt to enhance the predictability of the reasonableness test. Such position respecting the majority union's attitude also gives the parties an incentive to negotiate in good faith and reach an agreement.[28]

However, several Supreme Court decisions[29] issued in 2000 suggest that the Supreme Court does not necessarily respect the majority unions' attitude towards a work rules modification and it actively reviews the reasonableness of the modification on the basis of its own criteria.

Following these case law situations, the rule of reasonable modification in work rules was incorporated into the newly enacted Labor Contract Act in 2007. After the debate, the legislature did not explicitly adopt the said commentators'

---

26. The *Dai-ichi Kogata Haiya* case, July 13, 1992, *Hanrei Jiho* no. 1434 p. 133; The *Daishi Ginko* case, Supreme Court, February 28, 1997, *Minshu* vol. 51 no. 2, 705.
27. Kazuo Sugeno, *Shugyo Kisoku Henko to Roshi Kosho (Work Rules Modification and Labor-Management Negotiation)*, 718 Rodo Hanrei 6 (1997); Takashi Araki, *Koyo Sisutemu to Rodojoken Henko Hori (Employment systems and Variation of Terms and Conditions of Employment)*, 265 (Yuhikaku Publishing, 2001).
28. Yasuo Suwa, *Shugyo Kisoku no Kozo to Kino (Structure and Function of Work Rules)* 71 Nihon Rodoho Gakkai-shi 19 (1988); Araki, *supra* n. 27, at 267.
29. The *Michinoku Ginko* case, *supra* n. 22; the *Ugo (Hokuto) Ginko* case, 788 Rodo Hanrei 23 (Supreme Court, September 12, 2000); The *Hakodate Shinyo Kinko* case, 788 Rodo Hanrei 17 (Supreme Court, September 22, 2000).

position[30] respecting the majority unions' consent but simply lists factors taken into consideration for deciding reasonableness.[31]

11.6 CONCLUSION: DECENTRALIZED INDUSTRIAL RELATIONS WITH INTERNAL FLEXICURITY

11.6.1 Decentralized Industrial Relations

The first feature of the Japanese labor law system is decentralized industrial relations. Most labor unions in Japan are enterprise-based unions. Collective bargaining takes place between an individual company and its enterprise union. CBAs are thus concluded by those parties at the company level and their application is confined within the company.

The practice of decentralized bargaining can meet the grassroots needs of workers swiftly and flexibly. The keenest request made by workers employed by a company in bad shape in particular, is not a wage hike but a guarantee of their sustained employment. If their employment can be secured, such workers tend to agree to a lowering of their working conditions. In fact, many Japanese enterprise unions agreed to lower their wages across-the-board in order not to avoid the dismissal of any workers.

German centralized industrial relations in the 1990s witnessed a so-called "escape from the CBA" (*Fluch aus dem Tarifvertrag*). When sector-level CBA had set minimum wages that were too high for the ailing company, it was not possible for the company and workers to lower wages in order to avoid economic dismissals because they were bound by the normative effect of the CBA. To make what the decentralized parties wanted possible, they had to be freed from the binding effect of the sector-level CBA. Thus, some employers seceded from their employers' organizations.

In Japanese decentralized industrial relations, such a scenario is unlikely to arise, because decentralized parties can do whatever they want and need. This is a merit of the decentralized system.

However, there are also disadvantages to the decentralized system, since the negotiating power of the decentralized parties is weak compared to that of centralized parties. In Japan, this problem typically surfaces in the derogation scheme which allows deviation from the statutory minimum standards by means of an agreement between an employer and a worker elected to represent all in the establishment. Even if some degree of adaptation of minimum labor standards is needed, such adaptation or flexibilization must not be unjust and

---

30. Quoted note 27.
31. Article 10, LCA lists the following factors: "the change to the rules of employment is reasonable in light of the extent of the disadvantage to be incurred by the worker, the need for changing the working conditions, the appropriateness of the contents of the changed rules of employment, the status of negotiations with a labor union or the like, or any other circumstances pertaining to the change to the rules of employment."

unfair. In order to secure sound and fair flexibilization, the labor side party must be sufficiently resistant to pressure from the employer. On this point, the current Japanese law that allows derogation by the agreement with the person representing the majority of workers at the establishment requires reconsideration.

11.6.2 Internal Flexicurity

The second feature of the Japanese labor law system is internal flexicurity that balances employment security with flexible adjustment of working conditions. Japanese law has typically prioritized employment security, hence to compensate for the lack of numerical flexibility adjusting the size of workforces, Japan has introduced quantitative or internal flexibility to adjust working conditions.

When we analyze *traditional* American, European and Japanese employment systems from the perspective of flexibility and security in the external and internal labor market, they might be described as in Table 11.1.

Table 11.1 Flexibility versus Security

	Flexibility	Security
USA External Flexibility Model	At-will employment	
	Flexible adjustment by obtaining consent under at-will employment	
Japan Internal Flexibility Model	[Non-standard workers]	Security in employment
	Reasonable work rules modification	
Europe Security-Oriented Model	Relaxing dismissal regulations?	Security in employment
		Security in working conditions

Japanese flexicurity strikes a balance between security in employment and flexibility in the adjustment of working conditions in the internal labor market in a particular company. Therefore, this could be seen as a better-balanced system compared to the American flexibility-oriented model and the traditional European security-oriented model.

However, the pitfall of the Japanese system is this. The Japanese brand of flexicurity applies only to regular or standard workers. Non-standard workers such as part-timers, fixed-term workers, dispatched workers are excluded from the system. In 1990, the ratio of standard workers in Japan was 80% of the total workforce but by 2015, this had dropped to 62%. In other words, 38% of the current Japanese workforce are non-standard workers. For those unstable non-standard workers, the Japanese system is not at all well-balanced.

Chapter 11: Japan's Decentralized Industrial Relations, Internal Flexicurity

To address this problem, Japan started to develop new measures to protect non-standard workers. The 2007 and 2014 revisions of the Part-Time Workers Act prohibits discrimination against part-timers, the 2012 and 2015 revision of the Dispatched Workers Act strengthened protection for temporary workers, and the 2012 revision of the Labor Contract Act introduced new protections for fixed-term contract workers.

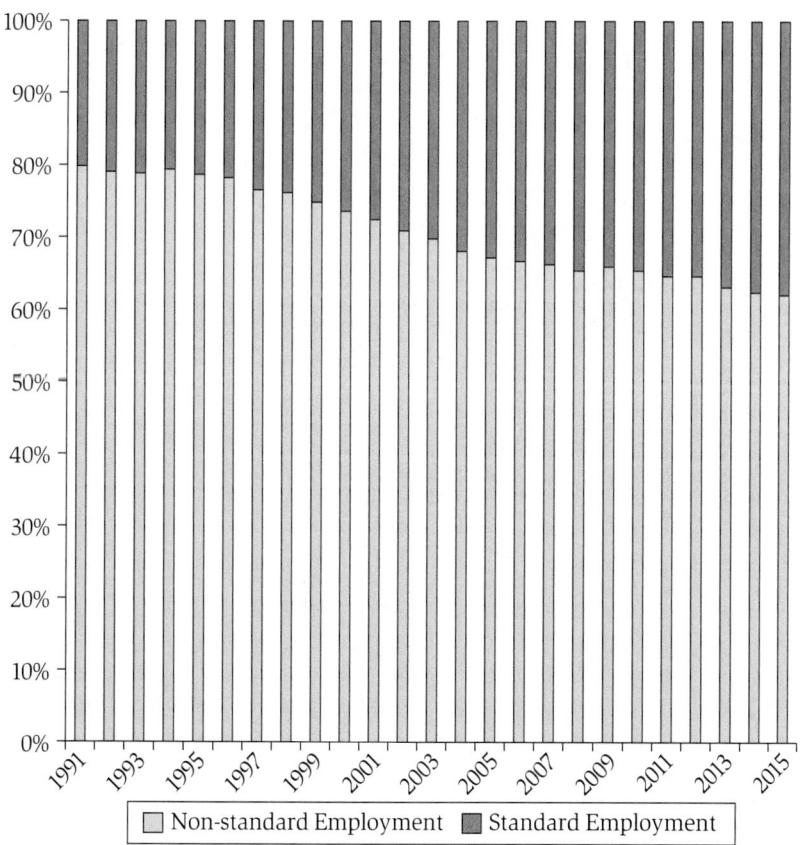

Figure 11.3 Ratio of Standard/Non-standard Workers in Japan

11.6.3 A Reconsideration of Statutory Regulations

Japan has four legal tools regulating working conditions: state law, CBA, work rules and labor contract. However, currently more than 80% of Japanese workers are unorganized. They are outside of the application of CBAs because collective agreements at the company level in Japan cannot have *erga omnes* effect, or an extension effect like in France. Nor is there any alternative practice to the CBA to refer to as a model of labor contract, like in Germany (*Bezugnamenklausel*). Therefore, in these unorganized sectors, the picture appears as shown in Figure 11.4. There is no CBA. Consequently the role of state law becomes more important in Japan than in other countries. However, in the contemporary diversified work environment with diversified workers with different interests, applying universal regulation by state law is very difficult and sometimes inappropriate.

Figure 11.4   Unorganized Japanese Workers

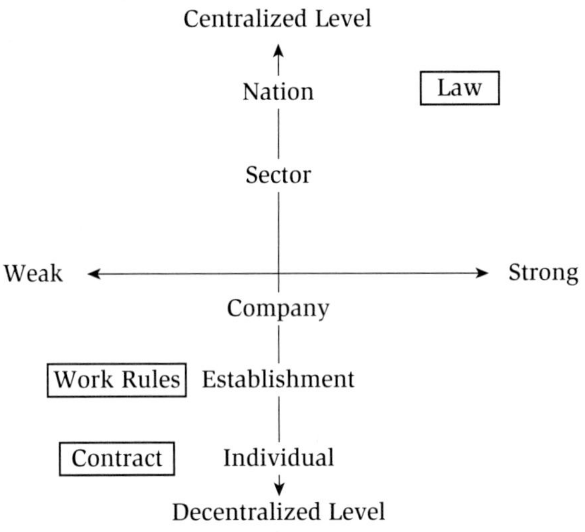

```
                    Centralized Level
                           ↑
                        Nation      | Law |
                           |
                         Sector
                           |
        Weak  ←────────────┼────────────→  Strong
                           |
                        Company
                           |
            | Work Rules | Establishment
                           |
               | Contract |  Individual
                           ↓
                    Decentralized Level
```

To cope with this challenge, first, we must reconsider the nature of state law. Traditionally, statutory norms are mandatory and imperative. However, we know that statutory norms that can be altered by the collective agreement (*Tarifdispositivesrecht*), and we may think of non-mandatory statute that will intervene only where the vacancy of the agreement between the labor contract parties trigger legal disputes. Soft law can also be a useful approach to establish new social norms. In the past, Japan has made much use of a "duty to endeavor" clause that has no direct legal effect, but is effective in practice to introduce new but necessary norms in society.[32] Such diversification of statutory norms should be considered.

Second, we must reconsider the method of regulation. Traditional labor law has been constituted of substantive regulations such as those for setting

---

32. See Takashi Araki, *Equal Employment and Harmonization of Work and Family Life: Japan's Soft-law Approach*, 21 Comparative Labor Law & Policy Journal 451–466 (2000); Takashi Araki, *The Impact of Fundamental Social Rights on Japanese Law*, in Bob Hepple (ed.), *Social and Labour Rights in a Global Context—International and Comparative Perspectives*, 215–237 (2002).

minimum wages and maximum work hours. However, in accordance with the decentralization and diversification of statutory norms, substantive regulations will be more entrusted to decentralized parties. The role of statutory regulation is to regulate proper and fair procedures of such derogation from the statutory norms. Of course, some norms related to fundamental human rights should be neither derogable nor diminishable. Therefore, the final result should be a hybrid form of regulation that incorporates both substantive and procedural regulation.

As already mentioned, in order to properly operate procedural regulations, it is vitally important to establish competent actors who can bear responsibility and make derogatory procedures function fairly. On this point, Japan needs to improve its current system to deal with the situation in which four fifths of the workforce are left unorganized, and introduce machineries to convey unorganized workers collective voices.

In this sense, the Japanese decentralized system is still seeking for a better, more sustainable balance between flexibility and security as well as efficiency and protection.

PART V Enterprises in EU Law

A Enterprises and the Courts

CHAPTER 12

The Enterprise, Labour and the Court of Justice*

Jeff Kenner

12.1 INTRODUCTION

There is a palpable disconnect between the standard bi-dimensional model of the employment relationship and the multidimensional mutations in contractual arrangements and the organisation of enterprises in the early decades of the twenty-first century.[1] European Union (EU) labour laws, originating from the 1970s, regulate the behaviour of the enterprise[2] and its workers, reflecting the standard model. Transnational labour regulations were drafted on the assumption that both the enterprise and its workforce were easily identified, were relatively static, were in a proximate physical space, and knew each other directly, or at least indirectly through representatives of management and labour. Over time, however, both enterprises and workers have become more frangible as a consequence of the phenomena of globalisation, liberalisation and

---

* This Chapter is based on a presentation made at Ca' Foscari University of Venice on 6 July 2015.
1. See Adalberto Perulli in the Introductory Chapter in this collection.
2. For the purposes of this Chapter, and to be consistent with the theme of the book, I have used the term 'enterprise' generically, to include 'an undertaking', which may be public or private, and also a 'business' or 'firm'. See R. E. Allen (ed.), *The Concise Oxford Dictionary of Current English*, 8th edn, 390 (Clarendon Press 1990). I also agree with Jean-Phillipe Robé that a 'multinational company' is also an 'enterprise' because it is 'an economic organization that produces goods or services and which has structured its business activities on the territory of numerous States'. See Jean-Phillipe Robé, *Globalization and Constitutionalization of the World Power System*, in Jean-Phillipe Robé, Antoine Lyon-Caen and Stéphane Vernac (eds), *Multinationals and the Constitutionalization of the World-Power System* 11, 13 (Routledge 2016).

privatisation. The standard enterprise model has undergone, what Hugh Collins has described as 'vertical disintegration', under which managers of large firms arrange, as a concerted strategy, 'subcontracting, franchising, concessions and outsourcing' of aspects of production.[3] Also, workspaces have become 'deterritorialised' as workers, under contracts for services, become disconnected and reconnected to national territory as labour markets integrate,[4] heightening concerns about, on the one hand, undercutting of labour standards or social dumping and, on the other hand, undermining the bonds of social solidarity. This process of transformation of the enterprise has been accelerated by liberalisation of services and rules on the establishment of companies in the EU's single market, leading to regulatory competition between Member States,[5] and a drive by the European Commission, under the European semester process of economic policy guidance,[6] to encourage labour market reforms in a policy climate that, as Catherine Barnard observes, prioritises 'the economic over the social'.[7]

As a consequence, EU labour law today simply does not fit with multidimensional globalised systems of corporate organisation and contracting where strategic decisions affecting continuing operations at subsidiaries or units of the enterprise, situated in Europe, are taken unilaterally, often without informing local management, and sometimes outside the territorial reach of EU regulation. Indeed, it is often difficult to identify the employer. Is it the global corporation, which may be domiciled outside the EU, or a group of enterprises linked by complex and often opaque organisational arrangements designed to avoid tax liabilities. Moreover, just as the decision-making processes of the enterprise have changed, so too have the methods for deploying its workforce. As a result, an increasingly diminishing *core* of workers fall under the protective umbrella of EU labour law, while an ever growing *contingent* workforce of outsourced or subcontracted labour, posted workers, agency workers, casual or on demand 'zero-hour' contract workers, or 'gig'[8] workers, have limited employment

---

3. Hugh Collins, *Independent Contractors and the Challenge of Vertical Disintegration to Employment Protection Laws* (1990) 10/3 OJLS 353, 353.
4. *See* Ines Wagner, *Posted Work and Deterritorialization in the European Union: A Study of the German Construction and Meat Industry* (2015) Jyväskylä Studies in Education, Psychology and Social Research 521, p. 26: https://jyx.jyu.fi/dspace/handle/123456789/45494
5. *See* Simon Deakin, *Legal Diversity and Regulatory Competition: Which Model for Europe?* Centre for Business Research, University of Cambridge Working Paper No. 323, March 2006: https://core.ac.uk/download/pdf/7151307.pdf.
6. *See* European Commission, 'The European Semester': http://ec.europa.eu/economy_finance/economic_governance/the_european_semester/index_en.htm
7. Catherine Barnard, *EU Employment Law and the European Social Model: The Past, the Present and the Future* (2014) 67 Current Legal Problems 199, 204–205.
8. Workers in the 'gig economy' have individual contracts to work, when required, usually via a mobile phone app. Examples include Uber taxis and Deliveroo drivers. *See* Will Hutton, *The Gig Economy Is Here to Stay. So Making It Fairer Must Be a Priority*, The Guardian (4 September 2016).

protection or none at all.⁹ Contingency, as Antonio Lo Faro observes, is synonymous with the flexibility of both the enterprise and the worker, and, in its most extreme form, the worker is 'not part of the organisational and productive "core" of the disintegrated firm'.¹⁰

This chapter addresses two specific issues arising from the transformation of the relationship between enterprises and workers with reference to case law of the Court of Justice of the EU (the Court). The first issue, discussed in Part 12.2, concerns the approach of the Court to interpreting and applying the concepts of 'employer', 'undertaking' and 'establishment' in complex corporate redundancy scenarios falling within the scope of the EU Collective Redundancies Directive (CRD).¹¹ It asks to what extent, if at all, in the light of this case law, the Directive is effective in its aim of protecting workers in a variety of redundancy contexts, such as strategic 'downsizing' decisions taken at the global or national level of the enterprise or insolvencies leading to mass redundancies in multiple local establishments.

The second issue, in Part 12.3, concerns the Court's rulings on the validity of national or local laws, or collective agreements, concerning terms and conditions of employment in contracts, such as a requirement to pay the applicable minimum wage, falling within the scope of EU directives on posted workers and/or public procurement. In particular, the cases discussed concern, mainly, the Posted Workers Directive (PWD), 96/71,¹² which provides a guarantee for workers posted to the territory of a Member State of, *inter alia*, minimum rates of pay as defined by law or applicable collective agreements, and, secondly, the Public Procurement Directive, now Directive 2014/24, which grants contracting authorities the right to lay down 'special conditions' relating to the performance of a contract which may concern 'social or employment-related considerations'.¹³ In the context of both directives, any national measure must be compatible with the freedom to provide services under Article 56 TFEU. Based on analysis of this case law, it asks, to what extent the relevant provisions in these directives can be used to provide minimum protection for workers, both core and contingent, and mitigate against the most harmful effects of social dumping. Finally, Part 12.4, adds some concluding remarks.

---

9. See generally, Edoardo Ales, Olaf Deinert and Jeff Kenner (eds), *Core and Contingent Work in the European Union* (Hart Publishing 2017).
10. Antonio Lo Faro, *Contingent Work: A Conceptual Framework*, in Edoardo Ales et al., *ibid*, 7-23, 8.
11. *Council Directive 98/59/EC of 20 July 1998 on the approximation of the laws of the Member States relating to collective redundancies*, OJ L 225, 12.8.1998, 16-21.
12. *Directive 96/71/EC of the European Parliament and of the Council of 16 December 1996 concerning the posting of workers in the framework of the provision of services*, OJ L 18, 21.1.1997, 1-6.
13. *Directive 2014/24/EU of the European Parliament and of the Council of 26 February 2014 on public procurement and repealing Directive 2004/18/EC*, OJ L 94, 28.3.2014, 65-242, Art. 70 (replacing Directive 2004/18, Art. 26).

12.2 COLLECTIVE REDUNDANCIES

12.2.1 Analysis of the CRD

The EU CRD, 98/59,[14] was first introduced as a crisis measure intended to alleviate the consequences for workers of economic decline in the mid-1970s, particularly in the private manufacturing sector where unemployment was rising fast as factories closed.[15] It was not intended to be interventionist. According to the European Commission, closing down some companies was 'an integral part of the evolution towards more promising activities'.[16] Ultimately the decision of the management to close down an enterprise, or drastically reduce the size of the workforce, is unfettered by the Directive. Instead, the Directive, as amended, provides a mechanism for constructive dialogue between the social partners to ensure that, where 'collective redundancies'[17] are contemplated by the employer in qualifying 'establishments', but the decision has not yet been made to terminate employment contracts, a process is followed whereby consultations begin with workers' representatives 'in good time with a view to reaching an agreement'.[18] Such an agreement should, at least, cover 'ways and means of *avoiding* collective redundancies or *reducing* the numbers of workers affected, and *mitigating* the consequences by recourse to accompanying social measures' such as redeployment or retraining.[19] In order to enable workers' representatives 'to make constructive proposals, the employers shall in good time during the course of the consultations' supply them with relevant information including specific details notified in writing.[20] It is only once the 'employer' is 'contemplating' redundancies that the procedural safeguards

---

14. Council Directive 75/129/EEC of 17 February 1975 on the approximation of the laws of the Member States relating to collective redundancies, OJ L 48, 22.2.1975, 29–30. *See also*, Council Directive 92/56/EEC of 24 June 1992 amending Directive 75/129/EEC on the approximation of the laws of the Member States relating to collective redundancies, OJ L 245, 26.8.1992, 3–5. The two directives were consolidated and replaced by *Council Directive 98/59/EC of 20 July 1998* on the *approximation* of the *laws* of the *Member States relating* to *collective redundancies*, OJ L 225, 12.8.1998, 16–21.
15. See Jeff Kenner, *EU Employment Law* 28 (Hart Publishing 2003).
16. European Commission, Explanatory Memorandum, 1972, reproduced in *Bulletin No. 4*, Institute of Labour Relations, University of Leuven, 206 (1973).
17. Directive 98/59, Art. 1(1)(a) defines 'collective redundancies' as 'dismissals effected by an employer for one or more reasons not related to the individuals concerned'. The Court has given a Union meaning to the concept of redundancy as 'any termination of [a] contract of employment not sought by the worker, and therefore without his consent', Case C-55/02 *Commission v. Portugal* [2004] ECR I-9387, para. 50. For further discussion, *see* Catherine Barnard, *EU Employment Law*, 4th edn, 630–642 (OUP 2012).
18. *Directive 98/59/EC*, Art. 2(1).
19. *Ibid*. Art. 2(2). Emphasis added.
20. *Ibid*. Art. 2(3). Under Art. 2(3)(b) the specified information includes: the reason for the projected redundancies; the number and categories of workers to be made redundant by reference also to the numbers normally employed; the period over which the projected redundancies are to be effected; the criteria proposed for the selection of workers to be

outlined above apply, introducing a subjective element into what is otherwise meant to be an objective process.[21]

Each Member State is left with considerable freedom to apply the Directive in a fashion that fits with their indigenous systems of labour law and industrial relations.[22] For example, Member States can choose between options for rules governing the size of qualifying 'establishments' and the timescale of the redundancies. These rules significantly limit the scope of the Directive. To count as 'collective redundancies' for the purpose of the Directive, the minimum number of redundancies relating to the size of the 'establishment' under Article 1(1)(a) is:

(i) Either, over a period of thirty days:

- at least ten in establishments normally employing more than twenty and less than 100 workers;
- at least 10% of the number of workers in establishments normally employing at least 100 but less than 300 workers;
- at least thirty in establishments normally employing 300 workers or more;

(ii) or, over a period of ninety days, at least twenty, whatever the number of workers normally employed in the establishments in questions.

Such flexibility demonstrates that the CRD 'carries out only a partial harmonisation of the rules for the protection of workers in the event of collective redundancies'.[23] Partial harmonisation allows for significant diversity in the transposition of the Directive, as a minimum standards measure, including the possibility of introducing 'provisions which are more favourable to workers or to promote or to allow the application of collective agreements more favourable to workers'.[24]

An important feature of the Directive, as amended in the early 1990s, is a transnational dimension whereby, under Article 2(4), the information and consultation obligations are applicable 'irrespective of whether the decision regarding collective redundancies is being taken by the employer or by an undertaking controlling the employer'. Also, it is not a defence on the part of the employer that 'the necessary information has not been provided to the employer by the undertaking which took the decision leading to collective redundancies'. The revised Article 2(4) was necessary to respond to 'accelerating corporate

---

made redundant in so far as this is a requirement of national law and/or practice; and the method for calculating any redundancy payments other than those arising out of national law and/or practice.
21. *See* Barnard, *supra* n. 17, at 631.
22. Case C-383/92 *Commission v. UK* [1994] ECR I-2435.
23. Case C-44/08 *Akavan Erityisalojen Keskusliitto AEK ry and Others v. Fujitsu Siemens Computers Oy* [2009] ECR I-8163, para. 60.
24. Directive 98/59, Art. 5.

restructuring' arising from mergers and takeovers often involving enterprises based outside the EU, but no further updating of the Directive has taken place over a twenty-five-year period in which there has been exponential growth in the power and influence of globalised enterprises using communication and trade networks, to distribute products and services worldwide, often operating outside the boundaries of State authority.[25]

The Directive contains a range of terms to describe the enterprise, or parts thereof, specifically: 'undertaking'; 'controlling undertaking'; 'establishments'; and 'employer'. Article 1, concerning definitions and scope, is silent on the precise meaning of these terms. It is therefore left to the Court to interpret them in the context of the Directive's overarching aim, whereby 'it is important that greater protection should be afforded to workers in the event of collective redundancies while taking into account the need for balanced economic and social development within the [Union]'.[26] Let us now turn to four cases that illustrate the difficulty of this judicial task.

12.2.2 Case Law

In the first case, *AEK v. Fujitsu Siemens Computers* ('*AEK*'),[27] a reference from the Supreme Court of Finland, the Court was asked to consider, for the first time, the scope of the obligations under the Directive, including the revised Article 2(4), in a situation where the decision to close an undertaking was taken by the board of directors of the undertaking's parent company. The redundancies arose following a merger between the computer businesses of Fujitsu and Siemens to form a new parent group of companies, Fujitsu Siemens Computers (Holding) BV (Netherlands). Following the merger, the board of directors of the parent company, based in the Netherlands, accepted a proposal from the company's executive council to 'disengage' from a production plant in Finland. On the same day, the local management of the parent company's Finnish subsidiary, Fujitsu Siemens Computers Oy, began a six-week period of consultations with the trade unions at the plant. Immediately after this process was complete, the board of the parent company took a final decision to terminate the company's operations in Finland with the exception of computer sales. Following this decision, the Finnish subsidiary dismissed 450 out of 490 employees at the plant. The main trade union at the plant, AEK, brought an action against the subsidiary claiming that it had infringed its obligations under the Finnish law transposing the Directive. It was argued that the parent company had separated the Finnish factory from the company group and it had, alone, made the decision to close the

---

25. *See* especially, Robé, *supra* n. 2, at 11.
26. Directive 98/59, recital 2 of the preamble.
27. Case C-44/08 *Akavan Erityisalojen Keskusliitto AEK ry and Others v. Fujitsu Siemens Computers Oy* (hereinafter '*AEK*')[2009] ECR I-8163.

factory. The national court asked a series of questions which can be distilled into three core questions, with subquestions, summarised below.[28]

Firstly, what is the meaning of the expression 'is contemplating redundancies' so as to determine the time at which the obligation to hold consultations starts? Is the obligation to start consultations triggered when the strategic decision to make collective redundancies is finally made or at an earlier stage at which a need for collective redundancies is expected?[29]

In its answer, the Court emphasised the temporal application of the Directive. The obligations of consultation and notification become operative when there is an intention to make 'projected' collective redundancies but prior to the employer's decision to actually terminate employment contracts.[30] This means that the notification by the employer is not a *fait accompli* but rather it is the commencement of a process under which there is a possibility of avoiding or at least reducing collective redundancies, or mitigating the consequences.[31] Once the employer has contemplated collective redundancies, or has a plan for them, the information and consultation obligations are triggered.[32] In the specific context of the case, the effect of the revised Article 2(4), concerning decisions taken by controlling undertakings, is to trigger the obligation to hold consultations 'where the prospect of collective redundancies is not directly the choice of the employer'[33] and 'even though the employer may not have been immediately and properly informed of that decision'.[34] Applying Article 2(4), therefore, ensures, in the context of 'an economic background marked by the increasing presence of groups of undertakings', there is 'greater protection for workers in the event of collective redundancies' in situations where there is a controlling undertaking.[35] It followed that, for this objective to be fully effective, 'the consultation procedure must be started by the employer once a strategic or commercial decision compelling him to contemplate or to plan for collective redundancies has been taken'.[36]

Secondly, in a case involving a group of undertakings, does the obligation to start consultations on the collective redundancies contemplated arise even

---

28. For the full set of questions *see*, AEK, para. 30.
29. AEK, para. 36.
30. AEK, paras 38–40, referencing Directive 98/59, Arts 2(1) and 3(1). *See* further, Case C-188/03 *Junk* [2005] ECR I-885, paras 36–37.
31. AEK, para. 38.
32. AEK, para. 41. *See* Case 248/83 *Dansk Metalarbejderforbund and Specialarbederforbundet i Danmark* [1985] ECR 553, para. 17.
33. AEK, para. 42.
34. AEK, para. 43.
35. AEK, para. 44, referencing recital 2 of the preamble cited above. *See* Case C-270/05 *Athinaïki Chartopoiïa* [2007] ECR I-1499, para. 25.
36. AEK, para. 48.

before the employer is able to supply all the required information to the workers' representatives?[37] Also, when is the consultation procedure to be concluded?[38]

In reply, the Court explained that the process is designed to be flexible, to ensure that even if the subsidiary, the 'employer', did not have all the required information at the start of consultations it would be possible to provide it 'during the course of the consultations'[39] and 'to enable the workers' representatives to participate in the consultation process as fully and effectively as possible and, to achieve that, any new relevant information must be supplied up to the end of the process'.[40] For the purposes of Article 2(4), 'the decision' has been taken by the parent company and it is obliged to provide the necessary information to the employer under its control so that the latter can fulfil the information, consultation and notification obligations.[41] Therefore, the obligation to start consultations does not depend on whether the employer is already able to supply the workers' representatives with the necessary information concerning, *inter alia*, the reasons for the projected redundancies, the number of redundancies, and the period over which they are to be effected.[42] Also, the employer must fulfil all of the consultation obligations in the Directive before any decision on the termination of contracts is taken.[43]

Thirdly, should the obligation to start consultations arise when the employer or the parent company, which controls the employer, is contemplating collective redundancies and, in order for the obligation to start consultations to arise, must the subsidiary, within which the redundancies are contemplated, be identified?[44]

The Court's answer was very specific. Under the scheme of the Directive only the employer, who is in an employment relationship with the workers, has the obligation to inform, consult and notify.[45] The fact that the parent undertaking controls the employer, even if it can take decisions which are binding on the employer, does not make it the employer.[46] As the Directive provides only partial harmonisation it does not restrict the freedom of a group of undertakings to organise their activities in a fashion that best suits their needs.[47] It followed, as a specific consequence of the introduction of Article 2(4), that the Finnish subsidiary, as the immediate 'employer' of the workers in the 'establishment', could not escape from its obligations under the Directive simply because the decision to disengage from the plant was taken by the parent company. Because

---

37. *AEK*, para. 50.
38. *AEK*, para. 66.
39. *AEK*, paras 52–53.
40. *AEK*, para. 53.
41. *AEK*, EU:C:2009:241, Opinion of Advocate General Mengozzi, para. 40.
42. *AEK*, judgment, para. 55, with reference to Art. 2(3)(b) of Directive 98/59.
43. *AEK*, paras 66–72, applying Case C-188/03 *Junk* [2005] ECR I-885, para. 45.
44. *AEK*, para. 56.
45. *AEK*, para. 57.
46. *AEK*, para. 58.
47. *AEK*, paras 59–60. *See also* Case C-449/93 *Rockfon*, EU:C:1995:420, para. 21.

the employer was part of a group of undertakings, the Court ruled, it was compelled to contemplate redundancies and initiate the consultation procedure, whether or not it had prior knowledge of the decision of the parent or controlling undertaking.[48] It is for this reason that it is not possible to start the consultations until the subsidiary has been identified.[49]

In its ruling in *AEK*, the Court demonstrated a strongly purposive reading of the scope of the CRD, specifically the gap-filling Article 2(4). The judgment recognises that the underlying teleology of the Directive, as amended, is to afford greater protection to workers in the event that collective redundancies are contemplated in situations where restructuring decisions are taken at the central headquarters of the parent enterprise, wherever it is located.[50] The provisions of the Directive are effective even where those decisions have been taken without the direct involvement, or even knowledge, of the subsidiary that is the immediate employer of the workers being made redundant. Nevertheless, deeming the subsidiary, once it has been identified, to be contemplating redundancies in situations where 'the decision' is unexpected and the subsidiary has little or no knowledge of the plan, is unlikely to lead to meaningful local consultations with workers' representatives. Although an obligation can be inferred on the parent company making 'the decision', that obligation is only valid between the parent company and the subsidiary, it does not affect the obligation to hold consultations which remains the responsibility of the subsidiary as 'employer'.[51] The employer may be able to supply the required information, at least during 'the course of the consultations', or even up to the end of the consultations,[52] but there is no corresponding obligation on the real decision-maker, the central undertaking, to participate in the consultations. Even if the reasons for the restructuring or closure decision are provided to the subsidiary, so long as it conducts the consultations in good faith and provides all the necessary information over the applicable timetable, the minimum requirements of the Directive will have been met without the subsidiary, as 'the employer', being able, in practice, to take any significant steps to avoid or reduce the redundancies or otherwise ameliorate their effects.

Three further cases on the scope of the CRD, decided in quick succession by the Court in the spring of 2015, each concerned the meaning of the terms 'establishment' or 'establishments', for the purpose of calculating the threshold and the time period for the number of redundancies to qualify as 'collective redundancies', depending on the option chosen by the Member State concerned under Article 1(1)(a). These cases also highlight the potential for broader

---

48. *AEK*, para. 62.
49. *AEK*, para. 63.
50. Although the restructuring decision was taken in another Member State, there is no territorial limit to Art. 2(4) and nothing in the judgment to suggest that the ruling would have been any different if the parent company had been located in a third country.
51. *AEK*, Opinion of Advocate General Mengozzi, para. 40.
52. *AEK*, judgment, para. 65.

protection of workers in Member States that choose to make use of Article 5 of the Directive, by introducing laws, regulations or administrative provisions, or allow the application of collective agreements, that are 'more favourable' to workers.

The first two cases, from the United Kingdom, *Lyttle*[53] and *USDAW and Wilson*,[54] concerned redundancies arising as a consequence of mass closures of retail stores after the owners had been declared insolvent. In both cases the central issue was whether each individual store was an 'establishment', for the purpose of calculating the threshold of 'at least 20' redundancies over a period of ninety days, to fall within the definition of 'collective redundancies' under Article 1(1)(a)(ii), *see* above, the option chosen by the UK under its implementing legislation.[55]

In *Lyttle*, Bluebird UK Bidco 2 ('Bluebird'), had taken over the ownership of Bonmarché following the insolvency of the previous owners. At the time when the business was transferred in January 2012, Bonmarché had 414 clothing stores in the UK employing around 4,200 workers. In the spring of 2012 Bluebird carried out a redundancy programme, reducing the number of stores to 273 with approximately 3,000 employees. The claimants, Ms Lyttle and others, worked at four different branches of Bonmarché in Northern Ireland each of which had fewer than twenty workers. The stores where they had been working were closed and the redundancies took effect in March 2012. It was not disputed that the redundancy consultation did not satisfy the requirements of the Directive.

USDAW and Wilson concerned the insolvency of the high street chains Woolworth and Ethel Austin in 2011. By contrast with *Lyttle*, there was a total liquidation of the businesses without a transfer of ownership leading to closure of all the stores and several thousand redundancies. In stores that had employed twenty workers or more, protective awards were made by the UK Secretary of State in accordance with the national legislation applicable where the employer has failed to comply with the requirements of the Directive.[56] However, 4,500 of the redundant workers, who had been working in stores employing fewer than twenty workers, were denied a protective award on the ground that each of those stores was a separate 'establishment' and therefore below the threshold for 'collective redundancies'. Ms Wilson, one of those affected, and her trade union, USDAW, contended that the dismissed workers at all the Woolworth and Ethel Austin stores were within the scope of the Directive and were entitled to protective awards on the basis that the stores, collectively, were 'establishments' for the purpose of Article 1(1)(a)(ii).

---

53. Case C-182/13 *Valerie Lyttle and Others v. Bluebird UK Bidco 2 Limited*, EU:C:2015:317, referred from the Industrial Tribunals (Northern Ireland) – hereinafter *Lyttle*.
54. Case C-80/14 *Union of Shop, Distributive and Allied Workers (USDAW), B Wilson v. WW Realisation 1 Ltd, in liquidation, Ethel Austin Ltd, Secretary of State for Business, Innovation and Skills*, EU:C:2015:291, referred from the Court of Appeal (England and Wales) – hereinafter *USDAW and Wilson*.
55. The Trade Union and Labour Relations (Consolidation) Act 1992, s. 188(1).
56. *Ibid.* s. 189(3), transposing Directive 98/59, Art. 6.

In each case, therefore, the crux of the issue raised in the questions referred to the Court, was either whether the term 'establishments' referred to the whole of the retail business, which should be treated as a single economic unit that was contemplating mass redundancies, or did it refer only to the particular units or stores to which the workers concerned had been assigned their duties? If the answer was the former, the protective awards would be payable to all workers dismissed in the course of the same restructuring exercise, irrespective of the size of the store at which they had worked.[57]

In separate judgments, which were essentially identical on the main issues, the Court followed its previous case law on the scope of 'establishment' in Article 1(1)(a)(i), the alternative option to the one chosen by the UK. In *Rockfon*,[58] a Danish case concerning the scope of Article 1(1)(a)(i), the Court had held that, as the term 'establishment' is not defined in the Directive, it must be interpreted autonomously and uniformly in the EU legal order and cannot, therefore, be defined independently in the laws of the Member States.[59] It followed that the term 'establishment' is defined by reference to the 'employment relationship' of the individual workers which is 'essentially characterised by the link existing between the worker and the part of the undertaking or business to which he is assigned to carry out his duties'.[60] From this perspective, the term 'establishment' in Article 1(1)(a) 'must be interpreted as designating ... the unit to which the workers made redundant are assigned to carry out their duties'.[61] Based on the Court's narrow view of an 'establishment' it is not necessary that 'the unit in question is endowed with a management that can independently effect collective redundancies'.[62] According to the Court, an 'establishment' is a 'distinct entity' from an 'undertaking' if the undertaking has several units each 'having a certain degree of permanence and stability, which is assigned to perform one or more given tasks and which has a workforce, technical means and a certain organisational structure allowing for the accomplishment of those tasks'.[63] The meaning of the term 'establishment' was

---

57. *See* Opinion of Advocate General Wahl, EU:C:2015:68, para. 47. The Advocate General's Opinion was issued for all three cases under consideration: *Lyttle*, *USDAW and Wilson*, and Case C-392/13 *Andrés Rabal Cañas v. Nexea Gestión Documental SA and Fondo de Garantía Salarial* (discussed below).
58. Case C-449/93 *Rockfon*, EU:C:1995:420.
59. *Lyttle*, para. 26, *USDAW and Wilson*, para. 45, applying Case C-449/93 *Rockfon*, EU:C:1995:420, para. 25 and Case C-270/05 *Athinaïki Chartopoiïa AE v. L Panagiotidis and Others*, EU:C:2007:101, para. 23.
60. *Lyttle*, para. 28, *USDAW and Wilson*, para. 47, applying Case C-449/93 *Rockfon*, EU:C:1995:420, para. 32.
61. *Lyttle*, para. 28, *USDAW and Wilson*, para. 47.
62. *Lyttle*, para. 28, *USDAW and Wilson*, para. 47.
63. *Lyttle*, paras 30–31, *USDAW and Wilson*, paras 49–50, applying Case C-270/05, *ibid*, para. 27.

identical regardless of which option the Member State had chosen under Article 1(1)(a). The two options were 'substantially equivalent' alternatives.[64]

The Court noted that the provisions of Directive 2002/14/EC, establishing a general framework for informing and consulting employees in the EU, contain a clear distinction between the terms 'undertakings' and 'establishments'.[65] Under that Directive an 'undertaking' is 'a public or private undertaking carrying out an economic activity, whether or not operating for gain, which is located within the territory of the Member States',[66] whereas an establishment is 'a unit of business *defined in accordance with national law and practice*'.[67] In Directive 2002/14, therefore, the term 'establishment' is not given an autonomous and uniform meaning unlike the term 'undertaking'. Large retailers, of the size of Bonmarché and Woolworths/Ethel Austin before insolvency, with a single owner, would fall within the very broad definition of 'undertaking' in that Directive. If, as the Court had already asserted in both *Lyttle* and *USDAW and Wilson*, an 'undertaking' covers 'all the separate employment units of the undertaking',[68] it is legitimate to suggest that the term 'establishments', plural, used in Article 1(1)(a) of Directive 98/59, is the same as 'undertaking'. The Court dismisses the use of the term 'establishments' in Article 1(1)(a), which is in, *inter alia*, the English, French, Italian and Spanish versions of the Directive, on the basis that the singular term 'establishment' is used in some language versions and the latter is deemed to preclude equating an 'establishment' with an 'undertaking'.[69] This is rather odd as it could, conversely, be suggested that the use of 'establishments' in several language versions, specifically, in context of Article 1(1)(a)(ii), which refers to 'the number of workers normally employed in the establishments in question',[70] points to the opposite interpretation. Unlike Directive 2002/14, the CRD makes no distinction between 'undertakings' and 'establishments' and, it is submitted, to include all workers in the undertakings' 'establishments' in the calculation of the number of redundancies in situations where redundancies are contemplated across multiple units of the enterprise, is more consistent with the protective aim of the Directive and should therefore be preferred.

---

64. *Lyttle*, para. 37, *USDAW and Wilson*, para. 56.
65. *Lyttle*, para. 50, *USDAW and Wilson*, para. 69. Directive 2002/14/EC of the European Parliament and of the Council of 11 March 2002 establishing a general framework for informing and consulting employees in the European Community – Joint declaration of the European Parliament, the Council and the Commission on employee representation, OJ L80, *23.03.2002, 29–34*.
66. Directive 2002/14, Art. 2(a).
67. Directive 2002/14, Art. 2(b). Emphasis added.
68. *Lyttle*, para. 47, *USDAW and Wilson*, para. 66.
69. *Lyttle*, para. 36, *USDAW and Wilson*, para. 55. Advocate General Wahl, at para. 53 of his Opinion, points to the Croatian, Danish, German, Finnish, Hungarian and Swedish versions.
70. Directive 98/59, Art. 1(1)(a)(ii).

What is remarkable is how the Court's very specific Union definition of 'establishment' in *Lyttle* and *USDAW and Wilson* has had the effect of excluding large numbers of workers from protection under the Directive in a situation where a single enterprise, or its administrator, is contemplating the dismissal of hundreds or, in the case of Woolworths and Ethel Austin, thousands of workers simultaneously. The only difference between these mass dismissals and a similar number of dismissals that might occur in a redundancy scenario in a single large factory, such as the Fujitsu Siemens plant in *AEK*, arises from the particular organisation of the retail trade into multiple store units.

According to the Court, the fact that, theoretically, an inclusive approach might cover a single worker of an establishment, would be contrary to the ordinary meaning of the term 'collective redundancy'.[71] This argument is erroneous because, even if there had only been a single worker in one of the stores, that worker would have been made redundant by a decision taken by central management of the enterprise to make all, or a substantial proportion of the workforce, redundant, providing a collective dimension. Ultimately, in both *Lyttle* and *USDAW and Wilson*, all the redundancies had been contemplated by central management and put into effect nationwide. It is difficult to rationalise how an interpretation, which has such inequitable effects between identically situated workers employed in different-sized stores, is justified.

In explaining its reasoning, the Court recognised that an *erga omnes* interpretation of the concept of 'establishment' to cover all affected workplaces within the undertaking and treat them as a single entity, would have significantly increased the number of workers eligible for protection, corresponding with one of the objectives in the Directive of affording greater protection to workers.[72] According to the Court, however, the objective of worker protection in the event of collective redundancies must be balanced with a need 'to ensure comparable protection for workers' rights in different Member States and to harmonise the costs which such protective rules entail for EU undertakings' and thus 'rendering comparable the burden of those costs in all Member States'.[73]

None of these arguments is convincing. The logical approach would be to apply the same interpretation of 'establishments' to all Member States, regardless of which option in Article 1(1)(a) applies, so as to include the total number of redundancies across all establishments of an enterprise where these are effected as part of a single management plan. It would also ensure comparable protection of workers in enterprises contemplating redundancies regardless of whether the workforce is in single or multiple locations. It might entail different costs for enterprises, depending on the method chosen to carry out consultations, but this would be a natural consequence of the organisation of the enterprise and does not justify inequitable treatment of the workforce. An inclusive interpretation would also be consistent with the Directive's core aim,

---

71. *Lyttle*, para. 45, *USDAW and Wilson*, para. 64.
72. *Lyttle*, para. 42, *USDAW and Wilson*, para. 61.
73. *Lyttle*, paras 43–44, *USDAW and Wilson*, paras 62–63.

which not only affords greater protection to workers in the event of collective redundancies, but also takes account of 'the need for balanced economic and social development'.[74] It would protect small businesses, or indeed autonomous franchises of retail chains, with fewer than twenty workers, who make their own decisions, and would be outside the scope of the Directive whichever option in Article 1(1) is chosen.[75]

Finally, the Court suggests that it would have been open to the UK to introduce 'more favourable' provisions under Article 5 in order to extend protection 'to all workers affected by redundancy in an undertaking or part of an undertaking of the same employer, the term "undertaking" being understood as covering all the separate employment units of that undertaking or that part of an undertaking'.[76] It would have been possible to lay down more favourable rules without affecting the 'autonomous and uniform' interpretation given to the term 'establishment'.[77] It is submitted that this is the wrong approach. The main purpose of EU social policy harmonisation is to extend the basic guarantee of directives as widely as possible to achieve a common standard,[78] which should, under the CRD, encompass all those affected by large scale redundancies initiated by an enterprise as part of a single plan. It should then be left to some Member States, who have chosen to avail themselves of the 'more favourable' provisions to workers, to improve the quality of protection when collective redundancies are contemplated by, for example, introducing more stringent rules to improve the quality of the information and consultation process and introduce more effective remedies.

The third case, *Rabal Cañas*,[79] referred from a Spanish court, concerned redundancies made by Nexea, an undertaking providing hybrid email services which formed part of a group of undertakings owned by the Spanish State. Nexea had two establishments: an administration department and production site in Madrid with 164 employees, and an operations centre in Barcelona with twenty employees. Although the Barcelona site was an extension of Nexea's Madrid operation carrying out substantially identical tasks, it did have its own manager. Following losses in 2011, and the forecast of further losses in 2012, Nexea gradually carried out dismissals at both locations from August 2012, reducing the number of workers employed at its Barcelona site to 16 by December 2012. At that point it decided to close its operation in Barcelona leading to the dismissal of Mr Rabal Cañas and twelve other workers on economic grounds.

---

74. Directive 98/59, recital 2 of the preamble.
75. Consistent with Art. 153(2)(b) TFEU.
76. *Lyttle*, para. 47, *USDAW and Wilson*, para. 66.
77. *Lyttle*, para. 48, *USDAW and Wilson*, para. 67.
78. *See* Kenner, *supra* n. 15, at 30–31 and Brian Bercusson, *European Labour Law* (Butterworths, 1996) 52.
79. Case C-392/13 *Andrés Rabal Cañas v. Nexea Gestión Documental SA and Fondo de Garantía Salarial*, EU:C:2015:318.

Spain's implementing legislation was, on the one hand, apparently more favourable to workers because it used 'undertaking' rather than the 'establishment' as the sole reference unit but, on the other hand, it was more restrictive, limiting the concept of collective redundancies to particular types of termination based on 'economic, technological, organisational or production grounds'.[80] Spanish law was somewhat aligned with the option in Article 1(1)(a)(i) but there were differences. The definition of 'collective redundancies' included, terminations, over a period of ninety days, affecting, *inter alia*, at least ten workers in undertakings employing fewer than 100 workers, or 10% of the workers in undertakings employing between 100 and 300 workers. It was argued by Mr Rabal Cañas that, at the time of his dismissal, the total number of dismissals over a period of ninety days was eighteen which amounted to 10% of the total personnel of the undertaking and therefore the threshold had been met for 'collective redundancies' under the national legislation. Conversely, the Spanish Government contended that the national legislation had to be interpreted consistently with the options in Article 1(1)(a)(i) and (ii), which required there to be at least twenty workers in 'establishments' for the dismissals to be deemed collective redundancies. By using the latter formulation, and treating the Barcelona site as an 'establishment', the threshold had not been met.

In its judgment, the Court addressed the question of whether the national legislation, which used only the undertaking as the reference unit, was compatible with the Directive. Applying its previous case law, including the recently decided *Lyttle* and *USDAW and Wilson* cases, the Court was satisfied that Nexea's operation in Barcelona was an 'establishment' as distinct from an 'undertaking'.[81] Having deemed it an 'establishment', the Court, without any further reasoning, accepted the argument of the Spanish Government that there had to be a minimum of twenty workers for the dismissals to count as 'collective redundancies'.[82] It appears, therefore, that the expression 'more favourable' provisions under Article 5 does not extend to lowering the threshold even though this would have benefited the workers concerned. On the central point behind the reference, the Court observed that replacing the term 'establishment' with 'undertaking' could be regarded as more favourable to the workers concerned, and thus compatible with the Directive, but only if it did not mean that the protection afforded to workers is lost or reduced.[83] It followed that national legislation was incompatible with the Directive if it had the effect of precluding the information and consultation procedure provided for in the Directive, when the dismissals would have been considered 'collective

---

80. 'Law on the Workers' Statute', Art. 51(1).
81. *Rabal Cañas*, para. 51.
82. *Rabal Cañas*, para. 55.
83. *Rabal Cañas*, para. 52.

redundancies' under the definition in Article 1(1)(a), had the establishment been used as the reference unit.[84]

Rabal Cañas highlights continuing difficulties with the Court's interpretation of the Directive in the context of restructuring. Nexea had chosen to establish an outreach operation in Barcelona when it was expanding its business. When the economic climate became more difficult, it was able to gradually reduce its workforce in Barcelona in stages and ultimately shut down the site over a period beyond the maximum ninety days stipulated in Article 1(1)(a), keeping below the threshold and thereby avoiding any obligations under the Directive. It would not have been able to avoid those obligations if it had slimmed down its staffing in Madrid instead of closing down its operation in Barcelona. If the Court had, instead, applied a literal interpretation of the national legislation, by treating Nexea as a single 'undertaking', the dismissals in Barcelona would have been subject to the national rules on information and consultation. The Spanish legislation was rather sloppily drafted and involved some 'cherry picking'[85] but it is somewhat contrary for the Court to suggest, in *Lyttle* and *USDAW and Wilson*, that the UK had the option of widening protection for workers, by using the freedom offered by Article 5 to introduce 'more favourable' provisions for workers, but then to proceed, in *Rabal Cañas*, to override Spain's exercise of its *'right'*[86] to introduce such provisions. The Court is correct in its desire to ensure that national legislation should not be interpreted in such a way as to deny workers the protection afforded by the Directive but this theoretical problem only arose because of its own narrow interpretation of the language contained therein.

12.2.3 Ways Forward

In the example of the CRD, partial harmonisation has led to a degree of convergence in the laws of the Member States but there is significant differentiation in protection arising from the choice of model for calculating and timing of redundancy decisions and the use of more favourable provisions to widen the scope of protection for workers in redundancy situations. As outlined above, the underlying purpose of EU regulation is not to question the employer's rationale for *contemplating* redundancies but rather to offer a process of information and consultation that may lead, after negotiations on constructive proposals from workers' representatives, to a rethink or at least a less unpalatable plan. The CRD, operating within a very narrow window, offers the prospect of a less harsh outcome, but only for those workers coming within its scope.

---

84. *Rabal Cañas*, para. 57.
85. *Rabal Cañas*, para. 57.
86. Directive 98/59, Art. 5. Emphasis added.

When the CRD was amended in the 1990s it extended its arc of coverage to 'cases where the redundancy decision is taken by a decision-making centre or an undertaking located in another Member State'.[87] Recognising that transnational restructuring was becoming increasingly common, arising in part by mergers of enterprises within the single market, the revised CRD 'eliminated' a loophole.[88] In *AEK*,[89] case analysis has shown that the Court met this basic challenge by upholding the revised Article 2(4) to ensure that workers were protected notwithstanding the fact that the decision taken to dismiss them was made by central management located in another Member State. The outcome of the case is, nevertheless, unsatisfactory because the full obligation for transmitting information and conducting consultations lies with local 'establishment' of the 'undertaking'. Formally the information and consultation requirements can be met, but the 'establishment' or 'employer' may have its hands tied and be able to offer little to ameliorate the scale or impact of the redundancies. Any improvements offered must be sanctioned by the central management at armslength from the consultation process. It is submitted that the CRD should be amended to ensure that, where the employer is unable to effectively negotiate on proposals from workers' representatives, in line with the protective aims of the CRD, responsibility should be placed on the shoulders of the real decisionmaker, the central management, to conduct the consultations.

In *Lyttle*[90] and *USDAW and Wilson*,[91] analysis demonstrates that the Court's adoption of a rigid formula for the concept of an 'establishment', to give this term a uniform meaning, has led to inequality of protection for otherwise identically situated workers made redundant, collectively, as a consequence of the transfer or liquidation of the enterprise after insolvency. By treating each unit of the organisation as a micro 'establishment' the CRD, as interpreted by the Court, allows for restructuring plans to be based on divide and rule, and worse still those who work in the units below the threshold of twenty workers can be excluded altogether. It is submitted that this runs contrary to the purpose of the Directive, not least language used at the time of restructuring that recognised that key corporate decisions are taken at a higher level than the place where the worker is employed, all pointing to a need for flexibility to ensure that where

---

87. European Commission, 'Proposal for a Directive amending Directive 75/129/EEC on the approximation of the laws of the Member States relating to collective redundancies', COM(91) 292 final, 3.
88. *Ibid.*
89. Case C-44/08 *Akavan Erityisalojen Keskusliitto AEK ry and Others v. Fujitsu Siemens Computers Oy* [2009] ECR I-8163.
90. Case C-182/13 *Valerie Lyttle and Others v. Bluebird UK Bidco 2 Limited*, EU:C:2015:317.
91. Case C-80/14 *Union of Shop, Distributive and Allied Workers (USDAW), B Wilson v. WW Realisation 1 Ltd, in liquidation, Ethel Austin Ltd, Secretary of State for Business, Innovation and Skills*, EU:C:2015:291.

mass redundancies are being contemplated by the central management across multiple sites of the enterprise within one or more Member States, the total number of employees in the combined 'establishments' of the 'undertaking' are brought with the umbrella of protection. At the very least, in order to escape from the inflexible meaning given to 'establishment' by the Court, the CRD should be revised to leave the definition to 'national law and practice' as is the case with the Framework Directive on Information and Consultation of Employees, 2002/14.[92] This approach would also ensure that workers in situations similar to those in the Spanish case, *Rabal Cañas*,[93] would be counted at both establishments, towards the threshold, although this could have been achieved by recognising the approach of Spain as a 'more favourable' provision.

To conclude on the CRD, it is necessary to carry out a further revision to ensure that its mechanisms are more robust. The Commission's proposed 'European Pillar of Social Rights',[94] contains references to the need for adequate compensation in the event of dismissal and strengthened involvement of workers in enterprises. It is necessary to convert this initiative into an EU-wide basis for reviewing labour law. An important reference point is Article 27 of the Charter of Fundamental Rights of the EU which, as EU primary law,[95] provides that workers or their representatives must 'at the appropriate level, be guaranteed information and consultation in good time in the cases and under the conditions provided by Union law and national laws and practices'. The Court has taken a restrictive approach to the interpretation of Article 27 in *AMS*,[96] ruling that it cannot be relied on by a private party in a dispute with another private party, limiting its use to the public sector. It is noticeable that Article 27 has not featured in the cases under discussion in this Chapter. In the absence of any prospect of judicial activism by the Court, it is submitted that EU law falls short of offering the guarantee promised by Article 27 and this should now be addressed.[97]

---

92. Directive 2002/14/EC of the European Parliament and of the Council of 11 March 2002 establishing a general framework for informing and consulting employees in the European Community – Joint declaration of the European Parliament, the Council and the Commission on employee representation, OJ L80, 23.03.2002, 29–34, Art. 2(b).
93. Case C-392/13 *Andrés Rabal Cañas v. Nexea Gestión Documental SA and Fondo de Garantía Salarial*, EU:C:2015:318.
94. European Commission, 'Towards a European Pillar of Social Rights', 14 September 2015: http://ec.europa.eu/priorities/deeper-and-fairer-economic-and-monetary-union/towards-european-pillar-social-rights_en.
95. Treaty on European Union, Art. 6(1).
96. Case C-176/12 *Association de médiation sociale v. Union locale des syndicats CGT*, ECLI:EU:C:2014:2.
97. *See* further, Filip Dorssement, '*Article 27*', in Steve Peers, Tamara Hervey, Jeff Kenner & Angela Ward (eds), *The EU Charter of Fundamental Rights: A Commentary* 749 (Hart 2014).

12.3 POSTED WORKERS, PUBLIC PROCUREMENT AND 'FAIR COMPETITION' IN THE EU'S SINGLE MARKET

12.3.1 The Posted Workers Directive

Although the PWD, 96/71,[98] has its roots in EU social policy[99] it operates within the framework of the provision of services in the Union's single market,[100] an ambiguity that has caused problems regarding both the perception of its essential purpose and the scope of its application to enterprises and labour. By the mid-1990s, services were rapidly liberalising. The dynamism of the single market had encouraged enterprises 'to develop their transnational activities and increasingly to provide transnational services'.[101] In turn, transnational services had led to transnational employment relationships and a deterritorialisation of labour law, raising questions about the best method of protecting workers posted temporarily to another Member State to perform work under a service contract and prevent social dumping so as to ensure fair competition in the single market.

Under the Rome Convention of 1980, and now the Rome I Regulation,[102] the presumption is that the employment contract is governed by the law of the country in which the employee habitually carries out his work, even if he is temporarily employed in another country,[103] but it permits 'overriding mandatory provisions' to be applied by the receiving country under certain

---

98. Directive 96/71/EC of the European Parliament and of the Council of 16 December 1996 concerning the posting of workers in the framework of the provision of services, OJ L 18, 21.1.1997, 1–6.
99. The source of the Directive is the draft of the European Community Charter of the Fundamental Social Rights of Workers, COM(89) 248, point 3. *See* Kenner, *supra* n. 15, at 138. At the time of its adoption, unanimity would have been required to adopt it as a social policy measure. Unanimity was not possible because the United Kingdom and Portugal were opposed. The legal bases for the Directive are TFEU Arts 53 and 62, relating to free movement of services, which only require a qualified majority vote in the Council of the EU. *See* further, Jonas Malmberg, *Posting Post Laval – International and National Responses*, Uppsala Center for Labor Studies, Working Paper 2010:5, 6. (2010).
100. Recital 4 of the preamble of Directive 96/71 explains that 'the provision of services may take the form either of performance of work by an undertaking on its account and under its direction, under a contract concluded between the undertaking and the party for whom the services are intended, or of the hiring-out of workers for use by an undertaking in the framework of a public or private contract'.
101. European Commission, *The Implementation of Directive 96/71/EC in the Member States*, COM(2003) 458 final 4.
102. Regulation (EC) No. 593/2008 of the European Parliament and of the Council of 17 June 2008 on the law applicable to contractual obligations (Rome I), OJ L 177, 4.7.2008, 6–16. For discussion, *see* Catherine Barnard, *The UK and Posted Workers: The Effect of 'Commission v. Luxembourg' on the Territorial Application of British Labour Law*, 38 ILJ 122 (2009).
103. Directive 96/71, Art. 8(2).

conditions.[104] In particular, if labour conditions, such as wages and working hours, are less advanced in the home country of the posted worker by comparison with the host country, the practice of posting, in an environment of liberalised services, will inevitably cause social dumping by undercutting. Indeed, as early as 1988, the Commission anticipated downward pressure on social conditions because of the demands of competition in the single market with a particular intensification of social dumping expected in areas such as public works contracts, construction and transport.[105] This was precisely the issue that arose in *Rush Portuguesa*,[106] a case involving Portuguese construction workers posted temporarily to France to perform a service contract, in which the Court made it possible, but not obligatory, for France, as host, to extend labour law rules, including provisions in collective agreements, to posted workers.[107]

The PWD seeks to address this problem by making obligatory the application by the host Member State of certain terms and conditions of employment to posted workers with the aim of providing 'a climate of fair competition and measures guaranteeing respect for the rights of workers'.[108] The PWD applies horizontally to undertakings established in any Member State that posts workers to another Member State.[109] It includes three types of posting by undertakings:[110]

(a) posting workers directly under a contract concluded between the undertaking and the party for whom the services are intended;
(b) posting to an establishment or an undertaking owned by the group; and
(c) posting by a temporary employment or posting agency.[111]

In each case the posted worker must have an employment relationship with the undertaking or agency. Additional provisions to identify genuine

---

104. Directive 96/71, Art. 9.
105. European Commission, *The Social Dimension of the Internal Market*, Social Europe, Special Ed., 65-66 (1988).
106. Case C-113/89, *Rush Portuguesa Ld^a v. Office national d'immigration*, EU:C:1990:142.
107. *See* Barnard, *supra* n. 17, at 218; Kenner, *supra* n. 15, at 15.
108. Directive 96/71, recital 5 of the preamble.
109. Directive 96/71, Art. 1(1). Under Art. 1(4) undertakings established in a non-member State must not be given more favourable treatment than undertakings established in a Member State.
110. Directive 96/71, Art. 1(3).
111. Also, under Directive 96/71, Art. 3(9), Member States can choose to extend the principle of equal treatment between temporary agency workers and workers of the user undertaking to posted agency workers. In practice this would mean that the rights of posted agency workers in those Member States would be equivalent to those provided by Directive 2008/104/EC of the European Parliament and of the Council of 19 November 2008 on temporary agency work, OJ L 327, 5.12.2008, 9-14.

posting and prevent abuse and circumvention of the Directive can be found in the subsequent Posted Workers Enforcement Directive adopted in 2014.[112]

In its core provisions, the PWD sets out a framework for the coordination of laws of the Member States 'in order to lay down a nucleus of mandatory rules for minimum protection to be observed in the host country by employers who post workers to perform temporary work in the territory of a Member State where the services are provided'.[113] These 'hard core'[114] rules, must be introduced by law and/or, in the case of activities involving building work,[115] by means of certain types of collective agreement or arbitration award,[116] to provide a 'guarantee' for 'posted workers'[117] of terms and conditions of employment[118] under Article 3(1) covering, *inter alia*:[119]

---

112. Directive 2014/67/EU of the European Parliament and of the Council of 15 May 2014 on the enforcement of Directive 96/71/EC concerning the posting of workers in the framework of the provision of services and amending Regulation (EU) No. 1024/2012 on administrative cooperation through the Internal Market Information System ('the IMI Regulation'), OJ L 159, 28.5.2014, 11–31.
113. Directive 96/71, recital 13.
114. Directive 96/71, recital 14.
115. Defined in the Annex of Directive 96/71 as including 'all building work relating to the construction, repair, upkeep, alteration or demolition of buildings' and certain particular types of building work listed therein.
116. Directive 96/71, Art. 3(8). In some Member States collective agreements or arbitration awards can be made 'universally applicable', which means that they 'must be observed by all undertakings in the geographical area and in the profession or industry concerned'. Alternatively, if a Member State does not have such a system, there are two alternatives for them to base their rules on. First, collective agreements or arbitration awards must be 'generally applicable to all similar undertakings in the geographical area and in the profession or industry concerned' and/or, second, 'collective agreements which have been concluded by the most representative employers' and labour organisations at national level and which are applied throughout national territory'. Both of these alternatives must apply to all the undertakings covered by the Directive and must ensure 'equality of treatment', meaning the same obligations between national undertakings and posting undertakings in a similar position as regards the matters listed in Art. 3(1) and also a requirement 'to fulfil such obligations with the same effects'.
117. Directive 96/71, Art. 2(1) defines a 'posted worker' as 'a worker who, for a limited period, carries out his work in the territory of a Member State other than the State in which he normally works'. Under Art. 3(6) the length of the posting shall be calculated on the basis of a reference period of one year from the beginning of the posting.
118. Social security coordination is excluded. It is covered by Regulation (EC) No. 883/2004 of the European Parliament and of the Council of 29 April 2004 on the coordination of social security systems, OJ L 166, 30.04.2004, 1–123.
119. Directive 96/71, Art. 3(1). Under Art. 3(3), if the posting is for less than one month, the provisions on work periods, rest periods and holidays can be waived by Member States, after consulting management and labour. Under Art. 3(5), it is possible to have an exemption from those provisions for a longer period on the grounds that the work to be done is not significant. Also, under Art. 3(4), if the posting is for less than one month it is possible to waive the provision on minimum rates of pay but only by means of a collective agreement as defined in Art. 3(8). These derogations do not apply to posted agency workers.

(a) maximum work periods and minimum rest periods;
(b) minimum paid annual holidays;
(c) minimum rates of pay defined by national law and practice of the host Member State;[120]
(d) the conditions of hiring-out workers, in particular the supply of workers by temporary employment undertakings;
(e) health, safety and hygiene at work;
(f) protective measures with regard to the terms and employment of pregnant women or women who have recently given birth, of children and of young people;
(g) equality of treatment between men and women and other provisions on non-discrimination.

Also, under Article 3(10), Member States, are not precluded from applying Treaty compatible terms and conditions of employment on matters not listed in Article 3(1) either by means of 'public policy provisions' or, in the case of activities other than building work,[121] by collective agreements or arbitration awards that meet criteria laid down in Article 3(8).[122] Such an extension of scope must be based on equality of treatment between national undertakings and undertakings of other Member States.[123] Finally, Article 3(7) 'shall not prevent' Member States applying terms and conditions of employment which are 'more favourable' to workers.

By contrast with social policy measures, the PWD coordinates but does not harmonise minimum standards for workers within its scope.[124] This reflects the fact that it was adopted on the basis of Treaty provisions concerned with the coordination of service provision.[125] In the absence of harmonisation, there have been significant variations in implementation, such as, differential approaches to the use of laws to put into the effect the mandatory terms and conditions, the application of collective agreements for this purpose, introducing 'more favourable provisions', and including terms and conditions on other matters as public policy provisions.[126] Differentiation has caused particular problems of interpretation for enterprises, social partners and the courts.

---

120. Under Directive 96/71, Art. 3(7) allowances specific to the posting shall be considered part of the minimum wage, unless they are paid in reimbursement of expenditure actually incurred on account of the posting, such as expenditure on travel, board and lodging.
121. As defined in the Annex, see supra n. 104.
122. See supra n. 116.
123. Directive 96/71, Art. 3(10).
124. See Barnard, supra n. 17, at 221.
125. TFEU Arts 53(1) and 62.
126. European Commission (n. 90) 8–9. European Parliament Directorate-General for Internal Policies, *Posting of Workers Directive – current situation and challenges: STUDY for the EMPL Committee*, June 2016, IP/A/EMPL/2016-07 PE 579.001, 9.

An additional factor, when considering the cases discussed below, is the competing visions of two broad groups of Member States: those who are the main recipients of posted workers, who tend to favour strong regulation; and those who are exporters of posted workers, who are seeking market access for their services. Also problematic has been the 'framework of services' context which provides the point of reference for the Court when it seeks to reconcile the 'inherent tension' within the PWD between 'a free relatively unrestricted cross-border provision of services, and guaranteeing a means with which to meet the objectives related to the social protection of posted workers'.[127] The next part offers analysis on selected case law of the Court in which it has had to address the 'regulatory balance' between these perhaps incompatible principles.[128] Also important are related cases where liberalisation of services, as a result of the application of EU public procurement rules, has increased the use of posted workers, or the transfer of jobs from one Member State to another. In such cases there is a complex interaction between provisions in the EU's Public Procurement Directive, now 2014/24, which allow for contract compliance in public works contracts concerning, *inter alia*, 'social and employment-related' considerations,[129] and the PWD, where the point of reference is only the 'hard core' terms and conditions.

12.3.2 Case Law

12.3.2.1 Laval, Commission v. Luxembourg *and* Rüffert: *Preventing or Promoting Social Dumping?*

In the short period from December 2007 to June 2008 the Court delivered a trilogy of powerful judgments – *Laval*,[130] *Commission v. Luxembourg*,[131] *Rüffert*[132] – that collectively demonstrate that the Court mainly views the PWD through the lens of free movement of services and not labour law. Indeed, following these cases, the PWD is so constrained in its application that, in its present form, and in isolation, it offers very limited potential to be used by the host Member State to prevent social dumping and may even be promoting it.

---

127. European Parliament, *ibid*, 9.
128. *Ibid*. 21.
129. Directive 2014/24/EU of the European Parliament and of the Council of 26 February 2014 on public procurement and repealing Directive 2004/18/EC, OJ L 94, 28.3.2014, 65–242, Art. 70 (replacing Art. 26 of Directive 2004/18).
130. Case C-341/05 *Laval un Partneri Ltd v. Svenska Byggnadsarbetareförbundet, Svenska Byggnadsarbetareförbundets avdelning 1, Byggettan and Svenska Elektrikerförbundet*, EU:C:2007:809.
131. Case C-319/06 *Commission v. Luxembourg*, EU:C:2008:350.
132. Case C-346/06 *Dirk Rüffert v. Land Niedersachsen*, EU:C:2008:189.

Any discussion of the Court's case law on the PWD has to begin with *Laval*,[133] a reference from the Swedish Labour Court issued by the Grand Chamber as a Christmas surprise on 18 December 2007. It is a case that has come to symbolise the free movement of services versus labour rights conundrum and when, ultimately, liberalised services won out, it led to demands to strengthen the PWD that continue to reverberate to this day.

Laval is mainly known, along with *Viking*,[134] its sister case on freedom of establishment, for its restrictive approach to the rights of trade unions to engage in collective action to resist the posting of workers on lower terms and conditions of employment than workers of the home Member State and other forms of social dumping.[135] For the purposes of this chapter, however, the main focus is on the extent to which national norms, including those derived from collective agreements, can be used to minimise differences between posted workers and workers of the host Member State or even to equalise labour standards.

Laval is a textbook case on the complex challenges of regulating the law on posted workers in the context of strongly contested single market rules on opening up public works' contracts for building work. It pitted the laws and industrial relations traditions of Sweden, a Member State mainly receiving posted workers, against the laws of Latvia, a mainly posting Member State that had recently joined the Union.[136] Swedish legislation implementing the Directive did not fix minimum rates of pay for posted workers and had no express provisions concerning the application of the terms and conditions in collective agreements in respect of building work. This approach reflected the Swedish and wider Nordic model of labour law in which as much autonomy as possible is left to management and labour to negotiate their own legally binding agreements.

Laval was a Latvian company that posted workers to Sweden to work on building sites operated by a Swedish company. Laval had signed a collective agreement with a Latvian construction union setting, *inter alia*, levels of pay. The posted workers were paid about 40% less than comparable Swedish workers who were covered by the national collective agreement for the construction sector.[137] Over a six-month period, Laval was responsible for a contract to build a school. The Swedish trade unions sought to extend the domestic collective agreement to Laval's workers. This collective agreement included not only rates of pay but also, *inter alia*, a 'special building supplement' to pay for insurance. One of the Swedish unions, Bygettan, threatened industrial action directed against Laval if they did not agree to a wage level for the workers based

---

133. Case C-341/05 *Laval un Partneri Ltd v. Svenska Byggnadsarbetareförbundet, Svenska Byggnadsarbetareförbundets avdelning 1, Byggettan and Svenska Elektrikerförbundet*, EU:C:2007:809.
134. Case C-438/05 *International Transport Workers' Federation and Finnish Seamen's Union v. Viking Line ABP and OÜ Viking Line Eesti*, EU:C:2007:772.
135. Such as the reflagging of ships in *Viking*, *ibid*.
136. Latvia joined the EU on 1 May 2004. Sweden had joined the EU nearly a decade earlier in 1995.
137. *See* Barnard, *supra* n. 17, at 223.

on Bygettan's estimate of average wages in the sector. When these negotiations were unsuccessful, the unions instigated a blockade of the building site that, when followed by sympathy action, made it impossible for Laval to perform the contract. The police would not intervene, as the industrial action was lawful under Swedish law. Eventually the workers returned to Latvia. Laval brought an action before the Swedish Labour Court seeking compensation directly from the unions for the damage suffered.

The central question referred to the Court was whether it is compatible with the freedom to provide services and the PWD for trade unions to attempt, by means of collective action, to force a foreign provider of services to sign a collective agreement in the host country with respect to terms and conditions of employment. In its reply, the Court emphasised that Member States have discretion to freely define the content of the 'hard core' of mandatory rules so long as their rules are compatible with EU law.[138] In the case of Sweden, the requirements in Article 3(1) regarding minimum rates of pay for posted workers were not laid down either by national law or an applicable collective agreement, and yet the dispute revolved around a requirement imposed on Laval to negotiate with trade unions on wage levels and to sign a collective agreement. Referring to Article 3(8), concerning collective agreements, the Court noted that it is possible for national rules in the construction sector to be based on rules that are 'generally applicable' to all similar undertakings in the industry concerned, covering the matters listed in Article 3(1), but this approach must be based on equality of treatment between national undertakings and undertakings that post workers from abroad.[139] The position was, therefore, quite different in Sweden from certain other Member States that have national laws or universally applicable collective agreements that guarantee such equality of treatment. In the absence of such provisions, the Court reasoned, Swedish law might still comply with the PWD so long as it did not hinder the provision of services between Member States.[140] Article 3(1), however, only refers to minimum rates of pay, but what the trade unions were seeking to impose was the whole framework of the Swedish system for pay in the sector. Because the minimum rates of pay were not determined by Swedish law, and the attempt to extend the collective agreement was applicable only to Laval and not to other undertakings in the construction sector, the Court concluded that Articles 3(1) and 3(8) did not entitle Sweden to impose wage negotiations on individual undertakings.[141]

Next the Court turned to the general aim of the Directive to provide for a 'climate of fair competition' between national undertakings and undertakings that provide services transnationally. According to the Court, the rules in Article 3(1), in relation to terms and conditions of employment, prevent service providers that post workers from other Member States from competing unfairly

---

138. *Laval*, para. 60.
139. *Laval*, paras 65–66.
140. *Laval*, para. 68.
141. *Laval*, para. 71.

against undertakings of the host Member State if the level of social protection in the host Member State is higher.[142] The workers concerned can then enjoy those better terms and conditions in the host Member State. However, the Court ruled that the provision in Article 3(7) allowing for 'more favourable' terms cannot be interpreted as allowing the host Member State to make the provision of services in its territory 'conditional' on the observance of terms and conditions of employment 'which go beyond the mandatory rules for minimum protection' in Article 3(1).[143] The Court proceeded to crystallise a new test that effectively boxes in Article 3(1) and (7) to protect service providers as follows:[144]

> the level of protection which must be guaranteed to workers posted to the territory of the host Member State is limited, in principle, to that provided for in [Article 3(1)(a)-(g)], unless, pursuant to the law or collective agreements *in the Member State of origin*, those workers already enjoy more favourable terms and conditions of employment as regards the matters referred to in that provision.

Article 3(7) is not, therefore, a weapon that can be used to prevent social dumping. Moreover, the public policy exception in Article 3(10) could not be called in aid either. Sweden had not had recourse to it in its implementing legislation and therefore it was not possible to include matters such as the insurance supplement because it had chosen to leave this to management and labour. The social partners are not bodies governed by public law and hence the trade unions could not avail themselves of that provision by citing grounds of public policy in order to maintain collective action.[145]

The Court proceeded to address collective action from the perspective of EU single market law. Emphasising that the free movement of services guarantee is one of the fundamental principles of EU law, the Court held that collective action by trade unions was a restriction on free movement that could only be warranted if it pursues a legitimate objective compatible with the treaties and is justified by overriding reasons of public interest.[146] The Court recognised that the right to take collective action for the protection of host State workers against 'possible social dumping may constitute an overriding reason of public interest', namely the protection of the interests of workers, which, if exercised proportionately, was capable of justifying a restriction on the free movement of services.[147] However, having adopted a restrictive approach to the scope of Article 3(1), the Court concluded that the collective action, specifically the blockade, had been taken for the purpose of forcing a provider of services established in another Member State to enter into negotiations with the Swedish union on rates of pay for posted workers and to sign a collective agreement, the terms of which laid

---

142. *Laval*, para. 75.
143. *Laval*, para. 80.
144. *Laval*, para. 81.
145. *Laval*, paras 82–84.
146. *Laval*, para. 101.
147. *Laval*, para. 105.

down more favourable conditions than those resulting from the relevant legislative provisions, while other terms, such as the insurance supplement, related to matters not referred to in Article 3(1). Also, Sweden had not activated Article 3(10) to extend the scope of protection. The Court held that, even though the trade unions were private parties, the form of collective action they had taken was precluded by both Article 56 TFEU and the PWD and could not be objectively justified.[148] Bizarrely the trade union could be held responsible for the impact of their collective action on free movement of services as though they were akin to a public body but, for the purposes of Article 3(10), as outlined above, they could not make 'public policy' even in a system that granted them autonomy to negotiate legally binding norms.

In its ruling in *Laval*, the Court took an extremely restrictive and, in many ways, unbalanced view of the protective provisions of the PWD vis-à-vis free movement of services. As a coordination rather than harmonisation measure, the PWD leaves considerable flexibility for host Member States to apply the 'hard core' rules in a fashion that fits with their own system of labour law and industrial relations with a view to 'guaranteeing respect for the rights of workers'.[149] Sweden, in accordance with the traditions of its system, had abstained from detailed regulation in order to allow for collective bargaining and, subject to certain restrictions, collective action was lawful. In this regard, the Court's restrictive approach to Article 3(7) and (10), provisions that might allow for stronger and wider protective employment measures, is problematic. Undoubtedly, the method of collective action in *Laval*, its impact on the enterprise and the workers concerned, and the breadth of equal treatment that the trade union was seeking, made this a hard case for the Court, which had, as its main reference point, the Union's fundamental economic freedoms. It would have been open for the Court to uphold the Swedish method of flexible implementation of the PWD and interpret Article 3 more broadly so as to avoid interfering with its labour law system, but still find that the method chosen by the unions was a disproportionate exercise of their members' right to take collective action.[150] Instead, as Catherine Barnard observes, the Court 'came close to making Article 3(1) not a floor but a ceiling'.[151] So long as the 'hard core' of mandatory rules' is applied by the host Member State there is deemed to be no unfair competition. Hence, as Jonas Malmberg notes, 'the idea of equal treatment of domestic and foreign service providers has been rejected in favour of *a principle of minimum protection*'.[152]

Before *Laval* it would perhaps seem obvious for a Member State to simply extend its domestic labour laws or applicable collective agreements to posted workers *en bloc* so as to cover the areas included in Article 3(1) and other

---

148. *Laval*, para. 111.
149. Directive 96/71, recital 5.
150. Charter of the Fundamental Rights of the EU, Art. 28.
151. Barnard, *supra* n. 17, at 224.
152. Malmberg, *supra* n. 99, at 8.

'matters' concerning terms and conditions of employment under the first indent of Article 3(10), as 'public policy provisions' on the basis that if such measures are compatible with EU law and ensure equality of treatment between home and host Member State undertakings, those other 'matters' are not precluded.[153] An all-embracing approach would provide consistency for all service providers and workers based on comprehensive equal treatment under labour law and would prevent social dumping. This was essentially the method of implementation adopted by Luxembourg, which relied primarily on Article 3(10),[154] as the basis for extending the whole body of its labour law, including collective agreements, to posted workers as 'mandatory provisions falling under national public policy'.[155] However, this broad method of implementation was contested by the Commission in an infringement action, *Commission v. Luxembourg*,[156] seeking to have the Luxembourg law declared invalid on the grounds that it went beyond the mandatory rules for 'minimum protection' in Article 3(1) and would, in practice, put service providers from other Member States, who would be unfamiliar with Luxembourg law, at a disadvantage, amounting to a discriminatory restriction on the free movement of services. Luxembourg contended that its labour laws were, collectively, provisions of 'public policy' that ensured equality of treatment between undertakings falling within the exception permitted by Article 3(10). The Commission countered that the notion of public policy could not be used by a Member State to unilaterally impose all mandatory provisions of its employment law.

In its judgment the Court went even further than it had in *Laval* in its strict approach to the scope of Article 3(1) by proclaiming that it 'sets out an exhaustive list of the matters in respect of which the Member States may give priority to the rules in force in the host Member State'.[157] This is somewhat incongruous given the reference in Article 3(10), first indent, to Member States not being precluded from adopting laws based on equality of treatment between undertakings, concerning terms and conditions of employment 'on matters other than those' referred to in Article 3(1) 'in the case of public policy provisions', which, in the light of the context of the PWD, relate to the protection of workers' interests. Luxembourg's case was that the body of its national labour law was 'public policy' by reference to what is now Article 9(2) of the Rome I Regulation,

---

153. Luxembourg's case was not helped by additional rules requiring a prior notification procedure for certain types of posting and also requiring documents necessary for monitoring purposes to be retained by an ad hoc agent registered in Luxembourg. It was inevitable that such a rule would be found likely to inhibit service providers from other Member States and be contrary to TFEU Art. 56. See Case C-319/06 *Commission v. Luxembourg*, EU:C:2008:350, paras 75–84.
154. Luxembourg also declared laws resulting from collective agreements to be universally applicable under Art. 1 of the Law of 20 December 2002, *Commission v. Luxembourg*, para. 4.
155. *Commission v. Luxembourg*, para. 4.
156. *Commission v. Luxembourg*, para. 4.
157. *Commission v. Luxembourg*, para. 26.

which authorises 'overriding mandatory provisions' of national law superseding the contract law of the home Member State.[158] The term 'overriding mandatory provisions' is defined in Article 9(1) of that Regulation as 'provisions the respect for which is regarded as crucial by a country for safeguarding its public interests, such as its political, social or economic organisation, to such an extent that they are applicable to any situation falling within their scope'.[159]

This argument did not help Luxembourg. The Court interpreted the first indent of Article 3(10) and the derogation in Article 9(2) of the Regulation as having an essentially identical application. This was not surprising as the Court's own previous case law in *Arblade*,[160] on the meaning of the 'public policy' exception to free movement of services,[161] was the basis for the text of Article 9(1) of the revised Regulation.[162] The Court applied *Arblade* directly by recalling its dictum that 'public-order legislation' applies to 'national provisions compliance with which has been deemed to be so crucial for the protection of the political, social or economic order in the Member State concerned as to require compliance therewith by all persons present on the national territory of that Member State and all legal relationships within that State'.[163] According to the Court, it followed that the term 'public policy', located in an EU legislative act within the framework of the provision of services, was 'a derogation from the fundamental principle of freedom to provide services which must be interpreted strictly, the scope of which cannot be determined unilaterally by the Member States'.[164] In light of the above, as the first indent of Article 3(10) is a derogation from the principle that the matters to be covered by laws and/or applicable collective agreements in the Member States are set out in the exhaustive list in Article 3(1), it must be interpreted strictly.[165]

In support of this interpretation the Court made express reference to Declaration No 10 on Article 3(10) of the Directive, which was recorded in the minutes of the Council of the EU as follows:[166]

> The Council and Commission stated: 'the expression 'public policy provisions' should be construed as covering those mandatory rules from which there can be no derogation and which, by their nature and objective, meet the

---

158. *See supra* n. 102.
159. *Ibid.*
160. Case C-369/96 *Criminal proceedings against Jean-Claude Arblade and Arblade & Fils SARL* and Case C-376/96 *Bernard Leloup, Serge Leloup and Sofrage SARL*, EU:C:1999:575.
161. TFEU Arts 62 and 52(1).
162. *See* Barnard, *supra* n. 17, at 230.
163. *Commission v. Luxembourg*, para. 29, applying *Arblade, supra* n. 160, at para. 30.
164. *Commission v. Luxembourg*, para. 30, applying Case C-503/03 *Commission v. Spain* [2006] ECR I-1097.
165. *Commission v. Luxembourg*, para. 31. The Court also found, at para. 65, that, to the extent that Art. 3(10) could be applied, provisions concerning collective agreements could fall under the definition of 'public policy'.
166. *Commission v. Luxembourg*, para. 31.

imperative requirements of the public interest. These may include, in particular the prohibition of forced labour or the involvement of public authorities in monitoring compliance with legislation on working conditions.

This Declaration has no formal legal status and was not published in the EU's Official Journal. As a unilateral declaration of intent, it is best described as a *travaux préparatoires* given formal recognition by these institutions at the final legislative stage.[167] In recent years, *travaux préparatoires* have become an increasingly important part of the Court's approach to interpretation, in particular in cases where the documentation is publicly accessible and there is a clear statement of intent.[168] With regard to a declaration of this kind, the Court has previously held that such declarations can be excluded where no reference is made to the content of the declaration in the wording of the provision in question.[169] Nevertheless, the Advocate General observed that, in his opinion, notwithstanding the lack of a reference to the Declaration in the text of the Directive, it is 'in conformity with the case-law developed by the Court on the inherent limits on the fundamental freedoms which are also applicable to cases of transnational posting of workers'[170] and, on this basis, it was admissible as an aid to interpretation. It is submitted that, in the absence of publication and express reference, this is an extremely shaky basis for such strong reliance by the Court and it has the potential to further shrink the scope for application of the first indent of Article 3(10). Moreover, the Court made no reference to recital 34 of the Rome I Regulation which makes express reference to the overriding mandatory provisions of the country to which workers are posted in the context of the PWD.[171] This implies that labour law provisions should be capable of falling within the scope of 'public policy' under the first indent of Article 3(10) indicating, at the very least, that the provision should be interpreted on a case by case basis and recital 34 should be taken into account.

Next the Court addressed a requirement in Luxembourg law relating to the automatic adjustment of rates of remuneration to the cost of living. Increasing the minimum wage by the cost of living fell squarely within 'minimum rates of pay' in Article 3(1)(c) but the indexation concerned all wages including those

---

167. See Eur-Lex, 'Preparatory acts': http://eur-lex.europa.eu/collection/eu-law/pre-acts.html
168. Koen Lenaerts, José A. Gutiérrez-Fons, *To Say What the Law of the EU Is: Methods of Interpretation and the European Court of Justice*, AEL 2013/9, Working Paper (Academy of European Law, European University Institute) 19–24: http://cadmus.eui.eu/bitstream/handle/1814/28339/AEL_2013_09_DL.pdf
169. *Commission v. Luxembourg*, Opinion of Advocate General Trstenjak, EU:C:2007:516, para. 45, citing: Case 429/85 *Commission v. Italy* [1988] ECR 843, para. 9; Case C-292/89 *Antonissen* [1991] ECR I-745, para. 18; Case C-329/95 *VAG Sverige* [1997] ECR I-2675, para. 23; and Case C-368/96 *Generics (UK) and Others* [1998] ECR I-7967, paras 25 to 28.
170. *Commission v. Luxembourg*, judgment, para. 45.
171. The recital states that: 'The rule on individual employment contracts should not prejudice the application of the overriding mandatory provisions of the country to which a worker is posted in accordance with Directive 96/71'. *See* further, Barnard (n. 17) 232.

above the minimum wage.[172] Once again the Court's reading was very strict. It found that the intention of the EU legislature was to limit intervention of Member States on the minimum rates of pay. It followed that the automatic adjustment of rates of pay other than the minimum wage fell outside the scope of Article 3(1)(c). The Court was not prepared to countenance any intention on the part of the Member States to allow for an interpretation of 'minimum rates of pay' that did not equate with the national or sectoral 'minimum wage', effectively lowering the ceiling further on Article 3(1). In a similar vein the Court found separately that rules governing equal treatment for part-time and fixed-term workers did not fall within Article 3(1) as these matters were not specifically listed therein, notwithstanding that there is a reference in Article 3(1)(g) to 'other provisions on non-discrimination'.[173]

Also, the wage indexation or living wage requirement could not be saved as a 'public policy' provision under the first indent of Article 3(10). Luxembourg had sought to justify it as aimed at ensuring 'good labour relations' and, on that basis, constituting a public policy imperative by protecting workers from the effects of inflation.[174] However, the Court took an even narrower view of 'public policy' noting that while Member States are, in principle, 'free to determine the requirements of public policy in the light of national needs, the notion of public policy in the [EU] context ... may be relied on only if there is a genuine and sufficiently serious threat to a fundamental interest of society'.[175] As Catherine Barnard has observed, this test is based on case law on justifications for deporting EU citizens 'transplanted ... to the very different context of labour law'.[176] Such an 'extraordinarily high standard', she adds, would perhaps only cover laws against slavery, referred to in Declaration No 10, and would be likely to exclude laws on, *inter alia*, freedom of association and collective bargaining, data protection and possibly even elimination of exploitative forms of child labour and forced labour.[177]

Moreover, the reasons invoked by a Member State to justify utilising the public policy exception must be accompanied by appropriate evidence or analysis of the expediency and proportionality of the measure in question and precise evidence to substantiate its position.[178] In this case, the Court found that Luxembourg had put forward generalised justifications, 'without adducing any evidence to enable the necessity for and the proportionality of the measures adopted to be evaluated'.[179] The Court held that this defence was insufficient to satisfy the strict requirements of the public policy exception.[180]

---

172. *Commission v. Luxembourg*, para. 45.
173. *Commission v. Luxembourg*, paras 54–55. *See* Barnard's critique, *supra* n. 17, at 233.
174. *Commission v. Luxembourg*, para. 48.
175. *Commission v. Luxembourg*, para. 50.
176. Barnard, *supra* n. 17, at 232.
177. *Ibid.* 232–233.
178. *Commission v. Luxembourg*, paras 50–51.
179. *Commission v. Luxembourg*, para. 53.
180. *Commission v. Luxembourg*, para. 55.

Finally, the Court addressed the use of collective agreements as 'public policy provisions' under the first indent of Article 3(10). The Court found that Luxembourg's approach was too wide-ranging. Although provisions in collective agreements could fall under this provision, it could not be used to apply the body of national collective agreements in their entirety.[181] Also, Luxembourg could not rely on the second indent of Article 3(10) as an alternative because this only applied to collective agreements that were 'universally applicable' which means, under Article 3(8), that they must be observed by all undertakings in all sectors,[182] which was not the case.[183]

The next case, Rüffert,[184] was the first of several challenges to social clauses contained in public procurement laws of German states and cities. The dispute arose when Lower Saxony awarded a contract to build a prison to Objekt und Bauregie (OuB) subject to a requirement in the tender that they must pay at least the minimum wage to construction workers pursuant to the collective agreement in force in the building and public works sector. OuB used a subcontractor based in Poland to carry out the work. After an investigation, the contract was terminated on the grounds that OuB had failed to fulfil its contractual obligation to comply with the collective agreement on the grounds that fifty-three posted workers on the building site were being paid less than 50% of the minimum wage laid down in the collective agreement.

The single question before the Court was, in essence, whether the requirement, when submitting tenders for building contracts, to pay at least the remuneration prescribed by the collective agreement in force at the place where those services were performed, amounted to an unjustified restriction on the freedom to provide services contrary to Article 56 TFEU?[185]

Even though the question was silent on the subject of posted workers, the Court decided that it was necessary to take the PWD into consideration because the subject matter fell within the scope of Article 1(3)(a) concerning the posting of workers, who are in an employment relationship with an undertaking, to a host Member State directly under a contract concluded between that undertaking and the party for whom the services are intended.[186] The fact that Lower Saxony's legislation was not intended to govern the posting of workers did not preclude a situation coming within the scope of the PWD.[187] Having established the locus of the case under the PWD, the next issue was to determine the status of the collective agreement, which was the means used to 'fix' the 'minimum rates of pay' as a guaranteed term and condition applicable to the posted

---

181. *Commission v. Luxembourg*, paras 64–65.
182. *See supra* n. 116.
183. *Commission v. Luxembourg*, para. 67.
184. Case C-346/06 *Dirk Rüffert v. Land Niedersachsen*, EU:C:2008:189.
185. *Rüffert*, para. 16.
186. *Rüffert*, paras 18–19.
187. *Rüffert*, para. 20.

workers.[188] In accordance with the second indent of Article 3(1), which concerns activities in the building work sector, it was necessary for this purpose for the collective agreement to be declared 'universally applicable' as defined in Article 3(8).

As the Court noted, there are two means by which a collective agreement can be regarded as 'universally applicable' under Article 3(8). Under the first subparagraph, 'universally applicable' collective agreements or arbitration awards are those that must be observed by all undertakings in the geographical area and in the profession or industry concerned.[189] Under the second subparagraph, in the absence of a system for declaring collective agreements to be of universal application, the possibility exists to base them on collective agreements or arbitration awards that are 'generally applicable' to all similar undertakings in the profession or industry concerned or agreements that have been concluded by the most representative employers' and labour organisations at the national level and are applied throughout the national territory.[190]

It was therefore necessary to establish whether the rates of pay had been fixed in accordance with one of these procedures. In relation to the first procedure, the national law implementing the PWD extended the application of provisions on minimum wages in collective agreements, which had been declared universally applicable, to employers established in other Member States which had posted workers to Germany. However, the collective agreement referring to Lower Saxony's law had neither been declared universally applicable, nor was their evidence that it was capable of being treated as such.[191] With regard to the second procedure, the Court held that it applies only where there is no system for declaring collective agreements to be of universal application, which was not the case in Germany.[192] In any event it would not have fallen within that procedure because it was not 'generally applicable', because its binding effect covered only part of the construction sector falling within the geographical area of the agreement as it only applied to public contracts.[193] As the collective agreement did not meet either of these requirements it could not be used to impose the rate of minimum pay on undertakings established in other Member States.[194]

With Article 3(1) precluded, the only fall back appeared to be Article 3(7), allowing for 'terms and conditions of employment which are more favourable for workers'. This was a possibility instantly rejected by the Court, which explained that, having already found the rate of pay set under the collective

---

188. *Rüffert*, para. 21. The Court also noted, at para. 24, that the regional legislation on the award of public contracts did not, of itself, fix the minimum rates of pay and therefore it was not a 'law' within the meaning of the first indent of Directive 96/71, Art. 3(1).
189. *Rüffert*, para. 21.
190. *Rüffert*, para. 22.
191. *Rüffert*, paras 25–27.
192. *Rüffert*, para. 28.
193. *Rüffert*, para. 29.
194. *Rüffert*, paras 30–31.

agreement to be outside Article 3(1), the 'more favourable' clause could not be used to impose it as a condition on providers of services from other Member States.[195] The host Member State is not 'entitled' to require undertakings to observe a degree of protection for workers beyond the matters listed in Article 3(1).[196] It would be different, however, if undertakings established in another Member State were to sign, of their own accord, a collective agreement in a host Member State the terms of which were more favourable.[197]

Making reference again to the ceiling imposed in *Laval*, the Court reiterated that, with the exception of the unusual instance of more favourable provisions emanating from the home Member State, there was no prospect 'in principle' of using Article 3(7) to enhance the minimum protection offered by Article 3(1)(a)–(g).[198] The point of 'principle' being economic – the rights of transnational services providers to unencumbered market access – ahead of the social, protection of the interests of workers both posted and domestic. Indeed, the Court went further, stating that the law of Lower Saxony was so restrictive on service providers from Member States where levels of pay were lower, that it 'may impose ... an additional economic burden that may prohibit, impede or render less attractive the provision of their services in the host Member State'. It followed that 'it cannot be considered to be justified by the objective of ensuring the protection of workers'. In these few words the Court in *Rüffert*, far from preventing social dumping, has effectively endorsed it, in the form of levelling down wages, as a price worth paying for opening of public work contracts and liberalising the market.

Finally, the Court took a direct swipe at the whole concept of ethical clauses in public works contracts citing a lack of evidence to support a policy applying such clauses solely to public contracts.[199] It made no mention of the EU public procurement rules because, on the facts, the situation was confined to the posting of workers.[200] It also found that such a restrictive measure could not be supported by the arguments put forward by Lower Saxony based on, firstly, protecting independence in the organisation of working life by trade unions, and secondly, ensuring the financial balance of social security systems, which are dependent on the level of wages, as an overriding interest.[201]

Rüffert, along with *Laval* and *Commission v. Luxembourg*, represent, collectively, an unwarranted intrusion into the autonomy of domestic labour law systems that have evolved as part of the social consensus in Member States at

---

195. *Rüffert*, para. 35.
196. *Rüffert*, para. 33, applying *Laval* para. 80.
197. *Rüffert*, para. 34.
198. *Rüffert*, para. 34, applying *Laval*, para. 81.
199. *Rüffert*, para. 40.
200. Sue Arrowsmith and Peter Kunzlik (eds), *Social and Environmental Policies in EC Procurement Law* Introduction, 6 (Cambridge 2009). For further analysis on this point, *see* Aristea Koukiadaki, *The Far-Reaching Implications of the Laval Quartet: The Case of the UK living Wage* (2014) 43 *International Law of Jouranl* 91, 101.
201. *Rüffert*, paras 41–42.

national, regional and sectoral levels. It is remarkable, and perhaps ironic, that whereas the social policy provisions in the Treaty on the Functioning of the European Union (TFEU) require that EU measures must 'take account of the diverse form of national practices, in particular in the field of contractual relations',[202] the free movement of services provisions, as the source of the Directive, have been applied as a blunt instrument by the Court, supported by the Commission, to Europeanise those social policy practices and relations that are regarded as restrictive. This logic applies even in cases where the measures are introduced for social reasons, such as guaranteeing the minimum wage, but the impact on posted workers is incidental. In its response to *Rüffert*, the European Trade Union Confederation (ETUC) remarked that the judgment was an 'open invitation for social dumping, which will not only threaten workers' rights and working conditions but also the capacity of local (small and medium) enterprises to compete on a level playing field with foreign (sub)contractors'.[203]

Rüffert has had a significant impact on the system of public procurement favoured by many federal states in Germany and more widely throughout the Union.[204] The extent to which it is a problem depends on the national system. For example, in Finland, the national law on employment contracts, which is declared as 'universally applicable', places an obligation on employers to observe the provisions of a national collective agreement considered representative in the sector in question on the terms and conditions of the employment relationship including a minimum wage to be paid to posted workers. In the subsequent Finnish case, *ESA*,[205] the relevant collective agreement for construction workers in the electricity sector, which included a minimum wage for posted workers, was found by the Court to be 'universally applicable' within the meaning of the second indent of Article 3(1) and Article 3(8), and therefore *Rüffert* could be distinguished.

The Finnish approach does not fit with the German constitutional system, which favours decentralisation to the federal state level. Detlef Sack points to three reforming responses in Germany.[206] First, several federal states have abolished state-specific contract compliance laws. Second, other federal states, including Lower Saxony, have amended their laws, in line with the Court's jurisprudence, to ensure that these laws are consistent with the 'hard core' of protection in the PWD. Third, certain federal states have repackaged their

---

202. TFEU, Art. 151.
203. ETUC, 'Rüffert case: ETUC warns that ECJ's judgement is destructive and damaging' (Press Release, 3 April 2008): https://www.etuc.org/press/rüffert-case-etuc-warns-ecj's-judgement-destructive-and-damaging.
204. *See* Detlef Sack, 'Europeanization Through Law, Compliance, and Party Differences – The ECJ's 'Rüffert' Judgment (C-346/06) and Amendments to Public Procurement Laws in German Federal States' (2012) 34/3 *European Integration* 241.
205. Case C-396/13 *Sähköalojen ammattiliitto ry v. Elektrobudowa Spolka Akcyjna (ESA)*, EU:C:2015:86.
206. Sack, *supra* n. 204, at 253.

contract compliance requirements to fit with the regime of EU public procurement. It is to the third of these responses that I shall now turn with reference to two recent cases referred from German courts that highlight the interplay between the laws on posted workers and public procurement.

12.3.2.2 Bundesruckerei *and* RegioPost: *Posted Workers and Public Procurement – Tilting the Balance Towards the Social?*

Public procurement as a concept encompasses 'the purchasing by government from private sector contractors, usually on the basis of competitive bidding, of goods and services that government needs'.[207] The EU public procurement regime provides minimum harmonised rules for the purchase of services, works and supplies by public authorities whose monetary value exceeds a specified European-level threshold in order to create a level playing field for all enterprises across the Union.[208] By means of the public procurement rules, the EU seeks, *inter alia*, to facilitate better use of public procurement through strategic use of public contracts and promote participation of small and medium-sized enterprises. It therefore recognises the important contribution of public authorities in driving forward the single market programme. The relevant instrument applicable at the time of the two cases discussed in this section was Directive 2004/18 on the coordination of procedures for the award of public work contracts, public supply contracts and public service contracts.[209] Directive 2004/18 has now been repealed and replaced by Directive 2014/24.[210] Under Article 1 of Directive 2004/18 contracting authorities 'shall treat economic operators equally and non-discriminatorily and shall act in a transparent way'. Article 26 provides that:

> Contracting authorities may lay down special conditions relating to the performance of a contract, provided that these are compatible with [Union] law and are indicated in the contract notice or in the specifications. The

---

207. Christopher McCrudden, *Buying Social Justice: Equality, Government Procurement, and Legal Change* 3 (Oxford 2007). In EU law, 'public procurement' is defined as 'the acquisition by means of a public contract of works, supplies or services by one or more contracting authorities from economic operators chosen by those contracting authorities, whether or not the works, supplies or services are intended for a public purpose': Directive 2014/24/EU of the European Parliament and of the Council of 26 February 2014 on public procurement and repealing Directive 2004/18/EC, OJ L 94, 28.3.2014, 65–242, Art. 1(2).
208. European Commission, 'Public Procurement': https://ec.europa.eu/growth/single-market/public-procurement_en. *See* further, Sue Arrowsmith and Peter Kunzlik (eds), *Social and Environmental Policies in EC Procurement Law* (Cambridge 2009).
209. Directive 2004/18/EC of the European Parliament and of the Council of 31 March 2004 on the coordination of procedures for the award of public works contracts, public supply contracts and public service contracts OJ L 134, 30.4.2004, 114–240. For detailed analysis, *see* Catherine Barnard, *Using Procurement Law to Enforce Labour Standards* in Guy Davidov and Brian Langille (eds), *The Idea of Labour Law,* 256 (Oxford 2011).
210. Directive 2014/24/EU of the European Parliament and of the Council of 26 February 2014 on public procurement and repealing Directive 2004/18/EC, OJ L 94, 28.3.2014, 65–242.

conditions governing the performance of a contract may, in particular, concern social and environmental considerations.

This provision has now been replaced by Article 70 of Directive 2014/24 which has been amended to specifically include, *inter alia*, 'employment related considerations' in the final sentence. As Éric Van den Abeele has noted, Article 26 (now Article 70) is part of a framework designed 'to integrate strong social and environmental dimensions and include provisions favourable to employment in the public procurement rules'.[211] Article 26 was relied on by German public authorities in two cases: *Bundesruckerei*[212] and *RegioPost*.[213]

The context of *Bundesruckerei* was as follows. In 2012, the Land of North Rhine-Westphalia introduced a law on compliance with collective agreements, social norms and fair competition in the award of public contracts. This law fell within the third category of responses to *Rüffert* identified by Sack, above.[214] It distinguished between, *inter alia*, those public service contracts within the scope of the application of the law on posted workers, which essentially replicated the 'hard core' terms and conditions in the PWD, and other public contracts, not covered by the posted workers law, which could only be awarded to undertakings which, at the time of submission of the tender, had agreed in writing to pay their workers EUR 8.62 as a minimum hourly wage for the performance of the service. The Land Rhine-Westphalian law, specifically the minimum wage rate, was applied by the City of Dortmund as a condition in a call for tenders for a public contract relating to data services for urban planning. The value of the contract, at EUR 300,000, brought the tender within the scope of Directive 2004/18 which covers higher value contracts. This means that under the EU public procurement regime, the tender must be advertised throughout the EU so as to guarantee that economic operators in the EU and the European Economic Area will be given genuine and equal opportunities to take part.[215]

Bundesruckerei, a German company, informed the City of Dortmund that, if it was awarded the contract, it would use a wholly owned subsidiary established in Poland as subcontractor. It would pay a lower wage to the workers in Poland in the light of the standard of living in that Member State. It was therefore seeking an assurance that the stipulated minimum wage would not apply to its subcontractor. The City of Dortmund was unable to give this assurance because it was bound by the Rhine-Westphalian law. Bundesruckerei brought a legal challenge against the City of Dortmund claiming that the

---

211. Éric Van den Abeele, *Integrating social and environmental dimensions in public procurement: one small step for the internal market, one giant leap for the EU?* European Trade Union Institute Working Paper 2014.08.
212. Case C-549/13 *Bundesruckerei GmbH v. Stadt Dortmund*, EU:C:2014:2235.
213. Case C-115/14 *RegioPost GmbH & Co KG v. Stadt Landau in der Pfalz*, EU:C:2015:760.
214. Sack, *supra* n. 204.
215. Kerstin Ahlberg and Niklas Bruun, *Public Procurement and Labour Law – Friends or Foes?* in Mia Rönnmar (ed.), *Labour Law, Fundamental Rights and Social Europe*, 89, 91–92 (Hart 2011).

tendering rules constituted an unjustified restriction on its freedom to provide services under Article 56 TFEU.[216] The City of Dortmund's defence was threefold. Firstly, the tender was compatible with *Rüffert*, as the requirement to pay the minimum wage was in a law consistent with the first indent of Article 3(1) of the PWD, secondly, the legislation was laid down as a 'special condition' relating to the performance of the contract in accordance with Article 26 of Directive 2004/18, cited above, and, thirdly, the statutory obligation was justified because it ensured that a reasonable wage was paid to the employees engaged for the performance of public works, which also reduced the burden on the social security system.[217]

The Court gave its judgment in September 2014. In essence, the national court had asked whether the application of the Rhine-Westphalian law to a subcontractor established in another Member State, having recourse exclusively to workers employed in that State, was precluded by Article 56 TFEU. If so, the minimum wage condition would be inapplicable.[218] It also asked about the application of the PWD but, because Bundesruckerei did not intend to perform the contract by posting the employees of its Polish subcontractor in German territory, the Court found that it was not a situation covered by one of the three transnational measures referred to in Article 1(3) of the PWD and therefore the Directive was not applicable.[219]

Turning to Article 26 of Directive 2004/18, the Court emphasised that, with reference to the language in that provision, any 'social considerations' relating to the performance of the contract could only be imposed as requirements, within the meaning of that provision, if they were 'compatible' with EU law. Once again, as EU public procurement law is based on single market objectives, the main reference point is free movement of services under Article 56 TFEU and also competition law.

The Court treated the situation as analogous to *Rüffert*. Applying the test laid down in that case, as the tenderer intended to carry out the work using subcontractors established in a Member State other than that to which the contracting authority belongs and in which minimum rates of pay were lower, this requirement 'constituted an additional economic burden that may prohibit, impede or render less attractive the provision of their services in the host Member State' and was, therefore, a restriction within the meaning of Article 56 TFEU.[220] Likewise, although such a measure might be justified in principle by the objective of protecting employees and also avoiding social dumping, the legislation of Land Rhine-Westphalia, applicable solely to public contracts, was not backed up by information 'to suggest that employees in the private sector are not in need of the same wage protection as those working in the context of public

---

216. *Bundesruckerei*, para. 13.
217. *Bundesruckerei*, para. 14.
218. *Bundesruckerei*, para. 29.
219. *Bundesruckerei*, para. 27.
220. *Bundesruckerei*, para. 30, applying *Rüffert* (n. 184), para. 37.

contracts'.[221] Also, in so far as the scope of the national legislation could extend to this situation, in which the contract was being performed in another Member State, the fact that wages were lower than in Poland, made the minimum wage requirement disproportionate.[222] It bore no relation to the cost of living in Poland and therefore prevented subcontractors established there 'from deriving a competitive advantage from the differences between the respective rates of pay, that national legislation goes beyond what is necessary to ensure that the objective of employee protection is attained'.[223] Finally, the objective of stability of social security systems could not be used to justify the minimum wage requirement because, again analogous to *Rüffert*, if the Polish workers did not receive a reasonable wage and needed to have recourse to social security, 'it would be to the Polish social assistance that they would have a right', which would not affect the German social security system.[224] It followed that the requirement in the tender was precluded by Article 56 TFEU[225] and, therefore, as it was incompatible with Union law, Article 26 of Directive 2004/18 was inapplicable.

Bundesruckerei is a case of posting in reverse with consequences that are in many respects even more negative for labour law than *Rüffert*. Labour, under the type of outsourcing proposed by the tenderers, is deterritorialised not by posting, in this instance, but by use of a subsidiary established in another Member State to shift the workspace to a national regulatory regime with lower wages. As a result, the contract compliance provisions have the reverse effect to that intended by national law. Rival tenderers proposing to use workers based in the national territory of the public procuring authority, are placed at a competitive disadvantage as they are bound by the minimum wage requirement under national law and therefore have higher costs. As the core principle of awarding contracts under Directive 2004/18 was to 'treat economic operators equally and non-discriminatorily and ... act in a transparent way',[226] it was extremely difficult for those rival tenderers to compete unless they too decided to use subcontractors established in Member States with lower costs. The effect is a kind of circular dumping of labour standards that leads to a general levelling down of wages and other terms and conditions of employment. *Rüffert* and *Bundesruckerei*, left unchecked, would create a climate of unfair competition wholly contrary to the social objectives of the EU directives under discussion. There is no doubt that this case law was influential in persuading the EU institutions to amend the principles of awarding contracts in Directive 2014/24, discussed below.

---

221. *Bundesruckerei*, paras 31–32, applying *Rüffert* (n. 184), paras 38–40.
222. *Bundesruckerei*, para. 33.
223. *Bundesruckerei*, para. 34.
224. *Bundesruckerei*, para. 35, applying, by analogy, *Rüffert* (n184), para. 42.
225. *Bundesruckerei*, para. 36.
226. Directive 2014/24, Art. 18(1).

The most recent case, *RegioPost*,[227] decided just over twelve months later, in November 2015, is an antidote to *Rüffert* and *Bundesruckerei*, and represents a significant shift in the Court's jurisprudence. The dispute arose after the town of Landau, situated in the Land of Rhineland-Palatinate, launched an EU-wide call for tenders for a public procurement contract for postal services in the municipality. Tenderers had to comply with a Rhineland-Palatinate law requiring them to guarantee a minimum wage of EUR 8.70 per hour when awarding public contracts. Specifically, when submitting the tender documents, enterprises were expected to present declarations that they and their subcontractors would pay the stipulated minimum wage. Unless the declarations were submitted the tender would be excluded from the evaluation. RegioPost did not submit a declaration with its tender, even after a reminder, but declarations by its subcontractors were submitted. When Landau refused to evaluate its tender for want of the declaration, RegioPost challenged the decision leading ultimately to a judicial referral to the Court.

In essence, the main question for the Court was whether, in a procedure for the award of a public procurement contract, tenderers and their subcontractors could be lawfully required to undertake to pay the statutory minimum hourly wage to the personnel who would be performing the work under that contract?[228] Reference was made to both Article 56 TFEU and the PWD, and also the fact that there was neither a national minimum wage, at the time of the case, nor a universally applicable collective agreement. The Court also asked whether, if the condition to pay the minimum wage met the requirements of Article 26 of Directive 2004/18, and was compatible with EU law, the tenderers would automatically be bound to pay that minimum wage rendering the declarations superfluous. Although the case might appear, at face value, to be fully covered by the *Rüffert*, *Bundesruckerei* line of case law, the referring court referred to the lively academic debate in Germany, which focused on the restrictive approach of the Court in those cases and the possibilities for refining the law at federal state level in a fashion that required payment of the applicable minimum wage as a condition for tendering to perform public contracts, in line with Article 26, and in conformity with 'hard core' of the PWD. In effect the Court was being asked to think again.

The Court found, as an initial point, that the case was admissible even though all the tenderers were established in Germany. The fact that Directive 2004/18 was applicable to the tender in this case meant that a question of interpretation of Article 26 was admissible. There was a cross-border interest because the value of the contract exceeded the threshold for the application of Directive 2004/18. An undertaking established in another Member State might have been deterred from submitting a tender by the requirement to undertake to

---

227. Case C-115/14 *RegioPost GmbH & Co KG v. Stadt Landau in der Pfalz*, EU:C:2015:760.
228. *RegioPost*, Opinion of Advocate General Mengozzi, EU:C:2015:566, para. 1.

pay the minimum wage set by the Land Rhineland-Palatinate because of lower prevailing wage levels in that Member State.[229]

Addressing the main question, the Court found that the minimum wage requirement was a 'special condition' concerning 'social considerations' for the purposes of Article 26 and its publication satisfied the procedural condition of transparency.[230] It was also neither directly or indirectly discriminatory.[231] In an important shift from its approach in *Bundesruckerei*, where the Court had considered Article 26 mainly in isolation from Directive 2004/18 as a whole, the Court ruled that where a national measure falls within a field 'exhaustively harmonised at EU level', in line with settled-case law, it 'must be assessed … in the light of the provisions of that harmonising measure and not in the light of the primary law of the European Union'.[232] However, because under Article 26 'special conditions' must be 'compatible' with EU law, the rules relating to that provision were not exhaustively enumerated and it was necessary also to consider the compatibility of the measure with primary law and other EU measures.[233] In particular, the measure had to be compatible with the minimum conditions laid down in the PWD, a requirement drawn from recital 34 of the preamble of Directive 2004/18,[234] directly linking the two provisions. Because, hypothetically, an undertaking established in another Member State, with a lower standard of living and a lower minimum wage in the sector, may have been interested in submitting a tender for the contract and envisaged posting workers to Germany, and such an undertaking might have been deterred by the minimum wage requirement, it was necessary to examine the national measure in the light of Article 3(1) of the PWD.[235]

With regard to the PWD, the Court distinguished *Rüffert* on the facts. Firstly, unlike the Law of Lower Saxony in that case, the Law of Rhineland-Palatinate laid down the minimum rate of pay bringing it within the first indent of Article 3(1) and also Article 3(1)(c), and secondly, at the time of the case, which was before Germany had introduced a national minimum wage law, national legislation did not impose a lower rate for the postal services sector.[236] Another important point of distinction was that the second indent concerning the requirement for collective agreements to be universally applicable was not relevant because this was not a contract for building works falling within that indent. As this condition did not apply, Article 3(8) was not relevant and categorisation of the Rhineland-Palatinate law under the first indent 'cannot be called into question on the basis that [it applied] to public contracts and not to

---

229. *RegioPost*, para. 51.
230. *RegioPost*, paras 54–55.
231. *RegioPost*, para. 56, referencing recital 33 of the preamble of Directive 2004/18.
232. *RegioPost*, para. 57, and the cases cited therein.
233. *RegioPost*, paras 58–59.
234. *RegioPost*, para. 60.
235. *RegioPost*, para. 61, cf Advocate General Paolo Mengozzi's Opinion, paras 51–59.
236. *RegioPost*, para. 62.

private contracts'.[237] Moreover, once again linking the PWD with Article 26 of Directive 2004/18, the Court added that, the national measure fell within the latter provision, 'which permits, subject to certain conditions, the imposition of a minimum wage in public contracts [and] that measure cannot be required to extend beyond that specified field by applying generally to all contracts, including private contracts'.[238] The Court concisely drove home the point by adding that the limitation of the scope of the measure to public contracts was 'the simple consequence of the fact that there are rules of EU law specific to that field, in this case, those laid down in Directive 2004/18'. In one bound, by firstly identifying this vital linkage between the directives and, secondly, giving precedence to the public procurement rules, based on the facts of the case, the Court was able to break free from the straightjacket it had imposed on itself in *Rüffert*.

The effect is to turn *Rüffert* on its head in cases where Article 26 (now Article 70 of Directive 2014/24) applies, thus:[239]

> It follows that Article 26 of Directive 2004/18, read in conjunction with Directive 96/71, permits the host Member State to lay down, in the context of the award of a public contract, a mandatory rule for minimum protection referred to in point (c) of the first subparagraph of Article 3(1) of that directive, such as that at issue in the main proceedings, which requires undertakings established in other Member States to comply with an obligation in respect of a minimum rate of pay for the benefit of their workers posted to the territory of the host Member State in order to perform that public contract. Such a rule is part of the level of protection which must be guaranteed to those workers.

Most significantly, in complete contrast to *Laval, Commission v. Luxembourg, Rüffert* and *Bundesruckerei*, in this specific instance, the rule prohibiting restrictions on the freedom to provide services in Article 56 TFEU, so often a negative from a labour law perspective, becomes more of a neutral factor. As the Court explains, Article 26 is to be read in the light of Article 56 TFEU 'since that directive [seeks] in particular to bring about the freedom to provide services'.[240] Viewed through this prism, although a minimum wage requirement in the context of an EU-level public procurement contract is 'capable' of constituting a restriction on the freedom to provide services, such a measure may, in principle, be justified by the objective of protecting workers.[241] Again, *Rüffert* could be distinguished. Even though *Rüffert* had appeared to rule out minimum wage rules relating solely to public contracts,[242] in that case what was at issue was a collective agreement applying solely to the construction sector that had not been

---

237. *RegioPost*, para. 63.
238. *RegioPost*, para. 64.
239. *RegioPost*, para. 66, also applying language from *Laval* (n. 133), paras 74, 80 and 81.
240. *RegioPost*, para. 67.
241. *RegioPost*, paras 69–70.
242. *RegioPost*, para. 71, referring to *Rüffert* (n. 184), paras 38–40, discussed in the previous section.

declared universally applicable.²⁴³ By contrast, in *RegioPost*, the Rhineland-Palatinate law on the minimum wage was 'a mandatory rule for minimum protection' that applied irrespective of the sector concerned and no other legislation, at the time, imposed a lower minimum wage for the postal sector. This was sufficient, in the context of the application of Article 26, to justify the measure.²⁴⁴

In briefly answering the second question in the reference, concerning the lawfulness of the declaration that Regiopost was required to sign, the Court found that such a requirement was not precluded in the light of its answer to the previous question.²⁴⁵ Once again the Court turned a possible negative into a positive from a labour law perspective. Exclusion from the evaluation for failing to supply the declaration was not a penalty, it was simply a failure to meet a requirement. Moreover, such a method was formulated 'in a particularly transparent manner' in the contract notice so as 'to emphasise, from the outset, the importance of compliance with a mandatory rule for minimum protection expressly authorised by Article 26 of Directive 2004/18'.²⁴⁶ It followed that Article 26 permitted such an exclusion which was appropriate and proportionate.²⁴⁷

After so many setbacks, *Regiopost* has been heralded as a belated stance by the Court against social dumping.²⁴⁸ Albert Sanchez-Graells observes that the Court has 'back-tracked' from its restrictive line of case law on the use of public procurement for social policy purposes but expresses concern that the judgment amounts to 'economic protectionism' and facilitates 'the politicised use of public procurement'.²⁴⁹ In my view, however, the Court has merely addressed an imbalance between the economic and the social dimensions of EU single market law. In certain, strictly circumscribed, situations it is possible to justify minimum wage requirements and other terms and conditions of employment in the tendering of higher value public contracts falling within the scope of the EU's public procurement regime so long as requirements applicable to posted workers are compatible with the PWD. *Rüffert* remains in place and continues to limit

---

243. *RegioPost*, para. 73.
244. *RegioPost*, paras 75–77.
245. *RegioPost*, para. 79.
246. *RegioPost*, para. 83.
247. *RegioPost*, paras 84–5 and 87–88, with reference to recital 34 in the preamble of Directive 2004/18 which allows for exclusion in such circumstances. The Court added, at para. 86, that the declaration imposed a 'negligible' burden on tenderers and their subcontractors.
248. *See* Daniel William Carter, 'CJEU (finally) takes stance against social dumping', Leiden Law Blog, 19 February 2016: http://leidenlawblog.nl/articles/cjeu-finally-takes-stance-against-social-dumping.
249. Albert Sanchez-Graells, *CJEU clarifies and minimises Rüffert, and expands the scope for minimum wage requirements in public procurement (C-115/14)*, How to Crack a Nut: A Blog on EU Economic law, 17 November 2015: http://www.howtocrackanut.com/blog/2015/11/cjeu-clarifies-and-minimises-ruffert.html.

measures that have an impact on posted workers in situations where either the public procurement rules are not applicable or laws or collective agreements do not satisfy the requirements in the Directive. In particular, the Court's test for universal applicability of collective agreements remains intact and would have rendered the type of minimum wage requirement relied on in *RegioPost* unlawful if the town had applied it to a construction contract.

12.3.3 Ways Forward

As the case law analysis has shown, the orientation of law on posted workers is single market law ahead of labour law, and the purpose of EU regulation is to coordinate rather than harmonise national laws. From the outset, therefore, any measure of national labour law seeking to regulate the posting of workers, or potentially impacting on them, must not infringe the principle of free movement of services. In practice this has led to a case by case rear guard action to defend the core principles and methodology of national labour laws that form part of the fabric of European social solidarity. The terms and conditions of employment in the PWD are perceived by the Court not as a reference point for upwards harmonisation, as would be the norm for social policy directives, but, instead, as an exhaustive list of rules providing a ceiling of minimum protection for posted workers who, outside of the free movement of workers' regime,[250] are only deserving of more favourable provisions in the host Member State when they already enjoy higher standards of employment protection in their *home* Member State. Preventing social dumping, which was the driving force for many Member States supporting the PWD, has been, in practice, a largely unsuccessful basis for objective justification of national rules, with the exception of *RegioPost*,[251] where the EU public procurement regime was the point of reference.

Laval,[252] *Commission v. Luxembourg*,[253] *Rüffert*,[254] and *Bundesruckerei*[255] highlight the extent of the squeeze placed by the Court on some of basic tenets of labour law in this context, including the right to take collective action, policies to ensure equality of treatment in employment contracts, and social clauses in public works contracts. Following *Rüffert*, and in response to widespread concern about the need to promote socially responsible public procurement,[256]

---

250. TFEU, Art. 45.
251. Case C-115/14 *RegioPost GmbH & Co KG v. Stadt Landau in der Pfalz*, EU:C:2015:760.
252. Case C-341/05 *Laval un Partneri Ltd v. Svenska Byggnadsarbetareförbundet, Svenska Byggnadsarbetareförbundets avdelning 1, Byggettan and Svenska Elektrikerförbundet*, EU:C:2007:809.
253. Case C-319/06 *Commission v. Luxembourg*, EU:C:2008:350.
254. Case C-346/06 *Dirk Rüffert v. Land Niedersachsen*, EU:C:2008:189.
255. Case C-549/13 *Bundesruckerei GmbH v. Stadt Dortmund*, EU:C:2014:2235.
256. *See* European Commission, *Buying Social: A Guide to Taking Account of Social Considerations in Public Procurement*, Staff Working Paper (SEC)2010 1258 final, 7. For discussion *see* Koukiadaki, *supra* n. 200, at 92.

the rules have been strengthened in Directive 2014/24.[257] In particular, environmental, social and labour considerations now form part of the principles of public procurement, as follows:[258]

> Member States shall take appropriate measures to ensure that in the performance of public contracts economic operators comply with applicable obligations in the fields of environmental, social and labour law established by Union law, national law, collective agreements or by the international environmental, social and labour law provisions listed in Annex X.

This provision, Article 18(2), has the effect of introducing a general obligation to comply with national, EU and international labour law. Annex X refers to the fundamental labour law conventions of the International Labour Organisation (ILO).[259] This is an important reference point as the ILO has been at the forefront of fostering the incorporation of social objectives into public procurement by seeking respect for minimum labour standards and seeking 'to ensure that public contracts do not exert a downward pressure on wages and working conditions'.[260]

Two paragraphs in the recitals add teeth to this provision. First, Recital 37 states, in reference to the scope of Article 18(2), and in the context of the PWD, as follows:

> With a view to an appropriate integration of environmental, social and labour requirements into public procurement procedures it is of particular importance that Member States and contracting authorities take relevant measures to ensure compliance with obligations in the fields of environmental, social and labour law that apply at the place where the works are executed or the services provided and result from laws, regulations, decrees and decisions, at both national and Union level, as well as from collective agreements, provided that such rules, and their application, comply with Union law. Equally, obligations stemming from international agreements ratified by all Member States and listed in Annex X should apply during contract performance. However, this should in no way prevent the application of terms and conditions of employment which are more favourable to workers.
>
> The relevant measures should be applied in conformity with the basic principles of Union law, in particular with a view to ensuring equal treatment. Such relevant measures should be applied in accordance with Directive 96/71/EC of the European Parliament and of the Council and in a way that ensures equal treatment and does not discriminate directly or indirectly against economic operators and workers from other Member States.

---

257. Directive 2014/24/EU of the European Parliament and of the Council of 26 February 2014 on public procurement and repealing Directive 2004/18/EC, OJ L 94, 28.3.2014, 65–242.
258. *Ibid.* Art. 18(2).
259. *Ibid.* Annex X lists the eight fundamental ILO Conventions: http://www.ilo.org/global/standards/introduction-to-international-labour-standards/conventions-and-recommendations/lang--en/index.htm.
260. ILO, *Labour Clauses in Public Contracts: Integrating the Social Dimension into Procurement Policies and Practices* (ILO 2008). See ILO Convention No. 94 of 1949 on Labour Clauses (Public Contracts). For discussion *see* Koukiadaki, *supra* n. 200, at 92.

This recital provides clarification of the application of the obligation in Article 18(2) at both national and Union level. However, where the PWD is the main frame of reference, as in *Rüffert*,[261] it is doubtful whether it will lead to any fundamental change in the law.

Also, Recital 39 provides a strong statement on the status of collective agreements as follows:

> It should also be possible to include clauses ensuring compliance with collective agreements in compliance with Union law in public contracts. Non-compliance with the relevant obligations could be considered to be grave misconduct on the part of the economic operator concerned, liable to exclusion of that economic operator from the procedure for the award of a public contract.

This clause adds weight to the interpretation of the previous Directive, 2004/18, in *RegioPost*.[262] Once again, however, it does not completely rule out a situation, such as in *Rüffert*,[263] where a restrictive interpretation of the PWD is the overriding issue on the facts. However, if both the PWD and Directive 2014/24 are in play, it is submitted that *RegioPost* is reinforced and is the preferred case to follow.

In response to widespread concerns about the inadequacy of the PWD as a mechanism to combat social dumping, and a growing awareness that the law needs to be improved,[264] the Commission published a 'targeted revision' of the Directive in March 2016.[265] One factor driving reform is an increase in postings in the EU. In 2014 there were over 1.9 million workers posted to perform service contracts amounting to 0.7% of the total EU labour force, representing increases of 10.3% on 2013 and 44.4% from 2010.

The Commission notes that some improvements will be achieved by means of the Enforcement Directive, 2014/67,[266] which reached its transposition date in June 2016. The Enforcement Directive is mainly concerned with improved administrative cooperation between national authorities in charge of posting and strengthening monitoring mechanisms at national level. It only addresses problems relating to the implementation of existing rules. It does, however, highlight the issue of so-called 'letter-box' companies that are created in Member

---

261. Case C-346/06 *Dirk Rüffert v. Land Niedersachsen*, EU:C:2008:189.
262. Case C-115/14 *RegioPost GmbH & Co KG v. Stadt Landau in der Pfalz*, EU:C:2015:760.
263. Case C-346/06 *Dirk Rüffert v. Land Niedersachsen*, EU:C:2008:189.
264. European Parliament, *supra* n. 115, at 9.
265. European Commission, 'Proposal for a Directive of the European Parliament and of the Council amending Directive 96/71/EC of The European Parliament and of the Council of 16 December 1996 concerning the posting of workers in the framework of the provision of services', COM(2016) 128 final, 8 March 2016.
266. Directive 2014/67/EU of the European Parliament and of the Council of 15 May 2014 on the enforcement of Directive 96/71/EC concerning the posting of workers in the framework of the provision of services and amending Regulation (EU) No. 1024/2012 on administrative cooperation through the Internal Market Information System ('the IMI Regulation'), OJ L 159, 28.5.2014, 11–31.

States where labour costs are low.²⁶⁷ Once established, these companies carry out little or no activity in their home country, because their main purpose is to post workers to other Member States and pay less in social security contributions. Under Article 4(2) of the Enforcement Directive, a series of factors can be used to determine whether an undertaking genuinely performs substantial activities, other than purely internal management and/or administrative activities. For example, this can be done by identifying: the place where the undertaking performs its substantial business activity and where it employs administrative staff; and the number of contracts performed and the size of the turnover.

The revision of the PWD would maintain its orientation as a single market measure and does not harmonise labour costs.²⁶⁸ The main proposed changes are as follows:

- when the anticipated or effective duration of the posting exceeds twenty-four months, the host Member State will be deemed to be the country where the work is habitually carried out. The law of the host Member State will apply to the employment contract of these long-term posted workers if no other choice of law was made by the parties;²⁶⁹
- it removes the Annex concerning building work. This has the effect of making collective agreements capable of being 'universally applicable' to posted workers in all sectors of the economy;²⁷⁰
- it replaces the reference to 'minimum rates of pay' with 'remuneration'. It is left to all Member States to apply rules on remuneration in accordance with their national law and practice;²⁷¹
- a new subparagraph is added to the listing of the mandatory rules placing an obligation on Member States to publish information on the constituent elements of remuneration;²⁷²
- a new provision concerning subcontracting chains. Member States will be permitted, subject to the principle of proportionality, to oblige undertakings to subcontract only to undertakings that grant workers certain conditions on remuneration applicable to the contractor, including those resulting from non-universally applicable collective agreements.²⁷³ The same obligations must be imposed on all national subcontractors;

---

267. European Parliament, *supra* n. 115, at 39.
268. COM(2016) 128, 4.
269. *Ibid.* Art. 2a(1). Under Art. 2a(2): 'in case of replacement of posted workers performing the same task at the same place, the cumulative duration of the posting periods of the workers shall be taken into account, with regard to workers that are posted for an effective duration of at least six months'.
270. *Ibid.* first indent of Art. 3(a)(1). The term 'universally applicable' continues to be interpreted in line with Art. 3(8).
271. *Ibid.* Art. 3(a)(1)(c).
272. *Ibid.* Art. 3(a), second subparagraph.
273. *Ibid.* Art. 3(b).

– temporary posted workers are guaranteed the terms and conditions provided for in the Temporary Agency Work Directive, 2008/104.[274]

These proposals, if implemented, would amount to a significant improvement in the law concerning posted workers. The proposed Directive would effectively provide for equality of treatment under national law for long-term posted workers. However, these long-term posted workers will continue to be in a rather anomalous position as service providers rather than 'workers' with full EU citizenship rights. Further strengthening of protection would come with the provisions on subcontracting and temporary posted workers, although there is a danger that, where it is feasible, more enterprises will resort to carrying out the performance of the service contract in the home Member State of the workers and thereby avoid the PWD, as in *Bundesruckerei*.[275]

Most contentious is the amendment to change 'minimum rates of pay' to 'remuneration' in the mandatory rules. 'Remuneration' is defined as 'all the elements of remuneration rendered mandatory by national law'. It is broadly in line with *ESA*,[276] the Finnish case, briefly discussed above, where a collective agreement with detailed rules on remuneration was found to be universally applicable and, therefore, within the scope of the PWD.[277]

The prospects for agreement on the revised PWD, on the basis of the content proposed by the Commission, do not look promising. In the Explanatory Memorandum accompanying the proposal, it is made evident that there is a clear split between countries receiving posted workers – seven Member States in northern Europe,[278] supporting 'modernisation' of the PWD; and countries exporting posted workers – nine Member States in central and Eastern Europe,[279] who argue that a review of the PWD is premature.[280] In the summer of 2016, the Commission was required to reconsider its proposal after receiving objections in reasoned opinions from parliaments in eleven Member States.[281] Under the so-called 'yellow card' procedure,[282] the Commission has been warned that, in the reasoned opinion of this group of national parliaments, the proposal is not compatible with the principle of subsidiarity,[283] as action can be

---

274. *Ibid.* Art. 3(c). *See* Directive 2008/104/EC of the European Parliament and of the Council of 19 November 2008 on temporary agency work, OJ L 327, 5.12.2008, 9–14, Art. 5.
275. Case C-549/13 *Bundesruckerei GmbH v. Stadt Dortmund*, EU:C:2014:2235.
276. Case C-396/13 *Sähköalojen ammattiliitto ry v. Elektrobudowa Spolka Akcyjna (ESA)*, EU:C:2015:86.
277. For further analysis of Directive 2014/24, *see* Van den Abeele, *supra* n. 211.
278. Austria, Belgium, France, Germany, Luxembourg, the Netherlands and Sweden.
279. Bulgaria, Czech Republic, Estonia, Hungary, Lithuania, Latvia, Poland, Slovakia and Romania.
280. European Commission (n. 265) 4–5.
281. In addition to several of the countries referred to above, n. 279, the list of objectors included the parliaments of Denmark and Croatia. *See* European Commission, COM(2016) 505 final.
282. Protocol 2 annexed to the treaties.
283. TEU, Art. 5(3).

taken at Member State level to secure the EU's objectives. Having analysed all of the objections, the Commission has resolutely concluded that action at Union level is necessary.[284] It will proceed with the proposal but it faces a difficult hurdle to secure sufficient support in the Council of the EU where a qualified majority vote is required among the Member States for the measure to be adopted.

12.4 CONCLUDING REMARKS

Analysis of the Court's case law on collective redundancies, posted workers and public procurement has demonstrated that EU labour law and social provisions in single market law, originally designed to provide a modicum of protection to workers in specific employment situations, including in contexts such as transnational restructuring and subcontracting, is no long effective in securing those objectives. EU legislation, enacted in the twentieth century, has been interpreted inflexibly by the Court, in its desire to preserve an autonomous EU interpretation of core concepts, in twenty-first century cases involving complex transnational restructuring, major insolvencies, and 'downsizing' by closing smaller units of the enterprise. Moreover, EU single market law has accelerated the pace of globalisation, especially in services, opening up opportunities for enterprises to deterritorialise their activities, by establishing subsidiaries, subcontracting, outsourcing and posting workers to perform service contracts in other Member States. In turn, this has brought about institutional changes in transnational workspaces,[285] leading to an increasing fragmentation of labour, and gaps in employment and social protection.

As the EU has expanded territorially, inequalities in both labour conditions and social security between Member States have widened rather than closed, reviving the problem of social dumping that EU social policy was designed to cure by means of partial harmonisation, where necessary, to achieve a 'gradual coalescence of social policies' as a consequence of market integration.[286] The challenge for the EU is to reform the law to adapt to regulatory competition and transformational changes in the organisation of enterprises in the single market because, as Simon Deakin has observed 'outcomes are critically dependent on the way in which the rules of the game are designed'.[287]

---

284. European Commission, COM(2016) 505 final.
285. *See* Wagner, *supra* n. 4.
286. *See* Otto Kahn-Freund, *Labour Law and Social Security*, in E. Stein and T. L. Nicholson (eds), *American Enterprise in the European Common Market. A Legal Profile*, 297, 299 (University of Michigan Press 1960). Kahn-Freund was discussing the 'Spaak Report': High Authority of the European Community for Coal and Steel, 'The Brussels Report on the General Common Market', June 1956 http://aei.pitt.edu/995/1/Spaak_report.pdf. *See* further, Stefano Giubboni, *Social Rights and Market Freedom in the European Constitution: A Labour Law Perspective*, 45–49 (Cambridge 2006).
287. S. Deakin, *supra* n. 5, at 1.

CHAPTER 13
Appeals for Constitutional Protection "Recurso de Amparo"

Fernando Valdés Dal-Ré

13.1 A NEW CONFIGURATION OF APPEALS FOR CONSTITUTIONAL PROTECTION "RECURSO DE AMPARO"

Following the reform of the Public General Act of the Constitutional Court (LOTC) by virtue of Public General Act 6/2007, of May 24, the various stages that have successively regulated the constitutional appeal process (filing, admissibility, processing and resolution of the claim) have undergone regulatory changes which, far from being merely formal, reflect (or are being interpreted as) a new configuration of this process, which pursues the protection of fundamental rights and freedoms recognized in Article 154 and section 1, Chapter 2, Title 1 of the Spanish Constitution (CE).

The "most distinctive characteristic" of the law, as affirmed by Constitutional Court Judgment (STC) 155/2009, of June 25, delivered by the Plenary Meeting of the Court, is the material requirement or merits related to "the specific constitutional relevance" imposed by Article 50.1 b) LOTC to admit the appeal, to be examined latter. It will suffice now to state that, according to constitutional case-law, said requirement has consolidated the legislator's option on the constitutional protection model offered, further to the powers entrusted by Article 161.1 b) CE, in relation to Article 53.2, the latter enshrining this process in constitutional terms.

This new characterization, following said reform, closely related to appellant citizens, means that the mere infringement of a fundamental light or public freedom eligible for constitutional protection will not be sufficient per se to admit the appeal; furthermore, this special constitutional relevance will also be indispensable. Consequently, this new model has challenged or, at least, transformed the configuration of former regulations, where it was undisputed that the appeal essentially pursued the damage caused to the plaintiff's fundamental rights and public freedoms.

As a result of this novelty, configuration discussions will be based on what is materially left- beyond generic statements of survival of its specific protection- of an appeal for constitutional protection as an instrument for the subjective protection of fundamental rights specifically damaged in a particular case; it will also be questioned whether this new requirement, in addition to altering the procedure and rules, has also transformed its nature.

Obviously this is not a minor issue, given that irrespective of a formalist interpretation ("if applicable," further to Article 53.2 CE, when referring to constitutional protection through this appeal process) the constitutional mandate and the task traditionally executed through these channels, to react against relevant infringements, means that we are clearly dealing with an effective instrument of subjective protection; it is not a device where remedy of an infringement is a circumstantial or accessory consequence, or conditioned by other preeminent purposes, such as the determination of constitutional doctrine or the Court's role as a guarantor of fundamental rights in objective terms.

Certainly, the Constitution provides that any citizen may apply for protection of these freedoms and fundamental rights before the ordinary Courts. It is also true that constitutional case-law has established that Judges and Tribunals are the first natural guardians of these rights (again, STC 155/2009, and previously STC 22/1999, of December 13, Legal Consideration (FJ) 11, to name a few). Furthermore, their task has been reinforced by new regulations arising from the 2007 reform, particularly due to the broadening of procedural nullity incidents (Article 241 LOPJ), which is currently able to mitigate any harm of these fundamental rights that was previously not reported (as opposed to former provisions that limited the incident to inconsistency or to repair the formal defects generating the lack of protection). However, it is equally undisputed that the TC is the ultimate guarantor of these rights and their maximum interpreter (Articles 53.2 and 123.1 CE and 1.1 LOTC); it is the body, albeit as a last instance, entrusted not only with determining, specifying and defining their content, but also with guaranteeing their singular coverage and protection, given that this is clearly the object covered by Article 53.2 CE, which does not refer to fundamental rights and freedoms in the abstract but to the existence of a procedure allowing a claim to be filed against any possible infringement.

Based on these essential and decisive observations, any attempt to convert the constitutional protection process into something unrelated to this institutional protection would, in our opinion, collide headlong with unequivocal constitutional mandates. This scenario would not only arise in a model that excludes subjective protection, but also where the constitutional protection process is interpreted as safeguarding citizen fundamental rights in appearance only, entailing irremediable hindrance or obstacles, or where subjective protection is merely subsidiary or conditioned by other prevailing purposes or tasks assigned to the process.

On the other hand, we must remember that the protection of fundamental rights and freedoms, in objective terms, enjoys additional strengthening devices foreseen in the CE, such as its binding effects on all public powers, the need to regulate the matter in a Public General Act and, above all, respect for essential content through unconstitutionality appeals foreseen in Article 161.1 a) CE (Article 53.1 CE). Consequently, characterizing constitutional protection as an objective process aimed at providing a guarantee "to interpret or apply the Constitution, or for its general effects, and to determine the content and scope of fundamental rights" (we are deliberately using the expression used in Article 50.1. LOTC- specific constitutional effects- for discussion purposes only), must be consistent with the defensive aim of Article 53.2 CE and, furthermore, must provide a rational and systematic explanation that is harmoniously included in the other protection mechanisms foreseen in the CE; at least in terms of restricting the traditional protection granted given that, as seen, there are other constitutional means available for supra-individual consideration and objective protection.

The foregoing function is precisely backed up by Article 161.1.a) CE. No further illustration is necessary, given that the TC itself has linked a verification of the constitutionality of regulatory devices- through unconstitutionality appeals- to an "objective public interest" beyond the applicants. This is not the only device that exists; there are other constitutional processes which, despite not being expressly referred to in Article 53.1 CE, also pursue an objective that is over and beyond individual harm, providing objective control and defining these rights. This is very clear in the case of unconstitutionality issues, no matter how related to a specific case, given that, as in the case of unconstitutional appeals, they are used to preserve the constitutionality of laws and, consequently, of any affected fundamental rights and freedoms.

The *raison d'être* of an objective appeal for constitutional protection is therefore not based on a lack of guarantees in other constitutional processes, when defining the supra-individual effects of fundamental rights and freedoms. This objective nature, if understood in conflicting or excluding terms or, otherwise, as a formula that limits subjective protection, would not be covered by Article 53.2 CE, or systematically included in the Constitution itself. In any case, we are not defending the idea that this characterization is inappropriate, or that appeals for constitutional protection cannot be subject to new admissibility requirements. Rather, we are claiming that irrespective of what the new requirements consist of in the abstract- that is specific constitutional effects they need to be interpreted and applied consistently with this subjective protection which, if not prevalent, will question any regulations intending to alter the pre-existing model.

These doubts are evidenced when analyzing the TC's interpretation of the new appeal for constitutional protection, particularly as regards the requirement for specific constitutional effects, which underlies this reformulation of the constitutional protection process. In fact, according to current Article 50.1 LOTC the following will be a requirement of the appeal:

1.b) That the content of the appeal justify a decision on the merits of the case, by the Constitutional Court, based on its specific constitutional effects; the foregoing will be examined in terms of its relevance for an interpretation or application of the Constitution, or for its general effects, and in order to determine the content and scope fundamental rights.

Further to this regulatory novelty, at the admissibility stage it will no longer suffice for the TC to verify the absence of causes for inadmissibility, as was previously the case; it will now be necessary to examine the appeal from another point of view, based on an objective approach that surpasses individual cases and is able to fulfill the interpretation mandate established in the CE, as well as its guaranteed application and general effects or a determination of the content and scope of fundamental rights, referred to above. In other words, the traditional negative verification of the absence of causes of inadmissibility is now replaced or, more accurately, complemented, with another positive verification, that is the existence of objective grounds for inadmissibility, endowing the appeal with special constitutional relevance.

As may be deduced from merely reading its pronouncements, the TC has interpreted Article 50.1.b) LOTC in terms of an objective process. Although it repeatedly affirms that constitutional protection is still a remedy to protect subjective rights, mitigating any harm caused, this requirement for constitutionality issues to be filed that exceed an individual case, rendering the constitutional issue objective, means that admissibility is totally conditioned and lowers the protection of the hindered right, to the point of becoming accessory or subordinate.

The foregoing is a likely consequence of interpreting this reform, as part of the growing quantitative strength enjoyed by constitutional protection prior to its approval, which was overburdening the Court and affecting its dedication to the control of legal constitutionality. According to some authors, this structural situation endangered the Court's identity as a constitutional body, given the totally irrational increase in the number of appeals for constitutional protection, which prevented the Court from efficiently exercising all its competences.[1]

The foregoing facts and this trend (which has currently changed to a large extent, as proven by the statistics) mean that, following the 2007 reform of the LOTC, a different idea of constitutional protection may be upheld, as opposed to the pronouncements basically resulting from STC 155/2009. This new idea is closer to the defensive nature of the appeal, and therefore better enshrines the protection of rights and freedoms foreseen in the Constitution. Certainly, the CE does not previously define a specific and clear appeal model; however, it may hardly be claimed that the most natural assimilation of Article 53.2 CE leads to basic constitutional protection. Although this conclusion does not exclude the objective purpose of the appeal process, it does in fact require a subjective guarantee, which is inherent to the appeal. Article 162.1.b) CE, by entitling any

---

1. See Marc Carrillo, *La objetivación del recurso de amparo: una necesidad ineludible*, 80, Revista Vasca de Administración Pública, 89 (2008).

natural or legal person to file an appeal for constitutional protection, if a legitimate interest is claimed, as well as the Ombudsman and Public Prosecution Office, simply confirms this.

Without prejudice to the foregoing, the TC has interpreted the new regulation more in line with the immediate objectives of the reform, without considering its interpretative potential, reducing the amount and extent of the defensive nature of the law, as it is currently drafted, in any case upholding the configuration foreseen in Article 53.2 CE. These other narrower conceptions of the guarantee entrusted to the Constitutional Court are still valid, founded on its extraordinary nature; however, we do not agree with the opinions linking this strict notion to a breach of the true grounds underlying this appeal process, to the point of disfiguring the same.

This is a basic but decisive idea: a reform is acceptable and, even, an interpretation of the recent reform, strictly structuring the constitutional protection process, strengthening the role of ordinary courts in protecting fundamental rights, as well as articulating constitutional protection as a truly extraordinary and final recourse, subject to strict access conditions and exhausting all prior remedies. However, we disagree with a view of this reform and its interpretation that converts constitutional protection, de facto, into an instrument where subjective protection is residual. The former position is reasonable, and certainly essential to uphold the TC's position, as it seeks to contain the avalanche of appeals and reduce the Court's task to this specific issue; however, the latter position, despite various interpretations of legal regulations and of Article 53.2 CE, reveals a denaturalization of the appeal process and constitutional mandate, which defines it as a remedy and means to protect citizens fundamental rights.

Our opinion is not only based on constitutional mandates; it is also based on the very wording of the law, which may and should be accordingly interpreted, consistent with these mandates. In fact, amongst the guidelines behind the specific constitutional effects foreseen in Article 50.1 LOTC, the LOTC is characterized as relevant for constitutional interpretation, application or general effects and, ultimately, to determine the content and scope of fundamental rights. Some of these parameters, subsuming an individual case into the rule of specific constitutional relevance, are openly applied as objective rules for inclusion or coverage; others, however, clearly allow a mixed view or double representation of the constitutional appeal process. Further to a systematic view of the law, constitutional protection is still being traditionally configured along with this new objective protection.

The reference to "application" of the CE, further to Article 50.1 LOTC, is, without a doubt, the clearest confirmation of this alternative interpretation. As a result, there is a possibility of constitutional protection remaining in traditional terms, albeit alongside a new objective protection. As an example, may a case where a judgment is clearly delivered against constant constitutional case-law in the matter entail a "constitutional application" difficulty? And, if so, why does the TC consider that any appeals against what has been equally upheld and confirmed in prior judgments lack specific constitutional relevance?

Unfortunately, the reply to this question has already been anticipated: the TC considers that the rule is stating what it expects it to do. The idea was to reduce its global role and the extent of constitutional protection, not the opposite. This was probably why this excluding notion arose, that is only objective protection is admissible although, once admitted, subjective protection may indirectly ensue. Despite the foregoing, the regulatory text allows a multi-faceted process, both aimed at strict subjective protection (those appeals simply affecting "constitutional application" in relation to subjective infringements), and aimed at settling objective constitutionality issues, over and beyond each individual case. Basically cases which, apart from an infringement, raise doubts about constitutional interpretation or the boundaries of the content and scope of fundamental rights.

Consequently, we need to continue reflecting on the regulations and the protection task entrusted by the new LOTC to the constitutional appeal process. We disagree and lack any satisfactory explanation, certainly any arising from mandatory law in the 2007 reform, for the fact that the TC, when faced with an unequivocal infringement based on preceding constitutional case-law, is unable to deliver decisions guaranteeing the application of its doctrine and of the CE itself: The foregoing is not imposed by law and there are no organizational reasons for the same. Rather, it would be easy and speedy to deliver resolutions merely applying doctrine that protects the fundamental right that is accurately proven as infringed to the Court. It is precisely this logic which underlies Article 52.2 LOTC, when providing that the Chamber may forward an appeal to a Section "if a decision entails consolidated Constitutional Court doctrine".

Basically, a radically objective view of constitutional protection does not conform to the 2007 reform. STC 155/2009, which has listed the causes of specific constitutional relevance, along these lines, has therefore become, instead of the LOTC, a way in which to define this model, based on an interpretation of this Public General Act. As a result, the TC has become an instance with a strong doctrinal, rather than defensive, purpose, forgetting that the latter is not only perfectly compatible with the former but, also, essential and enforceable. It suffices to review the important task performed by constitutional case-law, particularly initial cases but also, certainly, recent doctrine. This modern case-law has defined the essential content of these rights and has generated broad coverage. To overlook this task, which the law has not only not denied but, in our opinion, even demands, risks putting a distance between the Constitutional Court and its protected citizens, somehow waiving a role that no one but the Constitutional Court has been able to perform or perfect. A reinforcement of prior judicial channels, strengthening the material scope of procedural nullity incidents under Article 241 LOPJ (*see* below), is insufficient compensation. Experience has shown that the route traveled by this incident is not even remotely comparable to traditional protection and its more than satisfactory coverage of citizens fundamental rights.

13.2 ADMISSIBILITY REQUIREMENTS IN APPEALS FOR CONSTITUTIONAL PROTECTION

13.2.1 General Considerations

The appeal for constitutional protection foreseen in LO 6/2007, of 24 May, does not accurately reflect the German model, let alone the U.S. *certiorari* system.[2] As opposed to the latter, discretionary decisions on admission are excluded. Furthermore, the wording of the LOTC probably requires admission based on strictly subjective reasons, as explained above. In any case and based on the foregoing configuration of an appeal for constitutional protection, our comments below intend to examine the admissibility requirements of the appeal, according to the interpretation provided by constitutional doctrine.

Before, we should state that there is a very high percentage of dismissed appeals for constitutional protection. In 2011, according to TC statistics, 7,192 cases were filed (approximately a third less than before the reform) and only 137 were granted leave to proceed; or, relatively speaking, admission only represented 2% of the appeals filed. Subject to exceptions, this figure[3] is sufficiently indicative of both the volume of appeals for constitutional protection that are still being formalized before the Court, and how difficult it is to complete the initial admission stage, in order for the case to be processed and judgment delivered.

This high percentage of dismissals is often due to unawareness of the constitutional protection process, which is still being used by a large number of appellants, despite the 2007 reform of the LOTC, as if it were the next judicial instance, articulating claims that are unable to prosper due to using a means of protection in a way that is contrary to its institutional purpose. However, many appeals are also dismissed for other reasons, particularly due to procedural defects when the claim was tiled or in the prior judicial process. And, very often, this arises in matters that should have been granted leave to proceed, evidencing the need to understand the parameters applied by the Constitutional Court at the initial admissibility stage or when applying for constitutional protection.

The task is huge. There are many criteria and, particularly, specifications, laid down by the TC in its "procedural" case-law. We are consequently unable to

---

2. *See* Marian Ahumada Ruiz, *Certiorari* y criterios de selección de casos, in VV.AA.*La defensa de los derechos fundamentales: Tribunal Constitucional y Poder Judicial. Actas de las XV Jornadas de la Asociación de Letrados del Tribunal Constitucional*, Madrid, Tribunal Constitucional-Centro de Estudios Políticos y Constitucionales, 59–83 (2010); Marc Carrillo, Roberto Romboli, *La reforma del recurso de amparo*, 50 (Fundación Coloquio Jurídico Europeo, Madrid 2012) and Ana Espinosa Díaz, *El recurso de amparo: problemas antes, y después, de la reforma*, 2 InDret, 6(2010) to cite a few.
3. In statistic terms, there is a great difference between the total number of cases filed and those resolved at the admission stage, totaling 589 appeals. *See* Javier Garcia Roca, *La cifra del amparo constitucional y su reforma*, in Pérez Tremps (Coord), *La reforma del recurso de amparo*, 273–295 (Ed. Tirant lo Blanch 2003).

resolve these difficulties in this work, let alone remotely. Rather, we will specifically and thoroughly examine the two-fold requirement foreseen in Articles 49.1 and 50.1.b) LOTC, as worded by the 2007 reform, referring to the burden of proving specific constitutional relevance resting on the applicant for protection, and the principles governing this material requirement for the appeal, respectively, as well as factors to define and ascertain the same. Given that the rules are still relatively new and largely unknown, resulting in a high number of dismissals, this approach is recommendable.

After this study, constituting most of our work, we will analyze the traditional requirements of constitutional protection, which have nevertheless survived the 2007 reform in basic terms, despite some minor amendments. This latter issue, we should point out now, will not be systematically arranged or examined, let alone analyzed exhaustively. Each requirement would require a monographic analysis, making this unfeasible. Rather, we will adopt purely selective approach. We have decided to refer to certain constitutional constructions, related to traditional procedural requirements when applying for constitutional protection, which are largely unknown. However, this does not mean that admissibility requirements are less important. Any statistic investigation of decisions dismissing appeals for protection will in fact confirm that there is a very high number of cases dismissed due to not meeting these so-called traditional requirements (basically the appeal deadline, standing,[4] application and exhaustion of prior judicial channels).

Before examining the two-fold perspective of the new requirements articulated in Articles 49.1 and 50.1.b) LOTC, we will refer to our foregoing conclusion, as it directly affects any definition of admissibility requirements for the appeal. In fact, we have already indicated that there is an actual risk of appeals for constitutional protection being diluted if the extreme objectiveness occasionally affirmed by constitutional case law should materialize. To avoid this, before other factors, the TC should more thoroughly reflect on the reform, examining and distinguishing any short and medium term objectives from institutional functions, in defensive terms.

In any case and beyond the contrary versions potentially arising from the appeal, defining the constitutional project in terms of a meeting of minds or intersection with citizens, the idea that subjective protection is a structural component of the appeal process will allow us to reach other conclusions that are relevant for admissibility purposes. Although these magnitudes may seem

---

4. Due to constraints in the length of this article, standing will not be examined. On the matter, see Perez Tremps, *El acceso al recurso de amparo*, in VV.AA., *Estudios en Homenaje al Profesor Gregorio Peces-Barba, Teoría y A4etodología del Derecho*, vol. 11, 979–1004 (Dykinson, Madrid, 2008); Vincente Gimeno Sendra, *El recurso español constitucional de amparo*, in VV.AA., *La ciencia del Derecho Procesal Constitucional. Estudios en homenaje a Héctor Fix-Zamudio en sus cincuenta años como investigador del derecho,vol. VII, Procesos constitucionales de la libertad*, 301 (Marcial Pons, México, 2008) and Angel J. Gómez Montoro, *El interés legítimo para recurrir en amparo. La experiencia del Tribunal Constitucional español*, 9 Cuestiones constitucionales, 159–185(2003).

narrower due to their essentially practical nature, their potentiality is essential to ensure the actual effectiveness of the procedure and achievement of its declared purpose. Thus, we will first of all connect the LOTC's admissibility requirements, *mutatis mutandis*, to the constitutional principle applied to applications, as a form of effective judicial protection enshrined in Article 41.1 CE. Appeals for constitutional protection, needless to say, do not constitute a judicial appeal; the constitutional body examining these appeals is different, and the institutional purpose of its regulated procedures is individual and specific. However, this subjective protection would mean that the TC is embracing the appeal in very strict and restrictive terms and, specifically, an examination of procedural requirements for constitutional protection that departs from the rule ordinarily used in constitutional case-law in court access matters (Article 24.1 CE). This is why we do not agree with unreasonable interpretations of constitutional protection access requirements; nor do we uphold any formalist interpretations that are disproportionate when compared to the extent of the harm suffered by the appellant.

When understanding and applying this rule, the double sequence control executed in the right of access to the courts is often mixed up. Even the TC, which has fully defined it in some of its decisions, seems to occasionally contradict it. In fact, when the applicant for protection is alleging a harmful restriction of the right to access the courts, the TC has examined the reasonableness of the court's interpretation of the procedural requirement in question. In other words, it analyzes whether the interpretation of the procedural rule is manifestly unreasonable- basically inconsistent or illogical- or arbitrary- lacking legal considerations, without delving any further- and adds, as a third possible infringement, a factual misunderstanding of the cause leading to termination of the process. The proportionality rule does not yet play a leading role in the matter. The court may even apply a strict interpretation, as long as its interpretation of the procedural rules is acceptable.

Only if the decision adopted on the procedural requirement passes this first test will the second proportionality examination be triggered, where the *pro actione* principle is in fact involved. The proportionality test- which does not apply equally at other stages, except for criminal and sanctioning matters, both in successive jurisdictional levels and the procedural remedies available before the deciding courtuses another starting point, that is whether the procedural requirement has in fact been breached, given that, further to the first test (reasonable and non-arbitrary interpretation), it is previously concluded that the court's decision was possible. In short, the judge's interpretation is accepted (and so is the consequent procedural breach by the applicant) and it is now examined whether the cancellation effects of the suit, associated by the court to this breach, may be defined as excessively strict or disproportionate (second stage in access to the courts); if this latter point is ascertained, the same statement is reached as would have applied had the first stage in the control sequence not been completed (manifest unreasonableness, arbitrariness or a factual error): a declared violation of Article 24.1 CE.

In other words, at the first stage, harm may arise due to the absence of a cause ending the lawsuit—applicable to the applicant's procedural conduct (arbitrariness)—or because its application is unreasonable or mistaken, in factual terms; and it may arise at the second stage if the cancellation or restrictive consequence of the action is disproportionate, when compared to the relevance of the defect. The first part of the rule, furthermore, is not used for a legal correction of interpretation or, even, to encourage action against other less generous hermeneutic options, but as an indirect or external examination of manifest unreasonableness or arbitrariness in the court's response. In turn, the proportionality rule has been extended to many procedural matters. The parameters used for its verifications depend on the circumstances of the case; even if proportionality may be examined ex ante (prior representation is possible, as a control issue), its effective materialization must inevitably be based on the specific circumstances of the facts. Thus, depending on the case, the seriousness of the breach is examined, as well as the purpose of the infringed requirement, the clarity of the rule overlooked (given that one thing is the reasonableness of the court's interpretation, and another is the misleading effect of the law on the plaintiff which would affect the proportionality rule), the possibilities of remedying the breach, the clarity of the court's summons when the infringement has entailed mitigation measures or a preservation of the action or, ultimately, the object of the suit and the rights examined therein, amongst others.

This done, we will be in a position to apply this logic to the constitutional protection process. Certainly and as in any other jurisdictional procedure upholding the principle of legal certainty, an appeal for constitutional protection needs clear procedural rules. On the one hand, it is clear that an orderly procedure has a valuable purpose which, particularly in the case of proceedings brought before the Constitutional Court, involves strict, though not excessively strict, procedural doctrine. Thus, when interpreting these requirements (based on the first reasonableness and non-arbitrariness test inherent to Article 24.1 CE), an accurate and scrupulous examination is necessary, suitable to adequately govern a process involving this senior institution where essential rights are involved. It is therefore not suitable to allow vague or informal procedural conduct, not supportive of the constitutional justice requested, or to avoid the logic of the system, characterized by the TC's ultimate intervention, upholding the latter's exclusivity when protection fundamental rights, which begins way back at the prior administrative and judicial stages.

The formal seriousness inherent to the solemnness of a constitutional protection process is evidenced in the TC's pronouncements. This is apparent at the admissibility stage but is also evident in the provisions of the judgment delivered, which very often entail inadmissibility without examining the merits of the case. The loss of protection requested, on the grounds of the appellant's lack of diligence, is a threat that last until the end, given that any irremediable defects in the appeal for constitutional protection are not remedied with the initial leave to proceed, that is verification of procedural requirements for the admissibility of an action may again be examined or reconsidered when judgment is delivered ex officio or at the party's request, entailing a pronouncement of inadmissibility, as repeatedly stated by the TC (see, for example, recent STC 186/2012 of October 29, FJ 2).

However, this need for rectitude when complying with procedural requirements, which we agree with, cannot entail futile severity, inflexibility or hindering formalism. The second proportionality rule applicable to court access (Article 24.1 CE) should therefore fully come into play, applied *mutatis mutandi* when examining the procedural requirements of constitutional protection. This proposal is not vacant or voluntary; rather, as will be seen below, when specifically examining these requirements very often the TC's pronouncements reveal an internal discussion, interpretative tension that is also present in these procedural issues. The fact that this tension exists is worrying in itself given that, if concepts are eventually consolidated before the Court that deny the necessary coverage to this protection, through a formalist interpretation of the access requirements, the consequence would not be consistent with the defensive purpose of the appeal. The discussion goes beyond the granting of constitutional protection in one case or the other; the intensity and effectiveness are examined, m the reinforced protection of fundamental rights ordered by the Constitution.

This is a real risk that cannot be overlooked. It probably arose from the backlog of appeals that to a large extent triggered the 2007 reform, along with a trend to reduce constitutional protection, consolidated in greater procedural rigidity. All attempts to refute this, precisely on the grounds of the new requirements of the 2007 reform (a breach of requirements linked to the objectiveness of constitutional protection) were unsuccessful, particularly because this formalist tendency began way before the amendment of the LOTC. Further to the foregoing, we may ask ourselves whether constitutional protection is being limited or, rather, whether the Court is limiting this constitutional process in qualitative terms. These questions are very relevant, are not at all trivial or minor; despite the description made above, they are once again directly applicable when examining admissibility requirements.

13.2.2 Specific Constitutional Relevance as a Material Requirement or Condition for Admissibility[5]

Constitutional case-law since 2007 indicates that subjective protection will not be possible, and an appeal will be inadmissible, in the absence of specific

---

5. See Francisco Javier Matia Portilla, *La especial trascendencia constitucional del recurso de amparo*, 86 Revista Espmiola de Derecho Constitucional, 343–368 (2009); Ana Espinosa Díaz, *supra* 3; Ortega Gutiérrez (2010); Juan Carlos Cabañas García,*El recurso de amparo que queremos (reflexiones a propósito de la Ley Orgánica 6/2007, de 24 de mayo, de reforma parcial de la Ley Orgánica del Tribunal Constitucional)*, 88 Revista Elpmiola de Estudios Constitucionales, 39–81 (2010) and Magdalena Nogueira guastavino,*La trascendencia constitucional de la demanda de amparo tras la reforma de la Ley Orgánica del Tribunal Constitucional por la LO 6/2007*, 51 Revista de Derecho Social, 165–200 (2010), to cite a few.

constitutional relevance. We will now refer to the material requirement [regulated in Article 50.1 b) LOTC] and not to the burden of justifying the same, required from the appellant further to Article 49.1 in fine LOTC, to be examined in the next section.

The fact that specific constitutional relevance is ascertained at the admissibility stage, turning the requirement into a parameter of the initial decision to process the appeal or shelve the proceedings, does not prevent its characterization as something other than a mere procedural requirement. This has been highlighted by the Court in recent STC 178/2012, of October 15, where it states that this is not a purely formal requirement but a material and substantive requirement, despite being classified as an admissibility requirement of a claim further to Article 50.1.b) (Decision of the Constitutional Court (ATC) 264/2009, of November 16, single FJ).

Constitutional case-law has paid more attention to the scope of Article 49.1 LOTC (justification burden) than that of Article 50.1 b) LOTC. In relation to the latter, that is specific constitutional relevance in strict terms, STC 155/2009, of June 25, delivered by the Plenary Meeting of the TC, established in a non-exhaustive manner (the list is expressly stated as being open-ended) the situations where it may be upheld. This decision defined the concept and criteria established in the LOTC, linking appeals for constitutional protection, from this point of view, to "their relevance for constitutional interpretation, application or general effects, and to determine the content and scope of fundamental rights," providing, with a catalogue of situations covered by "specific constitutional relevance," a first step for the applicants of constitutional protection, in order to be able to fulfill the justification burden ordered by Article 49.1 in fine LOTC[6] in a legal certainty scenario.

Nevertheless and given that this requirement will be thoroughly analyzed during the 3rd course of this Seminar, it will not be examined here and reference will be made to our comments below.

13.2.3 Comments on the Traditional Requirements of Appeal Claims

In the foregoing section we already referred to our particular analysis of the requirements listed in Articles 49.1 *in fine* and 50.1 b) LOTC, due to their stiff recent nature and possible interpretation. Having completed this task, we will now examine the other admissibility requirements in appeals for constitutional protection, insisting on the endless specifications made by the TC throughout its extended lifetime, which would require a monograph for each requirement. As

---

6. The Court has been requested to specify the reason to admit an appeal for constitutional protection, as this will be very useful for future appellants. *See* Mario Hernández Ramos, *La especial trascendencia constitucional del recurso de amparo y su aplicación en la Jurisprudencia del Tribunal Constitucional. Luces y sombras en cuatro años de actividad*, 3 Aranzadi Doctrinal (2011).

this is not possible, we have decided in favor of a selective approach, highlighting some matters that may be unknown but which lead to a large number of inadmissibility decisions.

13.2.3.1 Deadline and Register Receiving the Appeal

Regarding where the appeal should be filed, the reference decision is STC 28/2011, of March 14, which states that the possibility foreseen in Article 85.2 LOTC (filing of writs to commence appeals for constitutional protection in places other than the General Register of the TC) is limited to writs which, in accordance with Article 135.1 of the Civil Procedure Act (LEC), are registered before 3:00 p.m. on the day following the expiration date, in such a way that any appeals for constitutional protection filed outside the TC Register at a time other than the one foreseen will follow the date they were deposited at the TC. This interpretation should certainly be revisited. In fact, STC 28/2011 distinguishes two situations: (i) the filing of writs commencing appeals for constitutional protection in a place other than the General Register of the TC, pursuant to Article 135.1 LEC, that is appeals registered before 3:00 p.m. on the day following the ordinary expiration date; and (ii) writs to commence appeals for constitutional protection that were formalized in a place other than said General Register but at a different time than the one foreseen in Article 135.1 LEC; that is also outside the TC Register but, unlike the previous case, within the appeal timeframe.

This constitutional doctrine is clearly contradictory, as it suggests that the first type of appeal would be timely, irrespective of the date of receipt, whereas the second would be untimely if not received by the Court within the timeframe foreseen in Articles 43.2 and 44.2 LOTC. As a result, an application filing an appeal within the timeframe foreseen in Articles 43.2 and 44.2 LOTC is in a worse position than the party filing it the day after its expiration, pursuant to Article 135.1 LEC, albeit in the same place (i.e., outside the TC Register). It is likely that the Court, in order to avoid this inconsistency, will change its doctrine sooner or later. In fact, Article 85.2 LOTC allows all writs of appeal registered outside the TC Register to be deemed as formalized on their filing date, irrespective of when they were received by the Court. The provision stating that "appeals for constitutional protection may also be filed before 3:00 p.m. on the business day following expiration of the timeframe, at the Constitutional Court register or at the office or central registry service of the Civil Courts in any town, pursuant to Article 135.1 of Civil Procedure Act 1/2000, of 7 January" may not be conceived only for writs delivered outside the ordinary expiration timeframe, but for all writs. Certainly, the reference made to Article 135.1 LEC would suggest otherwise, that is writs filed the day after expiration, the subject matter of this provision; but it is also true that the subject of the provision constitutes "appeals for constitutional protection," "not appeals for constitutional protection filed the day after expiration," which is why the possibility of their formalization before the Civil Courts exists in all appeals, not only those registered after the expiration date. This would avoid this paradoxical outcome.

Still in relation to calculation of the timeframe, we should point out the difference between appeals for constitutional protection brought under Articles 43 or 44 LOTC. In the first case, there is a twenty-day timeframe following notice of the resolution delivered in the preceding judicial process, in relation to appeals brought against violations of rights and freedoms as a result of provisions, legal acts, omissions or de facto situations involving the Government or its authorities or public officials, or collegiate executive bodies in autonomous communities or their authorities or public officials or agents; instead, in the second case, there is a thirty-day timeframe following notice of the resolution delivered in the judicial process, this time in appeals brought against violations of rights and freedoms eligible for constitutional protection that are immediately and directly caused by a court's actor omission.

This two-fold regulation of the timeframe may also entail significant risks at the admissibility stage. This is particularly the case whenever the appeal contains a merely formal challenge of a judgment delivered in a judicial process, where the claim is materially brought against an administrative resolution. In these cases, the twenty-day term of Article 43.2 LOTC applies, not the thirty-day term of Article 44.2 LOTC. In other words, the longer term will only apply to appeals brought against judicial resolutions under Article 44 LOTC, or if independent and differentiated complaints are brought against an administrative resolution or the judicial resolutions upholding it (combined protection under Articles 43 and 44 LOTC).

13.2.3.2 *Procedural Nullity Incidents*

Of particular interest are procedural nullity incidents (Article 241 Public General Act of the Judiciary (LOPJ)) which, following the 2007 reform, has extended its objective scope to any infringements of fundamental rights, not only, as was previously the case, to inconsistency and formal defects giving rise to lack of protection (Article 24.1 CE).[7]

Both the manifestly inadequate use of the incident foreseen in Article 241 LOPJ, as well as its omission if applicable, consequently affects the successive admissibility stage of the appeal. In the first case, the Court may consider the appeal untimely (Article 44.2 LOTC) due to artificially extending the prior judicial procedure. Whereas in the second case it may declare that Article 44.1.a) LOTC has not been exhausted, as the failure to use it breaches the principle of

---

7. For an analysis of the regulatory background of this procedural remedy, *see* Maria Emilia Casas, *Incidente de nulidad de actuaciones y recurso de amparo constitucional*, in VV.AA., *Derecho vivo del Trabajo y Constitución. Estudios en Homenaje al Profesor Doctor Fernando Suárez González*, 449–490 (La Ley & MTAS, Madrid 2003); M. Nogueira Guastavino (2003) and Lorena BACHMAIER WINTER, *La reforma dela LOTC y la ampliación del incidente de nulidad de actuaciones*, 13 Revista de Derecho Procesal, 45–67 (2007).

subsidiarity inherent to this constitutional process. Insofar as there are many pronouncements upholding these conclusions, we will point out some peculiarities of the system foreseen in Article 241 LOPJ.

One of them refers to the eventuality of independent infringements caused when resolving the incident. Constitutional Court Judgments 107/2011, of June 20, and 153/2012, of July 16, provide guidelines on the matter. Both pronouncements are compatible and explain the transformation of the institutional purpose of the incident foreseen in Article 241 LOPJ. If the appellant does not essentially base its complaint on a breach of the right to effective judicial protection due to the outright dismissal of a nullity incident, but on the infringement of other rights by the Judgment challenged through this procedural remedy (as in STC 107/2011), it is presumed that the channel foreseen in Article 241 LOPJ was merely used to exhaust prior judicial proceedings (Article 44.1.a) LOTC) and dismissal of the appeal, albeit irregular, does not constitute an independent infringement of any fundamental right whatsoever. However, if the appeal for constitutional protection exclusively covers the resolution adopted in the Decision dismissing a nullity incident, claiming that the court has evaded its palliative duty, as in STC 153/2012, it may be presumed that the right upheld has been individually infringed.

Of relevance here is the doctrine that started with STC 39/2003, which is relatively unknown. According to this decision, if an appellant claims a breach of fundamental rights before the Supreme Court (TS) in a motion to vacate for the unification of doctrine, but the complaint is not processed due to not meeting the requirements to access this extraordinary appeal (e.g., absence of *audi alteram partem*), following the decision to dismiss the appeal a nullity incident should be brought before the Higher Court of Justice (TSJ), if it is the judicial body accused of the infringement, in order to guarantee the subsidiarity of an appeal for constitutional protection. Many dismissals are also based on this cause.

Article 241 LOPJ also coexists with untimeliness. The most common cases are those where, once the incident is resolved, dismissing or rejecting the same, a new appeal is lodged or, even a new nullity incident, against what is expressly foreseen in this article. The same applies when it is used to report an infringement that was already examined in prior procedural stages or jurisdictional levels, ignoring the fact that this procedural remedy is only suitable for unchallengeable complaints. In these cases, unless the judicial body, despite the manifest inadequacy of the incident, responds to the issue raised and settles the claim (in which case the Court considers that the artificial extension of the process has been remedied), the outcome will be a declaration of untimeliness provided that, logically, the undue extension of prior channels has affected – as is usually the case without exception – expiration of the appeal (for calculation purposes, the notification date of the resolution challenged before the Court will be taken into account, that is the decision that was inadequately challenged through the procedure of Article 241 LOPJ.

13.2.3.3 Observations on the Exhaustion of the Means of Challenge Foreseen in Procedural Rules: Article 44.1.a) General Public Act of the Constitutional Court (LOTC)

Revisiting the issues related to exhaustion of prior judicial proceedings, albeit in different fields from the ones covered by procedural nullity incidents, we will now refer to situations where the judicial body may request a remedy that the summoned party deems unjustified. The scenario where this usually materializes is the remedy of an employment claim. On the matter, ATC 50/2000 established that it is necessary to challenge the order containing the remedy request deemed excessive; in the foregoing case, due to the request not referring to the employment claim requirements contained in Article 80 of the Labour Procedure Act (LPL), currently Article 80 of the Labour Jurisdiction Act (LJS). If the applicant for constitutional protection does not agree with the order demanding a remedy, but does not fulfill or challenge the same, it will be presumed that prior judicial channels have not been exhausted.

It could be claimed that an appeal for reversal brought against an order demanding a remedy of a claim does not guarantee the fundamental rights alleged in an appeal for constitutional protection. The foregoing may be based on the fact that the filing of an appeal for reversal does not suspend the challenged resolution (Article 186.3 LJS, formerly Article 184.1. LPL), in such a way that a challenge of the remedy order would not prevent the harm derived from the court's *ultra vires* conduct, as the appellant, irrespective of whether or not the order is challenged, would be obliged to fulfill it (in other words, an infringement would be confirmed that it was trying to avoid with an appeal for reversal). However, this risk does not exist, as proven by STC 10/2011. The Court declared in this case that, in similar situations, when a fundamental right is being discussed in an appeal for reversal, non-suspensive effects do not automatically apply and the constitutionality issue raised should first be settled; if the appellant's objection is dismissed, it should be granted a further term in which to fulfill the remedy order.

In short, both ATC 50/200 and STC 10/2011 respectively determine the need to challenge the order whereby the judicial secretary currently requests what it cannot do, being advised of the failure to exhaust prior judicial proceedings and, otherwise, the guarantee that such challenge will not affect the fundamental right in question given that the appeal for reversal has no suspension effects.

Still in relation to Article 44.1.a) LOTC, we will finally refer to the premature nature of appeals for constitutional protection, although the issue is more familiar than the previous ones. The Court has repeatedly established (e.g., STC 50/2001, of February 26, FJ 2) that, in principle and subject to the exceptions indicated below, if a complaint is brought against judicial resolutions delivered as part on an ongoing process, in the absence of a final and non-appealable resolution, prior judicial proceedings are not presumed exhausted and, consequently, it is not possible to bring an appeal for constitutional protection before the TC.

There are only exceptions to this general rule if an exhaustive completion of prior procedural steps, covering all stages or instances, entails an extra burden, extension or greater infringement of the right due to its continuation in time (e.g., STC 247/1994, of September 19, FJ 1), provided that, furthermore, the constitutional infringement "is immediately and irreversibly effective" (STC 52/2000, of February 28, FJ 4). On the other hand, in all those cases where an alleged infringement has no immediate effects and any consequential effect will only be evidenced in the outstanding judgment, it is the latter decision, once final, which should be challenged before the Constitutional Court. Otherwise, further to a material interpretation of the need to exhaust judicial proceedings (Article 44.1.a) LOTC), given the procedural stage where constitutional protection is raised, it may be concluded that there is still a possibility of reported infringements being repaired by the ordinary courts or to be ultimately devoid of material relevance. This would be the case, for instance, if the appellant obtains a favorable resolution on the merits of the case, which is still a possibility and would deprive complaints of any constitutional relevance.

Nevertheless and as already anticipated, there are some exceptions to this premature system, that is in the case of personal freedom (STC 247/1994), when a breach is claimed of the right to an ordinary judge predetermined by law (Article 24.2 CE) (STC 161/1995), and in certain habeas corpus cases, as pointed out in Constitutional Court Judgments 27/1997 and 136/1997. But apart from the foregoing, the other principle will apply. Furthermore, appeals for constitutional protection are not used for preventive or interim purposes only.[8]

13.2.3.4 *Untimeliness of Appeals and Unification of Doctrine*

To conclude, it is relevant to point out ATC 64/2007, of February 26. Traditionally, the TC has considered that attempts to unify doctrine, regardless of a subsequent inadmissibility decision, did not entail a manifestly inadequate use of appeals which, indirectly, determined the untimeliness of an appeal for constitutional protection, given that an application for unification of doctrine is not aimed at extending the timeframe available for the appeal (Constitutional Court Judgments 211/1999, of November 29, FJ 3; and 144/2005, of June 6, FJ 2, for example).

ATC 64/2007 questions this traditional premise. According to established doctrine, the filing of this extraordinary appeal will be manifestly inadequate if "it is in all respects incompatible with unification of doctrine as an institution,

---

8. Vicente Gimeno Sendra, *El recurso español constitucional de amparo*, in VV.AA., *La ciencia del Derecho Procesal Constitucional. Estudios en homenaje a Héctor Fix-Zamudio en sus cincuenta años como investigador del derecho*, vol. VII, 293 (Procesos constitucionales de la libertad, Marcial Pons, México, 2008).

pursuant to legal regulations and consistent case-law laid down by the Employment Chamber of the TS, that is whenever this procedural means of reaction is used in cases where a pursued standard application of the law, in the case of diverging doctrine, is not a likely possibility *ex ante* and according to TS criteria."

Please note that this ATC does not only refer to unequivocal determinations of procedural law, but also to a "constant interpretation of the case-law." Consequently, an appeal for constitutional protection will be untimely if during a motion to vacate the appellant has ignored reiterated and constant TS doctrine on appeal admissibility criteria. To give an example, constitutional protection sought after a decision is delivered dismissing a motion to vacate for the unification of doctrine due to the non-final nature of the comparative judgment.

It is also likely that this same logic may apply to other procedural appeals and remedies and to any jurisdictional order.

13.3 POSSIBLE PRONOUNCEMENTS, ENFORCEMENT OF APPEAL JUDGMENTS AND IRREGULARITIES IN PROCESSING THE APPEAL

A judgment delivered in appeals for constitutional protection is regulated by Articles 53–55 LOTC. The first article states that the Chamber or Section (in forwarded appeals)—to include the Plenary Meeting (when hearing and ruling on cases)—will grant or reject the protection sought. The next article, conceived for Article 44 LOTC appeals, includes a precaution about a declaratory judgment, point out that it will merely specify whether or not the plaintiff's rights or freedoms have been infringed, upholding or reestablishing such rights or freedoms, refraining from any other consideration on the conduct of jurisdictional bodies. In turn, Article 55 establishes the pronouncements that the Court's resolution may contain: (a) declared nullity of the decision, act or resolution preventing a full exercise of the rights or freedoms protected, determining the scope of its effects, as the case may be, (b) acknowledgement of the right or public freedom, according to its constitutionally declared content, and (c) restoring the appellant in its full right or freedom, adopting the necessary measures to preserve it, as the case may be.[9]

These provisions grant the Court a wide margin of discretion, as a result of which it is completely free to deliver its Rulings. This freedom, nevertheless, has occasionally given rise to controversial resolutions, such as STC 225/2001, of November 26 (despite a violation of a trade union as an institution, as a result of an employer's decision to regulate working conditions, which damaged and

---

9. Section 2 adds that any appeal for constitutional protection that is upheld on the grounds that the law applied breaches fundamental rights or public freedoms (third scenario from amongst those foreseen in la STC 155/2009) will be forwarded to the Plenary Meeting, suspending the timeframe in which judgment is delivered, pursuant to Arts. 35 et seq. of the Act.

avoided the binding nature of the CBA in force in the company (Articles 28.1 and 37.1 CE), excluding an entire group if workers and not following the internal channels foreseen in the CBA and any external channels, agreed upon or established by law, or related to the resolution of conflicts), which merely made a declaratory pronouncement of the breach, without nullifying the working conditions contained in the document that replaced the CBA and which had given rise to the breach, or overruling the Judgment that had upheld its validity.

Next, we will refer to Article 92 LOTC, the provision of this Public General Act in charge of enforcing the Court's resolutions:

> The Court may establish in its judgment or resolution, or in subsequent acts. who will enforce it and, if applicable, settle any enforcement incidents.
>
> It may also declare the nullity of any resolutions that contradict those delivered further to its competence, as a result of enforcing the latter, after hearing the State Prosecution Office and the deciding court.

Section 2 of the article was introduced by Public General Act 6/2007. ATC 1/2009, delivered in an incident to enforce STC 3/2007, of January 15 (which granted the protection requested by the appellant worker and, consequently recognized her fundamental right to no discrimination on the grounds of sex (Article 14 CE)), describes the essential components of this Article 92 LOTC incident and the right to enforce constitutional judgments, establishing the following criteria: (a) the enforcement of final Judgments in their own terms and upholding their final nature and intangibility of the legal situations declared therein is also applicable to Constitutional Court Judgments, (b) all public powers will be bound by constitutional Judgments, both as regards the ruling and legal grounds, (c) when a judicial body is fulfilling a constitutional Judgment, it may interpret its scope, as long as it does not contradict it or reduce the effectiveness of the subjective legal situation declared in the constitutional resolution, (d) the failure of ordinary courts to enforce Judgments in constitutional protection appeals will not only breach the enforcement and intangibility guarantee, but also the fundamental right acknowledged and restored by the Court in its ruling (i.e., the material fundamental right at play), and, finally, (e) in Article 92 LOTC enforcement incidents, the TC will merely check whether the constitutional Judgment has been adequately enforced, that is the understanding of the Judge as to the content of the constitutional Judgment, further to its enforcement mandate and, furthermore, whether it has been adequately fulfilled.

The foregoing claims may therefore be challenged through the Article 92 LOTC incident.

To end, we will refer to Act 13/2009, of November 3, on the reform of procedural laws to establish a new judicial office, published in the Otlicial State Gazette (BOE) on November 4, 2009. Article 9 included section 5 in Article 139 of Act 30/1992, of November 26, on the legal regime applicable to public administrations and common administrative procedure (LPC) as follows:

The Council of Ministers will determine the indemnification payable when the Constitutional Court has declared, at the request of an interested party, that appeals for constitutional protection or unconstitutionality issues have been irregularly processed. The procedure to establish the indemnification amount will be processed by the Ministry of Justice, after hearing the State Council.

Further to this rule, the Plenary Meeting of the Court delivered ATC 194/2010, of December 2, and subsequent Decisions 106/2012, of May 22, and 120/2012, of June 6, all in relation to this liability procedure that is still relatively unknown. The most important part of the Court's posture is its outright affirmation that it is the only competent instance to declare whether or not there has been an indemnifiable irregularity in the processing of appeals for constitutional protection and unconstitutionality issues, further to Article 139.5 LPC. Only if the Court believes that there was irregular processing will the second stage begin, where indemnification will be determined by the Council of Ministers after the relevant procedure. In other words, the Court does not make any pronouncement about the outcome of the suits in order for the Council of Ministers to issue a decision, but resolves on the irregularity claimed, and is the only one able to do so. Further to its jurisdictional supremacy (Article 1.1 LOTC) the Court's resolutions "may not be examined by any [other] jurisdictional body of the State (Article 4.2 LOTC)."

B Workers Participation in the Enterprise: Information and Consultation Rights, Codetermination Dynamics and Firms Welfare

CHAPTER 14
Workers Participation in the Firm: Trends and Insights

Tiziano Treu

14.1 DIVERGENT NATIONAL PATTERNS AND EUROPEAN HARMONIZATION

The concept and the practice of workers participation in the enterprise have a long and controversial history in the European countries.[1] Indeed the basic ideas and ideologies have been a matter of discussion and of bitter controversies within the labour movement throughout the twentieth Century. These controversies reflect the different position of the labour movement and of the (labour friendly) political parties on the role of workers and of trade unions in democratic countries.

Different unions and political strategies have shaped all the relations between the labour movement and the economic and social institutions of the European countries.[2] The divergence among the various strategies has been most acute on the role of workers and unions *vis-à-vis* the central economic

---

1. *See* in general Marco Biagi, Michele Tiraboschi, *Forms of Employee Representational Participation*, in Roger Blanpain (ed.), Comparative Labor Law & Ind. Rel. in Industrialized market economies, 585 et seq. (W. Kluwer, 2014).; Roger Blanpain (ed.), *Involvement of Employees in the European Works Councils, European Company Statute, Information and Consultation Rights,* 42 BCLR (2002); Manfred Weiss, *The European Community Approach to Workers' Participation: Recent Developments,* in Alan Neal (ed.), *The Changing Face of European Labour Law and Social Policy,* 39–53 (Kluwer Law International, The Netherlands, 2004).
2. These differences correspond to various models of national trade union movements: *see* the comparative analysis in Gian Primo Cella, Tiziano Treu, *National Trade Union Movements,* in Roger Blanpain (ed.), Comparative Labor Law, *supra* n. 1, Ch. 18, at 541 et seq.

institution of our societies, namely the firm in its various forms, and has influenced the major traits of the national systems of labour management relations.

The role of workers and of unions representatives within the firms, in particular the forms and the possibility of their participation to enterprise decision making, have been considered a significant element which characterizes the social model and indeed the different types of (national) capitalism.[3]

The difference between the various European systems, and their collectives actors, is well represented in the long dispute, which lasted for over two decades, concerning the European directives aimed at promoting different forms of workers participation in the enterprise.[4]

The directives approved between 1985 and 2009 on this issue represent the major attempt of the European institution to intervene directly in labour management relations; and are an exception to the mainly abstensionistic attitude of the European Union (EU) in this area.

This intensive regulatory action confirms the importance attributed by the EU to the internal dynamics of the firms and to the promotion of collaboratory labour relations as essential components of the European social model. More specifically it is assumed that collaborative industrial relations at firm level are conducive to both social peace and economic efficiency. Moreover the promotion of social peace and collaboration within the firms is considered to contribute positively to radiate similar participatory attitudes and strategies to the entire system of industrial relations and hence to reinforce social cohesion and economic stability.[5]

These reasons asserted by the European institutions during the preparation of the directives, were influenced by the most prominent model of workers participation at firm level, namely the German codetermination. But precisely on this point the European strategy had to face quite different positions not only of most national employers association, which are traditionally opposed or sceptical to all kind of workers participation, but also the reluctance of many national labour unions to adopt the German model of participation. The resistance was common to those unions which were not opposed in principle to workers participation, like the non-communist unions of Italy, France, Spain and even UK.

---

3. Peter Hall, David Soskice, *Varieties of capitalism: the institutional foundations of comparative advantage* (OUP, 2001); see also Raymond Markey et al. (eds), *Models of employee participation in a changing global environment. Directory and interaction* (Aldershot, Ashgate, 2001).
4. Different positions have emerged already in the first proposal of directive known as Vredeling (1980): see Roger Blanpain et al., *The Vredeling proposal* (Deventer, Kluwer, 1983).
5. Manfred Weiss, *Industrial Relations and EU Employment*, in John Craig, Michael Lynk (eds), *Globalization and the Future of Labor Law*, 181 et seq. (Cambridge, Cambridge University Press, 2010).

This opposition was consistent with the practices of labour management relations prevailing in these countries. Their national unions, which traditionally regarded collective bargaining as the primary way to govern labour management in general and at firm level, attributed to collective agreements, and not to the law, the decision to set up and to regulate workers information and participation, and shared different positions on the content and on the forms of these rights.

14.2 THE CONTINUUM OF WORKERS PARTICIPATION: FROM INFORMATION TO BOARD-LEVEL REPRESENTATION

The different forms of participation adopted in the national systems can be placed along a continuum, ranging from the right of workers and of their representatives to be informed about the major decisions of the enterprise, to that of being consulted on the same issues prior to employers decisions, to the various forms of 'institutional' participation,[6] including the presence of workers representatives in the governing bodies of the company. The definition of these participatory rights as a continuum indicates that they share common elements and differ for the modes and the intensity of their influence on enterprise decision making.

But the two poles of the continuum represent different policy and ideological approaches of the unions vis-à-vis the firm, a divergence linked to the general positions of the labour movement in industrial relations and in society. At one extreme the basic concept is that the unions and the forms of workers participation have to remain external to the firm, and the influence on firms decisions can be exerted through the various forms of collective action, including strike.

This position excludes the presence of employees representatives not only in the decision making process of the enterprise, but in principle also in bilateral institutions set up within the enterprise with the task of determining working conditions in conjunction with management.

A similar approach has inspired the general attitude of these Unions towards the private enterprise and indeed towards the functioning of the economy. Unions actions and collective bargaining had to be concerned exclusively with the representation and protection of workers interests mainly in the distribution of income, with no concern with the organization, the strategies and even the success of the firm.

These positions have deep roots in the political and labour union history of these countries. They are favoured by a system of industrial relations characterized by high level of political and ideological conflict and class consciousness of the labour movement, by the existence of strong left-wing parties, particularly the communist, and by the traditional weakness of organized labour which has

---

6. The term 'institutional' or 'organic' implies the formal presence of workers representatives within the enterprise as an 'institution'.

kept it away from the enterprise, and excluded the possibility of influencing from within the managerial decision making process.

Similar 'antagonistic' orientations were not confined to the most militant labour unions, but reflected the widely shared opinion that growth was a self-sustaining mechanism, in a linear direction of development. This opinion implied that labour law and at social policies in most countries, had the exclusive objective to protect workers in their employment conditions.

The profound transformations intervened in the last decades with the recurrent economic crisis and instability, have altered the very basis on which these assumptions were founded. These transformations have challenged the economic actors to change attitude and forced them to share the concern for the conditions of production and for the dynamics of the firms. For much the same reasons labour law is required to change its approach with respect to the economic conditions of growth. We will return of this point.

14.3 THE GERMAN MODEL AND ITS FOUNDATIONS

The other extreme of the continuum is represented by the 'institutional' or organic forms of workers participation, in which workers representatives are present in the governing bodies of the firms, more precisely of their legal expression, the corporation. Here too the development of these forms of institutional participation is rooted in the history of the political and industrial relations systems.[7] These systems, which are mainly concentrated in central and northern European countries, are characterized by a strong, united and politically integrated union movement, by a stable social and political structure of the country, by a civic attitude and ethos inclined to sustain social cohesion. All these elements are conducive to develop and to make acceptable non adversarial labour management relations. More specifically they are reinforced by a widely shared concept of the firm as an organic entity or as a community (*gemeinschaft*), which corresponds to the common feeling of the people and has been dominant also among the legal scholars. In fact this communitarian concept of the firm is most congenial for hosting some institutional or organic forms of participation of workers who are a decisive component of the enterprise community.

These favourable conditions have not removed all the obstacles to the introduction of the various forms of institutional participation in those countries. The difficulties are shown in the first experiments and in the subsequent events of the Weimar Republic, and after the second world by the introduction of *Mitbestimmung* in Germany by decree of the allied forces occupying the country.

---

7. In Germany the first set of proposals of workers participation in the enterprise and in the economy goes back to the Weimar republic and the socialist scholars of that period, from Sinzheimer to Naphtali.

These forms of workers participation have been introduced in the governance structure of the companies as existing at the time, without questioning its form and legitimacy. This decision appears to be consistent with the idea of the firm as *'Gemeinschaft'*, in so far as the workers representatives are an integral part of the community as it is. In fact this assumption has not been challenged in the subsequent experience of the *Mitbestimmung*. As we shall see it will have to be re-examined in view of the transformations of the companies' structure in the postfordist era.

One further element must be mentioned in order to qualify the forms of institutional participation adopted in central European countries: namely the presence of workers representative elected in the units of the firm having codetermination rights in a series of important enterprise decisions.[8] These powers of codetermination legally recognized are an essential part of the participatory model of German companies. They do not alter the hierarchical structure of firms but they shape their decision processes not by periodical pressures like in collective bargaining but by their presence and daily intervention in the work organization and practices.

14.4 EUROPEAN HARMONIZATION OF A MINIMUM COMMON DENOMINATOR

The various system of participation have developed in the European countries according to the national traditions and responding to the strategies of the national actors: the social parties, the governments and the relevant public institutions.

For this reason the original purpose of the European authorities to harmonize the national models of participation has met with strong obstacles. In fact the European Commission has promoted successfully the harmonization only of those forms of participation which were present and accepted in most European countries: first of all information and consultation, subsequently the European Works Councils (EWC), which are mainly instrumental to the practice of information and consultation rights.

The EU directives on these issues have managed to harmonize some common traits of national practices, that is, adopting and extending a sort of minimum common denominator. This result and these limits of the European harmonization are indeed common to other areas of European social law.

The unions and the EWCs have been granted the rights to previous information and consultation on the major firms initiatives and policies, but not the rights to codetermination, which have the most direct influence on the decision making process of the firms. The EU promotion of the rights of information and consultation had a direct impact in these countries whose national practices had never experienced statutory regulation of the matter. In

---

8. *See* the contribution of Manfred Weiss in this volume.

other countries, like Italy, where information and consultation rights were recognized by many national agreements, the European directives 94/45 and 2002/14 contributed to consolidate and to extend the existing practices. An important impact of these directives is that they have contributed to spread these practices among small and medium size firms which usually were not reached by collective agreements.

The scope of directive 2002/149 covers all European firms employing more than fifty employees in one member country; which means a coverage of 3% of firms and of 50% of the employees. Lower limits are sometime indicated in national systems, following the impulse of legislation and of unions' pressure.[9]

The impact of these directives on the actual practice of information and consultation has been uneven, depending not so much on the legal transposition of the European norms in the national legislations, but on trade unions influence in the workplaces and on the general conditions of national industrial relations.

The European directive 94/45 (revised by directive 2009/38) has been rather effective in promoting the diffusion of EWCS among firms operating in different European states. According to recent estimates[10] EWCs have been set up in 1071 firms and groups of enterprises, amounting to a considerable percentage of the large companies operating in Europe (employing over 17 million workers). These representative bodies have contributed to improve the effectiveness of information and consultation practices with regard to transnational issues.

Moreover the EWC have developed their functions often beyond the area indicated by the directive, because they tend the use their rights to information and consultation in order to behave informally as bargaining agents, making the most of their acquired knowledge of firms' decisions and strategies.[11]

As mentioned already the directives on EWCs and information and consultation rights have promoted the type of participation more in line with the tradition of Industrial Relation of many European countries, and less resisted by both the unions and the employers' associations precisely because these rights are asserted from 'outside' the firm. However the diffusion of information and consultation rights and of the representative bodies exercising these rights has contributed considerably to introduce participatory patterns in European labour management relations, and to influence in the same direction the practices of collective bargaining.

---

9. See in general Alan Neal, *Information and Consultation for Employees – Still Seeking the Philosopher's Stone?* in Marco Biagi (ed.), *Quality of Work an Employee Involvement in Europe*, 83–99 (The Hage-London-New York, 2002); Edoardo Ales, *Directive 2002/14/EC establishing a general framework for informing and consulting employees in the European Community*, Sinthesis report, Labour Asociados Consultores (October 2007).
10. Stan De Spiegelaere, Romuald Jagodzinsky, *European works councils and SE Works councils in 2015*, Facts and Figures (ETUI, 2015).
11. Romuald Jagodzinski (ed.), *The Implementation of the EWC Recast Directive*, (ETUI, Brussels, 2015); Sigurt Vitols, *European works Councils: an assessment of their social welfare impact* (ETUI, Brussels, 2009).

The collective rights of informations and consultation recognized by the directives concern the firms decisions not only on work organization and on the conditions of work, but also on the employment trends and on the major decisions and development plans impinging on employment and working conditions. The periodic exchange of information and of opinions between the parties on these issues has provided workers representatives with a systematic knowledge of the enterprise functioning and strategies, which is absent or even excluded in adversarial collective bargaining.

The norms of the directive provide that information and consultation must intervene in due time, that is since the initial formation of enterprise decisions, so to allow an effective dialogue between the parties and an influence on the final decisions of the firm: then norms are an explicit indication that these firms decisions must take into account the collective voice of the employees. The other provision of the directives whereby the rights to information and consultation must be exercised *vis-à-vis* 'the appropriate level of the enterprise decision making process', gives the workers representative an unprecedented opportunity to look into the structure of the enterprises and to verify the relevant centres of decision even beyond the 'legal veils' of the different companies which are part of the group.

The diffusion and the acceptance of the rights of information and consultation mark a substantial distance from the positions traditionally followed by some national unions which excluded any involvement in the enterprise. These rights, although asserted 'from outside' may be quite influential on enterprise behaviour.

This argument may be used and in fact is often advanced, to confirm the view that the various forms of participation should be analysed on a continuum and judged for their effective incidence on firms' decisions more than for their legal form.

14.5 THE COMPROMISE SOLUTION OF THE SE

The different positions of the actors of the national industrial relations systems are reflected in the long discussions which have brought to the approval of the European company statute in 2001 (directive 2001/86 and regulation 2157/2001). The final approval was based on a compromise among the different positions which had blocked the decision for years.[12] The initial proposal to

---

12. *See* in general, Filip Dorssemont, *The Adoption of the SE Directive: The EWC Directive Now Has 'Company'*, in Charlotte Villiers (ed.), *The Directive on Employee Involvement in the European Company: Its Role in European Corporate Governance and Industrial Relations*, in 2 IJCLLIR 209 et seq. (2006). A critical view of this compromise solution of the SE, in Paul L. Davies, *Workers on the Board of European Company*, 32, 2 IRJ 87 (2003); Kenneth W. Wedderburn of Charlton, *Employees. Partnership and company law*, 101 ILJ (2002); according to this author this directive represents the end of the community efforts to provide for representatives of the employees interest within the structure of company law.

adopt the German system of board-level employees' representation as the only model for the SE, was abandoned. Instead the European company was shaped as to allow other forms of employees participation practiced in the European countries: not only the presence of employees representatives in the governing bodies of the companies (board of directors, supervisory board), but also the election of workers representatives in a special body, distinct from those organs and enabled to exercise the rights to information and consultation.

The option between these different models was left in first instance to the parties negotiating the adoption of the SE (special negotiating body), according to the subsidiarity principle followed in other areas of European social policies. Lacking any agreement among the parties the directive indicates as subsidiary requirements two possible solutions: the adoption of a form of organic participation if pre-existing in the companies present in the SE or of a representative body distinct from the organs of the enterprise. This provision, based on the before/after principle implies that the rights of participation acquired in the original company are the basis for the same rights in the SE. More specifically it is intended to avoid that the adoption of the SE might reduce the rights of the employees of the countries where the institutional participation of workers in the companies was previously established.

The plurality of forms allowed by the directive and the conservation of previous employees' rights indicates the impossibility to fully harmonize the different systems present in the European countries. In particular it confirms the reluctance of the social parties of many countries, although for different reasons, to break with their national traditions and to accept a direct involvement in the governance structure of the firms.

On the other hand the directive recognizes to the representative bodies of the workers in the SE the same rights to information, consultation and participation which are granted to the trade unions and to the EWCs by the directives 2002/149 and 2009/38.

This latter solution can hardly be considered equivalent to the organic participation typical of the German model, because the presence of workers participation within the boards of the firm allows for a more stable and more significant exchange of information and of opinions between the boards and workers representatives. It may also facilitate greater workers influence on the decisions of the bodies where their representatives are present: the board of directors (*vorstand*) or the supervisory board (*aufsichtrat*).

14.6 FACTORS AFFECTING THE EFFECTIVENESS OF PARTICIPATION

In any case however the influence of workers representatives on company's decisions is limited because they are in a minority position within the boards, and even in the most advanced form of participation they can never determine the final decision of the board (*see* Manfred Weiss, in this volume).

The effective influence may depend on factors others than the legal composition of the boards, namely on the capacity of workers representatives to support their view with the authority derived from the pressure of their constituencies and possibly on the ability to establish alliances with other stakeholders, internal and external to the firm. Moreover the structure of the decision – making process and the distribution of competences among the various organs of the firm, even beyond the legal provisions, is relevant in determining the real impact of workers participation on the company strategy and organization.

The effectiveness of workers representation is also linked to the specific objects of firm decisions. The practice of participation indicates that workers representatives in the boards (and also the Work Directors provided by the German legislation of 1976 and 1951) usually concentrate their attention on those decisions which are directly relevant to working conditions. This represent a sort of tacit division of labour with the representatives of management which correspond to the skills and the traditional roles of workers and of managers in any type of company. Given this division of labour, the position of workers representatives in the institutional participation may resemble to that of unions representatives and of the EWCs in a well-functioning system of information and consultation in participatory bargaining.

Moreover informal arrangements are often adopted by companies in order to specify or to circumvent formal procedures, and to change the functions of the organs where workers representatives are present, with the effect of reducing their voice and influence. Indeed, as indicated by Manfred Weiss with reference to the Germany model, the actual value of institutional participation can be fully appreciated only by taking into account the entire system of labour management relations; particularly the presence of two levels of workers representation closely interrelated, where the workers representation in the supervisory board is a sort of extended arm of the works councils. Most employees' representatives in the board are usually also works council members and this link has strengthened both those instruments of participation. It has promoted communication through informal channels, between workers representatives and their constituencies contributing to build mutual trust and an organizational culture based on long lasting consultation practices. The success of the German model is grounded on these factors, and even more profoundly in common social values, including the idea of the firm a community: all elements which are not easily transferable in other national systems.

The impact of directive 86/2001 on the harmonization of participatory practices in Europe has been rather limited.[13] The number of SE has increased to around 600, but mainly in the countries of central Europe where large companies

---

13. Berndt Keller, *The European company statute: employee involvement and beyond*, 33 IRJ 439 (2002); Jan Cremers, Michael Stollt, Sigurt Vitols (eds), *A Decade of Experience with the European Company* (ETUI, Brussels, 2013).

had already adopted forms of organic participation and wanted to maintain them in the new European format.

In the other European countries the parties have continued to practice the forms of participation traditionally prevailing, and have avoided to adopt the SE even in the minimal version (subsidiary requirements) endorsed by the directive in case of non-agreement among the negotiating parties which does not innovate the traditional practices of information and consultation.

The practice of these countries confirms the reluctance of both social parties (although for different reasons) to cross the 'borders' of the company structure of governance. The unions are still opposed to be involved in the internal functioning of the enterprise, because they consider it an alien if not a hostile ground. The employers prefer to keep workers representatives off this ground; indeed in the case of SME they tend to exclude the very presence of these representatives.

14.7 THE IMPACT OF THE RECENT TRANSFORMATIONS OF WORK AND OF FIRMS STRUCTURE ON WORKERS PARTICIPATION

The great transformations occurred in recent years in the economic and social conditions of the world and in the structure of firms have exposed to new challenges all the components of industrial relations systems including the forms and practices of participation.

An extensive body of research has analysed the economic and social changes which have altered the traditional traits of Industrial relations and the power relations between the actors to the detriment of the labour movement. The impact of the new forms of organization of the firms, national and multinational, has also been analysed, but not yet fully explored.

The diversity and the increased volatility of the types of work induced by the new technologies, the competitive pressures, and the deregulation of markets have contributed to a general weakening of the labour movement, eroding the very basis of their representativeness and of collective action. These factors have a negative impact particularly on workers representative bodies in the workplace which are essential actors of collective action and are directly exposed to the pressure of these factors. The diversity of the new workforce has reduced its social cohesion and contributed to create favourable conditions for the individualization of labour management relations. It has reduced the appeal of all forms of collective action for the new workers and at the same time has made room for an innovative management to establish direct relations with the individual employees and/or groups of them with the aim of promoting their involvement in the enterprise.

The term 'involvement' has multiple connotations, but in these cases it implies that the participation of employees is shaped individually on management terms and is determined by management more strictly than those forms of participation based on collective or legal regulations.

14.8 MANAGEMENT-LED FORMS OF EMPLOYEES INVOLVEMENT

The forms and objects of these managerial initiatives are different. But they share a common character, that of being mostly concerned with the organization of work in the productive units, or even below, in the shop floor.

The involvement of employees as individuals and in team works, which are often being used particularly in the sectors of intelligent manufacturing, has proved to be an effective instrument for promoting innovations and productivity. Participatory teams are highly valued by management because they allow making the most of the experience and of the knowledge of the employees acquired in the daily life of the plants.[14]

The direct participation of employees to the organization of work has been recently promoted by Italian Legislation (Act 208/2015 and 232/2016) which has granted special fiscal incentives when the employers who negotiate productivity bonuses at company level, also establish this kind of bilateral forms of employees participation.

Recent research, concerned mainly with Italian cases, shows ambivalent implications of this type of involvement for labour management and industrial relation. It confirms that employees' involvement in participatory teams is gaining ground among high performance firms where it contributes to the firms' success and to the well-being of the people involved.[15] The initiation and the contents of these experiments are always in the hands of management. But their objective is not necessary anti-union, as it has been historically in many countries (US in the first place). Most often management initiatives seem to develop outside union channels, without any formal unions' intervention, particularly in the countries where they have no legal power to intervene in work organization. Union representatives particularly at plant level have been involved and contributed to their success in specific cases where the practice of collaborative labour relations was already established.

The success of these experiments confirms their importance for the quality of future labour management relations. The labour unions are called to respond to this new challenge on penalty of leaving to management an important ground

---

14. See Eurofound, *Work Organization and innovation* (Dublin, 2012), where various high performance workplace practices (Hpwp), are reported. These practices, inspired originally by managerial strategies developed in the US, have been mainly interested in their impact on productivity and on HRM innovation; the implications on workers participation have usually been considered instrumental to pursing those objectives. The body of research is vast: see Duncan Gallie (ed.), *Employment Regimes and the quality of Work* (Oxford, Oxford university press, 2007); Alex Bryson (ed.), *Advances in the Economic Analysis of participatory and Labor-managed firms*, 267–309 (Bingley (UK), Emerald Group, 2012); Inge Lippert, *Corporate governance, Employee Voice, and Work Organization* (New York, Oxford University Press, 2014); Federico Butera, *Options for the Future of Work*, in Federico Butera et al. (ed.), *Options for the Future* (London, Coogan 1987).
15. Luciano Pero, Anna Maria Ponzellini, *Il nuovo lavoro industriale tra innovazione, organizzazione partecipazione diretta*, in *La partecipazione incisiva*, Mimmo Carrieri, Paolo Nerozzi & Tiziano Treu (a cura), 45 et seq. (2015).

of action which may enrich the value of participation, particularly for employees who are not reached by traditional collective activities.

It is up to the unions to place these forms of 'micro participation' in the wider context of labour management relations, so that the scope and influence of collective participation may be extended to all business activities and strategies, as it has been in the most valuable national traditions.

14.9 SPECIALIZED AND FINANCIAL FORMS OF WORKERS PARTICIPATION

European firms have experienced in many countries other forms of employees' participation. A widely diffused type is represented by specialized representative bodies, often bilateral, dealing with matters of common interest of the parties directly influential on the quality of work.

The major areas of interest are professional training, health and safety at work and welfare benefits. The EU has not provided any general model of specialized workers representation.

Health and safety at work has been an area of extensive regulation by the European authorities. The council directive of 12 June 1989 recognizes the rights of employees and /or of their representatives to be consulted and to take part in all issues relating to health and safety at work. A similar right is sanctioned by many national legislations which regulate also various forms of specialized committees competent in these matters.[16]

It is also worth noting that the EU has recognized the opportunity to adopt various forms of workers participation to the economic results of the firm, in two directions: by promoting various kinds of bonuses and profit sharing and by favouring with fiscal incentives the distribution of shares among employees and Employees Stock Ownership Plans (ESOP).[17]

These types of participation have in common with other forms character that they may contribute to promote employees involvement within the enterprise, but they differ from the mainstream approach of workers participation for their sectorial or micro objects which reduces or exclude their impact on the overall balance of labour management relations.[18]

---

16. R. Eberlie, *The new health and safety legislation of the European community*, ILJ 81 (1990) ss.; *see also* directive 94/33 on the protection of youngsters at work; V. Morettini, *Le comité consultative pour la securité, l'hygiène et la protection de la santé sur le lieu de travail*, ES, 2/1990, p. 14 ss.
17. The contents and the diffusion of these forms of financial employees participation in the European Union are documented by the Pepper IV Report: (updated 2010), Jens Lowitsch (ed.), Institute for Eastern European Studies, Free University of Berlin. According to the latest estimates of the European federation of Employee share ownership (EFES) in 2015 the number of European employees holding shared has reached eight million, amounting to EUR 370 million.
18. *See* in general Pepper Report IV. Often these bonuses and stock ownership represent simply an economic supplement to the regular wages of the individual employee with no

For this reason they have usually attracted scarce interest or met with resistance from the labour movement; and in many cases have been promoted by managerial initiatives. On the other hand they have acquired greater importance also for the labour movement when, like in the field of health and safety and of professional training, they have been endorsed by legislation or when some forms of financial participation such as profit sharing and stock ownership have not remained a simply way of remunerating the work, but have implied some participation of workers to the governance of the firm. This has been the case for example in some Italian and French state controlled enterprises.[19]

14.10 ACCEPTANCE AND INNOVATION OF WORKERS PARTICIPATION: THE IMPACT OF THE INDIVIDUALIZATION OF EMPLOYMENT RELATIONS

The forms of workers participation analysed so far have come to be widely, if not unanimously, accepted in many European countries. But their long experience does not rescue them from the challenges deriving from the new environment in which they must operate, which is so different from that of their origins. On the contrary this acceptance might favour inertia or even prize conservation over innovation.

The major challenges to employees participation come from two factors, which are affecting all aspects of social and economic life: the diversity and the individualization of the working population; the changing structure and organization of the firms.

As I have already mentioned, the former trend poses a major threat to the very basis on which industrial relations and labour law have been built. How to re-launch the spirit and the strategies of collective action is an open question decisive for the future of the labour movement. The diffusion of workers participation at the enterprise and workshop level, may contribute to revitalizing the unions initiatives. This contribution may be more significant than that of adversarial collective bargaining which in the present contest of economic turmoil may be less attractive to the new labour force and possibly detrimental to the pursuance of common objectives of economic growth.

The importance of micro participation can increase if the legislator, as it has done in Germany will reinforce the presence of workers representative providing

---

involvement of the beneficiary in any aspect of enterprise decisions or organization. *See* the critical remarks of Jeremias Prassl, *Employee shareholders 'status', dismantling the contract of employment*, 4 ILJ, 323 (2013), who argues that the British legislation on employees shareholders may go to the detriment of the overall treatment of the beneficiaries.

19. In France workers participation in the governing bodies of state controlled enterprise has a long tradition. The last regulation, Act of 14 June 2013, is rather restrictive and provides the presence of a minority of workers representatives in the boards of enterprises with at least 5,000 employees in France or 10,000 worldwide (a very high threshold).

them with significant and even binding powers on the major issues of work organization. It remains to be seen if and under which conditions workers participation may keep this positive influence when it has to deal not with micro issues but with the general strategies of the firms and even more so with the directions and quality of economic growth; because these issues are less easily perceivable by the individualized constituencies of the unions.[20]

The second major trend of our time, that is the new forms of organization and of governance of the firm, have wide ranging implications on our social and economic systems and specifically on labour management relations. These implications are only partially explored by the actors of labour relations; because both the theoretical analysis and the practical consequences of the transformation of the firm (and of its legal form the corporation) have been for a long time neglected. Their impact has not been fully explored not only by unions representatives, but also by scholars, due to the traditional separation between the approach of labour lawyers and of business lawyers. The same separation is present in the two European legal sources, which have regulated the matter: a regulation on the statute of SE and a directive on workers participation in the SE. More specific research should be directed to analyse carefully, also on the basis of the existing practices, particularly these issues: how the functions and the structure of the various governing bodies of the firm influence the behaviour of the workers representatives, the interaction of these representatives with their constituency and with the representatives of management and of property; the distribution of roles, formal and informal, in respect to the different firm activities.

14.11 THE IMPACT OF CHANGING ENTERPRISE STRUCTURES: GROUP ENTERPRISES AND 'NETWORK CONTRACTS'

This neglect seems to be a residual manifestation of the traditional idea that the firm is not a matter of concern for the labour movement, but an entity to be taken as given and possibly to be changed by external action pressure.

Indeed one aspect of the enterprise transformation, namely the group of enterprises, has attached more attention than others by the legal doctrine and also by many national legislators. The aim has been mainly that of extending the area of labour law protections to the whole perimeter of the enterprise group and *vis-à-vis* the group itself. These attempts of the legal doctrine and of the national judges have not always been successful to break the 'corporate veil' and to identify the group as an entity responsible for labour law obligations. The identity and the responsibility of the enterprise group have been affirmed on

---

20. This is a critical point raised by the European unions with respect to similar forms of workers participation in the workplace, Due to their specific and narrow focus, they way prove more attractive for the personal interest of the individuals, but less for the general issues of union management relations; and consequently they may be easily captured by management logic and priorities.

various grounds only for specific issues, including the exercise of workers' rights of information, consultation and participation.[21]

The EU has pursued since the 1980s the objective of 'forcing' the centre of decision of the enterprise group with the aim of providing workers representatives with the relevant information concerning the whole group; in the Vredeling proposal even when this centre of decision was located outside the European community.[22]

Directives 2002/4 and 2009/38 confirm the same purpose by providing that the rights of workers representatives to consultation and information, must be exercised *vis-à-vis* the appropriate level of decision making. The EWC directive (Article 3) has also given an extensive definition of the controlling undertaking, in order to establish the body responsible for many duties of informations and consultation.

Similarly the norms on the institutional forms of participation take into account the specific character of the enterprise group, usually by providing that workers representatives must be present in the boards of the dominant firm of the group. The national and European regulation seem to indicate that the law is inclined to take into account the real power relations within the companies and the groups even beyond their legal structure. This factual approach is more easily followed here than in traditional employment regulation.

Such an approach seems in line with the need that these collective rights be measured precisely on their capacity to influence the power relations among the social parties. Complex problems of interpretation remain to be solved, particularly in order to identify the boundaries of the group of enterprises and the real centre of decisions among different legal entities. In fact the conclusion reached on this question by national and European courts are far from convergent.

Moreover the criteria adopted to solve this problem with respect to enterprise groups are not easily applicable to other forms of aggregation between firms, like the so called 'network contracts' where no dominant centre of power is identifiable because the units of the network are linked by contractual

---

21. The problems raised by the group enterprises are multifaceted. *See* for various aspects: José Baz Rodriguez, *Las relaciones de trabajo en la empresa de groupo*, (Granada, Editorial Comares, 2002); Gunther Teubner, *Unitas multiplex: problems of governance in Group enterprises from a system theory point of view* (Florence, EUS, 1988); Alain Supiot, *Groupes de societès et paradigme de l'enterprise*, RTD comm., 621 et seq. (1985); Simon Deakin, *The changing concept of employer in labor law*, ILJ 72 (2001); in Italy Marzia Barbera, *Trasformazioni della figura del datore di lavoro e flessibilizzazione delle regole del diritto*, GDLRI, 203 (2010).

22. *See* the Vredeling proposal quoted; the OECD guidelines on multinationals: Roger Blanpain, *The OECD guidelines for multinational enterprises and labor relations* (Deventer, Kluwer, 1983); Jorn Pipkorn, *The law of groups of enterprises in the European community* (ETUI, paper 1987); J. Vandamme, *L'information et la consultation des travailleurs dans la proposition de directive sur les enterprise a structure complexe*, RMC, 368 (1981); Chris Engels, Lisa Salas, *Transnational Information and Consultation; the European Works Council Directive*, in Roger Blanpain (ed.), *Comparative Labour Law, supra* n. 1, at 563 et seq. (2007).

relations established through consensus among peers. The practice of network contracts, is becoming less an exception, indeed quite common, as modern firms move away from the hierarchical structure of governance developed in the fordist model of production.

In fact the transformations of modern business enterprise have general implications for the legal theories of the firm and have spurred the legal doctrine to re-conceptualize the economic theorization of corporate law and of corporate governance.

14.12 PARTICIPATION IN THE 'FLUID ENTERPRISE'

The revision is underway with interesting but still uncertain results, some of which are presented in this volume.

Contributions to this debate are coming from the field of legal theory and of corporation law more than from labour lawyers for the reasons indicated above.[23] For the same reason the law and the practice of industrial relations have been predominantly interested in the firm as productive unit and have disregarded the importance of its governance structure. But the new configuration of the network firm and the theories which represent the enterprise as a more or less defined combination of contracts, have major consequences on both collective and individual employment relations because they blur the identity of the subject employer who is the necessary counterpart of the employees in individual and collective relations. The new character of the firm as a 'fluide sequence' of contract may require criteria for the identification of the employer different from those developed by traditional labour law.

The new criteria for this identification may be based on the major functions which underpins the notion of employer. It has been argued that the transformation of the firm's structure and organization may modify and even abolish the traditional subjects, but not the major functions and roles of business enterprises.[24] In the specific case of 'networks contracts' involving multiple units and firms, the definition of the various functions will depend in the first place on the contract which defines the powers and responsibilities of the parties, including those concerning employment relations. But the conditions for establishing these responsibilities will follow in principle the general rules of civil law. To avoid abuses the various types of responsibility will be attributed to the subjects who have exercised the functions of employer even beyond the wording of the contract.

These mutations of the firm structure have different implications on the forms of workers participation. Board-level participation has been based on the pattern of the large fordist corporation and on the notion of the enterprise as

---

23. *See* the contributions of Adalberto Perulli and Francesco Denozza published in this volume.
24. Denozza, quoted.

community. This form of participation may continue to operate as long as this type of enterprise exists. Its factual influence on labour management relations will depend on the importance that large corporations continue to have in the future systems of production. The various forms of subcontracting, outsourcing and fragmentation of productive activities will tend to reduce the scope of this type of participation. In any event workers institutional participation might have to adopt new instruments in order to function within the host corporation, which itself will be influenced by the changed economic and social scenario. For this reason the existing patterns of governance where workers representatives are elected cannot any long taken for granted as it has been so far. The very legal notion of establishment and of employees relevant to the application of workers participation might have to be redefined in view of the changing forms of organization of work and of the enterprise.[25]

Other patterns of participatory rights – mainly information and consultation – which have developed in Europe are less dependent on the structure of the enterprise. But even these rights have been mainly exercised – like most other collective rights – *vis-à-vis* the large enterprises and group enterprises assuming their existing governance and centres of decision.

The emergence of network firms and of multifunctional employers will require profound adaptation also of these forms of participation if they want to maintain economic and social effectiveness. In these cases the risk for workers representatives is to run after the multiple functions of the firm, as it happens with the micro forms of participation mentioned above, and to be captured by the interests of management or at best to reflect the 'partial rationalities' of the specific functions.

How to restore some unity of purpose among the various fragments of participation and finalize them, is an open question which must be faced with innovative answers by the collective actors in the first place and possibly by the legislator. A useful contribution could be to reinforce by law the powers of workers representatives at shop-floor level, which remains a decisive area of influence also in the new contest of multifunctional firms.

A second important condition is to strengthen the organizational and political links between shop floor representatives and the other levels of unions' organization present in the enterprise and beyond. This condition must be fulfilled by the labour movement itself and presupposes a search for unity beyond the boundaries of the individual firm. The pursuance of a unitary collective voice is the most important answer that the labour unions can oppose to the fragmentation of the employer. Indeed this is a general challenge facing the labour movement in the advanced economies; which implies not only a revision of strategies by the labour movement itself but also a reconsideration of the role of the law *vis-à-vis* the firm's governance.

---

25. *See* Effrosyni Bakirtzi, *The Role of the German Co-determination (mitbestimmung) in Balancing Interest at the Workplace*, in A. Perulli (eds), L'idea del diritto del lavoro, oggi. In ricordo di Giorgio Ghezzi (Cedam, 2016).

This issue can only be mentioned here because it has to be framed in the much boarder perspective of the horizontal effects of fundamental rights and of the scope of 'constitutionalism beyond the state'. The implications of this 'societal constitutionalism' on the new forms of firms governance should be explored following the suggestions of the authors who stress the importance of 'capillary constitutions' to counteract the 'totalization tendencies or the partial rationalities of the social subsystems' and of the multiple centres of powers present in our society.[26] It has to be remembered that the various forms of workers participation were among the forerunners of this idea of societal constitutionalism. Giving new instruments and strategies to workers participation in the enterprise will contribute to the expansion of constitutionalism in a critical area of social relations.

The impulse in this direction may come from an interplay of two process: of legal interventions and of the influence of social structures. The law can contribute to strengthen the autonomy and the powers of workers representativeness in the enterprise. But this process requires to be sustained by social actors 'by a self reflection' of the agents operating inside the firm of which workers representatives are an important element and by external actors (mention is made of NGOs, of social movements, and also of legal initiatives like the class action).[27]

14.13 PARTICIPATION IN THE CORPORATION AS 'COMMONS'

The necessary revision of participatory practices and strategies may receive new impulse and broader perspective if confronted with a recent reconceptualization of the corporations 'as commons'. According to this position the theory of commons, originally developed with respect to natural resources, better describes the legal structure of business enterprise that does the shareholder primacy model. The firms are to be seen as a shared resource whose sustainability depends on the participation of multiple constituencies in its governance: not just shareholders but employees, consumers and core suppliers.[28]

Viewing the corporation as a collectively managed resource by many stakeholders helps to understand the conditions on which the different actors can contribute both to the short term efficiency but also to long term sustainable development. Even more widely it can emphasize the role of business enterprise in generating the conditions for social and environmental sustainability.

---

26. Gunther Teubner, *Societal Constitutionalism: Alternatives to State-Centered Constitutional Theory?* in Christian Joerges, Inger-Johanne Sand and Gunther Teubner (eds) *Transnational governance and Constitutionalism*, 3–28 (Oxford Univ. Press, 2004); ID, *The many autonomies of private law*, 9 Soc. & Leg. Stud., 399 et seq. (2000) and already ID, *Substantive and reflexive elements in modern law*, 2 Spec. L. & Soc. Rev. 269 et seq. (1983).
27. Gunther Teubner, *Societal constitutionalism*, supra n. 26, at 9. et seq.
28. Simon Deakin, *The corporation as commons: rethinking property rights governance and sustainability in the business enterprise*, 37, 2 Queen's L. J., 367 et seq. (2012).

The growing interest in Corporate Social Responsibility (CSR) reflects the recognition that shareholder value model does not necessarily address social and environmental needs. The concept of sustainability, which involves generating value for stakeholders instead of just shareholders, is an alternative orienting principle which builds on the older concept of the company as a community of interest and connects it with wider concerns with the interests of society and of the environment as a whole.

It is true that institutional board-level workers participation has been originally based on the concept of the enterprise as a community. But the configuration of firm as commons has important difference with that historic precedent: both the German idea of community and the communitarian vision of Japanese firms.[29] They both refuse the shareholders primacy model. But the model of the German tradition is historically linked to the governance structure of the large fordist enterprises. The communitarian principle which support the participation of workers does not necessarily alter the hierarchical structure of the company, indeed it integrates workers representatives in the governing bodies of the corporation without changing their functioning. It may submit some workplace decisions to the controlling powers of the works councils, but without changing the primacy of the managers in the decision – making process and the control powers of the shareholders.

Consequently the scope and the actors of participation tend to coincide with the closed circuit of the corporation. Whereas the idea of commons describes the sphere of the business enterprise as being open to the influence of various stakeholders provided with different rights and claims.[30]

European documents have stated since the early years of the Community that legally supported employee participation is an expression of socially responsible management. The participation of stakeholders, in particular of workers, is needed to include a voice for long term interests in the company decision making process and to counterbalance the short- term interests of shareholders.

The argument, supported by (some) empirical evidence is that worker involvement can help create a win-win situation in which workers enjoy strong rights and the company operates efficiently in a sustainable manner.

A similar concept of 'sustainable company' has been recently analysed and proposed also by the European trade unions.[31] This indeed is the central meaning of CSR: that the essential values of the firm must be promoted not only by management but by all the stakeholders in their respective positions,

---

29. Ronald Dore, *Taking Japan seriously, a Confucian perspective on leading economic issues* (Stanford University Press, 1987); ID, *British factory Japanese factory – the origins of national diversity in industrial relations with a new afterwords* (Univ. of California Press, 1973).
30. Simon Deakin, *The corporation as commons*, supra n. 28, at 370 et seq.
31. Sigurt Vitols, Norbert Kluge (eds), *The sustainable company: a new approach to corporate governance*, I (ETUI, 2011); the author reports that a few companies have established formal stakeholders boards, including representatives of different interest groups.

included specifically the employees through their collective voice. This perspective has significant implications in the relations between workers representatives and other stakeholders.

A supportive legal framework is envisaged by the EUs in order to extend the sustainable model of companies beyond a few isolated cases. It is recognized that many aspects of the multidimensional concept of sustainability stretch beyond the traditional concerns of trade unions. In this respect the sustainable company presents a challenge to the unions capacity to take position on these issues and to advise works councils representatives at a decentralized level. For this reason a supportive legislation should not only introduce changes in various aspects of capital market regulation, but also provide an extended role for trade unions including expert capabilities on sustainability and on working with other stakeholders (e.g., NGOs).

In the open forum of the enterprise as commons, workers representatives may have to compete with the voice and claims of other stakeholders, particularly when workers interests overlap or do not coincide with those of other wider interests which are considered, as it is implied in the idea of the corporation as commons. The recent history of advanced economics present quite a few cases in which the positions of workers representatives go against the interests of wider communities, in particular the objective to keep a safe environment and to promote a sustainable development.[32] These conflicts of interest, are different from those which have traditionally been settled by trade unions and by workers representatives *vis-à-vis* the employers.

The need to face these new conflicts is acknowledged by those entrepreneurs who have adopted effective strategies and not simply generic formulas of social responsibility.

This is a further factor which requires a revision of workers participation at least in two directions. The contents and objective of workers representation will have to be reframed so as to include the consideration of a wider range of interests. Workers representatives will be challenged to be more selective in pursing their objectives and even to abandon traditional claims.

New channels of communication will have to be opened with the various constituencies in view of building common strategies not only on traditional labour issues, but also on matters of general interest.

Most European Unions has expanded in the past their action beyond the strict economic and normative contents of the employment contract and have sustained programs of social and economic reforms. But the collective action for social reforms was predominantly supported by the labour movement and reflected its priorities. The variety of stakeholders which must be considered by a socially responsible enterprise have a different and wider social agenda. The

---

32. Katrin Vitols, *Strengthening Cooperation Between NGOs and Trade Unions in the Interest of Sustainability*, in Sigurt Vitols, Norbert Kluge (eds), The Sustainable Company, supra n. 31, at 185, recognizes that the relationship between these actors may be competitive, but there is a growing common concern of them with the issue of sustainability.

workers representatives in the firms will have to interact with these stakeholders on new grounds and with new proposals. This diversified social interaction will contribute to enrich the objectives and the strategies of all kinds of participation. Moreover it will better equip workers representatives against the risk of being 'captured' by the logic of management and of pursuing corporatist short- term objectives.

Precisely to avoid these risks the European labour movement has always held that workers participation in the enterprise should not be practiced in isolation and be limited to micro issues. Instead participation in specific aspects of firm's organization should be combined with participation concerning the overall strategies of the companies. Moreover firm level workers involvement has to be connected with broader collective action and objectives of the labour unions.

The growing pressures toward the decentralization of labour relations are increasing the risks of micro corporatist drifts particularly for these workers representatives who are directly involved with management in consultation and participation within the firm.

Opening the practices of participation to new horizons and to the influence of other social actors might be useful to reinforce workers representatives at plant level, more than any attempt at recentralizing industrial relations from the top, by national unions initiatives and political appeals.

The long history and the diversified experiences of participation have contributed, particularly in the European countries, to consolidate it as an essential form of workers voice in the firms and as a fundamental component of the social model. The capacity of workers participation to adjourn its goals and instruments will be quite important for the future of the labour movement and of the social model.

CHAPTER 15

Workers' Participation in the Enterprise in Germany

Manfred Weiss

15.1 INTRODUCTION

Workers' participation in the enterprise has a long history in Germany. The origins date back to the nineteenth century. The system of workers' participation in management's decision-making normally is looked upon as being the backbone of German collective labour law and industrial relations. There are two channels: participation by works councils acting as counterparts of management and participation in supervisory boards of big companies.

Of course, workers' participation is only one element among others within a complex industrial relations structure in which collective bargaining and specified labour courts play a crucial role. Collective bargaining in Germany mainly takes place on sector level[1] which allows for a good division of labour between trade unions and works councils. The labour court system, organized on three levels by labour courts, labour courts of appeal and on top a Federal Labour Court,[2] guarantees the efficient application of the rights of works councils in cases where conflicts arise with the employer. The access to the labour court system, therefore, is a necessary precondition for the works council. Conflicts arising in the context of workers' representation in the supervisory boards are considered to belong to company law and, therefore, are treated by the ordinary civil law court system.[3]

---

1. For a detailed description *see* Manfred Weiss, Marlene Schmidt, *Labour Law and Industrial Relations in Germany*, 180 et seq. (4th edition Kluwer 2008).
2. For a detailed description *ibid.*, 149 et seq. and 261 et seq.
3. *Ibid.*, 264 et seq.

This article is supposed to briefly describe the basic elements and the functioning of the works council system 15.2 and the system of workers' representation in the supervisory boards 15.3, ending with an attempt to assess the system as a whole 15.4.

15.2 THE WORKS COUNCIL SYSTEM[4]

15.2.1 The Basic Organizational Structure

The present legal basis for the works council is the Works Constitution Act of 1972. This Act was significantly amended in 2001 to reflect the radical changes which the organizational structures of companies had undergone.[5]

Contrary to many other countries, works councils in Germany consist exclusively of employee representatives. Works councils act as counterparts to management. Works council members are elected by secret ballot by all employees over 18 years of age. Employees over 18 years of age, who have been employed for at least six months, may be elected for a term of four years; there are no term limits.

The law provides for the election of works council members in every establishment with more than five employees over 18 years of age, provided three of them have been employed for at least six months. Nevertheless, many Small and Medium-Sized Enterprises (SME) do not have a works council. Only larger companies fully comply with the law. Ultimately, it is up to the employees of the establishment to establish a works council. There is no sanction if they fail to do so, but employees who do not take the initiative relinquish all rights vested in the works council by law. In order to encourage the creation of more such councils in SME, the amendment of 2001 facilitated the election procedure. That change has led to a significant but by far not sufficient increase of work councils in SME.

As a matter of law, works councils are not affiliated with trade unions. They represent all employees of an establishment. But in spite of the institutional separation between unions and works councils, close links do exist. The large majority of works council members are union members.

The size of the works council depends on the number of employees in the establishment. Thus, in establishments with up to twenty employees there is only one council member. Works councils in firms with more than twenty and up to fifty employees are entitled to three members. Companies with more than 7,000 and up to 9,000 employees have thirty-one works council members. Above this level, the number of works council members increases by two for each additional 3,000 employees.

---

4. For a more detailed description Weiss, Schmidt, *supra* n. 1, at 222 et. seq.
5. Manfred Weiss, *Modernizing the German Works Council System: A Recent Amendment*, IJCLLIR 251 et seq. (2002).

Since the last amendment of 2001, blue-collar and white-collar employees are no longer treated as separate groups. According to a provision also introduced through this amendment, men and women must be represented in the works council according to their proportional rate within the workforce.

If works councils are established in different establishments of a multi-plant enterprise, they shall form a company works council. Each works council appoints two of its members to the company works council. The works councils of the individual establishments are not subordinate to the company works council. The company works council is only authorized to deal with matters which either cannot be resolved within the individual establishment or which are delegated to it by an individual works council.

If is up to the company works councils of enterprises belonging to one group of companies to establish a group works council at the level of the parent company. Each company works council would have to appoint two of its members.

The works council may delegate specific functions and rights to subcommittees which play an important role in practice. In enterprises with at least hundred employees, a committee dealing with economic affairs shall be appointed by the works council (or by the company works council in a multi-establishment enterprise).

According to the law all employees of an establishment should meet four times each year. These so-called works meetings take place during working hours and do not entail any loss of wages. Works meetings must be initiated and chaired by the works council. The works council is supposed to report on its activities. The employer shall be invited to the works meetings and is entitled to address the works meeting. At least once a year the employer shall report to the works meeting on matters of personnel policy and social affairs in the establishment, as well as on the present and prospective economic situation of the establishment. It is evident that the law attaches great importance to the works meeting as a communication link between works council and its constituency. Nevertheless, in this area the legal prescriptions do not correspond with reality. Empirical studies show that only in a small proportion of establishments all four works meetings are annually held, and that in quite a few establishments such meetings do not occur at all.

The Works Constitution Act 1972 also introduced a measure of representation for those workers who have not reached the age of majority. The organizational structure, as well as the election procedure, is very much identical to that of the works council, except that the juvenile delegation is not entitled to act directly as a counterpart to management.

According to the Works Constitution Act, executive staff is not covered by works council representation. Members of this group are neither permitted to participate in the election of works council members, nor can they be elected. The definition of this group was very controversial when the Act was promulgated in 1972. The legislature did not actually resolve the conflict but, instead, employed broad and unspecific language, thus forcing the courts to step in with their interpretation. The Courts strictly limited the scope of this group, and a 1989 amendment to the Act codified this jurisprudence. In the same year, an Act on a Representative Body for Executive Staff was passed, providing the legal basis for separate executive staff representation. Representative bodies of executive staff only enjoy information and consultation rights.

15.2.2 The Link to the Trade Unions

Works councils and trade unions are for historical reasons institutionally separated. Over time, however, trade unions have succeeded in overcoming the institutional pattern of dual representation due to the fact that a great number of works council members are also union members. In addition, the Works Constitution Act grants unions with at least one member in a company the right to become active within that company Thus in companies without works council, unions may take the initiative and call a works meeting during which the employees may decide whether they wish to establish a works council. Furthermore, if no works meeting has taken place for a certain period, unions may insist on having one. Considering the widespread non-existence of works councils and the low frequency of works meetings, it is apparent that these initiatives play only a marginal role in practice. More important, then, are the control functions unions assume. The unions are legally empowered to control the works council election procedure. They may even move for the nullification of a works council election by court decision if legal rules were disregarded. If a member of the works council or the works council as such has violated its duties of office, the union may obtain a court decision excluding a works council member from office or dissolving the works council. If the employer violates the duties imposed on him by the Works Constitution Act, unions are entitled to call for the imposition of sanctions by the labour courts. Although works meetings do not take place in public sessions, external union representatives have a right to be present. At the request of at least one fourth of the works council members, an external official of a union represented in the works council is entitled to participate in the works council meeting. The same rule applies to committee meetings, including meetings of the economic committee. Provided the employer was put on notice, agents of unions that are represented within an establishment must be granted access to the establishment.

Works council members are entitled to participate in training courses at the employer's expenses. These courses are supposed to impart the knowledge necessary for works council members to fulfil their task. Because these courses are almost exclusively offered by trade unions, they obviously serve as a powerful tool to bring works council members in line with union positions.

15.2.3 The Legal Position of the Works Council Members

During their term of office, works council members can only be recalled on the basis of a labour court decision, which may either be initiated by a union represented in the establishment or by one fourth of the employees, or by the employer. An individual works council member may be removed from office, or the works council as a whole may be dissolved, only if the member or the council severely violated the duties pertaining to the office. Such claims are hardly ever taken to court and are rarely successful. Works council members (as well as members of juvenile delegations) enjoy far reaching protection against dismissals.

Works council members may neither enjoy privileges nor may they suffer disadvantages as a consequence of holding office. Essentially, this general rule has three specific implications: first, works council members are not entitled to receive additional payments or benefits as a compensation for holding office. Second, it is guaranteed that their remuneration stays in lock-step with the wage increases they would have received had they not joined the works council. Third and perhaps most importantly, members are guaranteed to stay employed in a position that corresponds to their level of occupational skills. One corollary of this occupational standard guarantee is that works council members must not be excluded from further vocational training which other employees may enjoy. All these guarantees apply during the term of office and until one year after it has expired.

Works council members are entitled to be released from their duty to work without loss of pay 'to the extent that is necessary for properly carrying out their functions, taking into account the size and nature of the establishment'. In other words, the time to be released from work is not fixed, but depends on the circumstances of the particular case. According to the rules developed by the labour courts, the works council members decide what time is necessary to carry out their functions. The employer may refuse to release a works council member from his job duties only in cases of flagrant abuse.

Large enterprises are required to release a certain number of works council members entirely from their ordinary job duties for the full term of their office. The exact number varies with the number of employees, but the rule does not apply at all to firms with less than 200 employees. The possibility of a full release from work duties is one of the most important features of the works council system. Its effects are ambiguous. On the one hand, it leads to more professionalism and greater efficiency on the part of works council members. On the other hand, these professional works council members find it difficult, or unattractive, to be reintegrated in the rank and file when their term of office expires. This is why these members often work hard on their re-election and treat their status as a lifetime career. Thus, there is some valid concern that the system fosters a functionary-driven bureaucratic power structure with self-serving interests that distract from the original tasks.

15.2.4 The Financial Structure and the Basic Duties

It is the employer who bears all the expenses arising from the activities of the works council. In addition, the employer must provide the necessary accommodation, facilities and office staff required for meetings, consultations, and day-to-day operation of the works council. The exact scope of the duty to pay works council expenses is subject to many controversies. The decisive criterion is proportionality. It requires that there be a reasonable relationship between the costs on the one hand and the size as well as the financial resources of the company on the other hand.

The employer must provide the works council with all the information, including the files, the works council needs to carry out its tasks properly. Under certain, rather limited circumstances, the works council is entitled to call on the advice of experts. The restrictions on this choice are in place because all expenses are born by the employer. This is why in most cases union officials fulfil the function of providing expert advice to works councils free of charge.

Works councils are required by law to co-operate with the employer in good faith. Consequently, industrial action as a means of conflict resolution is explicitly prohibited. This, of course, does not mean that works council members are not allowed to participate in lawful strikes called by a trade union.

The works council is prohibited to from divulge information that was explicitly classified as secret by the employer. This applies only to information acquired by virtue of holding the office of a works council. The ban on disclosing information applies neither to the exchange of information between members of the works council nor to the communication with other bodies of workers' representation in the company. Not infrequently, this kind of information forms the basis for the decision of a works council on specific matters. On the other hand, the works council must not communicate such facts to its constituency. The resultant lack of transparency can be a source of alienation between the works council and the employees it represents.

15.2.5 The Arbitration Committee

Since strikes and lock-outs as means of conflict resolution are only legal in the context of collective bargaining, but are expressly prohibited under the Works Constitution Act, a special dispute settlement body has been created by law. This institution, the arbitration committee, can either be formed as a permanent committee or as an ad hoc committee for each case as necessary. In practice, the permanent committee is never used for fear that this body might be permanently biased in one way or another.

One half of the arbitration committee members are appointed by the employer, the other half by the works council. A neutral president, chosen by both sides, chairs the committee. There rarely is agreement over who this person should be. Absent an agreement, the Labour Court will appoint the president, typically a career labour judge. The total number of arbitration committee members is determined by agreement between the works council and the employer. If an agreement cannot be reached, either side may request the Labour Court to decide the matter. A special procedure regulates the formation and composition of an arbitration committee and expedites the resolution of conflicts. Decisions can be reached within a few days. The costs of the arbitration committee, as all other costs associated with the works constitution, are to be borne by the employer.

In reaching its decision, the arbitration committee must take into account the interests of the establishment and the interests of the employees concerned. Employer and/or works council may appeal to the Labour Court within two weeks of the date of notification of the award. On appeal, the Court may annul, but not rewrite, the decision of the committee only if the arbitration committee exceeded its discretionary powers. If that happens, the works council and the employer may again call on the arbitration committee. However, in practice, appeals are very rare so that, typically, the arbitration committee's first decision becomes final. The law requires that decisions of the arbitration committee be recorded in writing, signed by the chairperson, and forwarded to the employer and the works council. During the deliberations of the committee, outsiders are not admitted. The exclusion of the public is considered necessary to allow for compromises that may be necessary to reach equitable results.

15.2.6 The Works Council's Rights of Participation

The Works Constitution Act grants the works council an array of specific rights of participation, which include access to information, consultation and veto rights, and the most important right of all, the right to co-determination. In matters in which this right applies the decision-making process is no longer the prerogative of management. Co-determination in this context means that management cannot make any decisions without the consent of the works council. In the absence of consensus, any unilateral move by management would be illegal. However, co-determination means even more, it gives both sides an equal voice in the decision-making process.

The works council enjoys the right to participation in reference to important topics as are for example the beginning and termination of daily working hours, including breaks and allocation of working hours over the single days of the week, temporary reduction or extension of the usual working hours in the establishment, introduction and use of technical devices designed to monitor the employees' conduct or performance, regulations for the prevention of work accidents and occupational diseases or questions relating to remuneration arrangements which do not refer to the amount but to the distribution of remuneration within the workforce. Of course, the list is much more extended. But the few examples may be sufficient to show that these are matters which are not only important but can happen every day.

Of specific relevance are the rights of works councils in specific economic decisions which may cause substantial disadvantages to the workforce of the establishment or to a significant part of it. According to the law the works council enjoys these rights in companies with a minimum of twenty employees with respect to the following decisions: the reduction of operations, partial or total closings, a transfer of the establishment or transfer of essential parts of it, a merger with other establishments or the breaking up of establishments, basic organizational changes, basic changes of the purpose of the establishment, changes affecting the plant facilities, the introduction of new work methods and production processes. Furthermore, a reduction of the workforce is considered tantamount to a reduction of operations. Thus, the case of collective dismissal is, in principle, also included.

In all these cases, management must provide full information in advance in order to enter into negotiations with the works council. 'Information in advance' means that it has to be given at an early planning stage. 'Full information' means that management must not only disclose its plans but must supply information on all possible alternatives and modifications which were taken into account at any time. This obligation to disclose enables the works council to have some input in the decision-making process.

In addition to supplying information, management is required to reach a so-called 'reconciliation of interests' with the works council. This means that management must make an effort to reach an agreement with the works council on whether, and in what manner, the management plans will be carried out. If the parties fail to agree, either side can call on the President of the Regional Employment Office for mediation. If this mediation is not successful or does not occur because neither party called for it, either side may take the issue to the arbitration committee. But in this instance, the arbitration committee has no power to issue a binding decision. It can only present a proposal which may or may not be acceptable to the parties Thus, the law provides a procedure for the reconciliation of interests, but if the procedure fails, management has the final say. Ultimately, then, the works council has no legal power to force management in a certain direction.

Regardless of whether management has fulfilled its duties to inform the works council and has tried to reach a reconciliation of interests, the works council is always entitled to enforce a so-called 'social plan'. A social plan means nothing less than a special works agreement to compensate or reduce the disadvantages that employees suffer in the event of a substantial change of the establishment or in cases of insolvency. A social plan is not confined to financial compensation but may include important affirmative measures such as re-training programs and transfer of employees to other establishments of the enterprise. If an agreement on a social plan cannot be reached, either side is entitled to appeal to the arbitration committee which then acts as the final decision-maker. Its decision is binding on both sides. Except in cases of insolvency, which cannot be treated here, there are no minimum or maximum financial limits for a social plan.

15.3 WORKERS' REPRESENTATION IN THE SUPERVISORY BOARD[6]

15.3.1 Three Different Models

Workers' representation on company boards is understood to be one further step towards changing the power structure in the economic field. The first successes in implementing such change occurred in the coal, iron and steel industries. After World War II., the enterprises in these areas of industry faced the danger of being totally dismantled by the Allied Forces. To avoid what would have amounted to obliteration, these industries sought the support of the unions. Because the unions had not been affiliated with the Nazi regime, they had an important voice in this context. In order to gain the support of trade unions, the leaders of the coal, iron and steel industries offered equal representation of employees on the supervisory boards of the companies in exchange. After much controversy, this model featuring strong employees' representative rights, was established and confirmed by the legislature in 1951. This historical development explains why until today the representation rules in the coal, iron and steel industries differ from those applying to other German industrial sectors.

By 1952 the political and economic circumstances had changed: With the danger of dismantlement banned, employers were in no need to enlist the support of the unions and were no longer prepared to make concessions. Not surprisingly, then, the 1952 Works Constitution Act introduced a model of employee representation on the supervisory board which remained far below the level of representation reached in the coal, iron and steel industries. In the years following the adoption of the Works Constitution Act, the unions undertook great efforts to extend the 1951 model of the coal, iron and steel industries to all areas of industry. In 1976, these efforts led to a third model which represents a compromise between the previous two. All three different models still exist today and will be briefly described below

15.3.2 The Function of the Supervisory Board

In order to appreciate the impact of employee representation on the supervisory board, it is necessary to understand the general role of this board within the power structure of an enterprise. Under company law, the supervisory board is a company organ which must be present in companies with a specific company law structure. The Acts providing employee representation on the supervisory board did not create new institutions. They simply fit employee representation into the traditional corporate framework, modifying only the composition of the governing bodies. The supervisory and management boards, which existed prior to the introduction of employee participation, retained their traditional

---

6. For a more detailed description Weiss, Schmidt, *supra* n. 1, 248 et seq.

functions. The only difference is that these boards are no longer composed exclusively of individuals guided by the interest of the owners.

According to the German two boards system of company law, it is exclusively the management board which represents and manages the enterprise. The structure best may be explained by the example of the joint-stock company. The supervisory board has only two basic functions, to elect and recall the members of the management board, and to supervise the activities of the management board. In order to fulfil its monitoring tasks, the supervisory board has extended rights of access to information. At least once a year, the management board must supply the supervisory board with comprehensive information on all basic issues concerning the management of the enterprise. Furthermore, the supervisory board or any member of the supervisory board can request at any time additional information on matters of importance to the enterprise. The management board is statutorily required to meet such a request.

The shareholders' meeting, or even the supervisory board itself, may extend the powers of the supervisory board by majority vote. Either one can establish rules which require the consent of the supervisory board to certain types of managerial decisions. However, even if the supervisory board withholds its consent, the management board may nevertheless effectuate its decision by obtaining approval in the course of a shareholders' meeting. Such approval always remedies a lack of consent on the part of the supervisory board.

To make the point: the authority of the supervisory board is significant but it pales in comparison with any management board, because it is the latter that is actually in charge of the company's operations and in a position to employ a staff of experts who prepare its decisions.

15.3.3 The Model of the Coal, Iron and Steel Industries

This model is based on equal representation of shareholders and employees on the supervisory board, the chairpersonship being reserved for a 'neutral' person, elected by majority vote of both, employee representatives and shareholder representatives. The Act on Workers' Representation in the Coal, Iron and Steel Industries of 1951 applies to enterprises that were created as joint-stock corporations and private limited companies employing more than 1000 employees.

In general, the supervisory board consists of eleven members. In very large enterprises the number may increase to fifteen or even twenty-one members. Taking the normal case of a supervisory board with eleven members, shareholders and employees each appoint five members.

At least two of the five employee representatives must belong to the workforce of the enterprise. The remaining three employee representatives need not be employed by the enterprise, but may be external representatives. Whereas two of the three external members always are members of the respective unions, the third member (the so-called 'additional member') must neither be a trade union member nor an employee of the respective enterprise nor have economic interests in the enterprise. After consultation with the unions represented in the enterprise, the works council nominates the employee representative candidates belonging to the workforce of the enterprise by secret ballot. The unions represented in the enterprise propose the candidates for the remaining three seats, and the works council formally nominates these representatives, again by secret ballot. Finally, all nominated representatives must be elected and confirmed by the shareholders' assembly. However, the nominations are binding on the assembly. This election is only a formality which reflects the original structure of the electoral power of the shareholders' assembly.

The neutral chairperson of the supervisory board is nominated by a majority vote of the other members of the supervisory board (shareholder representatives and employee representatives). This nomination is again binding on the shareholders' meeting, which should formally elect and confirm the chairperson. If a majority decision on the supervisory board cannot be obtained, a rather complicated procedure provides alternative means for the nomination of the candidate. Should this procedure fail, it is up to the shareholders to decide. A neutral chairperson is deemed necessary to ensure that the supervisory board can overcome a deadlock between shareholder representatives and employee representatives.

The Act on Workers' Representation in the Coal, Iron and Steel Industries of 1951 does not only provide for employee representation on the supervisory board. It is the only Act that also provides for some employee representation on the management board. The elected representative, the 'work director in charge of personnel and social affairs of the enterprise', is a full member of the management board, who enjoys the same legal status as all other board members. This representative cannot be elected against the majority of votes of the employee representatives on the supervisory board.

In the period after 1951, it turned out that workers' representation in enterprises of the coal, iron and steel industries was not very effective if the representatives did not have access to the supervisory board of the parent company of the group. Several Acts introduced and expanded these representation rights at the level of parent companies. Today, it applies whether coal, iron and steel activities within a group amount to a share of at least 20% of all activities, or if at least 2000 employees are employed in those industries. This legal development notwithstanding, the number of companies and groups that are actually subject to the rules of this model is steadily decreasing.

15.3.4 The Model of 1952

Originally by the Works Constitution Act of 1952 and since 2004 transferred into a separate Act on One Third Workers Participation in the Supervisory Board this model also covers only enterprises related to specific types of company law. All enterprises covered by this model must employ at least 500 employees.

According to the Act, one third of the supervisory board members must be workers' representatives. The size of the supervisory board depends on the rules of company law. If only one or two employee representatives can be elected, these representatives must be employed by the enterprise. If more than two representatives are up for election, at least two must be employees of the enterprise. The additional representatives may, but do not have to, be elected from external candidates. Works councils as well as groups of one tenth of the employees (or at least 100 employees) of the enterprise are entitled to nominate candidates. Workers' representatives are elected by all employees of the enterprise who are over 18 years of age.

15.3.5 The Model of 1976

Like the other Acts concerning employee representation on the supervisory board, the Co-Determination Act of 1976 is applicable to enterprises organized according to specific types of company law, this time with a size of at least 2000 employees. As far as holding companies are concerned, the Co-Determination Act 1976 applies to enterprises employing less than 2000 employees, provided that the holding company and the German group entities employ in the aggregate at least 2000 persons. If an enterprise covered by the 1976 Co-Determination Act is a holding company, the employees of the subsidiaries participate in the election of the employee representatives to the supervisory board of the holding company. Therefore, the number of subsidiaries which are indirectly covered by the 1976 Co-Determination Act is significantly higher than the above mentioned number of directly affected enterprises.

Until recently it was taken for granted that foreign subsidiaries are not included. This view now is under attack. According to a recent judgment[7] employees of foreign subsidiaries are to be included in counting the necessary number of 2000 employees. This would mean a significant extension of workers' representation in supervisory boards. However, the appeal against this judgment is still pending. Linked to this question is an even more far reaching one. In recent scholarly writing some argue that the prevention of employees to participate in the election for the workers' representatives in the foreign subsidiaries within the European Union (EU) violates Article 18 (prohibition of discrimination) and 45 (freedom of movement for workers) Treaty on the Functioning of the European Union (TFEU). This was denied by several courts.[8] However, on appeal against the Berlin judgment the court[9] has handed over the respective questions to the Court of Justice of the European Union (CJEU) where the case now is pending.

---

7. LG Frankfurt, judgment of 16 February 2015.
8. LG Landau, judgment of 18 September 2013, LG Munich, judgment of 27 August 2015 and LG Berlin, judgment of 1 August 2015.
9. KG Berlin, decision of 16 October 2015.

In enterprises covered by the 1976 Co-determination Act, the supervisory board consists of an equal number of shareholder representatives and workers' representatives. The numbers are as follows: in enterprises with up to 10,000 employees twelve representatives, six from each side; in enterprises with more than 10,000 and up to 20,000 employees sixteen representatives, eight from each side; and in enterprises with more than 20,000 employees twenty representatives, ten from each side. The company statutes may provide for more representatives. A board consisting of twelve members may be enlarged to sixteen members, and a board consisting of sixteen members may grow to a maximum of twenty members.

On supervisory boards with twelve or sixteen members, two seats are reserved for external trade union representatives, and on supervisory boards with twenty members, there are three such seats. The remaining seats on the employees' side (four, six, or seven, depending on the size of the board) are reserved for the workers and the executive staff of the enterprise. Each group, if represented at all, is guaranteed at least one seat. Although the exact distribution depends on the proportion in which these groups are represented, executive staff is in fact almost always over-represented.

The chairperson and the vice-chairperson of the supervisory board are elected by a two-third majority of the board members. If an election fails to yield a two-third majority, a frequent result, the shareholder representatives elect the chairperson, and the employees elect the vice-chairperson from among their own group. In practice, then, the position of the chairperson is reserved to the shareholders' representatives. Thus, in contrast to the coal, iron and steel industries model, which features a neutral chairperson in charge of overcoming deadlocks on the board, the 1976 Co-Determination Act favours a shareholder-selected chairperson who has the casting vote.

The vast majority of employee representatives on the supervisory board are members of a trade union. This is not only true for the external representatives but also for those employed in the respective enterprise or group.

15.3.6 The Legal Position of Employee Representatives

Employee and shareholder representatives on the supervisory board are co-equals. The law assigns identical rights and obligations to either group. Employee representatives are privy to any information accessible to members of the supervisory board.

As under traditional company law, the members of the supervisory board are free to discuss company matters among themselves. However, they are strictly prohibited from disclosing this information to anyone else. This confidentiality requirement severely hampers the communication between the employee representatives and their constituency which, in turn, fosters alienation and the perception about employee representatives as an elitist, isolated group with limited legitimacy.

The so-called 'interest of the enterprise' is the crucial legal point of reference for the substantive board decisions which both shareholder representatives and employee representatives are called upon to make. While this criterion was formally understood as referring solely to the interests of the capital owners (shareholder value), it is today generally accepted as covering workers' interests as well (stakeholder value). However, the standard has become so malleable that it is difficult to delineate the permissible scope of the board's activities.

Equal status of employee and shareholder representatives also implies equal remuneration. For the former, this income is considered a threat to neutrality if not a source of corruption. Therefore, the standing rules of the unions require employee representatives on the supervisory board who are trade union members to transfer a high percentage of this income to a union foundation. Of course, this duty does not apply to non-union members.

Shareholder representatives obviously do not need protection against dismissal or a right to participate in vocational programs in order to become or stay qualified for their job. This is different for employee representatives. If they are employed in the enterprise, protection against dismissal may be just as necessary as for members of the works council. And if employee board members actually are to have an impact on the policy of the supervisory board, they must be highly qualified, particularly in view of the qualifications the shareholders' representatives usually bring to bear as qualified experts in economic and financial affairs. To create a level playing field, it would arguably be appropriate to let workers' representatives participate in educational programs without loss of pay. This is not an option, however, due to the principle of equal legal status of employee and shareholder representatives. On the other hand, it is generally agreed that employee representatives ought to be released from their ordinary job duties to participate in supervisory board meetings without loss of pay.

15.3.7 The Implementation in Practice

Within the relationship between the management board and the supervisory board the position of the latter has been weakened by the redefinition of the criterion 'interest of the enterprise' as outlined above. It has become more difficult to argue that specific measures taken or suggested by the management board do not comport with this rather vague formula. Nevertheless the supervisory board at least continues to be an important source of information for the employees' representatives. Thus, they have access to all relevant facts which give rise to management activities, to discuss these activities and to present their views. Of course, only the model of the coal, iron and steel industries actually enables them to overrule the shareholders' bench if the neutral chairperson sides with the workers' representatives.

However, to better appreciate the role and influence of workers' representation on the supervisory board, the works council system must be considered as well. In practice, the employee representatives on the supervisory board belonging to the workforce of the enterprise are almost exclusively also works council members. On the whole, this has strengthened both instruments of participation. In particular, it has promoted communication through informal channels. Because management has an interest to stay on good terms with the works council due to its co-determination power, it is likewise interested in avoiding conflicts with works council members who are also members of the supervisory board. Thus, before informing the supervisory board, management tends to discuss critical questions with at least the internal employee representatives in informal meetings. These informal communications are most important under the coal, iron and steel industries model in which the work director functions as a crucial link. It is primarily these informal structures which make employee representation on the supervisory board effective. This informal communication tends to soften the original position of management and the manner in which it presents questions to the supervisory board. As a result, most decisions on the supervisory board are reached unanimously. Notwithstanding the right of all supervisory board members to deal with all questions arising under its mandate, employee representatives focus primarily on the social aspects of company policies and less on economic and financial strategies that lead to basic management decisions. With little or no expert knowledge in economic and financial matters, employee representatives thus typically concentrate their efforts on preventing or mitigating the immediate negative consequences that basic business decisions would have for the workforce.

15.4 ATTEMPT OF AN ASSESSMENT

Workers' participation nowadays is uncontested and based on a broad consensus, even if there are always controversies referring to details of the institutional arrangements. It is considered to be one of the main pillars of economic success in Germany. This became particularly evident in the international financial crisis. Due to the mutual trust gained by the permanent dialogue between management and workers' representatives it was easy to agree on arrangements in order to prevent lay-offs of employees. Thereby in particular, working time was reduced, the free time was used to further train the workforce and the State helped to compensate the loss of remuneration. Thus skilled labour was on board when the effects of the crisis were over. This gave the German economy a significant advantage compared to other countries.

Compared to unilateral decision-making workers participation has many advantages. The mere fact that workers' representatives have a voice in decision-making increases significantly the legitimacy of management's decisions and it facilitates implementation. It absorbs conflicts, leads to better motivation of the workforce and, thereby, increases productivity. It also leads – at least in principle – to better decision-making because management prepares decisions more carefully in view of the fact that it has to give and discuss reasons for what is supposed to be done or – in case of co-determination – is dependent on the consent of the workers' representatives. And it favours long term strategies rather than short term effects.

Most helpful for the understanding of the system as a whole is the report on an empirical project which was conducted not only by social scientists, led by Wolfgang Streeck, but also by representatives of trade unions and employers' associations.[10] There it shows how closely the two levels of workers participation are interrelated and that workers' representation in the supervisory board has become a sort of 'extended arm' of the works council's activities.[11] The report not only confirms the already mentioned informal communication between management and works' council members in the supervisory board.[12] It also shows that management voluntarily gets the works councils involved much beyond the limits of the law in order to integrate them already in an early preparatory stage of decision-making.[13] A specific role of works councils is seen in the fact that they help to enforce necessary restructuring measures in order to make or keep the company competitive. In this context the report speaks of a culture of 'cooperative modernisation'.[14] The report insists that negative economic effects of workers' participation are not to be seen. However it favours an organizational culture which might imply long-lasting consultation procedures, but thereby eliminates as much as possible dramatic mistakes. The report concluded that 'in the past workers participation has repeatedly adapted to difficult conditions', that it 'has not been an obstacle to an internationalization of the strategic perspectives of German companies' and in particular that 'there is no need to re-regulate workers' participation in order to raise the effectiveness of the supervisory boards'.[15]

Not at all in line with the optimistic message of this report workers' representation in supervisory boards was put into question in the first decade of the new century by the confederation of employers' associations. The goal was to reduce the model established by the Act of 1976 to the level of the model introduced in 1952, now transferred to the Act of 2004.[16] Of course, this proposal was rejected by the trade unions. Even if the debate became rather heated, it remained to be an episode. After the success of workers' participation in the financial crisis nobody would dare any more to start such a fundamental attack

---

10. Kommisson Mitbestimmung, Bertelsmann Stiftung, Hans-Boeckler- Stiftung, *The German Model of Codetermination and Corporate Governance – Report from the Commission on Codetermination* (Bertelsmann Foundation Publisher 1998).
11. *Ibid.*, at 10.
12. *Ibid.*, at 103.
13. *Ibid.*, at 76.
14. *Ibid.*, at 77.
15. *Ibid.*, at 24 and 25.
16. For this debate *see* Manfred Weiss, *The Future of Employee Involvement in Company Boards in Germany*, BNyström et al. (ed.) *Liber Amicorum Reinhold Fahlbeck*, 633, 644 et seq. (Lund, 2005).

against the system of workers' representation in the supervisory boards. Just to the contrary: it never was as strong and widely accepted as presently.

In spite of this generally positive assessment there are problems. The law according to which works councils are to be elected in establishments of at least five employees still is not followed in many small and medium-sized companies. This leads to a very problematic segmentation of the labour market. In addition the works council system is endangered by the fragmentation and segmentation of the workforce as well as by the erosion of the traditional pattern of the workplace. The works council system is built on the assumption that there is a workplace where a collective of employees with more or less homogeneous interests is present. Not only the diversity of the interests of the workforce but also the erosion of the workplace concept have made it difficult for such bodies to function efficiently. This may still be possible for the core groups. However, for people in new forms of work it is very problematic. The question is whether and how the system of workers' participation by works councils can be restructured in order to integrate the whole diversity of interests of the workforce and take account of the new enterprise organization (outsourcing strategies and so forth). It may be doubted whether this is possible at all. And it may also be doubted whether the strength of a representative body composed of so many diverse groups with diverse interests would be as strong to defend and promote employees interests as before. Therefore, there is a question mark behind the future of the works council system.

The danger for workers representation in supervisory boards comes from EU law. For a long time, the headquarters of a company was considered decisive for the corporate law to be applied. Consequently, it was obvious that German corporate law including the rules for workers' participation in supervisory boards had to apply to a company headquartered in Germany. However, according to the CJEU this view is not consistent with the freedom of establishment guaranteed under EU law. It suggests that the applicable corporate law is that of the country where the company is established.[17] The company may then decide to have its headquarters registered in any country within the EU with no change relating to corporate law. This implies that German companies can establish companies abroad and operate at home disregarding workers' representation in supervisory boards. To date, however, this possibility has been exploited only to a moderate extent. It, however, cannot be ruled out that this might change.

Finally it should be insisted that workers' participation in Germany functions in a special historical, cultural and institutional context. Whether it would work the same elsewhere, may be doubted.

---

17. CJEU, judgment of 9 March 1999, case C-212/97, Rec. 1999, I-1459 et seq. (Centros); CJEU judgment of 5 November 2002 – case C-208/00, Rec. 2002, I-9919 et seq.(Überrseering);CJEU judgment of 30 September 2003 – case C-167/01 (Inspire Art).

CHAPTER 16

Workers Participation in the Enterprise: Welfare and Quality of Work

Agar Brugiavini

When speaking about 'workers participation in the enterprise' one implicitly thinks about workers' rights and hence gives mostly a 'juridical' significance/valence to this topic. Still the aspects related to this issue are multifaceted and hence deserve a more multidisciplinary treatment/approach.

An important aspect is the economic one. Economic research attempts to understand and evaluate the consequences of workers involvement in the firms' decisions, the impact of the rights to be informed and consulted with respect to issues related to firms' activity.

In the present analysis I first focus on evaluating the consequences of workers' participation on various aspects of individuals' lives and then I point to some shortcomings/limits of the current legislation.

The study is structured as follows: first I briefly revise the main forms of workers' involvement, then I present the European Participation Index as a possible measure of the strength of the workers' participation. I shortly summarize part of the existing evidence/literature on the effects of workers' participation and then I make a graphic analysis of the job quality and workers' satisfaction based on the data from the Survey on Health, Ageing and Retirement in Europe (SHARE). Finally, I discuss one important issue that is still subject to important limitations: women's rights and the gender gap in the labour market.

16.1 WORKERS PARTICIPATION

There is a multitude of ways in which workers can participate to an enterprise decision-making process and their classification is based on how this can be applied (directly or through representatives), on the level of influence that can be exerted (whether participation it is only 'consultative' or 'deliberative') as well as on the area in which the workers can intervene.

We can speak of direct participation, work councils, quality circles and total quality management, joint project-groups, semi-autonomous group work and team work, employee representation on supervisory board, employee shareholding, health and safety committee and representatives.

One of the issues on which workers are most frequently involved is that of health and safety at the work place. The European Law supports the participation of the employees to the enterprise decisions in this field, but there are wide differences among countries on how this right is exerted. While in Czech Republic, Greece, Italy representation of workers is guaranteed by employee representatives, in Belgium, Bulgaria, Denmark, France and Lithuania it is done by a joint employer/employee committee. A combination of the two alternatives above is present in UK, Spain, Sweden, Finland, Portugal and several East-European countries while work councils guarantee this right to workers in Austria, Germany, the Netherlands, Luxembourg and Slovenia.

16.2 EUROPEAN PARTICIPATION INDEX

Cross-country analysis make necessary to define a measure of the strength of workers participation. Researchers at the European Trade Union Institute developed and released a multi-dimensional index of the workers participation rights: the European Participation Index. In constructing this measure they took into consideration three aspects: board-level participation, plant-level participation and collective bargaining participation. The results revealed strong worker participation for Nordic European countries and very weak for countries as Estonia, Latvia, UK or Lithuania.

Chapter 16: Workers Participation in the Enterprise: Welfare and Quality of Work

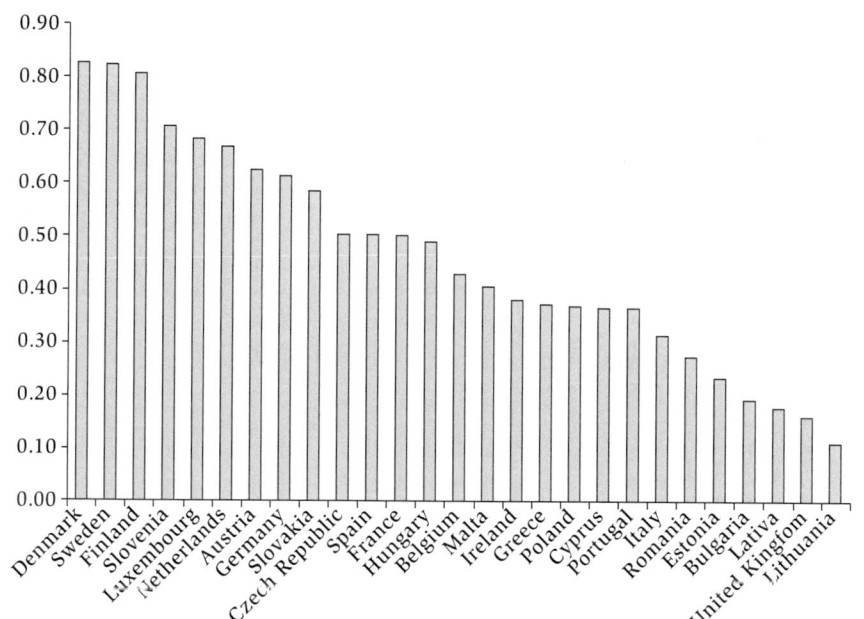

Figure 16.1 European Participation Index

16.3 LITERATURE REVIEW

The importance of workers' participation resides in the very fact that it empowers the workers, but it is also significantly related to its impacts on the enterprise as a whole and workers lives. Hence, it becomes very important to evaluate the effects that it has on the enterprise performance, the consequences on work quality, on job satisfaction, the impact on job safety and workers' health etc.

There are several studies, both at the academic level and in the form of policy reports, which focus on the effects of workers' participation on workplace risks, health in general and work accidents in particular. A safety and health report of the UK government documents that major involvement of workers with respect to health and safety lead to lower accidents rates (14% versus 26%) and overall, the health and safety conditions are better. The explanation may be that in the enterprises with stronger workers' participation there is a greater awareness of workplace risks, which determine a better control of these. Such findings confirm/enforce other studies such as Relly et al. 1995, which finds that the presence of joint consultative committees with all employees' representatives appointed by unions significantly reduces the frequency of workplace injuries with respect to the establishments where the management alone determines the health and safety arrangements. Still some authors observe that in order to be effective the participation should be supported by several 'preconditions' such as: strong legislative steer, commitment of managers to health and safety, competent risk evaluation and control and effective external inspection.

Another very important topic is that of the effects on firms' performance. There is important recent economic research that tries to assess the productivity impact of workers involvement at various levels. Many authors argue that workers participation can lead to better performance of enterprises (Ichinowshi, Shaw and Prennushi, 1997, Black and Lynch, 2001, Zwick, 2004, Wolf and Zwick, 2008). In revising the existing theory, Zwick (2004) identifies four channels through which productivity can improve by means of workers participation: (i) benefit of the specific knowledge/skills that workers have about the work process (ii) 'higher identification with enterprise' and hence more commitment to its objectives, (iii) 'balance production more effectively' and (iv) 'diminish waste and inefficiencies' and reduce redundancies. He finds that the involvement of shop-floor employees through the introduction of team work and autonomous work groups led to a significant increase in the average firms' productivity.

In what follows I am going to perform a graphic analysis that relates aspects as job quality, job satisfaction to the workers participation.

16.4 THE DATA

The individual-level data used in this analysis are drawn from SHARE (Survey of Health, Ageing and Retirement in Europe). SHARE, coordinated by the Mannheim Research Institute for the Economics of Aging (MEA), collects detailed information on a wide variety of factors, including the health status, health care access, work quality, and other socio-economic characteristics of people aged 50+ in Europe. The design is based on the Health and Retirement Study (HRS) and the English Longitudinal Study of Ageing (Borsh-Supan and Jurges, 2005).

Our analysis is based on waves 1, 2 and 4 of SHARE, whose data were collected in 2004, 2006 and 2010, respectively. We excluded the third wave (2008), named SHARELIFE, which is not a traditional wave. It was implemented to collect the retrospective histories of the SHARE respondents in order to obtain information about their lives before the baseline year of the survey (2004).

We decided to use these data because SHARE asks respondents a battery of questions that bear on the individuals' perceptions of work quality. The survey requires the participants to report their opinions about different dimensions of work quality, such as job satisfaction, level physical workload, job pressure, and level of freedom to perform specific tasks.

We focus on the following questions:

(1) All things considered I am satisfied with my job. Would you say you strongly agree, agree, disagree or strongly disagree?
(2) My job is physically demanding. Would you say you strongly agree, agree, disagree or strongly disagree?

Chapter 16: Workers Participation in the Enterprise: Welfare and Quality of Work

(3) I am under constant time pressure due to a heavy workload. (Would you say you strongly agree, agree, disagree or strongly disagree?)

(4) I have very little freedom to decide how I do my work. (Would you say you strongly agree, agree, disagree or strongly disagree?)

The questions were answered on a 4 point scale, from 'strongly agree' to 'strongly disagree' and we treated them as ordered categorical variables.

In addition to this first set of variables, respondents were also asked about whether they think their current job offers possibilities to improve skills, whether they receive support in difficult situations and recognition for their job. Specifically, we refer to the responses of the following set of questions:

(5) I have an opportunity to develop new skills. (Would you say you strongly agree, agree, disagree or strongly disagree?)

(6) I receive adequate support in difficult situations. (Would you say you strongly agree, agree, disagree or strongly disagree?)

(7) I receive the recognition I deserve for my work. (Would you say you strongly agree, agree, disagree or strongly disagree?)

Individual's opinions about the adequacy of the salary, possibilities to advance in career and perception about poor job security were also included in the analysis. The following are the questions reported in the SHARE survey:

(8) Considering all my efforts and achievements, my [salary is/earnings are/salary is] adequate. (Would you say you strongly agree, agree, disagree or strongly disagree?)

(9) My [job promotion prospects/prospects for job advancement/job promotion prospects] are poor. (Would you say you strongly agree, agree, disagree or strongly disagree?)

(10) My job security is poor. (Would you say you strongly agree, agree, disagree or strongly disagree?)

As for the first set of work quality indicators, all these additional questions were measured on a 4 point scale (from 'strongly agree' to 'strongly disagree').

Eventually, we also consider information on the individual eagerness to retire using a dichotomous variable, which assigns value 1 if the respondent declares to be willing to retire as early as he/she can from the current job.

16.5 DESCRIPTIVE ANALYSIS

As a first preliminary step we observe the degree of satisfaction of the individuals with their job, based on their answer to question 8 above, which puts into balance efforts and earnings. We define a scale with four categories based on the percentage of respondents who reported that their efforts were not compensated by their salary. The categories go from 'low quality of work' (the lowest step), in those countries where the shares of unsatisfied people were higher than 50% to high work quality (where the proportion of unsatisfied were lower than 30%), as is described in figure 16.2.

Figure 16.2   Quality of Work

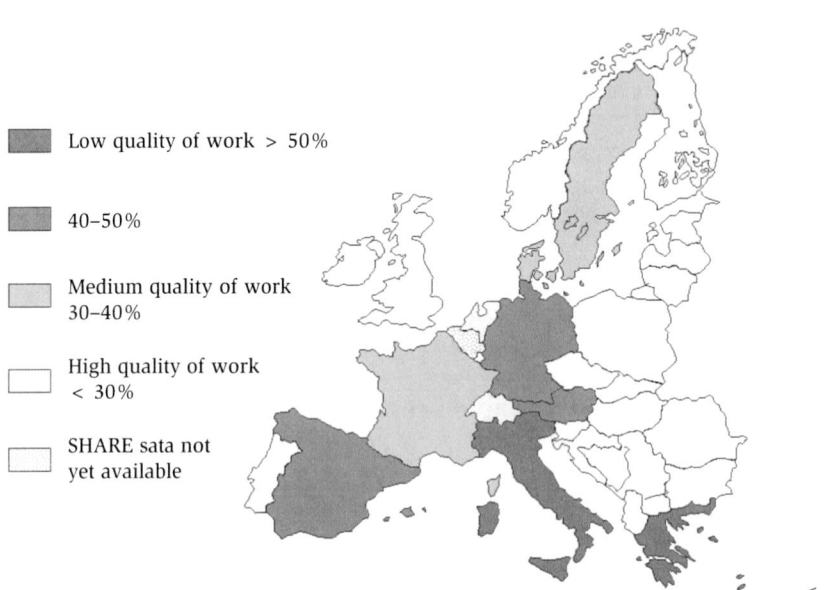

Figure 16.2 shows the percentage of workers aged 50 and over reporting low, medium and high quality of work, respectively. We observe that Switzerland and the Netherlands are the countries characterized by a high work quality (the percentage of unsatisfied individuals is lower than 30%). An intermediate level of work quality is perceived in France, Denmark and Sweden, while Germany, Austria and Spain report slightly lower levels of satisfaction (between 40% and 50% of workers declare that efforts were not compensated by reward). Finally, the worst levels are observed in Italy and Spain (>50%). Thus, a spurious geographic gradient can be identified from these results: while the Continental Europe is heterogeneously characterized, the figure clearly highlights a Northern European cluster where work quality is perceived as relatively high, and a Mediterranean cluster characterized by low work quality.

In order to synthetize the information from the whole battery of questions on work quality in a unique number/measure, we have constructed (starting from the eleven questions presented above) a job quality index via a Principal Component Analysis (PCA) method. The results are presented in figure 16.3 that displays the quality index by country and gender. The differences between men and women are rather small but there is high heterogeneity among countries.

Chapter 16: Workers Participation in the Enterprise: Welfare and Quality of Work

In Germany, Sweden, Spain, Italy, France, Denmark and Poland the index is slightly higher for men, while the opposite is true for Netherlands, Switzerland and Ireland. It is important to observe that when we consider the whole set of work quality variables the country ranking remains similar to the one we observed in figure 16.2. At the top, we find Switzerland and the Netherlands followed at close distance by Denmark, Sweden, Belgium and Ireland. The lowest work quality index is registered again in Italy followed by Poland. Analysing these results in relation to the EPI we can state that the highest quality of the work environment is registered in the countries with stronger worker participation. In fact, the EPI index is very high in Denmark, Sweden and the Netherlands while Italy and Poland are at the end of the list.

Figure 16.3 Job Quality Index

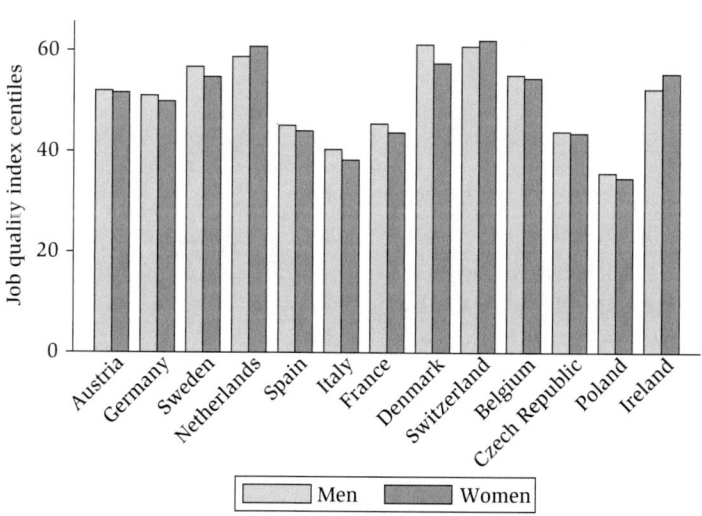

Next, I wanted to analyse whether the quality of the work environment deteriorated because of the economic crisis. Figure 16.4 presents the job quality index computed separately for the periods before and after 2008. We can observe that for a vast majority of countries the index is definitely higher for the years post-2008 (Austria, Germany, Sweden, The Netherlands, Denmark, Belgium), with just Italy and Czech Republic showing an opposite trend. However, it is difficult to come with a conclusion since the fact that work quality 'increased' after 2008 may be due to the fact that individuals less satisfied exited the labour market because they were not happy with their job. Such a trend may also mean that some low quality occupations disappeared after the start of the crisis because they were located in inefficient enterprises.

Figure 16.4   Job Quality Index

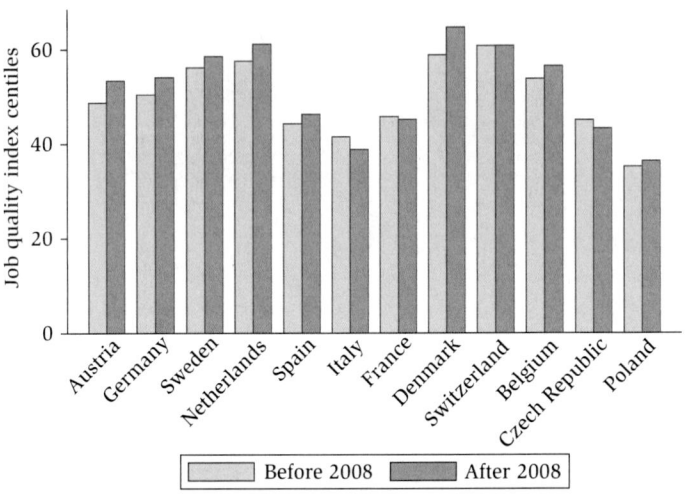

In order to get a better insight, we analyse separately some of the index components. Figure 16.5 shows the average shares of male individuals that report to receive adequate recognition for work. The resulting picture is slightly different from that of the overall index, with Poland, Italy and Spain overtaking France and the Czech Republic.

Figure 16.5   Percentage of Men Receiving Adequate Recognition for Their Job

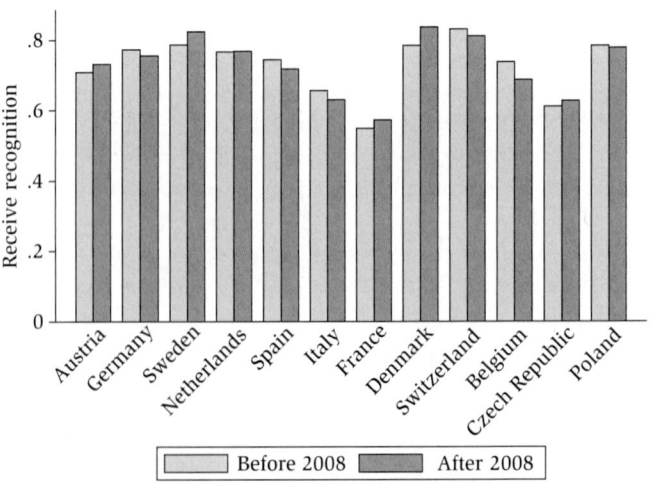

Chapter 16: Workers Participation in the Enterprise: Welfare and Quality of Work

In figure 16.6 we look at the prevalence of individuals reporting that their salary is adequate, separately before and after 2008 and by gender. It can be noted that in general men are more satisfied with their reward than women are (in almost all countries the share of respondents that report that their salary is adequate is higher for men than for women). While in countries such as Switzerland, Austria or Italy the differences between genders are very little, they are more significant in Sweden. In addition, it seems that men with their reward after 2008 than women are.

Figure 16.6   Salary Adequate

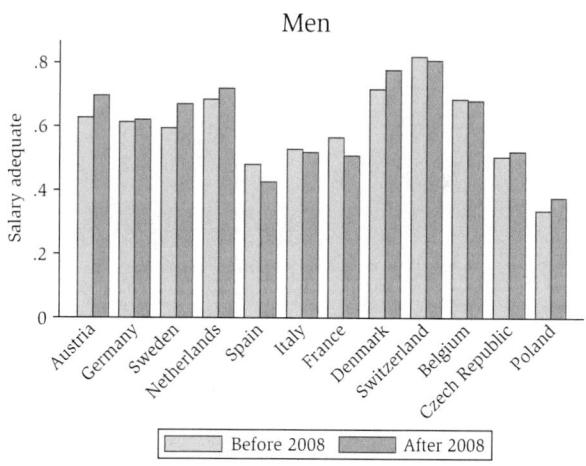

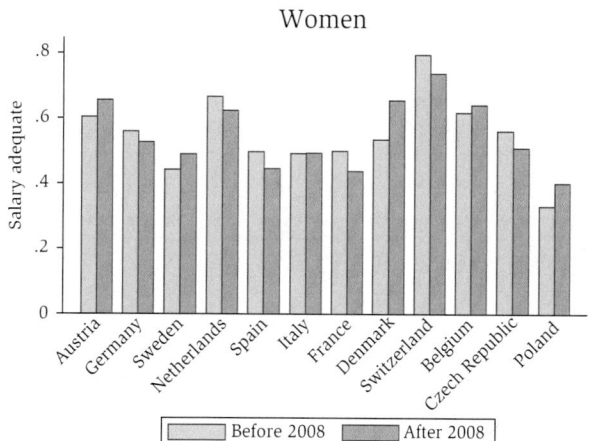

Interestingly enough, the reported heterogeneities in the job-quality index can be compared with the prevalence of permanent of temporary jobs in the considered set of countries. Figure 16.7 reports the ratio between temporary and permanent occupation for male and women, and shows that: (i) a relationship is visible between slightly low levels of this ratio (Spain, Italy, France, Greece, Poland) with lower job-quality levels; but at the same time (ii) the between countries ratios are quite similar so that the aforementioned relationship is not strongly supported.

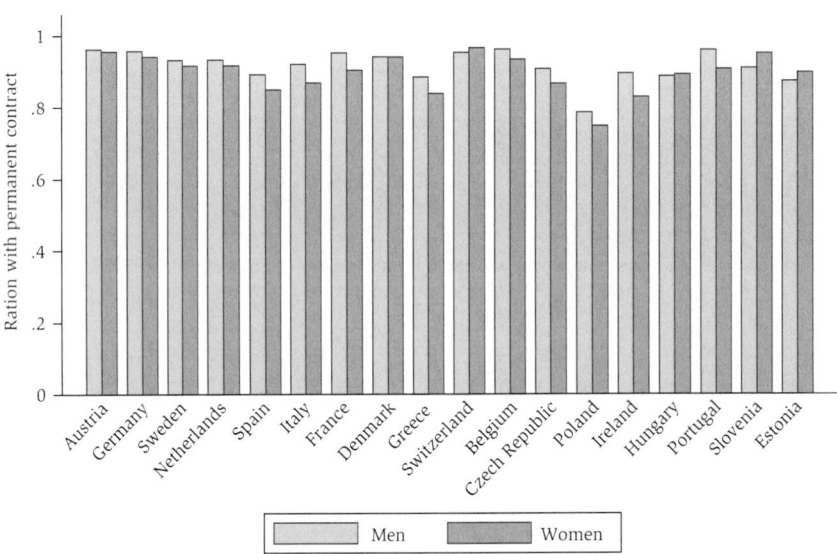

Figure 16.7   Ratio with Permanent Contract

Figure 16.8 reports the ratio between temporary and permanent occupation separately for male and women. At a first glance, we can notice that Northern European countries (Sweden, Netherlands, Denmark and Ireland) along with Switzerland show higher level of job satisfaction for both women and men compared to the Southern and Continental ones. Moreover, permanent workers from Nordic areas report a higher job satisfaction (with the only exception of Ireland) compared with temporary workers, irrespective of gender. The lower levels of the job quality index concern the Southern cluster (Italy, Greece, and Spain), in line with the previous evidence (*see*, for instance, figure 16.1). Interestingly, the gap in terms of job satisfaction between permanent and temporary workers tends to be less pronounced when we look at the women sub sample.

Chapter 16: Workers Participation in the Enterprise: Welfare and Quality of Work

Figure 16.8

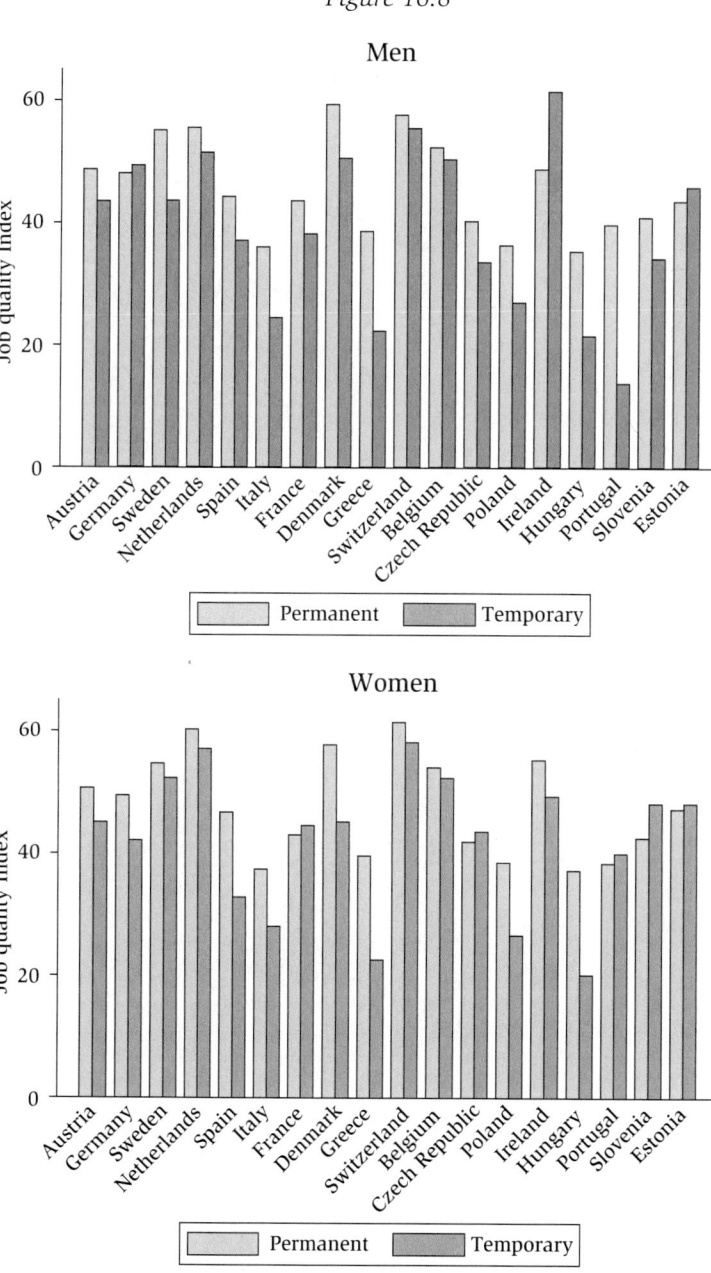

Similar results are found with respect to the individual's opinions about the adequacy of salary and the freedom at work to perform specific tasks. As you can note from Figures 16.9 and 16.10, the gap between permanent and temporary female workers tends to be smaller compared with the male workers.

Figure 16.9

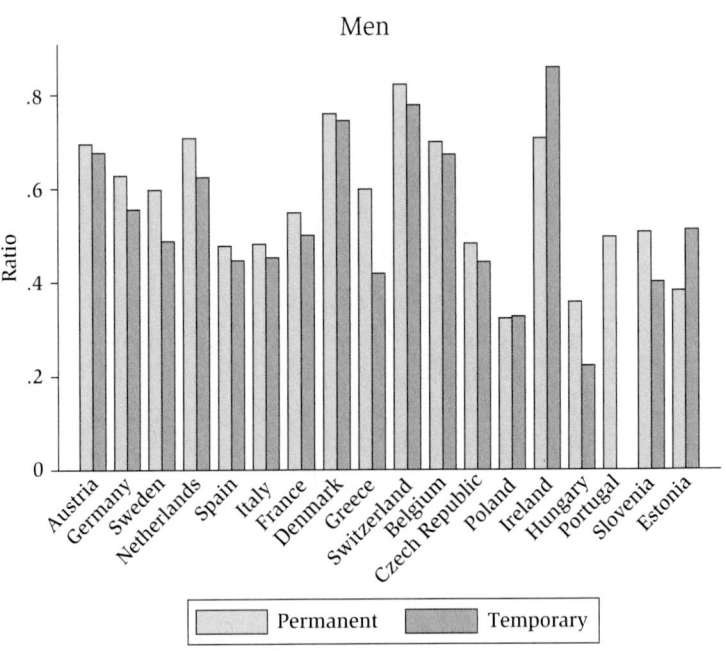

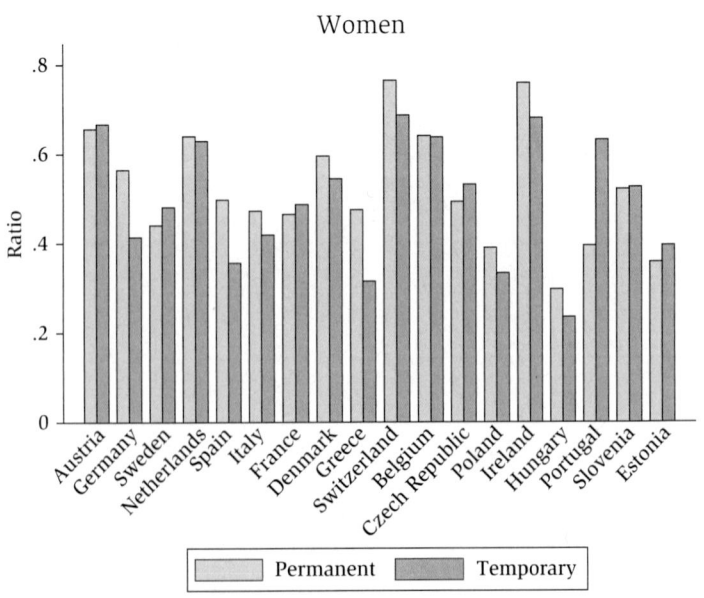

Chapter 16: Workers Participation in the Enterprise: Welfare and Quality of Work

Figure 16.10   Ratio

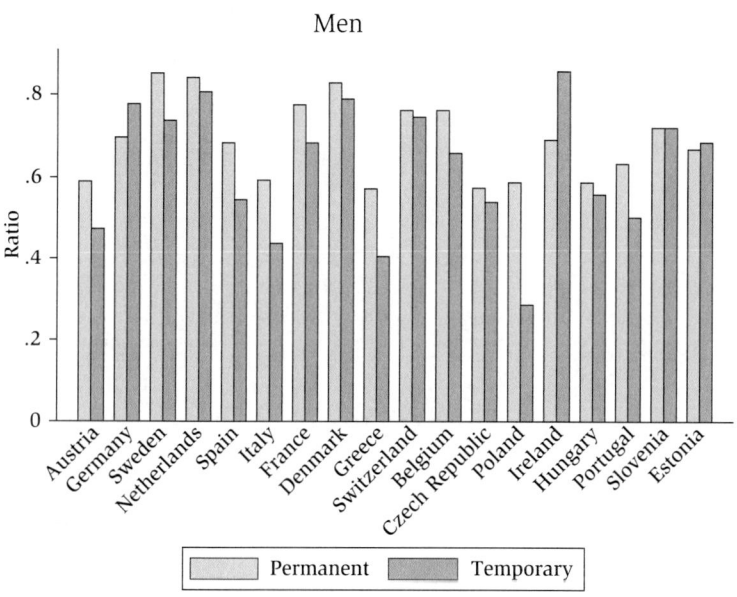

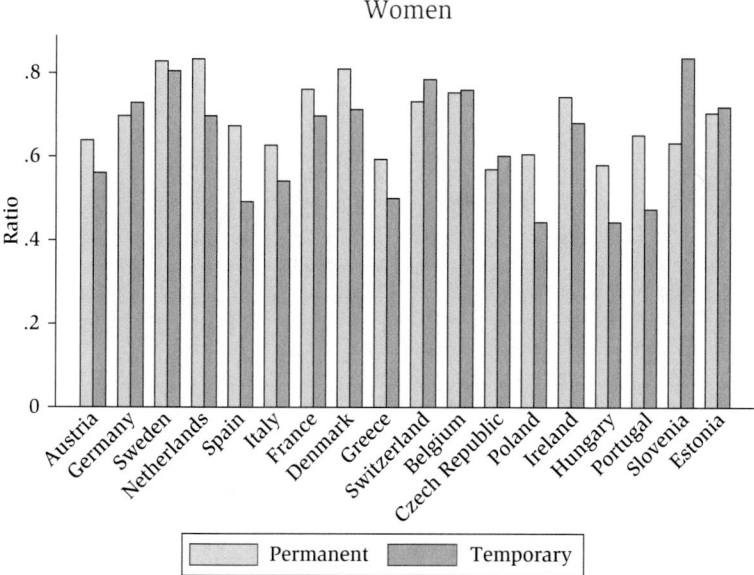

While much has been done with respect to the implementation of new employee participative practices there are still significant shortcomings with

respect to women's rights. In spite of the recent progresses in order to reduce the gender gap in the various aspects of the working life, yet there are many issues to be solved especially in certain countries. Of great importance is the problem on how maternity influences both the working career and, further on, the retirement of women. Due to childbearing and childcare, women often display discontinuous working career, episodes of part-time or temporary jobs. While female participation to the labour market increased significantly in all European countries recently, there are still discriminations that seem to take place even before a pregnancy episode occurs.

SHARE data document important differences both along time and among countries with respect to women's working careers. Figure 16.11, from Brugiavini, Pasini, Trevisan, 2011, shows the share of women not working at the time of the first childbearing. It is easy to observe that this quote reduced for most countries by about 18%–20% for the cohort born after 1941 with respect to the cohort of women born before 1941, with peaks for the Netherlands and Belgium, where the gap between the two cohorts is about 25%.

On the other hand, the graph points important and persistent differences among the various countries with Germany, Austria and the Nordic countries characterized by low rates of non-employment and Mediterranean countries that display important peaks: 62% in Italy, 65% in Greece and almost 80% in Spain.

Figure 16.11   Women That Do Not Work at the Time of the First Childbearing

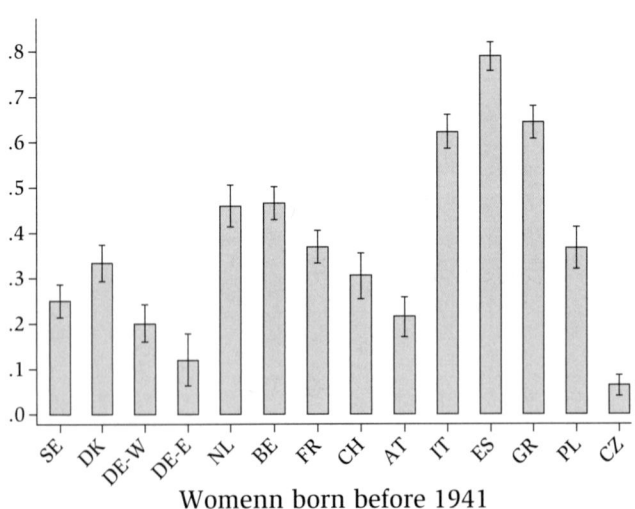

Womenn born before 1941

Chapter 16: Workers Participation in the Enterprise: Welfare and Quality of Work

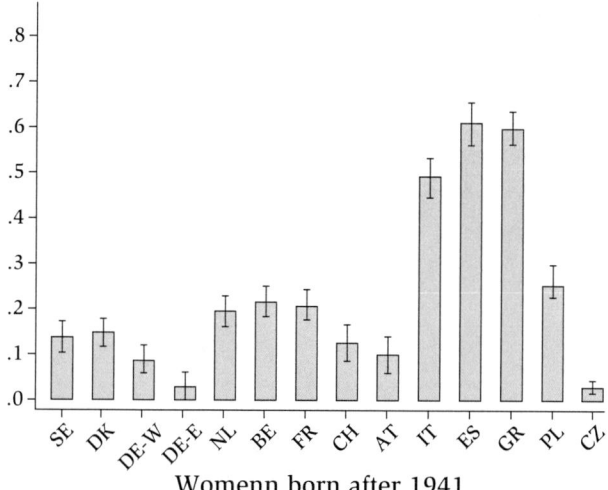

Womenn born after 1941

The fact that maternity/childcare influences women participation to the labour market is documented also by Organisation for Economic Co-operation and Development (OECD) data. Figure 16.12, below, shows that mothers' employment rate is ordinarily lower than that of all women. While there is almost no gap or a very little one in the North-European countries, the difference is rather significant for countries like United States or Germany.

We should also observe that although the gap is not so big in Italy as it is in Germany, it refers to significantly lower levels of employment, for in the first one both maternal and women employment rates are much lower indicating possible higher discrepancies between women and men in general.

Figure 16.12 Maternal Employment Rate versus Female Employment Rate

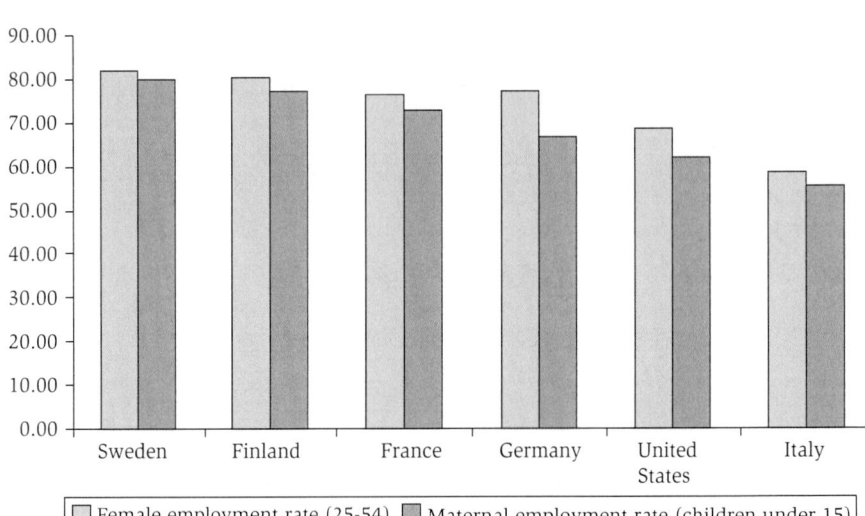

Source: OECD data.

These gaps may give an idea about the policies that countries promote/enact in support of families in general, of motherhood in particular and a hint about women's contractual power.

If we go deeper in the analysis, we observe in fact that mothers have a higher propensity to work if they receive maternity benefits. Figure 16.13 (Brugiavini, Pasini, Trevisan, 2011), displays women's behaviour/participation to the labour market after childbearing in the presence and in the absence of maternity benefits. The graph is constructed using SHARE data on women with two children, separately by countries and for the first and for the second child.

We can see important differences in the women's employment situation after childbearing in the two cases.

Chapter 16: Workers Participation in the Enterprise: Welfare and Quality of Work

Figure 16.13

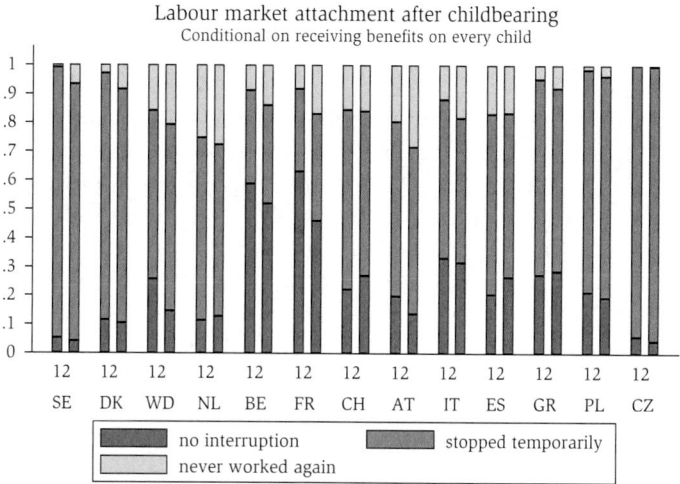

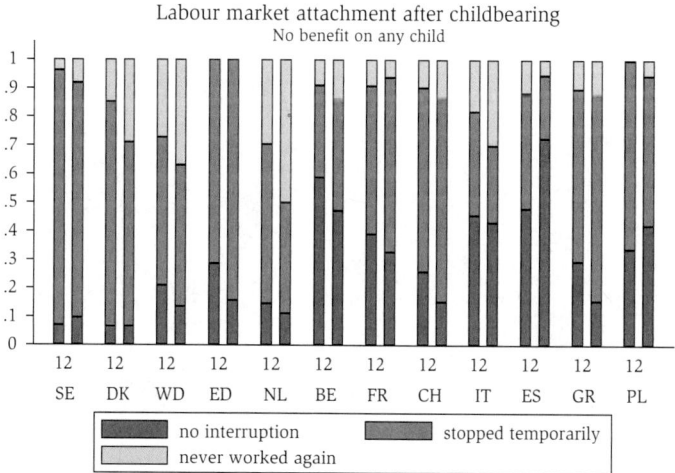

Source: Brugiavini, Pasini, Trevisan, 2011.

In almost all countries, if benefits were paid, the share of women that exited the labour market was significantly lower than in the situation with no benefits. While for the first child the gaps were smaller, for the second one they were much more important. In the Netherlands, for example, the difference in the drop-out rates is of around 5% for the first child but 20 percentage points for the second child, in West Germany, about 12% for the first and 15% for the second child. In Italy the drop-out rate was higher by 9% after the first childbearing and by 12% after the second when no benefits were paid with respect to the situation in which benefits were available.

The situations described above are extremely relevant because women represent an important resource for the labour market. But they are also the main providers of chid care as well as of long term care (which is of critical importance under the recent demographic trends). Consequently, governments and enterprises should promote measures meant to keep women in the labour market. On the one hand, provision of facilities *for children* such as employer provided childcare, out-of-school hours care, or *for elderly* (elderly care support) will allow women to avoid leaving the job or reduce their working hours as a consequence of care giving and to better concentrate to job tasks. On the other hand, flexible working programs or extra-statutory leave from work arrangements will allow women to better reconcile work and family life.

Using OECD data we constructed a graph showing the shares of various working arrangements (with different degrees of flexibility), figure 16.14. By comparing it with figure 16.12 we easily observe that the countries where employees have more flexibility in choosing their working schedule are those with higher rates of women/mothers employment. In fact Sweden and Finland are those that present higher percentages of flexible working arrangement and simultaneously higher women/mothers employment rates. They are followed by France and Germany while Italy performs worse (comes last) in both fields.

Figure 16.14   Working Arrangements by Country

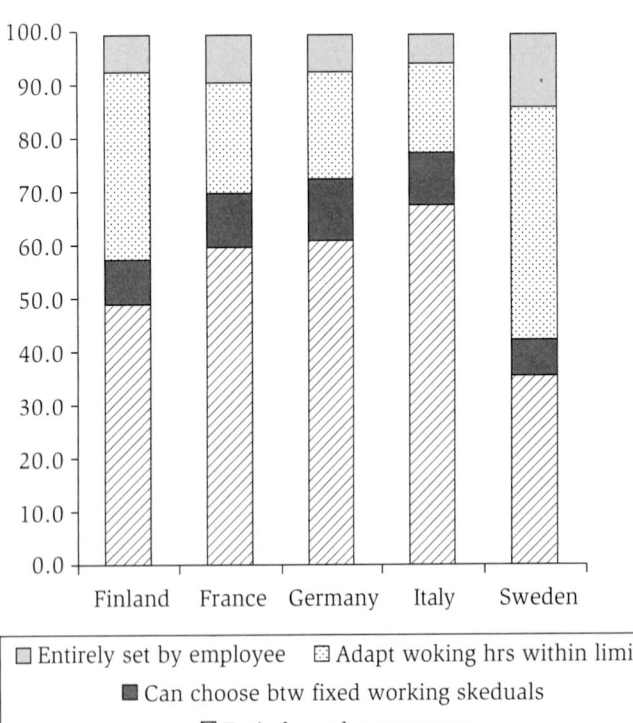

□ Entirely set by employee   ▨ Adapt woking hrs within limits
■ Can choose btw fixed working skeduals
▨ Entirely set by company

Source: OECD data.

Chapter 16: Workers Participation in the Enterprise: Welfare and Quality of Work

The same picture comes out when watching the proportion of establishments offering flexible working arrangements (figure 16.15). It is interesting to observe that both the flexibility in working arrangements and the women/mothers employment rate follow the same pattern as the EPI (figure 16.1). While the fact that workers participation and flexibility in working arrangements go in the same direction is to be expected, the relationship between EPI and women/mothers' employment rates is less obvious and is probably a consequence of the higher flexibility in the working schemes.

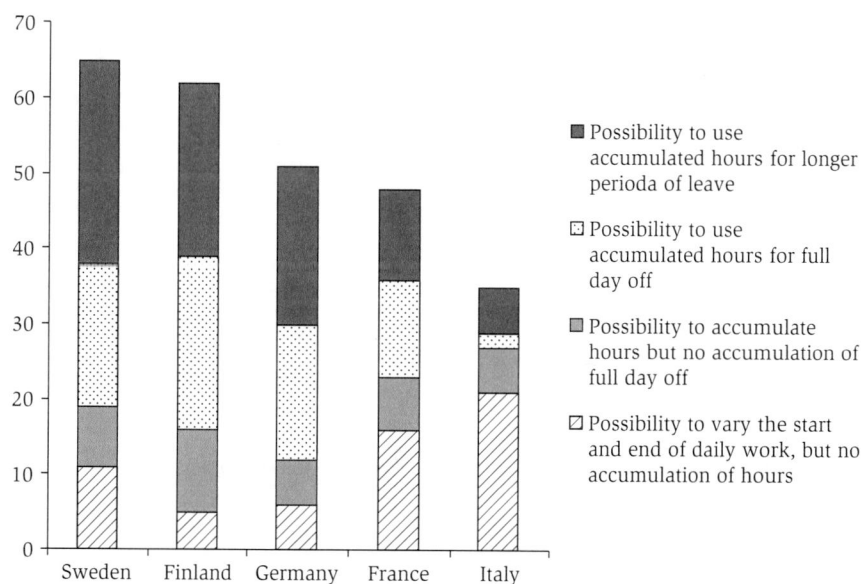

Figure 16.15 *Proportion of Establishments Offering Flexible Working Arrangements*

Source: OECD data.

Finally, we want to bring the attention towards two issues on which there still much to do in order to cancel out the discriminations between genders: the wage gap and the share of women in leaders' positions. OECD data (figure 16.16) document large differences among countries with respect to the wage differences between men and women. The peaks are attained in countries as Korea (almost 40%) and Japan (around 28%) but it is very significant also in many European countries. For example in the Netherlands, UK, Finland and Austria the pay gap is around 18–20 percentage points. Italy performs better, with around 11%, while the lowest difference is registered in countries such as Luxemburg, Hungary and Spain, around 6%–7%.

Figure 16.16 Wage Gap

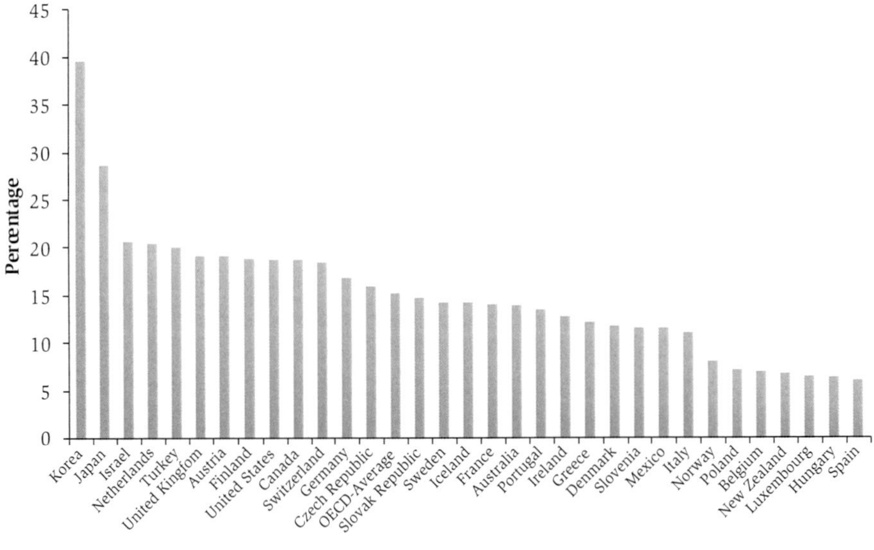

Source: OECD data.

Figure 17 presents the share of women on boards of directors in the Forbes Global 500 companies, by country.

Figure 16.17

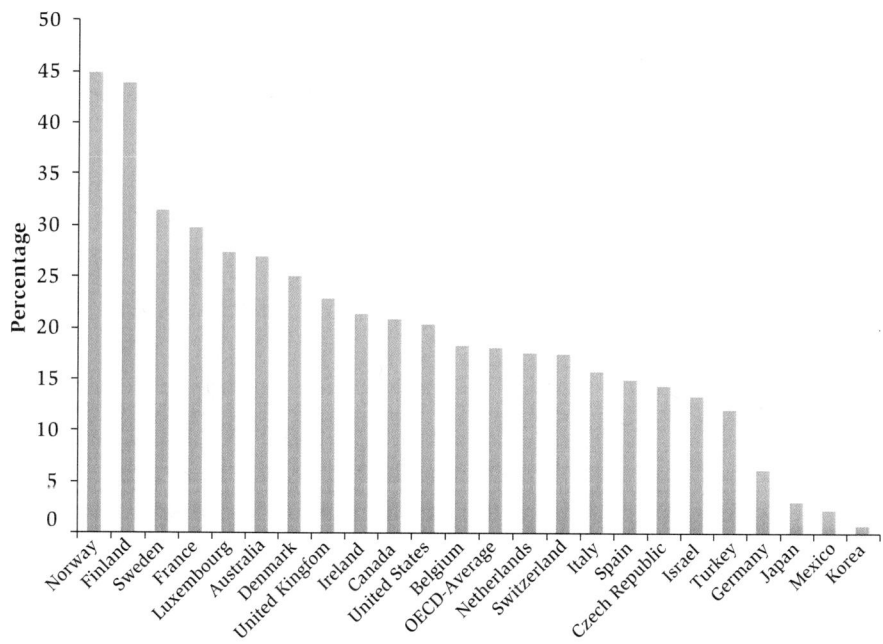

Source: OECD data, 2013.

We find again that the higher percentages of women in leading positions are in North-European countries (almost 45% in Finland and Norway), more menial positions for Belgium, the Netherlands or Italy while countries like Japan, Mexico or Korea are at the end of the list (with just around 2.5%).

16.6 CONCLUSIONS

This chapter looks at the consequences of workers' participation in the firm on various aspects of individuals' lives and the economy at large. Some shortcomings of the current legislation prevailing in Europe (and OECD countries) are identified and discussed.

There are several ways in which workers can be involved in the firm's governance and managerial activities, each presenting 'pros and cons': in this chapter the attention is focused on factual observations and some data, such as the European Participation Index as a possible measure of the strength of the workers' participation. The results show wide variability across countries, even beyond what is to be expected from differences in legislation, pointing to a potential role of the application of the rules in place in explaining the variability. This chapter provides also a graphical analysis of the job quality and workers' satisfaction based on the data from the Survey on Health, Ageing and Retirement in Europe (SHARE), which shows that the Nordic countries report higher quality of work vis-à-vis Southern countries in Europe, possibly also related to the effect of workers' participation in the organization of the workplace. One important issue in this context is the important limitations that women face in the work place, which do not seem to have voice even when participation is advocated: women's rights and the gender gap in the labour market are still quite remarkable.

PART VI The 'Constitutionalisation' of the Firm: Multinational Regulations in the Global Context between Hard and Soft Law

CHAPTER 17
The 'Constitutionalisation' of the Firm: The Corporation as a Legal System

Andrea Pin

> I'm saddened and offended by the idea that companies exist to enrich their owners... That is the very least of their roles; they are far more worthy, more honourable, and more important than that. Without the vital creative force of business, our world would be impoverished beyond reckoning.[1]

17.1 INTRODUCTION

This Chapter considers the hypothesis of the constitutionalisation of the firm from the viewpoint of constitutional law: namely, that such entities can be understood as micro-constitutional systems, which encompass several different sets of interests and develop proper dynamics and mechanisms. In doing so, it bears in mind the deep transformations that both the identity of the firm and the constitution have undergone through the decades.

This topic presupposes that considering the firm as a complex institution which is endowed with a constitutional structure would make sense transnationally. Such a discussion is one that is both necessary and challenging. Constitutionalising the firm is necessary because it addresses the growing traffic of legal concepts that has accompanied globalisation. Since firms have become increasingly transnational, giving shape to the idea that they can be seen as constitutional systems is both a useful task and an urgent need. The need to

---

1. Quotation from Michael Hammer, reported in Dennis Hevesi, *Michael Hammer, Business Writer, Dies at 60*, New York Times, 4 September 2008.

constitutionalise the firm is deeply connected with the contemporary understanding that law is economically-sensitive, to a degree that was likely non-existent in previous ages. While private law has constantly served economic agents, today it is the law that many scholars argue should follow the needs of the economy and of the market.[2]

This discussion, however, is rather challenging. In fact, there are many factors that make this process of constitutionalisation complex and even intricate. Several of these factors affect both the substance of the firm and of the constitution, both on a national and on a global scale. These factors mobilise the field and create many nuances. They therefore make it difficult to define the boundaries of the topic. In order to surmount this difficulty, this chapter will begin by taking a fresh look at the two main components of the constitutionalisation of the firm, in order to limit the field of investigation and create a coherent pattern.

The first component is the changing nature of the term firm. This term has expanded throughout time, and in doing so it has come to encompass a growing batch of interests. It has become a multi-layered idea with increasing numbers and types of shareholders and stakeholders. A firm's very rights have broadened alongside the often conflicting rights of its stakeholders, making the firm a complex environment in which several interests are at play.[3] This, in turn, means that the firm now has internalised conflicts of interests that were previously understood as lying outside the spectrum of the firm.[4]

The second component is the changing face of the constitution through time and space. The constitution is no longer a characteristic feature of the nation-state. Nor is it just a notion that refers to written texts or institutional engineering. Constitutionalisation is a phenomenon that now encompasses everything from private entities and their interests to international law. Constitutionalism itself is no longer a simple discipline: it is also an active practice of giving a definite shape to social and legal phenomena, which has powerful consequences. Constitutionalisation processes have drawn from domestic constitutional experiments as well as from supranational legal bodies such as the European Union (EU) and the European Convention of Human Rights, which have themselves developed in a piecemeal fashion (through the drafting efforts of international organisations and state governments, but mostly through the cooperative efforts of jurists and judges throughout the globe). Indeed, the more jurists and judges throughout the globe understand themselves as engaged in a transnational dialogue, the more they draw from other experiences, implement

---

2. Maria Rosaria Ferrarese, *Prima lezione di diritto globale*, 90 (Laterza 2012).
3. Marion Crain, John Inazu, *Re-Assembling Labor*, 5 U. Ill. L. R., 1791, 1846 (2015).
4. *See*, among many, Anastasia Telesetsky, *Beyond Voluntary Corporate Social Responsibility: Corporate Human Rights Obligations to Prevent Disasters and to Provide Temporary Emergency Relief*, 48 Vanderbilt J. Trans. L. 1003, 1005 and 1016 (2015).

foreign laws through adjudication, and bless international law with constitutional status. All these practices have developed a *generic constitutional law:*[5] a body of law that operates transnationally through the actions of judges and other legal players and that effectively implements laws that are already in place in other legal systems. This global phenomenon of constitutionalisation crystallises political processes and legal tendencies by giving them constitutional salience. But, since it consists of an interrupted development of concepts and ideas that are divorced from their original legal environments, constitutionalisation destabilises institutions that are firmly founded. Like a breezy wind, new ideas keep blowing through countries, thereby affecting the legal reasoning and the adjudications that take place in each of them.

The constitutionalisation of the firm is the crucible of many more factors than merely the concepts of the firm and of the constitution. But, above all the rest, these two factors seem to set the ground for the consideration of the whole project's foundation.

The dynamics of these two components suffice to illustrate that the idea of the constitutionalisation of the firm blends together the concepts of the firm and of the constitution, both of which our era has transformed into highly volatile realities. Their dynamics therefore sufficiently sound the alarm that it would be too confident to expect the idea of the constitutionalisation of the firm itself to be stable, uniform, and predictable. Yes, the idea of the constitutionalisation can be useful from an epistemological as well as normative standpoint. It still, however, derives its primary strength from extremely fluid concepts, and can hardly therefore be expected to be stronger and to last longer than these same concepts. Constitutionalisation can explain why and how the legal environment of the firm is changing, and it can orient political and legal players accordingly; it is less clear, however, to what extent this concept can square the circle of accommodating competing interests.

The idea of constitutionalising the firm captures the zeitgeist of the globalisation of trades, economy, and law. The general belief that there is some connection between societal changes and legal changes is a common feature of contemporary legal thought.[6] Contemporary legal theories that see social evolution both as a factor that impacts law and as criteria to which law itself should adjust,[7] accept that the law must necessarily follow social change and even lead it to the extent that this is feasible. One example of this is when contemporary legal theories support the law's attempt to insulate social changes in a positive way. Contemporary legal culture is a combination of the sunset of classic state

---

5. David S. Law, *Generic Constitutional Law*, 89 Minn. L. R. 652, 662 and 725 (2005).
6. Maria Rosaria Ferrarese, *Diritto sconfinato. Inventiva giuridica e spazi nel mondo globale*, 22 and 54 (Laterza, 2006).
7. Ferrarese, *supra* n. 3, at 44.

sovereignty,[8] the judicialisation of politics,[9] and the belief that the economy should be regulated. Supranational legal orders and transnational firms have set the new stage for constitutional ideas: concepts are able to cross state jurisdictions and draw global attention to themselves because, instead of distilling fully-fledged rules, they set minimal standards.[10]

It is worth noting, however, that the constitutionalisation of the firm is more than a mere product of contemporary legal tendencies; to some extent, constitutionalisation goes against the very wave of rights that has rolled onto the shores of the globalised legal world. In fact, contemporary constitutionalism and human rights language are inclined to dismantle institutions into constellations of separated, individualised rights. Claims and claimants operate independently, therefore exacerbating conflicts.[11] The constitutionalisation of the firm may, therefore, conceptualise the diversity of rights and rights owners that make up the firm's common framework. Rights normally place the individual against the community,[12] but in the scenario of the constitutionalisation of the firm rights are supposed to stem from the firm as an institution, one in which individual and collective rights owners may thrive and from which they take their force.

The idea of constitutionalising firms has been shaped by scholars such as Gunther Teubner, who drew from Habermas and Luhmann,[13] among others. The links between sociology, legal philosophy, and legal theory that are embedded in constitutionalising firms is evident in the connections between these great scholars' individual disciplines. While the origin of the idea of constitutionalising the firm does, in fact, have sociological roots, the second part of this Chapter will propose that the entire idea of constitutionalising firms be reconsidered in light of a broader and stronger understanding of legal orders.

Teubner develops his idea of constitutionalising the firm from his own understanding of the term constitution. In order, therefore, to consider the possibility of incorporating Teubner's idea of a constitution into the life and the very structure of the firm, a very brief sketch of his constitutional theory is needed.

For Teubner, the constitution performs two basic duties. First, it establishes the borders of a system: it says what lies in and what remain out of a system.[14]

---

8. Sabino Cassese, *Chi governa il mondo*, 35 (Il Mulino, 2013).
9. Ran Hirschl, *Towards Juristocracy. The Origins and Consequences of the New Constitutionalism* (Harvard University Press, 2004).
10. Cassese, supra n. 9, at 128.
11. See Christopher McCrudden, Brendan O'Leary, *Courts and Consociations* (Oxford University Press 2013).
12. Joseph H.H. Weiler, *Deciphering the Political and Legal DNA of European Integration: An Exploratory Essay*, J. Dickson, P. Eleftheriadis (eds), *Philosophical Foundations of European Union Law*, 155 (Oxford University Press, 2012).
13. See the reflections of Clemens Mattheis, *The System Theory of Niklas Luhmann and the Constitutionalization of the World Society*, 2 Goettingen J. Int'l. L., 625 (2012).
14. Gunther Teubner, *Substantive and Reflexive Elements in Modern Law*, 2 L. & Socy. Rev. 240, 269 (1983).

Second, it structures the system: it endows the system with a backbone,[15] it controls the system's functions, and it secures the preservation of the system through time. This last point implies that constitutions are supposed to last: they are not ephemeral combinations of factors that just take place and then quickly dissolve. On the contrary, the mechanisms of constitutions enjoy stability and predictability.

For Teubner, these basic assumptions about the constitution can – and actually should be – expanded to encompass firms as forms of societal constitutions. In fact, Teubner believes that constitutions are an epistemological device that adequately fulfils the need to describe how firms work.[16] We will explore, however, whether this expansion is simply a matter of fact or whether it also has normative implications.[17]

17.2 SOFT AND HARD LAW IN GLOBAL CONTEXT AND THE ROLE OF FIRMS

It is well known that firms and firms practice forum shopping. Various factors encourage firms to de-localise and mobilise their economic activities in search of places where they can more easily perform them.[18] Ease is a concept that encompasses several factors: it can mean that the market is more accessible, but also that labour law is more permissive, that labour unions are weaker, that human rights are less protected, that environmental concerns are neglected, and that corrupting public functionaries is feasible.[19] While the relevancy of each of these factors depends upon the respective place and market, all of them raise broad concerns on a global scale.[20]

Moreover, even though the above description of the rationale behind economic activities is partial, it is nonetheless consistent with a certain understanding of economic activities: firms operate as rational agents whose only interest is to maximise their own profits.

While this conception of the firm as a purely profit-maximising rational agent will be investigated more in depth later in this Chapter, some of the consequences that this depiction entails are immediately visible. If firms are purely maximising rational agents, then states can only attract them if they

---

15. Gunther Teubner, *Self-Constitutionalizing TNCs? On the Linkage of 'Private' and 'Public' Corporate Codes of Conduct*, 18 Ind. J. Glob. L. St. 617, 624 (2011).
16. Gunther Teubner, Anna Beckers, *Expanding Constitutionalism*, 20 Ind. J. Glob. L. St. 523, 540 (2013).
17. Larry Catà Backer, *Transnational Corporation's Outward Expression of Inward Self-Constitution: The Enforcement of Human Rights by Apple, Inc.*, 20 Ind. J. Glob. L. St. 805, 809 (2013).
18. This trend has made firms contemporary 'lawmakers:' Julian Arato, *Corporation sas Lawmakers*, 56 Harv. Int'l. L. J. 229, 230 (2015).
19. Teubner, *supra* n. 16, at 618.
20. *See* the reflections of Mattheis, *supra* n. 14, at 643.

relieve firms from the limitations and burdens that affect their decisions regarding where to locate their activities. A race to the bottom among states would then take place, in order for states to attract firms to their territories.

This race to the bottom, however, triggers a race to the top within global constitutional law scholarship. What this means is that, in the face of the relief promised by states to firms, lawyers commit themselves to spreading the highest level of human rights protection throughout the world because the insulation of human rights into legal orders is the only concrete way to force firms to obey human rights. If states do not share a minimum global standard of human rights which they enforce, then states will attract firms by putting human rights' protection to the side, since the firms will desert the legal orders that are most protective of human rights.

Albeit debatable, this understanding of the firm as a maximising rational agent and of how it operates presents a framework made of factors that pull the firm in different directions. When we apply the concept of the constitutionalisation of the firm to it, the framework appears to depict a constellation of rights and interests, some of which belong to the realm of soft law, which means that they work persuasively and are not legally binding.[21] Others, however, do rise to the level of hard law in their nature and enforcement. It will be useful to describe them here, if only briefly:

(a) Reputation and marketing policies can force companies to align themselves with human rights' standards. Within this context, firms do not implement corporate policies that comply with human rights in order to comply with human rights per se, but rather the implementation of these rights is an expedient way to facilitate business. This dynamic constitutionalises societal trends through the threat of a bad reputation: societal reputation forces companies to comply with rules even though they are not legally binding.[22]

(b) Some dynamics shape and crystallise not just the actions of, but also the structure of firms[23] by transforming firms' purely internal rules into state rules. Under some circumstances, a state can bless a purely internal protocol that some firms keep as their legal standard for a whole field of economic activities. Logical inference justifies this extension of the protocol. If the majority of firms follow a protocol that benefits human rights, then there would be no reason to believe that a rights-pejorative protocol is necessary for a company to stay in the market. On the contrary, if a majority of firms follow a protocol that benefits human rights, a state is justified in their expectation that all

---

21. Teubner, *supra* n. 16, at 630.
22. Teubner, *supra* n. 15, at 268.
23. Teubner & Beckers, *supra* n. 17, at 527.

companies can follow the most human rights-protective protocol without becoming unmarketable. Along similar lines, the need for the firm's internal coherence justifies a state sanction of a firm that does not respect the protocol that the firm itself has formally implemented. Lately some domestic judicial decisions have taken these aforementioned approaches,[24] transforming corporate laws into the hard law of states.

(c) A foreign rule that affects the structure or the functions of a firm can become a state rule. The transformation of a foreign rule into a state rule normally takes place when a judge draws from foreign sources to address a domestic problem: the judge imports foreign law and incorporates it into the state legal order. Many scholars have tried to explain and promote this phenomenon, which is normally referred to as transnational judicial dialogue or judicial globalisation.[25] One of the most famous theories underpinning this practice of borrowing foreign law stems from the so-called *Condorcet jury theorem*.[26] The judicial version of the theory of the French philosopher and mathematician says that the best way to deal with a legal problem is most likely in the way that the majority of a sample of independent agents happen to deal with it. Judges that exploit this practice understand themselves as being at the top of a tower of Babel, looking down on diverse laws and legal regimes,[27] and as involved in creating a common means of communication through the import of the legal rules that belong to other states or supranational bodies.

In reality, the very existence of multinational firms often prompts this global law approach, instead of a simple regulation according to the global paradigm of judicial borrowing. Judges tend to draw from foreign experiences exactly because they think they need to universalise the highest level of rights protection to the maximum extent possible throughout all world economies. Global law, in a sense, is the offspring of multinational firms and lawyers' commitment to human rights.[28]

(d) Finally, international pressures push states to implement environmental policies, labour relations policies, or anti-corruption penal sanctions[29] through processes that are, at least to some extent, political. This is particularly evident in Europe, where the stable legal and judicial network of state institutions has developed out of historical

---

24. *Kasly v. Nike, Inc.*, 45 P.3d 243 (Cal. 2002), *cert. denied*, 539 U.S. 654 (2003).
25. Anne-Marie Slaughter, *Judicial Globalization*, 40 Va. J. Int'l. L. 1103, 1112 (1999–2000).
26. Among many, *see* Paul H. Edelman, *On Legal Interpretations of the Condorcet Jury Theorem*, 31 J. Leg. St. 327, 328 (2002).
27. Sabino Cassese, *I Tribunali di Babele* (Donzelli, 2009).
28. Catà Backer, *supra* n. 18, at 823.
29. Teubner, *supra* n. 16, at 637.

diplomatic relationships.[30] European states normally implement the aforementioned policies under the command of supranational institutions; but it is safe to say that each state commits itself to protecting human rights either voluntarily or under peer pressure, since European institutions normally voice and formalise decisions that the states themselves are willing to implement. If this political and legal scenario includes states' concerns for how firms operate and for the interests that are affected by economic activities, then the supranational legal orders will reflect these state concerns and, in turn, push the states that are members of such supranational orders to implement them. Since the EU[31] and the Council of Europe both assign importance to human rights standards in the field of economic activities, when they shape shared commercial policies or consider state candidatures for memberships, they force the states to comply with their rules and with the protocols they encourage. The EU has also set up some preferential treatments for third states that comply with some basic standards of human rights protection. These preferential treatments, in turn, affect the inner policies of the firms that are interested in doing business in the EU zone.

This quick overview shows that specific features characterise the pattern of the constitutionalisation of the firm. The judicialisation of politics and the interaction of national and supranational legal orders normally instigate this approach, which combines soft law with hard law.

In order to increase their reputation, expand their markets, and gain public attention, firms may take the initiative and apply policies that consider several concerns such as the environment, labour conditions, or corruption:[32] interests that would otherwise lie outside the scope of the firm. In this scenario, soft law remains as it is, and reputation and marketability are the main drivers of the policies' enforcement within companies.[33] But corporate[34] protocols can also receive legal sanctions from the state, and foreign and international laws can be incorporated into state laws, thereby transforming soft law into hard law.

This scenario enlists and explains several related phenomena, but presumes that the constitutionalisation of the firm is a societal fact, which calls for

---

30. Armin von Bogdandy, Christoph Grabenwarter, Peter Huber, *Il diritto costituzionale nel diritto pubblico europeo. L'esempio della rete istituzionalizzata della giustizia costituzionale*, www.associazionedeicostituzionalisti.it 4 (2015).
31. *See* the European Commission resolution of November 2011, which encouraged member state to facilitate social business: http://ec.europa.eu/internal_market/social_business/index_en.htm.
32. Teubner, Beckers, *supra* n. 17, at 531.
33. Catà Backer, *supra* n. 18, at 805, and passim, describes the economic reasons that led Apple, Inc., to change its transparency policy.
34. Teubner, *supra* n. 15, at 278.

a sociological perspective, rather than a normative pattern. Moreover, it presumes that firms are rational agents willing to maximise their profits.

These two assumptions affect the constitutionalisation of the firm itself. In fact, if constitutions are dividing lines between what lies in and what lies outside of a system, and if they are the means that govern systems, then states' attempts to correct firms' internal dynamics are still perceived as outside efforts[35] to prompt an internal evolution.[36] Limiting firms' autonomy and securing some basic rights are the reasons for which states draw from both foreign and private rules to influence firms' policies. The state constitution does not control the state system anymore.[37]

Within this perspective, it is not the firm that changes its face; it is rather the face of the state that changes. While a firm has a given, stable structure that focuses on making profit and is permeable only to the extent that is necessary to remain in the market, the state is susceptible to foreign as well as economic pressures in its attempts to regulate the firm.

This shift in the understanding of the relationship between the state constitution and the firm's constitutional structure is extremely important. Contemporary constitutionalism is intrinsically normative. Its normativity derives from the values embedded within the constitution itself:[38] the reasons for a law affect its nature, its scope, and its importance. If a state law that promotes a public good – such as the environment – is enforced by the firm only because of its positive economic outcome for the firm, then the meaning of that law changes as soon as that law penetrates the firm. If the political reason for a state's enactment of a law gives way to purely economic reasons when the law enters the firm, then the legal environment is divided into the morally-driven, just legal order of the state, and the a-moral, economically-maximising order of the firm. In Teubner's lexicon, we should conclude that while state constitutionalism and firm constitutionalism[39] may not differ in their rules, they do unescapably differ in the way in which they understand those rules.

This shift, however, only entails powerful consequences if firms are rational agents merely interested in maximising their profit and impermeable to interests of a different kind. If firms are understood as being legal orders with interests that go beyond the purely economic forum, then more analogies can be drawn between state constitutionalism and societal constitutionalism, and the universes of the state and of the firm can speak with each other more fruitfully.

---

35. Riccardo Prandini, *The Future of Societal Constitutionalism in the Age of Acceleration*, 2 Ind. J. Glob. L. St. 731, 740 (2013).
36. Teubner, *supra* n. 15, at 278.
37. *See* the reflections of Mattheis, *supra* n. 14, at 637.
38. Michael J. Perry, *The Political Morality of Liberal Democracy* (Cambridge University Press, 2012).
39. Teubner, *supra* n. 16, at 620. *See also* Prandini, *supra* at 36, 731.

17.3 FIRMS AS LEGAL ORDERS: THEORIES AND COMPONENTS

The rest of this chapter develops the idea of the constitutionalisation of the firm as a legal concept, and not just as a sociological concept to which the state attaches legal implications.

If the firm is understood as a legal order, then the concept of the constitutionalisation of the firm is of normative salience: by virtue of the very existence of this order, the inner regulations that connect the firm's interests acquire the status of law. From this viewpoint, the state should be understood as enforcing laws that are already present within the firm: instead of merely trying to influence the internal organisation of the firm, the state enforces rules that are already a part of the firm. There may be disagreement about which interests are at stake, and therefore about which of these interests need to be taken into account by the firm and protected by the state, but the interests that are at play are already legal within the firm system. As a result, the constitutionalisation of the firm becomes an autonomous legal construct.[40]

Understanding the constitutionalisation of the firm not from a sociological perspective, but from a legal perspective requires two things: a deeper understanding of what a legal order is, and an understanding of the firm that suits contemporary needs and trends.

17.4 THE FIRM AS A LEGAL ORDER

A great Italian constitutional law scholar, Santi Romano, developed a theory of law that understands legal orders as plural. He framed his idea of the plurality of legal orders at the dawn of the twentieth century, when the state was still monopolising the legal scene. Romano challenged the state-centred legal edifice. Romano argued that statehood had reached a phase of crisis.[41] He also argued that legal thinking had to broaden its horizons: that it had to encompass more entities and that it must try to understand these phenomena as autonomous legal orders, and not just as derivative systems which depended on their state for their very existence.

Santi Romano's theory does not simply portray legal systems as intrinsically open and interactive; rather, it maintains that the very understanding of law must encompass all sorts of legal systems that exist. Moreover, in his theory, legal systems develop their normativity both through the existence of a set of norms, and through the institutions that their collectivities recognise as lawmakers and law-enforcers.[42] The subjects that obey the system's laws and recognise

---

40. On the autonomy of the firm, *see* Arato, *supra* n. 19, at 234.
41. He spoke of the crisis of the modern state in 1909; *see* Santi Romano, *Lo stato moderno e la sua crisi. Saggi di diritto costituzionale* (Giuffré, 1969).
42. S. Romano, *L'ordinamento giuridico*, 35 (Mariotti, 1917).

its institutions are conscious of the fact that they do so because they are following the rules of a legal order.[43]

What Romano basically suggested is that legal orders' existence does not depend on the official recognition of another legal system, which normally happens to be the state.[44]

There is no reason to exclude firms from qualifying as legal orders. Firms function as a system. Their institutions produce rules,[45] and their compliance with the rules is crucial for the firms' very existence. Santi Romano's theory of legal orders seems to be just what the doctor ordered for the theorisation of the constitutionalisation of the firm.

17.5 THE MORALITY OF FIRMS

Merely portraying the firm as a profit maximiser affects the possibility that interests and values other than those of the market may be associated with the firm. As detailed above, a market player that is only interested in increasing its profits may still behave in a way that is conducive to environmental protection, sound conditions of labour, and social responsibility. It will nonetheless, however, align its protocols to such values simply because its aim is to secure its reputation and the marketability of its products; it will only behave in a way that is positive for society at large because such behaviour entails positive economic consequences for itself.

Political philosophers such as Michael Sandel have brilliantly shown that political communities do not – and actually cannot – formulate questions and solve problems by only taking economic and financial perspectives into account.[46] Debates about justice should play – and certainly do play – a role in shaping policies and rules.

Michael Sandel's reflections tend to draw distinctions between markets and political communities. He seems to suggest that a markets' logic should not overwhelm political communities and replace concerns for justice with economic and financial concerns. Sandel understands the polity and the market as alternatives, and not substitutes for one another, since their structure and mechanisms would operate according to incommensurable values.

Michael Sandel's preoccupation addresses the heart of the case against technocracy, which tends to defer highly political questions to technicians under the mistaken belief that complex moral arguments can be isolated from plain economic issues, and that it is possible to make decisions according to the latter while leaving aside the former. But Sandel may be wrong in assigning very narrow goals and dynamics to the markets and their operators: even markets do

---

43. Ibid., 27. *See also* Santi Romano, *Frammenti di un dizionario giuridico*, 65 (Giuffré 1983).
44. S. Romano, *supra* n. 43, at 37.
45. This idea is present also in Teubner, *supra* n. 16, at 625.
46. Michael Sandel, *What Money Can't Buy. The Moral Limits of Markets* (Farrar, Straus and Giroux, 2012).

not necessary function with the sole goal of maximising their profits. Markets' operators can have a soul.

Economic operators can run businesses with a regard to non-economic concerns. Firms can frame the environment, working conditions, labour unions' claims, anti-corruption policies, and corporate social responsibility at large as inherent parts of their functions and as the core concerns of their activities.

This understanding of firms does not apply to non-profit firms alone. The understanding is, in fact, embedded in the very entrepreneurial spirit that characterises economic activities at large,[47] and some courts have already sanctioned this approach.

Here it will suffice to mention the American Supreme Court's recent trends, which are outstandingly important since this institution has normally followed a rather traditional approach to the relationship between law and economics,[48] focusing on profit as the overwhelming goal of firms. In 2014, the Supreme Court issued a decision of great relevance, plainly endorsing the idea that markets can – and actually are – composed by for-profit agents whose concern is not *only* the maximisation of profit.

In *Burwell v. Hobby Lobby*,[49] the Court dealt with a for-profit company's claim. *Hobby Lobby* sought exemption from the Affordable Care Act requirement that all employers provide their employees with an insurance coverage that includes abortifacient medicines. *Hobby Lobby* was and still is a company that operates nationwide, with thousands of employees, but it is also owned by a family whose religious beliefs oppose abortion and who believe that facilitating abortion for their employees through the insurance infringed upon their sincere religious belief. *Hobby Lobby* was therefore seeking exemption from providing abortifacients through the insurance they offered, and framed its claim under the *Religious Freedom Restoration Act*, which commands religious needs be accommodated whenever a Government action that imposes a substantial burden on religious exercise does not serve a compelling government interest and is not the least restrictive means of furthering that compelling interest.

In a sharply split decision, the Court decided that for-profit firms can claim such an exemption, as long as they are *closely held* by their owners: in other words, as long as the firm's owners share their beliefs, keep this distinctive approach to business, and run their business according to their beliefs.[50]

Here it is worth quoting the following passage from the opinion of the Court:

> While it is certainly true that a central objective of for-profit corporations is to make money, modern corporate law does not require for-profit corporations to pursue profit at the expense of everything else, and many do not do so.

---

47. Stefano Zamagni, *L'impresa civile responsabile*, www.fondazionelanza.it/forum/zamagni.php.
48. Hirschl, *supra* n. 10, 220.
49. 573 U.S. ___ (2014).
50. For a comparison, *see* Catà Backer, *supra* n. 18, at 811.

For-profit corporations, with ownership approval, support a wide variety of charitable causes, and it is not at all uncommon for such corporations to further humanitarian and other altruistic objectives. Many examples come readily to mind. So long as its owners agree, a for-profit corporation may take costly pollution-control and energy-conservation measures that go beyond what the law requires. A for-profit corporation that operates facilities in other countries may exceed the requirements of local law regarding working conditions and benefits. If for-profit firms may pursue such worthy objectives, there is no apparent reason why they may not further religious objectives as well.[51]

The Court in *Hobby Lobby* clearly acknowledged that non-economic concerns are normal components of the life of firms. The Court supplemented this empirical observation with deeper considerations on the nature of firms:

Not all corporations that decline to organize as nonprofits do so in order to maximize profit. For example, organizations with religious and charitable aims might organize as for-profit corporations because of the potential advantages of that corporate form, such as the freedom to participate in lobbying for legislation or campaigning for political candidates who promote their religious or charitable goals. In fact, recognizing the inherent compatibility between establishing a for-profit corporation and pursuing nonprofit goals, States [i.d., American States] have increasingly adopted laws formally recognizing hybrid corporate forms. Over half of the States, for instance, now recognize the 'benefit corporation,' a dual-purpose entity that seeks to achieve both a benefit for the public and a profit for its owners.[52]

This second excerpt is particularly relevant, since it acknowledges that firms – whether for-profit or non-profit – have a logic that can extend beyond that of a 'maximising rational agent'. This leads to a consequence that is powerful both for understanding the firm as a legal order and for understanding the place the firm occupies within legal orders of individual states. Applying the Court's reasoning, firms' compliance with human rights,[53] or with environmental standards, do not originate from mere economic calculations; they may also stem from a firm's very identity and purpose. When the Court speaks of the 'dual-purpose' of the firm that seeks to achieve both a benefit for the public and a profit for its owners', it does not see a conflict between two seemingly diverse driving forces of a firm's activities. Here, dualism isolates two different types of interests that together reside in the very entrepreneurial spirit of the firm.

This understanding that the purpose and structure of firms are multifaceted realities that consider public interests within the spectrum of their activities gives legal significance to the sociological fact that they obey laws. Firms may genuinely endorse and foster public interests because they acknowledge that such values are binding for them and for the system – the firm – to which they have given birth.

---

51. 573 U.S. ___, 28.
52. 573 U.S. ___, 31.
53. Teubner, Beckers, *supra* n. 17, at 524.

17.6 SOME POSSIBLE CONSEQUENCES OF THE CONSTITUTIONALISATION OF THE FIRM

The constitutionalisation of the firm has no stable or irreproachable consequences, especially if this process is understood in a legal and not in a sociological fashion. Nevertheless, the shift from a sociological to a legal perspective when considering the concept of the constitutionalisation of the firm can foster further developments that deserve some consideration here, as the conclusion of this Chapter.

The consequence of understanding the constitutionalisation of the firm from a legal standpoint means that the firm itself is given more legal protection.[54] The *Hobby Lobby* decision confirms this conclusion, since it expands the firm's freedom to encompass religious liberty.[55]

This expansion of constitutional rights to the firm does not result in an abnormal expansion of the right to do business. In fact, the expansion mainly concerns the nature of the firm itself, and the interests of the firm that go beyond economic purposes.[56] These interests can now be considered as within the framework of the firm itself. Environmental concerns, labour union treatment, working conditions, and human rights, are blended together in a systemic way. They form a legal order, whose aim is not only to maximise profits. The firm moves from a hierarchy of powers[57] that focuses only on profit, to an institutional structure[58] that is composed of different powers and interests. Such interests remain distinct and have an autonomous influence,[59] but they all participate in the life and functions of the firm. These interests, therefore, affect the firm's life along with others.

The exact effects of including new rights within the framework of the firm are not fully predictable or standardised: these effects depend on the structure of the individual firm and on the dynamics of the legal environment in which the firm operates.[60] Depending on the system in which not only the firm, but also its branches and factories operate and are located, the balance between competing interests will be different. A Brazilian plant of a German firm will need to address issues that are only partially the same as those that the same German firm will

---

54. Mark Tushnet, *Do For-Profit Corporations Have Rights of Religious Conscience?* Cornell L. Rev. Online 70, 71 (2013).
55. Ibid., 72.
56. Alan J. Meese, Nathan B. Oman, Hobby Lobby, *Corporate Law, and the Theory of the Firm: Why For Profit Corporations Are RFRA Persons*, 127 Har. L. R. Forum 273, 274 (2014).
57. Zamagni, *supra* n. 48.
58. Teubner, *supra* n. 16, at 621.
59. Ibid., 626.
60. Meese, Oman, *supra* n. 57, at 287 ('There is no single model of corporate governance and concomitant relationship between shareholder, managers, and creditors'); Anastasia Telesetsky, *Beyond Voluntary Corporate Social Responsibility: Corporate Human Rights Obligations to Prevent Disasters and to Provide Temporary Emergency Relief*, 48 Vand. J. Trans. L. 1003, 1021 (2015) ('The exact substantive content of a corporate duty to prevent disaster will depend on the hazards associated with the industry').

need to address in Germany, or that an Italian firm will need to address in Romania. Different factors will normally lead to different balances between interests.

The balance among different interests can also change due to the understanding of the role of the judiciary. One of the most common features of the rise of 'generic constitutional law' is the wide-spread recourse to the proportionality test.[61] Such a test has successfully spread throughout domestic and supranational jurisdictions, especially due to the fact that it addresses issues by combining different interests, weighing each of them against the others, and then looking for the most adequate solution within the precise context of the issue. The proportionality test has developed as a type of judgment *in concreto*, which shapes specific solutions that are supposed to only operate under specific circumstances. Proportionality rejects generalisations. In the context of the proportionality type of scrutiny, the constitutionalisation of the firm cannot entail the same consequences and balances among competing interests when circumstances vary and the interests that are at stake shift, whether transnationally or even within a given legal system.

All things considered, the constitutionalisation of the firm does not entail a uniform understanding of the components of the firm system, or of how conflicting interests should be balanced. But this is not a shortcoming of the constitutionalisation of the firm; rather, it is a distinctive feature of the contemporary understanding of law as a global product, but one that is yet fluid, malleable, and only partially predictable.

The constitutionalisation of the firm is only a useful model as long as it does not impose a stable, rigid structure and dynamic on firms, a structure which cannot change over time or from one place to another. This is an age in which state constitutionalism has largely lost its rigidity, predictability, and stability; it would be unreasonable to expect that firms now acquire these discarded characteristics.[62]

---

61. Moshe Cohen-Eliya & Iddo Porat, *Proportionality and Constitutional Culture*, 126 (2013).
62. This can partially explain the flaws of the recent state legislations on firms: *see*, e.g., Antonio Nuzzo, Paolo Tullio, *La legislazione d'impresa dell'ultimo quinquennio: quantità più che qualità, Analisi giuridica dell'economia* 395, 411 (2013).

CHAPTER 18
The Theories of the Firm between Economy and Law

Adalberto Perulli

18.1 THE THEORY OF THE FIRM: ECONOMIC AND LEGAL PERSPECTIVES

The firm is increasingly at the centre of the relationships among market, society, institutional and political spheres; it is growing more and more global and able to self-regulate, facing, on the other hand an increasing inability of States – despite their permanent relevancy within the international system of global economy[1] – to regulate the economic dimension of the market and firms. The firm, in market economy, is the basic organism of the productive and economic activity. In the contemporary world, the firm has gained global value, it is able to influence the legislator in several aspects (fiscal, commercial, labour, competition, etc.). The growing relevance of firms in the economic-social scenario reaches its peak with the form of the trans-national firm, risen to be the constitutive unit in global governance by virtue of the authority carried out through the private law of contracts and the *lex mercatoria*, conditioning the labour market, the common welfare, and the environmental law way more efficiently than the Resolutions and the Conventions of the United Nations (UN).[2] But while the firm is, as a matter of fact, the main point of reference of contemporary society and its prosperity, it seems to represents the prerequisite

---

1. Desmond King, Robert Lieberman, *Ironies of State Building: A Comparative Perspective on the American State*, Vol. 61, I 3, 550 (Cambridge University Press 2009).
2. John G. Ruggie, *Foreword: Constitutionalization and Regulation of Transnational Firms*, in Jean-Philippe Robé, Antoine Lyon-Caen & Stéphane Vernac (eds) *Multinationals and the Constitutionalization of the World Power System*, XIII (Routledge, London and New York, 2016).

in order to generate a general thrivingness and aggregate economic welfare according to the still dominating theory of the *shareholder value*, its social dimension appears more and more recessive and uncertain. The theories of the firm, generally enclosed within the paradigm of economic analysis that reduces the firm to a function of production,[3] or at most to the nexus of contracts, do not seem to offer adequate answers to the social and institutional complexity of the phenomena, to the necessity of balancing the prerogatives and the responsibilities within the organization and to re-organize the juridical nexus among firm, society, and responsibility of the economic actor.

The juridical analysis itself does not appear as able to outline a general theory of the firm. On the one hand, the law gives juridical form to the *company*, which is a juridical notion founded on the principles of the legal personality, of limited liability, of fully transferable shares, shared ownership by contributors of capital, and on governance structure. On the other hand, law knows to a lesser extent the *firm*; it does not have a general vision or a theory. Often, within the juridical tradition both of common law and civil law, the doctrine (but also the legislator) used to rely on the 'economic method', in order to identify and provide a juridical form to the firm. In reality, the doctrine of commercial law generally provides a more limited 'functional' reflection on corporations,[4] that is totally inadequate with respects to the increasingly perceived necessity to place the firm in a regulatory context that valorizes not only the private function connected to the profit and to the corporate governance based on the shareholder primacy, but also the social and institutional function, whereby we can find differentiated juridical situations and a rich and lively pluralism of values and interests (which concerns shareholders, managers, workers, but also suppliers and the other stakeholders).[5] We find the confirmation of this limitedness of the theoretical outlook of commercial law (especially regarding common law), and its collocation within the functional coordinates of the economic analysis, in one of the most authoritative manuals of corporate law, whereby is stated that: 'much of corporate law can usefully be understood as responding to three principal sources of opportunism: conflicts between managers and shareholders, conflicts among shareholders, and conflicts between shareholders and the corporation's other constituents, including creditors and employees. All three of these generic conflicts may usefully be characterized as what economists call

---

3. In particular, in the USA, the economic analysis is especially influent in the academic studies of corporate law; cf. William T. Allen, *Contracts and Communities in Corporate Law*, Washington and Lee Law Review, Vol. 50, 1395 ff. (1993); such an approach is widespread in the UK, Canada, and Australia, cf. ad es. Chris A. Riley, *Understanding and Regulating the Corporation*, Modern Law Review, 595 (1995).
4. Cf. among several sources, Reinier Kraakmnan, *The Anatomy of Corporate Law. A Comparative and Functional Approach* (Oxford University Press 2009).
5. On the firm as 'a resource which is subject to multiple overlapping and sometimes conflicting claims on its use' *see* Simon Deakin, *The Corporation as Commons: Rethinking Property Rights, Governance and Sustainability in the Business Enterprise*, Queen's Law Journal, Vol. 37, I. 2, 373 (2012).

'agency problems'. Reducing the complex regulative dynamic of the firm to a mechanism of decrease of opportunism among constituents, in a perspective of maximization of the shareholders' interests, or, in a broader angle, of the aggregate welfare for the society, evidently appears as a way of reading this phenomenon in a merely efficiency key, neglecting the pluralism of the regulation and its goals. Other sectors of the juridical system, while strongly influenced by the firm, have not even attempted to build a theory of the firm that may be equal to the regulative challenges that involve themselves, only intervening on highly significant crucial points for each juridical discipline. Labour law, for example, in the latest years, basically focuses only on the search for the employer, in order to attribute the individual employment relationship and to ascribe the relative responsibilities, re-composing in some way the subjectivity of an often elusive and 'liquid' economic actor, by reason of both the separation – made possible by the law – between economic entity and juridical entity (like in the case of joint employment),[6] and the complexity of the material and normative processes of the production and organization of labour (like in the case of the forms of triangular work relationships, in the cases of subcontractors, in the supply chain employment, etc.). In this way, labour law risks losing the constitutional nexus with corporate law and theory of the firm, abandoning, or neglecting, the possible transforming functions of the theory of the enterprise, which should, on the other hand, be re-oriented to the fundamental normative needs expressed by labour law, intended to harmonize the principles of freedom, equality and solidarity within productive organizations.[7]

In parallel to this increasingly economic-centric vision of the firm and its regulation, labour law – which in the firm finds its main environment of expression – tends to change its foundational paradigm. Once conceived as an instrument of 'democratization' of the firm in order to limit the power of the entrepreneur to protect values and people, it is transforming into 'the law of the labour market', functional to the changing needs of the firm and markets.[8] This paradigm changing might be conceived within wider coordinates, which regard the role of economy in the society: it does not simply act as a coordination factor within other factors, but it *sub-ordinates* all the other factors and reduces its autonomous contribution. This is happening to labour law, more and more inscribed into the spirit of the market, as the success of law-economic *analysis* shows, which proposes a very reductive cognitive perception of the normative situation; it does not take into account the complexity expressed by the juridical

---

6. See Jeremias Prassl, *The Concept of the Employer* (Oxford University Press 2015).
7. For a philosophical-political approach to these issues, *see* Axel Honnet, *Die Idee Des Sozialismus* (Suhurkamp Verlag, Berlin 2015).
8. For a discussion on these issues, *see* Guy Davidov, *A Purposive Approach to Labour Law* (Oxford University Press 2016), who affirms that is necessary to restore the connection between labour laws and the goals behind them; Ruth Dukes, *The Labour Constitution: The Enduring Idea of Labour Law* (Oxford 2014); Simon Deakin, Frank Wilkinson, *The Law of the Labour Market. Industrialisation, Employment and Legal Evolution* (Oxford 2005).

system conceived as not only normative, but value-oriented and not to be reduced to mere rational and purely economic quantities.

18.2 WHAT IS THE FIRM? THE INCOMPLETE ANSWERS OF ECONOMY AND LAW

We may try to start again from the question: what is the firm? Why does it exist? Which is its function? Which are its components and how does it work? The economy, especially institutionalist and neo-institutionalist (from Coase on), provides some answers, but they are not always complete or satisfying. Are there any new prospects of analysis of the firm within the economic thought? Which is the role of law in this search for identity of the firm? Starting from these questions, will we be able to conduct an inter-disciplinary discourse, comparing different disciplines (economy, law, other social sciences) in the attempt to define the firm?

Both in juridical and in economic literature, it is possible to find an original common interlacement of two different constitutive elements of the firm: activity and organization. The firm as an *activity* expresses in juridical terms the function of the entrepreneur's *judgment,* as Frank Knight argued, establishing a relationship between economic principles and intelligibility of the different forms of *business organization*: the entrepreneur is the subject that takes decisions in conditions of 'uncertainty' and in this activity we find the real function of the entrepreneur.[9] Even the oldest juridical doctrine linked the rising concept of firm to the activity of production, searching in the mediating function (labour related, or between the factors of production and consumption) the point of contact between exchange activity and production activity. If the firm is activity, it also includes organizing the production of material utility; it involves the systematic management of an *organized* and organizational activity. The idea of the firm as *organization* was already acknowledged by Alfred Marshall at the end of the nineteenth century.[10] Therefore, the firm will be conceived, also in juridical terms, as an economic organism gathering and systematically setting in function the essential factors, in order to obtain a product to be exchanged, to the risk of the entrepreneur, and commercial law 'will acquire this economic concept of firm'.[11] A great part of the economic thought on the firm in the second part of the twentieth century is focused on organization and on systemic relationships between organization and market (or competition). You may refer to the concept of 'structure' proposed by Chandler, which recalls the one of 'administrated association with economic aims'; as well as Coase's Institutionalist theory,

---

9. Frank H. Knight, *Risk, Uncertainty and Profit* (Harper & Row, New York 1965); Ludwig M. Lachmann, *Capital and Its Structure,* 16 (Kansas City 1956).
10. Alfred Marshall, *Principles of Economics* (London 1920).
11. These thoughts, which plastically express the debt of commercial law with regards to economic science related to the theory of the firm, also belong to an Italian Maestro, Cesare Vivante, *Trattato di diritto commerciale*, I, 100 (Milano 1922).

which reported the error of considering the firm '*without organization*' and the exchanges '*without markets*', going beyond the neo-classical theory, putting on the same level market and hierarchical organization.[12] While neo-classic and general equilibrium theories treat the firm as an individual agent, driven by a logic of profit maximization and inscribed into a 'function of production', starting from the 1970s, the firm starts being considered as a parallel way of coordination, separated from the market. Williamson's analysis of Coase allows shedding some light on the double economic function of the firm: as a modality of non-trade-related coordination *between* markets (products, labour, credit, capital). And at the same time, as an individual agent, thanks to the mediation of the juridical system, providing the legal status and organizing, with the instrument of the contract, the hierarchy within the company.[13] In this perspective, the organization will not be intended only as a notion abstractly opposed to the market, but as a founding principle of the market, since the latter is constituted by several organizations and arises from a '*behavioural relation*' between the participants.[14]

Both the firm and the market can be defined as an '*instituted order*', which cannot operate without certain normative and regulative processes.[15] Therefore, law, not only provides the form and the architecture of the firm, but it influences its structures and strategies (hence, its power), both providing solutions for different hypothesis of *market failures*, and positively contributing to its behavioural evolution in the field of wider *governance* processes and social responsibility. The promotion of the firm's allocative efficiency has been since long acknowledged as a justification of the regulative intervention in the field of transactions and market, achieving an aggregated increase in terms of social welfare.[16]

The relationship between the firm and the juridical dimension can be analysed also by using the 'strategy-structure' model, theorized by Chandler. On one hand, the strategy of the firm influences, or at most it determines, the juridical rules that govern the organization, as well as, more in general the orientation of the institutions that should regulate the behaviour of the economic actor. The strategic and structural evolution of firms is in fact a determining factor for the analysis of the normative processes in an era of economic

---

12. Cf. Ronald M. Coase, *The Firm, the Market and the Law*, 3 (Chicago and London 1988).
13. Cf. Baudoin Roger (ed.), *L'entreprise, formes de la propriété et responsabilités sociales* (Collège des Bernardins, Paris, editions Lethielleux 2012).
14. Cf. Paul Auerbach, *Competition. The Economics of Industrial Change*, 122 ff. (Oxford, 1988).
15. Cf. Karl Polanyi, *The Economy as Instituted Process*, in Karl Polany, Conrad Arensberg & Harry Pearson (eds), *Trade and Market in the Early Empires* (Chicago, 1957).
16. Cf. Anthony Ogus, *Regulation: Legal Form and Economic Theory*, 29 ff. (Oxford, Clarendon Press 1994); Michael Trebilcock, *The Limits of Freedom of Contract*, Cambridge, Mass. (Harvard Univ. Press. 1993); Paul Burrows, *Contract Discipline: In Search of Principles in the Control of Contracting Power*, European Journal of Law and Economics, 2, 128 ff. (1995).

globalization; its impact on juridical systems is nowadays considerable and appears as destined to increase. It is enough to think about to the role of the multinational corporation, or world-corporation,[17] able not only to choose the location of its productive activity in one or another normative environment, but also to considerably influence the legislation of the different juridical systems, put into competition in order to be economically attractive. In Europe, this perspective of regulatory competition is endorsed by the Court of Justice, which with its decisions has confirmed the principle of freedom of choice of the law to be applied to corporations. By virtue of this jurisprudence, the European Union (EU) Member States can limit the right of establishment only by reason of the necessity to protect specific public interests.[18] Again, think about, in social-organizational terms, to the answer that corporations provides in view of the global economic challenges (competitiveness of the markets, technological innovations, growing products diversification, etc.), tending to define their *strategies* in a trans-national sense (with effects of strategic centralization) and their *structures* in a reticular sense, oriented to the product (with consequent sectorialization and outsourcing by lines of product, from the level of the operational company to the single productive unit). Such model of behaviour, which may evolve into a race to the bottom, is interlocked with the competition of (national and supra-national) regulatory regimes and the co-existence of common standard rules and of differentiated juridical statutes by reason of the global productive diversification.[19]

On the other hand, yet in a weak way, the existing institutional obligations condition the structure and the strategy of the firm, imposing the respect of certain principles and values. Contrary to the *standard* economic theory, which places the firm within a conceptual scheme that is strictly lacking in values – a simple algorithm associating *input* and *output* – the firm does not act within a lawless space, and it is neither the result of a self-regulation of the market, nor of a reciprocal and spontaneous adaptation among the economic actors. The firm as well as the market is therefore an 'instituted order', which cannot operate without determined normative and regulative processes.[20] The juridical system, in its complex, not only provides juridical form to the firm and not only attributes specific capabilities (like in the case of corporations), but it conditions its structure and strategy, contributing to its behavioural evolution in the field of

---

17. Antoine Lyon-Caen and others, *Multinationals and the Constitutionalization of the World Power System*, supra n. 2.
18. CGE Daily Mail 27 September 1999; Centros 9 March 1999; Uberseering 5 November 2002; Inspire Art 30 September 2003; Sevic 13 December 2005; Cartesio December 2008. Cf. Maria B. Deli, Federico Pernazza, *Trasferimento della sede della società tra libertà di stabilimento e norme internazionali privatistiche*, in Le Società, 11, 1389 ff. (2009).
19. Cf. Anthony Ogus, *The Economic Approach: Competition Between Legal Systems*, in Esin Orucu & David Nelken (eds) *Comparative Law: A Handbook*, 155 ff. (Oxford & Portland, Oregon 2007); Andrea Zoppini (a cura di), *La concorrenza tra ordinamenti giuridici* (Bari, Laterza 2004).
20. Cf. Karl Polanyi, *The Economy as Instituted Process*, supra n. 15.

wider processes of *governance* and of social responsibility. An example is the provision introduced with the reform of the *company law* in the UK, whereby the section 156 (3) of the *Company Act 2006* establishes that in order to comply with their obligation to promote the success of the Company, the managers must take into account, among other matters, the interest of the company's employees and the impact of the company's operations on the community and the environments.[21] According to a neo-institutional vision of the firm as a social-juridical cell, which keeps on being taken into account also in *common law* systems, and despite the expansion of individualistic and utilitarian doctrines, the firm as an institution and historical subject cannot be conceived not being in relationship with its environment, with which it must interact.[22] This perspective poses the problem of the economy's social integration and of *Corporate Social Responsibility*;[23] further, it must also interact with the juridical sphere, which aims at the integration of the firm in the society, thanks to mechanisms of self-regulation and constitutionalization of economic power (*see* below).

The economic vision is narrower, also within the institutional perspective. The firm is basically conceived as an efficient answer to the problem posed by the costs of transaction, which find their basis on the impossibility to plan within a contract all the possible future 'states of the world', characterizing the human interaction.[24] They may refer both to the situations related to the sphere of control of the agent, and to the ones that are hard to control but predictable and finally to those which cannot be controlled nor predicted.[25] The theory of the transaction costs is based on the idea that the firm exists as it is able to provide an efficient answer to transaction costs, deriving from the use of the mechanism of prices to allocate the resources, which constitute an essential element of the total cost of production of a given commodity. The transaction costs originate in the negotiation and the definition of the terms of the transaction (*ex ante* costs) and also in the execution and/or the control of the losses related to a bad realization of the transaction (*ex post* costs).

Therefore, the basic idea is that the different structures of governance (organizational forms) justify themselves since they tend to save on the overall transaction costs. According to Coase's intuition, the firm is conceived as an

---

21. Cf. Diego Corapi, *The Contractual Dimension of Company Law in Europe*, Riv. Dir. Comm., 583 (2012).
22. Cf. John E. Parkinson, *Corporate Power and Responsibility: Issues in the Theory of Company Law* (Oxford 1993); William T. Allen, *Contracts and Communities in Corporation Law*, Washington and Lee Law Review, Vol. 50, 1395 (1993), which underlines how the theory of the firm as *nexus of contracts*, promoted by neo-classical economy, neglects an essential part of the empirical reality: the social interactions inside *corporations*.
23. Adalberto Perulli (ed.), *La responsabilità sociale dell'impresa: idee e prassi* (Bologna, Il Mulino 2013).
24. W. Bentley MacLeod, *Reputations, Relationships and the Enforcement of Incomplete Contracts*, Cesifo Working Paper No. 1730 (2006).
25. Cf. Melvin Eisenberg, *Probability and Chance in Contract Law*, UCLA Law Review, 45 (1998).

alternative institution in relation to the market, and the choice among different organizational forms is carried out on the basis of a fundamental criterion of efficiency: minimizing the transactions' costs (costs related to gathering information, price formation, negotiation and execution of contracts).

A firm will tend to expand as long as the organizational costs of an internal adding operation will not match the ones in the open market, that is to say the costs to set up another firm. The argument lying in the background of this approach is that resorting to the market entails an avoidable burden if we substitute the interactions among economic subjects tied by hierarchical relationships, with exchanges between offer and demand. 'Inside the firm' – Coase writes – 'the individual contracts among the various production factors are eliminated and each market transaction is constituted with an *"administrative decision"*, which may be interpreted as the directive-organizational power of the entrepreneur.' However, within the Coasian vision, the firm does not seem to be aimed to legitimate the power of the employer; in fact, its aim is to save on transaction costs. The firm, as an organization managed by the authority of the entrepreneur, exists to the extent of ensuring a saving in the costs linked to the external purchase of productive factors. As a consequence, the managerial hierarchy becomes the 'invisible hand' described by Chandler, able to replace the market exchanges and their relative costs.[26]

So, the theory of the transaction costs strictly interlocks with the theory of the contractual and exchange models. Starting from the assumption that being efficient means combining selectively governance structures and attributes of transactions,[27] this theory significantly innovates the traditional scheme of the *discrete transaction*. The starting point within the juridical-economical analysis is represented by the *'maladaptation'* in the intervals of execution of the contract, considered as a main source of inefficiency.[28] From a juridical point of view, what is put into discussion is, first of all, the centrality of the *spot* exchange contract as an isolated and 'discrete' operation instantaneously executed. However, on the other hand, the attitude of the contract to have an activity regulation function, most of all in the field of the relationships among companies, and in the variety of its states and in the multilaterality of the relationships, is being consolidated. In this perspective, the model of the 'incomplete' contract, allowing an efficient *ex post* negotiation, represents an answer to the problem of the mutation of the states in the world and their *governance*.[29]

---

26. Alfred D. Chandler, *The Visible Hand: The Managerial Revolution in American Business*, 1, 6 ff. (1977).
27. Cf. O. E. Williamson, *Le istituzioni economiche del capitalismo*, 155 (Franco Angeli, Milano 1987).
28. Cf. Oliver E. Williamson, *The New Institutional Economics: Taking Stock, Looking Ahead*, Journal of Economic Literature, 38, 595 ff. (2000).
29. Cf. Oliver Hart, John Moore, *On the Design of Hierarchies: Coordination versus Specialisation*, Journal of Political Economy, 113, 675 ff. (2005); Sanford Grossman, Oliver Hart, *The Costs and Benefits of Ownership: A Theory of Vertical and Lateral Ownership*, Journal of Political Economy, 94, 691 ff. (1986).

The organization of labour as well, representing an important aspect of the theory of the transaction costs, finds economic justification related to the same logic regulating the governance of the contractual trade relationships. The hierarchy of the firm, intended as 'command hierarchy', guarantees the incorporation of the labour relationship within a governance structure able to solve more efficiently the problems linked to uncertainty, protection of specific HR investments, control of performance, even to a larger extent than the contractual hierarchy allows.

The labour contract's structural *flexibility*, consisting in the creation of 'areas of acceptance', within which the orders shall be executed without resistance, especially guarantees the adaptability of the firm to the ever-changing market and technological conditions, in the same way the internal organization responds to those issues more efficiently than the inter-firm bargaining. The Law promotes the acquiescence to directives and disciplinary norms, but it does not encourage employees to lavish, to accept responsibilities or to take initiative.[30] However, an optimal task planning rarely entails the elimination of hierarchy and, 'both the logic of efficiency and the historical evidence show that non-hierarchical forms have short life'.[31]

18.3 TRANSACTION COSTS, RELATIONAL CONTRACTS, AND NEO-HIERARCHY

Despite the undeniable reshaping of the subordination in the field of the labour organization,[32] hierarchy has again found the interest of economists and of jurists, within the theory of the firm. In contrast to the contractual or *law and economics* visions, some authors argue that one of the most important aspects of *corporate law* is the creation of regulative mechanisms, the so-called *'mediating hierarchy'*, through which the control on important assets and the decisions related to *production teams* shifts from the *team* and is guaranteed by the internal hierarchy. Within an explicit neo-hobbesian vision, the team member workers decide to submit to the internal authority, not only to guarantee the interests of the hierarchy, but to ensure, through the mediation of itself, the investments in firm-specific resources, dedicated to the *team*.[33] Some authors that have dealt with the theory of the firm have focused on the role of hierarchy,

---

30. Peter M. Blau, Richard W. Scott, *Formal Organization*, San Francisco, 140 (1962).
31. O. E. Williamson, *The New Institutional Economics, supra* n. 28, at 413. By the way, within Williamson's perspective, not all the transactions related to labour are necessarily inscribed in a specialized and hierarchical governance structure: the discrete bargaining will be preferable by non-specific and itinerant manpower (*ibid.*, at 415).
32. Starting from Alchian e Demsetz's studies.
33. Cf. Margaret M. Blair, Lynn A. Stout, *A Team Production Theory of Corporate Law*, Virginia Law Review, Vol. 85, No. 2, 247 ff. (March 1999); Margaret M. Blair, Lynn A. Stout, *Specific Investment and Corporate Law*, UCLA School of Law, Law and Economics Research Paper Series, Working Paper Number 05-30 (2005).

developing a distinction between 'contractual' relationships and 'relational' relationships that involve a series of *'non-contractible rights'*, that have to be *'coordinated by relational managers'*.[34] The same authors, in the perspective of a *relational adaptation*, have reconsidered Simon's classic model, in which the two parties – *boss* and *employee* – attribute the *boss* the decisional power in function of the state changes in the World, in order to overcome the inefficiencies (and the costs) of the *ex post* decisions.[35] Once again, the problem of the optimal allocation of decisional and control power refers to the inadequacy of the *spot* contractual models – source of inefficiency in the intervals of contractual execution – underlining the importance of the *contracting for control* model, in which the parties use relational contracts in order to create endogenous *governance* structures, able to allocate in an efficient way the decisional power (*decision rights*).[36]

Other authors, complying with economic neo-institutional-oriented firm theories, have argued that the entrepreneurial organization not only exists to reduce the costs of transaction, but also as an instrument to exert the entrepreneurial power (*entrepreneurial judgment*). In this perspective, the mutations in the structure of the firm (and its boundaries) can be read as the result of a process of 'entrepreneurial experimentation', while on the internal side, the organization is interpreted as a model in which the entrepreneur delegates certain rights of decision to his employees, who exert them as derivative forms of directive power.[37] The firm differentiates from other governance structures for three characteristics, centred on the *nature of subordinate labour*: (i) the employee does not own the means of production; (ii) the employee is subject to *'low-powered'* schemes of subsidy (ex. fixed salary instead of hourly salary, or hourly salary instead of a salary related to the result); (iii) the employee is subject to the authority of the employer.[38] Oliver Hart himself, one of the founders of the theory of property rights,[39] has modified his original attention on *property rights* and on the relatives control mechanisms as an essence of the firm, building a model of comparison between *'employment'* versus *'contracting'*, based on the individuation of whom is to decide the method of production:

---

34. Cf. George Baker, Robert Gibbons e Kevin J. Murphy, *Relational Contracts and the Theory of the Firm*, The Quarterly Journal of Economics, Vol. 117, No. 1, 33 ff. (2002).
35. Herbert Simon, *A Formal Theory of the Employment Relationship*, in Econometrica, 19, 293 ff. (1951).
36. G. Baker, R. Gibbons e K. J. Murphy, *supra* n. 34.
37. Cf. Nicolai J. Foss, Peter G. Klain, *Organizational Governance*, in Rafael Wittek, Tom Snijders & Victor Nee (eds), *The Handbook of Rational Choice Social Research* (New York 2008).
38. Cf., also for other references to authors quoted in the text, Margaret M. Blair, Erin O'Hara & Gregg Kirchhefer, *Outsourcing, Modularity and the Theory of the Firm*, Vanderbilt University Law School Conference on Legal Issues in the Governance of Supply Chains, 30–31 October, (2008).
39. Oliver Hart, John Moore, *Property Rights and the Nature of the Firm*, Journal of Political Economy, 98, 1119 ff. (1990).

while in a trading contract, the seller establishes the means of production, in the labour contract it's the buyer (i.e., to say, the employer) that decides.[40]

Within the relational model, which qualifies not a contractual category, but a different approach to the theory of the contract, the discretion function is completely removed in favour of a sort of a micro-society with a vast apparatus of norms which goes beyond the ones centred on the exchange and on the immediate processes.[41] A system of long-lasting and complex relationships, inspired by collaboration, trust and regulated by social rules and common law, allows a flexible adaptation of the contractual relationship to any supervention. These contractual forms denote the different level of autonomy maintained by the parties, polarized between a maximum (discrete transactions), and a minimum (hybrid transactions). So, the relational contracts do not necessarily match to hierarchical relationships, even if within *long-term transactions* the tendency is to find almost-hierarchical mechanisms.

Commercial law, company law, and labour law offer paradigmatic examples of this approach. The contracts of *joint-venture, business group and trust*; the corporate matter, the franchising relationships, the long-term supply contracts, the relationships of funding; the contracts of employment and the network contracts constitute as many hypothesis of relational contracts, which are characterized by their incompleteness for different levels of strength on the market of contractors, and for economic dependency of a subject on another. The theory of relational contracts – and of firm itself as a sort of incomplete contract whose content is continuously adjusted in the course of time – is acknowledged also within *civil law*, though it has come to light within the *common law*, where the notion of contract is founded on the idea of bargain. However, in this field, the notion of contract as agreement *creating law among the parties* decreases the necessity to define the contract as an open structure, while the same organizational and governing rules derive from contractual relationships (*contrat de société, Gesellschaftsvertrag*, associative contract).

As we can infer by what we have analysed so far, it is no longer acceptable, in the sphere of scientific analysis, to recognize a neat contrast between market and hierarchy as instruments to regulate the interactions among economic subjects. The labour law regulation has since long been more or less consciously confronting with this acquisition of the theory of the firm, which undermined the dogmas of traditional labour law to their foundations: on one hand, we have the

---

40. Cf. Oliver Hart, John Moore, *Contracts as Reference Points*, Quarterly Journal of Economics (2008); O. Hart, *Reference Points and the Theory of the Firm*, NBER Working paper 13481, (October 2007).
41. Ian R. Macneil, *The Many Futures of Contracts*, Southern California Law Review, 691, 696 ff. (1973–74); Ian R. Macneil, *Relational Contract: What We Do and Do Not Know*, Wisconsin Law Review, 483 (1985). The traditional difference between juridical-labour doctrine and this construction arises from these characteristics. This construction seems to allude to denied conceptions of organic solidarity, as well as neglecting fundamental social rights.

employer coinciding with the chief of the vertically integrated fordist organization (founded on the firm/market binary vision), on the other hand, we have the respective belonging of subordinate labour to the dimension of hierarchy, and of autonomous labour to the one of the market. The law-economic studies from Williamson on,[42] have allowed to overcome these dichotomous visions that may refer to the distinction between market and hierarchy, considering how the contractual (and for this reason, market) logic is present also within the firm, while the relational cooperation among firms may lead to hierarchic mechanisms founded on forms of economic-juridical supremacy, through which the dominating firm attempts to extend to another external relation with another entrepreneur the same hierarchy that qualifies its internal relations of production with workers.

The transaction costs are not only related to the exchanges on the market, but also to the firm's internal relationships. The firm, which starts up as *anti-market* (since it entails lesser transaction costs) must deal with the *governance* costs of the network of contracts which structures the firm's internal hierarchy. The boundaries between market and organization tend to shift on the basis of the characteristics of the context of the transaction and according to the relative efficiency criteria. New hybrid forms are coming to light – almost-market and almost-hierarchy oriented – which offer to the firm a synthesis between the benefits (and the costs) of the *open market transactions* and the *internal ownership*.[43] The hierarchy's economic raison d'être keeps on being reconnected to transaction costs; but the relationship between employer and employee, for example, is no longer merely hierarchical, but it is structured on the basis of a continuous series of negotiations on the ways on how to conduct the activity and on everyone's contribution (goals, quality, performance, etc.). It results as an appropriate vision to the new labour law paradigm: it is no longer binding and more and more individualized. Intermediate or hybrid structures, like *offshore outsourcing, business alliances,* and *franchising agreements*, represent an efficient compromise in the wake of the *capital structure theory*, which suggests, on one hand to reduce the transaction costs by aggregating the intra-firm assets, on the other hand to limit the distortion deriving from the agency cost problem.[44]

---

42. Oliver E. Williamson, *Le istituzioni economiche del capitalismo*, supra n. 27; Walter Powel, *Neither Market Nor Hierarchy: Network Form of Organization*, in Larry L. Cummings & Barry M. Staw (eds), *Research in Organisational Behavior*, Jai Press, 295 ff. (Greenwich, 1990); Naomi R. Lamoreaux et al., *Beyond Markets and Hierarchies: Towards a New Synthesis of American Business History*, 108 American Historical Review, 404 ff. (2003).
43. Cf. George S. Geis, *The Space Between Markets and Hierarchies*, 95 Virginia Law Review (2009), where we can find a wide and useful discussion of contractual topics linked to outsourcing, and on the reasons that push firms to develop outsourcing agreements.
44. Cf. Edward M. Iacobucci, George G. Triantis, *Economic and Legal Boundaries of the Firm*, 93 Virginia Law Review, 515 ff. (2007), which underlines the role of intermediate structures a san efficient compromise in the wake of the *structure theory of the firm*. The property rights theory stresses some limits of the approach of the transaction costs,

18.4 CONTRACTUAL THEORY OF THE FIRM

Also the internal organization of the firm presents some limits that highlight its costs within the governance of transactions, to the point that one may consider the hypothesis of *hierarchy failure* and the return to the market (i.e., familiar with *market failures*, too) as the most economic form of transaction governance.

In reality, this return to the market assumes the form of acquisition and valorization of external human resources through processes of externalization, creation of cooperative and communicative linkages among subjects and autonomous firms. The transactional environment thus becomes the place where hybrid organizational formulas come to life, as well as forms of 'organized market', that are gaps between classical political economy pure market and other typical organizational forms, the hierarchic one and the 'clan'[45] one. To place one's trust to the intermediate forms of the market organized for the management of the labour factor can be a choice whose reasons not only lie in the mere reduction of costs, but in the will to safeguard or to increase professional talents and qualities otherwise difficultly manageable in the field of hierarchic relationships, such as the characteristics of autonomy, entrepreneurship and the innovative capability of subjects. In a growing number of cases, the entrepreneur satisfies his/her productive needs by utilizing forms of autonomous or outsourced labour. He/She needs less obedience (the one to be required in his/her role of creditor of the performance, authorized to exercise the directional power); his attention is focused on results. Great part of his typical activity – organization intended to achieve production – is directly concentrated in the use of the negotiating power (i.e., to say of the power exercised as a contractor). More in general, the para-subordination and the contracts of economically dependent autonomous labour, on which the Italian and European have been since long reflecting,[46] represent an elective ground to test possible connections between market and hierarchy, in the light of the theory of relational contracts and of the new fluctuating boundaries of the firm (*see below*).

The typical contractual coordination of the relational structure ensures, from the economic point of view, the qualitative homogeneity between the two models whereby the very image of the firm changes, becoming nexus of a multiplicity of negotiating obligations, not only being internal, but with all its

---

especially concerning the choice between *make* or *buy*. cf. Giuseppe Clerico, *Analisi economica del contratto*, 295 (Milano, 2008). The role of property rights and the definition of control and choice is essential with incomplete contracts, which tend to prefer extra-market solutions. Cf. Oliver Hart, John Moore, *Property Rights and the Nature of the Firms*, Journal of Political Economy, 98 (1990); Oliver Hart, *Firms, Contracts, and Financial Structure* (Oxford, Clarendon Press 1995).

45. Cf. Arnaldo Camuffo, Giovanni Costa, *Strategia d'impresa e gestione delle risorse umane*, (Cedam, Padova 1990).
46. Adalberto Perulli, *Study on Economically Dependent Work/Parasubordinate (quasi-Subordinate) Work*, (Brussels 2003).

external suppliers. The commercial contract constitutes the fundamental requisite in order to ensure the integration among economic subjects and therefore the coordination among productive factors, material goods and labour, which are necessary to the realization of the product to introduce in the market, guaranteeing the continuity of the relationships among firms, by means of agreements projected in the course of time. Basically, the idea of the de-hierarchized and de-materialized firm as a relational 'network of contracts' regains vigour. In this perspective, the firm is conceived as a counterparty-subject in each of the bilateral negotiating relations that are necessary to the realization of the productive activity.

The contractual theory is a more individualistic conception, which theorizes the firm not as a subject or entity, but as a mere aggregate of the various *inputs* interacting together, in order to produce commodities or services: the employees supply the labour, the creditors supply the *debt capital*, the shareholders supply the *equity capital*, etc. The firm is merely a *legal fiction* representing the combination of the contractual relationships among these various *inputs*.[47] The theory of the *nexus of contracts* introduces an innovative element, aimed to re-introduce a market-oriented vision inside the firm, denying the heuristic utility of the concept of authority, within the explanation of the relational phenomena inside the hierarchic structure. In the contractual viewpoint, in fact, these phenomena are not the result of an act of authority, but of a voluntary exchange among subjects searching for a satisfying arrangement of their own interests. In their famous 1972 research, Alchian and Demsetz wonder how the relationship between a shopkeeper and a customer differentiates from the relationship between the same shopkeeper and an employee: which is the content of the power to manage and assign to workers different tasks? The answer is that the diversity, which connotes the firm related to other mechanisms of market bargaining, is perceived only in the team utilization of *inputs* by the *production team*, and in the centralized position of a given party in the contractual structure of all *inputs*. Who characterizes the organization is the centralized contractual agent of a *team production* process, and not some higher authoritative directive, whereby the central agent 'is called firm-owner or employer'.[48] With the notion of *team production*, the final product of the working activity (*output*) is always superior to the sum of the separable outputs of each one of its members.[49] But we need a subject (the *residual claimant*) who monitors the activity of all the subjects involved in the *team productive process* and the marginal productivity of workers, exerting an organizational power

---

47. Cf. Frank Easterbrook, Daniel Fischel, *The Economic Structure of Corporate Law* (Harvard Univ. Press. 1991).
48. Armen A. Alchian, Harold Demsetz, *Production, Information Costs, and Economic Organisation*, American Economic Review, 777 ff. (1972), (Italian translation in Nacamulli, Rugiadini (eds), Organizzazione e mercato, 133 (Bologna, 1985).
49. A.A. Alchian, H. Demsetz, *supra* 49.

towards them (incentivized as employees not to exploit to a major extent their *marginal productivity*, hiding behind other *agents*). However, in this perspective, this power is not explained at all in terms of hierarchical authority, but as a prerogative which does not differ from the contractual choice power, exerted by the consumer when buying a certain product. Translated into labour law terms, the theory we are analysing states that the directional power of the employer differs in nothing from the power of any creditor with respects to his/her debtor; for this reason it is no longer possible to distinguish between the (market) contractual transactions and the orders of the authority that characterize the hierarchy (the firm): the owners of the factors of production that intend to make use of their human resources shall anyway dedicate themselves to an activity of bargaining, to be carried out in the market as traditionally intended or in the field of a firm.

The contractual revision of the theory of the firm will see its maximum expression with the application to companies of the *nexus of contracts* model, elaborated by Oliver Hart.[50] Further, with the overcoming of the notion of firm as a *real entity*, going beyond the identity of the participating subjects, in favour of a vision focused on the network of contractual relationships among human beings, which might be reproducible in all sectors of the company: from the relationships binding the company top managers to creditors, to the ones binding employees and managers. According to a famous definition: 'the private firm or firm is simply one form of legal fiction which serves as a nexus for contracting relationships and which is also characterized by divisible residual claims on the assets and cash flows of the organization which can generally be sold without permission of the other contracting individuals'.[51] The main consequence of this vision is the superficiality of the distinction, dating back to Coase, between models of allocation based on the authority and models of allocation based on prices. In this perspective, there is no difference between 'dismissing' your shopkeeper or your secretary; while what we define *open-ended employment contract* is actually a continuous process of implicit negotiation between employer and employee. The economists, in particular, together with the law-economic doctrine to them inspired, assume that the firm merely constitute a mechanism in order to facilitate the bargaining among the various parties involved in the productive process, hence there would not be any particular difference between the governance within the firm and the contractual governance among firms.[52] From a juridical point of view, the theory we are analysing considers as harmful each legislation which should intervene only in

---

50. Cf. Oliver Hart, *An Economist's Perspective on the Theory of the Firm*, Columbia Law Review, 89, 1757 ff. (1989).
51. Michael Jensen, William Meckling, *The Theory of the Firm: Managerial Behavior, Agency Costs and Ownership Structure*, Journal of Financial Economics, 3, 305 ff. (1976).
52. Cf. Frank Easterbrook, Daniel Fischel, *The Corporate Contract*, 89 Columbia Law Review, 1416 (1989).

cases of *market failure*, while the *company law* should be constituted only – or mainly – by the rules freely negotiated by the parties.[53]

The limits and even the errors of this theory are evident. Labour law proves, contrary to the above-mentioned assumptions, that the function of the contract essentially consists in avoiding the continuous re-negotiations of the terms of the contract in the course of time, thanks to the attribution to the contractor of a modifying power (*ius variandi*) able to adapt, within certain limits, the labour relationship to the future states of the world. It is not realistic to connect the complex of the obligations deriving from the labour contract, in terms of power and responsibility, to the market contractual relations: this explains neither the subordination of the worker, nor the complex of rights that derive from the subordination, and that are translated into as many as obligations of security on the part of the employer (e.g., the protection against physical, economic, and psychological risks deriving from the labour relationship).

More in general, it appears as false to pretend to exclude from the analytic scenario every normative weaving on the firm that may not be referred to the contracting relationships explainable with the theory of agency; this theory, as we will see in the next chapter, does not keep into account the function of the law at all (both in national, comparative, and international fields), and it has traced complex regulative systems that have co-evolved in parallel to the evolution of the firm and of the market within industrial and post-industrial societies.[54]

18.5 THE THEORY OF THE AGENCY

One of the main heuristic instruments, applied within the theory of *nexus of contracts* in the conception of the firm, as a pure contractual network, is based on the *agency theory*. This theory provides for an *agency relationship* in which the shareholders are the *principals* within the interest of whom the proxy is being executed, while the *managers* are the beneficiary *agents* of the mandate. These agents, benefiting the vertical distribution of the entrepreneur's power, take on themselves, as employers, the status of 'principals' related to subordinate workers, who become 'agents'. In this perspective, the labour contract, similarly to the obligation deriving from it, tends to lose power. The same is valid for the firm contract: the firm becomes a chain of *principal-agent* relationships, governed by the shareholder: the 'absolute principal'. He may legitimately require, as the owner, from the *managers* and all the other *agents* within the firm, the execution of activities apt to the maximization of the profit. According to this vision, the firm is a legal fiction, which acts as a point of reference for that

---

53. Cf. D. Corapi, *The Contractual Dimension of Company Law in Europe*, supra n. 21, at 580.
54. *See* S. Deakin, *supra* n. 5, at 345.

complicated process that leads back to equilibrium contrasting goals.[55] In addition to losing an individual identity, the organization can no longer be conceived as a mere profile of production plans and pertaining production costs, because the agency relationship generates three new typologies of costs. *Monitoring costs*, charged on the principal, for any unfair action by his agent; *bonding costs*, through which the agent offers guarantees and reassures the principal that he will not act unfairly; eventually, the *residual loss*, defined as a loss of value of the firm, charged on the principal, and deriving from the agent's mandate.

In this framework, the informative asymmetries, relative both to the actions and to the information owned by managers, determine the departure from competitive solutions of maximization of the value of the firm.

A typical *principal-agent* contract is the labour contract stipulated by the firm with its employees (however, possibly also with para-subordinate collaborators), through which the entrepreneur 'connects to him/herself' with a nexus of contracts the totality of the members of the team, justifying his/her own profit as being a remuneration of his/her activity of controller of the team itself. The existence of the firm bears some sense, then, to the extent that the entrepreneur's control service, in terms of profit, costs less than the service of control and measurement of the marginal *outputs* of each single member.

The moment when the entrepreneur can no longer manage the contractual relation, by perfectly and at-a-low-cost controlling the service due by the member of the team, there is the need to structure an adequate mechanism of subsidization intended to stimulate behaviours that may be coherent with the goals of the firm, avoiding those phenomena that in literature, borrowing from the theory of the insurances, have been called *moral hazard* and adverse selection:[56] while the latter derives from the non-observability of the information, of the certainties and of the values on which the decisions of the others before a contract is stipulated are based, the moral hazard has its origins in the difficulty to monitor the effective behaviour in the implementation of the contract.

The definition of the contract will thus be re-thought so that the agent carries out actions and transmits information useful to the employer, accepting a mechanism of control of his/her own actions. There is the need to apply to the relations with workers an incomplete contractual structure, open to revisions, extended in the long term in order to ensure the balance – recommended by the micro-economic theory – between remuneration and marginal productivity of labour, so that to obtain the maximization of the social production which is achieved, in the arena of the labour market, through the logic of 'implicit' contracts.

---

55. Michael Jensen, William Meckling, *Theory of the Firm: Managerial Behaviour, Agency Costs and Ownership Structure*, Journal of Financial Economics, col. 3, (1976).
56. Cf. Bengt Holmstrom, *Moral Hazard and Observability*, Bell Journal of Economics, 10, (1979).

The contract of subordinate labour represents, in this framework of ideas, a typical example of 'implicit' contract, counterpointed to 'explicit' contracts (e.g., the sales contract), since the parties agree on the exchange between a 'salary of employment' and a *range* of labour services submitted to the bond of authority and to *ius variandi*.[57] In particular, the contract of labour, within an environment characterized by informative asymmetry and uncertainty, is characterized by obligations of time (working hour) and of tasks for the agent (in order to avoid the moral hazard), low potential incentives for the agent (salary not co-related to the product), no rights of property on the *assets*.[58]

On the contrary, a contract of autonomous labour, or of external supply, is connoted by the property of the asset on the part of the agent, for the positive correlation of the compensation to the product (hence, the agent is pushed towards an optimal effort, if need be reducing the qualitative level of the commodity produced), and eventually, for the complete control of the agent on the process of production (as regards to the duration and execution of the work or service).[59]

These ideal-typical conditions of subordination and contractual autonomy, with the relative characteristics, matter-of-factly interlock, giving life to hybrid and blurred typologies. For example, in the para-subordinate, coordinated and continuing collaboration (which is a typical *performance* contract) the optimal result is obtained by specifying the goal and the quality of the performance, but not the necessary time in order to realize it, which should represent a discretional choice on the part of the agent (and, in civil terms, constitute an activity of pre-compliance). At the same time, the provider does not benefit from full autonomy in the executive process, being obligated by the coordination – also temporal – of the performance with the organization of the buyer.

Among the several criticisms that may involve the theory of the agency, there is its referability to the model of enterprise characterized by a neat separation between property and control, and not to the system of medium-small family enterprises that characterizes the productive fabric of a lot advanced economic systems. Consequently, this theory is not able to explain the mechanisms of corporate governance of non-Anglo-Saxon Countries, influenced by social-cultural factors that are not considered at all by the theory of the agency.[60] Further, from a strictly juridical point of view, it is not correct to affirm that shareholders are the principals and manager the agents, because company law considers managers as agents of the company in itself (as a juridical entity) and not of shareholders, since, however, one of the functions of the juridical

---

57. Cf. Herbert A. Simon, *A Formal Theory of the Employment Relationship*, Econometrica, 19 (1951).
58. Cf. G. Clerico, *supra* n. 45, at 296.
59. G. Clerico, *supra* n. 45, at 296.
60. Daniel I.Mc Carthy, Sheila M. Puffer, *Interpreting the Ethicality of Corporate Governance* (2008).

regulation is to protect the board of directors from the pressure of shareholders.[61] However, what is most interesting to observe is the methodological basic assumption modelled to a rigid individualism of the rational actor that excludes any social dimension, differently from other approaches focused on the protection of the interests of stakeholders,[62] as well as, as we have already mentioned above, the reduction of a relationship that is complex and rich in normative variations such as the one binding the worker to the firm, to a mere problem of moral hazard and of adverse selection.

18.6 THE THEORY OF THE FIRM BEYOND THE CONTRACT: RETICULAR AND SYSTEMIC THEORIES

The integration of the economic theory of the firm with the organizational theory does not totally overcome the contradictions pertaining to the *standard* vision deriving from the neo-classical doctrine. If the models deriving from economy, on one hand, better explain the evolutionary relationship among the market, the firm's boundaries and the internal organization, on the other hand they pay the limit of the environmental determinism in which the transactions and the employable organizational forms are realized. In this perspective, part of the contractual theory tends to abandon the contract-transaction in favour of the *treaty-negotiation*: the main constitutional elements of the model persist, and the organizational structure is still conceived through the analysis of the transaction costs. But the firm also opens up to *external contracts*, managing the complementary competences through the use of both social and economic inter-organizational incentives, based on trust, safeguarding of the relationship and on the use of 'supra-contractual' norms.[63]

The broadening to social and political sciences of this vision is integrated, within a *behavioural approach*, by matters of power, bureaucracy, coalition and study of political institutions. What transmits an additional evolution to the theory of the firm is, most of all, the representation of the firm as a 'coalitional entity', allowing to better understand the current paradigm, connoted by the confusion between the market and hierarchy principles and between contractual and social relationships.

An alternative path for the theory of the enterprise takes its form from the organizational studies, along parallel and even converging lines, with respects to the ones of the neo-classical theory and its contractual revisions. One of these paths leads to the systemic organizational theory: a starting point not only for the doctrinal developments in autopoietic-biological terms, but also for evolutionist

---

61. S. Deakin, *supra* n. 5.
62. Joan Fontrodona, Alejo Sison, *The Nature of the Firm, Agency Theory and Shareholder Theory: A Critic from Philosophical Anthropology*, Journal of Business Ethics, Vol. 66, 33 (2006).
63. T. Reve, *The Firm as Nexus of Internal and External Contracts*, in Masahiko Aoki, Bo Gustafsson & Oliver Williamson (eds), *The Firm as Nexus of Treaties* (Sage, London 1990).

theories, for which the firm represents a complex system in evolutionary symbiosis with the environment in which it is inserted, emphasizing as a relevant factor the ability to organize the strategic and operational interaction with the other organizations (suppliers, customers, subsidizers), with the final demand, as well as with the social and cultural environment, including the institutional and normative aspects linked to the public sphere. The greater attention to environment is linked not only to the need to control the external subjectivities the firm is depending on; it develops relationships of interaction with other firms that are characterized by the permeation of competitive and cooperative elements.

In this way, the *reticular* conception of the firm takes its form, which is founded on the coordination of its autonomous unities, in the wake of not only contractual-juridical relations, but also of an intense communicative interaction, able to allow the mutual definition of the respective goals, the possible complementarities and collaborations, and the possible common projects. We have thus seen the affirmation of the *network* principle, as an organizational form where to re-conduce the relations of cooperation (agreements, alliances...) that are being developed among the different economic subjectivities. If the answer of the theory of the transaction costs consists in broadening one's perspective to the intermediate organizational forms between market and hierarchy, or to involve market within the problem of the management of the *external contracts*, the evolutionary perspective gives life to a new organizational form precisely entitled to the network. Referring to the firm's behavioural studies, belonging to the behavioural sciences' research tradition concerning the treatment of information, and Arrow's research on the relation between science, information-communication and organization, the new reticular paradigm is characterized by the use of communication as an additional organizational principle, able to govern the complexity and to correct and integrate both the market and the hierarchy model.

The productive offshoring and the re-birth of the small-firm, and the more recent phenomena, which have led to the de-structuring and outsourcing of big firms, are unequivocally to be placed within these theoretical coordinates, polarized, on one hand, in a process of aggregation and formalization of the relations typical of the medium-small district firms (*network of firms* phenomenon), and on the other hand, in the progressive displacement, typical of big firms, from the hierarchy principle to the one of the cooperation, both in internal and in external relations (*network-firm* phenomenon).[64]

The polymorphism of the network has imposed differentiated social-economic and juridical conceptualizations. For example, we need to discern between asymmetric and bureaucratic networks, coordinated through a contract, and symmetric or equal social networks: the first are characterized by the presence of a 'central' firm, whose coordination with the firms of the network is

---

64. On the network firm in the labour law perspective, cf. the important thesis of Elsa Peskine, *Réseau d'entreprises et droit du travail*, L.G.D.J., (2008), as well as in this volume, s. II.

formalized in exchange contracts, by virtue of which, it exercises an activity of supervision ascribable to the one of the integrates network firm (typical example the sub-supply or subcontract network); the second qualifies the systems of cooperation among small dimension firms based on non-codified exchange relationships that are not necessarily referable to some form of explicit contract, according to the model of the industrial district, characterized by small firms that co-work in a local field that is defined by strong relations of collaboration and exchange. While the first dimension of the network is close to the group logic, of whose constitution it may represent an intermediate passage, the equal network expresses a logic opposed to the group one, with collective leadership and constitution of a collective network brand.[65] However, other typologies are to be included in the by now vast social-economic and juridical literature, that discerns from radial and chain networks,[66] hierarchical or equal networks, contractual or company networks (in their turn discernible according to the use of linked or multilateral contracts) or mixed networks, exclusively firms networks or networks with different subjects (administrations, foundation, professionals, etc.).[67]

The emersion of firm network integration forms, linked to innovative processes requiring co-decisions and iteration, lead the juridical-economic doctrine to formulate new theoretical and explicative hypothesis of the collaboration models, that are complementary to the ones of vertically integrated firms. This perspective, as an alternative to the conventional contractual theory, sees one of the most recent transpositions on the juridical plan of the *networking approach*, resulting in the *contracting for innovation* model.[68]

In this theory, the vertical disintegration along the *supply chain* is not implemented by stipulating 'explicit contracts', organizing the modular productive structure; nor by 'implicit' relational contracts.[69] The changes of the firm's boundaries are achieved through a new contractual form, called *contracting for innovation*, which aims to a technical and iterative collaboration among firms, as an answer to the uncertainty of the processes of innovation. The inability of the parties to *ex ante* specify the nature of the commodities to be produced, or its distinctive *performance*, imposes the research of a real governance of the whole productive process, to be created through contracts. Therefore, the overcoming of the contractual theories, which from Coase on has counterposed the transactions between the parties on the market to the internal hierarchy, is to be

---

65. Fabrizio Cafaggi, *Il contratto di rete nella prassi. Prime riflessioni*, in Contratti, 5, 504 ff. (2011).
66. Maria R. Maugeri, *Reti di impresa e contratto di rete*, in Contratti, 942 (2009).
67. Aurelio Gentili, *Una prospettiva analitica su reti di imprese e contratti di rete*, in Obbligazioni e contratti, 88 (2010).
68. Ronald J. Gilson, Charles F. Sabel & Robert E. Scott, *Contracting for Innovation: Vertical Disintegration and Interfirm Collaboration*, Columbia Law Review, 431 ff. (2009).
69. For this observation, cf. Charles F. Sabel, Jonathan Zeitlin, *Neither Modularity Nor Relational Contracting: Inter-Firm Collaboration in the New Economy*, Firm & Society, Vol. 5, 388 (2004).

implemented through the elaboration of a contractual model among firms. Further, it has to support the new transaction structure, as part of a *governance* no longer describable in the perspective of a bilateral 'One to One' relationship, but of a 'Many to Many' one. Contrary to what the theory of the transaction costs states, in this case the firm invests in the *co-design* of parts and components of the production, despite the risks that such investments entail, in particular the phenomena of *hold-up*.[70] So, *contracting for innovation* alludes to a new form of hybridization among contract, bilateral *governance* and hierarchical *management*, based on the will of collaboration among firms with common projects, not to be *ex ante* defined, but guaranteed by important investments in know-how. Such investments, increasing the costs for breaking the relationship (the so-called *switching costs*: costs that have to be incurred by one party to replace the other party of the contract[71]), unify the parties, reducing the risks of opportunistic behaviour. These costs, represented by specific investments in know-how and related to the respective *capacities*, decrease the level of opportunism and strengthen the reciprocity and other mechanisms of *self-enforcement* of the contract, in situations in which, given the high speed of adaptation, the use of standard *legal enforcement* results deeply ineffective. In juridical terms, the main consequence is a new inter-dependency characteristic linked to complementarity; it is actually different from both the one linked to the equivalence characterizing the contractual synallagma, and the economic dependency related to the contractual power and to the position on the contracting firm on the market.[72]

18.7 THE FIRM IN THE NON-STANDARD ECONOMY RESEARCHES

Some paths of economic research have yet contributed to highlight the importance of the institutions in the dynamic of the firm, overcoming those standard economic doctrines that persist in considering the institutions as useful structures only to overcome the failures of the market, and thus to be analysed only in terms of efficiency. The school of Regulation, for example, has carried out crucial researches in order to mark the return to a social-juridical vision in the explanation of economic phenomena, in particular concerning the functioning of the company and market organization, distinguishing itself for a double critique

---

70. The *hold-up* phenomena is determined when an firm which has incurred the cost of a specific investment, is subjected to the initiative of the counterpart, incentivized to downtrend the price of the supply, since the investment is no longer recoverable (*sunk cost*).
71. Cf. in general Joseph Farrell, Paul Klemperer, *Coordination and Lock-In: Competition with Switching Cost and Network Effects*, 3 Handbook of Industrial Organization, 1972 ff. (1967). (Mark Armstrong & Ronald H. Porter eds, 2007).
72. Cf. Fabrizio Cafaggi (ed.), *Il contratto di rete. Commentario*, 15 (Il Mulino, Bologna, 2009); id. *Il contratto di rete e il diritto dei contratti*, in I contratti, 917 (2009): 'In the network contracts, the parties do specific investments which discourage opportunism, on the contrary of what usually believed within the conventional approach of the industrial organization'.

to the neo-classical and Marxist economic theory. From this specificity, we have a series of interesting elements of the analysis of the institutions in terms of theory of regulation, that are developed around a basic model that includes the 'institutional forms' and the 'regimes of accumulation'. The theory of the Regulation claims that the essential matter is not the optimization of the institutions, but the practicability of an institutional architecture expressing the ways of regulations, insisting on the two basic dynamics that cause the institutions to evolve: one is represented by the impact of the institutional forms on the regime of accumulation and on the modalities of regulation, the other concerns the endogenous dynamics (structural and cyclical crisis) and the relative institutional compromises.

Also the new institutionalist economy that refers to Douglass North, has provided a decisive contribution in terms of explanation of the normative conditionings to the economic sphere. Starting from postulates of neo-institutionalism and of the theory of the costs of transaction (selection of the institutions according to their efficacy), the new institutionalist economy underlines the 'foundational' role of the institutions in economy, in the sense that they define the positions and the relations among the actors, with inciting, coercive, and uncertainty-reduction mechanisms. The institutions intervene on the constitutional foundations (in a juridical sense) of market economy, according to social and political compromises and arrangements, defining the place of the actors and their coordination process; therefore, they must (and can) not be selected according to a principle of mere economic efficiency. In this perspective, the firm is an entity to be analysed starting from the institutional context that influences in a determining way its foundation and its evolution, so as the rational and maximizing behaviour of the economic organizations influences the institutional change, using resources to change the obligations according to a tray and error logic, that is pertaining to the evolutionist thought.

In this continuous counterpoint between firms and institutions, we can therefore explain, at the same time, the institutional change and the evolution of the economic actors. According to a neo-institutionalist vision, which persists in being cultivated also in the systems of common law despite the expansion of individualistic and utilitarian doctrines, the firm as a historical subject and as institution cannot be thought but in relation to its environment, with which it interacts, posing the problem of social integration of economy and of Corporate Social Responsibility, and in its relationship with the juridical sphere, which aims to the integration of the firm in the society thanks to mechanisms of company self-normativity and of constitutionalization of the economic power, sometimes (however not always, nor necessarily) disciplined and institutionalized by the State or supra-national law (*see* below). The latter is not only conceived as a system of rules and procedures, but as a totality of substantial norms intended both to realize an equal distribution of the regulative power between the groups and the actors bearing the economic power, and to realize the coordination between the social process of confrontation and concentration, in the research of the achievement of a general interest defined step by step.

The Economy of the Conventions represents an additional path of research, very much promising for whoever wants to go beyond the dominating economic theory. The Conventionalists do not limit themselves to postulate the existence of institutions in a functionalist viewpoint, but they try to explain the ways individuals agree on the rules and how they implement them – in this sense the economy of the conventions is also a theory of action – avoiding the two traditional methods of explanation of social sciences, that is to say the methodological individualism and the methodological holism. The Conventionalists study how individuals, acting according to an 'interpretative' and not only 'calculating' rationality, modify and build what they call the 'common mechanisms of coordination': organization, market, institutions. Therefore, we need to institute a reciprocal linkage among these instruments, in the light of the idea of convention, which – in the wake of Keynes – represents the constitutional mechanism of an agreement of will and its result, equipped with mandatory normative force, which needs to be comprehended at the same time as the result of individual actions and as a framework imposed to the subjects. According to the Conventionalists, rules are more a resource than an imposition. It is not a contract, in the sense that it does not lie on an explicit commitment. A convention is definable rather as a 'system of reciprocal agreements' on the competences and behaviours conceived in order to act; often, it is an unspoken, unwritten, and non-prescriptive modality. In this perspective, rules are resources definable in terms of 'collective cognitive mechanisms' that represent the common knowledge of the members of the firm and they conjugate the research for efficiency with the research for justice, going back to the conduct of the agents and to their 'justification', that is a peculiar juridical-moral category elaborated by Boltanski and Thévenot, able to transmit the foundation of the rule in the various contexts (or 'quantities') where it finds its raison d'être (the 'grandeur' industrielle, marchande, domestique et civique). In this perspective, the firm ceases to be conceived merely under the profile of the efficiency of the coordination, as it occurs for the theory of the costs of transaction. On the contrary, it represents the place of intersection among multiple forms of coordination, where the public sphere (la grandeur civique), with its needs for collective and social solidarity, and the industrial sphere, where the common wellbeing is conceived starting from an efficient contribution of the functional labour (la grandeur industrielle), invite to interpretative and cognitive rapprochements among economy, law, and ethics.

18.8 GOING BACK TO LAW IN ORDER TO REFORM THE GOVERNANCE OF THE FIRM

The analysis we have so far carried out highlighted the limits of the economic and juridical theories of the firm that are nowadays dominating; they have colonized the theory of the firm in order to drive it towards the model of corporate governance centred on the shareholder value. However, the flaws of this colonization are evident, both in material and normative terms. The real processes of the economy themselves, characterized by a global crisis, show the fallacy of the dominating model, unable to mirror the reality of the firm as a social-economic actor and to juridify the different rationalities coexisting in it, pushing the doctrine towards new re-constructive hypothesis that are more suitable and coherent with the multiple functions that the firm carries out in the economic and social contemporary scenario. In order to deepen these aspects of the theory of the firm we shall leave the atemporal and deterministic dimension of the economic theory of the firm (transaction costs, agency costs, etc.), in order to getting closer to conceiving the firm as an historical subject: a mutation of perspective which arises from the consideration of the subjectivity of the modern firm as intrinsic to its role of fundamental institution in the contemporary world, as a social and political cell of the modern polyarchies.[73]

We do not need to re-propose the extension of the democratic processes and models of constitutional states to companies; or the mechanical re-proposition of contractualism among the active parties of the firm, nor old Community theories of the firm-institution. Rather, we may go back to the idea of *Unternehmensrecht*, in which the firm is, indeed, conceived as a coalition of different social groups, opening the way to an integrated vision, yet *functionally differentiated*, allowing obtaining the economy's social integration without losing the advantages of a high level of systemic differentiation. In this perspective, we should get back to reflect upon the integration between the economic organization in its autonomy and the constitutional systems within which the firm is 'embedded'. Here, for example, we have a connection with the sphere of social rights, particularly recalled within labour law. Labour law does not have a theory of the firm, but the widespread European constitutional model generally conceives the firm as an economic and social unity, as an intermediate social body in which the personality of workers develops.

There are at least four promising paths of research that must be cultivated and interlocked, experimenting virtuous contaminations between the theory of the firm and labour law, that are able to spread the best praxis of corporate governance and to induce legislative changes adequate to the necessity of a social governance of the firm.

The first of these paths leads us to a topic that is to some extent traditional in the research of social-natured institutional mechanisms able to condition the structure of the company governance: the participation of workers to the management of the firm. This perspective clashes with the vision centred on the shareholders' value, so as with the tendencies to the short term valorization of the firm, in the form of a liquid and financial capital. The most mature and complete models of participation, like the German one, have showed in these years of crisis an extraordinary vitality and adaptability to the changes of the firm and of the market, with a surprising ability to condition in a social

---

73. Giulio Sapelli, *Responsabilità d'impresa*, 51 (Guerini e Associati 1996).

perspective the governance of the firm even within the prevailing neo-liberalistic model that is driving the global market. You may refer, as an example, to the disarticulation of the borders of the firm and of the labour relations, which was better controlled thanks to mechanisms of conditioning deriving from the co-determination.

The German Works Constitution law could make a significant contribution in order to deal with such phenomena, as instrument to mediate the competitiveness needs of the companies with workers' rights protection. It is significant that even less advanced systems in matter of workers participation, like France, have in the latest years undertaken a path of valorization of the representation of workers in the boards of companies. If it is true that the current processes of internationalization of firms and of industrial relations create uncertainties on the dynamics of co-determination, within an evolutionary scenario where the process of progressive substitution of the steady labour relations with atypical relations is not necessarily to be effectively contrasted,[74] the frontier of participation persists in representing a fascinating perspective of change of the firm in a social sense, with the help of other vectors, pertaining the construction of the firm and to the values related to it, like collective bargaining. Two different, but historically relevant, ways of conditioning the firm from the point of view of workers; but also within a function of social re-validation of the firm as a social and not-only-economic institution.

The second path of research regards the development of new normative techniques of responsibilization of the firm in a social sense, in the perspective of a new 'corporate accountability', that is declinable in strategic terms (in the sense that the firm is strategically accountable when it intends in such a way to better pursue its own interests), in equitable terms (when the firm deliberately follows aims of social justice), and in ultimative terms (when the firm is facing dominant fundamental rights or prevailing public interests).[75] One of these techniques leads to re-launch of the role of the law as an instrument of hard regulation of the firm's responsibility, in view of a widespread – however often ineffective – calls for soft law mechanisms. A recent example of this possible path is offered by the French system: in the wake of the disdain following the disaster of Rana Plaza, the parliament has adopted a law that introduces an important principle of 'national diligence', that is applicable to multinational enterprises in relation to the linked companies that are collocated under their sphere of influence,[76] imposing the adoption of a vigilance plan and providing for sanctions to the non-complying firms.

---

74. *See* Effrosyni Bakirtzi, *The Role of the German Codetermination (Mitbestimmung) in Balancing Intererst at the Workplace*, in Adalberto Perulli (ed.), *L'idea di diritto del lavoro, oggi*, 537 (Wolters Kluwer-Cedam 2016).
75. For this approach, *see* Sheldon Leader, *Human Rights and the Consitutionalized Corporation, supra* n. 2, at 193 ff.
76. Antoine Lyon-Caen, Tatiana Sachs, *The Responsibility of Multinational Enterprises. A Constitutionalization Process in Action, supra* n. 2, at 204 ff.

Chapter 18: The Theories of the Firm between Economy and Law

The third perspective, strictly linked, leads us to ponder on the constitutionalization of the firm. Is this typically *constitutional* vision of the firm still relevant? In order to analyse this challenging perspective, law should free itself by its subordination to the 'economic method'. There are at least two theoretical perspectives to analyse, related to this topic. The first, Teubner-inspired, valorizes constitutionalization for private regimes. The prerequisite of this vision is that the constitution is not only what characterizes the normative structure of a national-state, but it is a phenomenon that involves both private entities and international law: an epistemological tool that can be applied to the firm. One of the main medium of this constitutionalization of the firm is the contract.

It is a curious use of the contract in a very different perspective from the use the economic analysis does, as we have seen before. The idea of civil constitution refuses the purely economic logic of the contract, to get it to carry out public functions, which once was the prerogative of a state. Therefore, civil constitutions carry out a social and protective function, providing responsibility for the social sub-systems in the field of the production of negative externalities. But, can the contract do all this? Even following this thesis, according to which it should assume all the autonomous declinations of the society and connect the different participants to the processes of *governance*, wouldn't we have the problem of the conflict of rationality and logic related to the contract? Won't the demand for self-regulation of all the parties accentuate the anarchic characteristics of a society, which will, yes, stipulate contracts, but on the other hand will impose to any institution menacing a regulative invasion, their non-intervention?

The second perspective, promoted by a group of French scholars, is strongly connected to the public idea of constitution. In this perspective the firm-economic party connects to the positive juridical system through the national constitutional norms, and in international terms, through a global constitutional mechanism, constituted by the network of National constitutions and international treaties.[77] The problem of the constitutionalization of the firm means to reconsider the value, not only private, and the goals expressed by the economic organization. Without imposing any 'functionalization' of the firm (typical, for example, of the corporatism ideology), the thesis of the constitutionalization faces the issue of the entrepreneurial power, by refusing the reductionistic vision of the economic theories, agency theory in particular (that, on the contrary, underlines only the function of the firm as a maximization of the profit of shareholders) in favour of a pluralistic vision of the common interest of its members, which might be respectful of fundamental rights of non-members, interested in its correct functioning. Also this vision, anyway, bears some risks and vulnerabilities: it is quite critical to invoke the constitutionalization of the private juridical systems as the firm, in a moment of great crisis of constitutionalism, on national and above all on supra-national or even global level. A crisis

---

77. J.-P. Robé, Antoine Lyon-Caen e S. Vernac, *L'entreprise et la constitutionnalisation du système-monde de pouvoir*, in L'entreprise, *supra* n. 2, at 304 ff.

that is well visible in the fragmentation of the constitutional systems and within the processes of sectorial 'self-constitutionalization' of single juridical systems. Partial international constitutions, limited to the respect of some human rights (again, a sort of bill of rights) might be individuated in a series of international obligations that several countries have adopted. However, even in these formations, the effectiveness, especially regarding the firm, is still at elementary level, and for this reason it would be premature to consider them even only as embryonic constitutions, even if limited to the cataloguing and to the protection of human rights.

The last path of research is the one opened by the theory of Commons applied to the firm.[78] We are dealing with one of the most difficult challenges for the theory of the firm, considering the scarce juridical literature dedicated to the topic and the almost utopian extent of a richer taxonomy than the one imposed by the public/private logic applied to the firm. However, the law itself states that private property can be decomposed in a formal property and a substantial property: who actually manages an asset may not be the same that has the formal title of owner, as it happens in the scission between property and control within corporations. Therefore, we may refer to not one exclusive property, but to several properties, with a plural model that well fits to the reconsideration of the model of firm exclusively governed by shareholders, in their exclusive interest as being entitled of property rights. On the other hand, the firm as a 'common asset' gives benefits to the different stakeholders and to the firm in its totality, as an object of property rights of which not only the investors of financial capital (in the form of stocks), but also different subjects (workers, suppliers, customers, etc.) are the owners, the latter expressing property rights and interests of different nature, whose participation as 'constituencies' to the common-corporation guarantees to the firm conditions of economic and social sustainability that may be equal to the global challenges of the present and the future.

---

78. Simon Deakin, *The Corporation as Commons: Rethinking Property Rights, Governance and Sustainability in the Business Enterprise*, supra n. 5.

Bibliography

Adner R., *Match Your Innovation Strategy to Your Innovation Ecosystem*, 84.4 Harvard Business Review, 98 (2006).

Agrawal A., Kapur D. & McHale J., *How Do Spatial and Social Proximity Influence Knowledge Flows? Evidence from Patent Data*, 64.2 Journal of Urban Economics, 258 (2008).

Ahlberg K. & Bruun N., *Public Procurement and Labour Law – Friends or Foes?*, in Mia Rönnmar (ed.), *Labour Law, Fundamental Rights and Social Europe* 89, 91–92 (Hart, 2011).

Ahumada Ruiz M., Certiorari *y criterios de selección de casos*, in VV.AA., *La defensa de los derechos fundamentales: Tribunal Constitucional y Poder Judicial. Actas de las XV Jornadas de la Asociación de Letrados del Tribunal Constitucional*, 59–83 (Madrid, Tribunal Constitucional-Centro de Estudios Políticos y Constitucionales 2010).

Alcacer J. & Oxley J., *Learning by Supplying*, 35.2 Strategic Management Journal, 204 (2014).

Alchian A. A. & Demsetz H. (1972), *Production, Information Costs, and Economic Organization*, in Peter J. Buckley & Jonathan Michie (eds), *Firms, Organizations and Contracts* 75 (Oxford University Press 2001).

Alchian A. A. & Demsetz H., *Production, Information Costs, and Economic Organisation*, American Economic Review, 777 ff. (1972), (Italian translation in Nacamulli, Rugiadini (eds), Organizzazione e mercato, 133 (Bologna, 1985).

Ales E., Deinert O. & Kenner J. (eds), *Core and Contingent Work in the European Union* (Hart Publishing, 2017).

Ales E., Engblom S., Jaspers T., Laulom S., Sciarra S., Sobczak A. & Valdes Dal-Re F., *Transnational Collective Bargaining: Past, Present and Future: Final Report* (European Commission, Brussels 2006).

Aliprantis N., *L'entreprise en tant qu'ordre juridique*, in *Le droit collectif du travail. Etudes en hommage à H. Sinay Bâle*, Peter Lang 185 (1994).

Allen R. E. (ed.), *The Concise Oxford Dictionary of Current English*, 8th ed. (Clarendon Press, 1990).

Allen W. T., *Contracts and Communities in Corporate Law*, 50 Washington and Lee Law Review, 1395 ff. (1993).

Alvino I., *Il lavoro nelle reti di imprese. Profili giuridici* (Giuffré, Milano, 2014).

Amin A. & Wilkinson F., *Learning, Proximity and Industrial Performance: An Introduction*, 23.2 Cambridge Journal of Economics, 121(1999).
Anselin L., Varga A. & Acs Z., *Local Geographic Spillovers Between University Research and High Technology Innovations*, 42.3 Journal of Urban Economics, 422 (1997).
Antonmattei P. H. & Sciberras J.-C., *Le travailleur économiquement dépendant : quelle protection?* Report to the French Minister of Labour, Social Relations, Family, Solidarity and City, (2008).
Aragón Reyes M., *El incidente de nulidad de actuaciones como remedio previo al recurso de amparo. La función del Ministerio Fiscal*, Teoría y realidad constitucional, n. 28, 371–380 (2011).
Aragón Reyes M., *Problemas del recurso de amparo*, Anales de la Academia matritense del Notariado, Tomo XLII, 139–153 (2005).
Araki T., *Accommodating Terms and Conditions of Employment to Changing Circumstances: A Comparative Analysis of Quantitative and Qualitative Flexibility in the United States, Germany and Japan*, in C. Engels & M. Weiss (eds), *Labour Law and Industrial Relations at the Turn of the Century, Liber Amicorum in Honour of Prof. Dr. Roger Blanpain*, 509 (Kluwer Law International, 1998).
Araki T., *Equal Employment and Harmonization of Work and Family Life: Japan's Soft-Law Approach*, 21 Comparative Labor Law & Policy Journal, 451–466 (2000).
Araki T., *Koyo Sisutemu to Rodojoken Henko Hori (Employment Systems and Variation of Terms and Conditions of Employment)*, (Yuhikaku Publishing, 2001).
Araki T., *Labor and Employment Law in Japan* (Japan Institute of Labor, 2002).
Araki T., *Rōdō-hō*, (Labor Law) (2nd edn), (Yuhikaku, 2013).
Araki T., *The Impact of Fundamental Social Rights on Japanese Law*, in Bob Hepple (ed.), *Social and Labour Rights in a Global Context—International and Comparative Perspectives*, 215–237 (2002).
Arato J., *Corporation sas Lawmakers*, 56 Harvard International Law Journal, 229, 230 (2015).
Aristea Koukiadaki A., *The Far-Reaching Implications of the Laval Quartet: The Case of the UK Living Wage*, 43 International Law Journal, 91, 101 (2014).
Arrowsmith S., & Kunzlik P. (eds), *Social and Environmental Policies in EC Procurement Law* (Cambridge, 2009).
Arrowsmith J., & Marginson P., *The European Cross-Border Dimension to Collective Bargaining in Multinational Companies'*, 12.3 European Journal of Industrial Relations (2006).
Atiyah P. S., *Vicarious Liability in the Law of Torts* (Butterworths, 1967).
Audretsch D. B., Maryann P., & Feldman M. F., *R&D Spillovers and the Geography of Innovation and Production*, 86.3 The American Economic Review, 630 (1996).
Auerbach P., *Competition: The Economics of Industrial Change* (Oxford, 1988).
Auzero G., *Coemploi: en finir avec les approximations*, 1 Revue de droit du travail, 27–31(2016).
Bachmajer Winter L., *La reforma dela LOTC y la ampliación del incidente de nulidad de actuaciones*, Revista de Derecho Procesal, 45–67 (2007).

Bailey D., Bellandi M., Caloffi A. & De Propris L., *Place-Renewing Leadership: Trajectories of Change for Mature Manufacturing Regions in Europe*, 31.4 Policy Studies, 457 (2010).
Bainbridge S., *Abolishing veil piercing*, Oklahoma Law Review, 497 (1998).
Baird D. G., *In Coase's Footsteps*, 14 Chicago John M. Olin Law & Economics Working Paper No. 175 (2003).
Baker G., Gibbons R. & Murphy K. J., *Relational Contracts and the Theory of the Firm*, 117.1 The Quarterly Journal of Economics, 33 ff. (2002).
Bakirtzi E., *The Role of the German Co-determination (Mitbestimmung) in Balancing Interest at the Workplace*, in A. Perulli (ed.), L'idea del diritto del lavoro, oggi. In ricordo di Giorgio Ghezzi (Cedam, 2016).
Baldwin R. E., & Evenett S. J., *Value Creation and Trade in 21st Century Manufacturing*, 55.1 Journal of Regional Science, 31, 31 (2015).
Barbera M., *Trasformazioni della figura del datore di lavoro e flessibilizzazione delle regole del diritto*, in La figura del datore di lavoro. Articolazioni e trasformazioni. Atti del convegno nazionale A.i.d.la.s.s., Catania, 21–23 maggio 2009, 5 (Giuffrè, Milano, 2010).
Barbera M., *Trasformazioni della figura del datore di lavoro e flessibilizzazione delle regole del diritto*, GDLRI, 203 (2010).
Barnard C., *EU Employment Law and the European Social Model: The Past, the Present and the Future*, 67 Current Legal Problems 199, 204–205 (2014).
Barnard C., *The UK and Posted Workers: The Effect of 'Commission v Luxembourg' on the Territorial Application of British Labour Law*, 38 International Law Journal, 122 (2009).
Barnard C., *Using Procurement Law to Enforce Labour Standards*, in Guy Davidov & Brian Langille (eds), *The Idea of Labour Law* 256 (Oxford 2011).
Barreiro González G., *Notas sobre la descentralización productiva en la empresa y su escisión interna*, 94 Revista Española de Derecho del Trabajo, 168 (1999).
Basdevant-Gaudemet B. (coord.), *Contrat ou Institution: un enjeu de société* (LGDJ, Paris 2004).
Baz Rodriguez J., *Las relaciones laborales en la empresas de grupo* (editorial Comares, Granada 2002).
Bercusson B., *European Labour Law* (Butterworths, 1996).
Berger S., *Making in America. From Innovation to Market* (Cambridge, Massachusetts: The MIT Press, 2013).
Berle A., *The Theory of Enterprise Entity*, Columbia Law Review (1947), http://www.shiftproject.org/resources/publications/the-corporate-responsibility-to-respect-human-rights-an-interpretive-guide/.
Biagi M., & Tiraboschi M., *Forms of Employee Representational Participation*, in Roger Blanpain (ed.), Comparative Labor Law & Industrial Relations in Industrialized Market Economies, 585 et seq. (W. Kluwer, 2014).
Biasi M., *Dal divieto di interposizione alla codatorialità: le trasformazioni dell'impresa e le risposte dell'ordinamento*, in Gaetano Zilio Grandi & Marco Biasi (eds), *Contratto di rete e diritto del lavoro*, 117 (Wolters Kluwer, Cedam, Padova, 2014).

Blair M. M., O'Hara E. & Kirchhefer G., *Outsourcing, Modularity and the Theory of the Firm*, Vanderbilt University Law School Conference on Legal Issues in the Governance of Supply Chains, 30–31 October (2008).

Blair M. M. & Stout L. A., *A Team Production Theory of Corporate Law*, 85.2 Virginia Law Review, 247 ff. (March 1999).

Blair M. M. & Stout L. A., *Specific Investment and Corporate Law*, UCLA School of Law, Law and Economics Research Paper Series, Working Paper Number 05-30 (2005).

Blanpain R. (ed.), *Involvement of Employees in the European Works Councils, European Company Statute, Information and Consultation Rights*, 42 Bulletin of Comparative Labour Relations (2002).

Blanpain R. (ed.), *The Actors of Collective Bargaining: A World Report. XVII World Congress of Labour Law and Social Security, Montevideo, September 2003* (Kluwer Law International, The Hague, 2004).

Blanpain R. et al., *The Vredeling proposal* (Deventer, Kluwer, 1983).

Blanpain R., Araki T. & Ouchi S. (ed.), *Labour Law in Motion. Diversification of Labour Force and Terms and Conditions of Employment*, 53 Bulletin of Comparative Labour Relations (2005).

Blanpain R., *The OECD Guidelines for Multinational Enterprises and Labor Relations* (Deventer, Kluwer, 1983).

Blat Gimeno F., *El marco socioeconómico de la descentralización productiva*, in *Descentralización productiva y protección del trabajo en contratas. Estudios en recuerdo de Francisco Blat Gimeno* (Valencia Ed. Tirant lo Blanch, Valencia, 2000).

Blau P. M. & Scott R. W., *Formal Organization* (San Francisco, 1962).

Blinder A. S., Alan B. & Krueger A. B., *Alternative Measures of Offshorability: A Survey Approach*, Part 2, 31.2 Journal of Labor Economics, S97 (2013).

Bobbio N., *Organicismo e individualismo: un'antitesi*, in Petroni, Viale (a cura di), *Individuale e collettivo. Decisione e razionalità*, 179 et seq. (Cortina, 1997).

Bodie M., *Employees and the Boundaries of the Corporation*, in C. Hill & B. McDonnel (eds), *Research Handbook on the Economics of Corporate Law* (Edward Elgar 2012).

Bodie M., *Participating as a Theory of Employment*, 89 Notre Dame Law Review, 661 (2013).

Boersch-Supan A. & Jürges H., *The Survey of Health, Ageing and Retirement in Europe – Methodology*. Mannheim, Germany: Mannheim Research (2005).

Borrajo Iniesta L., *Mitos y realidades de la jurisdicción constitucional de amparo: hechos, Derecho, pronunciamientos, admisión, costes*, Teoría & Derecho, n. 3, 159–203 (2008).

Boschma R., *Proximity and Innovation: A Critical Assessment*, 39.1 Regional Studies, 61 (2005).

Braakmann N. & Brandl B., *The Efficiency of Hybrid Collective Bargaining Systems: An Analysis of the Impact of Collective Bargaining on Company Performance in Europe*, https://mpra.ub.uni-muenchen.de/70025/1/MPRA_paper_70025.pdf.

Brakman S., Marrewijk C. & Partridge M., *Local Consequences of Global Production Processes*, 55.1 Journal of Regional Science, 1, 2 (2015).

Breschi S. & Lissoni F., *Mobility of Skilled Workers and Co-invention Networks: An Anatomy of Localized Knowledge Flows*, lbp008 Journal of Economic Geography (2009).

Bronstein A., *Current Challenges of Labour Law* (Geneva, ILO/Palgrave, 2009).

Bronstein A., *La subcontratación laboral*, ponencia presentada en el Seminario Internacional sobre Derecho del Trabajo ante el nuevo Milenio, Rep. Dominicana, abril, 1999. On line version June 2007: www.oit.or.cr/oit/papers/subcontrat.pdf.

Brugiavini, A., Pasini G. & Trevisan E., *Maternity and Labour Market Outcome: Short and Long Term Effects*, in The Individual and the Welfare State, MEA, 151-159 (2011).

Bryson A.(ed.), *Advances in the Economic Analysis of Participatory and Labor-Managed Firms*, 267-309 (Bingley (UK), Emerald Group, 2012).

Buciuni G., Corò G. & Micelli S., *Rethinking the Role of Manufacturing in Global Value Chains: An International Comparative Study in the Furniture Industry*, 23.4 Industrial and Corporate Change, 967 (2014).

Burrows P., *Contract Discipline: In Search of Principles in the Control of Contracting Power*, European Journal of Law and Economics, 2, 128 ff. (1995).

Butera F., *Options for the future of Work*, in Federico Butera et al., (ed.), *Options for the Future*, (London, Coogan, 1987).

Cabañas García J. C., *El recurso de amparo que queremos (reflexiones a propósito de la Ley Orgánica 6/2007, de 24 de mayo, de reforma parcial de la Ley Orgánica del Tribunal Constitucional)*, Revista E1pmiola de Estudios Constitucionales, n. 88, 39-81 (2010).

Cafaggi F. (ed.), *Il contratto di rete. Commentario*, 15 (Il Mulino, Bologna, 2009); id. *Il contratto di rete e il diritto dei contratti*, in I contratti, 917 (2009).

Cafaggi F., *Il contratto di rete nella prassi. Prime riflessioni*, in Contratti, 5, 504 (2011).

Cagnin V., *Il distacco intra-gruppo alla luce delle novità sul contratto di rete* (2014) available at http://www.diprist.unimi.it/Reti_impresa/papers/21.pdf.

Calabrò E., *Lavoro, impresa di gruppo, effettività della tutela* (Milano, Giuffrè 1991).

Camagni R. P., *Regional Competitiveness: Towards a Concept of Territorial Capital*, in Roberto P. Camagni, Roberta Capello, Barbara Chizzolini & Ugo Fratesi (eds), *Modelling Regional Scenarios for the Enlarged Europe*, 33 (Springer Berlin Heidelberg, 2008).

Camps Ruiz L. M., *La contratación laboral temporal* (Valencia, Tirant lo Blanch, 1995).

Camuffo A. & Giovanni Costa G., *Strategia d'impresa e gestione delle risorse umane* (Cedam, Padova, 1990).

Capello R. & Lenzi C., *The Knowledge–Innovation Nexus. Its Spatially Differentiated Returns to Innovation*, 46.3 Growth and Change, 379 (2015).

Carabelli U., *Impresa di gruppo e diritto del lavoro*, in VV.AA., *Gruppi di imprese e nuove regole*, in Zanelli P. (ed.), 191 (Milano, Angeli, 1991).

Carinci M. T. (ed.), *Dall'impresa a rete alle reti d'impresa* (Giuffrè, 2015).

Carinci M.T., *Introduzione. Il concetto di datore di lavoro alla luce del sistema: la codatorialità e il rapporto con il divieto di interposizione*, in Ead. (ed.), *Dall'impresa a rete alle reti d'impresa. Scelte organizzative e diritto del lavoro*, 1, 39 (Giuffrè, Milano, 2015).

Carrillo M., *La objetivación del recurso de amparo: una necesidad ineludible*, Revista Vasca de Administración Pública, n. 81, 87–109 (2008).
Carrillo M. & Romboli R., *La reforma del recurso de amparo*, Fundación Coloquio Jurídico Europeo (Madrid, 2012).
Carter D. W., 'CJEU (finally) takes stance against social dumping', Leiden Law Blog, 19 February 2016: http://leidenlawblog.nl/articles/cjeu-finally-takes-stance-against-social-dumping.
Casale D., *Joint Responsibility of Enterprises for the Health and Safety of their Contractor's Workers: Recent Trends in Italian Law*, 36.1 Comparative Labor Law & Policy Journal, 131–148 (2014).
Casale G.(ed.), *The Employment Relationship: A Comparative Overview* (Geneva, ILO, 2011).
Casas M. E., *Incidente de nulidad de actuaciones y recurso de amparo constitucional*, in VV .AA., *Derecho vivo del Trabajo y Constitución. Estudios en Homenaje al Profesor Doctor Fernando Suárez González*, La Ley & MTAS, 449–490 (Madrid, 2003).
Cassese S., *Chi governa il mondo* (Il Mulino, 2013).
Cassese S., *I Tribunali di Babele* (Donzelli, 2009).
Castellani D. & Pieri F., *Investimenti Esteri e Produttività: Le Regioni Italiane nel Contesto Europeo* (eds), in Zazzaro A., *Reti di imprese e territorio* (Il Mulino, 2010).
Castellani D. & Pieri F., *Outward Investments and Productivity: Evidence from European Regions*, (ahead-of-print) Regional Studies, 1 (2015).
Castronovo C., La nuova responsabilità civile (Giuffrè, Milano, ed. 2006).
Catà Backer L., *Transnational Corporation's Outward Expression of Inward Self-Constitution: The Enforcement of Human Rights by Apple, Inc.*, 20 Indiana Journal of Global Legal Studies, 805, 809 (2013).
Cella G. P. & Treu T., *National Trade Union Movements*, in Roger Blanpain (ed.), Comparative Labor Law and Industrial Relations in Industrialized Market Economies (Kluwer Law International, 2010).
Cesaro J.-F. & Peskine E., *Le coemploi sur la sellette*, Rev. Dr. Tr. 661 (2014).
Chandler A. C., *The Visible Hand: The Managerial Revolution in American Business*, 1, 6 ff. (1977).
Chaudron T., *Les tiers employeurs ou comment conjuguer compétitivité et responsabilité dans la France du XXIème siècle*, Report to Mr. Brice Hortefeux, French Ministry of Labour, Social Relations, Family, Solidarity and City (2009).
Clerico G., *Analisi economica del contratto* (Milano, 2008).
Coase R. H., *The Nature of the Firm*, 4 Economica, 392 (1937).
Coase R. H., *The Nature of the Firm. Influence*, 4 Journal of Law, Economics and Organizations, 33 (1988).
Coase R. H., *The New Institutional Economics*, 88 American Economics Review, 72 et seq. (1998).
Coase R. M., *The Firm, the Market and the Law* (Chicago and London, 1988).
Cohen-Eliya M. & Porat I., *Proportionality and Constitutional Culture* (2013).

Coiquaud U., *Le droit du travail : générateur de pauvreté ? Le cas du Canada*, in Philippe Auvergnon (ed.), *Droit social et travailleurs pauvres*, 334–335 (Brussels, Bruylant, 2013).

Collins H., *A Review of the Concept of Employer by Dr. Jeremias Prassl*, available at https://www.law.ox.ac.uk/content/labour-law-0/blog/2015/11/review-concept-employer-dr-jeremias-prassl.

Collins H., *Ascription of Legal Responsibility to Groups in Complex Patterns of Economic Integration*, 53 Modern Law Review, 731 (1990).

Collins H., *Independent Contractors and the Challenge of Vertical Disintegration to Employment Protection Laws* 10/3 OJLS 353, 353 (1990).

Conte A. & Vivarelli M., *One or Many Knowledge Production Functions? Mapping Innovative Activity Using Microdata*, IZA Discussion Papers, 1878 (2005).

Cooke P., *Global Bioregions: Knowledge Domains, Capabilities and Innovation System Networks*, 13.4 Industry and Innovation, 437 (2006).

Cooke P., *Regionally Asymmetric Knowledge Capabilities and Open Innovation: Exploring 'Globalisation 2' – A New Model of Industry Organisation*, 34.8 Research Policy, 1128 (2005).

Cooney S., du Toit D., Fragale R., Tonnie R. & Sankaran K., *Building BRICS of Success?*, in Finkin M. W. & Mundlak G. (eds), *Comparative Labor Law*, 440 (Edward Elgar Publishing, 2015).

Corapi D., *The Contractual Dimension of Company Law in Europe*, Rivista del Diritto Commerciale, 583 (2012).

Corazza L., *'Contractual Integration' e rapporti di lavoro. Uno studio sulle tecniche di tutela del lavoratore* (Cedam, Padova, 2004).

Corazza L. & Razzolini O. (2014), *Who is the Employer?*, WP C.S.D.L.E. "Massimo D'Antona".INT, 11072014, in http://csdle.lex.unict.it/workingpapers.aspx, p. 1 et seq.

Corazza L. & Razzolini O., *Who is an Employer*, Comparative Labor Law (Matthew V. Finkin & Guy Mundlak, eds) Research Handbooks in Comparative Law, 132–152 (Edward Elgar Publishing, Cheltenham, IK, Northampton, Ma. USA, 2015).

Corazza L. & Razzolini O., *Who is an Employer*, in Matthew W. Finkin & Guy Mundlak (eds), *Comparative Labor Law*, 132 (Edward Elgar, 2015).

Corò G., Schenkel M. & Volpe M., *International Offshoring, Local Effects: An Inquiry on Italian Firms*, 2 Symphonya, 1 (2013).

Courault B. & Doeringer P. B., *From Hierarchical Districts to Collaborative Networks: The Transformation of the French Apparel Industry*, 6 Socio Economic Review, 261 et seq. (2008).

Crain M. & Inazu J., *Re-Assembling Labor*, 5 University of *Illinois* Law Review, 1791, 1846 (2015).

Cremers J., Stollt M. & Vitols S. (eds), *A Decade of Experience with the European Company* (ETUI, Brussels, 2013).

D'Antona M., *La subordinazione e oltre. Una teoria giuridica per il lavoro che cambia*, in *Lavoro subordinato e dintorni. Comparazione e prospettive*, (a cura di) Marcello Pedrazzoli, 43 (Ed. Il Mulino, 1989).

Da Costa I. & U. Rehfeldt, *Transnational Collective Bargaining at Company Level: Historical Developments*, in K. Papadakis (ed.) *Cross-Border Social Dialogue and Agreements: An Emerging Global Industrial Relations Framework?* (ILO, Geneva 2008).

Davidov G., *A Purposive Approach to Labour Law* (Oxford University Press, 2016).

Davidov G., Freedland M. & Kountouris N., *The Subjects of Labor law: 'Employees' and Other Workers*, in Matthew W. Finkin & Guy Mundlak (eds), Research Handbook on Labor Law, (Cheltenham, Edward Elgar, 2015); Bernd Waas, *The Legal Definition of the Employment Relationship*, 1.1 European Labour Law Journal, January 45-47 (2010).

Davidov G., *Indirect Employment: Should Lead Companies Be Liable?*, 37.1 Comparative Labor Law and Policy Journal, 5-36 (2015).

Davidov G., *The Goals of Regulating Work: Between Universalism and Selectivity*, Labour Law Research Network (2012).

Davies P. L., *Workers on the Board of European Company*, 32.2 Industrial Law Journal 87 (2003).

De Luca Tamajo R., *Gruppi di imprese e rapporto di lavoro: spunti preliminari*, DRI, n. 2, 67 (1991).

De Luca-Tamajo R. & Perulli A., *Productive Decentralisation and Labour Law (Individual and Collective Dimensions)*. World Congress of the ISLLSS, Paris, 5-8 September 2006, General Report.

De Propris L. & Olivier Crevosier O., *From Regional Anchors to Anchoring*, in Phil Cooke, Bjorn T. Asheim, Ron Boschma, Ron Martin, Dafna Schwartz & Franz Tödtling (eds), *Handbook of Regional Innovation and Growth* 167, 171 (Edward Elgar Publishing, 2011).

De Propris L., *Re-territorialising Production: Global Value Chain,* Paper presented at the Annual Meeting of the SASE Annual Conference, held in Philadelphia, PA, USA (2010).

De Simone G. (2015), *Confini dell'impresa, esercizio dei poteri, responsabilità, nei gruppi e nelle*.

De Simone G., *Gruppi di imprese*, in Marina Brollo (ed.), *Il mercato del lavoro. Trattato di diritto del lavoro diretto da Mattia Persiani e Franco Carinci*, vol. VI, 1509 (Cedam, Padova, 2012).

De Simone G., *I gruppi di imprese*, in Persiani M. & Carinci F. (directed by), *Trattato di diritto del lavoro*, VI, *Il mercato del lavoro*, 1509 (Padova, Cedam 2012).

De Simone G., *Titolarità dei rapporti di lavoro e regole di trasparenza. Interposizione, imprese di gruppo, lavoro interinale* (Milano, Franco Angeli 1995).

De Spiegelaere S. & Jagodzinsky R., *European Works Councils and SE Works Councils in 2015*, Facts and Figures (ETUI, 2015).

De Stefano V., *Introduction: Crowdsourcing, the Gig-Economy and the Law*, Comparative Labour Law and Policy Journal, 10,14 (May 2016).

Deakin S., *The Complexities of the Employing Enterprise*, in Davidov G. & Langille B. (eds), *Boundaries and Frontiers of Labour Law,* 275 (Oxford and Portland: Hart Publishing, 2006).

Deakin S., Gillian Morris G., *Labour Law*, (6th ed., 2012).

Deakin S., *Labour Law*, 4th edn (Hart Publishing, 2005).
Deakin S., *Legal Diversity and Regulatory Competition: Which Model for Europe?*, Centre for Business Research, University of Cambridge Working Paper No. 323, March 2006: https://core.ac.uk/download/pdf/7151307.pdf.
Deakin S., *The Changing Concept of the 'Employer' in Labour Law*, 30 International Law Journal, 72 (2001).
Deakin S., *The Corporation as Commons: Rethinking Property Rights Governance and Sustainability in the Business Enterprise*, 37.2 Queen's Law Jouranl, 367 et seq. (2012).
Deakin S. & Wilkinson F., *The Law of the Labour Market: Industrialisation, Employment and Legal Evolution* (Oxford, 2005).
Deli M. B. & Federico Pernazza F., *Trasferimento della sede della società tra libertà di stabilimento e norme internazionali privatistiche*, in Le Società, 11, 1389 ff. (2009).
Denozza F., *Il rapporto di lavoro subordinato nell'impresa neoliberale*, Riv. it. dir. lav. 41, I (2015).
Denozza F., *Law and Power in a World with No Transaction Costs: An Essay on the Legitimating Function of the Coasian Narrative*, http://ssrn.com/abstract=1361613 or http://dx.doi.org/10.2139/ssrn.1361613 (accessed 17 March 2009).
Despax M., *L'entreprise et le droit* (Paris LGDJ, 1957).
Dickson J. & Eleftheriadis P. (eds), *Philosophical Foundations of European Union Law*, 155 (Oxford University Press, 2012).
Dore R., *British Factory Japanese Factory – The Origins of National Diversity in Industrial Relations with a New Afterwords* (University of California Press, 1973).
Dore R., *Taking Japan seriously, a Confucian Perspective on Leading Economic Issues* (Stanford University Press, 1987).
Dorssement F., *'Article 27'*, in Steve Peers, Tamara Hervey, Jeff Kenner & Angela Ward (eds), *The EU Charter of Fundamental Rights: A Commentary*, 749 (Hart, 2014).
Dorssemont F., *The Adoption of the SE Directive: The EWC Directive Now Has 'Company'*, in Charlotte Villiers, *The Directive on Employee Involvement in the European Company: Its Role in European Corporate Governance and Industrial Relations*, in 2 IJCLLIR 209 et seq. (2006).
Drouin R.-C-, *Le développement du contentieux à l'encontre des entreprises transnationales : quel rôle pour le devoir de vigilance ?*, 3 Droit social 246–255 (2016).
Drouin R.-C., *Responsabiliser l'entreprise transnationale: portrait d'une normativité du travail en évolution*, in PierreVerge (ed.), *Droit international du travail. Perspectives canadiennes*, Cowansville, 306 (Ed. Yvon Blais, 2010).
Dukes R., *The Labour Constitution: The Enduring Idea of Labour Law* (Oxford, 2014).
Easterbrook F. & Fischel D., *The Corporate Contract*, 89 Columbia Law Review, 1416 (1989).
Easterbrook F. & Fischel D., *The Economic Structure of Corporate Law* (Harvard University Press, 1991).
Easterbrool F. H. & Fischel D. R., *L'Economia delle Società per azioni* (Giuffrè, Milano, 1996).

Eberlie R., *The New Health and Safety Legislation of the European Community*, International Law Jouranl, 81 ss. (1990)

Edelman P. H., *On Legal Interpretations of the Condorcet Jury Theorem*, 31 Jouranl Legal Studies 327, 328 (2002).

Eisenberg M. A., *The Conception That the Corporation Is a Nexus of Contracts, and the Dual Nature of the Firm*, 24 Iowa Jouranl Corporation Law, 819 (1999).

Eisenberg M., *Probability and Chance in Contract Law*, UCLA Law Review, 45 (1998).

Eisenhardt K. M. & Graebner M. E., *Theory Building from Cases: Opportunities and Challenges*, 50.1 Academy of Management Journal, 25 (2007).

Eisenhardt K. M., *Building Theories from Case Study Research*, 14.4. Academy of Management Review, 532 (1989).

Elia S., Mariotti I. & Piscitello L., *The Impact of Outward FDI on the Home Country's Labour Demand and Skill Composition*, 18.4 International Business Review, 357 (2009).

Ellison G., Glaeser E. L. & Kerr W.R., *What Causes Industry Agglomeration? Evidence from Coagglomeration Patterns*, 100.3 The American Economic Review, 1195 (2010).

Engels C. & Maes S., *La mise à disposition de travailleurs en Europe*, in Thomas Chaudron, *Les tiers employeurs ou comment conjuguer compétitivité et responsabilité dans la France du XXIème siècle*, Report to Mr. Brice Hortefeux, French Ministry of Labour, Social Relations, Family, Solidarity and City (2009).

Engels C. & Salas L., *Transnational Information and Consultation; the European Works Council Directive*, in Roger Blanpain (ed.), *Comparative Labour Law*, supra n. 1, at 563 et seq. (2007).

Espinosa Díaz A., *El recurso de amparo: problemas antes, y después, de la reforma*, InDret, n. 2, 1–21 (2010).

Esteve Segarra M. A., *Grupo de sociedades y contrato de trabajo* (editorial Tirant Lo Blanch, Valencia, 2002).

Etzkowitz H. & Leydesdorff L., *The Dynamics of Innovation: From National Systems and "Mode 2" to a Triple Helix of University–Industry–Government Relations*, 29.2 Research Policy, 109 (2000).

Eurofound, *New Forms of Employment* (Luxembourg, EU publications office, 2015).

Eurofound, *Private Employment Agencies*, Dublin, European Foundation for the Improvement of Living and Working Conditions, 23, 34 (2008).

Eurofound, *Work Organization and Innovation* (Dublin, 2012).

European Commission, *Adapting and Promoting the Social Dialogue at Community Level*, COM (1998) 322 final, 20 May 1998 (Brussels, 1998).

European Commission, *Buying Social: A Guide to Taking Account of Social Considerations in Public Procurement*, Staff Working Paper (SEC)2010 1258 final, 7.

European Commission, *Communication from the Commission to the European Parliament, the Council, the European Economic and Social Committee and the Committee of the Regions* (2012).

European Commission, *Communication of the Commission of Concerning the Development of the Social Dialogue at Community Level*, COM (96) 448 final, 18 September 1996 (Brussels, 1996).

European Commission, *Europe 2020: A Strategy for Smart, Sustainable and Inclusive Growth* (2010).
European Commission, *European Commission Competitiveness Report 2013: No Growth and Jobs Without Industry*, MEMO/13/815 25/09/2013, http://europa.eu/rapid/press-release_MEMO-13-815_en.htm (accessed 10 September 2013).
European Commission, Explanatory Memorandum, 1972, reproduced in *Bulletin No. 4* (1973) 206 (Institute of Labour Relations, University of Leuven, 1973).
European Commission, *Industrial Relations in Europe 2008* (2008).
European Commission, *Industrial Relations in Europe 2010* (2011).
European Commission, *Industrial Relations in Europe 2014* (2015).
European Commission, *Partnership for Change in an Enlarged Europe – Enhancing the Contribution of European Social Dialogue*, COM(2004) 557 final, 12 August 2004 (Brussels, 2004).
European Commission, *The Development of Transnational Agreements* (2006).
European Commission, *The European Social Dialogue, a Force for Innovation and Change – Proposal for a Council Decision establishing a Tripartite Social Summit for Growth and Employment*, COM (2002) 341 final, 26 June 2002 (Brussels, 2002).
European Industrial Relations Observatory on-line, *Temporary Agency Work and Collective Bargaining in the EU*, http://www.eurofound.europa.eu/eiro/studies/tn0807019s, (28 May 2009).
European Labour Law Network, *New Forms of Employment and EU Law*, 7th Annual Legal Seminar, The Hague, 27–28 November 2014.
Eurostat, Industrial production (volume) index overview, European Commission (2016), http://ec.europa.eu/eurostat/statistics-explained/index.php/Industrial_production_(volume)_index_overview (accessed 7 September 2016).
Eurostat, *Manufacturing statistics – NACE Rev. 2 – Data extracted in November 2015*, http://ec.europa.eu/eurostat/statistics-explained/index.php/Manufacturing_statistics_-_NACE_Rev._2 (Last modified on 24 February 2016).
Everatt D., Tsai T. & Cheng B.-S., *The Acer Group's China Manufacturing Decision*, Version A. Ivey Case Series #9A99M009, Richard Ivey School of Business, (University of Western Ontario, 1999).
Eymard-Duvernay F., *Economie politique de l'entreprise*, Collection Repères (La Découverte, 2004).
Fabre A., *La responsabilité délictuelle pour faute au secours des salariés victimes d'une société tierce*, Revue de droit du travail 672 (2014).
Fadeuilhe P. & Joubert F., *Quelle utilité des groupements d'employeurs?*, Revue de Droit du Travail, 84–90 (février, 2015).
Fanelli G., *Introduzione alla teoria giuridica dell'impresa*, 75,116 (Giuffrè, Milano, 1950); Paolo Grossi, *Scienza giuridica italiana. Un profilo storico 1860-1950*, 306 et seq. (Giuffrè, Milano, 2000).
Farrell J. & Klemperer P., *Coordination and Lock-In: Competition with Switching Cost and Network Effects*, 3 Handbook of Industrial Organization, 1972 ff. (1967). (Mark Armstrong & Ronald H. Porter eds, 2007).
Favereau O., *Entreprise: la grande déformation*, Parole et silence, 11 (Paris, 2014).

Favereau O., *Quelle gouvernance pour l'entreprise post-crise*, Entreprise et histoire, n°57, 239 (2007).

Feldman M. & Lowe N., *Consensus from Controversy: Cambridge's Biosafety Ordinance and the Anchoring of the Biotech Industry*, 16.3 European Planning Studies, 395 (2008).

Feldman M., *The Locational Dynamics of the US Biotech Industry: Knowledge Externalities and the Anchor Hypothesis*, 10 Industry and Innovation, 3 (2003).

Ferrarese M. R., *Diritto sconfinato. Inventiva giuridica e spazi nel mondo globale*, 22 and 54 (Laterza, 2006).

Ferrarese M. R., *Prima lezione di diritto globale* (Laterza, 2012).

Ferro Luzzi P. & Piergaetano Marchetti P., *Riflessioni sul gruppo creditizio*, Giur. comm., I, 419 ff. (1994).

Fontrodona J. & Sison A., *The Nature of the Firm, Agency Theory and Shareholder Theory: A Critic from Philosophical Anthropology*, 66 Journal of Business Ethics, 33 (2006).

Foss N. J. & Klain P. G., *Organizational Governance*, in Rafael Wittek, Tom Snijders & Victor Nee (eds), *The Handbook of Rational Choice Social Research* (New York, 2008).

Foss N., *Strategy, Economic Organization, and The knowledge Economy* (Oxford University Press, 2006).

Freedland M., *The Personal Employment Contract* (Oxford, OUP, 2003).

Freeman C., *Technology Policy and Economic Performance: Lessons from Japan* (London: Frances Printer Publishers, 1987).

Fudge J., *The Legal Boundaries of the Employer, Precarious Workers and Labour Protection*, in Guy Davidov & Brian Langille (eds), *Boundaries and Frontiers of Labour Law*, International Institute for Labour Studies (Oxford and Portland, Oregon, 2006).

Fulton L., *Health and Safety Representation in Europe*, Labour Research Department and ETUI (online publication prepared for worker-participation.eu) (2013).

Galgano F., *Le società. Trattato diretto da F. Galgano. I gruppi di società* (Utet, Torino, 2001).

Gallie D., (ed.), *Employment Regimes and the quality of Work* (Oxford, Oxford University Press, 2007).

Gallin, D., *International Framework Agreements: A Reassessment*, in K. Papadakis (ed.) *Cross-Border Social Dialogue and Agreements: An Emerging Global Industrial Relations Framework?* (ILO, Geneva, 2008).

García Quiñones J. C., *El impacto laboral de los grupos de empresa: una asignatura pendiente en el Derecho del Trabajo español*, vol. 4 (1) Revista Internacional y Comparada de relaciones laborales y derecho del empleo, (January-March 2016).

Garcia Roca J., *La cifra del amparo constitucional y su reforma*, in Pérez Tremps (Coord.), *La reforma del recurso de amparo*, Ed. Tirant lo Blanch, 273-295 (Valencia, 2003).

Gaudu F., *Entre concentration économique et externalisation: les nouvelles frontières de l'entreprise*, Droit Social, 474 (2001).

Geis G. S., *The Space Between Markets and Hierarchies*, 95 Virginia Law Review (2009).

Gentili A., *Una prospettiva analitica su reti di imprese e contratti di rete*, in Obbligazioni e contratti, 88 (2010).

Gereffi G., Humphrey J., Kaplinsky R. & Sturgeon T., *Introduction: Globalisation, Value Chains and Development*, IDS Bulletin, 32.1 DOI: 10.1111/j.1759-5436.2001.mp32003001.x (2001).

Gereffi G., *International Trade and Industrial Upgrading in the Apparel Commodity Chain*, 48.1 Journal of International Economics, 37 (1999).

Gereffi G. & Lee J., *Economic and Social Upgrading in Global Value Chains and Industrial Clusters: Why Governance Matters*, 133.1 Journal of Business Ethics, 25 (2016).

Gereffi G. & Sturgeon T., *Globalization, Employment, and Economic Development: A Briefing Paper*, Sloan Workshop Series in Industry Studies, Rockport, Massachusetts, 1, 2 (2004).

Giblin M., *Managing the Global–Local Dimensions of Clusters and the Role of 'Lead' Organizations: The Contrasting Cases of the Software and Medical Technology Clusters in the West of Ireland*, 19.1 European Planning Studies, 23 (2011).

Gil y Gil J. L., *La negociación colectiva en los grupos de empresas:marco jurídico*, Working paper, (Bordeaux, April 2009).

Gilly J.-P. & Torre A., *Dynamiques de Proximité* (Paris: L'Harmattan, 2000).

Gilotta S., *Interesse di gruppo e nuove regole sulle operazioni con parti correlate: una convivenza difficile*, Giur. comm., 254 (2012).

Gilson R. J., Sabel C. F. & Scott R. E., *Contracting for Innovation: Vertical Disintegration and Interfirm Collaboration*, Columbia Law Review, 431 ff. (2009).

Gimeno Sendra V., *El recurso español constitucional de amparo*, in VV.AA., *La ciencia del Derecho Procesal Constitucional. Estudios en homenaje a Héctor Fix-Zamudio en sus cincuenta años como investigador del derecho*, Tomo VII, Procesos constitucionales de la libertad, Marcial Pons, México, 277–315 (2008).

Giubboni S., *Social Rights and Market Freedom in the European Constitution: A Labour Law Perspective* (Cambridge, 2006).

Glassner, V., *Transnational Collective Bargaining Coordination at the European Sector Level: The Outlines and Limits of a 'European' System*, 1.2 International Journal of Labour Research (2009).

Glynn T., *Taking the Employer Out of Employment Law? Accountability for Wage and Hour Violations in an Age of Enterprise Disaggregation*, 15 Employee Rights and Employment Policy Journal, 201 (2011).

Goldin A., *La libertad sindical y las iniciativas voluntarias; el caso de Jerzees de Honduras* in the article *El Derecho a la Negociación Colectiva*, Liber Amicoru Profesor Antonio Ojeda Avilés (Juan Gorelli Hernández, Coordinador) Colección Monografías de Temas Laborales, Consejo Andaluz de Relaciones Laborales, 191 (Junta de Andalucía, 2014).

Goldin A., *Normas laborales y mercados de trabajo argentino: seguridad y flexibilidad*, CEPAL, División de Desarrollo Económico Santiago de Chile, 32 (December 2008).

Goldin A., Seminar on Freedom of Enterprise and Labour Relations (*Seminario sobre Libertad de empresa y Relaciones Laborales*), La Toja-Santiago de Compostela

April 12–16, 1993 on the issue *Las empresas de trabajo temporal en la Argentina*, 1031 (published in DT LIII B).

Gómez Montoro A.J., *El interés legítimo para recurrir en amparo. La experiencia del Tribunal Constitucional español*, Cuestiones constitucionales, n. 9, 159–185 (2003).

Gordon M. E. & Lowell Turner L. (eds), *Transnational Cooperation among Labor Unions* (ILR Press, Ithaca, NY, 2000).

Greco M. G., *La ricerca del datore di lavoro nell'impresa di gruppo: la codatorialità al vaglio della giurisprudenza*, RGL, I, 117 (2013).

Grossman S. & Hart O., *The Costs and Benefits of Ownership: A Theory of Vertical and Lateral Ownership*, Journal of Political Econom, 94, 691 ff. (1986).

Haipeter, T. & Lehndorff, S., *Collective Bargaining on Employment*, Working Paper No. 3, (ILO, Geneva, 2009).

Hall P. & Soskice D., *Varieties of Capitalism: The Institutional Foundations of Comparative Advantage* (OUP, 2001).

Hanami T., Komiya F. & Yamakawa R., *Labour Law in Japan* (2nd edn.), (Wolters Kluwer, 2015).

Hardin G., *The Tragedy of the Commons*, 162.3859 Science, 1243 (1968).

Harpur P., Phillip H. & James P. H., *The Shift in Regulatory Focus from Employment to Work Relationships: Critiquing Reforms to Australian and UK Occupational Safety and Health Laws*, 36.1 Comparative Labor Law & Policy Journal, 111–130 (fall 2014).

Hart O., *An Economist's Perspective on the Theory of the Firm*, 89 Columbia Law review, 1757 ff. (1989).

Hart O., *Firms, Contracts, and Financial Structure* (Oxford University Press, 1995).

Hart O., *Incomplete Contracts and the Theory of the Firm*, in O. Williamson & S. Winter (eds), *The Nature of the Firm: Origins, Evolution Development*, 141 (Oxford University Press, 1993).

Hart O. & Moore J., *Contracts as Reference Points*, Quarterly Journal of Economics (2008).

Hart O. & Moore J., *On the Design of Hierarchies: Coordination Versus Specialisation*, Journal of Political Economy, 113, 675 ff. (2005).

Hart O. & Moore J., *Property Rights and the Nature of the Firm*, Journal of Political Economy, 98, 1119 ff. (1990).

Hart O., *Reference Points and the Theory of the Firm*, NBER Working paper 13481 (October 2007).

Hartley J. F., *Case Studies in Organizational Research*, in Cathy Cassell & Gillian Symon (eds), *Qualitative Methods in Organizational Research* (London: Sage, 1994).

Heerma van Voss G., *The 'Tulip Model' and the New Legislation on Temporary Work in the Netherlands*, 15.4 The International Journal of Comparative Labour Law and Industrial Relations, 80–84 (1999).

Hernández Ramos M., *La especial trascendencia constitucional del recurso de amparo y su aplicación en la Jurisprudencia del Tribunal Constitucional. Luces y sombras en cuatro años de actividad*, Aranzadi Doctrinal, n. 3/20 11.

Hervas-Oliver J.-J. & Boix-Domenech R., *The Economic Geography of the Meso-Global Spaces: Integrating Multinationals and Clusters at the Local–Global Level*, 21.7 European Planning Studies, 1064, 1077 (2013).

Heymann E. & Vetter S., *Europe's Re-Industrialisation: The Gulf Between Aspiration and Reality*, Frankfurt: Deutsche Bank EU Monitor (2013).

Hirschl R., *Towards Juristocracy: The Origins and Consequences of the New Constitutionalism* (Harvard University Press, 2004).

Hodgson G. M., *Evolutionary and Competence-Based Theories of the Firm*, 25.1 Journal of Economic Studies, 25 (1998).

Hoffmann, J. et al., *The Europeanisation of Industrial Relations in a Global Perspective: A Literature Review*, Publications Office of the European Union (Luxembourg, 2002).

Holmstrom B., *Moral Hazard and Observability*, Bell Journal of Economics, 10 (1979).

Honnet A., *Die Idee Des Sozialismus* (Suhurkamp Verlag, Berlin, 2015).

Hopkins, M., *Corporate Social Responsibility: An Issues Paper*, Working Paper No. 27, International Labour Office (Geneva, 2004).

Humphrey J. & Schmitz H., *How Does Insertion in Global Value Chains Affect Upgrading in Industrial Clusters?*, 36.9 Regional Studies, 1017, 1017 (2002).

Hutton W., *The Gig Economy Is Here to Stay: So Making It Fairer Must Be a Priority*, the Guardian (4 September 2016).

Iacobucci E. M. & Triantis G. G., *Economic and Legal Boundaries of the Firm*, 93 Virginia Law Review, 515 ff. (2007).

Ichino P., *Il diritto del lavoro e i confini dell'impresa*, in *Diritto del lavoro e nuove forme di decentramento produttivo. Atti delle giornate di studio di diritto del lavoro, Trento, 4–5 giugno 1999*, 3 (Giuffrè, Milano, 1999).

ILO, (Visser J., Hayter S. & Gammarano R.), *Labour Relations and Collective Bargaining Coverage: Stability, Erosion or Decline?*, 5 (2015) http://www.ilo.org/public/english/iira/pdf/labourrelations.pdf.

ILO, survey *La situación sociolaboral en las zonas francas y en las empresas maquiladoras del istmo centroamericano y República Dominicana*, (1996).

ILO, *Combining flexibility and security for decent work*, Document GB.306/ESP/3/1, §4 (Ginevra, November 2009).

ILO, *Labour Clauses in Public Contracts: Integrating the Social Dimension into Procurement Policies and Practices* (ILO, 2008).

ILO, *Non-standard Forms of Employment*, Document MENSFE/2015 (Geneva, 2015).

ILO, *The Employment Relationship*, Report V (I), International Labour Conference (95th session, 2006), (Geneva, 2005).

ILO, *The Scope of the Employment Relationship*, Report V, International Labour Conference (91st session), (Geneva, 2003).

ILO, *World Employment and Social Outlook Trends 2016* (Geneva, 2016).

International Labour Organisation (ILO), *A Fair Globalization: The Role of the ILO: Report of the Director-General on the World Commission on the Social Dimension of Globalization* (ILO, Geneva, 2004).

International Training Centre (ITC), *Key Issues for Management to Consider with Regard to Transnational Company Agreements (TCAs). Lessons Learned from a*

Series of Workshops with and for Management Representatives. December 2010, VP 2009 003, (ITC-ILO, Turin, 2010).

Jaeger P. G., *Direzione unitaria» di gruppo e responsabilità degli amministratori*, Riv. soc. 817 (1985).

Jagodzinski R. (ed.), *The Implementation of the EWC Recast Directive* (ETUI, Brussels, 2015).

Jagodzinski, R., *Involving European Works Councils in Transnational Negotiations – A Positive Functional Advance in Their Operation or Trespassing?*, Industrielle eziehungen, 14 (4) (2007).

Jakobsen S.-E. & Onsager K., *Head Office Location: Agglomeration, Clusters or Flow Nodes?* 42.9 Urban Studies, 1517 (2005).

Jaspers T., *Flexiguridad: ? es la respuesta acertada a la modernización del Derecho del Trabajo? Una perpectiva holandesa* in Juan Pablo Landa Zapirain (ed.), *Estudios sobre la estrategia europea de flexiseguridad: una aproximación crítica*, 25–56 (Albacete, Ed. Bomarzo, 2009).

Jault-Seseke F., *La détermination des accords collectifs applicables aux relations de travail international*, in *Le droit international privé : esprit et méthodes. Mélanges en l'honneur de Paul Lagarde,* Paris, 455–473 (Dalloz, 2005).

Jensen M. & Meckling W., *The Theory of the Firm: Managerial Behavior, Agency Costs and Ownership Structure*, Journal of Financial Economics, 3, 305 ff. (1976).

Joint study by the Foundation for European Progressive Studies (FEPS) and UNI Europa, carried out by the University of Hertfordshire and Ipsos MORI: http://www.feps-europe.eu/en/publications/details/363.

Kahn-Freund O., *'Spaak Report': High Authority of the European Community for Coal and Steel*, 'The Brussels Report on the General Common Market', June 1956 http://aei.pitt.edu/995/1/Spaak_report.pdf.

Kahn-Freund O., *A Note on Status and Contract in British Labour Law*, 30 Modern Law Review, 635 et seq. (1967).

Kahn-Freund O., *Labour Law and Social Security*, in E. Stein & T. L. Nicholson (eds), *American Enterprise in the European Common Market: A Legal Profile* 297, 299 (University of Michigan Press 1960).

Keller B., *The European Company Statute: Employee Involvement and Beyond*, 33 Industrial Law Journal, 439 (2002).

Kenner J., *EU Employment Law* (Hart Publishing, 2003).

Ketokivi M. & Ali Yrkkö J., *Unbundling R&D and Manufacturing: Post-Industrial Myth or Economic Reality?*, 26.1-2 Review of Policy Research, 35 (2009).

Keynes J. M., *The General Theory of Employment, Interest and Money* (1936).

King D. & Lieberman R., *Ironies of State Building: A Comparative Perspective on the American State*, vol. 61, I 3, 550 (Cambridge University Press, 2009).

Kiss G. (ed.), *Recent Developments in Labour Law* (Akademiai Kiado, 2013).

Klages P., *Die Wiederentdeckung shlafender Alternativen in der Rechtlehre: Der Begriff 'Aktiengesellschaft'*, 18 Berliner Debatte Initial, 75 (2007).

Knight F. H., *Risk, Uncertainty and Profit* (Harper & Row, New York 1965).

Kocher M., *Le notion de groupe d'enterprises en droit du travail*, LGDJ, (2013).

Kolben K., *Dialogic Labor Regulation in the Global supply Chain*, 36.3 Michigan Journal of International Law, 425–465 (2015).

Kommisson Mitbestimmung, Bertelsmann Stiftung & Hans-Boeckler- Stiftung, *The German Model of Codetermination and Corporate Governance – Report from the Commission on Codetermination* (Bertelsmann Foundation Publisher, 1998).

Körner M., *La transformation du contrat de travail*, in *Tendances actuelles du droit social allemand*, Bulletin de droit comparé du travail et de la sécurité sociale, 29–30 (1998).

Koukiadi A., Távara I. & Martinez Lucio M., *Joint Regulation and Labour Market Policy in Europe during the crisis* (Brussels, ETUI, 2016).

Kraakmnan R., *The Anatomy of Corporate Law. A comparative and Functional Approach* (Oxford University Press, 2009).

Kroker R. & Lichtblau K., *'Industrieland Europa': Die europäische Industrie im internationalen Vergleich* (Eds Cologne Institute for Economic Research, Die Zukunft der Industrie in Deutschland und Europa, IW-Analysen No. 88 (Cologne, 2013).

La Torre M., *Law as Institution* (Springer Netherlands, 2010).

Lachmann L. M., *Capital and Its Structure* (Kansas City, 1956).

Lalande A., *Vocabulaire technique et critique de la philosophie* (Paris, PUF, 1962).

Lamoreaux N. R. et al., *Beyond Markets and Hierarchies: Towards a New Synthesis of American Business History*, 108 American Historical Review, 404 ff. (2003).

Langille B. & Guy Davidov G. (eds), *Boundaries and Frontiers of Labour Law* (Oxford, Hart Publishing, 2006).

Lars Hakanson, *The Firm as an Epistemic Community: The Knowledge Based View Revisited*, www2.druid.dk/conferences/viewpaper.php?id=500937&cf=43.

Law D. S., *Generic Constitutional Law*, 89 Minnesota Law Review 652, 662 and 725 (2005).

Leader S., *Human Rights and the Consitutionalized Corporation*, in Jean-Philippe Robé, Antoine Lyon-Caen & Stéphane Vernac (eds) *Multinationals and the Consitutionaliuzation of the World Power System*, XIII, 193 ff (Routledge, London and New York, 2016).

Lenaerts K. & Gutiérrez-Fons J. A., *To Say What the Law of the EU Is: Methods of Interpretation and the European Court of Justice*, AEL 2013/9, Working Paper (Academy of European Law, European University Institute) 19–24: http://cadmus.eui.eu/bitstream/handle/1814/28339/AEL_2013_09_DL.pdf.

Lippert I., *Corporate Governance, Employee Voice, and Work Organization* (New York, Oxford University Press, 2014).

Lo Faro A., *Contingent Work: A Conceptual Framework*, in Ales E., Deinert O. & Kenner J. (eds), *Core and Contingent Work in the European Union* 7-23, 8 (Hart Publishing, 2017).

Loffredo A., *Sobre las transformaciones de la figura del empresario: entre contractualismo y sugerencias institucionalistas*, in *Los empresarios complejos; un reto para el Derecho del Trabajo*, Lorenzo Gaeta, Rosario Gallardo Moya (coords), (Bomarzo, 2010).

López Ahumada E., *Le contenu des conventions collectives des groupes d'entreprises*, Working paper, Comptrasec, Montesquieu -Bordeaux IV University (2009).

Lòpez Sànchez C., *El empleador en la organizaciones complejas* (CES, Madrid, 2007).
Lunardon F., *Autonomia collettiva e gruppi di imprese* (Torino, Giappichelli, 1996).
Lyon-Caen A. & Lyon-Caen G., *La doctrine de l'entreprise*, in *Dix ans de droit de l'entreprise* (Litec, 1978).
Lyon-Caen A. & Perulli A., *Transformazioni dell'impresa e rapporti di lavoro* (CEDAM, 2004).
Lyon-Caen A. & Sachs T., *Multinationals and the Constitutionalization of the World Power System*, 204 (Routledge, 2016).
Lyon-Caen A. & Sachs T., *The Responsibility of Multinational Enterprises. A Costitutionalization Process in Action*, supra n. 2, at 204 ff.
Lyon-Caen G., *Le droit du travail non salarié* (Paris, Sirey, 1990).
Macchi M., *Le reti Gucci ed Esaote: un'analisi economica*, Giorn. dir. lav. rel. ind. 79 et seq. (2016).
MacLeod W. B., *Reputations, Relationships and the Enforcement of Incomplete Contracts*, Cesifo Working Paper No. 1730 (2006).
Macneil I. R., *Relational Contract: What We Do and Do Not Know*, Wisconsin Law Review, 483 (1985).
Macneil I. R., *The Many Futures of Contracts*, Southern California Law Review, 691, 696 ff. (1973-1974).
Malmberg J., *Posting Post Laval – International and National Responses*, Working Paper 2010:5, 6 (Uppsala Center for Labor Studies, June 2010).
Mangarelli C., *Descentralización empresarial y responsabilidad laboral en Uruguay*, included in *La descentralización empresarial y la responsabilidad laboral en América Latina y España* (coordinators Tomás Sala Franco, Cristina Mangarelli & Francisco J. Tapia Guerrero), 349-396 (Ed. Tirant lo Blanch, 2nd ed. Valencia, 2011).
Marginson, P., *The Transnational Dimension to Collective Bargaining in a European Context*, Industrial Relations Research Unit, University of Warwick, UK (2008).
Mariucci L., *Il lavoro decentrato. Discipline legislative e contrattuali* (Franco Angeli, 1979).
Markey R. et al. (eds), *Models of Employee Participation in a Changing Global Environment: Directory and Interaction* (Aldershot, Ashgate, 2001).
Marshall A., *Principles of Economics* (London: Macmillan and Co., 1890).
Martin I., *Corporate Governance Structures and Practices: From Ordeal to Opportunities and Challenges for Transnational Labour Law*, in Blackett A. & Trebilcock A. (eds), *Research Handbook on Transnational Labour Law*, 51-64 (Edward Elgar, 2015).
Marx K., *Preface to Critique Political Economy* (London: Lawrence and Wishart, 1968).
Matía Portilla F.J., *La especial trascendencia constitucional del recurso de amparo*, Revista Espmiola de Derecho Constitucional, n. 86, 343-368 (2009).
Mattheis C., *The System Theory of Niklas Luhmann and the Constitutionalization of the World Society*, 2 Goettingen Jouranl of International Law, 625 (2012).
Maugeri M. R., *Reti di impresa e contratto di rete*, in Contratti, 942 (2009).
Maugeri M., *Interesse sociale, interesse dei soci e interesse del gruppo*, Giur. comm., 66 (2012).

Mazzotta O., Divide et impera: *diritto del lavoro e gruppi di imprese*, LD, 365 (1988).
Mazzotta O., *Gruppi di imprese, codatorialità e subordinazione*, RGL, I., 3 (2013).
Mc Carthy D. I. & Puffer S. M., *Interpreting the Ethicality of Corporate Governance* (2008).
McCann D., *Regulating Flexible Work* (Oxford University Press, 2006).
McCrudden C., *Buying Social Justice: Equality, Government Procurement, and Legal Change* (Oxford, 2007).
McCrudden C. & O'Leary B., *Courts and Consociations* (Oxford University Press, 2013).
McMaster R. & Michael White M., *An Investigation of Williamson's Analysis of the Division of Labour*, 37 Cambridge Journal of Economics, 1283 (2013).
Meese A. J. & Oman N. B., *Hobby Lobby, Corporate Law, and the Theory of the Firm: Why for Profit Corporations Are RFRA Persons*, 127 Harvard Law Review Forum, 273, 274 (2014).
Meliadò G., *Il rapporto di lavoro nei gruppi di società. Subordinazione e imprese a struttura complessa* (Milano, Giuffré, 1991).
Mengoni L., *Contratto e rapporto di lavoro nella recente dottrina italiana*, Riv. Soc., I, 684 et seq (1965).
Mercader Uguina J., *La contratación temporal en la jurisprudencia del Tribunal Supremo*, 29 et seq. (Valencia, Tirant lo Blanch, 1999).
Mignoli A., *Interesse di gruppo e società a sovranità limitata*, Contratto e impresa, 730 (1986).
Monereo Pérez J. L., *El trabajo autónomo, entre autonomía y subordinación*, Aranzadi Social, no. 5/2009 (Estudio, 2009).
Montalenti P., *Conflitto di interessi nei gruppi di società e teoria dei vantaggi compensativi*, Giur. Comm., I, 710 et seq. (1995).
Moore J. F., *The Death of Competition: Leadership and Strategy in the Age of Business Ecosystems* (New York: Harper Business, 1996).
Moreno G. J., *Aspectos juridico-laborales de las empresa filiales. La identificatiòn del empresario responsable* (editorial Tecnos, Madrid, 2003).
Morettini V., *Le comité consultative pour la securité, l'hygiène et la protection de la santé sur le lieu de travail*, ES, 2/1990, p. 14 ss.
Morin M. L., *Labour Law and New Forms of Corporate organization*, 144.1 International Labour Review (2005).
Mudambi R., *Location, Control and Innovation in Knowledge-Intensive Industries*, 8.5 Journal of Economic Geography, 699 (2008).
Murray J., *Transnational Labour Regulation: The ILO and EC compared* (The Hague, Kluwer, 2002).
Navas-Alemán L., *The Impact of Operating in Multiple Value Chains for Upgrading: The Case of the Brazilian Furniture and Footwear Industries*, 39.8 World Development, 1386 (2011).
Neal A., *Information and Consultation for Employees – Still seeking the Philosopher's Stone?*, in Marco Biagi (ed.), *Quality of Work an Employee Involvement in Europe*, 83–99 (The Hage-London-New York, 2002); Edoardo Ales, *Directive 2002/14/EC establishing a general framework for informing and consulting employees in the*

European Community, Sinthesis report, Labour Asociados Consultores (October 2007).
Nogler L., *Gruppo di imprese e diritto del lavoro,* LD, 291 (1992).
Nogler L., *Metodo tipologico e qualificazione dei rapporti di lavoro subordinato,* Riv. it. dir. lav. 182, I (1990).
Nogueira Guastavino M., *Contracciones y dilataciones en la reforma de la Ley Orgánica del Tribunal Constitucional: parto prematuro del incidente de nulidad de actuaciones e incongruencia omisiva,* Teoría & Derecho, n. 3, 206–232 (2008).
Nogueira Guastavino M., *La trascendencia constitucional de la demanda de amparo tras la reforma de la Ley Orgánica del Tribunal Constitucional por la LO 6/2007,* Revista de Derecho Social, n. 51, 165–200 (2010).
Novitz T., *Trading in Services: Commmodification and Beneficiaries,* in Adelle Blackett & Anne Trebilcock(eds), *Reseach Book on Transnational Law,* 497–508 (Cheltenham, E; Elgar, 2015).
Nüchter B.S., *Betrieb, Unternehmen und Konzern im Kündigungsschutzgesetz. Eine Untersuchung der Begriffe und systematischen Zusammenhänge* (Marburg, Tectum Verlag, 2006).
Nuzzo A. & Tullio P., *La legislazione d'impresa dell'ultimo quinquennio: quantità più che qualità,* Analisi giuridica dell'economia (2013).
OCED, *Territorial Outlook 2001,* 15 (2001).
OECD, *OECD Guidelines for Multinational Enterprises* (Paris 1976 and 2000).
Ogus A., *Regulation: Legal Form and Economic Theory* (Oxford, Clarendon Press, 1994).
Ogus A., *The Economic Approach: Competition Between Legal Systems,* in Esin Orucu & David Nelken (eds), *Comparative Law: A Handbook,* 155 ff. (Oxford & Portland, Oregon, 2007).
Ojeda Avilés A., *La 'externalización' del derecho del trabajo,* vol. 148, n. 1-2, Revista Internacional del Trabajo, 49–70 (2009).
Ostrom E., *Beyond Markets and States: Polycentric Governance of Complex Economic Systems,* 2.2 Transnational Corporations Review, 1 (2010).
Ostrom E., *Governing the Commons: The Evolution of Institutions for Collective Action* (Cambridge: Cambridge University Press, 1990).
Ozaki M. & Trebilcock A., *Forms of Workers' Participation,* in Anne Trebilcock (ed.), *Labour Relations and Human Resources Management*; Jeanne Mager Stellman (Editor-in-Chief), *Encyclopedia of Occupational Health and Safety* (International Labor Organization, 2011).
Pagnerre Y., *Regard comparatiste sur le co-emploi,* Revue de droit compare du travail et de la sécurité sociale 1, 84–90 (2016).
Papadakis, K. (ed.), *Cross-Border Social Dialogue and Agreements: An Emerging Global Industrial Relations Framework?* (ILO, Geneva, 2008).
Papadakis, K., Casale G. & Tsotroudi, K., *International Framework Agreements as elements of a Cross-Border Industrial Relations Framework,* in K. Papadakis (ed.), *Cross-Border Social Dialogue and Agreements: An Emerging Global Industrial Relations Framework?* International Institute for Labour Studies (ILO, Geneva, 2008).

Papadakis, K., *Globalizing Industrial Relations: What Role for International Framework Agreements?*, in Hayter, S. (ed.) *The Role of Collective Bargaining in the Global Economy. Negotiating for Social Justice* (ILO, Geneva, 2011).

Parkinson J. E., *Corporate Power and Responsibility. Issues in the Theory of Company Law* (Oxford, 1993).

Perez Tremps P., *El acceso al recurso de amparo*, in VV.AA.; *Estudios en Homenaje al Profesor Gregorio Peces-Barba, Teoría y A4etodología del Derecho*, vol. 11, 979–1004 (Dykinson Madrid, 2008).

Pero L. & Ponzellini A. M., *Il nuovo lavoro industriale tra innovazione, organizzazione partecipazione diretta*, in *La partecipazione incisiva*, Mimmo Carrieri, Paolo Nerozzi & Tiziano Treu (a cura).

Perry M. J., *The Political Morality of Liberal Democracy* (Cambridge University Press, 2012).

Persiani M., *Contratto di lavoro e organizzazione* (Cedam, Padova, 1966).

Perulli A. (ed.), *La responsabilità sociale dell'impresa: idee e prassi* (Bologna, Il Mulino, 2013).

Perulli A., *Contratto di rete, distacco, codatorialità, assunzioni in agricoltura*, in Luigi Fiorillo, Adalberto Perulli (eds), *La riforma del mercato del lavoro*, 463, 503 (Torino, Giappichelli, 2014).

Perulli A., *Diritto del lavoro e decentramento produttivo in una prospettiva comparata: problemi e prospettive*, RIDL, I, 29 (2007)

Perulli A., *Gruppi di imprese, reti di imprese e codatorialità: una prospettiva comparata*, RGL, I, 83 (2013).

Perulli A., *Study on Economically Dependent Work/pArasubordinate (Quasi-Subordinate) Work*, (Brussels, 2003).

Peruzzi M., *Il distacco di personale tra imprese che hanno sottoscritto un contratto di rete. Nozione di codatorialità e questioni aperte* (2014), available at http://www.diprist.unimi.it/Reti_impresa/papers/11.pdf.

Peskine E., *Réseaux d'entreprise et droit du travail* (LGDJ Paris, 2004).

Peskine E., *L'imputation en droit du travail. A propos de la responsabilité des sociétés mères en matière de licenciement pour motif économique*, Revue de droit du travail, 347 (2012).

Peskine E., *Réseau d'entreprises et droit du travail*, L.G.D.J. (2008).

Peskine E. & Wolmark C., *Droit du travail 2013* (Paris, Dalloz, 2013).

Piergiovanni R., Santarelli E. & Vivarelli M., *From Which Source Do Small Firm Derive Their Innovative Inputs? Some Evidence from Italian Provinces*, 12 Review of Industrial Organization, 243 (1997).

Pinto V. (2013), *Profili critici della teoria della codatorialità nei rapporto di lavoro*, RGL, 1, 55 (2013).

Pinto V., *I gruppi imprenditoriali tra diritto dell'Unione europea e diritto nazionale*, ADL, 4-5-, 890 (2011).

Pinto V., *I gruppi societari nel sistema giuridico del lavoro*, (Bari, Cacucci, 2005).

Pipkorn J., *The Law of Groups of Enterprises in the European Community* (ETUI, paper, 1987).

Pisano G. P. & Shih W. C., *Producing Prosperity. Why America Needs a Manufacturing Renaissance* (Boston: Harvard Business School Press, 2012).

Pisano G. P. & Shih W. C., *Restoring American Competitiveness*, 87.7-8 Harvard Business Review, 114 (2009).

Polanyi K., *The Economy as Insituted Process*, in Karl Polany, Conrad Arensberg & Harry Pearson (eds), *Trade and Market in the Early Empires* (Chicago, 1957).

Porter M. E. & Kramer M. R., *Creating Shared Value*, 89.1/2 Harvard Business Review, 62, 6 (2011).

Porter M. E., *The Competitive Advantage of Nations* (New York: The Free Press, 1990).

Powel W., *Neither Market Nor Hierarchy: Network Form of organization*, in Larry L. Cummings & Barry M. Staw (eds), *Research in Organisational Behavior*, Jai Press, 295 ff. (Greenwich, 1990).

Prandini R., *The Future of Societal Constitutionalism in the Age of Acceleration*, 2 Indiana Journal of Global Legal Studies, 731, 740 (2013).

Prassl J., *Employee Shareholders 'Status', Dismantling the Contract of Employment*, 4 International Law Jouranl, 323 (2013).

Prassl J., *L'emploi multilatéral en droit anglais. A la recherche du patron perdu*, Revue de droit du travail 236 (2014).

Prassl J. & Risak M., *Uber, Taskrabbit, & Co: Platforms As Employers? Rethinking The Legal Analysis of Crowdwork*, Comparative Labour Law and Policy Journal (May 2016).

Prassl J., *The Concept of Employer* (Oxford University Press, 2015).

Raimondi E., *Il datore di lavoro nei gruppi imprenditoriali*, Giorn. Dir. Lav. Rel. ind. 287 (2012).

Raimondi E., *Rapporto di lavoro e gruppi imprenditoriali. La figura del datore di lavoro e le tecniche di tutela*, (Torino, Giappichelli 2016).

Ramirez P. & Helen Rainbird H., *Making the Connections: Bringing Skill Formation into Global Value Chain Analysis*, 24.4 Work, Employment & Society, 699 (2010).

Raso Delgue J., *La contratación atípica del trabajo*, Montevideo, AMF (2009).

Ratti L., *Agency Work and the Idea of Dual Employership: A Comparative Perspective*, 30 Comparative Labor Law Journal & Policy Journal, 835 (2009); Id., *Réseaux d'entreprises et coemploi*, Rev. dr. tr. 72 (2015).

Ratti L., *Intorno al/i concetto/i di datore di lavoro. A proposito di* The Concept of the Employer *di Jeremias Prassl*, DLRI, 381 (2016).

Ratti R., *Réseaux d'entreprises et coemploi, perspectives comparatives*, Rev. Dr. Tr. 72 (2015).

Rawls J., *Lectures on the History of Political Philosophy* (Harvard University Press, 2007).

Razzolini O., *Contitolarità del rapporto di lavoro nel gruppo caratterizzato da 'unicità di impresa'*, DLRI, 263 (2009).

Razzolini O., *Impresa di gruppo, interesse di gruppo e codatorialità nell'era della flexicurity*, Riv. giur. lav. 29 (2013).

Razzolini O., *Network Forms of Organisation and Network Agreements in a Labour Law Perspective: Two Tuscan Case Studies*, in Edoardo Ales et al. (eds), *Employment Relations and Transformation of the Enterprise in the Global Economy*, 67 et seq. (Giappichelli, Torino, 2016).
Reilly B., Paci P. & Holl P., *Unions, Safety Committees and Workplace Injuries*, 33 British Journal of Industrial Relations, 273–288 (1995).
reti, *Studi in memoria di Giovanni Garofalo*, t. I, 273 (Bari, Cacucci 2015).
Reve T., *The Firm as Nexus of Internal and External Contracts*, in Masahiko Aoki, Bo Gustafsson & Oliver Williamson, *The Firm as Nexus of Treaties* (Sage, London, 1990).
Riley C. A., *Understanding and Regulating the Corporation*, Modern Law Review, 595 (1995).
Rivero Lamas J., *La descentralización productiva y las nuevas formas organizativas del trabajo*, published in Asociación Española de Derecho del Trabajo y de la Seguridad Social, X Congreso Nacional Español de Derecho del Trabajo y de la Seguridad Social, Ministerio de Trabajo y Asuntos Sociales, 22 (Madrid, 2000).
Robé J.-P., Antoine Lyon-Caen A. & Stéphane Vernac S. (eds), *Multinationals and Constitutionalization of the World Power System* (Routledge, 2016).
Robé J.-P., *Globalization and Constitutionalization of the World Power System*, in Jean-Phillipe Robé, Antoine Lyon-Caen & Stéphane Vernac (eds), *Multinationals and the Constitutionalization of the World-Power System*, 11, 13 (Routledge, 2016).
Robé J.-P., *L'entreprise et le droit*, coll. 'Que sais-je' (Paris PUF, 1999).
Robé J.-P., *La constitutionnalisation du système-monde de pouvoir* (College de Berardin. Département économie, homme et société, 2011).
Robé J.-P., *Le temps du monde de l'entreprise*, Coll. A droit ouvert (Paris Dalloz, 2015).
Robé J.-P., Lyon-Caen A. & Vernac S., *L'entreprise et la constitutionnalisation du système-monde de pouvoir*, in Jean-Philippe Robé, Antoine Lyon-Caen & Stéphane Vernac (eds) *Multinationals and the Consitutionaliuzation of the World Power System*, XIII (Routledge, London and New York, 2016).
Robin-Olivier S., *Les contrats de travail flexibles. Une comparaison internationale* (Paris, Presses de Sciences-Po, 2015).
Rodière P., *Droit social de l'Union européenne* (Paris, LGDJ, 2002).
Rodriguez J. B., *Las relaciones de trabajo en la empresa de groupo* (Granada, Editorial Comares, 2002).
Roger B. (ed.), *L'entreprise, formes de la propriété et responsabilités sociales*, (Collège des Bernardins, Paris, editions Lethielleux 2012).
Roger Blanpain R., Shinya Ouchi S. & Takashi Araki T. (eds), *Decentralizing Industrial Relations and the Role of Labour Unions and Employee Representatives*, no. 61 Bulletin of Comparative Labour Relations (Kluwer Law International, 2007).
Romano S., *Frammenti di un dizionario giuridico* (Giuffré, 1983).
Romano S., *L'ordinamento giuridico* (Mariotti, 1917).

Romano S., *Lo stato moderno e la sua crisi. Saggi di diritto costituzionale* (Giuffré, 1969).

Rönmmar M., *Labour Policy on Fixed-Term Employment Contracts in Sweden*, no. 76 Bulletin of Comparative Labour Relations, 159 (2010).

Rosioriu F., *Legal Acknowledgement of the Category of Economically Dependent Workers*, 5.3/4 European Labour Law Journal, 279–305 (2015).

Rueda-Cantuche J. M., Sousa N., Andreoni V. & Arto I., *The Single Market as an Engine for Employment Growth Through the External Trade*, Joint Research Centre, IPTS, (Seville 2012).

Ruggie J. G., *Foreword: Constitutionalization and Regulation of Transnational Firms*, in Jean-Philippe Robé, Antoine Lyon-Caen & Stéphane Vernac (eds) *Multinationals and the Consitutionaliuzation of the World Power System*, XIII (Routledge, London and New York, 2016).

Sabel C. F. & Zeitlin J., *Neither Modularity Nor Relational Contracting: Inter-Firm Collaboration in the New Economy*, Firm and Society 5, 388 (2004).

Sanchez-Graells A., *CJEU Clarifies and Minimises Rüffert, and Expands the Scope for Minimum Wage Requirements in Public Procurement (C-115/14)*, How to Crack a Nut: A Blog on EU Economic law, 17 November 2015: http://www.howtocrackanut.com/blog/2015/11/cjeu-clarifies-and-minimises-ruffert.html.

Sandel M., *What Money Can't Buy: The Moral Limits of Markets* (Farrar, Straus and Giroux, 2012).

Sanguinetti Raymond W., in *Las transformaciones del empleador y el futuro del derecho del trabajo*, published in No. 1 Relaciones laborales 389–416 (Madrid, 2009).

Sanguinetti Raymond W., *La dependencia y las nuevas realidades económicas y sociales: ¿un criterio en crisis?*, published in no.2 Doctrina Judicial Laboral (Rosario, Argentina), 5 et seq. (July 2000).

Sapelli G., *Responsabilità d'impresa* (Guerini e Associati, 1996).

Schömann, I., A. Sobczak, E. Voss & P. Wilke, *Codes of Conduct and International Framework Agreements: New Forms of Governance at Company Level*, Publications Office of the European Union (Luxembourg, 2008).

Schömann, I., *The Impact of Transnational Company Agreements on Social Dialogue and Industrial Relations'*, in K. Papadakis (ed.) *Shaping Global Industrial Relations: The Impact of International Framework Agreements* (ILO, Geneva, 2011).

Sciarra S., Corazza L., *Reti di imprese e sostenibilità sociale della filiera* (2013), available at www.nelmerito.com/index.php?option=com_content&task=view&id=1906&Itemid=1.

Sciarra, S., *The Evolving Structure on Collective Bargaining in Europe 1990–2004*, research project co-financed by the European Commission and the University of Florence (VS/2003/0219-SI2. 359910), (2003).

Segrestin B., Roger B. & Vernac S. (eds), *L'entreprise. Point aveugle du savoir* (Editions Sciences Humaines, 2014).

Sen A., *The Idea of Justice* (London, Penguin Books, 2009).

Servais J.-M-, *International Labour Law*, §§ 714–719 (4th edn, The Hague, Kluwer, 2014).

Sigurt V., *The European Participation Index (EPI): A Tool for Cross-National Quantitative Comparison*, European Trade Union *Background Paper* (2010).

Silvi R. & Cuganesan S., *Investigating the Management of Knowledge for Competitive Advantage: A Strategic Cost Management Perspective*, 7.3 Journal of Intellectual Capital, 309 (2006).

Simitis S., *Il diritto del lavoro ha ancora un futuro?*, 79 Giornale di Diritto del Lavoro e di Relazioni Industriali 617 (1997), cited by Fernando Valdes dal Re in the paper *Descentralización productiva y desorganización del Derecho del Trabajo*, published in 2 Revista Universitaria de Ciencias del Trabajo, 41–63 (2002).

Simon H., *A Formal Theory of the Employment Relationship*, in Econometrica, 19, 293 ff. (1951).

Slaughter A.-M-, *Judicial Globalization*, 40 Virginia Jouranl of International Law 1103, 1112 (1999–2000).

Speziale V., *Gruppi di imprese e codatorialità: introduzione ad un dibattito*, RGL, I, 3 (2013).

Speziale V., *Il datore di lavoro nell'impresa integrata*, DLRI, 1 (2010).

Speziale V., *Il datore di lavoro nell'impresa integrata*, in *La figura del datore di lavoro. Articolazioni e trasformazioni. Atti del convegno nazionale A.i.d.la.s.s., Catania, 21–23 maggio 2009*, 77 et seq. (Giuffrè, Milano, 2010).

Stevis, D., *International Framework Agreements and Global Social Dialogue: Parameters and Prospects*, Employment Working Paper No. 47 (Geneva, ILO, 2010).

Stone K. V. W. & Arthurs H. (eds), *Rethinking Workplace Regulation: Beyond the Standard Contract of Employment* (New York, Russell Sage Foundation, 2013).

Storper M., *The Resurgence of Regional Economies Ten Years Later: The Region as a Nexus of Untraded Interdependencies*, 2 European Urban and Regional Studies, 191 (1995).

Sugeno K., *Japanese Employment and Labor Law* (Carolina Academic Press, 2002).

Sugeno K., *Shugyo Kisoku Henko to Roshi Kosho (Work Rules Modification and Labor-Management Negotiation)*, Rodo Hanrei 6 (1997).

Supiot A. (ed.), *Au-delà de l'emploi. Transformations du travail et devenir du droit du travail en Europe*.

Supiot A., *Groupes de societès et paradigme de l'enterprise*, RTD comm., 621 et seq. (1985).

Supiot A., *L'avenir d'un vieux couple: travail et sécurité sociale*, Droit social, Nos 9–10, 823–831 (September-October 1995).

Supiot A., *Les nouveaux visages de la subordination*, no 2 Droit social, 131–145 (February 2000).

Suwa Y., *Shugyo Kisoku no Kozo to Kino (Structure and Function of Work Rules)* 71 Nihon Rodoho Gakkai-shi 19 (1988).

Tapia Guerrero F. J., *Descentralización empresarial y responsabilidad laboral en Chile*, included in *La descentralización empresarial y la responsabilidad laboral en América Latina y España* (coordinators Tomás Sala Franco, Cristina Mangarelli & Francisco J. Tapia Guerrero), 85–118 (Ed. Tirant lo Blanch, 2nd Ed. Valencia 2011).

Telesetsky A., *Beyond Voluntary Corporate Social Responsibility: Corporate Human Rights Obligations to Prevent Disasters and to Provide Temporary Emergenc Relief*, 48 Vanderbilt Journal of Transnational Law 1003, (2015).

Telljohann, V., I. da Costa, T. Müller, U. Rehfeldt & R. Zimmer, *European and International Framework Agreements: Practical Experiences and Strategic Approaches*, Publications Office of the European Union (Luxembourg, 2009).

Teubner G. & Beckers A., *Expanding Constitutionalism*, 20 Indiana Journal of Global Legal Studies, 523, 540 (2013).

Teubner G., *Enterprise Corporatism: New Industrial Policy and the 'Essence' of the Legal Person*, 36 The American Journal of Comparative Law, 130, 134 (1988).

Teubner G., *Networks as Connected Contracts* (Oxford: HartPublishing, 2011).

Teubner G., *Self-Constitutionalizing TNCs? On the Linkage of 'Private' and 'Public' Corporate Codes of Conduct*, 18 Indiana Journal of Global Legal Studies, 617, 624 (2011).

Teubner G., *Societal Constitutionalism: Alternatives to State-Centered Constitutional Theory?*, in Christian Joerges, Inger-Johanne Sand & Gunther Teubner (eds), *Transnational Governance and Constitutionalism*, 3–28 (Oxford University Press, 2004).

Teubner G., *Substantive and Reflexive Elements in Modern Law*, 2 Law & Society Review 240, 269 (1983).

Teubner G., *The Many Autonomies of Private Law*, 9 Social and Legal Studies, 399 et seq. (2000).

Teubner G., *Unitas Multiplex: Corporate Governance in Group Enterprises* (Bremen/Firenze, 1988).

Teubner G., *Unitas Multiplex: Problems of Governance in Group Enterprises from a System Theory Point of View* (Florence, EUS, 1988).

Tirado Estrada J.J., *Requisito particular de admisión del recurso: la especial trascendencia constitucional* (I), Diario La Ley, n. 7838, (2012).

Toennies F., *Community and Civil Society* (Jose Harris, Cambridge University Press, 2001).

Torre A. & Rallet A., *Proximity and Localization*, 39.1 Regional Studies, 47 (2005).

Trebilcock M., *The Limits of Freedom of Contract* (Cambridge, Mass. Harvard Univ. Press, 1993).

Treu T., *Trasformazioni delle imprese: reti di imprese e regolazione del lavoro*, Merc. conc. reg. 19 (2012).

Tushnet M., *Do For-Profit Corporations Have Rights of Religious Conscience?*, Cornell Law Review Online 70, 71 (2013).

Ushakova T., *Derecho de la OIT para el trabajo a distancia: ¿una regulación superada o todavía aplicable?*, Vol. 3, no 4 Revista Internacional y Comparada de Relaciones Laborales y Derecho del Empleo 74-92 (october-december 2015).

Vacarie I., *Le travail dans un marché sans frontières*, 10 Revue de droit du travail, 634–64 (2015).

Valdés Dal-Ré, F., *Freedom of association of workers and employers in the countries of the European Union*, Ministerio de Trabajo y Asuntos Sociales (Madrid, 2006).

Valle Muñoz F. A., *El contrato en prácticas incentivado como mecanismo de inserción laboral*, 42 Revista General de Derecho del Trabajo y de la Seguridad Social (2016).
Van den Abeele E., *Integrating Social and Environmental Dimesnions in Public Procurement: One Small Step for the Internal Market, One Giant Leap for the EU?* (European Trade Union Institute Working Paper 2014.08).
Van Ho T., *Corporate Liability in a New Setting: Shell and the Changing Legal Landscape for the Multinational oil Industry in the Niger Delta* (2011) by the Essex Business and Human Rights Project https://www.essex.ac.uk/ebhr/documents/niger-delta-report.pdf.
Van Hoek, A. & F. Hendrickx, *International Private Law Aspects and Dispute Settlement Related to Transnational Company Agreements*. Study undertaken on behalf of the European Commission (Contract number VC/2009/0157), (Brussels 2009).
Vandamme J., *L'information et la consultation des travailleurs dans la proposition de directive sur les enterprise a structure complexe*, RMC, 368 (1981).
Vardaro G., *Prima e dopo la persona giuridica: sindacati, imprese di gruppo e relazioni industriali*, Giorn. dir. lav. rel. ind. 211 (1988).
Veneziani B., *Gruppi di imprese e diritto del lavoro*, LD, 609 (1990).
Veneziani, B., *Right of collective Bargaining and Action*, in B. Bercusson (ed.) *European Labour Law and the EU Charter of Fundamental Rights* (Nomos, Baden-Baden, 2006).
Verge P. (with the collaboration of Sophie Dufour), *Configuration diversifiée de l'entreprise et droit du travail*, (Saint Nicolas (Québec), P U Laval, 2003).
Vernac S., *L'avenir sauvegardé du coemploi*, Revue de droit du travail 560 (2016).
Vernac S., *Le pouvoir d'organisation. Au croisement du droit du travail et du droit des sociétés*, (LGDJ Paris 2016), pending publication.
Villalòn J. Cruz, *Notas acerca del régimen contractual laboral en los grupos de empresa*, Tema laborales, 38, 31 (1996).
Villalòn J. Cruz, *Los cambios en la organizaciòn, de la empresa y sus efectos en el Derecho del Trabajo: aspectos individuales*, in AA. VV., *El empleador en el Derecho del Trabajo*, XVI Jornadas Universitarias Andaluzas de Derecho del Trabajo y Relaciones Laborales, (editorial Tecnos, Madrid, 1999).
Vitols K., *Strengthening Cooperation Between NGOs and Trade Unions in the Interest of Sustainability*, in Sigurt Vitols & Norbert Kluge (eds), *The Sustainable Company: A New Approach to Corporate Governance*, I, 185 (ETUI, 2011).
Vitols S., *European Works Councils: An Assessment of Their Social Welfare Impact* (ETUI, Brussels, 2009).
Vitols S. & Kluge N. (eds), *The Sustainable Company: A New Approach to Corporate Governance*, I (ETUI, 2011).
Vivante C., *Trattato di diritto commerciale*, I (Milano, 1922).
Vogt V., *Arbeitsrecht im Konzern* (Baden Baden, Nomos, 2014).
Von Bogdandy A., Grabenwarter C. & Huber P., *Il diritto costituzionale nel diritto pubblico europeo. L'esempio della rete istituzionalizzata della giustizia costituzionale*, www.associazionedeicostituzionalisti.it 4 (2015).

Vosko L., *Managing the Margins:Gender, Citizenship and International Regulation of Precarious Employment* (New York (NY), Oxford University Press, 2010).
Wagner I., *Posted Work and Deterritorialization in the European Union: A Study of the German Construction and Meat Industry* (2015) Jyväskylä studies in education, psychology and social research 521, p 26: https://jyx.jyu.fi/dspace/handle/12345 6789/45494.
Walker P., *Contracts, Entrepreneurs, Market Creation and Judgement: The Contemporary Mainstream Theory of the Firm in Perspective*, Journal of Economic Surveys, published online, 7 February (2014).
Walters D., T. Nochols, Connor J., Tasiran A. C. & Cam S., *The Role and Effectiveness of Safety Representatives in Influencing Workplace Health and Safety*, Health and Safety Executive, Research Report 363 (2005).
Wedderburn of Charlton K. W., *Employees: Partnership and Company Law*, 101 Internaitonal Law Jouranl (2002).
Weil D., *The Fissured Workplace: Why Work Became So Bad for So Many and What Can Be Done to Improve It* (Harvard University Press, 2014).
Weiler J. H.H., *Deciphering the Political and Legal DNA of European Integration: An Exploratory Essay*.
Weinstein O., *The Current State of the Economic Theory of the Firm: Contractual, Competence-Based, and Beyond*, in Biondi Y., Canziani A. & Kirat T. (eds), *The Firm as an Entity*, 42 (Routledge, 2007).
Weiss M., *Industrial Relations and EU Employment*, in John Craig & Michael Lynk (eds), *Globalization and the Future of Labor Law*, 181 et seq. (Cambridge, Cambridge University Press, 2010).
Weiss M., *Modernizing the German Works Council System: A Recent Amendment*, IJCLLIR 251 et seq. (2002).
Weiss M., *Négociation collective et groupe de sociétés en Allemagne*, Working paper (Bordeaux, April 2009).
Weiss M. & Schmidt M., *Labour Law and Industrial Relations in Germany* (4th edition, Kluwer, 2008).
Weiss M., *The European Community Approach to Workers' Participation: Recent Developments*, in Alan Neal (ed.), *The Changing Face of European Labour Law and Social Policy*, 39–53 (Kluwer Law International, The Netherlands, 2004).
Weiss M., *The Future of Employee Involvement in Company Boards in Germany*, in B. Nyström et alii (ed.) Liber Amicorum Reinhold Fahlbeck, Lund (2005).
Williamson O. E., *Le istituzioni economiche del capitalismo* (Franco Angeli, Milano, 1987).
Williamson O. E., *The New Institutional Economics: Taking Stock, Looking Ahead*, Journal of Economic Literature, 38, 595 ff. (2000).
Williamson O. E., *Transaction-Cost Economics: The Governance of Contractual Relations*, in Peter J. Buckley & Michie J. (eds), *Firms, Organizations and Contracts*, 168 (Oxford University Press, 2001).
Williamson O., *The Economic Institutions of Capitalism: Firms, Markets, Relational Contracting* (New York, Free Press, 1985).

Williamson O., *The Vertical Integration of Production: Market Failure Considerations*, 61 American Economic Review, 112 (1971).
Williamson O., Watcher M. & Harris J., *Understanding the Employment Relation: The Analysis of Idiosyncratic Exchange*, Bell Journal Economics, 1 (1975).
Windbichler C., *Arbeitsrecht und Konzernrecht, Recht der Arbeit* (1999).
Wolf E. & Zwick T., *Reassessing the Productivity Impact of Employee Involvement and Financial Incentives*, 60 Schmalenbach Business Review, 160–181 (2008).
World Commission on the Social Dimension of Globalization, *Report, A Fair Globalization: Creating Opportunity for All* (ILO, Geneva, 2004).
Yin R. Y., *Case Study Research: Design and Methods* (Newbury Park, CA: Sage Publications, 3/e 2003).
Zamagni S., *L'impresa civile responsabile*, www.fondazionelanza.it/forum/zamagni.php.
Zimmermann J.-B., *L'Ancrage Territorial des Activités Industrielles et Technologiques: Une Approche Méthodologique* (Commissariat Général du Plan, Paris, 1995).
Zoppini A. (a cura di), *La concorrenza tra ordinamenti giuridici* (Bari, Laterza, 2004).
Zwick T., *Employee Participation and Productivity*, 11.6 Labour Economics, 715–740 (February 2004).

Index

A

Accountability, 123-129, 376
AEK v Fujitsu Siemens Computers (Case), 9, 204
Agency problems, 353
Agency Theory, 366-369
Agency work, 66-71, 79, 85, 88-90, 246
Albron (Case), 154
Allocation, 36-37, 78, 79, 104, 142, 299, 360, 365
Appalto di manodopera, 96
Apprenticeship, 64
Arbitration, 219, 220, 231, 298-300
Arblade (Case), 227
Argentina, 43, 86-91, 150
Article 2094, 97
Associated employer, 137, 152
Association, 8, 27, 44, 50, 52, 55, 67, 68, 161, 164, 165, 170, 174, 229, 272, 276, 308, 354
Associative contract, 361
Asymmetry, 8, 32, 165, 166, 368
Atypical forms of dependent work, 45-46
Austria, 54, 70, 71, 149, 312, 313, 316-324, 330

B

Bargaining power, 4, 8, 41
Belgium, 51, 52, 54, 60, 67, 69, 71, 108, 312, 313, 317-324, 330, 331

Benefits, 4, 8, 11, 34, 46, 47, 53, 54, 57, 63-65, 67, 70, 73, 83, 88, 94, 103, 104, 108, 112, 113, 115, 149, 153, 154, 164, 174, 240, 282, 297, 314, 326, 327, 340, 347, 362, 378
Biagi Decree (no. 276/2003), 96, 97
Borders, 3, 6, 20, 98, 107, 121, 163, 167, 169, 221, 238, 280, 338, 376
Brazil, 86-91, 153
Bundesruckerei (Case), 234-242, 246
Business, 28, 29, 42, 48, 54, 69, 73, 75, 76, 78, 79, 81, 82, 85, 94, 103, 107, 109, 111, 112, 114, 116, 123-126, 128, 131, 132, 137, 141, 143, 150-153, 161, 182, 183, 190, 204, 208-210, 212, 214, 245, 261, 282, 284, 286, 288, 289, 307, 340, 342, 346, 348, 354, 361, 362
Business Alliances, 362
Business group, 361
Business organization, 137, 152, 354

C

Canada, 61, 150, 152, 330, 331
Capital boundaries problem, 132
Capital structure theory, 362
Chains of production, 56
Chandler v Cape Industries (Case), 123
Charter of Fundamental Rights, 170, 171, 216
Child labour, 44, 52, 229
Childbearing, 324, 326, 327
CJEU, 55, 57, 65, 304, 309

Index

Co-determination, 10, 157, 299, 304, 305, 307, 308, 376
Co-employer, 22, 56, 70, 73, 157
Co-employeurs, 138
Co-employment, 3, 6, 7, 22, 151, 154-157
Coase (Ronald), 2, 32-37, 132, 354, 355, 357, 358, 365, 371
Coasean idea, 25
Codatorialità, 138, 142
Code(s) of conduct, 1, 57
Codetermination, 272, 275
Collective agreement(s), 7, 9, 49, 54, 55, 59, 62, 69-71, 167, 169, 170, 178-180, 183, 187, 193, 194, 201, 203, 208, 218-220, 222-227, 230-233, 235, 238-240, 242-246, 273, 276
Collective Dismissals, 9, 10, 148-150, 152, 157, 300
Collective redundancies, 55, 58, 201-216, 247
Commercial law, 2, 43, 56, 73, 80, 122, 129, 148, 352, 354, 361
Commission v Luxembourg (Case), 10, 221-234, 240, 242
Commodity, 35, 357, 368
Common law, 31, 32, 69, 137, 139, 352, 357, 361, 373
Company, 69-71, 90-91, 111-115, 147-158, 164-165
Competition, 3, 19, 20, 58, 73, 81, 169, 200, 217-247, 351, 356
Competitive advantage(s), 6, 105, 111, 117, 147, 237
Competitiveness, 101, 107, 116, 136, 356, 376
Constitutional Court, 9, 10, 249, 252-255, 258, 260, 261, 263-265, 267, 268
Constitutionalization (of the firm), 134, 377
Contitolarità, 138
Contract law, 28, 227

Contractor(s), 3, 5, 21, 28, 32, 72, 76, 78, 79, 82, 83, 87-89, 95-97, 141, 233, 245, 361, 363, 366
Contractual network, 135, 142, 366
Contractual relations, 5, 18, 58, 154, 170, 189, 233, 360, 361, 364-367
Contrat de société, 361
Contratto di rete, 136
Convention(s), 44-46, 50, 52-54, 62-69, 89, 165, 169, 170, 217, 243, 336, 351, 371, 374
Core labour standards, 165
Corporate accountability, 376
Corporate Governance, 18, 286, 352, 368, 374, 375
Corporate group(s), 21, 122-126
Corporate law, 20, 122-124, 129, 286, 309, 341, 346, 353, 359
Corporate personality, 122, 151
Corporate Social Responsibility (CSR), 7, 48, 57, 94, 162, 289, 346, 357, 373
Crisis, 3, 11, 21, 34, 75-77, 141, 152, 167, 202, 274, 307, 308, 317, 344, 373, 375, 377
Czech Republic, 312, 313, 317-323, 330, 331

D

Decent work agenda, 166
Decentralization, 41-91, 95, 162, 173-195, 291
Decentralized Industrial Relations, 173-195
Deconstruction, 78, 80
Degradation, 81-83, 87
Denmark, 70, 71, 108, 312, 313, 316-323, 331
Dependence, 51, 61, 72, 76, 81, 83, 88, 121, 151, 232
Deterritorialization (of labour law), 217
Developing countries, 41, 60, 75
Digital innovation, 104
Directive 2001/23/EC, 58, 59, 154

Directive 2004/18/EC, 234-241
Directive 2009/38/EC, 57, 148, 168, 276, 278, 285
Directive 2014/24/EU, 9, 201, 221, 234, 235, 237, 240, 243, 244
Directive 2014/67/EU, 50, 55, 73, 144, 244
Directive 96/71/EC, 9, 49, 50, 55, 144, 201, 240, 243
Discrimination, 52, 65, 193, 304, 324, 330
Disintegration, 3, 21, 200, 371
Dismissals, 9, 10, 45, 63, 88, 139, 148-154, 157, 174, 175, 187-189, 191, 192, 211-214, 216, 255, 256, 263, 297, 300, 306
Distribution, 6, 20, 21, 22, 36-37, 60, 100, 147, 182, 187, 273, 279, 282, 284, 299, 305, 366, 373
Diversification, 150, 183, 194, 195, 356
Double employer, 152
Duties of the entrepreneur, 31
Duty of care, 6, 121-129, 139
Duty of loyalty, 157

E

Economic freedom, 27, 73, 225
Economic subordination, 44
Economic theory, 3, 17, 356, 369, 373-375
Economically dependent autonomous labour, 363
Economically-dependent (work), 5, 83
Efficiency, 3, 25, 26, 31-33, 36, 195, 272, 288, 297, 353, 355, 358, 359, 362, 372-374
Emerging countries, 105
Emerging economies, 100, 101, 105, 106
Employability, 144, 145
Employees participation, 278, 281-283
Employer's responsibilities, 31, 140
Employment agencies, 54, 66, 67, 69-71, 93, 96, 97

Employment law, 20, 23, 139, 143, 226
Employment relationship, 21, 25-37, 44, 19, 50-52, 54, 55, 59, 61, 62, 65, 66, 68, 69, 72, 78, 80, 84, 94, 148, 152, 153, 182, 188, 199, 206, 209, 217, 218, 230, 233, 353
Enforcement of labour standards, 93, 94
Enterprise Unionism, 175, 178-182, 185
Enterprise(s), 17-23, 75-91, 121-145, 161-332
Entrepreneur(s), 29-30
Entrepreneurial opportunities' test, 32
Equal treatment, 70, 71, 88-89, 95-96, 162, 225, 226, 229, 243
Equality of treatment, 62, 70, 220, 223, 226, 242, 246
ESA (Case), 233, 246
Establishment, 50, 53, 54, 57, 65, 72, 87, 95, 174, 176-178, 183-185, 187, 191, 192, 194, 200-204, 206-216, 218, 222, 287, 294-297, 299, 300, 309, 313, 329, 356
EU Charter of Fundamental Rights, 170, 171, 216
EU Directive 2001/86, 277
EU Directive 2002/14, 55, 71, 210, 216, 276, 278
EU Directive 2002/149, 276, 278
EU Directive 2008/104, 66, 68, 71, 246
EU Directive 91/533, 52, 68
EU Directive 94/45, 276
EU Directive 98/59, 58, 148, 202, 210
EUCJ, 50, 58
Europe, 11, 12, 21, 51, 56, 95, 98, 108, 109, 112, 114, 137, 162, 164, 174, 183, 185, 192, 200, 246, 276, 279, 287, 311, 314, 316, 331, 332, 341, 342, 356
European Industry Federations (EIFs), 165
European Participation Index, 12, 311-313, 331
European Social Charter, 169-170
European social dialogue, 167-169

Index

European Social Law, 41, 275
European Social Model, 272
European Trade Union Confederation (ETUC), 233
European Union, 9, 19, 48, 148, 164, 199, 239, 272, 290, 304, 336, 356
European Works Council(s), 57, 148, 162, 275
External workers, 94
Externalization process(es), 41, 43, 75–91

F

Family work, 53
Finland, 54, 108, 204, 233, 312, 313, 326, 328–331
Fixed-term, 59, 66–67, 192, 193, 229
Flexibility, 5, 7, 8, 36, 66, 67, 95, 143, 144, 150, 173, 174, 192, 195, 201, 203, 215, 225, 328, 329, 359
Flexibility clauses, 44
Flexibilization, 78, 173–175, 182–185, 191, 192
Flexicurity, 4, 8, 67, 72, 144–145, 173–175, 186–195
Fluid enterprise, 286–288
Fordist model, 5, 75, 286
Formal employer, 140, 151, 153, 155, 157
Fragmentation, 3, 5, 6, 10, 21, 73, 75, 79, 89, 93, 99, 108, 121, 149, 247, 287, 309, 378
Fragmented Responsibility, 121–125
France, 42, 43, 51, 52, 54, 55, 57, 58, 67, 69–71, 108–110, 124, 151, 162, 193, 218, 272, 312, 313, 316–323, 326, 328–331, 376
Franchising agreements, 362
Free movement of services, 221, 222, 224–227, 233, 236, 242
Freedom of association, 8, 44, 50, 52, 68, 161, 165, 229

Freedom to provide services, 201, 223, 227, 230, 236, 240
Functional employer, 139, 287

G

Gender Gap, 311, 324, 332
Genuine groups, 153
Germany, 9–11, 43, 51, 52, 54, 57, 61–63, 71, 108, 109, 162, 175, 194, 231, 233, 238, 239, 274, 279, 283, 293–309, 312–313, 316–331, 349
Gesellschaftsvertrag, 361
Gig workers, 200
Global Union Federations (GUFs), 162, 165
Global Value Chains (GVCs) (GVC), 99–118
Global Work Councils, 164
Globalization, 77, 161, 163–165, 356
Governance of the firm, 283, 284, 374–378
Greece, 69, 312, 313, 320–324, 330
Grossman-Hart-Moore model, 29
Grouping of enterprises, 55–56
Groups of companies, 90–91, 131, 135, 137, 138, 145, 147–158
Groups of enterprises, 6, 7, 42, 57–58, 276
Gucci, 136, 141

H

Harmonisation, 203, 206, 212, 214, 220, 225, 242, 247
Harmonization, 181, 271–273, 275–277, 279
Health and safety 45, 47, 57, 69, 94, 123, 124, 128, 162, 165, 282, 283, 312–314
Human rights, 47, 48, 73, 123, 127, 195, 336, 338–342, 347, 348, 378
Hungary, 313, 320–323, 330

I

ILO (International Labour Organization), 8, 43, 44, 45, 47, 50-57, 59, 61, 62, 65, 66-70, 72, 80, 89, 161, 162165-167, 169, 170, 243
ILO Committee of Experts, 170
ILO Convention(s), 44, 54, 67, 68, 89, 165, 169, 170
ILO Recommendation No. 198, 51, 61, 72
ILO standards, 44, 45, 69
Industrial commons, 4, 99-118
Industrial Relations, 82-83, 173-195
Industrialised countries, 100, 105
Informal economy, 41, 42
Informal sector, 45
Information and consultation, 55, 139, 162, 167, 171, 203, 205, 212-216, 275-280, 287, 296
Integrated Production, 6, 111, 121-124, 129
Interests, 3, 4, 12, 13, 25, 28, 29, 32, 37, 42, 43, 69, 71, 134, 144, 145, 156, 157, 164, 166, 169, 174, 190, 194, 224, 226, 227, 232, 273, 287, 289, 290, 297, 299, 300, 303, 306, 309, 335-337, 340, 342-345, 347-349, 352, 353, 356, 359, 364, 369, 376, 378
Interfirm Network Agreement, 132, 136, 140-144
Interim, 66, 187, 265
International Framework Agreements (IFAs), 8, 162, 165-166
International Labour Standards, 44, 45, 54, 162, 165, 166
Investment fund, 21, 22, 114
Investment(s), 21, 22, 33-35, 37, 101, 102, 107, 113, 114, 116, 359, 372
Invisible hand, 358
Ireland, 313, 317, 320-323, 330, 331
Italy, 51, 54, 59, 69-71, 108-113, 149, 150, 162, 272, 276, 312, 313, 316-331

J

Jabir and others v KiK Textilien und non-food GmbH (Case), 128
Japan, 7, 8, 173-195, 330, 331
Job satisfaction, 313, 314, 320
Job(s), 12, 23, 41-46, 52, 58, 60, 68, 69, 70, 77, 81, 82, 85, 94, 105, 107, 109, 134, 144, 145, 148, 150, 156, 157, 178, 221, 297, 306, 311, 313-318, 320, 321, 324, 328, 332
Joint employment (relationship), 137, 138, 142, 143, 148, 151, 353
Joint-employers, 6, 138, 142
Joint-employment, 137, 138, 142, 143
Joint-venture, 361
Jurisdiction(s), 124, 127, 169, 257, 258, 263, 264, 266, 268, 338, 349

L

Labor-management agreement, 177, 184
Labour contract, 5-9, 25, 149, 151, 359, 361, 366, 367
Labour cost(s), 78, 89, 100, 105, 106, 112, 245
Labour market, 8, 36, 89, 93, 109, 116, 145, 161, 200, 309, 311, 317, 324-328, 332, 351, 353, 367
Labour power, 26
Labour relationship, 41, 72, 359, 366
Labour Standard(s), 5, 6, 44, 45, 54, 56, 93-95, 98, 127, 142, 145, 162, 165, 166, 200, 222, 237, 243
Laval (Case), 10, 50, 221-234, 240, 242
Lavoro parasubordinato, 80
Learning by supplying, 101
Lex mercatoria, 351
Liberalisation, 4, 9, 199, 200, 221
Liberalization, 41, 162
Lock-out(s), 298
Luxembourg, 64, 226-230, 312, 313, 330, 331
Lyttle (Case), 208, 210, 211, 213-215

Index

M

Management power, 20, 67
Management theory, 18
Manager, 1, 3, 11, 27, 34, 57, 96, 100, 111, 113–115, 134, 141, 200, 212, 279, 281, 283, 289, 302, 314, 331, 352, 357, 358, 360, 365–368
Manufacturing, 4, 5, 42, 99–102, 104–112, 116, 117, 202, 281Market, 2, 186–191, 217–247
Market actors, 27
Market system, 26, 27
Maternity, 45, 63, 65, 324–326
Mercosur, 5, 83–91
Micro-enterprises, 42, 52
Migrant workers, 46, 68
Minimum wage, 55, 67, 177, 182, 187, 191, 195, 201, 228–231, 233, 235–242
MNEs, 162–167
Multinational companies, 47, 99, 101, 106, 108, 116, 117
Multinational firms – Multinational companies, 43, 47, 99–118, 341

N

Network, 121–145, 284–286
Network agreement, 132, 136, 140–144
Network companies / Network of companies, 5, 76, 77
Network contracts, 7, 284–286, 361
Network of contracts, 25, 29, 133, 362, 364, 365
Network of firms, 132–136, 370
Network responsibility, 128
Network-firm, 286, 287, 370, 371
Nexus of contracts, 1, 2, 27–30, 352, 364–367
Normativity, 3, 20, 343, 344, 373
Notion of employer, 21, 22, 29, 286

O

OECD, 48, 54, 103, 174, 325, 326, 328–331
Offshore outsourcing, 98
Offshoring, 98, 99, 102, 105–110, 370
Organised irresponsibility, 132, 140, 142, 145
Outsourcing, 3–8, 80, 84, 90, 95, 98, 108, 200, 237, 247, 287, 306, 359, 362, 370
Owner, 28, 48, 54, 58, 69, 79, 94, 134,

P

Parasubordinated, 80
Parasubordinazione, 44, 59, 61, 72, 80
Parent companies, 58, 79, 90, 114, 121–127, 150–152, 155, 204, 206, 207, 295, 303
Part-time, 59, 64–65, 81, 192, 193, 229, 324
Plural or complex employer, 56, 91, 137, 138, 142
Plural Unionism, 180–181
Poland, 69, 70, 110, 230, 235, 237, 313, 317–323, 330
Posted worker(s), 49–50, 217–247
Posting, 50, 55, 73, 143, 144, 187, 218–219, 222, 228, 230, 232, 236, 237, 239, 242, 244, 247
Precarization, 81–82
Privatisation, 9, 200
Productive decentralization, 41–91
Purchasers(s), 122, 126–128

R

Rabal Cañas (Case), 9, 212, 213, 216
Rana Plaza, 376
Reclassement (obbligation of), 138
Redundancies, 58, 202–216
RegioPost (Case), 234–242, 244
Regulation, 84–91, 193–195, 335–378
Regulatory competition, 200, 247, 356

Remuneration, 51, 60, 63, 67, 70, 90, 228, 230, 245, 246, 297, 299, 306, 307, 367
Renewals, 66, 76
Restructuring, 162, 165, 182, 204, 207, 209, 214, 215, 247, 308
Right to dismiss, 35, 37, 188
Rights of the employee, 25, 278, 282
Risk, 7, 8, 21, 22, 30, 31, 45, 54, 59, 63, 68, 69, 80, 85, 88, 95, 106, 126, 132, 136, 140, 142, 143, 153, 174, 184, 254, 256, 259, 262, 264, 287, 291, 313, 314, 353, 354, 366, 372, 377
Rockfon (Case), 209
Rome Convention of 1980, 217
Rome I Regulation, 217, 226, 228
Rüffert (Case), 10, 50, 221–234, 236–242, 244
Rush Portuguesa (case), 218

S

Safety and health, 45, 50, 53, 54, 59, 62, 64, 66, 70, 187, 313
Salary, 46, 60, 81, 315, 316, 319, 321, 360, 368
Scientific organization of work, 75
Self-employed, 42–45, 52, 57, 60–62, 72, 73, 77, 81, 83, 85
Self-employment, 25, 31, 51, 59–61, 72, 80, 81
Self-employment relationship, 31–32
Self-regulation, 356, 357, 377
Shareholder, 1, 11, 21, 22, 27, 31, 133, 134, 288, 289, 302, 303, 305–306, 336, 352, 353, 364, 366, 368, 369, 374, 375, 377, 378
Shareholder value, 31, 289, 306, 352, 374
Short-termism, 34–35
Single Market, 10, 200, 215, 217–247
Skills, 33, 89, 97, 100, 101, 103, 105, 106, 109, 111–113, 115, 116, 144, 145, 279, 297, 314, 315

Small and medium-sized enterprise(s) (SME(s)), 42, 44, 52–53, 103, 135, 234, 280, 294
Social Dumping, 10, 73, 200, 201, 217, 218, 221–234, 236, 241, 242, 244, 247
Social model, 272, 291
Social partners, 63, 66, 67, 70, 164, 165, 169, 174, 202, 220, 224
Social policies, 48, 57, 212, 217, 220, 233, 241, 242, 247, 274, 278
Social protection, 10, 47, 62, 73, 83, 85, 174, 221, 224, 232, 247
Social security, 46, 47, 50, 53, 60, 61, 63, 65, 67, 72, 82, 87, 89, 90, 149, 150, 232, 236, 237, 245, 247
Societal constitutionalism, 288, 343
Society, 26, 28, 29, 35, 37, 60, 194, 229, 272, 273, 288, 289, 345, 351–353, 357, 373, 377
Spain, 10, 54, 61, 69–71, 108, 110, 149, 152, 213, 214, 216, 272, 312, 313, 316–324, 330, 331
Stakeholders, 1, 4, 11, 72, 117, 134, 279, 289–291, 306, 336, 352, 369, 378
Strike, 49, 50, 68, 89, 174, 180, 181, 192, 273, 298
Subcontracting, 42, 43, 52–56, 72, 76, 77, 80, 81, 85–89, 93, 95–97, 106, 200, 245–247, 287
Subcontractor(s), 5–6, 47, 54, 55, 79, 81, 82, 85, 87–89, 95–97, 141, 230, 235–238, 245, 353
Subordination, 43, 44, 50, 51, 67, 72, 81, 90, 95–97, 140, 156, 359, 366, 368, 377
Subsidiaries, 58, 72, 87, 88, 106, 121–128, 138, 139, 151, 167, 171, 200, 204, 206, 207, 235, 237, 246, 247, 250, 263, 278, 280, 304
Supplier(s), 54, 76, 79, 82, 85, 100, 101, 103, 106, 107, 111, 112, 116, 122, 125–128, 141, 288, 352, 364, 370, 378

Index

Supply chain, 56, 122, 125–129, 353, 371
Survey on Health, Ageing and Retirement in Europe (SHARE), 311, 314, 315, 316, 324, 326, 332
Sustainability, 48, 101, 108, 115, 288–290, 378
Sustainable development, 288, 290
Sweden, 51, 69–71, 108, 149, 222–225, 312, 313, 316–323, 326, 328–331
Switching costs, 372
Switzerland, 54, 56, 316–323, 330, 331

T

Team Production Theory, 30, 32, 134–136, 141
Temporary Work Agencies, 53, 67–70, 89–90
Temporary workers, 45, 66, 67, 69, 71, 82, 85, 89, 90, 193, 320
Termination of employment, 58, 65, 66
The firm as organization, 354
The Netherlands, 51, 54, 67, 70, 71, 204, 312, 313, 316–324, 327, 330–331
The power of organisation, 20, 22
Theory of the firm, 25–37, 351–378
Trade Unions, 41, 44, 49, 50, 59, 69, 71, 74, 82, 83, 90, 142, 162–166, 168, 170, 171, 204, 208, 222–225, 232, 266, 276, 278, 290, 293, 294, 296, 298, 301, 302, 305, 306, 308
Transaction costs, 29, 103, 133, 357–362, 369, 370, 372, 375
Transactions, 26, 29, 32, 33, 35, 36, 103, 131, 133, 355, 357–363, 365, 369–375
Transfer of Undertaking, 154
Transnational, 42, 48, 49, 50, 60, 161–172, 199, 203, 215, 217, 223, 228, 232, 236, 247, 276, 335–338, 341, 349
Transnational collective bargaining (TCB), 162–171

U

Undertaking, 42–45, 48–50, 52–59, 61, 66–71, 85, 88, 105, 136, 143, 149–151, 153–155, 157, 168, 169, 201, 203–207, 209–216, 218, 220, 223, 224, 226, 230–232, 235, 238–240, 245, 285
Unemployment, 46, 64, 174, 202
Unions representatives, 272, 279, 284
United Kingdom, 55, 61, 108, 152, 208
United States, 56, 70, 71, 325
USDAW and Wilson (Case), 208, 210, 211, 213–215

V

Vertical Disintegration, 200, 371
Vertical firm, 131–132
Viking (Case), 222
Violations of labour standards, 94
Vocational training, 59, 64, 70, 187, 297

W

Wage, 42, 45–47, 50, 54, 55, 57, 60–63, 65, 67, 70, 72, 94, 144, 162, 183, 184, 186, 187, 191, 195, 201, 218, 222, 223, 228–233, 235–243, 295, 297, 330
Welfare, 271–332
Well-being, 31, 36, 281
Williamson (Oliver), 35, 133, 355, 362
Work organization, 41, 42, 55, 63, 275, 277, 281, 284
Workers participation, 271–332
Workforce, 34, 80, 82, 94, 100, 106, 109, 110, 115, 149, 166, 183, 192, 195, 199, 200, 202, 209, 211, 214, 280, 295, 299, 300, 302, 307, 309
Working conditions, 45, 175–178, 186–191
Workplace, 32, 33, 52, 59, 69, 94–95, 97, 173, 174, 176, 177, 183, 184, 187, 211, 276, 280, 309, 313, 332

Works Constitution Act, 294–296, 298, 299, 301, 303
Works Council Agreements (WCA), 175–177
Works Council System, 178, 182, 185, 294–300, 306–307, 309

World-corporation, 356

Z

Zero-hours contracts, 43, 65, 71, 200

STUDIES IN EMPLOYMENT AND SOCIAL POLICY

1. W. Beck, L. van der Maesen & A. Walker (eds), *The Social Quality of Europe*, 1997 (ISBN 90-411-0456-9).
2. R. Blanpain, M. Colucci, C. Engels, F. Hendrickx, L. Salas & E. De Smyter, *Institutional Changes and European Social Policies after the Treaty of Amsterdam*, 1998 (ISBN 90-411-1018-6).
3. V. Lo: *Law and Industrial Relations: China and Japan after World War II*, 1998 (ISBN 90-411-1075-5).
4. A. Den Exter & H. Hermans (eds), *The Right to Health Care in Several European Countries*, 1998 (ISBN 90-411-1087-9).
5. M. Biagi (ed.), *Job Creation and Labour Law from Protection towards Pro-Action*, 2000 (ISBN 90-411-1432-7).
6. W. Beck, L. van der Maesen, F. Thomése & A. Walker (eds), *Social Quality: A Vision for Europe*, 2000 (ISBN 90-411-1523-4).
7. F. Pennings, *Introduction to European Social Law*, 3rd ed., 2001 (ISBN 90-411-1628-1).
8. J. Murray, *Transnational Labour Regulation: The ILO and EC Compared*, 2001 (ISBN 90-411-1583-8).
9. R. Blanpain & C. Engels (eds), *The ILO and Social Challenges of the 21st Century*, 2001 (ISBN 90-411-1572-2).
10. M. Biagi (ed.), *Towards a European Model of Industrial Relations? Building on the First Report of the European Commission*, 2001 (ISBN 90-411-1653-2).
11. J. Clasen (ed.), *What Future for Social Security? Debates and Reforms in National and Cross-National Perspective*, 2001 (ISBN 90-411-1671-0).
12. A. Numhauser-Henning (ed.), *Legal Perspectives on Equal Treatment and Non-Discrimination*, 2001 (ISBN 90-411-1665-6).
13. R. Blanpain (ed.), *Labour Law, Human Rights and Social Justice* 2001 (ISBN 90-411-1697-4).
14. M.-C. Kuo, H.F. Zacher & H.-S. Chan (eds), *Reform and Perspectives on Social Insurance: Lessons from the East and West*, 2002 (ISBN 90-411-1819-5).
15. P. Foubert, *The Legal Protection of the Pregnant Worker in the European Community*, 2002 (ISBN 90-411-1842-X).
16. M. Biagi (ed.), *Quality of Work and Employee Involvement in Europe*, 2002 (ISBN 90-411-1885-3).
17. F. Pennings, *Dutch Social Security Law in an International Context*, 2002 (ISBN 90-411-1887-X).

18. T. Carney & G. Ramia, *From Rights to Management: Contract, New Public Management and Employment Services*, 2002 (ISBN 90-411-1889-6).
19. R. Blanpain & M. Colucci, *European Labour and Social Security Law, Glossary*, 2002 (ISBN 90-411-1905-1).
20. I.U. Zeytinoglu (ed.), *Flexible Work Arrangements: Conceptualizations and International Experiences*, 2002 (ISBN 90-411-1947-7).
21. J. Berghman, A. Nagelkerke, M. Boos, R. Doeschot & G. Vonk (eds), *Social Security in Transition*, 2002 (ISBN 90-411-1969-8).
22. R. Blanpain, *The Legal Status of Sportsmen and Sportswomen under International, European and Belgian National and Regional Law*, 2003 (ISBN 90-411-1980-9).
23. R. Blanpain & M. Weiss (eds), *Changing Industrial Relations & Modernisation of Labour Law, Liber Amicorum in Honour of Professor Marco Biagi*, 2003 (ISBN 90-411-2008-4).
24. J. Malmberg (ed.), *Effective Enforcement of EC Labour Law*, 2003 (ISBN 90-411-2160-9).
25. M. De Vos (ed.), *A Decade Beyond Maastricht: The European Social Dialogue Revisited*, 2003 (ISBN 90-411-2163-3).
26. M. Sewerynski (ed.), *Collective Agreements and Individual Contracts of Employment*, 2003 (ISBN 90-411-2190-0).
27. R. Blanpain & M. Van Gestel, *Use and Monitoring of E-Mail, Intranet and Internet Facilities at Work: Law and Practice*, 2004 (ISBN 90-411-22-66-4).
28. A. C. Neal (ed.), *The Changing Face of European Labour Law and Social Policy*, 2004 (ISBN 90-411-2312-1).
29. E. Sol & M. Westerveld (eds), *Contractualism in Employment Services: A New Form of Welfare State Governance*, 2005 (ISBN 90-411-2405-5).
30. F. Pennings (ed.), *Between Soft and Hard Law – The Impact of International Social Security Standards on National Social Security Law*, 2006 (ISBN 978-90-411-2491-3).
31. L. Dickens & A. C. Neal (eds), *The Changing Institutional Face of British Employment Relations*, 2006 (ISBN 978-90-411-2541-5).
32. G. Sebardt, *Redundancy and the Swedish Model in an International Context*, 2006 (ISBN 978-90-411-2503-3).
33. A.M. Świątkowski, *Charter of Social Rights of the Council of Europe*, 2007 (ISBN 978-90-411-2608-5).
34. M. Sargeant (ed.), *The Law on Age Discrimination in the EU*, 2008 (ISBN 978-90-411-2522-4).
35. G. Di Domenico & S. Spattini (eds), *New European Approaches to Long-Term Unemployment: What Role for Public Employment Services and What Market for Private Stakeholders?*, 2008 (ISBN 978-90-411-2614-6.)
36. C. Welz, *The European Social Dialogue under Articles 138 and 139 of the EC Treaty: Actors, Processes, Outcomes*, 2008 (ISBN 978-90-411-2744-0).
37. M. Rönnmar (ed.), *EU Industrial Relations v. National Industrial Relations: Comparative and Interdisciplinary Perspectives*, 2008 (ISBN 978-90-411-2770-9).

38. F. Pennings, Y. Konijn & A. Veldman (eds), *Social Responsibility in Labour Relations: European and Comparative Perspectives*, 2008 (ISBN 978-90-411-2783-9).
39. F. Pennings & C. Bosse (eds), *The Protection of Working Relationships: A Comparative Study*, 2011 (ISBN 978-90-411-3289-5).
40. S. Devetzi & S. Stendahl (eds), *Too Sick to Work?: Social Security Reference in Europe for Persons with Reduced Earnings Capacity*, 2011 (ISBN 978-90-411-3426-4).
41. U. Becker, F. Pennings & T. Dijkhoff (eds), *International Standard-Setting and Innovations in Social Security*, 2013 (ISBN 978-90-411-3233-8).
42. E. Ales (ed.), *Health and Safety at Work: European and Comparative Perspective*, 2013 (ISBN 978-90-411-4661-8).
43. F. Pennings, T. Erhag & S. Stendahl (eds), *Non-public Actors in Social Security Administration: A Comparative Study*, 2013 (ISBN 978-90-411-4917-6).
44. A. Neal (ed.), *Cross-Currents in Modern Chinese Labour Law*, 2014 (ISBN 978-90-411-4763-9).
45. B. Waas (ed.), *The Right to Strike: A Comparative View*, 2014 (ISBN 978-90-411-5007-3).
46. A. Ojeda-Avilés, *Transnational Labour Law*, 2015 (ISBN 978-90-411-5858-1).
47. A. Numhauser-Henning & M. Rönnmar, *Age Discrimination and Labour-Law: Comparative and Conceptual Perspectives in the EU and Beyond*, 2015 (ISBN 978-90-411-4979-4).
48. Adalberto Perulli & Tiziano Treu (eds), *Enterprise and Social Rights*, 2017 (ISBN 978-90-411-8234-0).